Architectural
Working Drawings

Architectural Working Drawings

Residential and Commercial Buildings

William P. Spence

John Wiley & Sons, Inc.

New York • Chichester • Brisbane • Toronto • Singapore

Library of Congress Cataloging in Publication Data:
Spence, William Perkins, 1925–
    Architectural working drawings: residential and commercial
buildings/William P. Spence.
        p.   cm.
    Includes index.
    ISBN 0-471-57488-0
    1. Architecture—Working drawings. 2. Architecture, Domestic—
Designs and plans. 3. Commercial buildings—Designs and plans.
NA2713.S64   1992
720′.28′4—dc20   92-1507

Printed in United States of America

10 9 8 7 6 5 4 3 2 1

Contents

Preface

This text is designed for those preparing for a career in architecture, architectural drafting, architectural engineering, construction engineering, construction engineering technology, and construction management. While designed for community college, technical institute, university, or college level instruction it could serve well for senior high school classes composed of above average students. It can also be of value to those preparing for construction-related careers.

This text presents a detailed study of typical methods of construction and the preparation of architectural working drawings for residential and commercial buildings. While those using this book will most likely have had beginning manual drafting and computer drafting courses, basic tools and techniques in each are presented for those who may need them. Chapters 1 and 2 cover the use of drafting tools and materials and sketching techniques. Ability to sketch rapidly and accurately is an important skill for architects and architectural drafters. Computer drafting is finding increasing use in architectural firms. A detailed discussion of computer graphics hardware is covered in Chapter 3, while the software and basic operating procedures are discussed in Chapter 4.

The design and drafting of residential and commercial buildings require a knowledge of drafting standards, the architectural design process, and the related construction documents. These are covered by separate chapters.

The basic methods of construction are covered in a series of chapters. This begins with foundation design considerations and presents various foundation designs for buildings large and small. Separate chapters are used to present floor, wall, and roof construction for light construction and commercial buildings.

The final 11 chapters give detailed instructions and illustrations on how to prepare architectural drawings. Included are the title sheet, site plan, floor plan, foundation plan, architectural sections, architectural details, elevations, roof plans, framing plans, schedules, electrical plans, heating and air-conditioning plans, and plumbing plans.

A study of this text will give the reader a detailed overview of methods of construction as well as the needed information on preparing architectural working drawings. Each chapter is of sufficient detail that it can stand alone as an area of study. Students should be able to learn the material with a minimum of instructor effort. Each chapter has a series of student activities the instructor may use to help reinforce the learning experience. Each chapter contains many photographs and illustrations which aid the reader in understanding the material.

WILLIAM P. SPENCE
Pinehurst, North Carolina
June 1992

Drafting Tools and Materials

The selection of professional quality drafting tools is important because the quality of the drawing depends partially upon them. The skill of the drafter plus quality tools complete the cycle for producing professional architectural drawings.

Architectural working drawings are drawn manually using a wide variety of tools or can be drawn using computer drafting hardware and software. In this chapter, the commonly used manual drafting tools and materials are described. Computer drafting is discussed in Chapters 4 and 5.

Drafting Tables

A wide variety of drafting tables are manufactured. The older style has four legs and an adjustable top. New models use a single or double pedestal base that has controls to enable the drafter to raise and lower the height of the top above the floor and tilt it on various angles (Fig. 1-1). Typical tops range from 30 × 48 in. to 30 × 60 in. Large size tops are used for architectural drawing.

The pedestal type tables permit the drafters to sit in a chair with a comfortable back. This enables them to work with less fatigue than when the old long legged drafting stools were used. Since the height of the top can be adjusted the drafter can work sitting or standing (Fig. 1-2).

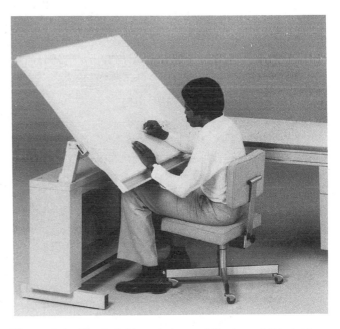

Figure 1-1. The height and slope of the top of this table can be adjusted to suit the drafter. (Courtesy The Mayline Company.)

Table tops are usually wood or hardboard over a cellular core. Most drafters prefer to cover this with a vinyl drawing-board cover.

Parallel straightedges or drafting machines are used with drafting tables.

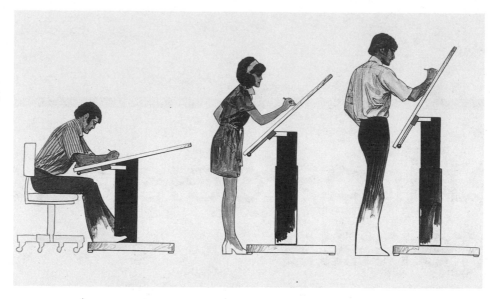

Figure 1-2. *Drafters can work seated or standing. (Courtesy The Mayline Company.)*

The Parallel Straightedge

The parallel straight edge runs on wires which move over pulleys inside the straightedge. When properly installed it can be moved up and down the board and always remain parallel with the top of the drawing table (Fig. 1-3). Many architectural drafters like the parallel straightedge be-cause architectural drawings are long and it permits drawing long horizontal lines.

Drafting Machines

The two basic types of drafting machines are the arm type and the track type.

Figure 1-3. *The parallel straightedge is used to draw horizontal lines and serves as a base for the triangles. (Courtesy Keuffel and Esser Co.)*

The arm type clamps to the top edge of the drafting table. It has two arms that pivot in the center and a head at the end of the lower arm. The head is moved by the drafter up and down and right and left. The scales on the head remain parallel to their original setting (Fig. 1-4).

The track type has a track on the top of the table. A vertical track slides left and right along the top track. The head is fastened to the vertical track and slides up and down on it (Fig. 1-5).

Drafting machines are a combination of several conventional drafting tools. The vertical and horizontal blades serve as scales for linear measurement and replace the triangle and T-square for drawing vertical and horizontal lines. The head has a scale in degrees which replaces the protractor.

Drafting machines are made right-handed and left-handed. Right-handed people hold the head in their left hand. Left-handed people hold the head in their right hand and have scales facing opposite those in Figs. 1-4 and 1-5.

The scales are set on angles by releasing a lock, pressing a release button and turning the head. Positive set points are located at frequently used angles such as 30°, 45°, and 60°. Other angles are held by tightening the lock handle (Fig. 1-6).

Scales are available in plastic and aluminum. They can be purchased in several lengths and all of the commonly used scales (architectural, metric, etc.) are available.

Triangles

Triangles are used with the parallel straightedge for drawing vertical and inclined lines. The 45° and 30°–60° triangles are available. Their size is specified by giving the

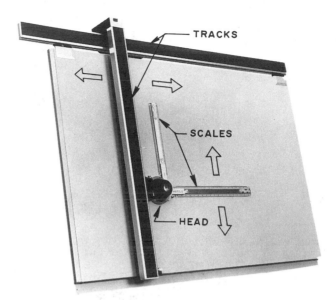

Figure 1-5. A track-type drafting machine. (Courtesy Keuffel and Esser Co.)

length of the longest side of the right angle (Fig. 1-7). Some triangles have recessed edges for use when inking. This keeps the ink from running under the triangle. They are available in clear and colored plastic. It is easy to nick the edges so triangles must be carefully used and stored.

Scales

Scales are tools with markings on the edge in inches or millimeters. The markings are also referred to as scales. These scales are available in a variety of sizes permitting

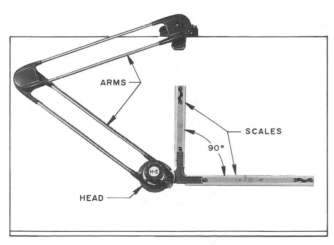

Figure 1-4. An arm-type drafting machine. (Courtesy Keuffel and Esser Co.)

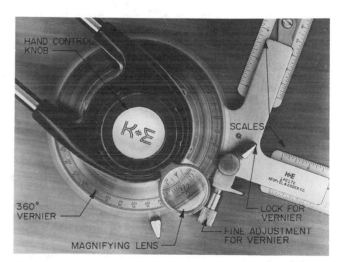

Figure 1-6. The head of the drafting machine. (Courtesy Keuffel and Esser Co.)

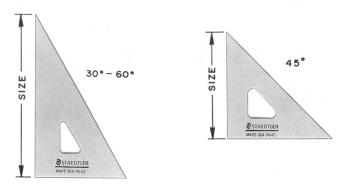

Figure 1-7. *Triangles used with the parallel straightedge to draw vertical lines and angles. (Courtesy Staedtler, Inc.)*

an object to be drawn larger, smaller, or the same size as the object to be drawn.

Scales may be flat or triangular in shape (Fig. 1-8) and may be fully divided or open divided. *Open-divided scales* have a unit on the end that represents one foot divided into inches and fractions of an inch or millimeters. The remainder of the scale is marked in feet only. *Fully divided scales* are marked in feet and inches or millimeters their entire length. Metric scales are usually fully divided (Fig. 1-9).

Drafters have to use several types of scales. These include the architect's scale, mechanical drafter's scale, engineer's chain scale, and metric scale. Notice in Fig. 1-9 they each have different types of subdivisions. Architectural drafters use the architect's scale, engineer's chain scale and the metric scale.

The *architect's scale* is used most frequently. It is used when laying out architectural working drawings in feet and inches. Each major division on the scale represents 1 ft. Subdivisions on the foot represent inches and fractions of an inch. For example, a major subdivision is divided into units each representing 1 in. The in. division can be divided into 1/2 or 1/4 in. units. The fineness of the subdivisions available depends upon the size of the major unit.

Architectural scales used are indicated as 3/32, 1/8, 3/16, 1/4, 3/8, 1/2, 3/4, 1, 1 1/2, and 3. Each of these lengths represent one foot on the scale. For example, on the 1/2 scale, 1/2 in. on the scale represents 1 ft.

When reading the architect's scale, begin at the 0 point. Count off the number of feet along the length of the scale using major subdivisions. Then count off the inches using the fully divided scale on the other side of the 0 point as shown in Fig. 1-10.

The *engineer's chain scale* is also called the civil engineer's scale. It has the inches along its edge divided into decimal parts of an inch (Fig. 1-11). These divisions are 10, 20, 30, 40, 50, and 60 parts to an inch. The 40 scale has subdivisions which equal 1/40 of an inch. It is used by architects and engineers when drawing site plans and maps. If a site plan is drawn to the scale 1″ = 40′-0″ the 40 scale will be used. Each of the 40 subdivisions represents one foot on the drawing. It can also be used to represent large units such as 400 or 4000 ft./in. (Fig. 1-12).

Metric scales are used when making architectural drawings in metric units. Architectural working drawings use only millimeters. Therefore, this is the basic unit of the scale. Metric scales are based on a ratio such as 1:50. This means 1 mm on the scale represents 50 mm on the object. Metric scales used on architectural drawing that reduce the size of the drawing are 1:10, 1:25, 1:50, 1:100, 1:200, and 1:500. Scales that enlarge a drawing are 2:1 and 5:1 (Fig. 1-13). There is a 1:3 scale available but it has not found wide use in the United States. It is used in other countries.

Metric scales may contain one or two ratios on one edge. In Fig. 1-14 the scales indicated are 1:1 and 1:100. When buying metric scales the drafter must decide which ratios will be most likely to be used. Scales are available in 150 and 300 mm lengths.

Single-ratio metric scales can be used to lay out other related ratios even though they are not marked on the scale. The metric system uses the base 10 and this makes it possible to use single-ratio scales for other ratios. For example, when using the 1:1 scale the 1-mm marking could be used to represent 1 mm, 10 mm, 100 mm, or 1000 mm. In Fig. 1-14 the indicated 100-mm distance could be used to represent 1000 mm or 10 000 mm. The 1:2 scale could be used to allow 1 mm to represent 20 mm, 200 mm, and so forth (Fig. 1-15). The metric scales used for various parts of architectural drawings are in Fig. 1-16.

Templates

Templates are available for many types of architectural drawings. They are used to draw various symbols, letter-

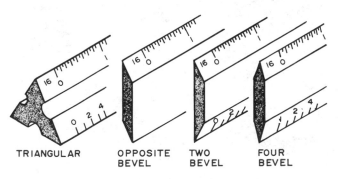

TRIANGULAR **OPPOSITE BEVEL** **TWO BEVEL** **FOUR BEVEL**

Figure 1-8. *Shapes of drafting scales.*

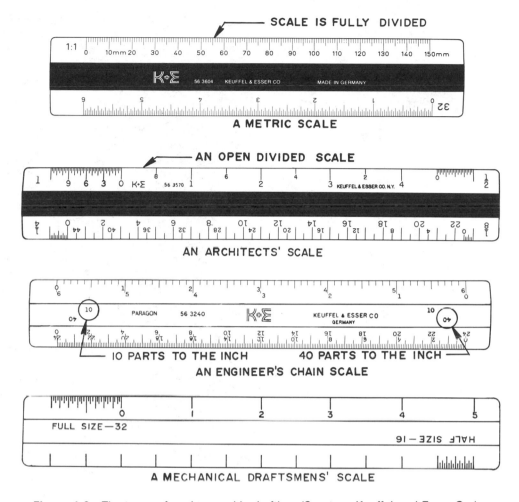

SCALE IS FULLY DIVIDED

A METRIC SCALE

AN OPEN DIVIDED SCALE

AN ARCHITECTS' SCALE

10 PARTS TO THE INCH   40 PARTS TO THE INCH

AN ENGINEER'S CHAIN SCALE

FULL SIZE—32

HALF SIZE—16

A MECHANICAL DRAFTSMENS' SCALE

Figure 1-9. *The types of scales used in drafting. (Courtesy Keuffel and Esser Co.)*

ing, and geometric shapes. For example, they are used to draw electrical symbols, plumbing symbols, doors and windows, circles, squares, and hundreds of other features. They speed up the manual drafting process and produce accurate drawings. A typical template used when drawing floor plans is in Fig. 1-17.

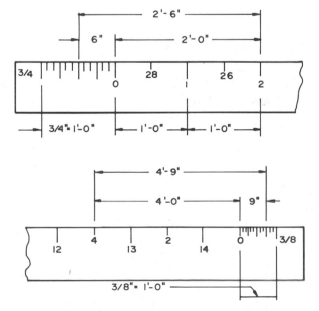

Figure 1-10. *How to read an architect's scale.*

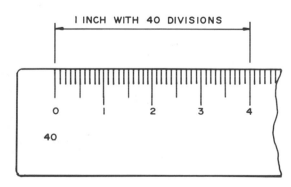

1 INCH WITH 40 DIVISIONS

Figure 1-11. *How to read an engineer's chain scale.*

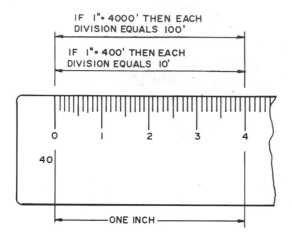

Figure 1-12. *The divisions on the engineers scale can be used to represent various distances.*

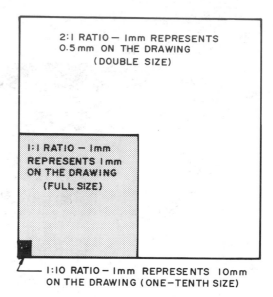

Figure 1-13. *Metric scale ratios are used to enlarge and reduce drawings.*

Instrument Sets

Sets of drawing instruments vary from small sets containing basic tools to larger sets having a wider variety of tools and several sizes of some. Typical sets contain a divider, compass, bow compass, small beam compass and a variety of points for pencil and ink drawing (Fig. 1-18). The compasses are used to draw circles and have a pin on one leg and a lead holder on the other. Compasses may be a friction or center wheel type.

The divider has a pin in both legs and is usually a friction type. It is used to transfer distances from one part of a drawing to another and for stepping off equal distances (Fig. 1-19).

Irregular Curves

Irregular curves are thin plastic tools used to draw irregular curved lines (Fig. 1-20). The line called an irregular curve is one that does not have a constant radius. It is often called a noncircular curve because it does not have a center.

Irregular curve tools are sold singly or in sets. There are many special use sets of curves such as those used in mechanical engineering. There are also flexible tapes which can be bent to fit an irregular curved surface and held in place as the line is drawn.

Drawing Pencils

The three types of pencils available include the wood-cased pencil, a fine line pencil, and a mechanical pencil. The fine line pencil is most widely used (Fig. 1-21).

Wood-cased pencils have the lead inside a wood shell. The wood is cut away to expose the lead. The mechanical lead holder uses large diameter leads the same size as those in wood-cased pencils. The lead is inserted in the

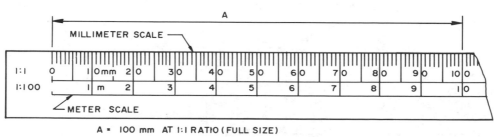

Figure 1-14. *A metric scale can be used to measure in several different ratios.*

Metric Scale Ratio	Meaning	Other Applications
1:1	1 mm = 1 mm (full size)	1 mm = 10 mm, 100 mm, 1000 mm
1:2	1 mm = 2 mm (half size)	1 mm = 20 mm, 200 mm, 2000 mm
1:3	1 mm = 3 mm (one-third size)	1 mm = 30 mm, 300 mm, 3000 mm
1:5	1 mm = 5 mm (one-fifth size)	1 mm = 50 mm, 500 mm, 5000 mm
1:10	1 mm = 10 mm (one-tenth size)	1 mm = 100 mm, 1000 mm, 10 000 mm
2:1	2 mm = 1 mm (double size)	
5:1	5 mm = 1 mm (enlarged 5 times)	

Figure 1-15. The meaning and applications of basic metric scales.

	Residential Drawings	Commercial Drawings
Floor plan	1:50	1:100
Foundation plan	1:50	1:100
Elevations	1:50	1:100
Construction details	1:20 and 1:10	1:20 or 1:110
Wall sections	1:20 and 1:10	1:25
Cabinet details	1:50 and 1:25	1:50 and 1:25
Site plan	1:100	1:100, 1:200, 1:500

Figure 1-16. Metric scales used for architectural drawings.

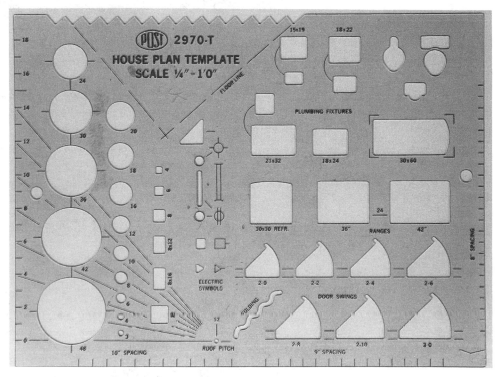

Figure 1-17. This template is used to draw various symbols on architectural floor plans.

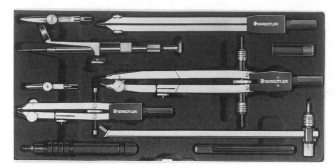

Figure 1-18. *A set of drafting instruments. (Courtesy Staedtler, Inc.)*

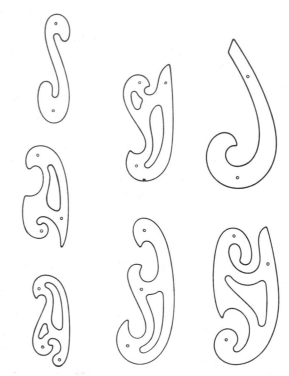

Figure 1-20. *A few of the many forms of irregular curves. (Courtesy Staedtler, Inc.)*

body of the pencil. Wood-cased and mechanical pencils require the lead be pointed with some type of lead pointer.

The fine-line lead holder uses leads that have very small diameters. The lead diameters available are 0.3, 0.5, 0.7, and 0.9 mm. Fine line pencils do not have to have the lead pointed. The diameter of the lead produces the desired line width. The leads are inserted in the holder and pushed out the tip by pressing a button on the end of the pencil.

The leads used on drafting vellum and tracing paper are graphite. The softer the lead the larger is its diameter. Graphite leads are specified from 9H, very hard, to 6B, very soft (Fig. 1-22). Most drafters use H and 2H leads for finished drawings. F and HB leads are used for sketching. B grade leads are used for pencil renderings and shading. 3H and 4H leads are used for light, preliminary layout work.

If drawing on plastic drafting film with pencils, special leads designed for that purpose are required. They bond well to the plastic and are water-resistant. A special vinyl eraser is used to remove them. These leads are available in five degrees of hardness, E1, soft, E2, medium, E3, hard, E4, extra hard, and E5, super hard.

Figure 1-21. *The types of pencils used in architectural drafting. (Courtesy Staedtler, Inc.)*

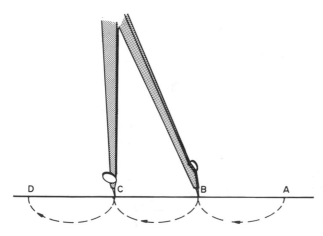

Figure 1-19. *Using a divider to step off equal distances.*

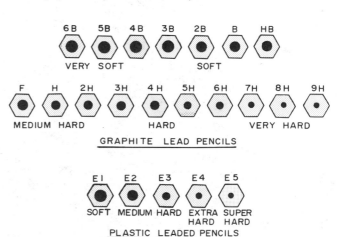

Figure 1-22. *The grades of graphite and plastic leaded pencils.*

Sharpening Drafting Pencils

Wood-cased pencils have the wood pointed with a draftsmen's pencil sharpener. It points the wood but does not touch the lead (Fig. 1-23). The lead is pointed with a lead pointer as shown in Fig. 1-24. This forms a conical point. For some jobs a wedge point might be used. It is formed by rubbing the lead on sandpaper (Fig. 1-25). When using sandpaper work over a wastebasket. If the carbon gets on the drawing or your hands it will dirty the drawing.

Ink

Ink drawings are made using a waterproof drawing ink. If inking on vellum a different ink is used than when inking on plastic drafting film. Vendors have a variety of products available. Inks are available in several colors.

One advantage to ink drawings, especially on plastic drafting film, is that they last for many years, do not smudge, and produce excellent reproductions.

Drawings are inked using a technical fountain pen (Fig. 1-26). There are a variety of point diameters as shown in

WOOD CUT AWAY — **LEAD NOT SHAPED**

Figure 1-23. Wood-cased pencils are sharpened by first cutting away only the wood.

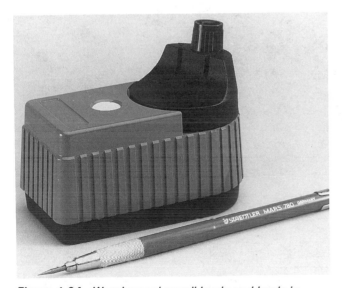

Figure 1-24. Wood-cased pencil leads and leads in mechanical lead holders are pointed in a lead pointer. (Courtesy Staedtler, Inc.)

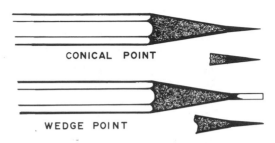

CONICAL POINT

WEDGE POINT

Figure 1-25. Two ways to point drafting pencil leads.

Fig. 1-27. These sizes correspond to ANSI line-width designations and are coordinated with metric sizes.

Erasers

Various types of erasers are available. Generally the softer rubber erasers are used on drafting vellum and vinyl erasers on plastic drafting film. There are several erasers designed to remove ink including one that has a solvent incorporated into the eraser.

Erasers are available in stick and block form (Fig. 1-28). Electric erasers are available and use long round lengths of eraser material that are rotated by the machine (Fig. 1-29).

Protractors

Protractors are available in metal and plastic and may be circular (360°) (Fig. 1-30) or a half circle (180°). They are used to lay out angles or measure angles on a drawing.

Computers

The computer is finding increasing use in architectural design and drawing (Fig. 1-31). The computer program permits the designer to develop a solution on the screen of the monitor and has the capacity to let the designer enter changes easily and rapidly. It is becoming a major tool in architectural design and drafting. More information on computer use can be found in Chapters 4 and 5.

Figure 1-26. A technical fountain pen. (Courtesy Staedtler, Inc.)

.13/5x0 .18/4x0 .25/3x0 .30/00 .35/0 .45/1 .50/2 .70/2½ .80/3 1.0/3½ 1.2/4 1.4/5 2.0/6

● IS O LINE WIDTHS
LINE WIDTHS CODE: .13/5XO MEANS LINE WIDTH
IS .13 mm OR AMERICAN STANDARD SIZE OOOOO.
METRIC WIDTHS FROM .13 TO 2.0 mm
AMERICAN STANDARD WIDTHS FROM OOOOOO TO 6.

Figure 1-27. Standard widths of ink lines used on architectural drawings. (Courtesy Staedtler, Inc.)

Drafting Papers, Film, and Grids

Architectural drawings can be produced on paper, film, or cloth.

Papers

The variety of drafting papers available provides a range of qualities such as cost, stability, translucency, permanence, and strength. The two major types are opaque and translucent papers. Opaque papers are thick and available in white, cream, and green colors. They are not suitable for working drawings because most reproduction machines cannot produce duplicate copies from them. Some are smooth on one side and rough on the other. The smooth side is for inking and the rough side for pencil drawings. Papers are sold in standard sheet sizes.

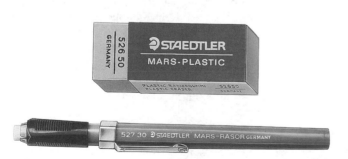

Figure 1-28. Block and stick erasers. (Courtesy Staedtler, Inc.)

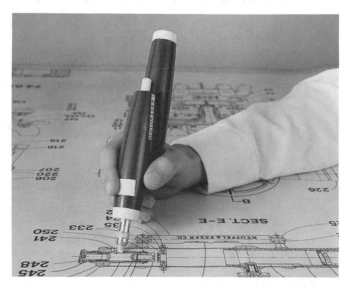

Figure 1-29. A cordless electric eraser. (Courtesy Keuffel and Esser Co.)

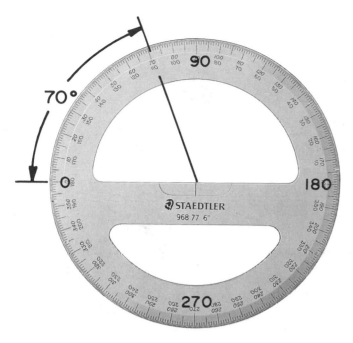

Figure 1-30. *This is a 360° protractor. Some contain only 180°. (Courtesy Staedtler, Inc.)*

Translucent papers are used for drawings that must be reproduced. They are of two major types: natural tracing paper and vellum.

Natural tracing paper is an untreated, translucent paper that is fairly strong and durable but not as transparent as vellums.

Vellum tracing papers are treated to improve their strength and transparency. They have a high rag content

Figure 1-31. *Computer-aided drafting is being used by many architectural drafters. (Courtesy Hewlett-Packard Company)*

giving good strength and can withstand erasing. Vellum can be used for either ink or pencil drawings. Tracing papers are sold in standard sheet sizes and in rolls.

Cloths

Tracing cloth is treated so it has a degree of translucency. There are different qualities. Some types work best for pencil drawings while others are excellent for ink. They are strong and durable but are being replaced by plastic drafting film.

Films

Plastic drafting film is a polyester material that is tough and translucent. It is sold in thicknesses such as 0.002, 0.003, 0.004, 0.005 and 0.0075 in. and in 0.05, 0.08, 0.10, 0.14, and 0.19 mm. The sheets may be single or double matt which means they may be frosted on one or both sides. The drawings are made on the frosted side.

Plastic drafting film is used for pencil and ink drawings. Special pencils are used and a special ink is available. It is sold in standard sheet sizes and in rolls.

Drafting Sheet Sizes

The standard sheet sizes of vellum and plastic drafting film are in Fig. 1-32. The inch sizes are identified by letters A through E. The metric sizes are identified by the letter A and a number. The metric sizes are very close to the inch sizes. Notice that the inch paper sizes for architectural drawing are larger than those for mechanical drawing.

Technical Vocabulary

Following are some important technical terms used in this chapter. Write a brief definition for each.

Parallel straightedge
Drafting machine
Open-divided scale
Fully divided scale
Architect's scale
Engineer's chain scale
Metric scale
Template
Drafting vellum
Drafting film

Type	Mechanical Drawing Sizes (in.)	Architectural Drawing Sizes (in.)	Type	Metric Sizes (mm)
A	$8\frac{1}{2} \times 11$	9×12	A4	210×297
B	11×17	12×18	A3	297×420
C	17×22	18×24	A2	420×594
D	22×34	24×36	A1	594×841
E	34×44	36×48	A0	841×1189

Figure 1-32. Standard drafting sheet sizes.

Study Questions

Answer the following study questions without referring to the text. Then check your answers with the text and correct those that were wrong.

1. Explain how the two types of drafting machines work.

2. What tools does the drafting machine replace?

3. What are the types of scales used in architectural drafting?

4. List the scales found on a metric scale.

5. What divisions are used on the engineers chain scale?

6. List the scales found on the architect's scale.

7. What is the term used to describe a noncircular curve?

8. List the degrees of hardness of drafting leads for use on vellum.

9. For what purpose does the architect use a protractor?

10. What type of paper is generally used for architectural drawings?

11. What is the difference between single matte and double matte polyester drafting film sheets?

12. List the sizes of sheets of drafting vellum and the letter identifying that size.

2

Technical Sketching

Technical sketching is used extensively as solutions are sought to all aspects of architectural projects. These projects can range from attempts to find the best use of space to decisions on construction details. Good sketching skills are essential for architectural designers, drafters, and builders.

The same principles apply for preparing good technical sketches as for preparing finished drawings. They are neatly prepared, kept in proportion but not necessarily to scale, and while the lines are a little irregular, they are of a respectable quality. Curves should be reasonably smooth and circles fairly round. The lines should be dark and the proper widths and symbols should be used. All of the principles of good manual drafting should be observed. Manual drafting techniques are discussed in Chapter 3.

Tools

The basic tools are soft lead pencils, a soft rubber eraser, and paper. Architectural sketches are generally made on a low-cost tracing paper called canary because of its light yellow color. Low-cost standard tracing paper is also used. Other implements, such as a ball point or felt tip pen, can be used, but pencils produce the most professional sketch.

Any soft pencil will do. A B or HB drafting pencil is excellent. A conical point produces the best line. As you sketch, rotate the pencil in your fingers to keep it round (Fig. 2-1). Do not make the point too sharp because it will break. A rounded point is better. If the pencil is too pointed, dull the lead by rubbing it on scrap paper. While any paper will do for sketching, drafting vellum or canary

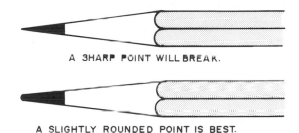

A SHARP POINT WILL BREAK.

A SLIGHTLY ROUNDED POINT IS BEST.

Figure 2-1. Use a slightly rounded point on the pencil.

tracing paper are best. They have a hard surface and erase easily. The sketch can be reproduced on a whiteprinter is necessary.

The eraser is used sparingly when sketching. Ideally, the sketch is developed quickly without the need to erase. Errors or changes can be corrected easily with an eraser if vellum or canary paper is used.

Sketching Techniques

The architect and engineer develop many of their original design solutions by sketching. This permits them to quickly make several variations of the possible design (Fig. 2-2). The sketch selected is used as the basis for producing the finished drawing.

The final sketch should be laid out using light construction lines and when completed the lines are drawn dark and to the proper thickness. The corners are usually crossed a little. Never leave a gap between intersecting lines on a sketch.

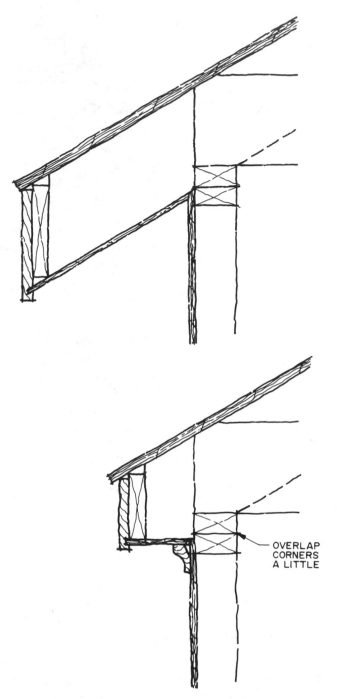

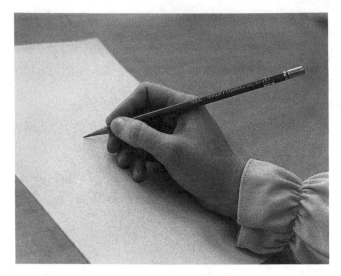

Figure 2-3. When sketching hold the pencil in a comfortable position, not too close to the point. (William P. Spence, Engineering Graphics, 2e, © 1988, Reprinted by permission of Prentice Hall, Englewood Cliffs, New Jersey.)

OVERLAP CORNERS A LITTLE

Figure 2-2. These cornice details were worked out quickly by sketching.

Holding the Pencil

The pencil should be held $1\frac{1}{2}$ to 2 in. from the end and in a comfortable, natural position. The hand should rest lightly on the paper and slide across as lines are drawn. Rotate the pencil to keep the point conical (Fig. 2-3).

Line Quality

The original layout will be made with light lines. The finished sketch will have dark lines of the proper thickness. Make the visible lines about twice as wide as dimension, hidden, and extension lines. Use the standard alphabet of lines as are used on the finished drawing (Fig. 2-4).

Sketching Straight Lines

Straight lines on a sketch should be relatively straight but will have minor irregularities. They must run directly from

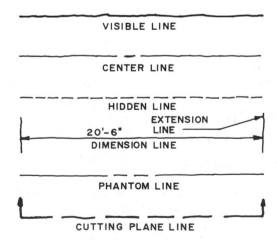

Figure 2-4. Thickness and symbols used on sketches.

Figure 2-5. *Using graph paper when sketching helps keep lines straight and aids in keeping the drawing in proportion. (William P. Spence, Engineering Graphics, 2e, © 1988, Reprinted by permission of Prentice Hall, Englewood Cliffs, New Jersey.)*

Figure 2-6. *Sketching horizontal lines from left to right. (William P. Spence, Engineering Graphics, 2e, © 1988, Reprinted by permission of Prentice Hall, Englewood Cliffs, New Jersey.)*

their starting point to their end point. Some prefer to place the sketching vellum over a sheet of graph paper and use the printed lines as a guide. Proportions can be maintained by counting the squares (Fig. 2-5).

Sketching Horizontal Lines

There are two methods for sketching horizontal lines. One involves locating the end points of the line. Sketch from left to right looking toward the right point as you make the line. Left-handed persons may find it easier to sketch from right to left. Move your hand and arm in a single smooth stroke (Fig. 2-6). You can practice by passing the pencil from one point to the other keeping the point slightly above the paper. After several tries lower the pencil and draw the line.

Another way some use is to sketch a series of short lines using short pencil strokes. The hand is moved from left to right but in a series of short strokes rather than one continuous movement. This produces a more irregular line.

It is necessary to move the hand and arm as you sketch otherwise a crowned line will be drawn.

Short lines can be sketched with only the movement of the fingers and wrist.

Sketching Vertical Lines

Most people can sketch vertical lines best by moving from a top point to a bottom point using the same technique as for horizontal lines (Fig. 2-7).

Any straight line can be sketched by using the edge of the sketch pad as a guide. Hold the pencil with the tip at the location of the line. Place several fingers on the edge of the pad and slide them along toward your body as shown in Fig. 2-8. This can also be used to draw parallel lines.

Sketching Inclined Lines

Techniques for sketching inclined lines are shown in Fig. 2-9. The same procedures are used as described for horizontal lines. Some prefer to slant the paper and sketch the slanted lines facing them in a horizontal position.

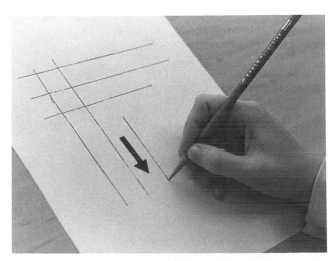

Figure 2-7. *Sketch vertical lines toward you.*

Figure 2-8. *A finger sliding along the edge of the sketch pad can be used as a guide when sketching straight lines. (William P. Spence, Engineering Graphics, 2e, © 1988, Reprinted by permission of Prentice Hall, Englewood Cliffs, New Jersey.)*

Sketching Basic Geometric Shapes

Items to be drawn are made up of a variety of geometric forms, such as cylinders, cones, pyramids, and prisms (Fig. 2-10). When sketching an object notice how it is made up of these forms. This will help when sketching it be-

Figure 2-9. *How to sketch inclined lines. (William P. Spence, Engineering Graphics, 2e, © 1988, Reprinted by permission of Prentice Hall, Englewood Cliffs, New Jersey.)*

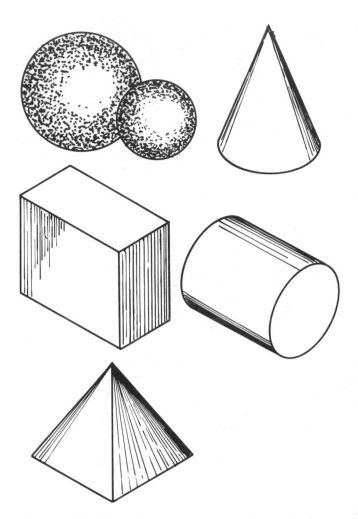

Figure 2-10. *The basic geometric shapes found in objects to be drawn. (William P. Spence, Engineering Graphics, 2e, © 1988, Reprinted by permission of Prentice Hall, Englewood Cliffs, New Jersey.)*

cause it can be broken up into the several forms involved (Fig. 2-11).

Sketching Squares and Rectangles

The easiest way to sketch a square or rectangle is to lay out the center lines and mark half the width and length on them. Then lightly sketch horizontal and vertical lines completing the shape. Darken the lines to finish the drawing (Fig. 2-12).

Sketching Circles and Arcs

Circles can be sketched using the center line or square technique. The center line technique involves sketching the center lines and several radial lines through the center. Mark the radius on a piece of paper and use it to mark

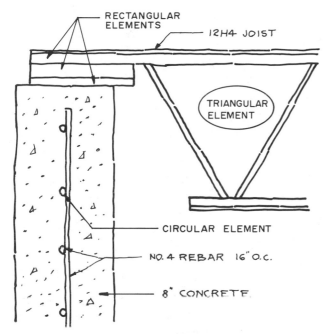

Figure 2-11. *Notice how this sketch is made up of several basic geometric shapes.*

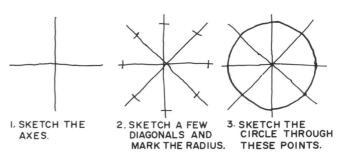

1. SKETCH THE AXES. 2. SKETCH A FEW DIAGONALS AND MARK THE RADIUS. 3. SKETCH THE CIRCLE THROUGH THESE POINTS.

Figure 2-13. *How to sketch a circle using the radius as a guide.*

the radius on each line. Then sketch the circle through these points (Fig. 2-13).

The square method involves lightly sketching a square with sides equal to the diameter of the circle. Sketch the center lines and a few diagonals. Mark the radius on the diagonal and sketch the circle through the points (Fig. 2-14).

Large-diameter circles can be sketched by laying out the center lines. Mark the radius on a piece of paper. Hold one end on the center and rotate the paper marking the

radius at several points around the center. Then sketch the circle through the points (Fig. 2-15).

Arcs can be sketched in the same manner as circles. A square could be laid out as described above. Locate points on the diagonals and sketch the needed arc through these points (Fig. 2-16).

Sketching Ellipses

Lay out the major and minor axes of the ellipse. Locate the ends of the ellipse on each other. Sketch a rectangle through these end points. Now sketch the end and side curves as shown in Fig. 2-17. Connect these curves with curved lines.

Proportion

Technical sketches are not drawn to scale but the various parts must be in proportion to each other. For example, the windows and doors on an elevation drawing must be

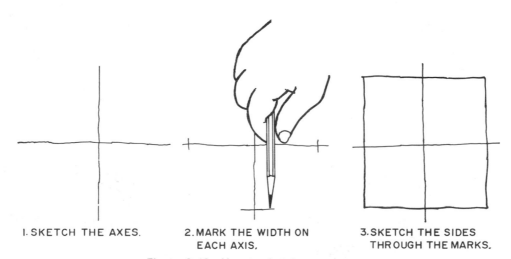

1. SKETCH THE AXES. 2. MARK THE WIDTH ON EACH AXIS. 3. SKETCH THE SIDES THROUGH THE MARKS.

Figure 2-12. *How to sketch a square.*

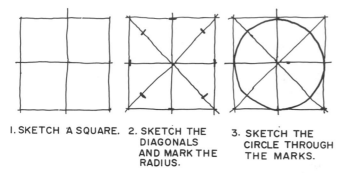

1. SKETCH A SQUARE. 2. SKETCH THE DIAGONALS AND MARK THE RADIUS. 3. SKETCH THE CIRCLE THROUGH THE MARKS.

Figure 2-14. *How to sketch a circle using a square with sides equal to the diameter.*

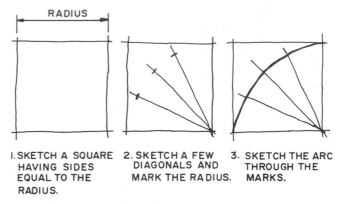

1. SKETCH A SQUARE HAVING SIDES EQUAL TO THE RADIUS. 2. SKETCH A FEW DIAGONALS AND MARK THE RADIUS. 3. SKETCH THE ARC THROUGH THE MARKS.

Figure 2-16. *Sketch an arc by locating radii.*

in proportion to each other and the overall size of the house exterior. Usually relationships are based on some ratio. A window 30 in. wide and 48 in. long has an approximate 2 to 3 proportion (Fig. 2-18).

One way to keep a drawing in proportion is to sketch a rectangle the overall size of the object. Then begin breaking it down into its major divisions. Then subdivide these into minor parts (Fig. 2-19).

If the sizes of an object are known they can be used in establishing proportions or the object can be measured. Graph paper is excellent for sketching an object of known size because the squares can be counted to help establish proportions (Fig. 2-20).

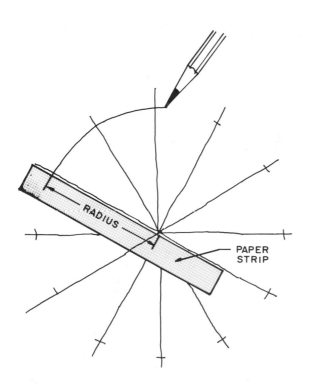

1. SKETCH AXES AND SEVERAL DIAGONALS.
2. MARK THE RADIUS ON A STRIP OF PAPER AND USE IT TO LOCATE THE RADIUS ON THE CENTERLINES AND DIAGONALS.
3. SKETCH A CIRCLE THROUGH THE MARKS.

Figure 2-15. *How to lay out and sketch a large-diameter circle.*

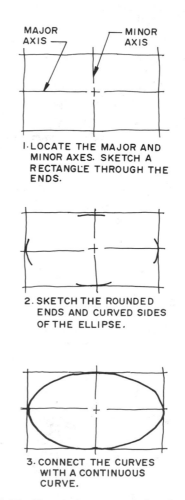

1. LOCATE THE MAJOR AND MINOR AXES. SKETCH A RECTANGLE THROUGH THE ENDS.

2. SKETCH THE ROUNDED ENDS AND CURVED SIDES OF THE ELLIPSE.

3. CONNECT THE CURVES WITH A CONTINUOUS CURVE.

Figure 2-17. *How to lay out and sketch an ellipse.*

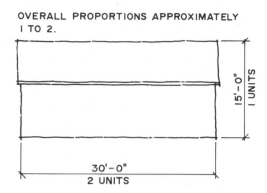

OVERALL PROPORTIONS APPROXIMATELY
I TO 2.

15'-0"
I UNITS

30'-0"
2 UNITS

Figure 2-18. Sketches must retain the basic proportions of the object.

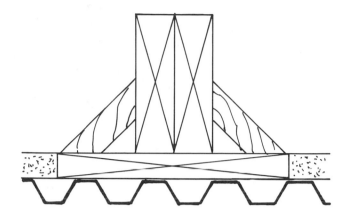

THIS SECTION DRAWING THROUGH AN AREA DIVIDER ON A BUILT-UP ROOF IS THE OBJECT TO BE SKETCHED.

Large objects can have sizes estimated for sketching purposes by using the pencil-and-eye procedure. Hold the pencil at arms length from your eye and line it up with the thing to be measured. Mark the sighted length on the pencil with your thumb. Transfer this distance to the sketch. Then sight and find another size until all needed measurements are taken (Fig. 2-21).

Angles are sketched by locating the ends and connecting them as shown in Fig. 2-22. Make an estimate as to how close it is to angles frequently used such as 30°, 45°, or 60°.

The size of the sketch depends upon the object and the detail required. In architecture few things can be sketched or drawn full size so establishing proportion is very important if the drawing is to be useful.

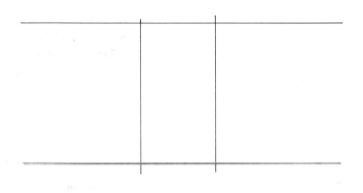

I. SKETCH A RECTANGLE GIVING THE OVERALL LENGTH AND WIDTH. BLOCK IN THE MAJOR ELEMENTS.

Pictorial Sketches

Pictorial sketches are an effective way to present technical information. They show several sides of the object and present it in a rather lifelike way. The most commonly used pictorials are isometric, oblique, and perspective. Perspective sketches are more lifelike.

Oblique Sketches

An oblique sketch is started by first sketching a normal front view. Then the depth is added by sketching parallel slanting receding lines for the sides. The receding lines are generally 45° with the horizontal, but other angles can be used. Oblique sketches are often used when a round component faces the front because it is drawn round rather than elliptical.

The steps to make an oblique sketch are in Fig. 2-23.

Circles in oblique drawings are sketched by first drawing a box with sides equal to the diameter of the circle. Then sketch the circle as shown in Fig. 2-24.

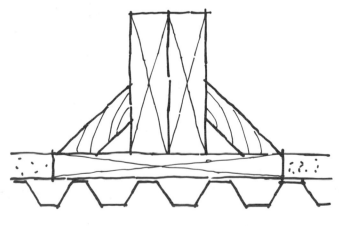

2. SUBDIVIDE MAJOR AREAS INTO SMALLER UNITS AND SKETCH DETAILS.

Figure 2-19. An example of breaking an object down into several parts and keeping these in proportion.

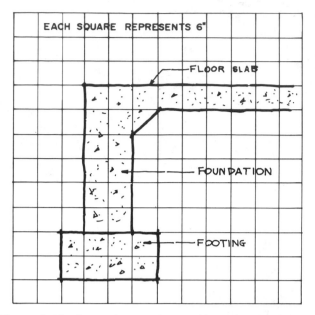

Figure 2-20. *Proportion can be established when using graph paper by counting the squares. If each square on this sketch equals 4 in. what are the sizes of the footing, foundation, and floor slab?*

Isometric Sketches

An isometric sketch is built around isometric axes which can take several positions (Fig. 2-25). The position chosen will influence what is shown on the drawing.

First sketch the isometric axes. You can measure or estimate distances along these lines. Sketch an isometric box the overall size of the object. Then begin locating edges that are parallel with the sides of the box. Edges that are on angles are drawn by first locating each end on an isometric line and connecting the two points. See the steps in Fig. 2-26.

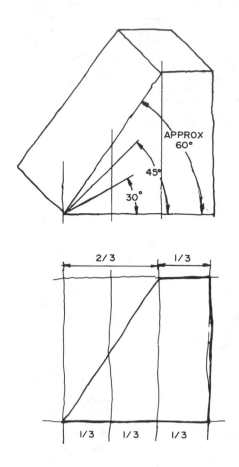

DRAW ANGLES BY LOCATING THEIR ENDS

Figure 2-22. *Angles can be sketched by locating the ends of the angles and connecting them or by estimating the angles.*

Circles in isometric are sketched by first sketching an isometric square with sides equal to the diameter of the circle. Then sketch the circles as shown in Fig. 2-27.

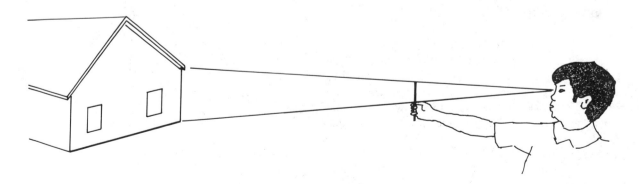

Figure 2-21. *Proportions can be approximated by sighting the object.*

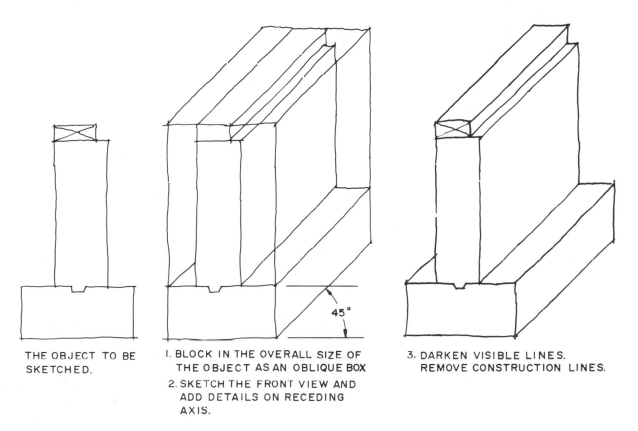

THE OBJECT TO BE
SKETCHED.

1. BLOCK IN THE OVERALL SIZE OF
   THE OBJECT AS AN OBLIQUE BOX

2. SKETCH THE FRONT VIEW AND
   ADD DETAILS ON RECEDING
   AXIS.

45°

3. DARKEN VISIBLE LINES.
   REMOVE CONSTRUCTION LINES.

Figure 2-23. *The steps to make an oblique sketch.*

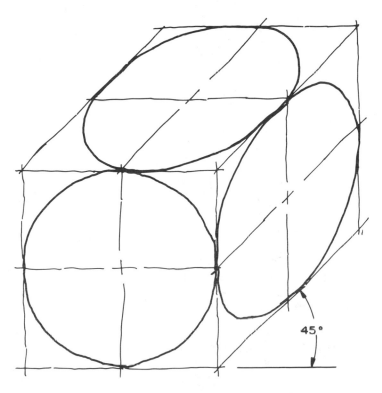

45°

Figure 2-24. *How to sketch an oblique circle.*

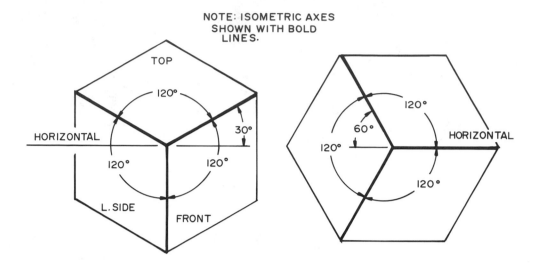

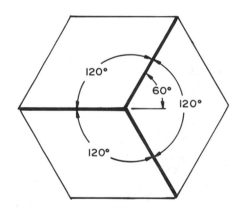

Figure 2-25. *Commonly used isometric axes.*

Perspective Sketches

Perspective sketches are more lifelike than oblique or isometric because they take into account the fact that as things move away from the viewer they get smaller. In perspective sketches, the receding lines converge to an imaginary spot on the horizon called a vanishing point.

The two commonly used types of perspectives are one point and two point. The view produced by both types is influenced by the location of the horizon. In Fig. 2-28 it shows how the location of the horizon changes the one-point perspective.

To draw a *one-point perspective* (Fig. 2-29):

1. Sketch the front surface of the object. Then decide where the horizon and vanishing point will be located. With experience you will learn to choose locations that give a desirable perspective.

2. Sketch the receding edges to the vanishing point.

3. Estimate the depth and mark it on the receding lines creating a box the overall size of the object.

4. Locate and sketch the details. Darken the visible lines and remove unneeded construction lines.

When drawing a two-point perspective the location of the horizon and vanishing points influences the sketch as shown in Fig. 2-30.

To draw a *two-point perspective* (Fig. 2-31):

1. Draw a vertical line representing the front corner of the object. Locate the horizon and vanishing points. One is to the right of the object and the other is to the left.

2. Locate the depth and width by estimation. The vertical front corner is the only true size line so the depth, width, and the size of details can be estimated. Each edge

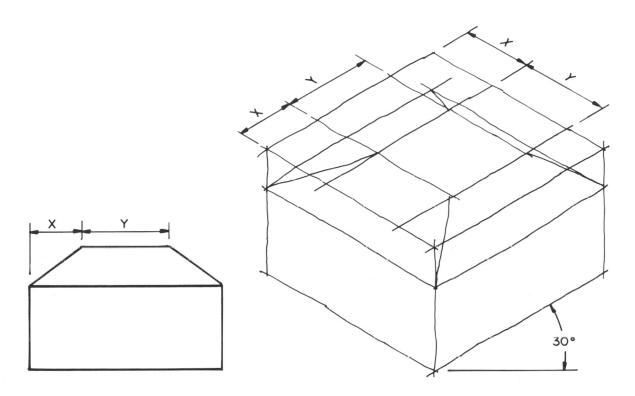

COLUMN FOOTING TO
BE SKETCHED.

1. SKETCH THE ISOMETRIC AXES AND DEVELOP
   AN ISOMETRIC BOX THE OVERALL SIZE OF
   THE OBJECT.
2. LOCATE DETAILS BY MEASURING ALONG
   LINES PARALLEL WITH ISOMETRIC AXES.

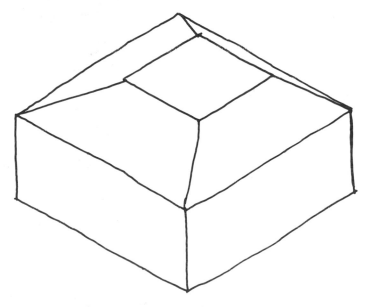

3. DARKEN THE VISIBLE LINES.
   REMOVE UNNEEDED LINES.

Figure 2-26. *The steps to make an isometric sketch.*

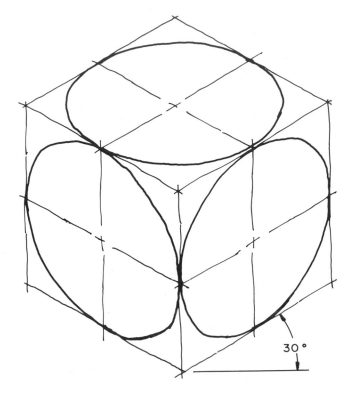

Figure 2-27. *How to sketch circles on isometric drawings.*

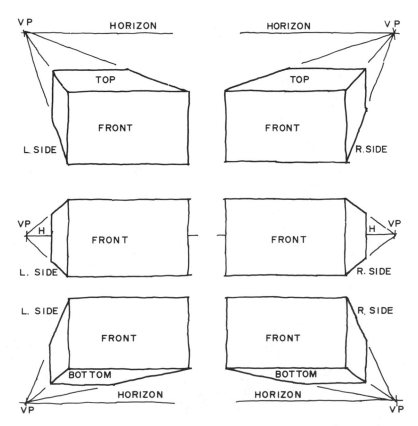

Figure 2-28. *The location of the horizon influences the appearance of one-point perspectives.*

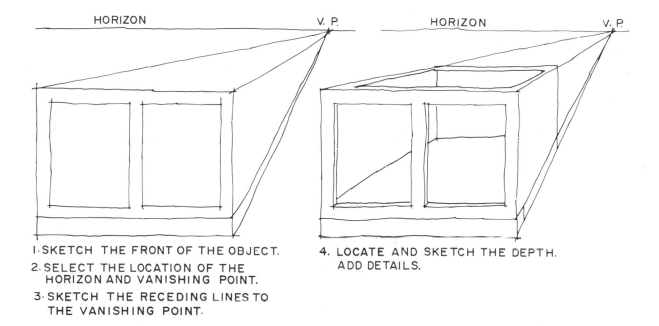

HORIZON   V. P.   HORIZON   V. P.

1. SKETCH THE FRONT OF THE OBJECT.

2. SELECT THE LOCATION OF THE HORIZON AND VANISHING POINT.

3. SKETCH THE RECEDING LINES TO THE VANISHING POINT.

4. LOCATE AND SKETCH THE DEPTH. ADD DETAILS.

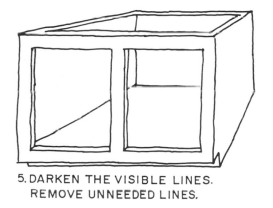

5. DARKEN THE VISIBLE LINES. REMOVE UNNEEDED LINES.

Figure 2-29. The steps to sketch a one-point perspective.

located is projected to a vanishing point. All edges parallel with the right side project to the right vanishing point. All edges parallel with the left side project to the left vanishing point.

3. After blocking in the details darken the visible line and remove unneeded construction lines.

Study Questions

Answer the following study questions without referring to the text. Then check your answers with the text and correct those that were wrong.

1. What type of paper is often used by the architect for preliminary sketches?

2. Explain how to hold the pencil for best results when sketching.

3. In which direction should right-handed people sketch horizontal lines? Left-handed people?

4. What is the best direction to sketch vertical lines?

5. Explain how to sketch circles.

6. What is meant by keeping a sketch in proportion?

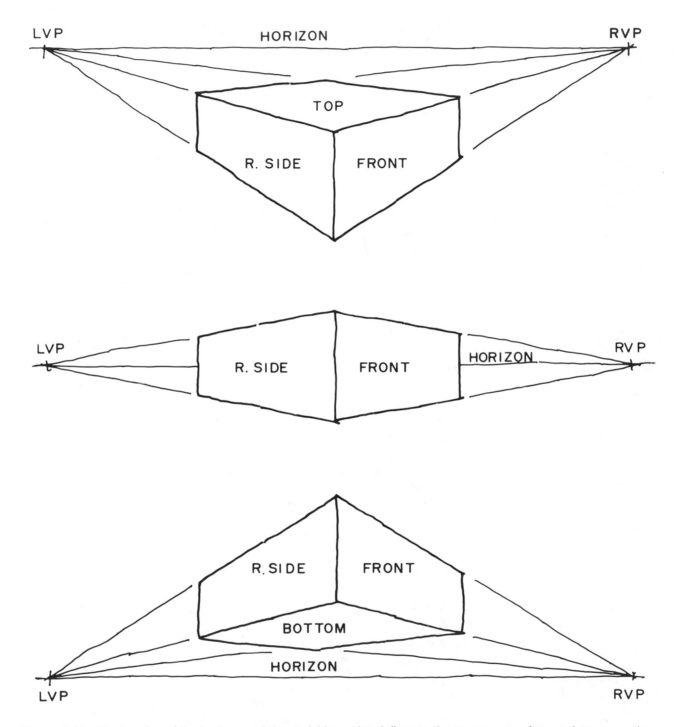

Figure 2-30. *The location of the horizon and the vanishing points influence the appearance of two-point perspectives.*

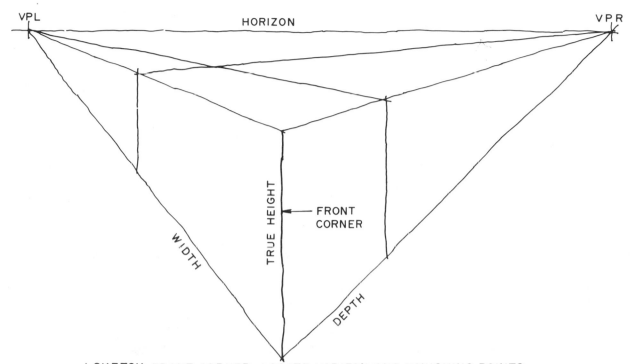

1. SKETCH FRONT CORNER. LOCATE HORIZON AND VANISHING POINTS.
2. PROJECT TOP AND BOTTOM EDGES TO VANISHING POINT. LOCATE OVERALL DEPTH AND WIDTH BOXING IN THE OBJECT.

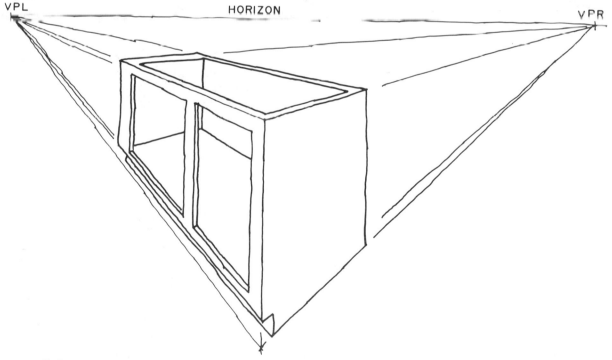

3. BLOCK IN THE DETAILS. DARKEN THE VISIBLE LINES.

Figure 2-31. *The steps to sketch a two-point perspective.*

SKETCH FOUR TIMES AS LARGE AS PRINTED.

Laboratory Problems

1. Divide a sheet of $8\frac{1}{2} \times 11$ in. graph paper into squares as shown in Fig. 2-32. Sketch the border of each square and the designs four times larger than printed.

2. Sketch architectural symbols as assigned by your instructor. These can be materials in section, electrical symbols, heating and air conditioning symbols, and others. These are listed in the appendix. Lay these out neatly on the sheet.

3. Try sketching Fig. 2-18 on vellum. Mark this A. Then sketch it again on vellum with a sheet of graph paper below. Mark this B. Which was easier?

4. Sketch the window and door in Fig. 6-3 four times as large as printed. Keep in proportion.

3

Drafting Techniques

Construction drawings are large and detailed and require a great deal of effort to draw. When finished they must be accurate, and have high quality lines, legible dimensions, and notes. Since time is money these drawings must be produced as rapidly as possible. The basic techniques in this chapter will assist in producing quality drawings.

Making Quality Lines

Proper line width and darkness are necessary to produce a quality drawing. The width varies with the symbol drawn. Architectural drawings use two line widths, thick and thin. Thick lines are 0.030 in. ($\frac{1}{32}$ in.) or about 0.8 mm wide. Thin lines are 0.015 in. ($\frac{1}{64}$ in.) or 0.4 mm wide. A rule of thumb is to make thick lines twice as wide as thin lines. Lines on pencil drawings tend to be made a bit thinner than those on ink drawings. All lines, thick and thin, must be as black and dense as possible so they will reproduce quality copies. Just because a line is thin does not mean it should be drawn light. Actually it is more important for thin lines to be dark.

Generally finished lines are drawn with an H or 2H grade pencil. Some prefer to use an F grade but it does smear more. The softer the lead the more that it will smear.

Many symbols are used on architectural drawings and they must be carefully drawn. Dashed lines must have the length of the dashes and the spaces between them the proper size. Dashes must be kept a uniform width. Commonly used line symbols are shown in Fig. 3-1.

Each finished line should be drawn to its proper length, width, and color in a single stroke. If this is not accomplished go over the line again, but be certain to keep the second try directly on top of the first line. As you try to increase the darkness remember to control the line width.

Mechanical and wood-cased pencils must be rotated as they are used so the point remains cone-shaped. If this is not done a flat spot develops and the line width increases (Fig. 3-2). Fine-line mechanical pencils have the diameter of the lead the width desired for the line, therefore they are not rotated.

Mechanical and wood-cased pencils have their lead pointed in a lead pointer. Do not get the lead to a needle point. If it is too sharp rub it on a piece of scrap paper until it has the right size tip. Thick lines require the lead be dulled more than for thin lines.

Hold the lead close to the edge of the straightedge or triangle. Hold the pencil about 1 in. (25 mm) from the tip and place the hand in a comfortable position. Keep the pencil at right angles to the paper and slant it back about 60° in the direction the line is to be drawn (Fig. 3-3). Fine-line mechanical pencils are held almost perpendicular to the paper (Fig. 3-4). If you slant this pencil the metal tip will cut the paper or the line width will be wider than the diameter of the lead.

If it is necessary to press down hard to get a dark line switch to a softer pencil. Heavy pressure produces grooves in the paper that will remain if the lines are erased.

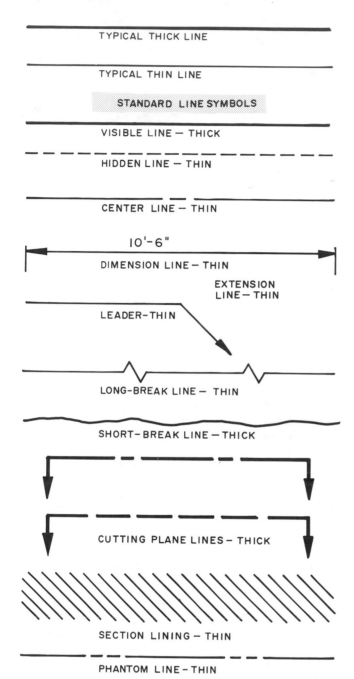

Figure 3-1. *Standard line symbols and their recommended widths.*

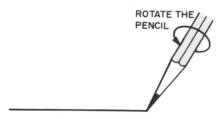

Figure 3-2. *When drawing lines with a wood-cased or mechanical pencil, rotate the pencil to get a uniform line width.*

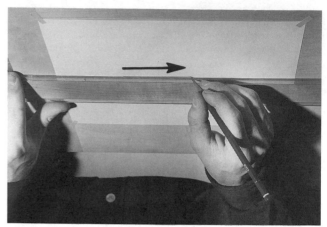

Figure 3-3. *Slant wood-cased and mechanical pencils 60° to the surface of the paper.*

Drawing Lines

The lines used on drawings include horizontal, vertical, inclined, regular curves, and irregular curves.

Drawing Straight Lines

Horizontal lines are drawn using the top edge of the parallel straightedge or the top edge of the horizontal scale on the drafting machine. Right-handed persons should draw horizontal lines from left to right while left-handed persons go from right to left (Fig. 3-5). Remember to slant the mechanical or wood-cased pencil 60° in the direction the line will be drawn. Keep the fine-line automatic pencil perpendicular to the paper.

In Fig. 3-6 it shows how to draw a horizontal line using the top edge of the horizontal scale. Notice the head is held in the left hand.

Drawing Vertical Lines

Vertical lines can be drawn using triangles resting on the top edge of the parallel straightedge or the vertical scale

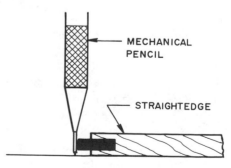

Figure 3-4. *Fine-line pencils are held perpendicular to the paper.*

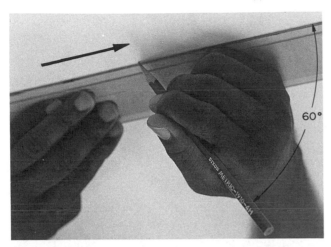

Figure 3-5. *Right-handed persons draw horizontal lines left to right. (William P. Spence, Engineering Graphics, 2e, © 1988, Reprinted by permission of Prentice Hall, Englewood Cliffs, New Jersey.)*

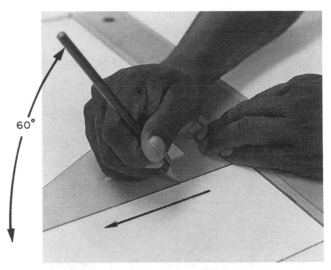

Figure 3-7. *Right-handed people draw vertical lines from bottom to top. (William P. Spence, Engineering Graphics, 2e, © 1988, Reprinted by permission of Prentice Hall, Englewood Cliffs, New Jersey.)*

on the drafting machine. Right-handed people find it easier to draw from the bottom to the top (Fig. 3-7). Left-handed people prefer to draw from the top to the bottom. Slant the pencil 60° in the direction the line will be drawn unless you are using a fine-line mechanical pencil.

In Fig. 3-8 it shows how to draw a vertical line using a drafting machine.

Drawing Inclined Lines

Inclined lines can be drawn using triangles or by rotating the scales on the drafting machine. It is easiest to draw lines sloping down to the right in the downhill direction.

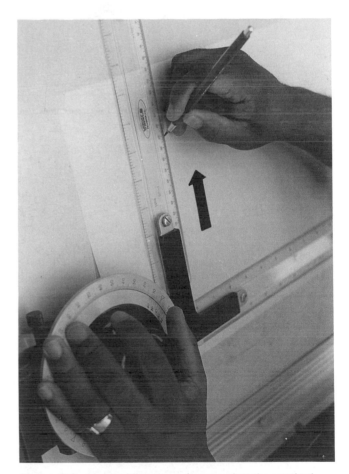

Figure 3-8. *Vertical lines are drawn using the vertical scale on the drafting machine. (William P. Spence, Engineering Graphics, 2e, © 1988. Reprinted by permission of Prentice Hall, Englewood Cliffs, New Jersey.)*

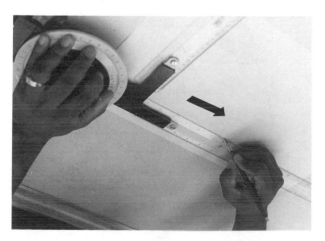

Figure 3-6. *When using a drafting machine horizontal lines are drawn along the edge of the horizontal scale. (William P. Spence, Engineering Graphics, 2e, © 1988, Reprinted by permission of Prentice Hall, Englewood Cliffs, New Jersey.)*

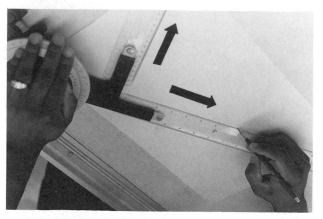

Figure 3-10. *To draw inclined lines with a drafting machine, rotate the head so the scales are on the desired angle. (William P. Spence, Engineering Graphics, 2e, © 1988. Reprinted by permission of Prentice Hall, Englewood Cliffs, New Jersey.)*

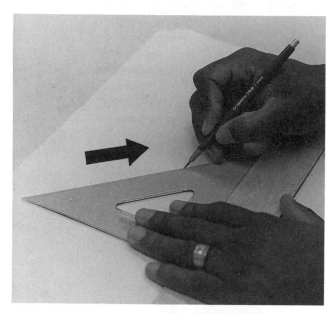

Figure 3-9. *How to draw inclined lines. (William P. Spence, Engineering Graphics, 2e, © 1988. Reprinted by permission of Prentice-Hall, Englewood Cliffs, New Jersey.)*

Lines sloping to the left should be drawn uphill (Fig. 3-9). The same directions are used when using a drafting machine (Fig. 3-10).

Drawing Angles

The size of angles can be laid out with triangles, a protractor, or the vernier scale on the head of the drafting machine. Triangles can be placed together in various ways to produce some angles (Fig. 3-11). Angles are laid out

with a drafting machine by unlocking the head and rotating it until the angle desired is indicated on the scale. Then lock the head and draw the angle. This is the same technique as drawing inclined lines.

The protractor in Fig. 3-12 is marked in degrees. To lay out an angle place the center point on the tool on the point from which the angle will be measured. Read the angle on the scale and mark it on the paper. Draw a line connecting these two points.

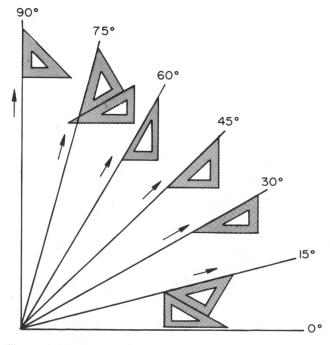

Figure 3-11. *How to draw commonly used angles by combing the triangles.*

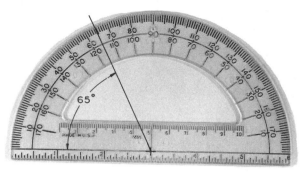

Figure 3-12. *Degrees are laid out using a protractor.*

Drawing Lines Perpendicular to Each Other

Lines perpendicular to horizontal lines can be drawn using a triangle on a parallel straightedge (Fig. 3-13) or the vertical scale on a drafting machine (Fig. 3-14).

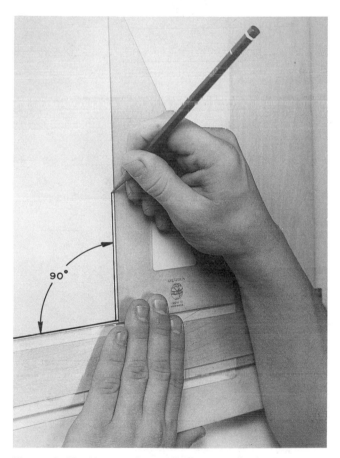

Figure 3-13. *How to draw a line perpendicular to a horizontal line with a triangle and parallel straightedge. (William P. Spence, Engineering Graphics, 2e, © 1988. Reprinted by permission of Prentice Hall, Englewood Cliffs, New Jersey.)*

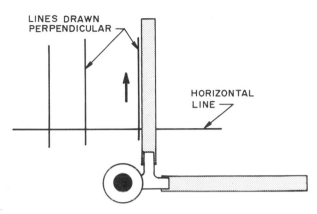

Figure 3-14. *Drawing perpendicular lines with a drafting machine.*

Perpendiculars to inclined lines can be drawn by placing a triangle along the line and another triangle on the edge of the first triangle as shown in Fig. 3-15. Using a drafting machine requires that the horizontal scale be placed parallel with the inclined line and locked in position. Then move the head until the vertical scale crosses the inclined line at the place desired. Draw the line as shown in Fig. 3-16.

Drawing Parallel Lines

Using triangles first place a triangle with one edge on the line. Place another triangle or straightedge below the first triangle. Slide the first triangle along the straightedge until it reaches the location for the parallel line. Draw the line as shown in Fig. 3-17.

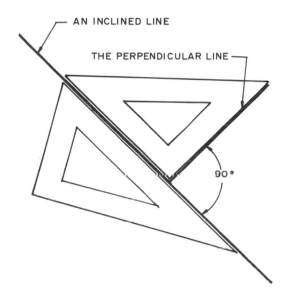

Figure 3-15. *A perpendicular can be drawn to an inclined line using two triangles.*

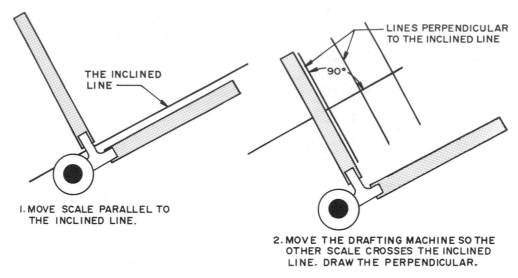

Figure 3-16. *Drawing a line perpendicular to an inclined line using a drafting machine.*

Using a drafting machine begin by rotating the head until one scale is parallel with the line and lock the head. Wherever you move the head this scale will be parallel with the original line (Fig. 3-18).

Drawing Curves

The two types of curves used are regular and irregular. Regular curves have a center point and all points on the curve are the same distance from this point. Irregular curves are noncircular and have no center or fixed radius.

Regular curves are drawn with a compass or circle template and irregular curves are drawn with tools called irregular curves.

Using a Compass

Set the compass to the desired radius. The best way to do this is to mark the radius on a piece of paper and adjust the compass to that measurement.

Draw the circle by placing the leg of the compass with

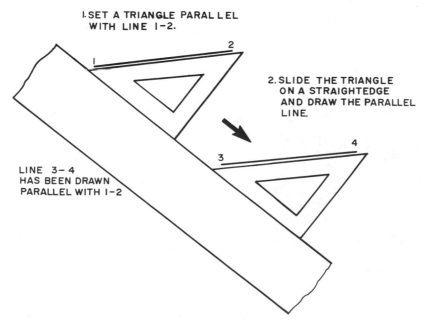

Figure 3-17. *Drawing parallel lines with triangles and a straightedge.*

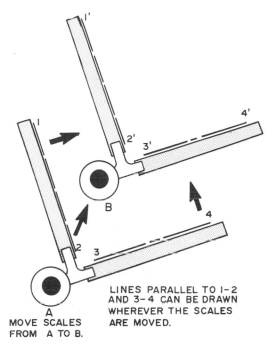

Figure 3-18. Drawing parallel lines with a drafting machine.

FIRST SAND LEAD ON A BEVEL.   NEXT SAND ON EACH SIDE.   FINALLY ADJUST LEAD A LITTLE SHORTER THAN THE PIN.

Figure 3-20. *How to sharpen a compass lead. (William P. Spence, Engineering Graphics, 2e, © 1988. Reprinted by permission of Prentice Hall, Englewood Cliffs, New Jersey.)*

a pin on the center point. Push it firm enough to hold but try to not produce a hole in the paper. Hold the compass at the top, lean it a little in the direction the circle will be drawn, and rotate it. Most find it easier to rotate clockwise. Press hard enough to get the desired dark line and if necessary insert a softer lead (Fig. 3-19). Try to complete the circle or arc in one continuous movement.

The lead in the compass is generally sharpened to a wedge point using a sandpaper pad. After forming the wedge sand each side lightly to flatten the edges (Fig. 3-20). Do not sand over the drafting table because the carbon will smudge the drawing. As the lead wears its length will have to be adjusted.

Using a Beam Compass

A beam compass is shown in Fig. 3-21. One leg holds a piece of lead or an ink pen and the other is a pin. They slide along the bar to set the desired radius. Hold the pin on the center with one hand and rotate the other end clockwise.

An adjustable ruler is shown in Fig. 3-22. It is used to draw large-radius curves. It will draw arcs with radii from $6\frac{3}{4}$ to 200 in. and the metric model ranges from 170 to 5000 mm.

Using Irregular Curves

Irregular curves are usually laid out on a drawing by a series of points. These are then connected by using various irregular curve tools. A set of irregular curves contains an extensive array of curves. It is necessary to select those that have curves that will smoothly connect several of the points. The more points that can be connected with one part of a curve the better. You must connect at least three points. As you connect points move the tool along the series of dots or select another curve that fits better. Continue drawing each section until the desired curve is complete (Fig. 3-23).

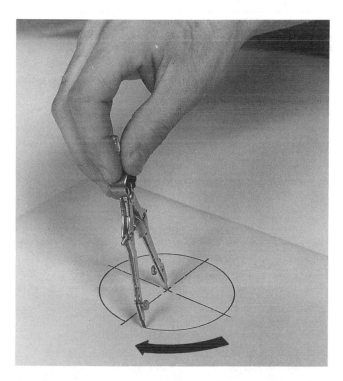

Figure 3-19. *Hold the compass at the top and lean in the direction it is rotated. (William P. Spence, Engineering Graphics, 2e, © 1988. Reprinted by permission of Prentice Hall, Englewood Cliffs, New Jersey.)*

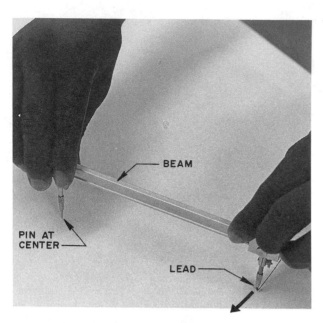

Figure 3-21. *Drawing a large diameter circle with a beam compass. (William P. Spence, Engineering Graphics, 2e, © 1988. Reprinted by permission of Prentice Hall, Englewood Cliffs, New Jersey.)*

Irregular curves can also be drawn using a flexible curve. They are made from plastic, rubber, or metal and are bent to fit the series of dots forming the curve (Fig. 3-24).

Using a Circle Template

Be certain to align the center lines of the circle to be drawn with the center line marks on the template (Fig. 3-25). Right-handed people generally draw the circle clockwise.

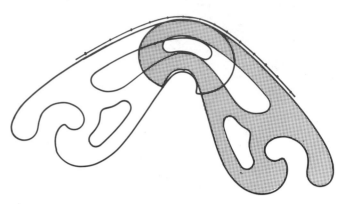

Figure 3-23. *Irregular curves are drawn by connecting points on the curve with a tool called an irregular curve.*

Rotate the pencil as you draw the circle to keep the line width uniform. Keep the pencil lead perpendicular to the edge of the template so the hole drawn is round and the correct diameter. A slanted pencil will produce an elliptical hole (Fig. 3-26).

Templates are made with the holes slightly larger to allow for the lead. If the drawing must be very accurate draw the hole on scrap paper to check the size.

Using a Divider

A divider is like a compass but has pins on both legs. It is used to transfer distances from one part of a drawing to another or to layout equally spaced distances. To step off equal distances locate the end point on the drawing. Set the divider on the distance desired. Place one pin on the first point and swing the other leg to locate the second

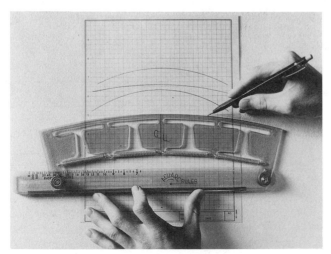

Figure 3-22. *An adjustable rules is used to draw large diameter arcs. (Courtesy Hoyle Products, Inc.)*

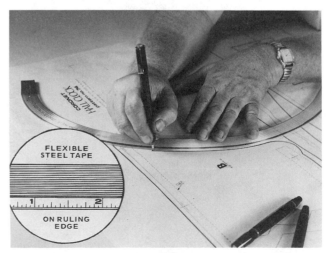

Figure 3-24. *Drawing an irregular curve with a flexible curve. (Courtesy Hoyle Products, Inc.)*

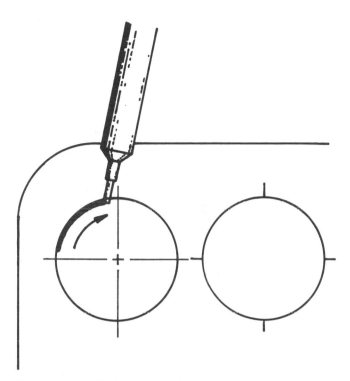

Figure 3-25. *Circles can be drawn using a circle template.*

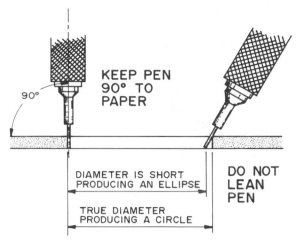

Figure 3-26. *When using a template, keep the pencil perpendicular to the paper.*

point. Continue stepping the divider down the line until the required spaces have been located (Fig. 3-27).

Inking

Drawings are inked using a technical fountain pen. The ink is stored in a plastic tube in the handle. It holds an ink supply that lasts quite a while. Remember to keep the cap on the pen when it is not in use (Fig. 3-28). Ink dissolving solvents are available for cleaning pens and an ultrasonic cleaner is also used (Fig. 3-29). Avoid taking the pen tip apart because the fine feed flow wire is easily damaged and hard to get back in the tip.

When starting to use the pen, see if the ink will flow by trying it on a piece of scrap paper. The clicking noise is the flow-regulating device sliding up and down in the point. This causes the ink to flow. If it will not flow clean the point with pen cleaner.

Tools used for inking, as triangles and straightedges,

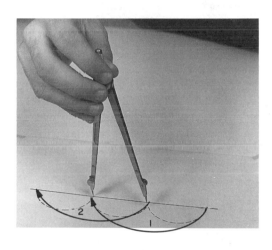

Figure 3-27. *Using a divider to step off equal distances. (William P. Spence, Engineering Graphics, 2e, © 1988. Reprinted by permission of Prentice Hall, Englewood Cliffs, New Jersey.)*

should have recessed edges to prevent ink from flowing under them. Pieces of cardboard can be taped to the back to provide a space (Fig. 3-30).

When ink smears let it dry before trying to erase it. Use an eraser designed to remove ink. Do not use gritty erasers because they damage the drawing surface.

Let inked lines dry normally. Some use electric hair

Figure 3-28. *The parts of a technical fountain pen. (Courtesy Staedtler, Inc.)*

Figure 3-29. *An ultrasonic cleaner for cleaning ink pen points. (Courtesy Keuffel and Esser Co.)*

driers to speed up the drying. Do not blot because this removes ink from the line and often causes smears. If an ink line is shining it is still wet. When it dries it is a dull flat color.

When inking over pencil construction lines, center the ink line on the pencil line. This is necessary so straight and curved lines will meet (Fig. 3-31).

Keep the pens reasonably full of ink because this helps the flow. Hold the pen perpendicular to the paper and as soon as it touches the paper move it in the direction desired. Do not delay the start or finish. When the end of the line is reached lift the pen off the paper (Fig. 3-32).

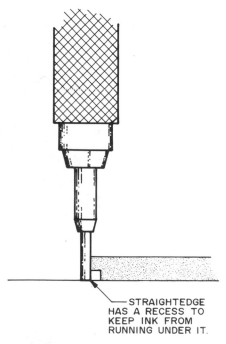

STRAIGHTEDGE HAS A RECESS TO KEEP INK FROM RUNNING UNDER IT.

Figure 3-30. *When inking, use tools that have recessed edges.*

PROPER TECHNIQUE   IMPROPER TECHNIQUE

Figure 3-31. *Ink lines should be centered on the pencil construction lines.*

Order of Inking

Following is a recommended order for inking a drawing.

1. Ink all centerlines. Do the circular lines first, then the horizontal lines, then the vertical straight lines.
2. Ink all arcs and circles.
3. Ink all horizontal visible lines.
4. Ink all vertical visible lines.
5. Ink all inclined visible lines.
6. Ink all hidden lines.
7. Ink section lines, extension lines, and dimension lines.
8. Ink arrowheads.
9. Ink all dimensions, notes, and titles.

Geometric Constructions

The basic geometric forms occur frequently on architectural drawings. Often they can be drawn using templates containing the needed form such as a hexagon or ellipse.

Figure 3-32. *The proper way to hold a technical fountain pen. (William P. Spence, Engineering Graphics, 2e, © 1988. Reprinted by permission of Prentice Hall, Englewood Cliffs, New Jersey.)*

If these are not available it becomes necessary to lay out the form. The following examples are only a few of the more frequently used geometric constructions.

Square

A square can be drawn by constructing tangents to the sides of a circle having a diameter equal to one side of the square (Fig. 3-33).

Hexagon

A hexagon can be drawn by constructing tangents to the side of a circle using the 30°–60° triangle. It can also be drawn by stepping off the radius along the circumference of the circle and connecting the points (Fig. 3-34).

Octagon

An octagon can be drawn by drawing tangent lines to a circle having a diameter equal to the across the flats dimension of the octagon using a 45° triangle (Fig. 3-35).

Approximate Ellipse

Lay out the major and minor diameters of the ellipse. Continue construction as shown in Fig. 3-36.

Divide into Equal Parts

Draw a line at any angle with the element to be divided. Then measure along this line using any convenient unit the

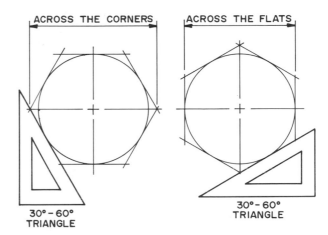

Figure 3-34. *Hexagons can be constructed around a circle having a diameter equal to the across the flats dimension.*

number of divisions wanted. Connect the end to the end of the element being divided. Draw lines through each part parallel with the end line (Fig. 3-37).

Orthographic Drawing

Architectural drawings are made according to the principles of orthographic projection. In this system an architectural object is drawn as viewed by the observer from the top and sides (Fig. 3-38). If these views were drawn on the sides of the box and the box unfolded the relationship between the views can be seen (Fig. 3-39). Since buildings are so large it is not possible to draw the views in relation to each other in this way so each is drawn separately.

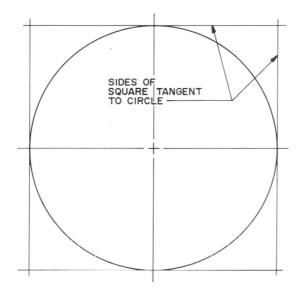

Figure 3-33. *A square can be constructed by drawing tangents to a circle.*

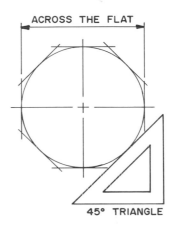

Figure 3-35. *An octagon can be drawn around a circle having a diameter equal to the across the flats dimension of the octagon.*

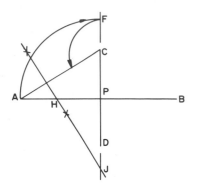

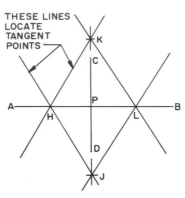

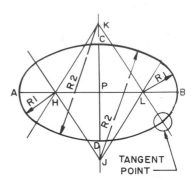

1. Draw axes *A-B* and *C-D*.
2. Connect *A* with *C*.
3. Swing radius *A-P* to *F*.
4. Swing *C-F* to *G*.
5. Draw perpendicular bisector of *A-G* and extend to *H* and *J*.

6. Transfer distance *P-J* to upper part of axis forming *E-K*.
7. Transfer *P-H* to right side of axis forming *P-L*.
8. Connect *H, J, K,* and *L*. These are centerpoints for drawing the ellipse. These also locate the tangent points for the curved sides.

9. Using radii *R1* and *R2* swing arcs to each tangent point.

Figure 3-36. How to draw an ellipse using the four-center method.

Sections

Sections are cut through parts of a building or entirely through a building to show hidden details (Fig. 3-40). A section is located by a cutting plane line with arrows indicating the direction of sight. Since there may be several sections they are identified by letters of the alphabet (Fig. 3-41).

A floor plan is actually a section cut through the house parallel with the floor. This reveals interior walls, stairs, windows, doors, and other details (Fig. 3-42).

Sometimes a section is cut just part way through a build-

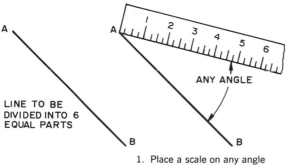

1. Place a scale on any angle and mark off the number of parts wanted. Any size division can be used. It was the 6–in. mark in this example.

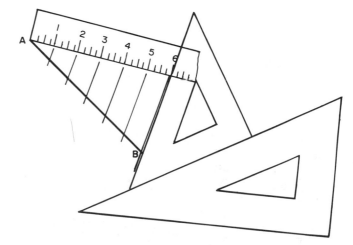

2. Connect the end of the line (*B*) with the last point on the scale (6). Draw lines parallel to this through the other points on the scale until they cross line *A-B*.
3. This divides the line into six equal parts.

Figure 3-37. How to divide a line into equal parts.

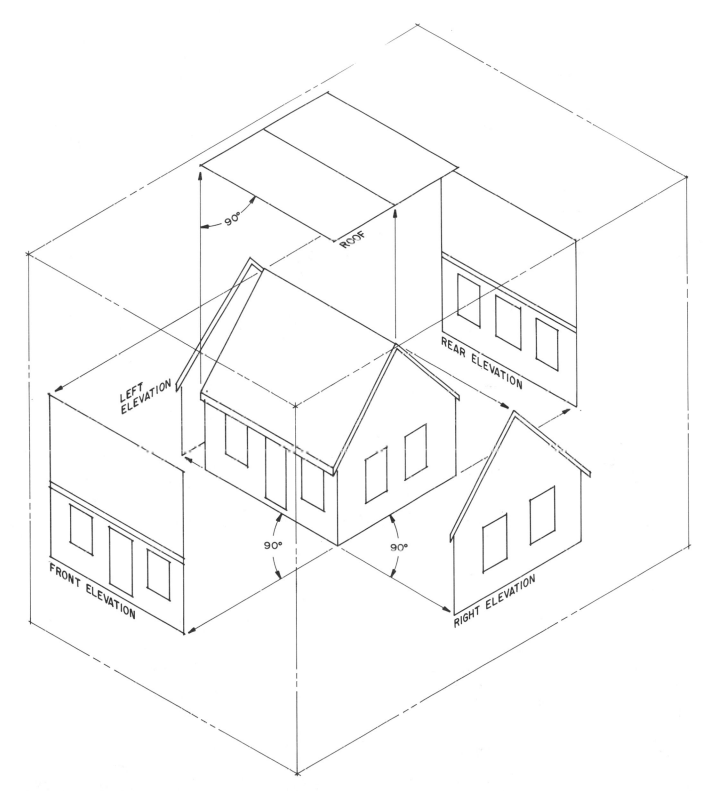

Figure 3-38. *Orthographic protection involves projecting each side of an object perpendicular to planes parallel with that side.*

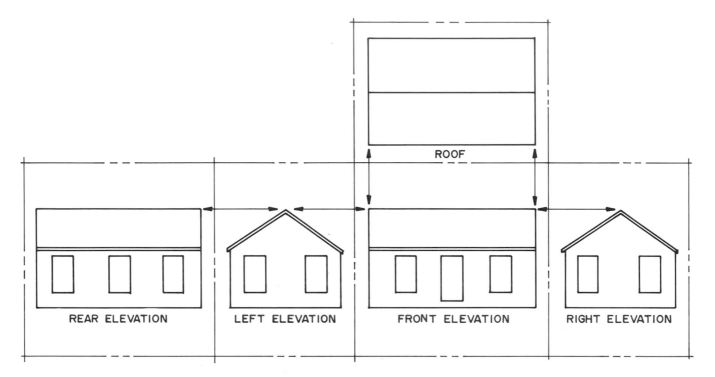

Figure 3-39. *This shows the relationship between orthographic views.*

ing to show details of construction in one area. A wall section, Fig. 3-43, is one example. These are drawn large so the details are clear.

Lettering

Dimensions and notes are an important part of the working drawings. If they are incorrect or not easily read, serious and expensive mistakes can occur.

The style of lettering used by manual drafters will depend upon that required by the employer. Since several drafters work on different parts of a set of working drawings, it is necessary that the lettering on all appear about the same. For that reason some firms demand the use of vertical, capital Gothic letters with the vertical strokes made with a triangle. Usually a small triangle placed against the bottom edge of the parallel straightedge is used for the vertical strokes (Fig. 3-44). The horizontal strokes may be parallel with the guide lines or slope slightly since it is easier to make them this way. Some firms use slant lettering with the vertical stroke leaning to the right at an angle of about 68°.

The correct way to form capital, Gothic letters is shown in Figs. 3-45 and 3-46.

Following are some basic fundamentals that all lettering should meet (Fig. 3-47).

1. Notes and dimensions are lettered $\frac{3}{32}$ or $\frac{1}{8}$ in. (2.4 to 3.0 mm) high. Major titles and drawing numbers are $\frac{1}{4}$ in. (6 mm) high. Lesser titles as room names are $\frac{1}{8}$ in. (3 mm).

2. Form the letters as shown in Fig. 3-45. Keep in the proportions shown. Note that most letters are almost as wide as they are high. The width of M and W is greater than their height.

3. Letters with divisions in the center, as B, should have the division slightly above center.

4. Draw guidelines to locate and set the height of the letters. Guidelines should be very light so they do not print, but if they do they should be barely visible. The Ames lettering guide is often used to rule the guidelines (Fig. 3-48).

5. Letters such as M and W should have the center portion touch the guidelines.

6. Keep the line thickness uniform in all letters. To do this keep the pencil sharp and rotate it in your fingers frequently to keep the point uniform.

7. All lettering should be as dark as possible.

8. Since several people will work on the same drawing, lettering styles must be the same to give the finished drawing a professional look. To do this some companies

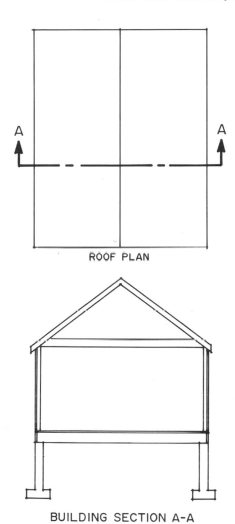

ROOF PLAN

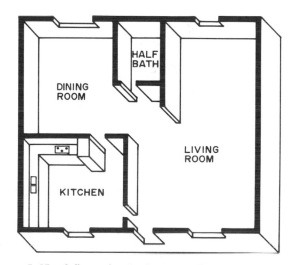

BUILDING SECTION A-A

Figure 3-41. *A building section is located by a section line and identified by letters of the alphabet.*

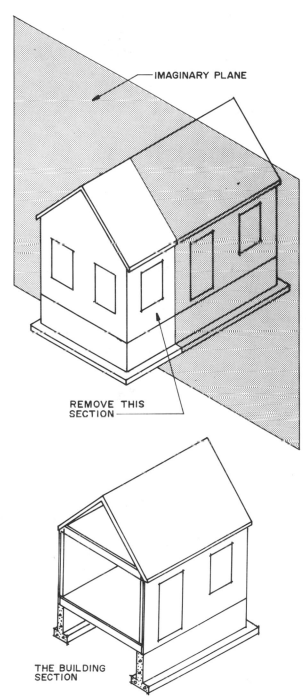

THE BUILDING SECTION

Figure 3-40. *A section is formed by an imaginary plane passing through the building. One segment of the building is removed revealing the construction details.*

require the use of vertical lettering and require all vertical strokes to be made mechanically (Fig. 3-44). The drafter slides a triangle or lettering guide along the straightedge making vertical strokes along the edge of the triangle and drawing horizontal and curved elements freehand. With practice, a good rate of speed can be developed.

Figure 3-42. *A floor plan is drawn as if an imaginary plane is passed horizontally through the building and the top half is removed.*

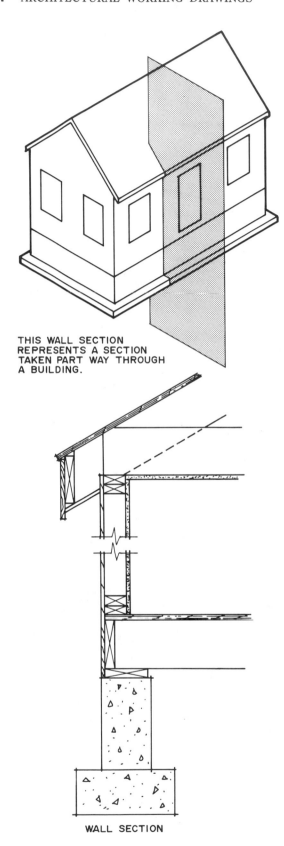

THIS WALL SECTION
REPRESENTS A SECTION
TAKEN PART WAY THROUGH
A BUILDING.

WALL SECTION

Figure 3-43. Sections may pass through only part of a building.

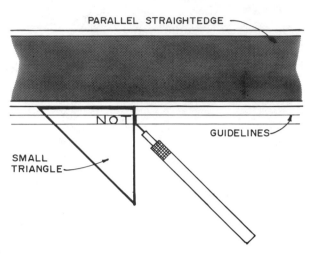

Figure 3-44. Vertical strokes on letters are often made using a small triangle placed on the bottom of the parallel straightedge.

9. Hold the pencil in a comfortable manner and place your arm on the table so you are comfortable. You may slant the paper or angle of your body to the table if it helps.

10. Some variations of lettering used on architectural drawings are in Fig. 3-49).

Pressure Sensitive Letters

Large letters for titles and other headings can be placed on the drawing using pressure sensitive tape. The letters are available in sheets with an adhesive on the back. They are removed from the sheet and pressed in place on the drawing. Another type of device producing pressure sensitive letters is shown in Fig. 3-50. The words are composed on the machine. They appear as composed on pressure sensitive tape.

Typewriters

Words can be placed on drawings with typewriters. One special kind has a long carriage that is open on both ends. The dimensions and notes are typed in the normal manner.

Ink

Mechanical inking devices can be used to letter from very small to quite large letters. The ink pen is held in a scriber. The pin leg on the scriber follows the letters incised into a template (Fig. 3-51). The template is held steady against the straightedge. Another type of template has the letters cut out and the pen follows these pierced openings (Fig. 3-52).

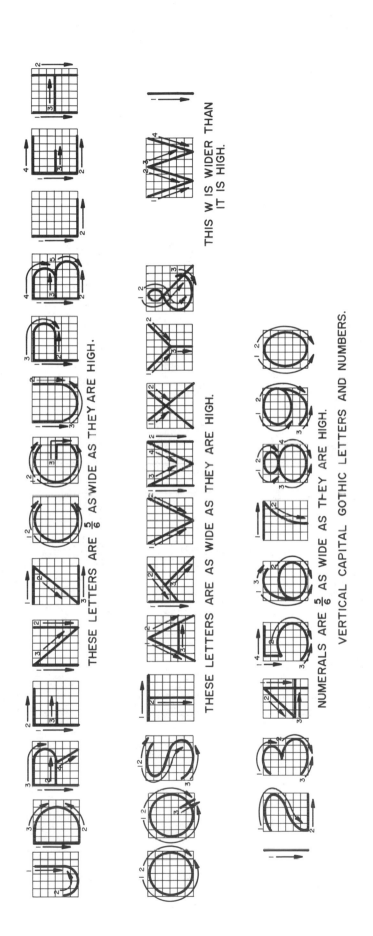

THESE LETTERS ARE $\frac{5}{6}$ AS WIDE AS THEY ARE HIGH.

THESE LETTERS ARE AS WIDE AS THEY ARE HIGH.

THIS W IS WIDER THAN IT IS HIGH.

THESE LETTERS ARE AS WIDE AS THEY ARE HIGH.

NUMERALS ARE $\frac{5}{6}$ AS WIDE AS THEY ARE HIGH.

VERTICAL CAPITAL GOTHIC LETTERS AND NUMBERS.

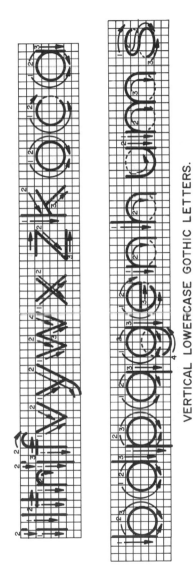

VERTICAL LOWERCASE GOTHIC LETTERS.

Figure 3-45. *Vertical capital and lower case Gothic lettering. (William P. Spence, Engineering Graphics, 2e, © 1988. Reprinted by permission of Prentice Hall, Englewood Cliffs, New Jersey.)*

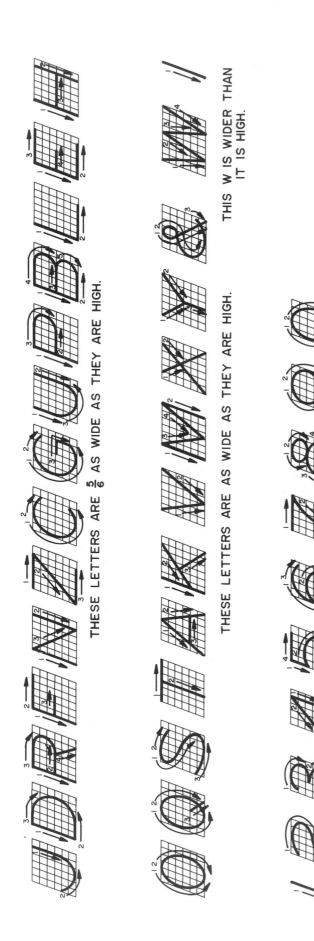

THESE LETTERS ARE $\frac{5}{6}$ AS WIDE AS THEY ARE HIGH.

THESE LETTERS ARE AS WIDE AS THEY ARE HIGH.

THIS W IS WIDER THAN IT IS HIGH.

NUMERALS ARE $\frac{5}{6}$ AS WIDE AS THEY ARE HIGH.

INCLINED CAPITAL GOTHIC LETTERS AND NUMBERS.

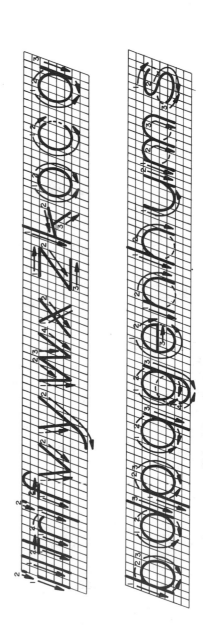

Figure 3-46. *Inclined capital and lowercase Gothic lettering. (William P. spence, Engineering Graphics, 2e, © 1988. Reprinted by permission of Prentice Hall, Englewood Cliffs, New Jersey.)*

INCLINED LOWERCASE GOTHIC LETTERS.

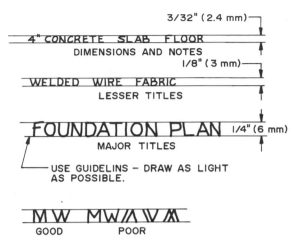

Figure 3-47. *Some basic lettering fundamentals.*

ABCDEFGHIJKLMNOPQR
STUVWXYZ 1234567890
PLYWOOD CONCRETE

VERTICAL STROKES WITH INCLINED HORIZONTAL
ELEMENTS

ABCDEFGHIJKLMNOPQRS
TUVWXYZ 1234567890
PLYWOOD CONCRETE

VERTICAL STROKES WITH HORIZONTAL ELEMENTS

ABCDEFGHIJKLMNOPQRS
TUVWXYZ 1234567890
PLYWOOD CONCRETE

SLANTED VERTICAL STROKES WITH HORIZONTAL
ELEMENTS

Figure 3-49. *Some acceptable variations for architectural lettering.*

Computers

When drafting using computers, the dimensions and notes are produced on the screen of the monitor. When the drawing is run off the plotter all the lettering is done also. Plotters use various types of ink pens.

HOW TO USE THE AMES LETTERING GUIDE

With your Ames Lettering Guide it is possible to draw guide lines and slope lines for lettering and numbering from $\frac{1}{16}$ to 2 in. in height.

The numbers on the disc from 10 through 2 denote the height of letters in thirty-seconds of an inch. Assume you want letters $\frac{1}{4}$ in. high. Rotate the disc so the 8 is at the frame index.

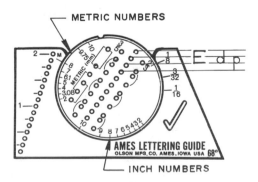

Figure 3-48. *Guidelines can be ruled with this lettering guide. (Courtesy Olson Manufacturing Co.)*

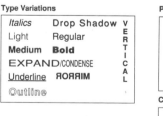

Figure 3-50. *This unit produces words on pressure-sensitive tape. The tape is pressed into place on the drawing. (Courtesy of Kroy, Inc.)*

Figure 3-51. *The template guides the scriber to form each letter. The scriber can be adjusted to form vertical and inclined letters. (Courtesy of Keuffel and Esser Co.)*

Lettering Techniques

Always draw guidelines to help locate and set the size of the lettering. They should be so light that they will not print. Vertical guidelines can also be drawn if necessary (Fig. 3-53).

The space between letters must appear to be equal. Because the letters are different shapes, the space cannot

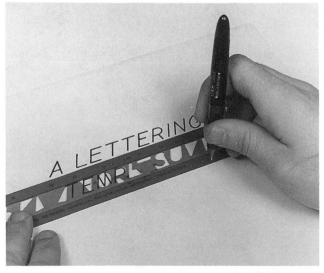

Figure 3-52. *This lettering guide has the letters cut out like a stencil. The technical fountain pen is used to form the letters.*

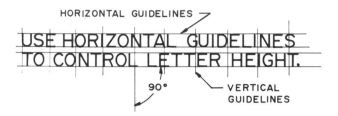

Figure 3-53. *Always use guidelines when lettering.*

actually be equal. When letters with tall vertical parts, such as H and I, come next to each other, more space is allowed than when letters having open space around them, such as A and V, fall together. The spacing is done by eye. Through experience letters can be placed so that they appear to be equally spaced (Fig. 3-54).

The space between words equals the size of the letter O (Fig. 3-55).

Figure 3-54. *Space the letters in each word so that they appear to be an equal distance apart.*

Figure 3-55. *The space between words equals the width of one letter.*

Figure 3-56. A drafter's brush. (Courtesy Staedtler, Inc.)

Cleanliness

Cleanliness is important in drafting. As tools move across the drawing they pick up carbon and begin to smear on the paper. Never sharpen a pencil over a table. After sharpening a pencil the loose carbon can be removed by wiping the point with a cloth or sticking it into a piece of Styrofoam. Wipe your triangles, straightedges, drafting machine head and scales, irregular curves, drafting table tops, and other tools frequently with a soft, clean cloth. Wash them and your hands with water and a mild cleaner as needed.

Some drafter like to use a drafting brush. It is used to remove eraser crumbs from the surface of a drawing without smearing the lines (Fig. 3-56).

You can cover the completed part of a drawing with a clean piece of paper. This prevents instruments from smearing finished lines.

Some people use eraser crumbs to clean a drawing. These are available in small bags. The crumbs are powdered over the drawing and lightly rubbed. They are brushed away with a drafting brush. While this cleans a drawing, it does reduce the darkness of the lines at the same time.

Study Questions

Answer the following study questions without referring to the text. Then check your answers with the text and correct those that were wrong.

1. What line thicknesses are used on architectural drawings?

2. Explain the difference in holding wood-cased and fine-line mechanical drawing pencils.

3. Name three ways to locate and draw angles.

4. Name two tools used to draw circles.

5. Name two tools used to draw irregular curves.

6. Explain what to do if the ink does not flow out of the pen.

7. List the steps in the order of inking.

8. What height letters are generally used for notes and dimensions on architectural drawings?

9. List some things you can do to help keep your drawing clean.

Computer Graphics Workstations

Introduction

The use of computers by architectural firms is gradually increasing though much drafting is still by the traditional manual methods. The development of desk-top computers has lowered the cost of such systems enabling the smaller offices to use them in their daily operation (Fig. 4-1).

Current systems have many applications for an architectural firm. The mathematical capabilities of computers make them useful for engineering design, such as structural systems design. Even a small firm can do a great deal of engineering work which makes the system cost effective. In addition, computers can be used for specification writing, cost estimating, scheduling, filing, typing, and even bookkeeping. A major use is computer-aided design and drafting (CADD). Architectural drawings of all kinds can be rapidly prepared on a CADD system.

The following sections will illustrate the components of a computer system. Basically, a computer system has two major groups of components, *hardware* and *software*. The *hardware* is the physical components, including input devices, the computing unit, and output devices. Computer programs are referred to as *software*. The program contains the commands that direct the functions of the computer. A computer system is assembled to perform certain tasks. These are brought together as a unit which is referred to as a *workstation*.

Workstations

Workstations contain the components that make up a system. They have input devices, output devices, and the computing unit (Fig. 4-2).

The Computer

The heart of a computer-aided design and drafting system is the computer. There are three main categories of computers—mainframe, minicomputers and microcomputers. *Mainframe* computers are very large, centrally located units to which many terminals can be connected. They are expensive and only used by large companies. *Minicomputers* are smaller than mainframe computers but still have considerable memory. They will accept several terminals and therefore can be used by several people at the same time. *Microcomputers* (sometimes called personal or desktop computers) have less memory than minicomputers but still have sufficient capacity to handle a high percentage of the computing tasks in an architectural firm. They are less expensive to buy and use.

The heart of the computer is the *computing unit*. It performs the thousands of calculations very rapidly. It is made up of an arithmetic logic unit (ALU), a memory, and a control unit that manages the interactions of these components and the input and output devices.

The *arithmetic logic unit* performs the calculations for

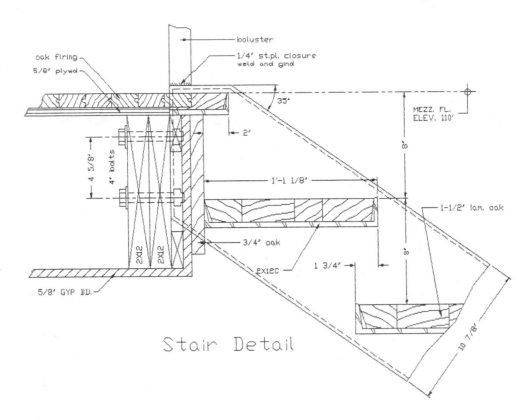

Stair Detail

Figure 4-1. *This stair detail was drawn with a CADD system. (Courtesy of Autodesk, Inc.)*

Figure 4-2. *A workstation containing all of the hardware needed for computer-aided design and drafting. (Courtesy of Hewlett Packard Company)*

the computer. The *memory* retains the information that the ALU or control section will need. The *control section* keeps all of the information moving in the proper order and enables it to arrive at the proper place at the proper time.

To develop a drawing on a computer, the software (an architectural program) that directs the computer in making the drawing is stored in the computer's memory. Storage in the memory is also needed for the instructions given to produce the drawing or other images. If many drawings have to be made, the storage may not be large enough to hold them. In this case, *auxiliary memory* devices are needed. Most commonly used storage devices are magnetic disks and magnetic tape.

Storage Devices

The magnetic disk is used to store data that will be retrieved and frequently updated. The two types of magnetic disks are hard disks and floppy disks. The hard disk is a set of platters much like long playing records. They are generally sealed in a dust-free casing. They have considerable storage for software and projects in progress.

Floppy disks are flexible plastic disks that have a magnetic coating and are mounted in a square vinyl jacket.

They are used primarily in microcomputer systems. They provide limited storage. When in use the disk rotates at about 300 revolutions per minute and the information is read through an opening in the jacket. The two sizes are a minifloppy that is $5\frac{1}{2}$ inches in diameter and a microfloppy that is $3\frac{1}{2}$ inches in diameter.

Magnetic tape is used to store CADD data that is not frequently retrieved. It appears much the same as reel-to-reel audio tape. Data from a magnetic disk is transferred to magnetic tape as a backup. If the magnetic disk is damaged or erased, the data are safe on the magnetic tape. Once the data are on the tape, the magnetic disk can be cleared, providing space for the generation of new input.

Input Devices

Input devices are used to make data available to the system. The *keyboard* is the most commonly used device (Fig. 4-3). It is similar to a typewriter keyboard but has additional keys needed to perform special functions. These functions might include instructing the computer to do specific calculations, to adjust the walls on a floor plan, or to save or erase input data.

A *digitizer* is another input device that is a square or rectangular unit with a smooth, flat surface (Fig. 4-4). Below the surface is a grid of hundreds of electronically sensitive points. It contains a variety of symbols and an area used to lay out the drawing (Fig. 4-5).

Figure 4-4. *A digitizer table with a tablet cursor that is used to enter commands. (Courtesy of Summagraphics © Corporation).*

Figure 4-3. *The keyboard is one of the most frequently used input devices. (Courtesy of Hewlett Packard Company).*

The digitizer is well suited for graphical use. The command is sent from the digitizer to the computer by touching the surface with a stylus (Fig. 4-6) or a tablet cursor (Fig. 4-7). When these touch the surface and their activation key is pressed, a signal is sent to the computer. If a spot on the blank area is touched, it appears as a point on the screen of the monitor. If one of the symbols or command areas are touched, this signal is sent to the computer and appears on the screen. This is much like traditional drafting. The commands to perform certain drafting functions are sent by positioning the stylus or tablet cursor (sometimes called a puck) over the symbol or area on the surface of the digitizer. For example, a line can be drawn by positioning the stylus at the beginning and ending points and commanding it to draw the line. This line not only appears on the screen of the monitor but is stored in the memory of the computer.

Other input devices used to control the cursor on the screen include a track ball, joystick, and mouse. A track ball (Fig. 4-8) has a ball that when moved relays information to the computer, resulting in moving the cursor on the screen. A joystick is similar to the track ball except it has a small handle, that when moved controls the movement of the cursor (Fig. 4-9). A mouse is a handheld con-

Figure 4-5. *This tablet overlay contains a variety of architectural symbols. (Courtesy of Autodesk, Inc.)*

Figure 4-6. *This is a digitizer table with a stylus. (Courtesy of Computervision Corporation).*

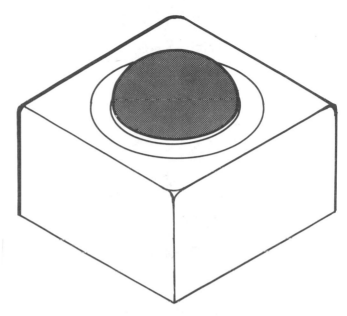

Figure 4-8. *A track ball.*

trol that is moved about on a flat surface. There are two kinds, optical and mechanical. The optical mouse which uses LED's and light detectors is moved across a special pad with a grid of wires over a reflective surface. A light signal from the mouse reflects back from the pad into a photo detector which translates the signal into signals sent to the computer. The computer converts these data into cursor movements on the screen.

The mechanical mouse has two wheels at 90° to each other that when moved by rolling the device over a flat surface send signals to the computer which enable it to control the movement of the cursor on the screen (Fig. 4-10).

Another input device is the *light pen*. It is used to add or change information directly on the screen (Fig. 4-11). While they are called light pens, they do not emit light but detect the presence of light. The operator controls the pen with a switch located on its tip. The switch can be held on and a line can be drawn. It can be momentarily turned on to identify a single element on an image. When

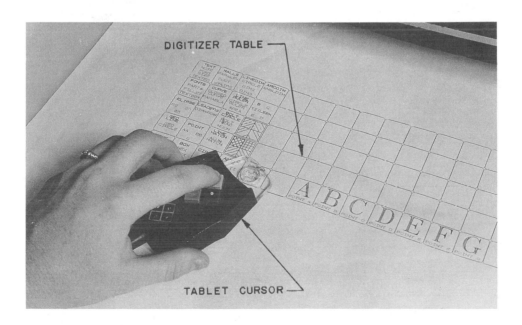

Figure 4-7. *Commands are sent from the digitizer to the computer using a tablet cursor or stylus.*

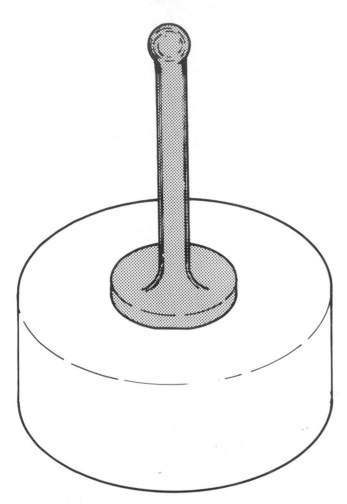

Figure 4-9. *A joystick.*

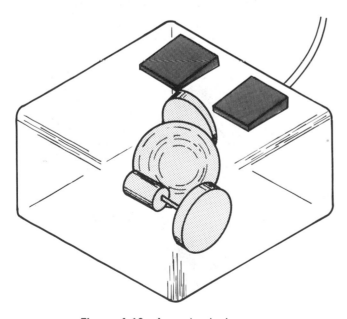

Figure 4-10. *A mechanical mouse.*

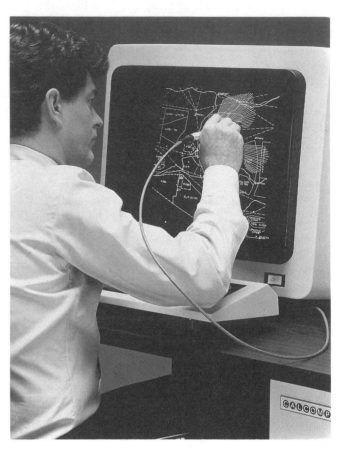

Figure 4-11. *Light pens are used to produce images on a CRT. (Courtesy of CalComp, Inc.)*

the switch is on the pen detects light from the screen and sends a signal to a digital pulse generator which sends this signal to the computer.

The light pen has the advantage of permitting an operator to interact directly with the displayed image by pointing to it. It has the disadvantage of requiring elaborate programming. It is also difficult to aim and requires much practice. The pen must be moved at a constant speed or it will lose contract.

Output Devices

Output devices useful in architectural design and drafting include visual displays and hard copy. *Visual display* refers to the developed images appearing on the CRT of the monitor. The monitor is a cathode ray tube (CRT) similar to that found in television sets. It is used with the input devices, such as the keyboard or digitizer, to show an image of the drawing, words, or numerical information as a video display. Monitors produce better images than ordinary television sets because they have a higher resolution (Fig. 4-12). Resolution is a measure of the precision and

Figure 4-12. *The image being developed appears on the monitor. (Courtesy of Hewlett Packard Company).*

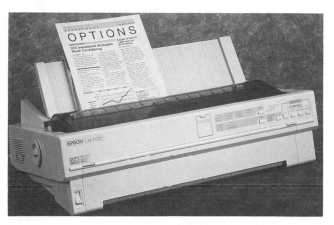

Figure 4-13. *A dot matrix printer. (Courtesy of Epson America, Inc.)*

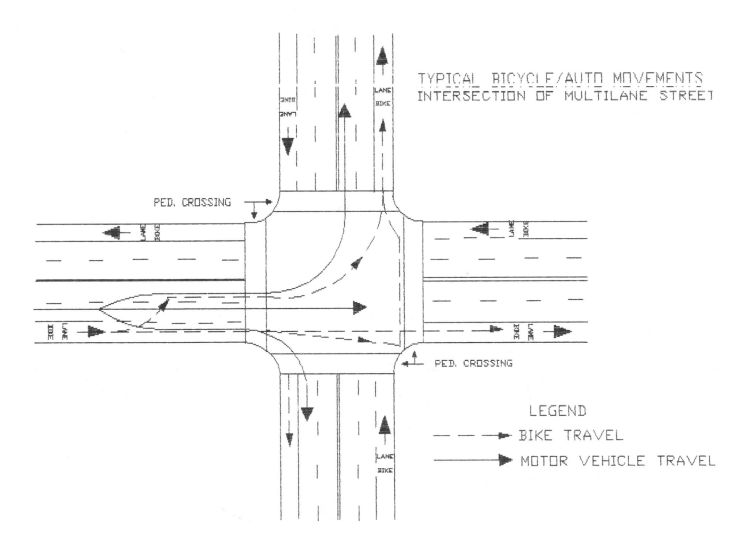

Figure 4-14. *This drawing of a intersection was produced by a dot matrix printer. (Courtesy of Autodesk, Inc.)*

A letter quality printer
produces typewriter quality
characters using a daisy
wheel as shown by this text.

Figure 4-15. Output from a daisy wheel printer.

clarity of the display. It is much like a television screen because it contains many dots. The more dots per unit area the clearer and more uniform the image, therefore the higher the resolution.

Drawings, text, specifications, spread sheets, and other developed images appear on the monitor as they are developed. As such, they can be examined but have limited use in that form. To be useful, the images must be transformed into hardcopy (paper form). This is done using printers and plotters.

Printers

Printers produce typewritten copy much like that from a standard typewriter. Some types of printers can produce graphic output such as charts and diagrams.

Two widely used printers for text material are the *dot matrix printer* (Fig. 4-13) and the *daisy wheel printer*. The dot matrix printer is faster than the daisy wheel and produces text and small graphics using a series of small dots

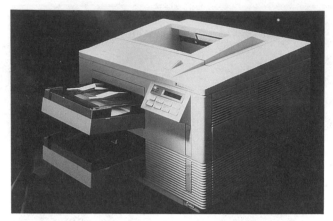

Figure 4-17. This laser printer uses a variety of font cartridges. (Courtesy of Hewlett Packard Company).

(Fig. 4-14). The daisy wheel produces what is often referred to as letter quality text (Fig. 4-15). The daisy wheel has the characters on the ends of a spoke-like wheel which revolves as the text is reproduced on the paper (Fig. 4-16).

Laser printers are often used to output images produced by the integration of CADD graphics with computer-aided publishing systems. They produce small black and white graphics and text (Fig. 4-17). *Ink jet* printers produce images by spraying fine jets of ink on the paper (Fig. 4-18).

Plotters

Plotters are used to print graphical output such as architectural drawings. In addition, they will letter notes and dimensions but are slow by comparison to printers.

Electromechanical plotters are of two types, flat-bed and drum. *Flat-bed plotters* are made in a variety of sizes corresponding to standard drafting paper sizes. They can have more than one pen and therefore can draw in several

Figure 4-16. A daisy wheel has the characters at the ends of the spokes.

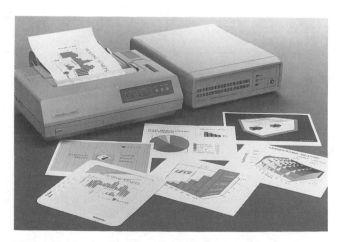

Figure 4-18. An ink jet printer. (Courtesy of Tektronix, Inc.)

Figure 4-19. A flat bed plotter. (Courtesy of Houston Instrument, A Summagraphics Co.)

colors. On the unit in Fig. 4-19 the pen travels along the horizontal bar while the bar moves along the length of the table.

Drum plotters roll the paper over a cylindrical drum. Drums are made in different widths that correspond with standard sizes of drafting paper. The plotter draws by moving the pen left and right on a horizontal bar running parallel with the drum and on top of it. To draw lines perpendicular to these, the drum rotates in both directions, moving the paper back and forth under the pen (Fig. 4-20). When these two movements are coordinated, the plotter can draw lines on angles or draw curves (Fig. 4-21).

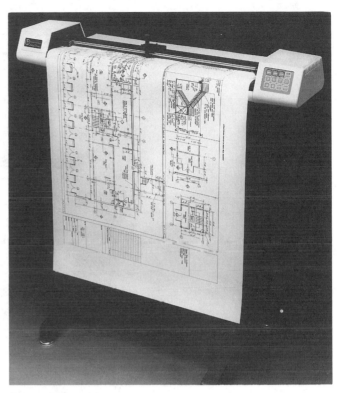

Figure 4-20. A drum plotter. (Courtesy of Houston Instrument, A Summagraphics Co.)

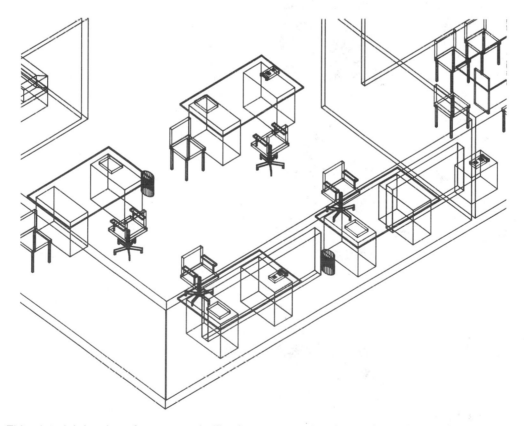

Figure 4-21. This pictorial drawing of a proposed office layout was printed on a drum plotter. (Courtesy of Autodesk, Inc.)

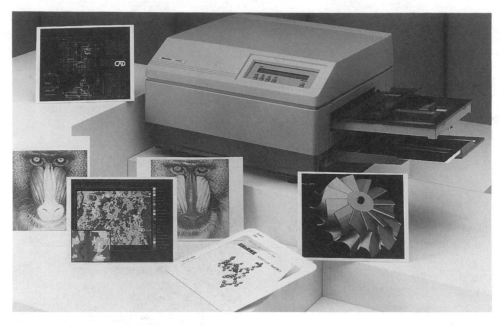

Figure 4-22. *A thermal plotter. (Courtesy of Tektronix, Inc.)*

Figure 4-23. *An electrostatic plotter. (Courtesy of Computervision Corporation.)*

Two other types of plotters are thermal and electrostatic. *Thermal plotters* use heat to produce lines and solid areas on a drawing (Fig. 4-22). The image for the *electrostatic plotter* may appear on the CRT or be stored in the computer memory. It is reproduced in the form of an electrostatic charge on paper, vellum, or plastic film. This electrical charge attracts a black powder to produce a visible image. The image is made permanent by passing it through a fixer.

Electrostatic plotters have a quality close to that of the electromechanical types. Usually they start printing at one end of the sheet and progress to the other as the paper moves through the machine (Fig. 4-23).

Pens

Drum and flat bed plotters use a variety of pens. Felt or fiber tip (Fig. 4-24) and ink pens (Fig. 4-25) are commonly used. Some types are refillable while others are disposable (Fig. 4-26). The ink pen produces the highest quality drawings but the felt and fiber tip pens run at higher speeds. Ink pens run at speeds up to 20 in./sec. These pens will draw on vellum, tracing paper, high-quality bond paper, and drafting film. Line widths are changed by using pens producing different line widths.

Linetypes and Text Founts

There are a variety of linetypes that can be drawn by a plotter (Fig. 4-27). Colored lines can be drawn by using

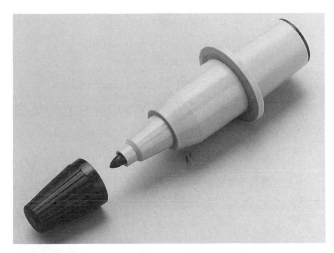

Figure 4-24. *A fiber-tip plotter pen. (Courtesy of Koh-I-Noor, Inc.)*

Figure 4-26. *Disposable ink-type plotter pens. (Courtesy of Koh-I-Noor, Inc.)*

NAME	SAMPLE
Dashed	----------------------
Hidden	----------------------
Center	--- - --- - --- - ---
Phantom	--- -- --- -- ---
Dot	....
Dashdot	--- · --- · --- · ---
Border	--- --- · --- --- ·
Divide	--- · · --- · · ---

Figure 4-27. *Some of the styles of linework drawn on a plotter. (Courtesy of Autodesk, Inc.)*

pens with colored ink. A variety of text founts are available (Fig. 4-28). The number and type of symbols available depends upon the software. Some programs have extra memory so additional symbols can be drawn and stored on the program. These are all rapidly reproduced by the plotter.

Figure 4-25. *Refillable ink plotter pens. (Courtesy of Koh-I-Noor, Inc.)*

!"#$%&'()*+,-./01234567
89:;<=>?@ABCDEFGHIJKLMNO
PQRSTUVWXYZ[\]^_'abcdefg
hijklmnopqrstuvwxyz{|}~°±ø

TXT font

!"#$%&'()*+,-./01234567
89:;<=>?@ABCDEFGHIJKLMNO
PQRSTUVWXYZ[\]^_'abcdefg
hijklmnopqrstuvwxyz{|}~°±ø

SIMPLEX font

!"#$%&'()*+,-./01234567
89:;<=>?@ABCDEFGHIJKLMNO
PQRSTUVWXYZ[\]^_'abcdefg
hijklmnopqrstuvwxyz{|}~°±ø

COMPLEX font

!"#$%&'()*+,-./01234567
89:;<=>?@ABCDEFGHIJKLMNO
PQRSTUVWXYZ[\]^_'abcdefg
hijklmnopqrstuvwxyz{|}~°±ø

ITALIC font

Figure 4-28. *Some of the types of lettering available on CAD software. (Courtesy of Autodesk, Inc.)*

Technical Vocabulary

Following are some important technical terms used in this chapter. Write a brief definition for each.

Hardware
Software
Workstation
Mainframe computers
Minicomputers
Microcomputers
Arithmetic logic unit
Control section
Input devices
Keyboard
Digitizer
Cathode ray tube
Monitor
Printer
Plotter

Study Questions

Answer the following study questions without referring to the text. Then check your answers with the text and correct those that were wrong.

1. What are some of the applications of a computer in architecture?

2. Give examples of computer hardware.

3. What is the purpose of computer software?

4. What functions does the computing unit perform?

5. Name the various devices used to store information.

6. Describe the operation of a digitizer.

7. Explain how light pens input commands.

8. What function does the monitor perform?

9. What are the commonly available types of printers?

10. Describe the commonly used types of plotters.

Laboratory Problems

1. Visit your computing center or computer-drafting laboratory and have the instructor or an advanced student show you the CADD hardware introduced in this chapter.

2. Take a computer-drafting class and learn how to prepare architectural drawings, write specifications, make estimates, and perform other duties required of the architect and constructor.

5

Using the Computer for Architectural Design and Drafting

Computer Software

The computer system is of little use without programs to direct its operation. Programs are available from companies specializing in design and production of computer software. A wide range of programs are available for use in architectural offices to perform tasks such as drafting, surveying, statics, estimating, and specification writing. If a special program is needed, it can be written. Programs are also available from other sources such as professional engineering groups and government agencies. There are user groups comprised of people working in a specific area which provide information about sources of programs. Whatever programs you select, it is essential that you make certain they will run on the equipment available and that they will do the work you require. Software manufacturers have technical representatives who help determine the programs needed for a particular application.

When new programs are received, it is necessary to train those who are to use them. While previous experience is helpful even an experienced operator will need training on new software. Some software manufacturers provide training sessions for customers either at the manufacturer's office or the architectural firm's office.

Following are examples of some of the major uses of computers in architecture and construction.

Office Uses

All correspondence can be generated on the computer using a word processing program and copies run off on a printer. A daisy wheel printer produces high-quality copy. For faster reproduction and the production of graphics, a dot matrix or laser printer can be used. The copy can be stored on a floppy disk, rather than stored as paper carbons in a file cabinet.

The writing of specifications is a major task made easier by the computer. The general practice has been to cut up an old set of specifications and tape in the new sections needed. Then it is usually necessary to retype the entire document. By using the computer, the basic information is available in a software package. The new material is typed in where needed. The final copies of the specifications are then reproduced by the printer.

All *office functions* such as payroll, billing, and bookkeeping can be performed by the computer. This information can be called up on the monitor, and newer data added and stored again until needed.

Cost estimates can be produced using an estimating program. Very accurate estimates of the costs of each segment of the building can be calculated rapidly. Changes, such as a new price, can be made at any time.

Project scheduling can be expedited by using the computer to make decisions as well as keeping a record as the job progresses. Scheduling involves tasks such as establishing the time required to do each part of a job, setting the expected rate of progress, and establishing a planned sequence for the use of manpower, machines, material, and funds.

The depth of analysis that can be carried out at the *feasibility study* stage of an architectural project is almost unlimited. Such a project requires the architect to list the key decision variables, parameters, and constraints (such as maximum height, cost, and code restrictions). Using a mathematical model that interrelates these key variables, feasible solutions are developed.

Computers are extremely useful as the architect works on the problem-structuring stage. *Problem structuring* is defined as organizing all the information gathered about a proposed project into a precise problem description and breaking it down into manageable subproblems.

A *space-needs analysis* involves gathering data about people, activities, and equipment to be included in a building, and developing from the analysis a set of spatial requirements. Computer-based techniques are now used in this phase of design.

The computer is also used to develop an interaction analysis. *Interaction analysis* is a format used to represent data describing the interactions and interrelations between activities or space in a building.

Computer-Aided Design

The computer enhances the design process because it enables the designer to quickly lay out a preliminary design and change it as often as necessary. For example, the designer can enter into the computer the criteria selected for a floor plan arrangement. The computer can then be instructed to find the best arrangement of the spaces and present this on the monitor. This is done so rapidly it appears the computer is thinking through the situation; however, it is only reacting to the criteria entered and the mathematical relationships involved. Therefore, it can be seen that while the computer can save much time on routine operations, the actual design process is still the function of the human mind of the architect.

Figure 5-1 shows the plan view of a proposed commercial building and the related streets. The designer can enter the plan and elevation data into the computer and have

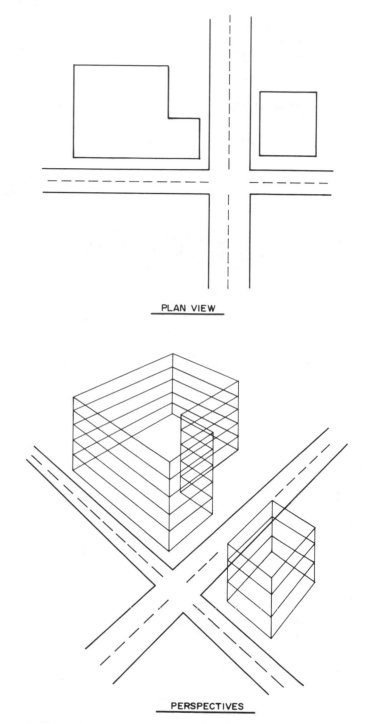

PLAN VIEW

PERSPECTIVES

Figure 5-1. *The computer can quickly produce plan and elevation data and show elevations from many directions.*

schematic perspectives appear on the monitor. The computer can be instructed to turn the building around on the screen so the designer can view it from all sides. This not only helps the designer to finalize plans but enables the client to get a good look at the building. Any of the views can be run off on the printer. They then can be overlaid with plastic drafting film or vellum and used as the basis for a rendering. The exterior of the building can be modeled on the computer. This gives a finished view of the proposed building. (Fig. 5-2).

Before attempting to use the computer to assist in the design process, it is important to have selected a program that will perform the analysis needed. The architects of the future will need to know how to select and analyze computer programs so reliable results will be obtained.

Computer-Aided Design and Drafting

Computer-aided design and drafting is used to produce the final architectural drawings after the design has been established. The software gives the CADD system the ability to draw site plans, floor plans, foundation plans, elevations, details, and other drawings commonly a part of a

set of architectural drawings. The architect develops the drawings on the monitor, generally with a digitizer or mouse as an input device. Once the drawing on the screen is finished and notes and dimensions are generated, hard copies can be produced with a plotter. The original design is stored in the memory of the computer or on a floppy disk or magnetic tape. It can be called up when revisions are necessary. Then the corrections are made, new copies run on the plotter, and the revised data are once again stored.

Following is a discussion to show in a general way how drawings are produced.

Getting Ready to Draw

Before a drawing can be started, the operator must select the units to be used, the limits and scale.

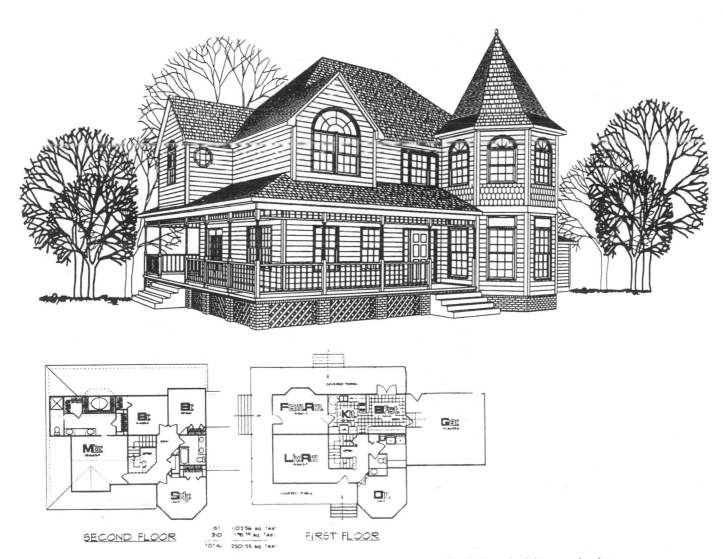

Figure 5-2. *Building exteriors can be modeled using the computer and used for design decisions and sales programs. (Courtesy Home Planners, Inc. © 1992 and Integrated Computer Graphics Acquisition Corporation © 1992.)*

Units are used when measuring linear *distances*. Various areas of engineering, architecture, and science use different notations for coordinates, distances, and angles. In architecture, one unit usually represents one inch. A measure of 17.50 units could equal 17.50 in. or 1'–5.5" or 1'–5 1/2". The operator must choose the fractional denominator to be used, such as $\frac{1}{8}$ in., or if in decimals, the number of decimal places, such as .01 in.

The system of *angle measurement* and its accuracy must be selected. The angle could be in decimal parts of a degree, degrees/minutes/seconds, grads, or radians.

Limits are used to establish the boundaries of the area in which the drawing can be made. The limit command (shown in the menu) is used to set these distances. Limits are specified in units such as 200 units on the *X* axis (horizontal) and 160 units on the *Y* axis (vertical).

Scaling establishes what one unit represents. Drawings are laid out in units. If it is decided to let one inch equal 10 units and it is decided to use *one unit* to represent *one foot*, the scale of the drawing will be 1" = 10'–0".

As you consider this, you need to know the size that can be drawn on your plotter. If your plotter will hold 18 × 24 in. paper and you have a half-inch border on all sides, the free area will be 17 × 23 in. Since the scale is 1" = 10'–0" the plotting area will be 10 ft × 17 in. or 170 by 10 ft × 23 in. or 230 ft (Fig. 5-3).

Coordinates

The Cartesian coordinate system is used to locate points on a drawing. The *X-axis* is in the *horizontal* direction. The *Y-axis* is in the *vertical* direction. Points are located by giving them *X* and *Y* values such as 8,6. The *X* value, 8, is always given first (Fig. 5-4). The *X* and *Y* axes intersect at the lower left corner of the drawing. This is point 0,0 in Fig. 5-4.

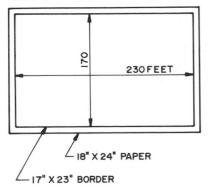

Figure 5-3. The size drawing that can be produced on the plotter depends upon its size, and the free drawing area on the paper.

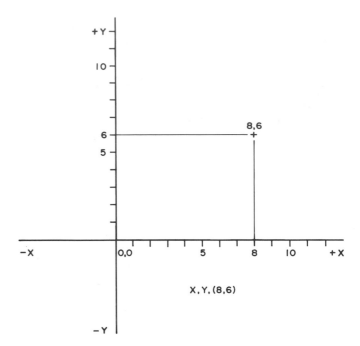

Figure 5-4. Points on a drawing are located using Cartesian coordinates.

Making Drawings on a CADD System

The following is a generalized explanation of how drawings are made with a CADD system using a digitizer. Specific details will vary from one manufacturer's program to another.

The CADD system must be told by the operator exactly what tasks it is to perform. However, it can only perform those tasks it has been programmed to do. For architectural drawing, the program is required to have graphic and alphanumeric data. *Graphic data* include things such as points, lines, and planes and geometric figures made up of these such as circles, triangles, ellipses, rectangles, arrowheads, and arcs. *Alphanumeric data* include letters, numbers, and special characters as found on the keyboard.

The graphics available appear on a menu. A *menu* is a listing of the drawing and support commands that a CADD operator can select from in order to produce a drawing. Menus either appear on the screen of the monitor or are as templates mounted on the surface of a digitizer (Fig. 5-5).

The positions of each symbol on the digitizer menu match electronic positions in the computer memory. When the symbol is touched with a stylus or tablet cursor, the computer is instructed to perform that function. Commands can also be typed in using the symbols that appear on the menu on the screen. This is much slower than using the digitizer tablet.

A *cursor* is a small crosshair mark that appears on the screen when the CADD system is operational. It is used

ELEVATION TEMPLATE (VELEV)

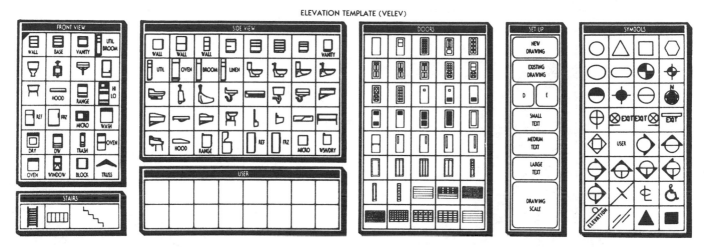

Figure 5-5. *This is an architectural elevation template containing elevations of various interior and exterior parts of buildings. (Courtesy of Computervision Corporation).*

by the operator to locate and identify data on the screen. For example, if it is desired to draw a circle, the cursor locates where it is to be drawn. If a line is to be drawn, the cursor locates the beginning and end and the line is drawn with a "line command." The cursor is moved about the screen with the stylus, tablet cursor (puck), or a mouse.

CADD Commands and Functions

The names used to identify CADD commands and functions vary somewhat from one program to another. The following examples reflect some of the features available in existing CADD software.

Most of these commands and functions are used when the CADD system is in the graphics editor mode. This allows the drafter to create and change drawings. When a CADD system is in the graphics editor mode, the computer screen for a system with a single monitor will appear similar to that in Fig. 5-6. As the drawing is made it will appear in the drawing area of the monitor. Some computers use two display monitors. One is for graphics and the other for text.

The drafter enters the commands and functions by typing them on the computer keyboard, picking them from a digitizer tablet with stylus or tablet cursor or picking them from the screen menu.

Following are examples of typical CADD commands and functions.

Graphic Creation Commands

The following commands are selected examples of those used to create architectural drawings.

Point Command. The *point command* is used to draw a point. Select the command "point" from the menu. Then enter the coordinates of the point's location, such as 8,6 giving the *X* coordinate first and the *Y* coordinate second.

Line Command. The *line command* is used to draw a line. Select the command "line" from the menu. A line can be drawn using a keyboard as follows.

First enter the *XY* coordinates of the first point locating one end of the line. Then enter the *XY* coordinates of the point locating the other end of the line. A line will be drawn on the screen connecting these points. As an example, the following commands will draw a line as shown in Fig. 5-7. The items shown in **boldface** type are what the drafter types on the keyboard.

Command: *Line*
From point: *4,2*
To point: *4,10*

The CADD program will draw a line from point 4,2 to point 4,10.

A line can also be drawn using a digitizer and a tablet cursor. Place the cross lines on the tablet cursor on the "line" indication on the menu and press the proper button. Then move the table cursor on to the drawing area. A lighted + (cursor) will appear on the monitor. Locate this + where you want the line to begin and press the proper button on the tablet cursor. Move the lighted cursor to the end of the line and press the button again. A line will be stretched between the two points (Fig. 5-8).

Double Line Command. Floor plans and parts of section drawings require double lines. These are drawn with the *double line command*. The distance between the

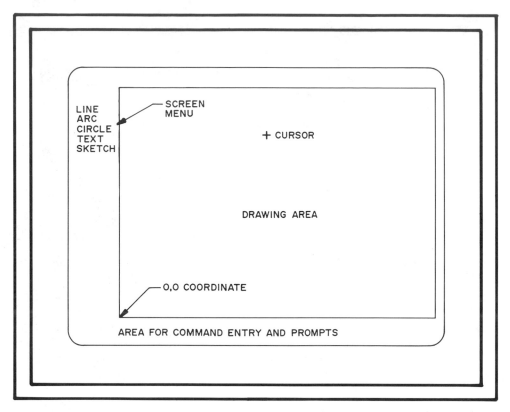

Figure 5-6. *This is how the screen on a system with a single monitor will appear when the CADD system is in the graphic editor mode. It switches to text display when it is necessary to output a large amount of information.*

lines, as the width of an exterior wall, is typed on the keyboard (Fig. 5-9).

Circle Command. Common ways to draw circles include center and radius, center and diameter, two-point, and three-point.

The **center and radius** method requires that you specify the center point and the radius of the circle (Fig.

5-10). The following is a typical command sequence:

Command: ***CIRCLE, CEN RAD***
Locate center: ***5,5***
Specify radius: ***4***

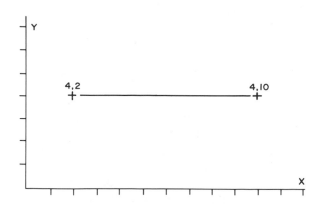

Figure 5-7. *A line is drawn using the line command and the coordinates of each end of the line.*

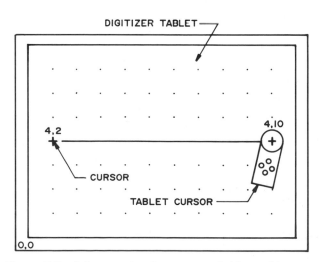

Figure 5-8. *A line can be drawn on a digitizer tablet using a tablet cursor to locate each end.*

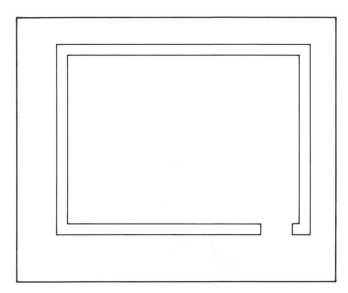

Figure 5-9. *The double line command is useful when drawing walls on floor plans.*

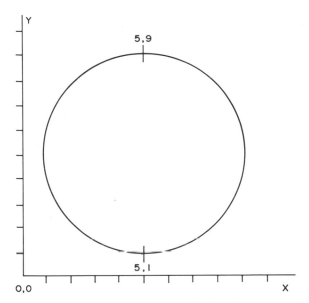

Figure 5-11. *A circle can be drawn by locating two points on its circumference.*

The **center and diameter** method requires you to specify the center point and the diameter of the circle. The following is a typical command sequence:

Command: *CIRCLE, CEN DIA*
Locate center: *5,5*
Specify diameter: *8*

The **two-point** method requires you to specify and locate two points on the circle's circumference (Fig. 5-11).

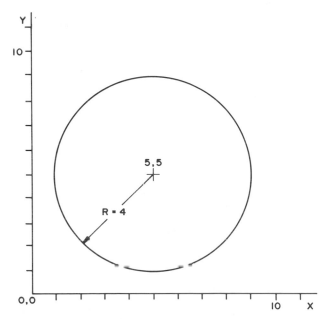

Figure 5-10. *A circle can be drawn by specifying the coordinates of the center and the length of the radius.*

These points are actually the ends of a diameter. The following is a typical command sequence:

Command: *CIRCLE, 2 POINT*
Enter first point on diameter: *5,1*
Enter second point on diameter: *5,9*

The **three-point** method requires you to locate three points on the circumference of the circle.

Arc Command. There are many ways to draw an arc using the **arc command**. The following illustrates some of them. Note that arcs are drawn counterclockwise.

The **start, center,** and **end** (SCE) method requires that you locate the center of the radius of the arc and the starting and ending points. The radius is equal to the distance from the center to the starting point (Fig. 5-12). The following is a typical command sequence:

Command: *ARC, SCE*
Enter center point: *8,7*
Enter starting point: *2,7*
Enter ending point: *8,1*

The **start, end, radius** (SER) method uses the length of the radius and the coordinates of the starting and ending points.

Linetype Commands. A variety of **linetypes** (hidden, visible, etc.) are used on drawings. The CADD program will permit you to call up on the screen the linetypes avail-

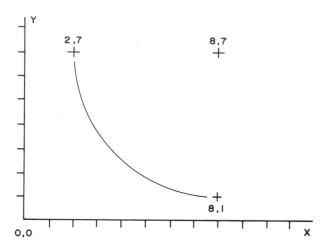

Figure 5-12. *An arc can be drawn giving the coordinates of its center, beginning point, and endpoint.*

able. The user's manual explains how you select linetypes from the menu.

Trace Command. On architectural drawings, you draw visible lines wider than hidden lines. The *trace command* is used to draw lines to the desired width. You enter the trace command and indicate the desired line width. Then you enter point-to-point coordinates for the lines that are to be widened. The lines are drawn wide on the plotter by having the pen redraw (trace) them several times, moving to one side a little more each time.

Polygon Command. A polygon is a closed geometric figure bounded by three or more line segments. The *polygon command* is used to draw regular polygons quickly. You specify the center point of the polygon, the number of sides, and the radius. The polygon is described as being inscribed in a circle or circumscribed about a circle (Fig. 5-13).

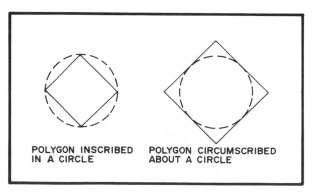

POLYGON INSCRIBED IN A CIRCLE   POLYGON CIRCUMSCRIBED ABOUT A CIRCLE

Figure 5-13. *Polygons can be created in two ways.*

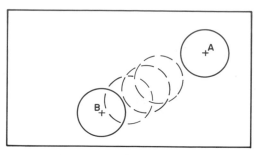

Figure 5-14. *Objects on the screen can be dragged to a new size or location. The circle has been dragged from location A to B.*

Drag Function. The *drag function* makes it possible to dynamically drag an image on the screen. It lets you move an object, rotate it, or scale it to size visually. When dragging begins, tentative images are drawn as you move the pointing device. When you are satisfied with the appearance of the image you press the pointer's pick button (Fig. 5-14).

Fillet Command. The *fillet command* is used when two lines must be connected with an arc having a specified radius. You have to indicate which lines are to be connected and give the radius of the fillet (Fig. 5-15).

Chamfer Command. A chamfer is a flat surface formed by cutting off the edge or corner of an object. To draw the chamfer, indicate the locations of its ends on the monitor. When the *chamfer command* is given, the two lines will be trimmed by the specified amount and connected with a straight line (Fig. 5-15).

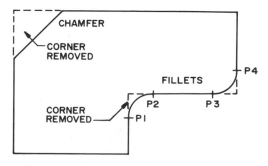

CHAMFER
LOCATE POINTS AT ENDS OF THE CHAMFER. THE CHAMFER COMMAND WILL DRAW THE CHAMFER

FILLETS
INDICATE LINES TO MEET IN A FILLET AS P1,P2 AND P3,P4. INDICATE RADIUS. FILLET COMMAND WILL DRAW THE FILLETS.

Figure 5-15. *Corners can be quickly chamfered or have fillets drawn.*

Pictorial Drawings

Isometric Drawings. An *isometric drawing* is a pictorial drawing that has equal angles between its axes. Some CADD programs have a mode that uses the three planes needed to draw using these three axes. Once the three axes are established, you must indicate whether you are drawing on the right, left, or top plane. Then the lines are drawn and edited in each plane using the normal commands. A typical isometric drawing is in Fig. 5-16.

3-D Drawings. Some CADD programs have a three-dimensional (3-D) facility which enables you to create lines and planes in three-dimensional space using *X*, *Y* and *Z* coordinates (Fig. 5-17).

Some 3-D programs produce **shaded solids modeling**. This places shades of color and shadows on and next to the object, giving a most realistic appearance. The direction of the light source can be chosen. For example, a building could be shaded to represent how it looks when the early morning sun strikes it. Figure 5-2 is an example of this technique.

Symbol Libraries

A **symbol library** is a group of frequently used symbols and details stored on a disk. For example, when making a heating diagram, you would use the symbol for a heat

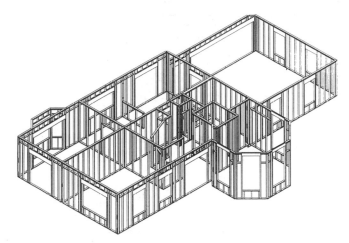

Figure 5-17. This is a 3-D drawing showing the wall framing of a small house. (Courtesy Home Planners, Inc. © 1992 and Integrated Computer Graphics Acquisition Corporation © 1992).

emitter many times. Rather than redraw it each time, you can call it up out of the library (storage), indicate its location, and it will automatically be drawn there. CADD programs are available with libraries for special fields such as architectural drawing. They also provide commands that enable the drafter to add additional items to the existing library.

Drawing Aids

Grid Command. The **grid command** produces a grid of dots on the monitor with a specified spacing. You can turn it on and off as needed and you can change the dot spacing quickly. The grid is for visual reference as you make a drawing and will not print when the drawing is produced by the plotter.

Axis Command. The **axis command** is used to place a ruler line on the lower and right borders of the screen. The spacing of the tick marks can be specified. You may find it helpful if they have the same spacing as the grid dots (Fig. 5-18).

Snap Command. Points entered on the screen can be aligned to an imaginary grid using the **snap command**. If a point is entered on the screen that is not aligned with a snap point on the grid, the point is automatically forced to the nearest snap point.

Ortho Command. It is difficult to draw lines that are exactly vertical or horizontal. The **ortho command** is used to make them exactly vertical or horizontal. This means that all lines and traces will be drawn horizontally

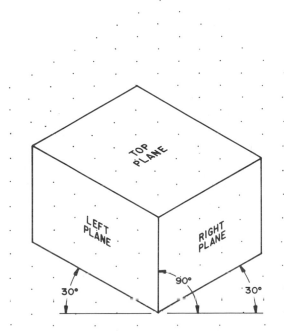

Figure 5-16. An isometric drawing has three planes. This drawing is on an isometric grid.

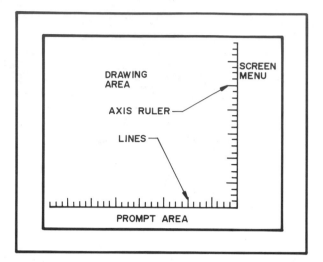

Figure 5-18. *The axis command is used to place ruler lines on the screen.*

or vertically but never on a diagonal. If the end point of a line makes it more nearly horizontal than vertical, the line will be forced into a horizontal position.

Dimensioning

When using CADD, a drawing can be dimensioned semi-automatically. This means that the program can construct a dimension line, measure the distance, and enter it in a break in the dimension line. While dimensions can be drawn using other commands, semiautomatic dimensioning is faster and simpler.

There are four basic types of dimensioning: linear, angular, diameter, and radius (Fig. 5-19). Each one of these has specific dimensioning commands. Linear dimensions can be horizontal, vertical, aligned with a sloping side, rotated to a specified angle, drawn from the baseline of the previous dimension, or continued from the second extension line of the previous dimension (Fig. 5-20). The angular dimensioning command draws an arc to show the angle between two lines. The diameter command shows the diameter of a circle or an arc. Radius dimensioning commands show the radius of a circle or arc (Fig. 5-21).

The dimensioning menu lists the commands for the four basic types of dimensioning. For example, these might be the words *linear*, *diameter*, *angular*, and *radius*. You pick the command for the type of dimension, such as linear–horizontal, and indicate its location on the drawing. The computer calculates the numerical value of the dimension, and the number, dimension line, and required extension lines appear on the monitor.

Other features available enable you to indicate whether you want arrows or tick marks at the ends of dimension lines, specify their size, and select the height of the text

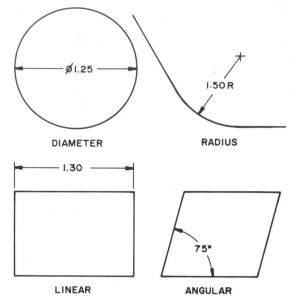

Figure 5-19. *The four basic types of dimensioning.*

(words and numerals). With associative dimensioning, the dimension value is automatically updated if an object's size is altered.

Diameter and radius commands automatically provide leaders for simple applications. When more complex situations arise, the leader command must be used. It enables you to route the leader where necessary.

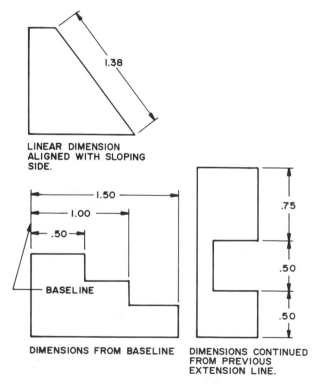

Figure 5-20. *Applications of linear dimensions.*

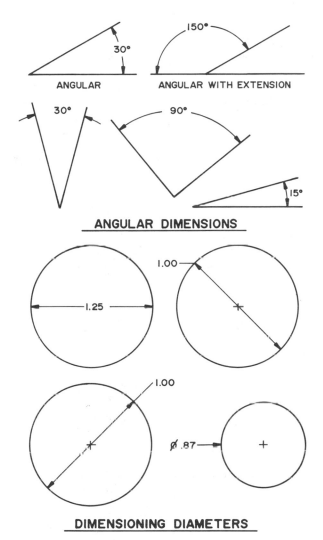

Figure 5-21. *Applications of circular and arc dimensions.*

Text Creation

Text is placed on a drawing using the **text command**. It is typed using the keyboard just like using a typewriter. The text style can be chosen from several that the program makes available. It can be stretched, compressed, obliqued, mirrored, or drawn in a vertical column. It can be of any size. Text is placed in several ways. One method is to show the starting point on the screen with the cursor and type the text. Another adjusts the text size to fit between two designated points. Text can be centered and justified (aligned) on the right side if desired.

Layers and Colors

Layers are similar to the transparent overlays used in manual drafting. A drawing may contain several layers with different data on each. For example, an architectural floor plan could be drawn on layer 1, the electrical system on layer 2, and the plumbing system on layer 3.

Each layer is given a name such as WALLS, ELECTRICAL, and PLUMBING. The layers can be turned on or off. Layers that are turned off are not displayed on the monitor or plotted, but they remain a part of the drawing file.

Each layer is assigned a **color**. If you have a color monitor, the layer will appear in the assigned color. Each layer is also assigned **linetype** (continuous, hidden, etc.). Entities will be drawn in their layer's linetype unless otherwise specified.

Editing Commands

Frequently it will be necessary to make changes in a **drawing**. First decide what part of a drawing you need to edit, or change and isolate it. This is done using the object selection process.

Object selection is accomplished by placing the cursor on the item you want to change or by drawing a window around it. A window is a box produced on the screen by indicating its lower left and upper right corners. Because a window can contain more than one entity, this method of object selection can save time if several related parts of a drawing are to be changed.

Erase Command. The **erase command** is used to remove arcs, lines, and other items from a drawing. The item to be erased is selected by placing the cursor on it or by drawing a window around it. This causes it to be highlighted. The item will disappear when the **enter** or **return** key is pressed.

Unerase Command. If you erase something and see immediately that it was a mistake to do so, the **unerase command** will restore the part just erased. This command should be executed before you initiate another command after erasing.

Break Command. The **break command** is used to erase part of a line, circle, or arc leaving an opening or break in it. You select points locating the beginning and end of the break. In Fig. 5-22, a semicircular recess is needed in the center of the object. The ends of the opening for the recess are located and the line removed with the break command. Then the arc is drawn using normal techniques.

Redraw Command. When a drawing is being developed, a number of markers are used and remain on the screen. If they become a distraction, they can be removed by using the **redraw command**. This clears the screen of all marks and redraws the drawing without the markers appearing on the screen.

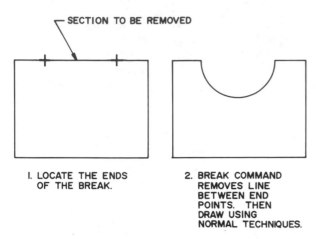

Figure 5-22. *The break command is used to remove unneeded sections of lines.*

Move Command. The *move command* is used to move one or more items on a drawing from their present location on a drawing to a new location without changing their orientation or size. You indicate what is to be moved and the distance it is to be moved (Fig. 5-23).

Copy Command. The *copy command* makes it possible to copy something on the drawing, such as a hole, in another place on the drawing. It is similar to the move

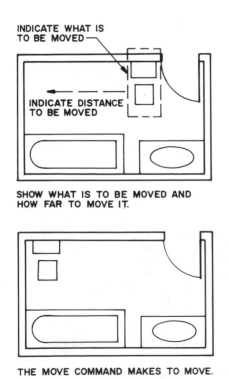

Figure 5-23. *The move command moves an item on a drawing from one location to another without changing its orientation or size.*

command except it copies the item in a new location and leaves the original in place. The coordinates of the new position are given and the material is copied at this new position (Fig. 5-24).

Mirror Command. The *mirror command* is used to produce a mirror image of something drawn on the monitor. A *mirror image* is the reverse of the original image.

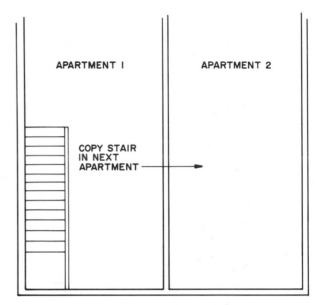

Figure 5-24. *The copy command enables you to reproduce something on a drawing in another location while the original remains in place.*

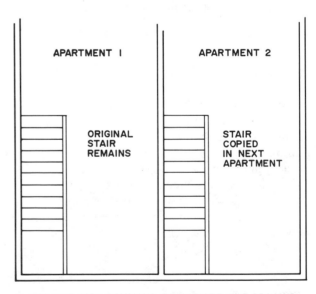

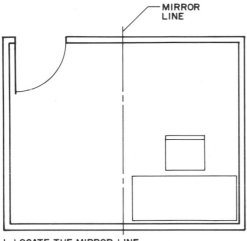

1. LOCATE THE MIRROR LINE.

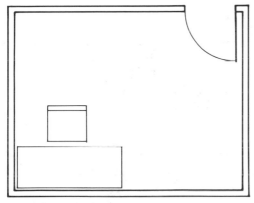

2. USE THE MIRROR COMMAND TO PRODUCE THE IMAGE.

Figure 5-25. *The mirror command produces a reverse of the original image.*

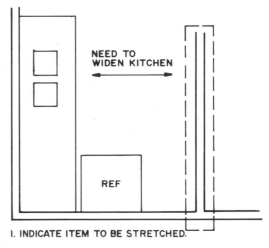

1. INDICATE ITEM TO BE STRETCHED.

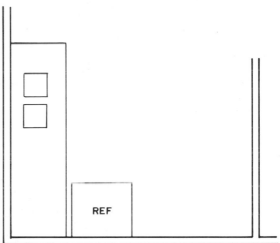

2. USE THE STRETCH COMMAND TO ENLARGE THE KITCHEN.

Figure 5-26. *The stretch command will permit you to move a part of a drawing without changing its connections.*

You place a mirror line on the drawing that becomes the axis about which the selected object is mirrored (Fig. 5-25).

Scale Command. The *scale command* permits the enlargement or reduction of an existing object. For example, if a factor of 3.0 is entered, the object will be enlarged to three times its original size.

Stretch Command. The *stretch command* is used to move a selected part of a drawing without changing the connection to parts of the drawing left in place. Connections with lines, arcs, traces, and solids can be stretched. To stretch an object, place a window around the part to be stretched, then select a base point and a destination. (Fig. 5-26).

Array Command. The *array command* is used to produce multiple copies of one or more objects in a circular or rectangular pattern. The rectangular array requires that the number of rows and columns be specified

and the distance center to center between the items be given (Fig. 5-27). The circular array requires that you specify the angle between the items from center to center and the number of items to draw (Fig. 5-28).

Display Drawing Commands

Zoom Command. The *zoom command* is used to increase or decrease the size of items appearing on the monitor without changing their actual size on the final drawing. When a drawing is small it can be difficult to draw some details because the lines run together on the screen. Using the zoom command the drawing can be enlarged on the screen. The zoom command is followed by a *magnification factor* such as 2. This results in a zoom magnification that shows the drawing twice its original size on the

RECTANGULAR ARRAY

1. DRAW THE ITEM TO BE REPRODUCED. INDICATE THE NUMBER OF ROWS AND COLUMNS, AS 3 ROWS AND 4 COLUMNS, .75 CENTER TO CENTER.

2. THE ARRAY COMMAND WILL REPRODUCE THE ORGINAL IN THE ARRAY INDICATED.

Figure 5-27. *This is a rectangular array.*

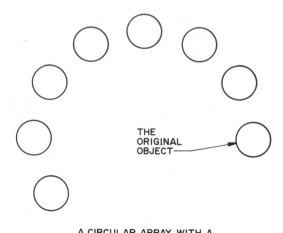

THE ORIGINAL OBJECT

A CIRCULAR ARRAY WITH A 30° ANGLE AND 8 ITEMS.

Figure 5-28. *This is a circular array.*

screen (Fig. 5-29). The drawing is continued at this size and zoomed back to the original when it is finished. It is also possible to use a zoom window command. This permits only a part of a drawing to be enlarged. You draw a window around the area to be enlarged and give the desired magnification. The enlarged area appears on the screen.

Pan Command. The **pan command** allows you to see a different portion of a drawing without changing its magnification. If some details of a drawing are off the screen you can use the pan command to move the drawing, so that you can see and draw on the area that was off the screen (Fig. 5-30).

View Command. When it is necessary to repeatedly switch from one section of a large drawing to another, use the view command. The views involved are stored zooms that are identified by a name. Whenever needed, a view can be recalled by using the **view command** and giving the name of the view. This is faster than zooming and panning repeatedly.

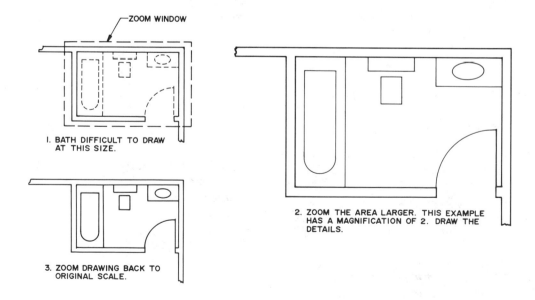

ZOOM WINDOW

1. BATH DIFFICULT TO DRAW AT THIS SIZE.

3. ZOOM DRAWING BACK TO ORIGINAL SCALE.

2. ZOOM THE AREA LARGER. THIS EXAMPLE HAS A MAGNIFICATION OF 2. DRAW THE DETAILS.

Figure 5-29. *The zoom command permits you to enlarge a detail, draw in the features, and reduce it to the original size.*

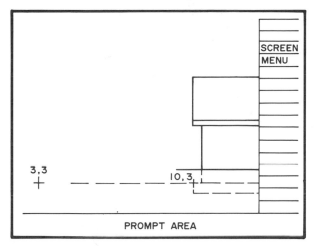

I. MOVE FROM 10,3 TO 3,3.

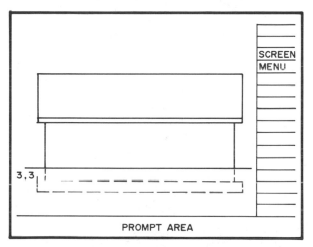

2. THE PAN COMMAND TELLS HOW FAR AND IN WHAT DIRECTION THE OBJECT IS TO BE MOVED.

Figure 5-30. The pan command will move a view across the screen the distance and direction indicated.

Facilitation Commands

Save Command. The *save command* is used to permanently store the work completed on the drawing since it was last saved. If, after starting a drawing, there is a power failure or you forget and turn off the computer, all of your work will be lost. It is wise to stop and save what you have done every so often so that it will not all be lost accidentally.

End Command. The *end command* is used when you are finished working on a drawing. It saves the drawing and exits to the main menu. Save also writes the drawing on a disk but also keeps it available for additional work.

Quit Command. The *quit command* discards all the work performed on a drawing since the last save command. The original drawing will still be intact.

Making An Architectural Drawing

The following is a generalized example used to illustrate the basic process. The project selected was a simple floor plan.

It is assumed that the special graphic symbols used when drawing floor plans are in the symbols library of the architectural drafting program. This includes symbols like materials in section and door and window symbols. If needed symbols are not in the program, the operator can create the symbol and add it to the library or draw it each time using the basic geometric commands.

Following are typical steps which are illustrated in Fig. 5-31:

1. Start the system. Log-on to the system and create a file. How this is done depends somewhat upon your system. Give the file a descriptive name. Determine the size paper to be used for the drawing. Establish the borders, and decide on the unit and scale to be used.

2. Lay out the exterior and interior walls using the CONSTRUCTION LINE function. Switch to the SOLID LINE function when the floor plan layout is finished. Since these are thick lines, it will be necessary to use the LINE WIDTH command. This command lets you set the width of the lines.

3. Add doors, windows, and openings in walls between rooms. These can be drawn from the symbols in the symbol library.

4. Add other interior details such as cabinets, stairs, appliances, and bath fixtures. These are thin lines. Their width can be specified using the LINE WIDTH command.

5. Use the *circle* function to draw the circles for the marks on doors and windows.

6. The electrical symbols could now be added. Add switches, outlets, lighting fixtures, and any special features. Connect switches to lights. To do this use the HIDDEN LINE and the IRREGULAR CURVE command to connect the lights to the switches.

7. Now switch to *dimension* mode and add the dimensions.

8. Switch to the TEXT mode and add room names, door, and window mark labels in the circles, titles, scale, electrical identification, and any needed notes.

9. Hit the SAVE command so the work is not accidently lost. It is now permanently in memory.

10. Ready the plotter. Make certain it has the proper paper in place and is turned on. Hit the PLOT command to produce the drawing.

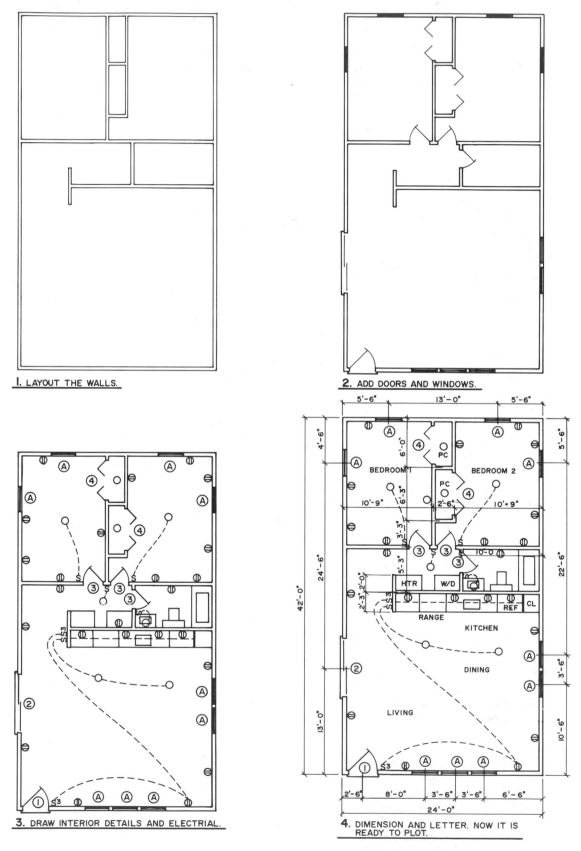

Figure 5-31. *The basic steps followed when making a CADD drawing.*

Other drawings such as foundation plans, wall sections, kitchen details, elevations, heating and air conditioning plans, plumbing plans, and schedules are produced in the same manner. The appropriate commands and symbols from the library are used.

Glossary

Address. The location in computer storage that contains a computer word.

Alphanumeric. Numbers (0–9), alphabetic characters (A–Z), and special symbols (such as *) that are used to form computer words.

Arithmetic-logic unit. The section of the central processing unit that performs the mathematical operations (addition, subtraction, etc.).

Basic. Beginners' All-purpose Symbolic Instruction Code. A popular computer language incorporated in most small computers now on the market.

Binary. A number system, used by digital computers, that requires only two symbols, 0 and 1, for the processing and storing of information.

Bit. A single binary digit that can take the value of 0 or 1.

Byte. A group of adjacent bits that form one alphanumeric character.

CAD (computer-aided design). Using computers in the design process to speed the flow of information, store data, increase analytical capabilities, and speed the decision-making process in the creation or modification of a design.

CAM (computer-aided manufacturing). The utilization of computer technology in the management, control, and operations of a manufacturing facility.

Circle generator. An electronic device that is part of the display device (CRT). It receives the data supplied by the computer, such as the center-point coordinates and the numeric length of the radius and calculates the coordinates for the points on the circumference of the circle.

CNC (computer numerical control). Using a dedicated computer within a numerical control unit to input data.

COBOL. Common Business-Oriented Language.

COM (computer output microfilm). The automated drawing is stored on microfilm by feeding the computer-produced signals through a COM recorder. This produces a microfilm for permanent storage of the drawing or report.

Command. The part of a computer program that specifies an operation, such as addition.

Computer graphics. A human-oriented system that uses the capabilities of a computer to create, modify, and display pictorial and symbolic data.

Core. The main storage area in a computer.

CRT (cathode ray tube). A display device resembling a television tube.

Cursor. A movable symbol, such as a cross, that shows the current position on a CRT.

Data. Information entered into the computer.

Digitizing. Entering information into the computer as electrical signals. Digitizing may be done by using a light pen or a digitizing tablet.

Digitizer board. A flat surface that is used to convert positional locations, such as points on a drawing, to XY coordinates.

Disk. A coated circular disk upon which information is recorded using a magnetic read–write head.

Floppy disk. A flexible disk used to store information from a computer.

Fortran. FORmula TRANslation. A computer language.

Hard copy. A computer printout or drawings produced on a plotter.

Hardware. Computer equipment.

I-CAB (interactive computer-aided design). The designer works directly with the computer design system to design, draft, detail, and document a drawing, in two or three dimensions. The designer works at a digitizer station much the same as at a drafting board. Working at a computer terminal with a video display screen and a digitizing table, the designer moves a cursor from point to point on an engineer's drawing to pick up the details of the drawing and feed them into a computer. Drafting instructions are also typed into the system on a terminal keyboard.

Once the information is in the computer system, the designer can recall it onto the screen for updating and editing. The system is linked to plotters for producing hard copies. The information is stored on computer disks or tapes and can be used by others for reports and documentation.

Input. Programmed instructions and related data put into a computer by human beings.

Interactive system. A system that permits the user to receive output immediately and edit or change the original print.

Interface. Electronic circuitry that changes the output of one piece of hardware so that the signal can be received by another.

I/O (input/output). Information that is put into or received from a computer.

Joystick. An input device that allows the user to plot points on the CRT screen.

Keyboard. The main input device, which resembles the keyboard of a typewriter.

Language. A set of symbols, conventions, and rules used to communicate information.

Library. A collection of programs and subroutines in a form that is readily usable.

Location. An area of computer storage that is identified by an address.

Loop. A series of instructions that can be executed repetitively.

Magnetic tape. A plastic tape upon which data can be stored by means of magnetized spots on its surface.

Megabyte. One million bytes.

Memory. The storage in a computer.

Menu. A list of options displayed either on a CRT or on a printed sheet placed over a digitizing table. The operator can select options for program action by keyboard, cursor, or other digitizing device.

Microprocessor. The electronics of a minicomputer miniaturized onto a single integrated-circuit (IC) chip.

Microsecond. One-millionth of a second.

Microcomputer. A microcomputer is essentially a small, low-cost single-user and single-task computer built around a microcomputer.

Minicomputer. A minicomputer is a multiuser and multitask machine with the capability of supporting up to 80 terminals (usually two to eight), together with essential peripheral devices.

Mirroring. A drawing capability of some computer drafting systems to provide mirror images of symmetrical objects. This ability permits the user to draw one-half of an object and then add the other half by using the mirror-image function.

MODEM. MOdulator–DEModulator. A device that connects a computer system to a communication channel, such as a phone line, leased line, and so forth.

Mouse. A hand-held data input device used to position a cursor.

Output. Any information produced by a computer.

Plotter. An output device used to present data in graphic form, such as a line drawing.

Program. Instructions to a computer that enable it to perform a specified task.

Programmer. A person who sets out computer instructions and numbers in their correct sequence. A programmer also allocates addresses to each instruction and each number.

Printer. A typewriter-like device for output that produces a printed copy of processed data.

RAM (random-access memory). A type of memory used for temporary storage of data and programs which can be randomly accessed while the computer is in operation.

Software. The programs and documentation that enable a computer system to operate and perform specific tasks.

Statement. A generalized instruction to a computer.

Storage. Any device in a computer system that holds information until needed.

Software. Computer programs.

Storage CRT. A CRT that maintains a steady image until the image is erased.

Subroutine. A part of a program designed for a specific operation. Sometimes called a subprogram.

Terminal. A point in a system where data may be put into it or received from it.

Tablet. A digitizing board that is used for inputting graphical data. The computer-drafting technician may draw on the surface of the tablet using a stylus, with the position of the stylus being transmitted to the computer.

Terminal. An input and output station consisting of a CRT and keyboard. Often, the terminal may be connected to a computer in another city via a telephone line.

Time-sharing. The use of a single computer by several users at separate terminals at the same time.

User-friendly. Software designed so as to provide easy use of the computer by persons who know very little about programming. Such software instructs and guides the user by offering questions and choices.

Video Display. A TV-like device that shows both input to a computer and the resulting output.

View Port. A view port is a user-selected bounded area which presents the contents of a window on the CRT screen. The view port determines how much of the screen is to be taken up by a specific window.

Window. A bounded area on the CRT screen, usually rectangular, selected by the operator.

Technical Vocabulary

Following are some important technical terms used in this chapter. Write a brief definition for each.

Computer-aided design
Units
Limits
Scaling
Cartesian coordinates
Alphanumeric data
Graphic data
Menu
Cursor
Commands
Symbol library
Layers

Study Questions

Answer the following study questions without referring to the text. Then check your answers with the text and correct those that were wrong.

1. List the office functions that can be performed with a computer.

2. What is meant by computer-aided design?

3. How are the drawings developed on the computer stored for future reference?

4. If 1 in. on a drawing equals 10 units and one unit represents 1 ft, what is the scale of the drawing?

5. If the clear drawing area on a paper is 17 × 23 in. and the scale used is 1″ = 5′-0″, what are the overall dimensions of the plotting area?

6. Draw Cartesian coordinates with horizontal and vertical scales of ±10. Plot the following points: 8,6; 5,10; −4+4; 6,−3; −5,−5.

7. Explain how to give the "line" command.

8. List the ways available to draw circles.

9. How do you command the plotter to draw wide lines?

10. What command do you use if you want to move an image already on the screen?

11. What is meant by the term semiautomatic dimensioning?

12. What command would you use when you want to put notes on a drawing?

13. Explain how layers are used on architectural drawings.

14. What command do you use when you want to change a drawing?

15. How do you enlarge or reduce the size of the image on the screen.?

Laboratory Problems

1. After you have studied the manuals and have had instruction in operating your computer drafting system, try to draw some of the figures in Chapter 6 such as 6-3, 6-5, 6-19, and 6-21. Copy figures in other chapters as assigned by your instructor.

2. Draw the finished floor plan in Fig. 5-31.

6

Architectural Drafting Standards

Architects and engineers prepare construction drawings. The purpose of these drawings is to communicate to others, such as contractors, subcontractors, owners, and financial officials, the specific details necessary to construct an acceptable building. Actually the drawings become part of the legal contract drawn up when a building is to be built. In order to communicate effectively, uniform drafting standards and symbols are used.

Architectural Symbols

Uniform symbols are used on architectural drawings to represent things that would be difficult or impossible to represent as they actually appear. For example, a simplified symbol is used to represent a casement window on a floor plan. To draw the actual window on a floor plan would be a difficult job. Also it would not add to the clarity of the drawing. The same can be said for other features such as a light, lavatory, or switch. Therefore, they are represented by standardized symbols.

Sections through various parts of the construction are necessary to clarify details. Standard symbols are used to indicate the *materials* in each part cut by the section (Fig. 6-1). Materials in elevation are also indicated by symbols (Fig. 6-2). A detailed listing of materials in elevation and section are in the Appendix. Additional material symbols

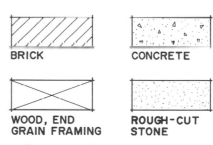

Figure 6-1. *Examples of symbols for materials in section.*

are available in architectural standards publications and the chapters in this text.

Building components, such as doors and windows, are represented by symbols showing them in plan view and elevation (Fig. 6-3). *Electrical symbols* greatly simplify the work of showing the components and electrical circuits (Fig. 6-4). *Plumbing fixtures* and *piping* of various kinds would produce complex drawing without the use of symbols (Fig. 6-4). The design of heating, ventilating, and air conditioning systems requires a careful study of the building and many calculations. Once the system has been designed, it is shown on the drawing with symbols (Fig. 6-5). The more commonly used symbols in these areas are shown in the chapters where these types of drawings are discussed. Additional symbols are found in architectural standards references and publications of the American National Standards Institute.

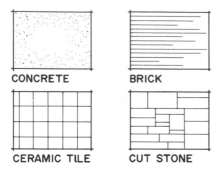

Figure 6-2. Examples of symbols for materials in elevation.

Architectural Standards Publications

There are a large number of publications the architect must have for reference purposes. It is impossible to remember the hundreds of thousands of details needed for design and drafting purposes. Information used frequently can be stored in the memory of the computer but the extent and type of information makes this impractical. Following are some of the major sources.

Published architectural standards references are available from a number of major publishing companies. These cover the total range of architectural design.

Publications of the American National Standards Institute, 1430 Broadway, New York, N.Y. 10018 cover standards applicable to appliances, acoustics, building construction, electrical components, concrete, building materials, insulating materials, graphic symbols, solar components, and pipe.

The companies manufacturing and selling materials,

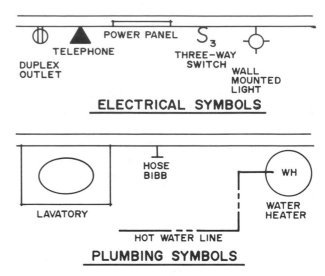

Figure 6-4. A few of the electrical and plumbing symbols used on floor plans.

components, systems, and services are another source of design data. Information about these companies is available in the dozens of magazines published which relate to the building industry. Up-to-date product information is provided by the various sets of Sweets Catalog Files.

Other organizations publish considerable material bearing on the design and construction of buildings. Typical of these are organizations such as the Portland Cement Association, American Institute of Steel Construction, Con-

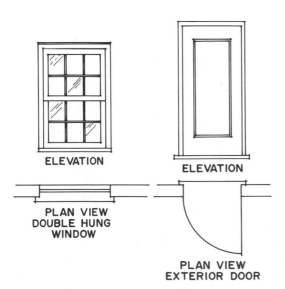

Figure 6-3. Examples of door and window symbols in elevation and in section.

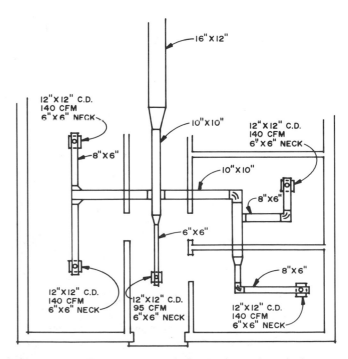

Figure 6-5. This shows symbols used on a hot-air duct system.

crete Reinforcing Steel Institute, Underwriter's Laboratories, Inc., American Society for Testing and Materials, National Forest Products Association, The American Plywood Association, and the U.S. Department of Commerce. These are but a few of the hundreds of trade, professional, and government organizations doing research and testing in building components, design, systems, and materials.

Lines and Line Quality

Two widths of lines are used on architectural drawings, thick and thin. In the following chapters, line widths will be mentioned but following are typical examples. The outline of a foundation is a thick line. The hidden lines representing the footing and any symbols, as for brick or concrete, are thin lines. The thick line is usually about 0.030 in. wide (a little under $\frac{1}{32}$ in. or 0.8 mm). A thin line is usually half the width of the thick line or 0.015 in. (or about $\frac{1}{64}$ in. or 0.4 mm). Border lines, title block frames and schedule outlines, are usually very wide, 0.035 in. (or $\frac{1}{32}$ in. or 0.9 mm).

All lines should be drawn as sharp and black as possible. Since the original drawing will be used to produce copies, the lines must be black enough to permit good reproduction. Additional information on reproduction is in the next chapter.

Sometimes the drafter likes to lighten up a bit on material symbols used to represent materials in elevation, such as brick on a building. This gives a lighter, broken line which some prefer. However, all working drawings must be drawn as dark as possible, even the thin lines.

Good line quality means using the proper hardness of lead, applying the proper pressure, and keeping the pencil point in good condition. Wood-cased and mechanical pencils require frequent pointing. Thin-line pencils require no pointing. In general, a 2H lead produces a quality line.

Borders

The size of borders used on architectural drawings varies according to the standards of the firm. Typically a 1-in. (25-mm) to 1.5-in. (38-mm) border is on the left edge and $\frac{1}{2}$-in. (12 mm) borders on the other three sides. The left edge has a larger border because the drawings are bound on that side (Fig. 6-6).

Title Blocks

The location, size, and information contained in the title block is standardized for each architectural firm. Typically it will contain the name of the job and its location, sheet title, the name and address of the architect, the name of the client, the names and addresses of consulting engineers, names or initials of drafters and checkers, revision blocks, professional seal, and drawing number.

The title block can be placed along the bottom edge of the sheet but most often is placed up the right side (Fig. 6-6). Typical title blocks are shown in Fig. 6-7 and 6-8.

A firm may have the border and title block printed on their sheets. The drafter can fill in the needed information using adhesive letters, Leroy lettering, rubber stamps, or templates, or letter it freehand.

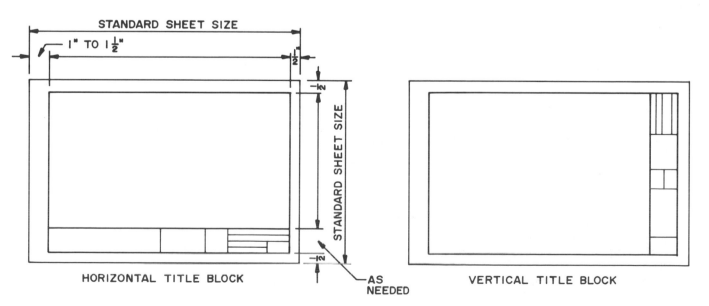

Figure 6-6. *Commonly used border and title block placement.*

| ADDITION TO UNION CHRISTIAN CHURCH 5673 HILL ST. ST. JOSEPH, OH. 51423 | R. WILL · ARCHITECT 1234 OAK ST. AURORA, KS. 66762 PHONE: 316-231-7000 | JOB NO. 327 / DATE ISSUED: 6-7-91 / DRAWN BY: W. P. S. / CHECKED BY: L. D. C. | SEAL | M2 |

Figure 6-7. *A typical title block placed along the bottom edge of the paper.*

| E3 | ADDITION TO UNION CHRISTIAN CHURCH 5673 HILL ST. ST. JOSEPH, OH. 51423 | R. WILL · ARCHITECT 1234 OAK ST. AURORA, KS. 66762 PHONE: 316-231-7000 | THIRD FLOOR ELECTRICAL DETAILS | CHECKED BY L.D.C. / DRAWN BY W.P.S. / DATE ISSUED 6/7/91 / JOB NUMBER 327 | SEAL |

Figure 6-8. *A typical vertical title block.*

Titles

The height of the lettering normally used for drawings to be reproduced the same size as the original, as is done by the diazo process is:

Main titles under drawings $\frac{3}{16}$–$\frac{1}{4}$ in. (5–6 mm)
Subtitles, as room names $\frac{1}{8}$–$\frac{3}{16}$ in. (3–5 mm)
Normal lettering as notes and dimensions $\frac{3}{32}$–$\frac{1}{8}$ in. (2.4–3 mm)
Sheet number in title block $\frac{1}{2}$ in. (12 mm)

If the drawing is to be reduced in size as can be done by xerography, the larger sizes of lettering should be used. If the reduction is to be great, even larger sizes may be necessary.

Measurement

The architect must thoroughly understand both the customary and metric systems of measurement.

The Customary System

The basic linear unit is the yard. It is divided into three units called feet. The 1-ft unit is divided into common fractions or decimal fractions.

Common fractions are specified in units such as $\frac{1}{2}$, $\frac{1}{4}$, $\frac{1}{8}$, $\frac{1}{16}$, $\frac{1}{32}$ and $\frac{1}{64}$. Decimal fractions are specified in one or more decimal parts of an inch such as 0.1 (one-tenth), 0.05 (five-hundredths), and 0.009 (nine-thousandths). A comparison of these scales with a metric scale is shown in Fig. 6-9).

SI Metric Measurements

The SI metric system has seven basic units, meter, candela, kilogram, second, kelvin, ampere, and mole. Of these the measure for linear distance, the meter, has the most application to the development of architectural drawings.

SI Units of Length

The meter is the basic metric unit of length. The linear system is built on base 10, therefore all subdivisions of the meter are divided by 10. The subdivisions of a meter are in Fig. 6-10. The meter (which is about 39.4 in.) is divided into 10 units called decimeters. Decimeters are divided into 10 units called centimeters. Centimeters are divided into 10 units called millimeters.

A metric unit can be changed from one unit (as centimeters) to another (as decimeters) by moving the decimal point. For example, 20 m equals 200 dm or 2500 cm or 25 000 mm.

Architectural working drawings are usually dimensioned in millimeters or meters. Decimeters and centimeters are rarely used.

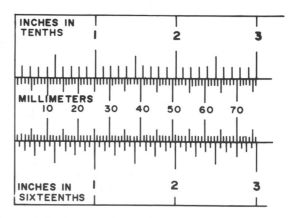

Figure 6-9. *A comparison of a metric scale with common fractions and decimal fractions of an inch.*

one kilometer (km) = 1000 meters (m)
one hectometer (hm) = 100 meters (m)
one decameter (dam) = 10 meters (m)
one meter is the base unit
one decimeter (dm) = 1/10 meter (m)
one centimeter (cm) = 1/100 meter (m)
one millimeter (mm) = 1/1000 meter (m)

Figure 6-10. *The subdivisions of a meter.*

Metric Notations

The standard placement for a decimal point is in the center of the line, as 35·40 mm; however, it is acceptable to place it at the bottom, 35.40, as used in customary dimensioning.

Spaces are used instead of commas between numbers in a long series. Numbers of five digits or more are separated into groups of three starting from the right or left of the decimal marker, 5 350.100 205 mm. Four-digit numbers do not require a space, 1530 mm.

All abbreviations for metric linear measurement units are lettered lower case. A space is left between the dimension and the abbreviation. Abbreviations do not have a plural. For example, 75 millimeters is written 75 mm.

Metric Conversion

The conversion from Customary to metric units is not frequently required, however, should the need arise, selected metric conversion factors are in the Appendix.

Drawing to Scale

A description of the architect's, engineers, and metric scales is in Chapter 1. The following will show where these are used.

The scale to use for various drawings in a set of architectural drawings varies with the size of the unit being drawn. Following are commonly used scales.

Scales for Small Buildings

	Customary (inches)	Metric (millimeters)
Floor plan	$\frac{1}{4}'' = 1'-0''$	1:50
Foundation plan	$\frac{1}{4}'' = 1'-0''$	1:50
Elevations	$\frac{1}{4}'' = 1'-0''$	1:50
Construction details	$\frac{3}{4}''$ to $1\frac{1}{2}'' = 1'-0''$	1:20 and 1:10
Wall sections	$\frac{3}{4}''$ to $1\frac{1}{2}'' = 1'-0''$	1:20 and 1:10
Cabinet details	$\frac{3}{8}''$ to $\frac{1}{2}'' = 1'-0''$	1:50 and 1:25
Site plan	$1'' = 20.0', 30.0',$ or $40.0'$	1:100

Scales for Large Buildings

	Customary (inches)	Metric (millimeters)
Floor plan	$\frac{1}{8}'' = 1'-0''$	1:100
Foundation plan	$\frac{1}{8}'' = 1'-0''$	1:100
Elevations	$\frac{1}{8}'' = 1'-0''$	1:100
Construction details	$\frac{1}{2}''$ to $3'' = 1'-0''$	1:25 or 1:10
Interior details	$\frac{1}{2}'' = 1'-0''$	1:25
Building sections	$\frac{1}{8}''$ or $\frac{1}{4}'' = 1'-0''$	1:50
Framing details	$\frac{1}{8}'' = 1'-0''$	1:100
Lighting, electrical, heating, plumbing, air conditioning plans	$\frac{1}{8} = 1'-0''$	1:100
Site plan	$1'' = 20.0', 30.0', 40.0', 50.0',$ or $60.0'$	1:100, 1:200, or 1:500

Abbreviations

Abbreviations are used to save time and space and still clearly indicate the intended message. The architect, engineer, drafter, and contractor must all know the meaning of these abbreviations. Some types of special work may use abbreviations that have a different meaning for those working in a different trade area. For example, R can identify a range and also a riser. If there is possible doubt in reading the abbreviation, a legend indicating the meanings of abbreviations can be placed on the drawings.

Selected standard abbreviations recommended for use on architectural drawings are shown in the Appendix.

8" 12" 2'-0 1'-03/4" 2'-6"

INCH DIMENSIONS

570   1375   15 762

METRIC   DIMENSIONS

Figure 6-11. How to measure distances in millimeters.

Dimensioning

At the present, most architectural drawings are dimensioned in feet and inches. Parts of an inch are given in

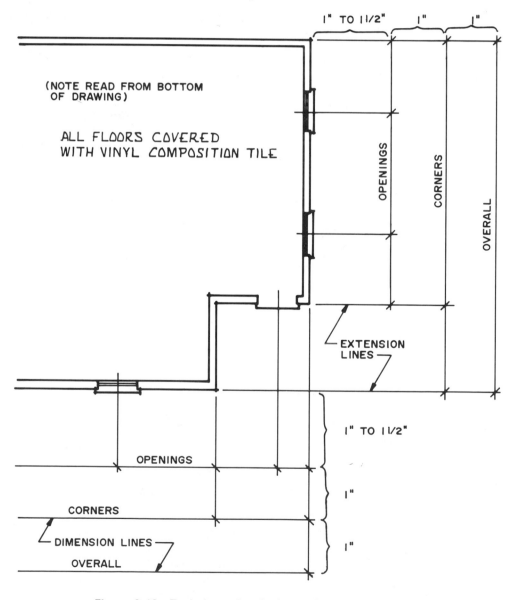

Figure 6-12. Techniques for placing and spacing dimensions.

common fractions. If the drawing is metric, all dimensions are in millimeters.

When dimensioning in feet and inches the symbols (') for feet and (") for inches are used. Any dimensions 12" and under are specified in inches with no zero before them. Dimensions over 12" are specified in feet and inches as 1'-5". A dash is always placed between the feet and inches. When a common fraction appears without a whole number before it, some prefer to put a zero before it. If the distance is an even number of feet, the inches are shown with a zero, 6'-0. Some prefer to leave the inch mark off when inches are zero. Metric drawings require no unit dimension because all dimensions are millimeters (Fig. 6-11).

There are usually three levels of dimensioning on plan views and related drawings. The dimensions locating *doors and windows* are placed nearest to the building. The next level locates *major corners* and the farthest out level shows the *overall* dimension. On sections and details usually only two levels are needed. The dimensions in each level are kept in line with each other. They are sometimes called *strings*.

The first level of dimensions should be placed 1 to $1\frac{1}{2}$ in. away from the building. Additional rows should be at least $\frac{1}{2}$ in. apart. The first level of dimensions should clear porches, decks, and other items that may protrude from a plan. All dimensions are placed so they are read from the bottom and right sides of the drawing. All notes are lettered so they are read from the bottom (Fig. 6-12).

When there is not enough room to letter the dimension, place the dimension outside the space and connect it to the space with a leader. When identifying something on a drawing, such as a concrete floor, the name is lettered near the item and connected to it with a leader. Two types of leaders, straight and curved, are commonly used as shown in Fig. 6-13. Whichever is chosen, they always start from the beginning or end of a word or note and are centered on that word. Straight line leaders always begin with a short horizontal line and then angle to the part. Generally one type or the other is used on a drawing rather than using both on the same drawing.

When possible, dimensions are placed off the drawing. The points between which dimensions are to be placed are extended out with extension lines. *Extension lines* must clear the building about $\frac{1}{16}$ in. They should extend beyond the dimension line about $\frac{1}{16}$ in. A solid *dimension line* runs between the extension lines and is parallel with the edge of the building. The dimension is lettered above the line. The numerals must not touch the dimension line (Fig. 6-14). Dimension and extension lines are drawn as thin lines. Since architectural drawings are complex it is necessary to place many dimensions directly on top of the drawing. In this case, dimension lines are used and sometimes interior parts are located using extension lines.

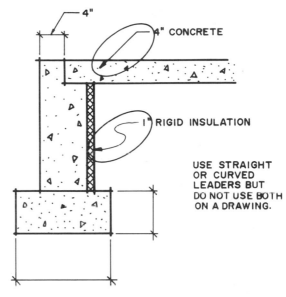

Figure 6-13. *How to use leaders.*

Other times, it is necessary to dimension directly to the surface being located (Fig. 6-15).

Where the dimension line touches an extension line or the surface, it is terminated with an arrow, a dot, or a 45° slash. When using the slash some prefer to let the dimen-

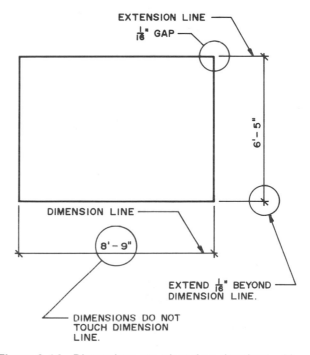

Figure 6-14. *Dimensions are placed on drawings with extension and dimension lines.*

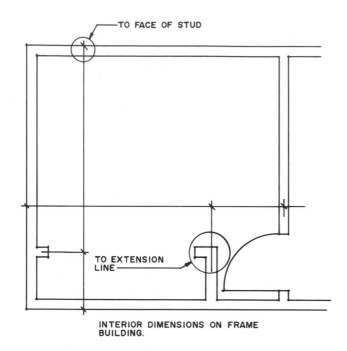

INTERIOR DIMENSIONS ON FRAME BUILDING.

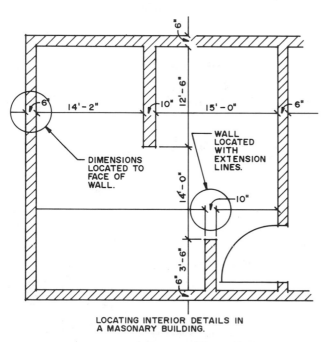

LOCATING INTERIOR DETAILS IN A MASONARY BUILDING.

Figure 6-15. Locating interior details.

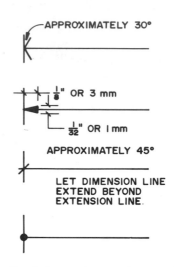

Figure 6-16. Symbols used to terminate a dimension line.

FLOOR PLAN
SCALE 1/4" = 1'- 0"

WALL SECTION
SCALE 1/2" = 1'-0"

SITE PLAN
SCALE 1"= 40.0'

Figure 6-17. Scales are indicated below the title of a drawing.

Every drawing on a sheet must have a title and a scale. Since architectural drawings located together on one sheet may have different scales, it is not possible to put a single scale in the title block as is done on engineering drawings. Occasionally one or more dimensions are shown on a drawing where the size was changed but the drawing was not redrawn. These dimensions are not to scale. They are so indicated by placing the abbreviation N.T.S. beside the dimension (Fig. 6-18). The specific application of dimensions to architectural drawings is in the chapters on drawings.

sion line extend a little beyond the extension line (Fig. 6-16). The one to be used is usually established by the architectural firm so all drawings have the same symbol.

The scale used when making the drawing must always be indicated. It is usually lettered below the drawing title in letters the same height as the dimensions. The title uses higher letters, often around $\frac{3}{16}$ in. (5 mm) (Fig. 6-17).

36'-9" (N.T.S.)

Figure 6-18. Dimensions that are no longer to scale must be so indicated.

Keeping the Drawing Clean

It is essential that the drawing be kept clean. Carbon from pencils is smeared by the drafting instruments and sticks to them. This produces smudges which sometimes make sections of prints run from these drawings hard to read. Following are some things to do to help keep the drawing free from smudges.

1. Wash the instruments and your hands frequently.

2. In hot weather, keep a piece of scrap paper under your hand to keep perspiration off the drawing.

3. When possible, start drawing at the top of the sheet and work down.

4. Use a drafters brush to dust away carbon left after drawing a line.

5. Do not slide the drafting instruments across the paper. When possible pick them up and move them.

6. Cover all completed work with a piece of clean paper. Tape it lightly in place (Fig. 6-19).

7. Use eraser crumbs to clear light smudges. They are sold in a sack made from porous cloth. Shake the sack over the drawing to lay down a very light sprinkling of eraser crumbs. Brush these off on the floor as you work because they will get dirty. Be careful to not overuse these because they could reduce the density of the lines on the drawing (Fig. 6-20).

8. If drawing on plastic drafting film use plastic-based lead pencils. These are designed to adhere to the plastic, and thereby reduce smudging. Regular graphite pencils will draw on plastic film but they dull rapidly and smear easily.

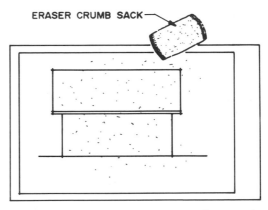

Figure 6-20. *Lightly sprinkle eraser crumbs over the drawing as you work. Brush off as they get dirty.*

9. After a drawing is finished, it can be given permanent protection from smearing by a spraying with a fixative (Fig. 6-21). A fixative is an invisible plastic spray sold in aerosol cans. It is available in a matte or gloss finish. Once a drawing has been sprayed, it cannot be changed. The fine coating is almost impossible to remove without damaging the paper.

When applying the spray, hold the can 12–18 in. from the surface. Start at one side of the drawing near the top. Start the spray and move the can rapidly across the drawing. Move down and repeat until the drawing is covered. It is better to put on several very light coats than one heavy coat. Before attempting to use a fixative, practice on scrap paper because it is difficult to use correctly.

Technical Vocabulary

Following are some important technical terms used in this chapter. Write a brief definition for each.

Architectural symbols
Architectural standards

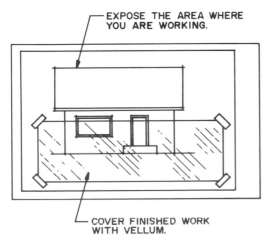

Figure 6-19. *Cover the completed area of the drawing to prevent smudging the pencil lines.*

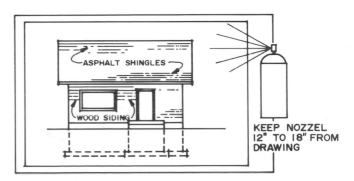

Figure 6-21. *After the drawing is finished it can be sprayed with a fixative.*

Title block
Customary system of measurement
Metric system
Architectural scales

Study Questions

Answer the following study questions without referring to the text. Then check your answers with the text and correct those that were wrong.

1. Why are architectural symbols used on drawings?

2. Name a major source of drafting and material standard publications.

3. What is the desired width of thick and thin lines used on architectural drawings?

4. What information is commonly found in a title block?

5. What are the recommended heights of lettering for notes, dimensions, and main titles?

6. What is a common fraction? A decimal fraction?

7. What is the base metric unit for linear measure?

8. How many millimeters are there in 1 ft?

9. What do the metric terms "kilo" and "milli" mean?

10. What metric units are used to give the area of a surface or piece of land?

11. Which of the following is correct spacing for a five-digit metric number: (a) 13160, (b) 13 160, (c) 13,160?

12. Why are different scales used for residential and commercial drawings?

13. What symbols are used for residential and commercial drawings?

14. What purpose does an extension line serve?

15. List some things you can do to help keep your drawing clean.

7

Reproduction of Drawings

Copies of preliminary drawings and check prints are needed for examination and revision before the final approved drawings are completed. Multiple copies of the final drawings are made for bidding and construction purposes. There are several systems in use for drawing reproduction.

Whiteprints

Whiteprints are copies of the original drawing that are reproduced with blue, black, or maroon lines on a white background. Those with blue lines are commonly referred to as 'blue lines.' A brown line product on a cream colored paper is also available. The choice of color is made when purchasing the diazo paper. The reproduction paper is coated with a diazo compound. This process is often referred to as the diazo process.

Whiteprints are produced by feeding the original drawing on top of a sheet of diazo paper into a whiteprint machine (Fig. 7-1). The diazo paper is placed with the yellow diazo dye side up and the drawing is placed on top of this with the pencil side up. As they are fed into the whiteprinter they are exposed to ultraviolet light. The pencil lines keep the light from hitting the dye and destroying it. The dye on unprotected areas is destroyed by the light. As the two sheets leave the exposure unit they are separated (Fig. 7-2). The diazo copy is then fed into the de-

Figure 7-1. A whiteprinter showing the original drawing on top of the diazo paper entering the exposure section. (Courtesy of Blue-Ray, Inc.

veloping unit. There are two diazo processes used for developing—the dry process and the moist process.

The *dry process* developer passes the exposed diazo paper into an atmosphere of heated ammonia vapor. When the vapor hits the diazo lines on the sheet, they are developed (Fig.7-3).

The *moist process* uses the same exposure system as the dry process. The exposed diazo copy is developed by feeding it into the developing section of the whiteprinter

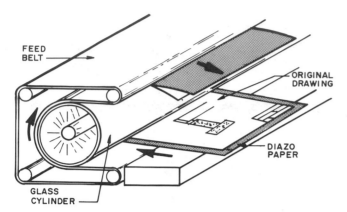

Figure 7-2. *A whiteprinter exposes the original drawing to the diazo paper.*

where it passes between rollers that are moistened with a liquid developing solution.

The appearance of the copy depends upon the speed at which the original drawing and the diazo paper are fed together past the light source. The slower the rate of feed the lighter the color of the background. If run too slow, the lines will begin to disappear. If run too fast, the background will be very blue. Diazo copies will fade rapidly if exposed to sunlight. They can sometimes be "refreshed" by running them through the developer.

Sepias

Sepias (often called brown lines) are used to produce a copy of the original drawing which is translucent and can be used to produce whiteprints, thus preserving the original drawing. Sepias can have changes made on them, leaving the original drawing intact.

Sepias are made using the diazo process. The dye is on a translucent material such as vellum and polyester film and when developed the film has brown lines.

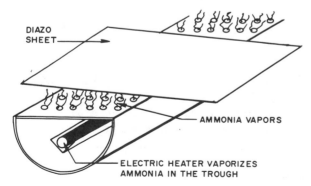

Figure 7-3. *The dry diazo process develops the reproduction with heated ammonia vapor.*

Blueprinting

The use of blueprints has diminished with the development of other reproductive methods. Basically blueprinting involves exposing a blueprint paper with the original drawing to a light source. The blueprint paper is separated from the drawing and developed in a solution of potassium dichromate and then dried. This produces a copy with a blue background and white lines. The chemicals in the protected areas (lines) wash away during developing. Blueprints are more durable than white prints and do not fade as readily.

Electrostatic Reproduction

Electrostatic reproductions are produced by the xerographic process. This produces copies with a black line on a white background. Copies can be produced on vellum, bond paper, polyester drafting film, and other papers.

The basic office copier can be used to produce reproductions of drawings. These are available in a variety of sizes. Xerographic units can reproduce almost any image that is fed into them, including line drawings and photographs. The image to be copied does not have to be on translucent paper. Xerographic printers will make enlarged or reduced copies. Xerographic engineering printers reproduce large drawings clearly and rapidly (Fig. 7-4). Prints on translucent materials can be used to produce additional copies using the diazo process if so desired.

Figure 7-4. *This is a high-speed electrostatic printer. (Courtesy of Xerox Corporation.)*

Figure 7-5. *This transceiver operates without an attendant, receiving and sending documents by telephone. It records the image on plain paper. (Courtesy of Xerox Corporation.)*

Drawings and reports can be transmitted over long-distance xerography networks using special telephone lines, microwave transmission, and coaxial cable. The images (drawings) are sent from one location to another very rapidly. These transmissions are made and received by a xerographic transceiver. It converts the images on the drawing to video transmission signals which when received by the printer converts them back and prints out a black line on white paper (Fig. 7-5).

Another way to transmit drawings and reports is with a *fax machine*. These transmit copy over a telephone line to a receiver which reproduces the copy on fax paper. The quality of these prints is low but is improving.

Pressure-Sensitive Reproductions

Drawings frequently used, especially detail drawings, can be reproduced on a material with an adhesive back. The protective surface is peeled away and the drawing is ad-

hered to the original. These materials are available with both the diazo and electrostatic systems.

Microfilm

A microfilm is a small negative. The drawing or document is photographed with a microfilm camera. The film is then developed in a film processor (Fig. 7-6). The negative produced contains the reduced image. It is inserted in an aperture card. An aperture card is a computer card with a window in which the negative is mounted (Fig. 7-7). The aperature card is keypunched with data needed for automated filing, sorting, and information retrieval. It contains printed information about the material on the negative.

Information on a microfilm can be retrieved by placing it in a reader–printer (Fig. 7-8). This unit will project an enlarged version of the drawing on the screen. If desired it will produce a hard copy on white paper. Also available is a microfilm *card duplicator* which produces additional aperature cards so many people can have copies of the drawing. Microfilm is available in 16-, 35-, and 105-mm sizes.

Some advantages to a microfilm system is that large numbers of drawings can be stored in a small file cabinet, information can be rapidly retrieved, multiple copies are available, and the original drawings are preserved (Fig 7-9)

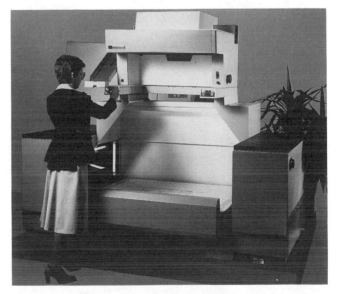

Figure 7-6. *A microfilm processor camera that has three reduction ratios: 16×, 24× and 30×. The copy board permits up to fifteen $8\frac{1}{2} \times 11$ in. single sided documents to be filmed simultaneously. (Courtesy of 3M Engineering Document Systems Division.)*

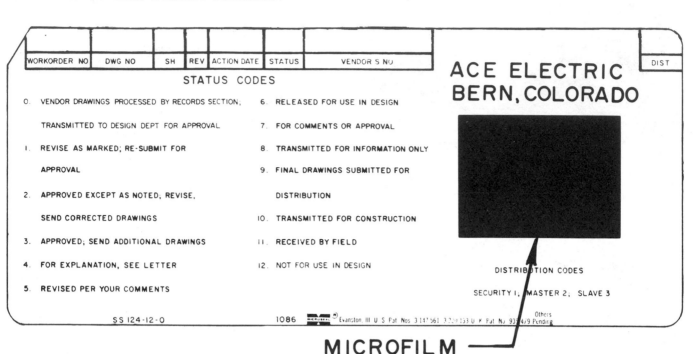

Figure 7-7. A tab-size aperature card. (Courtesy of Microseal Corporation.)

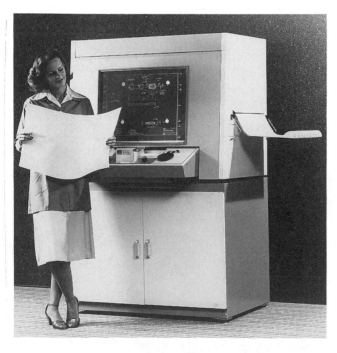

Figure 7-8. A reader–printer creates an enlarged view of the drawing on the screen and can print a large size hard copy of the drawing. (Courtesy of 3M Engineering Document Systems Division.)

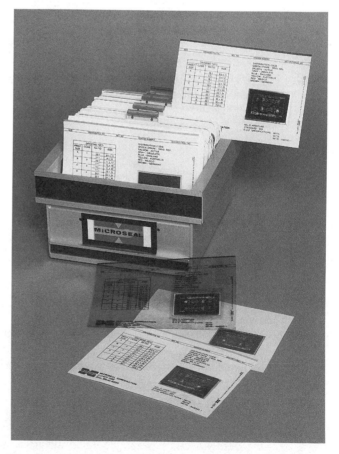

Figure 7-9. Microfilm aperature cards are stored in small file drawers. One drawer can hold hundreds of large drawings. (Courtesy of Microseal Corporation.)

Customary (in.)		Metric (mm)	
Size of Opening	Minimum Letter Height	Size of Drawing	Minimum Letter Height
9 × 12 (A)	0.125	A4, A3	3.5
12 × 18 (B)	0.125	A2	4.0
18 × 24 (C)	0.125	A1, A0	4.5
24 × 36 (D)	0.125	Titles	7.0
36 × 48 (E)	0.125	Drawing Number	8.0
Titles	0.250		
Drawing Number	0.250		

Figure 7-10. *Recommended lettering heights for drawings to be put on microfilm.*

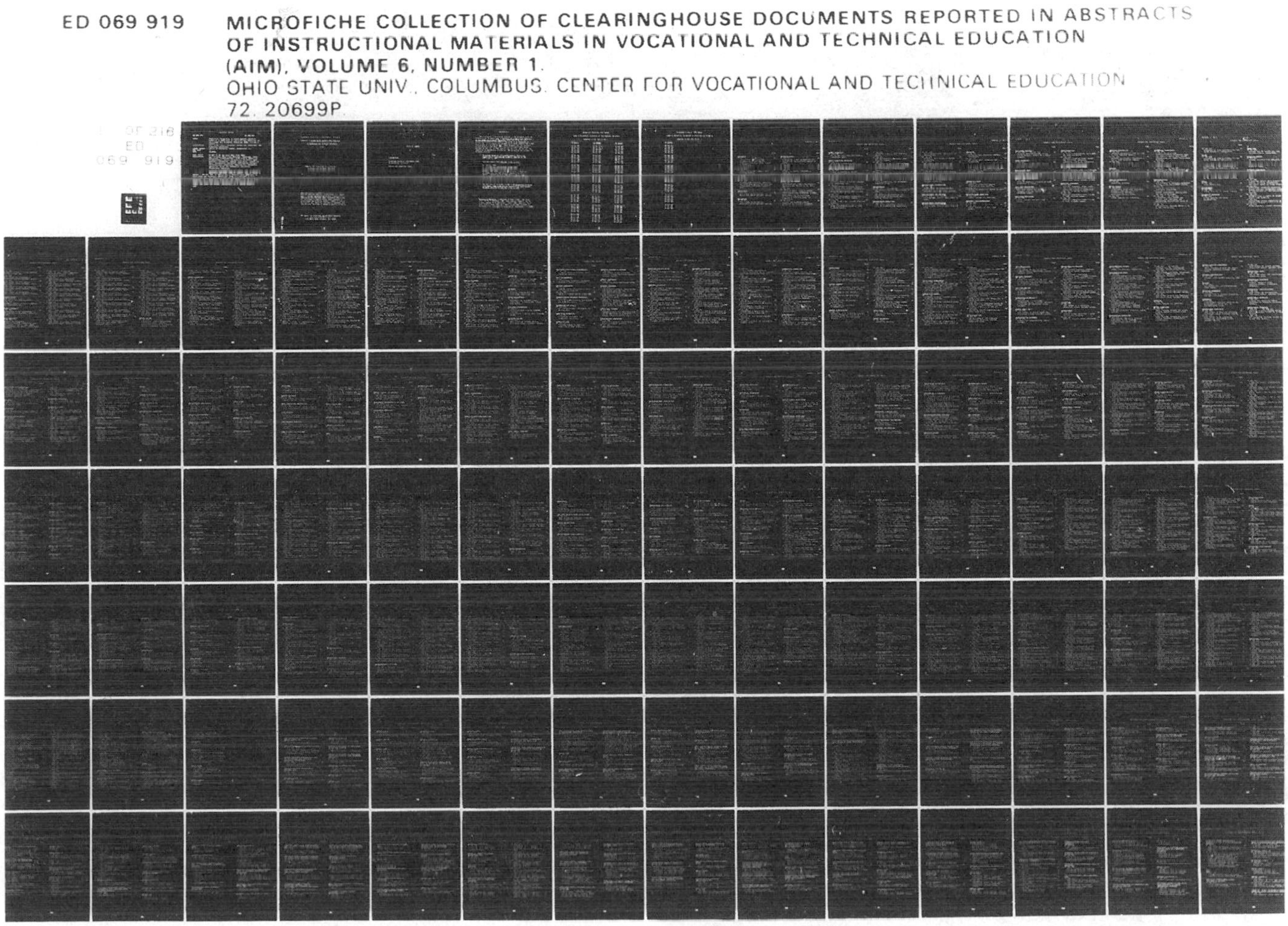

ED 069 919   MICROFICHE COLLECTION OF CLEARINGHOUSE DOCUMENTS REPORTED IN ABSTRACTS
OF INSTRUCTIONAL MATERIALS IN VOCATIONAL AND TECHNICAL EDUCATION
(AIM), VOLUME 6, NUMBER 1.
OHIO STATE UNIV., COLUMBUS. CENTER FOR VOCATIONAL AND TECHNICAL EDUCATION
72 20699P.

Figure 7-11. *A microfiche contains many pages of material.*

Drawings to be microfilmed require careful preparation. Line widths must be uniform, dense, and wide enough to permit reduction to the negative. Ink drawings produce the best microfilms. Lettering must be large enough to allow for reduction without losing clarity. Recommended lettering sizes are in Fig. 7-10.

Microfiche

A microfiche is a microfilm negative that is 4×6 in. and can hold up to 98 $8\frac{1}{2} \times 11$ in. pages (Fig. 7-11). They are used to store reports and other data and protect the originals. They can be read on a microfiche reader–printer and hard copy can be produced (Fig. 7-12).

Storing Drawings

Original drawings must be stored flat in drawers or by hanging (Fig. 7-13). Reproductions are often folded to help in handling and mailing. Various size sheets are folded in

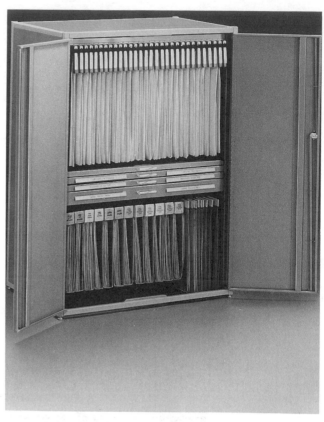

SUPERFILE 81-05

Figure 7-13. A typical drawing storage unit. (Courtesy of Plan Hold Corporation.

Figure 7-12. A microfiche reader–printer permits each page to be read on a screen. It also produces a hard copy of each page. (Courtesy of 3M Engineering Document Systems Division.)

different ways. The title block must always be on the front of the folded drawing. One method for folding architectural drawings is in Fig. 7-14.

Technical Vocabulary

Following are some important technical terms used in this chapter. Write a brief definition for each.

Whiteprint
Electrostatic reproductions
Microfilm
Microfiche

Study Questions

Answer the following study questions without referring to the text. Then check your answers with the text and correct those that were wrong.

1. Describe how a whiteprint is produced using an original drawing on vellum.

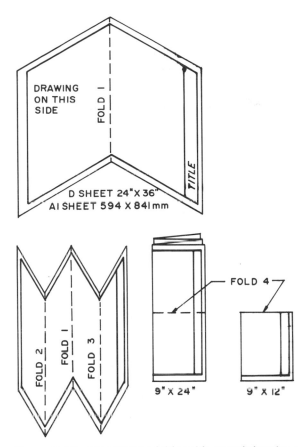

Figure 7-14. One way to fold architectural drawings.

2. How does the dry electrostatic process produce a copy of the original drawing?

3. What is the advantage of storing drawings on microfilm?

4. How do you get copies of drawings stored on microfilm?

5. List some important things to consider as you prepare drawings to be stored on microfilm.

Laboratory Problems

1. Run an original drawing on vellum through the white-printer. Set it to run on various speeds and note which gives the best copy. Explain why the very fast and very slow speeds do not produce satisfactory copies.

2. Prepare a small detail drawing for storage on micro film. If you do not have equipment available, take it to a local industry that does and have them run a film. Using the film, produce full-size whiteprints. Check your work for quality.

8

The Preliminary Design Process

Factors Influencing the Design

The preliminary design involves making preliminary design studies and schematic drawings for site utilization to determine relationships between the areas to be within the building and to establish possible structural design concepts. In addition, it involves consideration of exterior designs and proposals to meet the needs of those who will be using the building.

As the preliminary designs are developed, the architect must consider the following factors:

1. Site shape and orientation
2. Topography of the site
3. Soil conditions
4. Regional influences
5. Codes, zoning ordinances
6. Approval procedures
7. Economic considerations
8. Mechanical systems within the building
9. Occupancy
10. Special needs of the occupants

Site Shape and Orientation

The size and shape of the site are two factors to be considered first. They can influence the shape of the building and its relationship to streets and utilities. Related to these is the orientation of the building on the site. This depends upon the desired exposure to sun and wind and the need to utilize a pleasant view if one exists. Figure 8-1 shows a site that definitely influences the shape of the building. The set back plus side yard requirements severly restrict the area upon which a building can be built. In Fig. 8-2 the site is larger and permits a variety of building sizes and shapes. However, the orientation of the building to the wind, sun, and view will provide some limiting conditions.

Topography of the Site

Topography refers to the natural grade of the site before construction is started. It is highly desirable to have the site before the building is designed because grade conditions can directly influence the proposed design. It is desirable to keep the grading after construction to a mini-

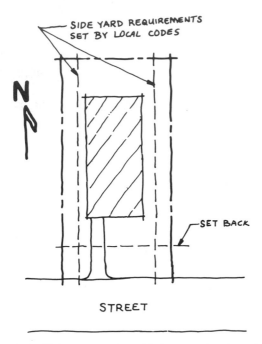

Figure 8-1. *This narrow site with front set-back and side yard requirements limits the shape of the building.*

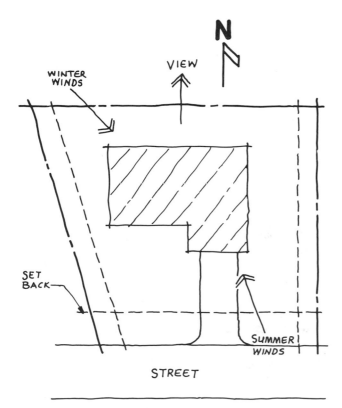

Figure 8-2. *A larger site permits a variety of building sizes and shapes to be considered.*

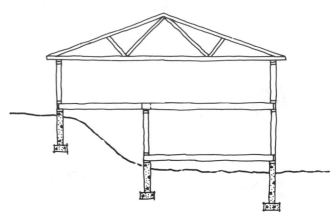

Figure 8-3. *This sketch shows how a steeply sloping lot can be used to advantage.*

mum. Often what may appear to be an undesirable slope can be utilized to produce a unique and very satisfying solution (Fig. 8-3). The design utilizes the slope by putting it into useful building space and provides more square feet of space per lineal foot of footing than a single-story building would provide.

Soil Conditions

It is important to have soil tests made and exploratory holes drilled to footing depths. The soil tests can reveal unstable conditions that would require expensive piers or other foundation construction. Also revealed would be the presence of rock or voids which would increase construction costs and create severe design problems. It is important to watch for filled areas and high water tables (Fig. 8-4).

Regional Influences

Climatic conditions related to the region must be considered. These include snow, high winds, the range of temperatures, and annual rainfall. In areas with heavy snow the roof will be designed to carry the heavy loads and perhaps be pitched steeply (Fig. 8-5). In southern regions the design must include sun control devices, such as a large roof overhang (Fig. 8-6).

Codes and Zoning

Local governing bodies legislate zoning ordinances that regulate the use of land within their jurisdiction, and include restrictions regarding the use of the building, the

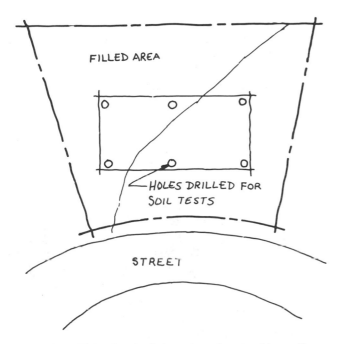

Figure 8-4. *This sketch shows plans for checking soil conditions and locates a previously filled area.*

area of the site available for construction, parking, and building heights. Codes regulate the design of the building in areas such as structure, electrical, plumbing, fire, safety, and materials. In addition, some buildings are subject to regulation by other state and federal agencies, such as Department of Health regulations on nursing homes and HUD regulations on single and multifamily housing. Additional information on zoning and codes is in Chapter 9.

Figure 8-7 illustrates a typical land use situation for zoning for single-family residences. Figure 8-8 shows zoning restrictions for a site to be used for multifamily housing. This requires open spaces and minimum parking be provided.

Figure 8-5. *Climatic conditions sometimes influence the design of the roof.*

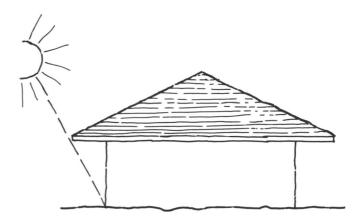

Figure 8-6. *Sun control devices are important design considerations in some regions.*

Approval Procedures

As the design is developed approval must be sought from the client. The client could be a single person, as the sole owner of the property, or a committee, as a building committee for a church. Clients often put restrictions on the design. For example, the church committee may want an A-frame type building with the high vaulted ceiling in the

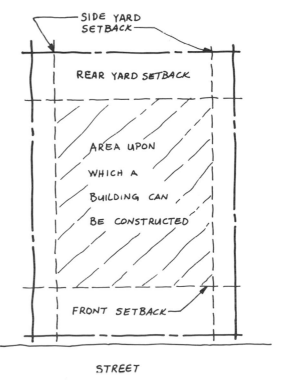

Figure 8-7. *Local zoning regulations regulate the area upon which a building can be built.*

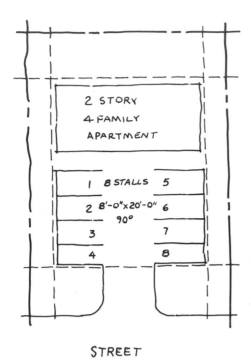

STREET

Figure 8-8. Buildings of various occupancies are regulated by zoning regulations. This four-family apartment building and required parking are restricted by requirements for setback from the street and side and rear yards.

sanctuary. They also may have firm choices on the materials to be used such as a native stone and rough sawed redwood exterior siding.

Economic Considerations

Usually the client has a maximum cost beyond which he or she is not willing to go. As the design progresses cost must be constantly considered. It may be necessary to reduce the size of the building or use less costly materials. Other factors, such as soil conditions, which are beyond the control of the client or designer may arise. In some cases, it is less costly to seek a better site than pay the extra costs due to unexpected problems such as rock or unstable soil.

Mechanical Systems

As the building is designed, the systems that will be required to control the interior environment must be examined. This includes heating, ventilating, air condition-

ing, electrical, plumbing, and fresh water. Their installation cost, effectiveness, and operation costs are factors to assess. Some buildings require special environments which deserve careful individual analysis. The environmental conditions in a hospital operating room is one example.

Occupancy

The occupancy refers to the use of the building. This dictates much about what the designer is allowed to do. For example, if it is a residence the desires of the owner are clearly identified before design begins. If it is a commercial building, an analysis of the activities to occur and the relationship between them must be completed. For example, in an office the number of workers, the required workstations, and the flow of work through the office must be established. This certainly establishes limitations on the work of the designer. The finished product must be one that satisfactorily meets the needs of the client.

Special Needs

Many buildings have unique requirements which require individual analysis. This could be things such as ingress (entrance) and egress (exit) requirements which need extra high or wide doors, extensive soundproofing of portions of a building, or the ability to withstand high temperatures. As the design progresses, the client must be contacted frequently and input from the client considered as the preliminary design progresses.

Consultants

Consultants play an important role in the planning and preparation of working drawings. Structural, mechanical, electrical, and civil engineering consultants become involved early in the design process. Adjustments are necessary in the overall design to permit the inclusion of their design requirements. These consultants must work in close cooperation because a decision made by one can influence that made by another. For example, the mechanical system may require a network of ducts. Some structural systems, such as open web joists, permit these to be run between or through the floor and ceiling joists. If a different system is used, they may have to run below the structure. The electrical consultant may require floor space to install electrical equipment or electrical raceways. This would necessitate some redesign if not planned early.

A Design Problem

It is desired to plan a building to house the medical practice of two dentists. The designer will have to study the site selected and determine the needs of the occupants and other activities related to the practice of dentistry.

Prepare a Vicinity Map

The solution to an architectural design problem begins with the *general* and moves to the *specific*. Begin by studying the site and noting the access routes, topography, and orientation features. In Fig. 8-9 is a vicinity map showing the proposed building site and the surrounding area. Observe the relationships between the site and its surroundings. The north side of the site faces an undeveloped tract. A

two-story building is on the lot to the east. The prevailing winds are from the northwest and southwest. An undeveloped tract is across the street and to the west of the site. The site slopes gradually to the northwest corner. Across Pine Street the property is occupied by retail shops and a shopping mall.

Access to the Site

One of the first problems to consider is access to the site. Since the site borders only on Oak street all patients must enter from that side. Notice that curb parking is not permitted in front of the site. Patients must park across the street or in the Mall Shopping Center across the street. There are crosswalks and electric traffic lights that will help those choosing to park in these areas. It is logical to

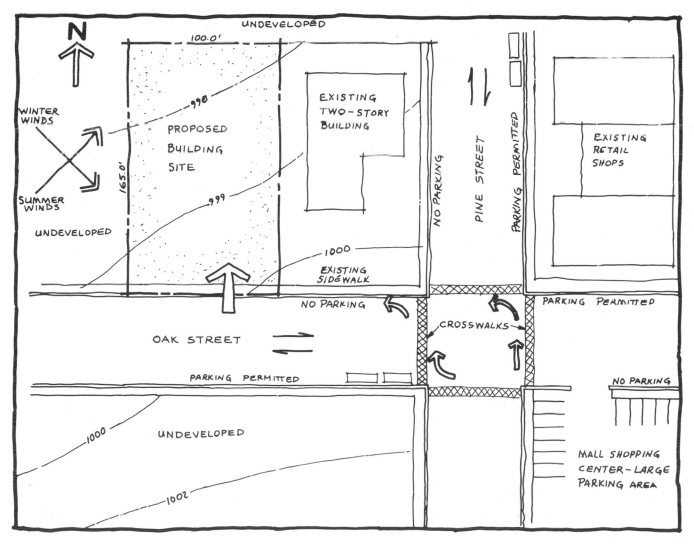

Figure 8-9. *The relationship between the site for the dentist office and the immediate surroundings and access routes must be studied.*

attempt to provide some parking on the building site. Any deliveries will also have to have access to the building from the on-site parking area (Fig. 8-9). Therefore, patients will reach the building from the site parking area or by one of the crosswalks. This locates the potential pedestrian access and vehicle access. City ordinances regulate how close to a corner a drive can enter a street. It is much safer to have the drive as far from the corner as possible.

Study the Site

Next study the building site (Fig. 8-10). Mark off the setbacks as specified by zoning ordinances. Remember, some

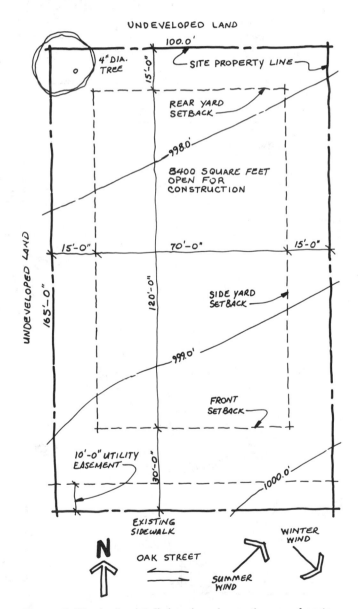

UNDEVELOPED LAND

4" DIA. TREE

SITE PROPERTY LINE

REAR YARD SETBACK

998.0'

8400 SQUARE FEET OPEN FOR CONSTRUCTION

100.0'

15'-0"

15'-0"   70'-0"   15'-0"

120'-0"

SIDE YARD SETBACK

999.0'

FRONT SETBACK

10'-0" UTILITY EASEMENT

30'-0"

1000.0'

EXISTING SIDEWALK

165'-0"   UNDEVELOPED LAND

N

OAK STREET

WINTER WIND

SUMMER WIND

Figure 8-10. *A site detail drawing shows the area free to accommodate the dentist building, parking, and needed access.*

permit parking in the setbacks and others do not. We will assume that parking is not permitted in the setback area.

Now determine if the site is large enough to accommodate the one-story building desired plus adequate parking. An analysis of the needs of the occupants revealed the following: four operatories, 320 ft^2, 2 offices, 200 ft^2, 2 toilets, 60 ft^2, 2 storage rooms, 200 ft^2, 2 laboratories, 200 ft^2, 2 dark rooms, 50 ft^2, 1 waiting room, 200 ft^2, 1 business office 100 ft^2, 1 reception area, 100 ft^2, and 1 furnace room, 50 ft^2. The building itself will occupy 1480 ft^2. The parking lot should accommodate 6 patients, 2 dentists, 4 technicians, and 1 receptionist. Therefore, 13 parking spaces are required. Using 90° parking with stalls 9'-0" × 20'-0" and an 18'-0" backing lane, 4800 ft^2 will be required for parking. Therefore, the building plus parking will occupy 6280 ft^2 of the site. The area inside the setbacks is 8400 ft^2. Therefore, this site will accommodate the required building and parking.

Orientation Factors. Now examine the factors that will influence the orientation of the building. On one side is a two-story building that will block any view but also serve as a barrier against wind, snow, and summer sun. Since it is on the east it will block the morning sun. The prevailing winds are from the northwest in winter and southwest in the summer. The two-story building will not block these so other plans must be made. Since the back of the lot faces north it should be easy to block off the extreme cold from that direction. The building will most likely face south with the front entrance and waiting room on this side to take advantage of the cheer and warmth of the southern exposure. Since the summer winds are from the southwest some provision might be made to use them for natural ventilation. The rear and west sides of the lot face undeveloped areas. Keep in mind what will be built there is unknown. Zoning ordinances will reveal the limitations to be imposed on buildings on these sites (Fig. 8-11). The lot slopes to the rear about 3 ft. This will provide natural drainage.

Establish the Scale of the Spaces

Each individual space can be drawn to scale so that relative size relationships can be seen. These can be simple rectangular shapes that represent area, not the actual shape of the room (Fig. 8-12).

Hallways are usually figured in as 15 to 20% of the total square feet in the building so we would have 222 to 296 ft^2 for this purpose. An examination of these areas enables the designer to realize the relative size of each. In this case the waiting room was the largest single space. It is helpful to list any other areas needed to support the activities in the structure, as our parking lot.

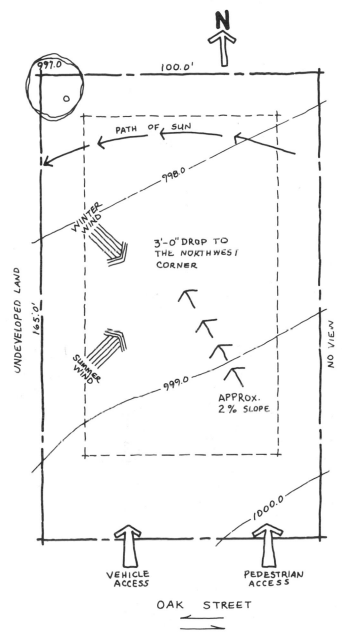

Figure 8-11. This sketch shows the orientation factors that could influence the design.

Determine the Functional Relationships

Now it is necessary to determine the relationships between activities to be housed in the building. This is accomplished with a concept or bubble diagram (Fig. 8-13). Each individual space is represented by a circle. The actual size of the circle is of no great significance. Then those that have a functional relationship are connected with arrows. For example, in Fig. 8-13, the waiting room has a direct connection to the reception and business area. It is

also related to the operatories but not the laboratory or darkroom.

As you prepare this diagram, analyze what occurs in each space and note the relationships. For example, x-rays are taken in the operatory and developed in the darkroom. This diagram is not a floor plan but reveals the relationships that should be considered as the floor plan is developed.

Sometimes the activities can be grouped into two or more major clusters. These clusters can then be rearranged into possible relationships which could lead to a basic floor plan arrangement (Fig. 8-14). In this example, we have four major clusters: waiting, business, reception, and facilities for doctors 1 and 2. They can be placed into a variety of arrangements until the most suitable is found. This is pretty much a trial-and-error process.

Select the best solution and prepare a schematic arrangement still utilizing the major clusters. Get them into scale and try out the arrangement (Fig. 8-15). It was decided to accept plan 2 and try to develop a floor plan utilizing these major relationships. One advantage to this plan is the close relationship between the waiting, business, and reception activities. Also the parallel relationship between doctors' facilities means less walking for staff and a close relationship between laboratories, darkrooms, and x-ray facilities.

Refine the Design

Once the areas needed for activities have been determined and the functional relationships between the major clusters of activities have been established, the design can be refined. Each cluster can be refined to show the individual areas needed in each. As the final design is developed, remember to check to see that no needed aspect has been overlooked. Figure 8-16 shows the design developed for this dental office building. Notice that the relationship between rooms reflects the relationship in the bubble diagram. Access is clearly shown by sidewalks and driveways.

Other Considerations

As this final plan is being developed, other decisions are being made. For example, ceiling heights, structural design, and details for the mechanical systems must be decided. Sometimes a quick three-dimensional sketch showing the basic mass of the structure is helpful (Fig. 8-17). This need not be a perspective. This is a place to show how roof and ceiling heights and possibly structural decisions influence the proposed design.

Sometimes a section through the building revealing its major areas is helpful in analyzing the final design (Fig.

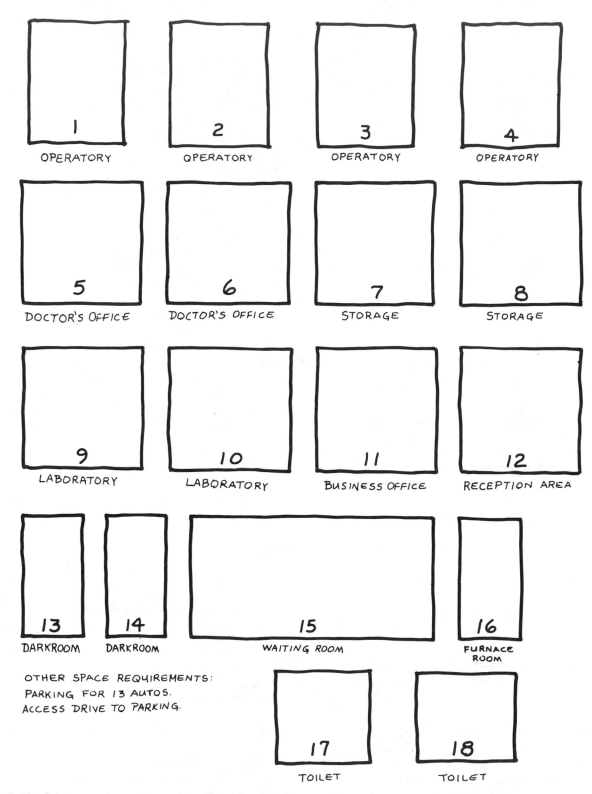

Figure 8-12. *Space requirements can be utilized by sketching scale templates representing the areas needed for each activity.*

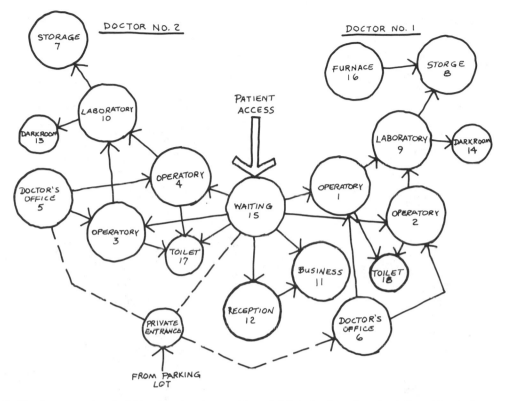

Figure 8-13. *A concept or bubble diagram is used to establish the functional relationships between areas.*

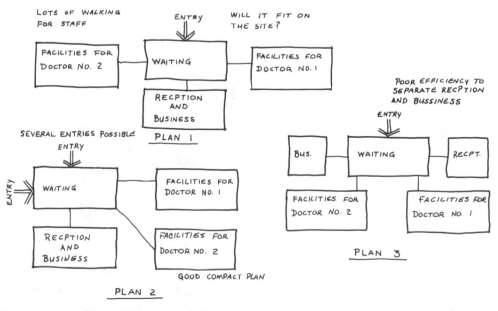

Figure 8-14. *These plans are using clusters of activities to concentrate on the major relationships that exist. Four clusters were identified for the dentist office building.*

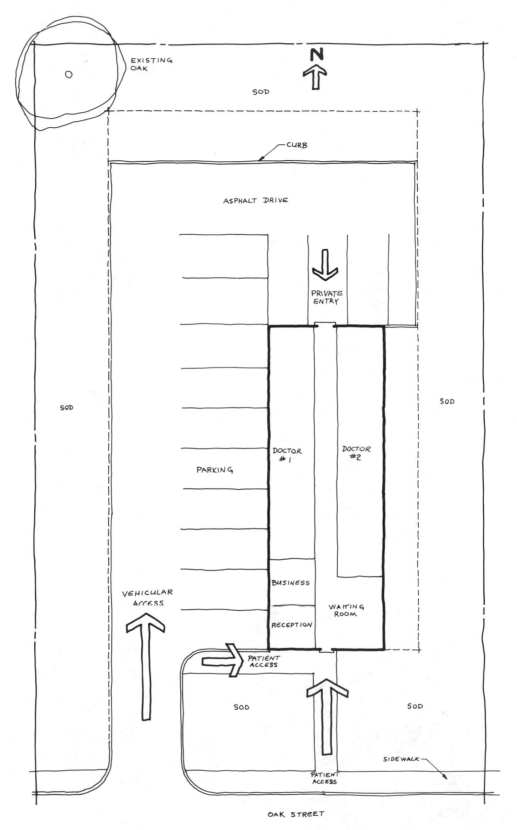

Figure 8-15. *A trial arrangement drawn to scale showing the relationship between areas. This is based on plan 2 in Fig. 8-14.*

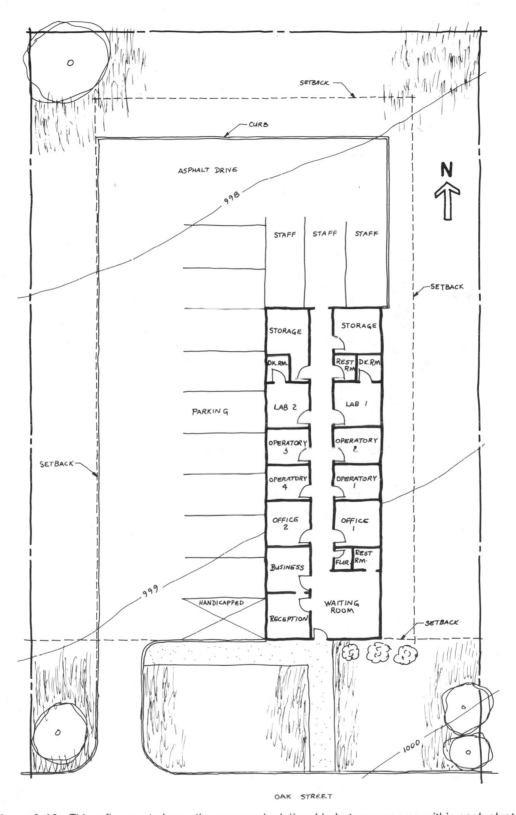

Figure 8-16. *This refinement shows the proposed relationship between rooms within each cluster.*

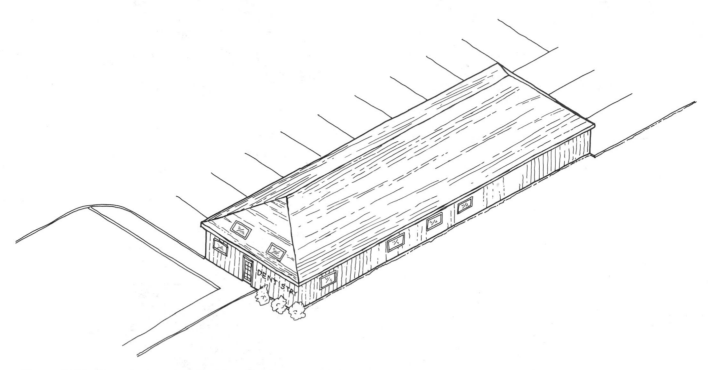

Figure 8-17. *Sometimes a drawing showing the mass of the proposed building helps with the analysis of the proposed solution.*

8-18). This can also reveal the profile of the mass and structural details.

Finally sketches of the proposed exterior help to show details of this part of the building. A variety of sketches can be made using different materials and windows and occasionally several different roof designs (Fig. 8-19).

Before the preliminary solution is finalized, a roof framing plan can be helpful (Fig. 8-20). On this building the roof is simple. Other buildings may require a rather extensive sketch showing column placement, main roof members, and purlins. The bearing walls must be clearly indicated. The various members are not sized but simply identified by notes.

Mechanical Considerations

As part of the preliminary planning, it is helpful to make a rough layout of the heating and air conditioning system. If special units are needed, such as a heat exchanger, they should be noted. This layout is not sized because a heat

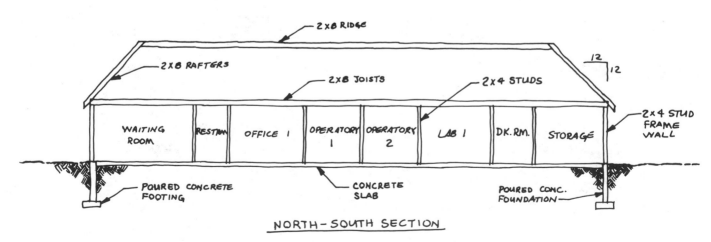

Figure 8-18. *Building sections help analyze the layout and structural requirements.*

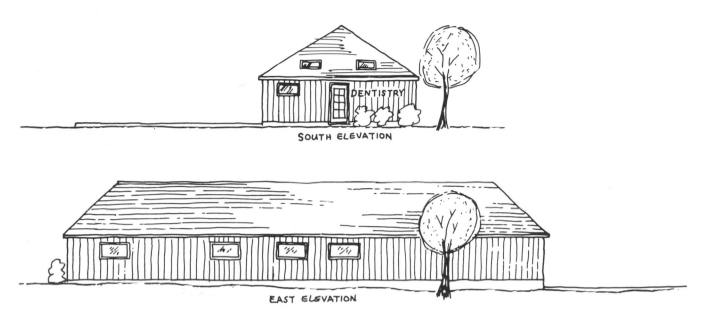

Figure 8-19. These trial elevations are used to confirm the proposed solution or lead to a reexamination of the project.

loss–gain study has not been made at this point (Fig. 8-21). In this solution a down draft gas-fired hot air furnace is placed in the furnace room. The electric air conditioner condensor is outside the building on the ground. The heat ducts are run in the slab floor with outlets on the outside walls.

Skylights are placed in the roof over the waiting room area. This provides a little solar heat but more importantly serves as a means of natural ventilation.

A Final Check

After the various facets of a preliminary design are complete, it helps to make a schematic illustration showing the circulation of traffic including people and automobiles. The plan should keep traffic patterns separated. Notice the special entrance and parking area for some of the staff. Internal circulation can also be checked with this schematic (Fig. 8-22). This shows that the operations of the two doctors are separate and there should be a minimum of conflict in the hall.

The Next Step

The preliminary designs must be accepted by the client and government agencies that grant building permits. To help the client understand the total design concept, a preliminary floor plan and site development are drawn. (Fig.

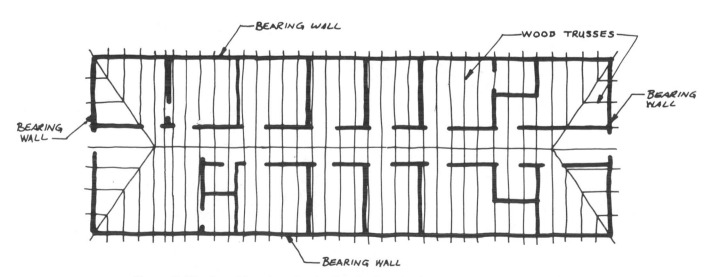

Figure 8-20. A roof framing plan is sketched to check on problems that may arise.

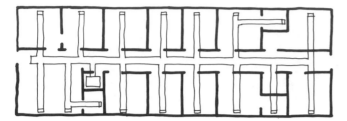

Figure 8-21. *This preliminary hot-air duct system helps to see if there are any unusual problems heating and cooling the proposed building.*

8-23). In addition three-dimensional models may be built, (Fig. 8-24), architectural perspectives produced (Fig. 8-25), and three-dimensional representations of interior and exterior space can be generated manually or by a CADD system (Fig. 8-26).

The early working drawings are really preliminary. Prints are run and used by those involved to see how their part of the design will fit. Eventually, everyone will be in general agreement on the use of space and the client satisfied with the detailed preliminary drawings. Even some specifications can be recorded during this phase. Finally, the final working drawings are prepared, checked for accuracy and completeness, and are ready for bidding and construction. Even during these processes changes may occur, which must be reflected on the drawings and in the specifications.

Technical Vocabulary

Following are some important technical terms used in this chapter. Write a brief definition for each.

Topography
Zoning ordinance
Building codes
Mechanical systems
Occupancy
Orientation
Functional relationships

Study Questions

Answer the following study questions without referring to the text. Then check your answers with the text and correct those that were wrong.

1. What factors must be considered during the preliminary design process?

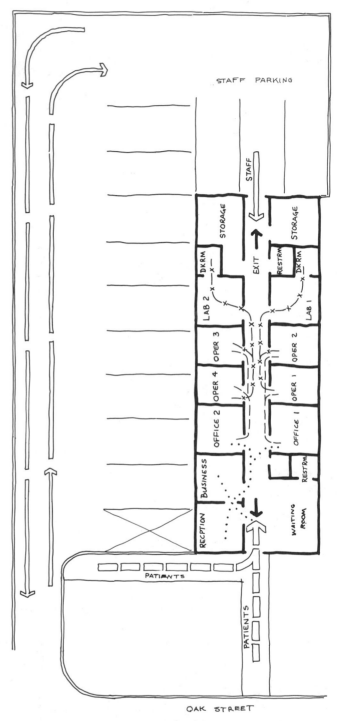

Figure 8-22. *Make a check of the traffic flow to see if it can be improved.*

2. Why should soil tests be made before the design is finalized?

3. What climatic conditions influence design solutions?

4. How does the occupancy influence the work of the architectural designer?

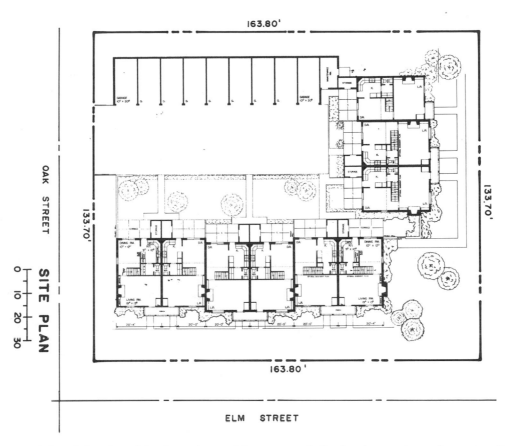

163.80'

OAK STREET

133.70'

133.70'

133.70'

SITE PLAN

0 10 20 30

163.80'

ELM STREET

Figure 8-23. A presentational drawing of the floor plan and the proposed site development are shown together on a single drawing. This is the plan for the building in Fig. 8-25. (Courtesy of Home Planners, Inc.)

Laboratory Problem

Following the steps of the design process prepare a preliminary design proposal for the following situation.

1. A retail store selling cameras and related equipment requires a total of 2000 ft² of floor space. This is to be divided into 1200 ft² of sales area and 800 ft² for stor-

age, a small office for one person to do the book work for the business, and one restroom for the staff. Ease of access to bring stock into the building to storage and from there into the sales area is important. It is necessary to dispose of packing materials and other trash.

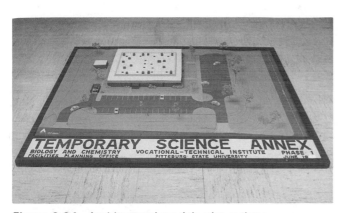

Figure 8-24. Architectural models give a three dimensional view of the project and relate it to the site.

Figure 8-25. An architectural perspective enables the client to understand the intent of the proposed exterior design. (Courtesy of Home Planners, Inc.)

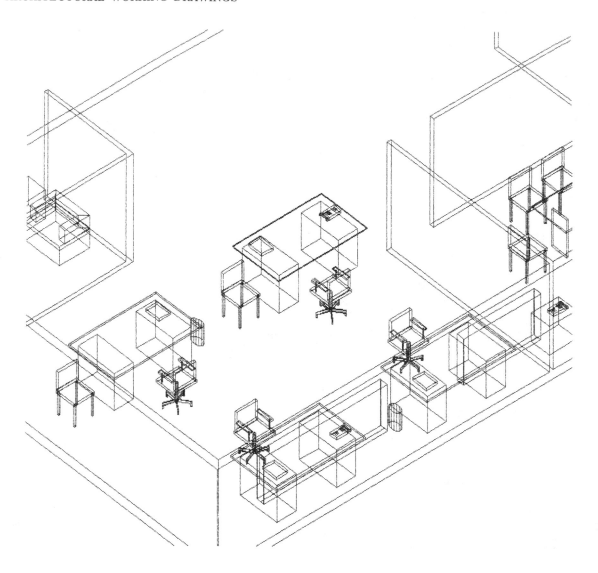

Figure 8-26. *A pictorial representation of an office layout for use during preliminary planning and client approval. (Courtesy of Autodesk, Inc.)*

Provide parking for two employees and customers. Site conditions are shown on the sketch in Fig. 8-27.

Each class member should present his or her solution and the graphics developed to the class. The presentation should be limited to 10 minutes or less. If this is too time consuming, the solutions could be posted and the class can examine them and vote on the best two or three solutions.

2. Design a single family residence with a maximum cost of $100,000. This does not include the price of the land, driveway, or landscaping. It should have at least two bedrooms, one full bath, a kitchen, eating area, living area, and a one-car garage. If you can exceed these and stay within the budget, you may expand the plan.

To ascertain costs, contact a local bank or savings and loan real estate loan officer or a local contractor and get estimated square foot costs for your area. Get figures for the average cost per square foot for the heated area, porches, and garages. Get the costs of kitchen appliances and plumbing fixtures from a local building supply store. The final cost of the building for our purpose will include the total of these items. Remember, this is only a rough estimate but your building must stay within the $100,000 limit.

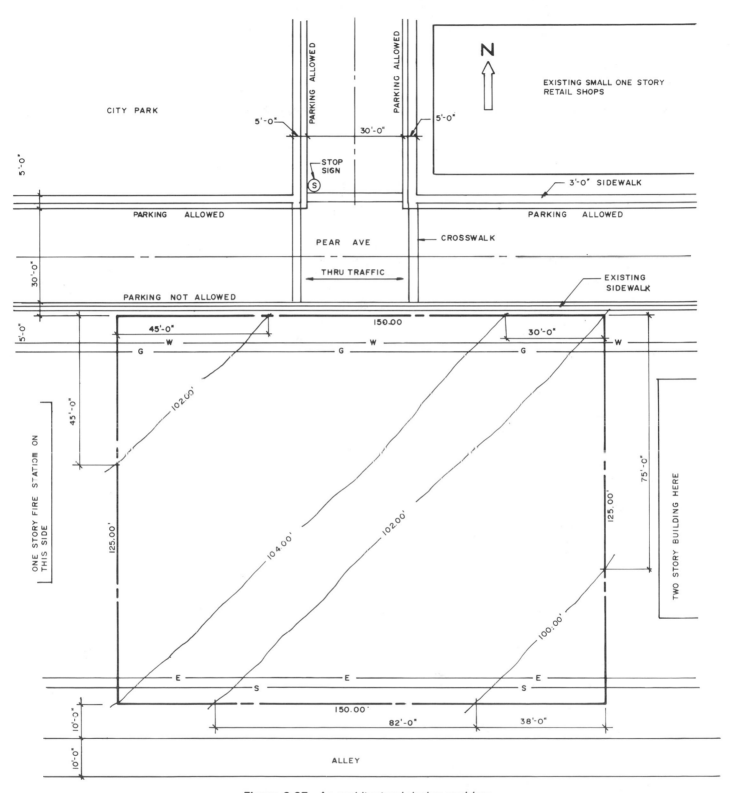

Figure 8-27. *An architectural design problem.*

9

Contract Documents

A construction project normally begins with the owner contracting for the services of an architect to do the design. After this has been completed, the project is usually placed out for bids.

Owner–Architect Agreement

The owner–architect agreement includes a listing of the architectural services expected and the owner's obligations. Different forms may be used but forms supplied by the American Institute of Architects are often used. One major difference in agreements is how the architect is to be paid. Commonly used methods include:

1. Percentage of construction cost
2. Fixed fee or lump-sum fee
3. Total expense plus a professional fee
4. Multiple of salary cost
5. Multiple of salary cost plus nonsalary expense

Architectural Payments

This is a schedule specifying how payments are to be made to the architect which are negotiable. The following is a typical schedule:

	Individual Payment (%)	Cumulative Payment (%)
1. Execution of agreement (retainer)	10	10
2. Preliminary design	5	15
3. Completion of schematic designs	5	20
4. Completion of contract documents	55	75
5. Receipt of bids	5	80
6. Contract administration	20	100

Construction Contract Documents

The normal construction contract consists of several different documents. Those required can vary but the following are those generally considered essential to the bidding, negotiation, and construction process:

1. Invitation to bid
2. Instructions to bidders
3. Bid form
4. Owner–contractor agreements
5. Performance bond
6. Labor and material bond
7. Architectural payments
8. General conditions
9. Supplementary conditions

10. Specifications
11. Working drawings
12. The agreement

Invitation to Bid

Bid invitations for *public contracts* are advertised in newspapers, magazines, trade publications, and other public media. The legal requirements vary across the country but typically require that advertisements be placed for two, three, or four consecutive weeks. The advertisement includes a description of the work, its location, where to obtain plans, the required deposit on the plans, and the time and place for the delivery of the bid (Fig. 9-1).

Advertising for bids for private contracts is not usually done by public advertising. Private owners can choose a contract any way they like. When competitive bidding is used, the private owner often uses *invitational bidding*. This procedure allows the owner to select the contractors considered capable of doing the job and invite them to bid on the project.

Instructions to Bidders

All contractors bidding on a project must bid under exactly the same conditions for an identical end result. The bidding procedure must be established and all bidders are required to adhere to it.

10—The Morning Sun, Pittsburg, Kan., Tuesday, February 10, 19

classifieds

LEGALS

COMMISSIONERS on or before 10:00 AM (CST), Friday, Feb. 27, 1992 at the COMMISSION ROOM, located at the CRAWFORD COUNTY COURTHOUSE, GIRARD, KANSAS at which time and place the bids will be publicly opened and considered. Any proposal received subsequent to the time specified will be promptly returned to the Bidder unopened.

The Plans and Specifications, together with all other necessary forms and documents for bidders, may be secured from STUART OWSLEY & ASSOCIATES, P.A., ARCHITECTS, at 408 N. Walnut, Suite 3, Pittsburg, Kansas (Mailing address: P.O. Box Z, Pittsburg, Kansas Zip Code 66762) upon deposit of $40.00 for each set, with any unsuccessful bidder, upon returning each set within 14 days after the date of bid opening, and in good condition, being given a full refund for the first set and $30.00 refund for each additional set thereafter. The plans and specifications may be examined at the office of STUART OWSLEY & ASSOCIATES, P.A., ARCHITECTS, in Pittsburg, Kansas and the office of the COUNTY CLERK, COUNTY COURTHOUSE in Girard, Kansas.

Bid Security Equal to 5% of the Base Bid will be required. 100% Performance and Payment Bonds will be required.
CRAWFORD COUNTY, KANSAS
Owner
/S/ Dean McFarland,
County Clerk

Date: _____
(Published in The Morning Sun February 3, 10, 17, 1992)

Figure 9-1. A typical advertisement for bids. (Courtesy of The Morning Sun, Pittsburg, KS.)

The instructions to bidders typically include:

1. Where to get the construction documents needed to bid the job and their cost.
2. The type of forms upon which the bid is to be submitted.
3. How to submit bids on alternates.
4. How to modify or withdraw the bid including the time frame within which this must be done.
5. Where and when to deliver the bids.
6. Where and when the bids will be opened.
7. Conditions under which a bid can be rejected such as an incomplete bid or one with erasures.
8. Instructions detailing how to seek approval to substitute materials for those specified on plans and specifications.
9. An explanation of how the winning bid will be determined.
10. Proposal and performance guarantees such as a cashiers check for five percent (5%) of the total amount of the bid must accompany each proposal.
11. The procedure for the acceptance of a proposal.
12. A list of the governing laws and regulations the bidder must be ready to observe.
13. How discrepancies between prices in words and those in figures are to be handled. Usually those in words are accepted.
14. The requirements for the performance bond and the labor and material bond.
15. The requirements for examination of the drawings and specifications and the site. Failure to do this does not release the bidder from existing conditions.
16. How interpretations and questions about the project are to be handled. Usually these must be in written form.
17. The time for executing the contract and providing needed bonds.

Bid Form

A bid form is a sample bidding letter from the bidder to the owner. It contains blank spaces where the bidder fills in the requested information such as the lump-sum price, the prices of bids on alternates, the signature of the bidder, and the corporate seal if one exists (Fig. 9-2).

General Conditions

The general conditions set forth the manner and procedures to be used to implement the provisions of the contract. In Fig. 9-3 is the cover of "Standard General Con-

```
PROPOSAL of ____Construction Services, Inc.____,a corporation
organized and existing under the laws of the State of _Kansas_ ,
a partnership _____



            _____

an individual doing business as _____

TO: Ace Manufacturing Co., 1323 E. Quincy, Butler, Ohio

PROJECT: Plant Addition, Project 735

Gentlemen:

       The Undersigned, in compliance with your Invitation for Bids
for  the  General  Construction of the above-described  project,
having  examined  the  drawings  and  specifications  with related
contract documents carefully,  with all addenda thereto,  and the
site of the work,  and being familiar with all of the conditions
surrounding the construction of the proposed project,  hereby
proposes  to furnish all  plant,  labor,  equipment,  appliances,
supplies,  and  materials  and  to  perform  all  work  for  the
construction  of  the  project  as  required  by  and  in  strict
accordance  with  the  contract  documents,  specifications,
schedules,  and  drawings with all addenda issued by the Architect-
Engineer, at the prices states below.

       The Undersigned hereby acknowledges receipt of the following
Addenda:

_____ Addendum #1,  Dated Jan. 2 _____

_____ Addendum #2,  Dated July 3 _____

BASE   PROPOSAL:   For  all  work  described  in  the   detailed
specifications  and  shown  on  the  contract  drawings  for  the
building, I (or We) agree to perform all the work for the sum of

_One Hundred Seventy Five Thousand and 00/100 ($175,000.00)_____

_____ dollars.  (Amount shall be shown in both written form
and figures the written amount will govern:)

       The  above-stated  compensation covers all expenses  incurred
in  performing the work,  including premium for  contract  bonds,
required under the contract documents,  of which this proposal is
a part.
```

Figure 9-2. A sample bid form (continued on next page).

ditions of the Construction Contracts.'' This is one of the most important construction documents. General Conditions contain contractual-legal requirements not covered by other contract forms. This is a very lengthy and detailed standard. The articles contained in this standard include:

1. Definitions
2. Preliminary matters
3. Contract documents: intent, amending, and reuse
4. Availability of lands: physical conditions; reference points
5. Bonds and insurance
6. Contractor's responsibilities
7. Other work
8. Owner's responsibilities
9. Engineer's status during construction
10. Changes in the work
11. Change of contract price
12. Change of contract time
13. Warranty and guarantee; tests and inspections; correction, removal, or acceptance of defective work
14. Payments to contractor and completion
15. Suspension of work and termination
16. Arbitration
17. Miscellaneous

ALTERNATE NO. 1: QUARRY TILE IN PLACE OF TERRAZZO IN SALES ROOM:
If the substitutions specified under this alternate are made, you
may ~~(deduct from)~~ (add to) the base proposal the sum of _____

__Four Hundred Eighty and 00/100 ($480.00)__ dollars.

ALTERNATE NO. 2: CHANGE STRUCTURAL GLAZED TILE TO BRICK IN OFFICE:
If the substitutions specified under this alternate are made, you
may (deduct from) ~~(add to)~~ the base proposal the sum of _____

__One Hundred Seventy Five and 00/100($175.00)__ dollars.

BID SECURITY: Attached cashier's check ~~(certified check)~~ (Bid
Bond) payable without condition, in the sum of __Eight Thousand Seven__

__Hundred and 00/100 ($8,700.00)__ dollars (equal to 5% of the
largest possible combination) is to become the property of the
Ace Manufacturing Company, Johnson, TN, in the event the Contract
and   contract bonds are not executed within the time set forth
hereinafter, as liquidated damages for the delay and additional
work caused thereby.

CONTRACT SECURITY: The Undersigned hereby agrees, if awarded the
contract, to furnish the contract bonds, as specified, with the

_____Howard_____ Surety Company of __Joplin, Missouri__ .

     Upon receipt of notice of the acceptance of this bid, the
Undersigned hereby agrees that he will execute and deliver the
formal written Contract in the form prescribed, in accordance
with the bid as accepted and that he will give contract bonds,
all within ten days after the prescribed forms are presented to
him for signature.

     If awarded the Contract, the Undersigned proposes to
commence work within 10 calendar days after receipt of notice to
proceed and to fully complete all of the work under his Contract,
ready for occupancy, within 380 calendar days thereafter.

                              Respectfully submitted,

                              __John C. Turner, Owner__

                 John C Turner
                 William R. Smith
            Witness

SEAL: (If bid is by a Corporation) _____

Figure 9-2. (Continued)

Supplementary Conditions

The general conditions cover a broad range of construction and must be amended or supplemented occasionally due to some unusual feature of a project. These changes are written up in the *supplementary conditions* section. This could include things such as a change in needed insurance or the substitution of materials.

Specifications

The specifications document gives a detailed explanation of the required materials, finishes, and workmanship (Fig. 9-4). They are grouped by trades. Many architects use the specification system recommended by the Construction Specifications Institute. The code used is a five digit number, such as 04100. The first two digits identify the division (masonry) and the last three, the product information (mortar in this example). Following are the major divisions in a typical specifications document:

Division 1—General requirements (alternatives, quality
control, etc.).
Division 2—Site work (clearing, drainage, etc.).
Division 3—Concrete (reinforcement, cast-in-place,
etc.).
Division 4—Masonry (mortars, stone, etc.).

This document has important legal consequences: consultation with an attorney is encouraged with respect to its completion or modification.

STANDARD
GENERAL CONDITIONS
OF THE
CONSTRUCTION CONTRACT

Prepared by

Engineers' Joint Contract Documents Committee

and

Issued and Published Jointly By

PROFESSIONAL ENGINEERS IN PRIVATE PRACTICE
A practice division of the
NATIONAL SOCIETY OF PROFESSIONAL ENGINEERS

AMERICAN CONSULTING ENGINEERS COUNCIL

AMERICAN SOCIETY OF CIVIL ENGINEERS

CONSTRUCTION SPECIFICATIONS INSTITUTE

This document has been approved and endorsed by

The Associated General Contractors of America

These General Conditions have been prepared for use with the Owner-Contractor Agreements (No. 1910-8-A-1 or 1910-8-A-2, 1983 editions). Their provisions are interrelated and a change in one may necessitate a change in the others. Comments concerning their usage are contained in the Commentary on Agreements for Engineering Services and Contract Documents, No. 1910-9, 1981 edition. For guidance in the preparation of Supplementary Conditions, see Guide to the Preparation of Supplementary Conditions (No. 1910-17, 1983 edition). When bidding is involved, the Standard Form of Instructions to Bidders (No. 1910-12, 1983 edition) may be used.

EJCDC No. 1910-8 (1983 Edition)

Reprinted 8/86

Figure 9-3. A "Standard General Conditions of the Construction Contract" document. (Printed with permission of the Engineers Joint Contract Documents Committee, National Society of Professional Engineers.)

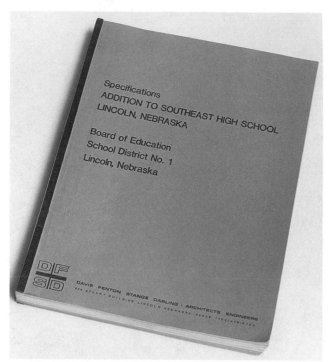

Figure 9-4. *Specifications for a construction job.*

Figure 9-5. *A set of architectural working drawings.*

information about the materials and workmanship (Fig. 9-5).

The Agreement

The agreement is a document that formalizes the construction contract. It brings together all of the contract segments by reference and it functions for the formal execution of the contract. It includes:

1. a statement of the work to be done
2. the agreed upon price for this work
3. signatures of the involved parties
4. the completion time
5. liquidated damages
6. method of payment to the contractor
7. a list of the contract documents

In Fig. 9-6 is a "Standard Form of Agreement Between the Owner and Construction Manager" which details the relationship between the manager and the owner. The articles included in this agreement are:

1. The Construction Team and Extent of Agreement
2. Construction Manager's Services
3. The Owner's Responsibilities
4. Trade Contracts
5. Schedule
6. Guaranteed Maximum Price
7. Construction Manager's Fee
8. Cost of the Project
9. Changes in the Project
10. Discounts

Division 5—Metals (joists, decking, etc.).
Division 6—Wood and plastics (rough carpentry, plastic fabrications, etc.).
Division 7—Thermal and moisture protection (waterproofing, etc.).
Division 8—Doors and windows (metal, wood, glazing, etc.)
Division 9—Finishes (tile, plaster, carpet, etc.).
Division 10—Specialties (fireplaces, lockers, etc.).
Division 11—Equipment (food service, laboratory, etc.).
Division 12—Furnishings (artwork, furniture, etc.).
Division 13—Special construction (clean room, vault, etc.).
Division 14—Conveying systems (elevator, hoists, etc.).
Division 15—Mechanical (plumbing, heat generation, etc.).
Division 16—Electrical (service, distribution, lighting, etc.).

Working Drawings

The architectural working drawings include the entire range of drawings needed to describe a project. They include such things as the floor plan, foundation plan, numerous sections, elevations, special details, schedules, electrical, plumbing, heating, and air conditioning plans, and the site plan. They show the design, location, and dimensions of all parts of the project. The specifications give

THE ASSOCIATED GENERAL CONTRACTORS

STANDARD FORM OF AGREEMENT BETWEEN OWNER AND CONSTRUCTION MANAGER

(GUARANTEED MAXIMUM PRICE OPTION)

(See AGC Document No. 8a for Establishing the
Guaranteed Maximum Price)

This Document has important legal and insurance consequences; consultation with an attorney is encouraged with respect to its completion or modification.

AGREEMENT

Made this   day of   in the year of Nineteen Hundred and

BETWEEN   the Owner, and

                                                         the Construction Manager.

For services in connection with the following described Project: (Include complete Project location and scope)

The Architect/Engineer for the Project is

The Owner and the Construction Manager agree as set forth below:

AGC DOCUMENT NO. 500   •   OWNER CONSTRUCTION MANAGER AGREEMENT   JULY 1980
©1980 Associated General Contractors of America

Figure 9-6. *A "Standard Form of Agreement Between the Owner and Construction Manager" document. (Represented with permission of the Associated General contractors of america (AGC). Copies of current forms may be obtained from AGC's Publication Department, 1957 E. Street, NW, Washington, D.C. 20006)*

11. Payments to the Construction Manager
12. Insurance, Indemnity, and Waiver of Subrogation
13. Termination of the Agreement and Owner's Right to Perform Construction Manager's Obligations
14. Assignment and Governing Law
15. Miscellaneous Provisions
16. Arbitration

A Standard Form of Agreement Between the Owner and Contractor on the Basis of a Stipulation Price is shown in Fig. 9-7. The articles included in this agreement are:

1. Work
2. Engineer
3. Contract Time

This document has important legal consequences; consultation with an attorney is encouraged with respect to its completion or modification.

STANDARD FORM OF AGREEMENT BETWEEN OWNER AND CONTRACTOR ON THE BASIS OF A STIPULATED PRICE

Prepared by

ENGINEERS' JOINT CONTRACT DOCUMENTS COMMITTEE

and

Issued and Published Jointly By

PROFESSIONAL ENGINEERS IN PRIVATE PRACTICE
A practice division of the
NATIONAL SOCIETY OF PROFESSIONAL ENGINEERS

AMERICAN CONSULTING ENGINEERS COUNCIL

AMERICAN SOCIETY OF CIVIL ENGINEERS

CONSTRUCTION SPECIFICATIONS INSTITUTE

This document has been approved and endorsed by

The Associated General Contractors of America

This Standard Form of Agreement has been prepared for use with the Standard General Conditions of the Construction Contract, No. 1910-8, 1983 edition. Their provisions are interrelated and a change in one may necessitate a change in the others. The suggested language for instructions to bidders contained in the Guide to the Preparation of Instructions to Bidders, No. 1910-12, 1983 edition, is also carefully interrelated with the language of this Agreement. Comments concerning their usage are contained in the Commentary on Agreements for Engineering Services and Contract Documents, No. 1910-9, 1981 edition. See also Guide to the Preparation of Supplementary Conditions, No. 1910-17, 1983 edition.

EJCDC No. 1910-8-A-1 (1983 Edition)

Reprinted 9/86

Figure 9-7. *A "Standard Form of Agreement Between Owner and Contractor on the Basis of a Stipulated Price" document. (Printed with permission of the Engineers Joint Contract Documents Committee, National Society of Professional Engineers.)*

4. Contract Price
5. Payment Procedures
6. Interest
7. Contractor's Representations
8. Contract Documents
9. Miscellaneous

Addenda and Change Orders

Addenda and change orders are issued whenever it is necessary to correct or make a change in the original construction documents. An *addendum* is issued before a contract is awarded and is sent to the bidders so they can incorporate this in their bid. A *change order* is issued after the contract is awarded. Usually the building is under construction and for some reason a change is desired. Each change is given a number and the amount it adds to or subtracts from the bid price is listed.

Technical Vocabulary

Following are some important technical terms used in this chapter. Write a brief definition for each.

Construction documents
Invitational bidding
Performance bond
General conditions
Supplementary conditions
Specifications
Working drawings
Addendum
Change order

Study Questions

Answer the following study questions without referring to the text. Then check your answers with the text and correct those that were wrong.

1. How are invitations for bids on public contracts advertised?
2. How does invitational bidding differ from bids for public contracts?
3. What is commonly included in the instructions to bidders?
4. What is included in the owner–architect agreement?
5. Why do contractors carry a performance bond on a job?
6. What does a material and labor bond guarantee?
7. What is included in the "General Conditions of the Construction Contract" document?
8. What type of information is given in the specifications?
9. What items are included in the agreement between the owner and the contractor?
10. What is the difference between an addendum and a change order?

Laboratory Problem

Write a legal advertisment requesting bids for the commercial building designed in Chapter 8. The owners are advertising. Set times, dates, and so on to suit your conditions.

Foundations and Footings

The foundation and footings of a building support the superstructure and are generally below grade. Foundations are walls or columns that extend to footings that rest directly upon the soil. The purpose of the footing is to spread the weight of the structure so that the bearing capacity of the soil will support the load. Since most soils permit some settlement as a building is built it is important that the settlement, if it occurs, be uniform throughout the structure. In addition to carrying structural loads, the foundation must be watertight to keep the area below the building dry. It must also resist lateral forces such as subsurface water pressure, wind, and soil pressure (Fig. 10-1).

Design Considerations

The design of footings and foundations varies considerably due to regional circumstances. The architect or engineer must know the local conditions and how local codes influence design. They must design footings and foundations to meet these specific conditions. Sizes shown in this chapter are typical of those commonly used but should not be used without examining the actual situation.

Conditions that influence footing and foundation design are:

Soil conditions
Rain

Wind, normal and unusual, such as hurricanes
Temperature ranges including frost lines and permafrost
Seismic conditions
Termites
Type of floor

Soil Conditions

Soil conditions can be obtained from a soils engineer. A major factor is the amount of weight the soil is capable of carrying. To ascertain this, borings are made at each corner of the building and the soil samples are tested for load-bearing capacity. The depth of the borings is determined by the soils engineer. The soils engineer reports findings to the architect and the structural engineer. The soil-bearing capacity varies according to the composition of the soil.

The load-bearing capabilities of soil are expressed in pounds per square foot or kilograms per square meter. In Fig. 10-2 are bearing values of commonly identified soils. In reality soils do not occur in such clearly defined classes but are mixtures of these. It is necessary to have a soil engineer take soil samples and test them to find the bearing capacity for a particular site. Even then the nature of soil on a single site will vary so soil samples are taken at a number of places in the area where the building is to be built. Figure 10-2 also shows maximum bearing pressures

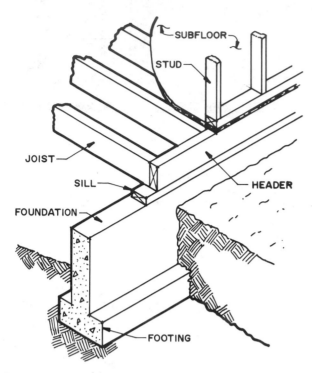

Figure 10-1. *The weight of the structure rests on the footing and foundation.*

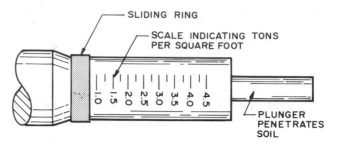

Figure 10-3. *A penetrometer is used to find the load-bearing capacity of the soil.*

on foundations per square foot per foot of depth below the surface.

One method of making an on-site test of the bearing capacity of the soil is to use a penetrometer (Fig. 10-3). The device has a ring around the barrel. The barrel has a scale marked in tons per square foot. The plunger is

Allowable Bearing Capacities of Various Foundation Beds, (lb/ft²)

Alluvial soil	1,000
Soft clay	2,000
Firm clay	4,000
Wet sand	4,000
Sand and clay mixed	4,000
Fine dry sand	6,000
Hard Clay	8,000
Coarse dry sand	8,000
Gravel	12,000
Gravel and sand, well cemented	16,000
Hardpan or hard shale	20,000
Medium rock	40,000
Rock under caissons	50,000
Hard rock	160,000

Figure 10-2. *Typical load-bearing capacities of various soils.*

pushed into the soil until the barrel touches the surface. The ring moves up the barrel along the scale. The instrument is removed and the bearing capacity of the soil is read on the scale.

Another method is to use a nuclear tester to determine density and moisture. The plate of the nuclear tester is placed on the soil. It gives an almost instant digital reading.

To determine the weight on a footing, the weight of materials and live loads to be applied (snow, furniture etc.) is calculated for a 1-ft-wide section of the structure (Fig. 10-4). This weight is compared with the bearing capacity of the soil. For example, if a 1-ft section of a building weighs 2000 lb and the soil will support 2000 lb/ft², a footing 12 in. long by 12 in. wide would meet the minimum design requirements. This is explained in detail later in the chapter.

Rain

In an area with excessively *high levels of rainfall*, the floors of buildings must be above the ground or have special provisions for repelling the moisture. Plastic moisture barriers are often used under concrete floors. Provision for removing moisture, such as pumps or sloping the lot, also helps. In areas of heavy rainfall, the subsurface moisture can be near the surface of the ground. This applies considerable hydrostatic pressure to the outside surface of the foundation.

Subsurface moisture can be carried away from the footing with perforated plastic pipe. The pipe has holes in one side which is placed down in a bed of gravel. It is covered with a fabric filter to keep soil out of the gravel bed. The

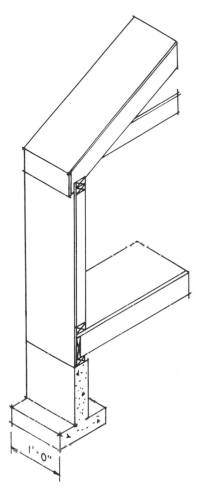

Figure 10-4. *The weight of a 1-ft-wide slice of the building is used when calculating the footing size.*

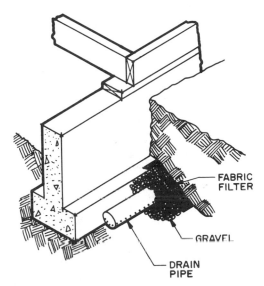

Figure 10-5. *Subsurface water is removed from the footing area with perforated plastic pipe.*

pipe is sloped so it drains to a dry well or storm sewer (Fig. 10-5).

Subsurface moisture also makes it necessary to place 6-mil polyethylene plastic sheets over the gravel base under concrete slab floors. The gravel bed below the slab helps drain moisture from under the slab. The vapor barrier keeps moisture from penetrating the slab (Fig. 10-6).

In areas with sandy soils, the moisture drains away rapidly; therefore, gravel fill below a concrete slab is often not used. In some areas, 2 to 3 in. of sand is placed over the gravel bed, then the vapor barrier is placed over this, and an inch or two of sand is placed over the vapor barrier to protect it during construction. The vapor barrier also helps protect the building against radon entering.

Wind

Foundations extending above grade are subjected to *wind loads*. The higher the foundation, the more the wind load becomes a factor. This is a special problem during periods of unusually strong winds, such as those from a hurricane. In addition, provision must be made to secure walls and wood floors to the foundation to resist wind pressures which may separate them. Anchor bolts and a variety of metal strap anchors are available to be set in the foundation to hold the sill and floor assembly in place. The foundation can be keyed to the footing or they can be tied together with metal reinforcing bars extending from the footing into the foundation to help resist lateral pressure from the wind, soil, and subsurface moisture.

Temperature

The major problem with ranges in *temperature* is freezing. Moisture tends to collect under footings. If this freezes it lifts the entire structure causing cracks in the footing,

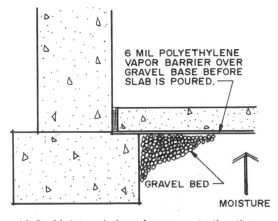

Figure 10-6. *Moisture is kept from penetrating the concrete slab by a plastic vapor barrier.*

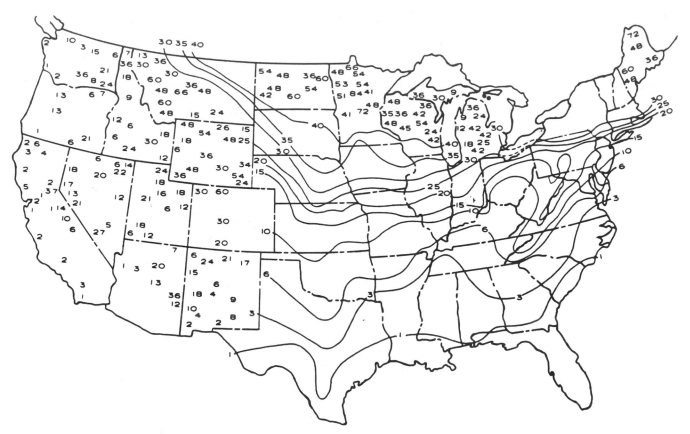

Figure 10-7. *Average depths of frost penetration. (Courtesy U.S. Department of commerce, National Climatic Data Center, Asheville, N.C.)*

foundation, walls, and floor. Doors and windows stick. The footing should be located below the *frost line*. The frost line is the lowest level below grade to which the ground freezes (Fig. 10-7). This map shows regional averages. Some parts of these regions will have a deeper frost line because of geographic conditions such as mountains. Always check with local authorities to determine actual frost depth.

Some prefer to place the footing 12 in. below the frost line to be ready for the rare occasion when unusual conditions cause freezing below the normal depth. Interior footings do not have to be placed below the frost line.

Colder climates usually have considerable snow. This requires a larger footing to carry the periodic increase in snow load. Foundations in cold climates also require insulation around the perimeter of the foundation, under the perimeter of a concrete slab floor, or below a wood floor.

Seismic Conditions

Earthquakes are clearly a possibility in many places. *Seismic risk maps* locate these areas. Local building officials can provide information on these high risk areas. Local building codes will contain detailed design regulations.

Termites

Termites are located almost everywhere. They are small ant-like insects that destroy wood members. Foundation design can help reduce their access to the wood parts of a building. Poured concrete walls are less likely to be breached than the hollow concrete block wall. Termite shields on top of the foundation help in some cases. The top course of a concrete block foundation should be a solid block. The best control technique is to treat the soil around the foundation with chemicals that kill and repel these insects.

Types of Floors

The two types of floors are wood framed and concrete. The joists on wood-framed floors must be held at least 18 in. above grade. The area below must be kept dry and well ventilated. Concrete floors are used in areas where there is a low water table and good drainage for the soil. They are usually cast on a gravel bed laid on the ground. The foundation acts as a barrier to keep water from getting under the concrete or wood floor. The concrete floor may rest on the footing or be completely clear of it. Footings

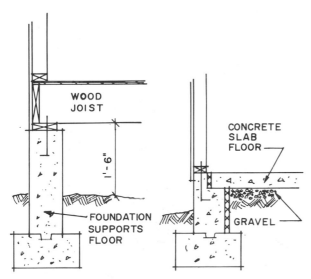

Figure 10-8. *Common types of floors.*

are sometimes used inside a large slab to stabilize it or to carry concentrated loads inside the building (Fig. 10-8).

Underfloor areas must be ventilated by mechanical means or openings in the exterior foundation. These openings should have a net area of not less than 1 ft^2 for each 150 ft^2 of underfloor area. They should be located as near the corners as possible.

Footings

A *footing* distributes the weight of a structure to the ground. It is much like a snowshoe that spreads a person's weight over a large area permitting the person to walk on snow.

The wall footing supports the foundation, floors, walls and roof. The foundation rests directly on the footing. The footing is a cast-in-place concrete member that rests on undisturbed soil and is wide and thick enough to carry the imposed weight. The size of the footing is determined by the weight it carries and the load-bearing capabilities of the soil upon which it rests. It is strengthened with reinforcing bars. All of these sizes must be calculated so the footing will not fail. Figure 10-9 shows a typical two-pour footing and foundation and the factors influencing its design.

There are a variety of ways a building can be supported (Fig. 10-10). The most common way is either a monolithically poured or a two-pour footing and foundation. With the monolithically poured type the footing and foundation are cast in one pour. This type is required by codes in some areas. The two-pour type has the footing formed and poured. A key is formed by cutting a groove in it before it hardens. After the footing hardens the foundation is formed and poured. A cast concrete footing is used to sup-

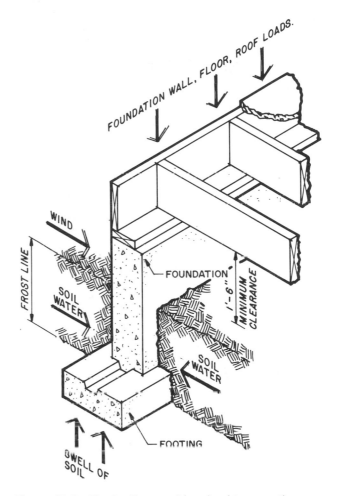

Figure 10-9. *The footing must be sized to carry the imposed loads on the existing soil*

port masonry foundations such as those made from concrete block or brick. When interior walls on a slab floor building must carry a load, a footing is formed under the wall area as the floor is poured.

When soil conditions are poor, piles are used to support a building. They can be steel, concrete, or wood. They are driven into the earth until they stop on hard strata. They also resist loading due to the friction between the soil and the surface of the piling. Some are held in place entirely by friction. Others are formed by boring holes into the earth, placing steel reinforcing in them, and filling them with concrete.

When piles are used, a grade beam serves as a foundation. It is cast in place on top of a row of piles. Examine Fig. 10-37.

Footings can be stepped up a hill to save excavating and concrete costs (Fig. 10-11). The maximum steepness of the footing is $\frac{3}{4}$ of the length of the horizontal step. The horizontal step must be at least 2'-0" long. If a concrete block foundation is to be built, the footing should be adjusted to fit standard blocks so they do not have to be cut. The horizontal and vertical footing members must be the

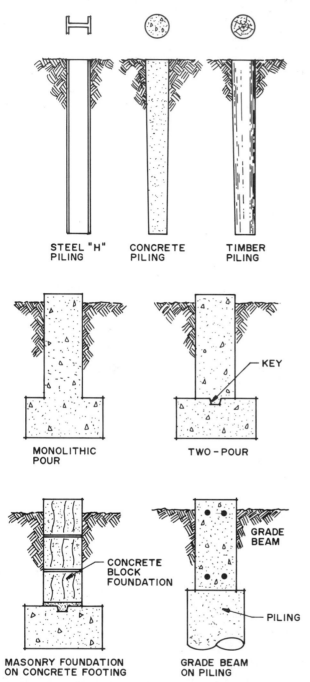

Figure 10-10. *Common load-bearing designs used to support a variety of structures.*

same thickness and the entire footing should be poured at the same time.

Column Footings

Many buildings have structural systems made up of wood, steel, or concrete columns and beams. Each column transfers part of the weight of the building and its contents to a footing. Under certain conditions, the column can be mounted on a cast-in-place concrete footing. Several con-

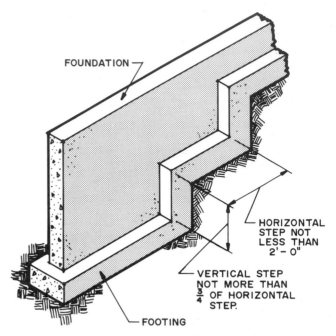

Figure 10-11. *A footing can be stepped up a hill.*

struction details for securing wood columns to a footing are in Fig. 10-12. Precast concrete columns are bolted to their concrete foundation. The column has a thick steel plate on the bottom through which the bolts pass. A nut is located above and below the plate. The nuts are used to raise and lower the column the correct level. After the column is correctly located, the space between the plate and the foundation is drypacked with a nonshrink grout (Fig. 10-13). A cast-in-place concrete column is secured to the footing with metal dowels. The dowels are set in place in the footing before it is cast and extend above the top of the footing. When the column is formed the dowels are cast in it (Fig. 10-14). Steel columns are joined to footings using some form of base plate and anchor bolts. The base plate may be welded to the column or be loose. Selected details are in Fig. 10-15.

When soil conditions are unstable, it is not possible to use a concrete footing cast directly upon the soil. In these cases piles are used to support the column. Examine Fig. 10-37. The piles are driven until they reach a solid strata. Then footings called pile caps are cast on top of the piles. Examples are shown in Fig. 10-16.

Footings are also required when constructing piers, chimneys, and fireplaces. They must be sized to carry the expected load.

Foundations

Foundations usually rest upon a footing. The floor, walls, and ceiling loads are passed through them to the footing. They must withstand the vertical loads due to these mem-

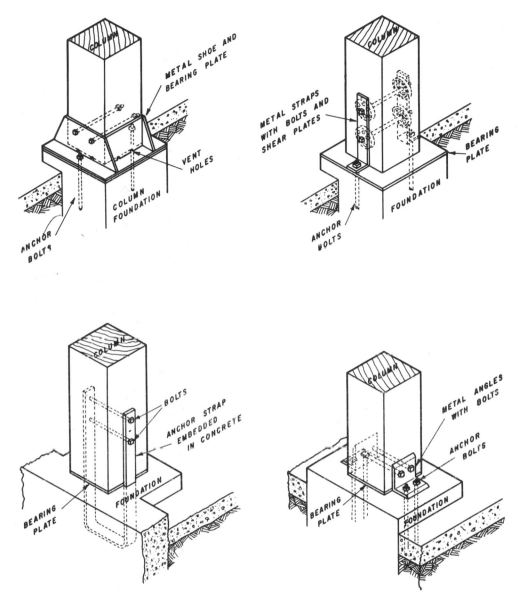

Figure 10-12. *Footing details for joining wood columns to concrete foundations. (Courtesy of National Forest Products Association.)*

bers. In addition they must withstand horizontal loads due to pressure from the soil and hydrostatic pressures from subsurface water. They should not leak and must withstand freezing and thawing conditions (Fig. 10-17). If a high water table exists, a water stop may be needed to seal the union between the footing and foundation. A water stop is a plastic diaphragm used across a joint between two adjoining concrete members to prevent the passage of water in the joint (Fig. 10-18).

The footing and poured concrete masonry foundations are joined by forming a groove in the top of the footing before the concrete hardens. The foundation is poured, filling this groove to form a key to help resist horizontal pressures. Reinforcing bars are sometimes placed in the footing and extend up into the foundation. In the founda-

tion, they are placed horizontally and vertically (Fig. 10-19). Reinforcing bars can also be placed in concrete block foundation walls and the cores in the blocks filled with concrete. The size and spacing of reinforcing bars is determined by an engineer who calculates the forces on the foundation.

Foundations are either cast-in-place concrete, concrete block, masonry, or wood. When used with a wood floor they hold the floor above the ground. When used with a concrete floor they usually support the outside edge of the floor slab, but slabs independent of the foundation are sometimes used. Poured concrete foundations are less likely to crack, leak, or be penetrated by termites.

Foundations require that a waterproofing material be applied to the exterior before the earth is backfilled.

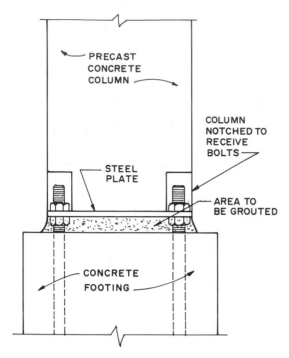

Figure 10-13. *Footing detail for a precast concrete column.*

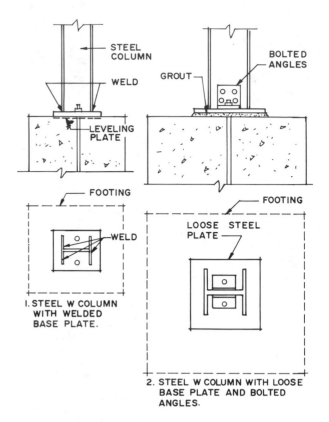

Figure 10-15. *Footing details for W-type steel columns.*

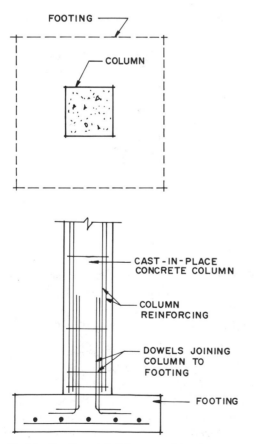

Figure 10-14. *Footing detail for a cast-in-place concrete column.*

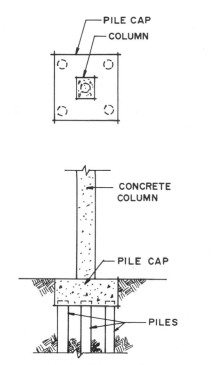

Figure 10-16. *Footing detail for a column resting on a pile cap.*

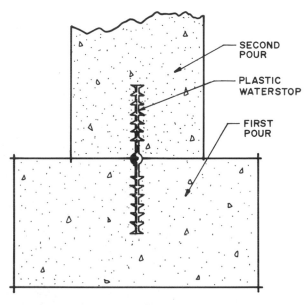

Figure 10-18. *A waterstop is used to seal joints between two abutting pours.*

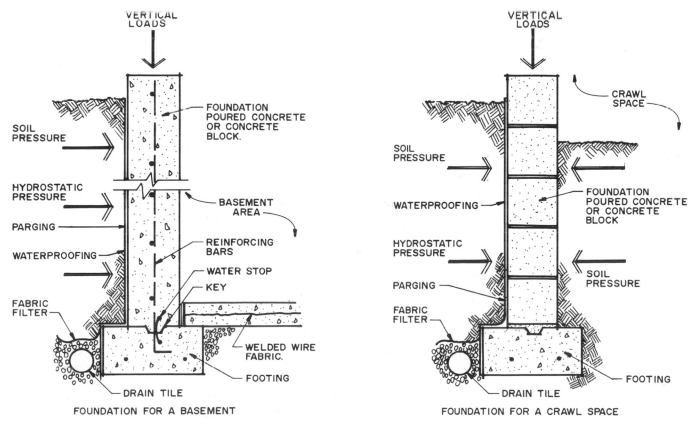

Figure 10-17. *Foundations are subject to a variety of vertical and horizontal forces.*

Figure 10-19. *These workers are installing reinforcing bars in the forms for a foundation. The vertical bars were cast in the footing and extend up the height of the wall.*

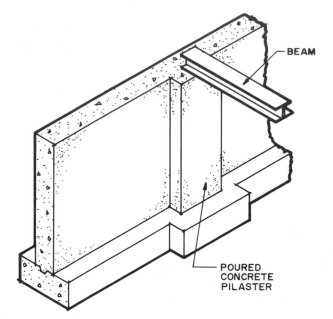

Figure 10-20. *A pilaster is used to stiffen a foundation and provide support for beams.*

on the foundation and the other on a ledger. Another solution is to cast a step in the side of the foundation (Fig. 10-23). Notice the step is formed by changing the shape of the footing. A third solution is to build a short stud wall on top of the lower floor (Fig. 10-24).

Sometimes a $\frac{1}{2}$-in. layer of cement plaster (called parging) is applied to the outside of concrete block foundations. The waterproofing membrane is applied over this. Subsurface moisture is drained away from the foundation by placing perforated plastic drain pipe around the outside next to the footing. The pipe is run to a dry well or out the side of a hill.

If a foundation is long, pilasters are needed to stiffen and brace it. In concrete block foundations, an 8 × 16 in. pilaster is built every 16 ft. In poured concrete walls, a 2 × 12 in. pilaster is built every 20 ft. The size and spacing can be changed to meet existing conditions. Pilasters are also used to thicken the foundation at each point a beam is to rest if additional width or strength is needed (Fig. 10-20 and 10-21).

A foundation for a building where the wood floor must change levels is shown in Fig. 10-22. Here one floor rests

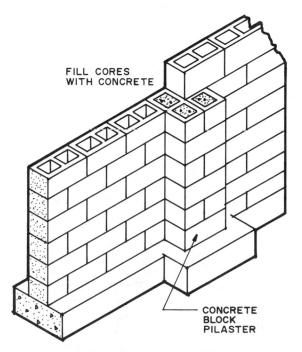

Figure 10-21. *A pilaster in a concrete block wall. It is usually filled with concrete.*

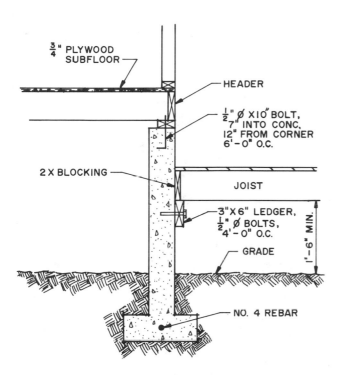

Figure 10-22. *Details for framing wood floors on different levels using a ledger*

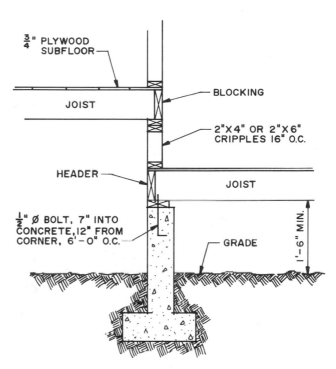

Figure 10-24. *Details for framing wood floors on different levels using cripples.*

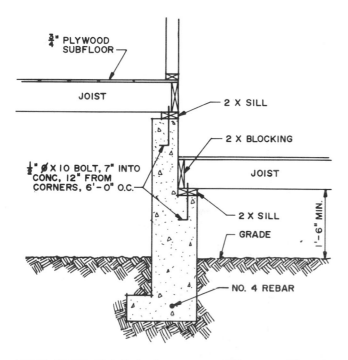

Figure 10-23. *Details for framing wood floors on different levels by forming a ledge in the foundation.*

Garage Foundations

Garage footings do not usually carry loads as great as those on the house footing. They also must permit the garage floor to be near the existing grade unless considerable fill is to be used. On a house with a concrete slab floor, the garage floor is usually 6 to 8 in. below it. When a house has a wood-framed floor, the garage floor is often 1 to 2 ft below the house floor.

The garage floor should be slightly above grade and slope toward the door to control the flow of surface water. When the floor is above grade, normally 3 or 4 in., an apron is poured sloping the area outside the garage to grade. A concrete footing is often poured below the slab in the door opening (Fig. 10-25).

When the garage floor is to be poured separately from the wall footing and foundation, a design as shown in Fig. 10-26 is used. The wood exterior wall must be kept at least 8 in. above grade. This design raises the wall the required distance above grade yet permits the slab floor to be the required 3 to 4 in. above grade.

If the garage floor is to be poured monolithically with the footing and foundation, the design would be like that shown in Fig. 10-27.

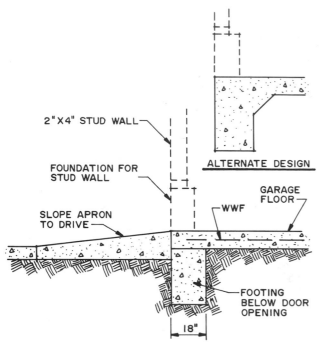

Figure 10-25. *A footing supports the garage floor at the door opening and an apron slopes to the surface of the driveway.*

Porch Construction

Porch construction on buildings with concrete slab floors is easier than on those with wood-framed floors because the slab is usually only 6 to 8 in. above grade. Also flashing is not needed because the concrete porch contacts the

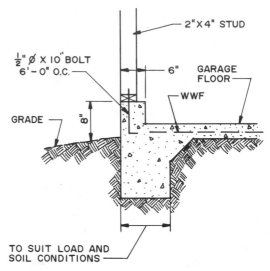

Figure 10-27. *This design shows the garage floor poured monolithically with the footing.*

concrete foundation. If fill is required under the porch, it should be firmly compacted. One design is in Fig. 10-28. Here a step was cast in the foundation to support the back edge of the porch. The other three sides have footings as shown. Another design connects the porch to the foundation with metal dowels. The rear edge of the porch is thickened and has a small footing (Fig. 10-29). These designs are important if there is much fill under the porch or the soil is unstable.

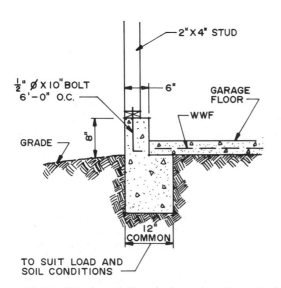

Figure 10-26. *This foundation design raises the exterior wall the required 8 in. above grade and places the garage floor slightly above grade.*

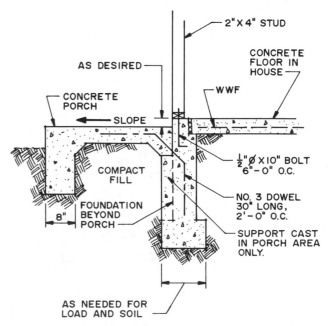

Figure 10-28. *This monolithically poured porch rests on a ledge cast in the foundation.*

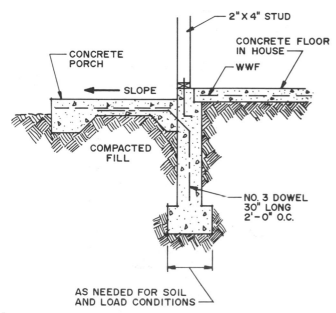

Figure 10-29. *This porch slab is supported by compacted fill, a small footing, and metal dowels tying it to the building.*

A porch built on a house with a wood-framed floor can be constructed as shown in Fig. 10-30. Metal dowels are used to connect the porch to the foundation. Flashing must be used over the wood sill to protect it from moisture. Since the wood floor is often 1 to 2 ft above grade, several

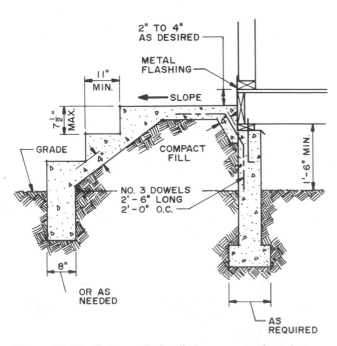

Figure 10-30. *This porch detail shows a porch and steps monolithically poured. It is often used on buildings with wood-framed floors.*

steps are necessary. In this design the porch floor and steps are poured monolithically. The minimum tread size is 11 in. and the maximum riser allowed is $7\frac{1}{2}$ in.

When a house has a basement the soil where the porch is to be built is removed when the foundation is dug. After it is backfilled, it is not suitable to support a porch, even if compacted. The porch must have footings that rest on undisturbed soil. This requires that footings and a foundation be built just like those for a house. They can be smaller because the loads are less (Fig. 10-31).

Another technique is to pour concrete supports that are keyed and tied to the foundation with metal dowels (Fig. 10-32).

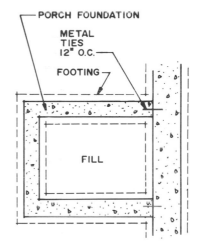

TOP VIEW WITH CONCRETE SLAB REMOVED.

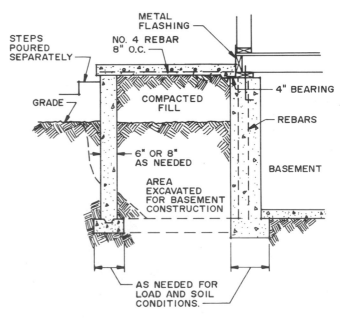

Figure 10-31. *This porch has a footing and foundation similar to that used for the building itself.*

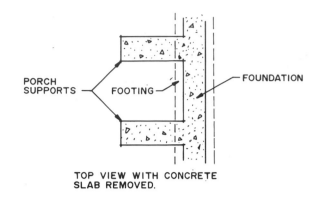

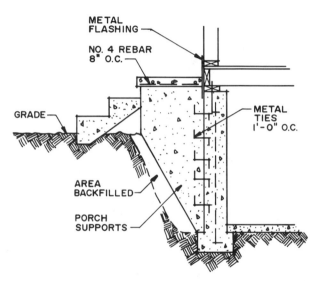

Figure 10-32. *Concrete supports tied to the foundation with metal ties can be used to support a porch deck.*

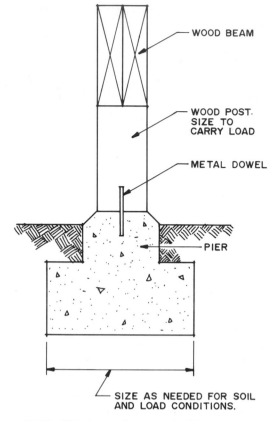

Figure 10-33. *This beam is supported by a concrete pier and a wood post.*

Beams, Columns, and Piers

There are many times when it is not practical to span long distances with wood floor joists. Their size and cost is prohibitive. The span can be reduced by placing one or more beams between the exterior foundation walls, thus dividing the long span into two or more shorter spans. The beam is run perpendicular to the floor joists and is supported in the center on piers or columns. In a building with a crawl space, the beam can be supported with a wood post set on a concrete pier (Fig. 10-33) or a concrete block pier (Fig. 10-34). When using concrete blocks fill the cores with concrete to form a solid pier. Cast-in-place concrete piers can also be used.

When putting beams over a basement, steel columns set on a footing are generally used (Fig. 10-35). For light construction 3½- and 4-in.-round steel columns are used. Square and rectangular steel columns and W and S shapes are used for heavy loads (Fig. 10-36). Wood posts can also be used.

Piles and Grade Beams

When the soil is very poor and will not support a standard poured concrete footing, piles can be used. They are drilled or driven until they reach a strata of stable soil. Often a hole the diameter of the pile is bored, reinforcing bars properly spaced are inserted in the hole, and the hole is filled with concrete. In some cases, the friction between the pile and earth provides the needed support. Once the piles are in place a grade beam is built on top of them. It spans the distances between the piles. Generally the grade beam is below the surface of the earth so it is poured concrete. If it is above the earth, wood or steel members could be used. The building is built on the grade beam in the same manner as described for foundations. In effect, the grade beam becomes the foundation (Fig. 10-37). Generally the soil is not filled up to touch the bottom of the grade beam. That way when the soil in that area freezes it will not swell and lift the grade beam.

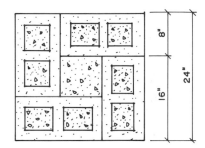

LARGER PIER—ALTERNATE BLOCKS
IN EACH LAYER.

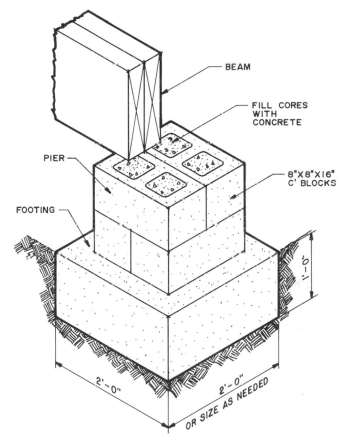

Figure 10-34. *Concrete block piers are often used in light construction.*

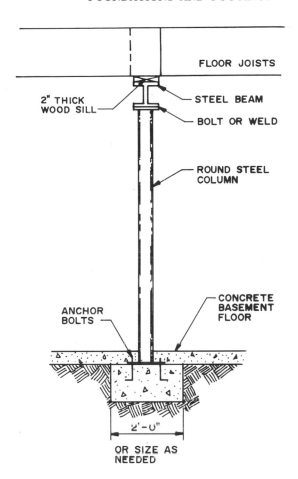

Figure 10-35. *Steel columns are used to support beams.*

Wood Foundations

The *wood foundation* is a load-bearing wood frame wall system designed for below-grade use as a foundation for light frame construction. It is basically the same as above-ground frame construction except for several factors. The lumber and plywood used in framing are stress-graded to withstand the lateral soil pressures. The foundation also carries the usual live and dead loads. Vertical loads on the foundation are distributed to the supporting soil be a footing made of a wood footing plate and a structural gravel layer.

The wood foundation does not require the customary concrete footing. This reduces the overall weight and cost of construction. Since it can be assembled in a shop and erected on the site it permits builders to install foundations in any kind of weather. Installation is fast and does not require the usual crew of concrete workers.

The basement tends to be warmer because the wood wall provides good insulation. In addition, it can be insulated on the inside in the same manner as above-grade frame construction. This tends to reduce heating costs.

Since considerable attention is given to waterproofing and handling below surface water, the basement produced is dry. This reduces the mildew often associated with basements.

The basement area is easier to finish into a living area. Normal procedures are used to apply wall finish over the insulation. It is easy to install electrical outlets around the basement walls.

A typical foundation panel is shown in Fig. 10-38. The

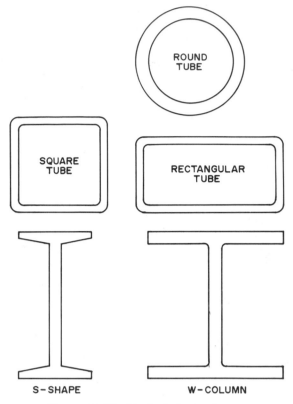

Figure 10-36. *Typical steel columns.*

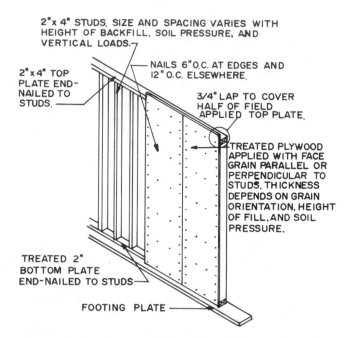

Figure 10-38. *A typical all-wood foundation wall panel. (Courtesy of National Forest Products Association.)*

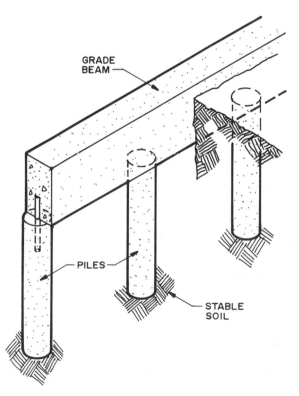

Figure 10-37. *Grade beams are cast on top of piles and serve as a foundation.*

thickness of the plywood depends upon the grain direction, height of soil, and soil pressure.

If the wall has openings for doors or windows, support members around them should be doubled.

In Fig. 10-39, the details for forming a corner are shown. Notice that after the panels are joined, a top plate is nailed in place. The method for joining panels in the wall is shown in Fig. 10-40.

Detailed structural design procedures to cover items such as soil types, transverse lateral loads against the wood foundation, racking loads (loads parallel to the wall), footing design, and design of load-bearing walls are available from the National Forest Products Association, 1619 Massachusetts Ave., N.W., Washington, D.C., 20036.

Complete construction details for a foundation wall for frame and a masonry veneer wall for houses with basements are shown in Figs. 10-41 and 10-42. Details for houses with crawl spaces are shown in Figs. 10-43 and 10-44.

The wall for frame construction rests on a footing plate that sits on a gravel bed. The masonry veneer wall is much the same except that it adds a knee wall to hold the masonry veneer. The footing plate is considerably larger because it has to support the foundation wall and the knee wall. The knee wall should also be used to support a concrete porch (Fig. 10-45).

A section through a typical sump is shown in Fig. 10-46. This concrete lined unit could require an electric sump pump to keep the water level down. This is required in poorly drained soil. In areas where the soil permits easy

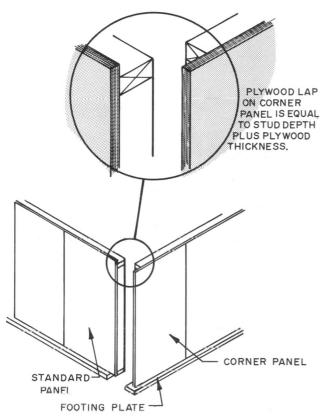

Figure 10-39. *Details for forming the wood foundation corner. (Courtesy of National Forest Products Association.)*

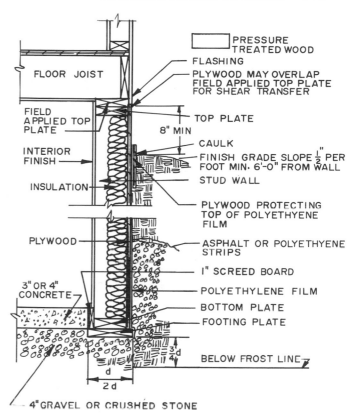

Figure 10-41. *Construction details for wood foundation used with frame construction and full basement. (Courtesy of National Forest Products Association.)*

drainage of moisture, a perforated pipe in a pit of gravel is adequate. The water collects in the pit and flows out the drain by gravity.

Figuring Footing Sizes

A footing is designed to distribute the weight of a structure uniformly to the soil beneath it. As explained earlier, soil conditions determine its bearing capacity. This limits

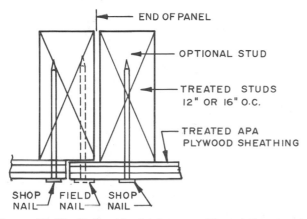

Figure 10-40. *Method for joining wood foundation panels. (Courtesy National Forest Products Association.)*

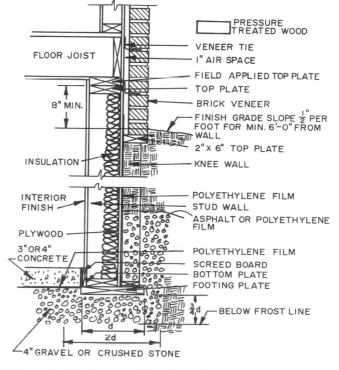

Figure 10-42. *Construction details for wood foundation with brick veneer construction and full basement. (Courtesy National Forest Products Association.)*

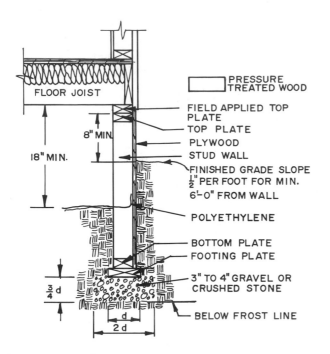

Figure 10-43. Construction details for wood foundation with frame construction over a crawl space. (Courtesy of National Forest Products Association.)

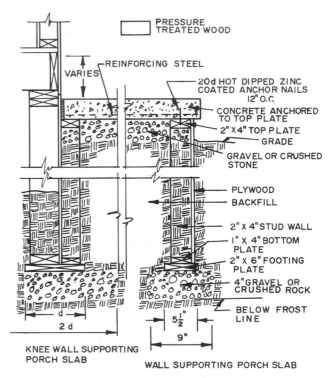

Figure 10-45. A wood foundation can support a concrete porch. (Courtesy National Forest Products Association.)

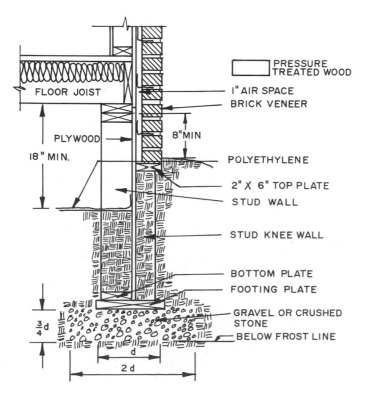

Figure 10-44. Construction details for wood foundation with brick veneer construction over a crawl space. (Courtesy of National Forest Products Association.)

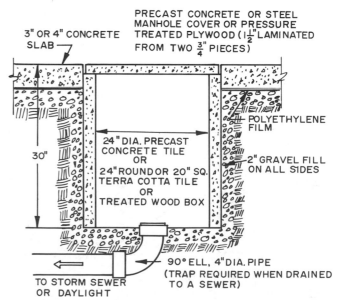

Figure 10-46. A recommended pit for collecting water to be removed with a sump pump. (Courtesy of National Forest Products Association.)

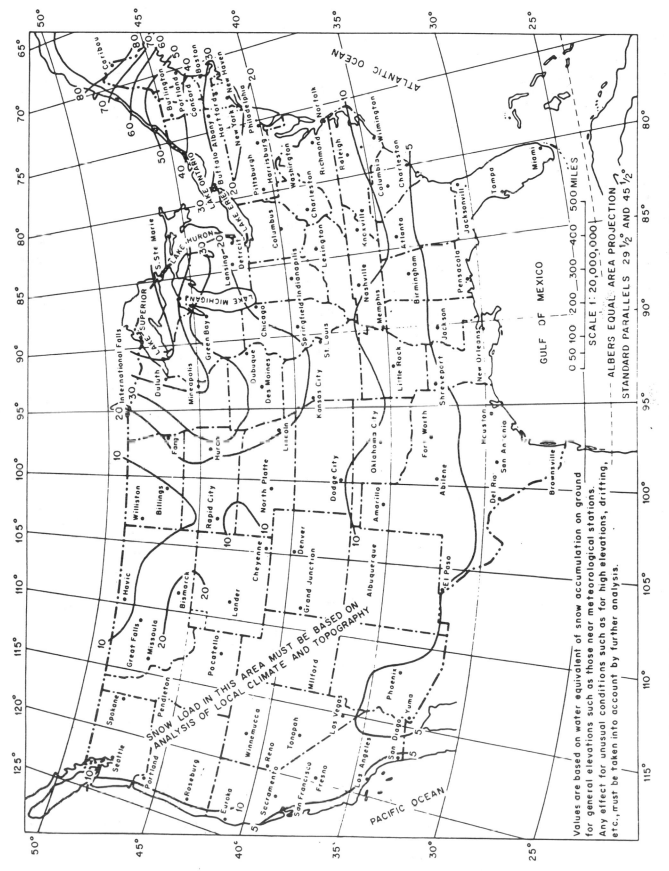

Figure 10-47. Average snow loads in pounds per square foot. (Courtesy of the National Climatic Data Center.)

Values are based on water equivalent of snow accumulation on ground for general elevations such as those near meteorological stations. Any effect for unusual conditions such as for high elevations, drifting, etc., must be taken into account by further analysis.

SNOW LOAD IN THIS AREA MUST BE BASED ON ANALYSIS OF LOCAL CLIMATE AND TOPOGRAPHY

SCALE 1:20,000,000

0 50 100 200 300 400 500 MILES

ALBERS EQUAL AREA PROJECTION
STANDARD PARALLELS 29½ AND 45½

147

the size of the footing. Typical soil-bearing capacities are in Fig. 10-2. For example, if a soil has a bearing capacity of 2000 lb/ft² 1 ft² of footing will support 2000 lb of building.

Soils vary widely on the same site and often have pockets of poor, weak, and compressible materials. Soil samples are often taken 50 or more feet apart so variances could occur between test borings. For this reason, it is common practice to apply a safety factor of at least 3 when doing soil engineering. This safety factor is built into the tables used that indicate the allowable soil pressure in pounds per square foot for various soils.

Exterior Wall Footings

1. Calculate the weight of a 1-ft-wide slice through the building. On most designs for light construction the roof is supported by the outside wall. On large commercial buildings interior load-bearing walls may be used or a system of steel, wood, or concrete columns may carry some of the roof load. In this case, the load on the columns would be figured separately from the wall load.

2. The weights include both live loads (snow, furniture, etc.) and dead loads (weight of the building materials). Dead loads used for design purposes are listed in the Appendix. Snow and wind loads vary with the locality.

Check local codes for these requirements. Generalized snow load conditions are in Fig. 10-47.

3. Add up the total weight of materials for one lineal foot of building (Fig. 10-48). Notice that only half the joist spans are used to calculate the load because the other half bears upon the beam through the center of the building. The partition load for light construction is 20 lb/ft² of floor area. This is added to the live and dead loads on the floors.

4. For light construction, a typical design solution is to make the footing twice the width of the foundation and the same thickness as the foundation. In Fig. 10-48 the foundation is 8 in. so the footing is 16 in. wide and 8 in. thick.

5. The total load on the footing in Fig. 10-48 is 2197 lb/lineal ft. To find the width of the footing required first try the normal proportions mentioned in step 4. If the soil supports 3000 lb/ft² and a 1-ft slice of footing (1'-4") contains 1.3 ft², then this footing will support $3000 \times 1.3 = 3900$ lb/lineal foot. This exceeds our requirements of 2197 lb so a standard footing is adequate.

If the soil-bearing capacity had been 1600 lb/ft² the standard footing would have been too small. If the footing was increased to 18 in. the footing would have a surface area of 1.5 ft². This would equal $1600 \times 1.5 = 2400$ lb/lineal ft which would be adequate. This procedure is

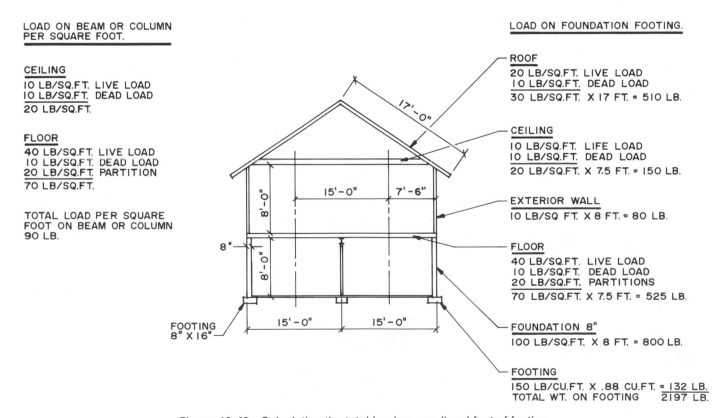

Figure 10-48. Calculating the total load on one lineal foot of footing.

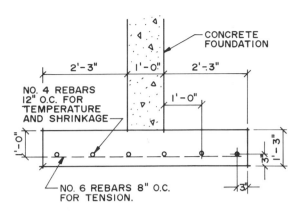

Figure 10-49. *A typical wall footing with reinforcement for tension and temperature and shrinkage reinforcement.*

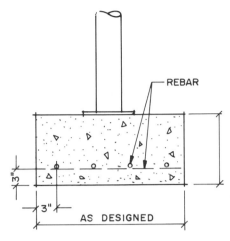

Figure 10-51. *A typical column footing.*

adequate for light framed buildings such as a typical residence because the loads are small. When heavier loads are present, more detailed calculations are necessary. A typical footing for a heavy commercial building is in Fig. 10-49. Since it is wider than the 2/1 proportion mentioned, the structural engineer must calculate its size and the size and location of reinforcing.

Pier and Column Footings

The design of pier and column footings is much like that discussed for wall footings. A major difference is that the total load is concentrated upon the column or pier. The following example is useful for light construction where loads are not great. Calculate the weight per square foot that will bear on the part of the building supported by the column. Refer back to Fig. 10-48. Then calculate the number of square feet the column or pier will support. This is

called the tributary area. They will carry half the load to the next supporting element as a foundation wall or another pier or column (Fig. 10-50). Multiply the area supported by the weight per square foot. In Fig. 10-44 the weight per square foot on the column was 90 lb/ft^2. The column therefore carries 90 lb × 300 ft^2 or 27 000 lb. If the soil supports 3000 lb/ft^2, the column footing must contain 9 ft^2. Columns and pier footings are square so the load is uniformly distributed. To find the size of the sides of the footing, take the square root of its area. In this example, it would be the $\sqrt{9}$ which is 3 ft. For light construction, pier and column footings are normally 1 ft thick with no. 4 rebar 8 in. O.C. both ways forming a grid. A typical design is in Fig. 10-51. For most soils and loads a 2'-0" × 2'-0" × 1'-0" column or pier footing is adequate for light construction.

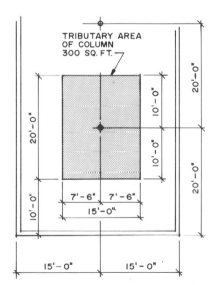

TRIBUTARY AREA 15'-0" X 20'-0" = 300 SQ/FT.
TOTAL LOAD = AREA X WEIGHT PER/FT.
= 300 SQ/FT. X 90 LB/SQ/FT.
27,000 LB. ON COLUMN.

LOOK AT COLUMN TABLES. IF THIS COLUMN IS 8'-0" LONG IT MUST CARRY 27,000 LBS. STANDARD WEIGHT, 3½" ∅ COLUMN WILL CARRY 32,000 LB. SO IS ADEQUATE.

9 SQ/FT. OF FOOTING REQUIRED.
3000 LB. SOIL ⟌ 27,000 LB. LOAD

$\sqrt{9}$ = 3 FT. FOOTING SIDE
FOOTING 3'-0" X 3'-0" X 1'-0".

Figure 10-50. *How to figure the tributary area on a column.*

Maximum Loads for Steel Columns*							
	Outside Diameter of Column (in.)	Weight Per Foot of Column (lbs.)	Maximum Load for Length of Column				
			length (ft)				
			6	7	8	9	10	12
Lightweight steel columns	$3\frac{1}{2}$	12	23	21	19	17		
	4	15	30	28	26	24		
Standard weight steel columns	$3\frac{1}{2}$	15	38		32		27	
	4	20	49		43		37	31

Safe concentric load for unbraced length in kips (thousands of pounds).
NOTE: Girder may be offset from centerline of house width up to one foot

Figure 10-52. *Design loads for selected round steel columns.*

Selecting Column Sizes

After the total load that bears upon a column is known its size can be selected. Typical loads for $3\frac{1}{2}$- and 4-in. steel columns are shown in Fig. 10-52. The longer the column the less load it can carry. Design loads for wood columns are in Fig. 10-53. Load carrying capacities of W, S, square, and rectangular steel columns can be found in a structural steel handbook.

Selecting a Beam

A beam is often run from one side of a foundation to the other to provide support for floor or ceiling joists. It makes it possible to use smaller joists because it cuts down the distance they must span.

Following is a typical way to determine the load a steel beam must carry. In Fig. 10-54 the beam must span 20 ft from one support to the next. It will carry half the floor load to the foundation on each side. This gives a tributary area of 15 × 20 or 300/ft². The floor load as found for the column is 90 lb/ft². The beam must carry 90 lb × 300

ft² or 27 000 lb. The size of beam is determined by selecting one from a table that will carry that load over that distance.

The load on wood beams in light construction is based upon the width of the building and if the building is one or two stories. The data in Fig. 10-55 assume that no roof load is transmitted to the wood beam.

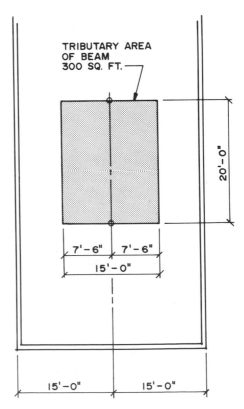

Figure 10-54. *How to figure the tributary area on a beam.*

Table of Maximum Loads to be Imposed on Columns Made From Douglas Fir or Southern Pine, No. 1 Grade						
Nominal Size	3″ × 4″	4″ × 4″	4″ × 6″	6″ × 6″	6″ × 8″	8″ × 8″
Height of Column	Imposed Load in Pounds					
4′-0″	8,720	12,920	19,850	30,250	41,250	56,250
5′-0″	7,430	12,400	19,200	30,050	41,000	56,250
6′-0″	5,630	11,600	17,950	29,500	40,260	56,250
6′-6″	4,750	10,880	16,850	29,300	39,950	56,000
7′-0″	4,130	10,040	15,550	29,000	39,600	55,650
7′-6″		9,300	14,400	28,800	39,000	55,300

Figure 10-53. *Design loads for selected wood columns.*

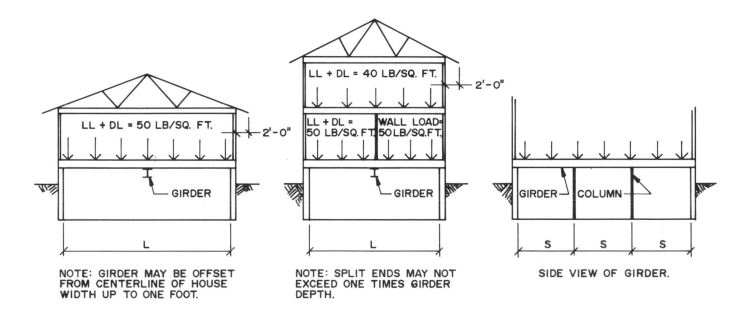

Maximum span designs for girders supporting one-story floor loads using lumber having an allowable bending stress not less than 1500 psi*

Nominal Lumber Sizes	House Widths = L (ft)								
	20	22	24	26	28	30	32	34	36
2—2 × 6	5'-3"	4'-10"	4'-5"	4'-1"	—	—	—	—	—
3—2 × 6	6'-9"	6'-5"	6'-2"	5'-11"	5'-8"	5'-3"	4'-11"	4'-8"	4'-5"
2—2 × 8	7'-0"	6'-4"	5'-10"	5'-4"	5'-0"	4'-8"	4'-4"	4'-1"	—
3—2 × 8	8'-11"	8'-6"	8'-1"	7'-9"	7'-5"	7'-0"	6'-6"	6'-2"	5'-10"
2—2 × 10	8'-11"	8'-1"	7'-5"	6'-10"	6'-4"	5'-11"	5'-7"	5'-3"	4'-11"
3—2 × 10	11'-4"	10'-10"	10'-4"	9'-11"	9'-6"	8'-11"	8'-4"	7'-10"	7'-5"
2—2 × 12	10'-10"	9'-10"	9'-0'	8'-4"	7'-9"	7'-2"	6'-9"	6'-4"	6'-0"
3—2 × 12	13'-9"	13'-2"	12'-7"	12'-1"	11'-7"	10'-10"	10'-2"	9'-6"	9'-0"

Linear interpolation within the above table for house widths not given is permitted.

Maximum span designs for girders supporting two-story floor loads using lumber having an allowable bending stress not less than 1000 psi*

Girder Spans = S (ft)*

Nominal Lumber Sizes	House Widths = L (ft)								
	20	22	24	26	28	30	32	34	36
3—2 × 8	4'-7	4'-2"	—	—	—	—	—	—	—
2—2 × 12	4'-9"	4'-4"	4'-0"	—	—	—	—	—	—
3—2 × 10	5'-10"	5'-4"	4'-11"	4'-7"	4'-3"	4'-0"	—	—	—
3—2 × 12	7'-1"	6'-6"	6'-0"	5'-6"	5'-2"	4'-10"	4'-6"	4'-3"	4-0"

Linear interpolation within the above table for house widths not given is permitted.

Figure 10-55. *Design data for built-up wood girders. (Courtesy of National Association of Home Builders Research Center.)*

Technical Vocabulary

Following are some important technical terms used in this chapter. Write a brief definition for each.

Foundation
Footing
Wind loads
Frost line
Seismic risk maps
Piles
Monolithic
Beam
Column
Pier
Grade beam

Study Questions

Answer the following study questions without referring to the text. Then check your answers with the text and correct those that were wrong.

1. What purpose does a footing serve?

2. What factors must be considered as the foundation and footing are designed?

3. What is the architect trying to find out when a soil test is run?

4. What provisions must be made to protect the foundation and footing in areas of high rainfall or subsurface water?

5. How does temperature effect the foundation and footing?

6. How can a building be protected against termites?

7. How does a two-pour footing and foundation differ from those monolithically poured?

8. When are piles used?

9. What types of materials are used to construct foundations?

10. How can you reduce the size of a beam needed over a long span?

11. When are grade beams used?

12. What supports a grade beam?

Laboratory Problems

1. Design a foundation for the residence planned in Chapter 8. Plan foundations for each of the following conditions:

   (a) Concrete slab on grade construction with a frame exterior wall
   (b) Brick veneer over frame wall with the floor over a crawl space
   (c) Frame construction with a full basement

2. Design a foundation for the retail store building planned in Chapter 8. Plan foundations for each of the following:

   (a) Concrete slab on grade with exterior wall of 4-in. brick and a 4-in. concrete block
   (b) Full basement with 4-in. concrete floor supported by bar joists.

Floor, Wall, and Roof Construction for Light Construction

This chapter covers the design of buildings, such as residences and similar size buildings, classified as light construction. While there are many variations the systems presented are typical of those most commonly used.

Design Considerations

As walls, floors, roofs, and ceilings are being designed their *fire rating, sound transmission class, and impact isolation class* must be considered. These are discussed in Chapter 12 and design data related to them are in the Appendix.

Wood-Framed Floors

Wood-framed floors can be built using solid wood joists, wood beams, manufactured and laminated joists, or truss joists.

Solid Wood Joists

The use of wood joists as the structural members for the floor and plywood as the subfloor is the most common system used. Solid wood floor joists are most often spaced 16 in. O.C. (on center). However, other spacings, such as 12, 13.7, 19.2, and 24 in. O.C. are used. These spacings divide the 8-ft length of plywood subflooring into even divisions so no waste occurs. In areas having heavier than normal loads, such as a bath or kitchen, joists are often spaced 12 in. O.C. Typical joist sizes are 2×8, 2×10, and 2×12 in. The size used depends upon the grade and species of lumber and the spans. A partial design table for floor joists is in Fig. 11-1. Complete data are in the Appendix.

The spans shown in this figure are the maximum clear spans. In residential construction bedrooms and attics are assumed to have a 30 lb/ft^2 live load and other rooms, as the living room and kitchen, are designed with a 40 lb/ft^2 live load. The live load is the weight of people and furniture bearing on the floor.

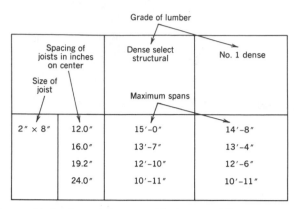

Size of joist	Spacing of joists in inches on center	Grade of lumber Dense select structural Maximum spans	No. 1 dense
2″ × 8″	12.0″	15′–0″	14′–8″
	16.0″	13′–7″	13′–4″
	19.2″	12′–10″	12′–6″
	24.0″	10′–11″	10′–11″

Figure 11-1. *A partial span table for wood floor joists. (Courtesy of Southern Pine Marketing Council).*

The wood floor joists are supported by the concrete foundation (Fig. 11-2). Since most buildings are wider than the available joists can span, a beam or concrete foundation is constructed in the interior of the building to help support the joists. The design of the foundation and beams and the necessary supporting piers or columns is shown in Chapter 10.

A detail showing a wood-framed floor on a concrete foundation with an exterior stud wall and wood siding is shown in Fig. 11-3. Notice the wood sill must be 8 in. above the grade. This is required by building codes. While this shows a basement the sill construction is the same for a building with a crawl space. If the building is to have a brick or stone exterior veneer it will be built as shown in Fig. 11-4. This shows the design with a crawl space. Most building codes required the floor joists be at least 1′–6″ above the ground and the bottom of a beam 1′–0″ above the ground. Notice the veneer is at least 2 in. above the outside grade.

When the exterior wall is solid masonry, several design possibilities exist. Probably the most common is shown in Fig. 11-5. Here the joists are placed so they bear 4 in. on the masonry wall and the masonry units are laid around each joist. The joist has a fire cut on the end. This cut makes it possible for the floor to cave in during a fire without bringing down the masonry wall. The cut enables the floor to fall free.

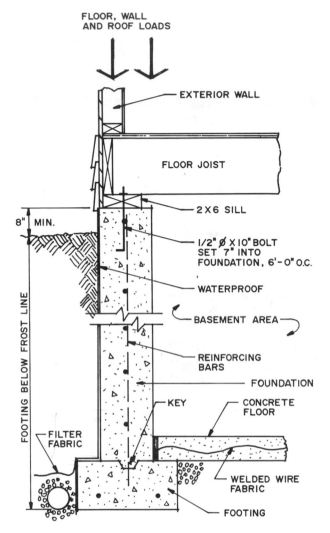

Figure 11-3. *Typical construction of a wood framed floor over a basement for a building with a wood-framed exterior wall.*

Another design has the foundation widened to provide a bearing surface for the wood sill upon which the joists are fastened (Fig. 11-6). This example shows a concrete block foundation; however, a poured concrete foundation could also be used.

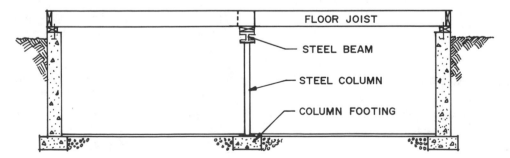

Figure 11-2. *Floor joists are supported by the foundation and beams. Beams may require support by columns or piers.*

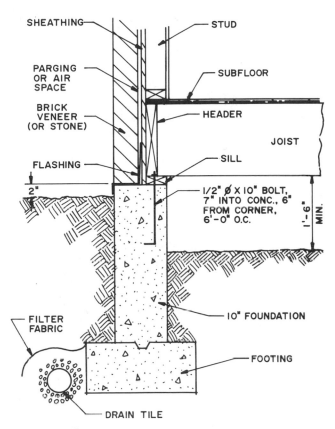

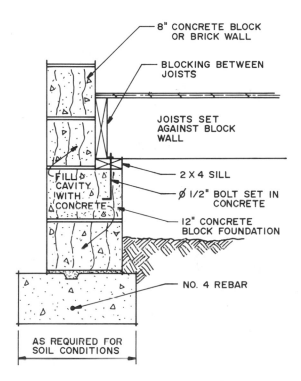

Figure 11-4. *Typical construction of a wood-framed floor over a crawl space for a building with a brick veneer over wood-framed exterior wall.*

Figure 11-6. *Wood joists can be secured to masonry walls by building a supporting ledge in the foundation.*

The use of wood ledgers to carry wood floor joists is shown in Figs. 11-7 and 11-8.

Floor Framing Details

The examples that follow show the typical way floors with solid wood joists are framed. Figure 11-9 shows a beam set into a pocket in the foundation. The pocket should have at least $\frac{1}{2}$ in. air space on all sides of the beam so it can remain dry. The beam is set flush with the top of the sill. Figure 11-10 shows the same construction using a steel beam. Notice it has a wood plate secured to the top so the wood joists can be nailed to the beam. Floor joists can be butted (Fig. 11-11) rather than lapped. If it is desired to have a flat ceiling in the area below the beam the floor joists are framed into the side of the beam as shown in Figs. 11-12, 11-13, and 11-14.

When codes permit the wood floor joists can be placed directly on top of the steel beam. They are held in place with a nail or metal clip (Fig. 11-15). When this is done remember that the top of the beam must be flush with the wood sill bolted to the foundation.

When an interior partition is to carry a load, such as the ceiling, the joists under it are doubled. They can be spaced apart so heat ducts and plumbing can be run in the wall (Fig. 11-16). Joists are also doubled and often spaced closer together under floor areas where a heavy load is known to be located (Fig. 11-17).

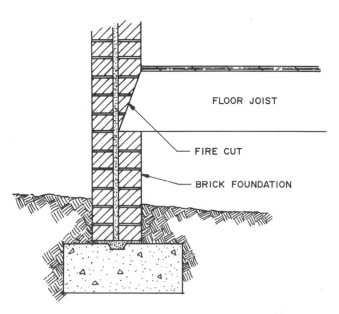

Figure 11-5. *Joists set in masonry wall should have a firecut.*

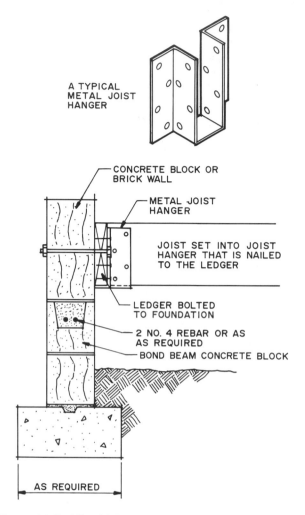

Figure 11-7. *Wood joists can be secured to masonry walls by using a wood ledger and metal joist hangers.*

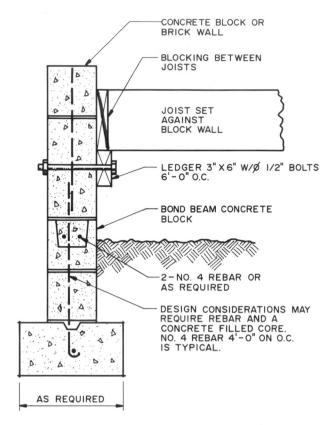

Figure 11-8. *This wood joist is supported by a ledger which is bolted to the foundation.*

Girder Framed Floor

This system of floor construction uses wood girders supported by piers as floor joists. They are generally spaced 4'-0" O.C. The subfloor is $1\frac{1}{8}$-in.-thick tongue-and-groove

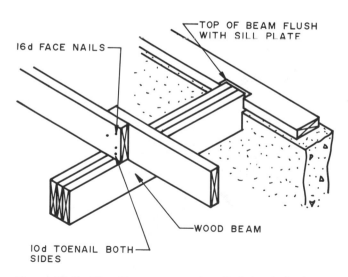

Figure 11-9. *Wood beams are set so their top is flush with the sill plate.*

Openings in the floor that are 4 ft or more must have double headers and double trimmer joists on each side (Fig. 11-18). When a floor is expected to cantilever (project over the foundation), it is framed as shown in Fig. 11-19.

Many codes require that bridging be installed between floor joists. Bridging is used to stiffen the floor, hold joists in place, and help distribute a concentrated floor load over several joists. This can be wood diagonal, metal diagonal, or solid wood blocking (Figs. 11-20 and 11-21). Usually it is placed in rows 8 ft apart (Fig. 11-22). Another form permitted by some codes uses 1×2 to 1×4 strips nailed to the bottom of the joists on each side of the beam.

Subflooring is usually 4×8 ft sheets of plywood $\frac{1}{2}$ to $\frac{3}{4}$ in. thick. Thicker types are available when joists have wider spans (Fig. 11-23). Underlayment is a smooth sheet, such as plywood or hardboard, which is placed on top of the subfloor if a smoother surface is needed. Plywood underlayment data are in Fig. 11-24.

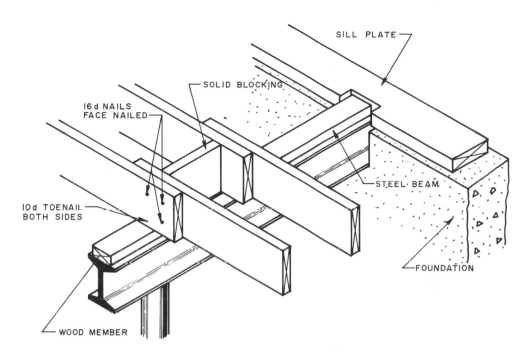

Figure 11-10. *Wood floor joists are toenailed to the wood member below and face nailed where they overlap.*

plywood (Fig. 11-25). This plywood is designed to carry normal floor loads in light construction (40 lb/sft²) over a 4'-0" span. A typical box sill is used at the foundation.

The floor panels are installed with the face grain perpendicular to the girders. The end joints are staggered. Since the panels have tongue-and-groove edges, blocking of panel edges is not necessary (Fig. 11-26).

Planking can also be used as a floor decking on this system. The decking is usually 2 in. thick but is available up to 4 in. thick. The wood members are laid flat on the girders. Usually they are tongue and grooved on the 2 in. edge (Fig. 11-27).

The spacing between girders varies according to the load-carrying capacity of the decking. Spans of 6'-0" O.C. are common.

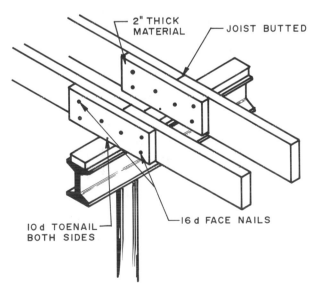

Figure 11-11. *Joists can be butted over the beam and joined with a wood scab.*

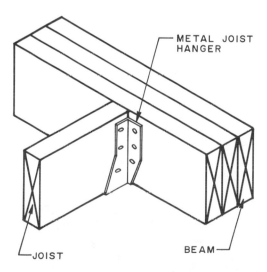

Figure 11-12. *Metal joist hangers are used to join joists to the sides of wood beams.*

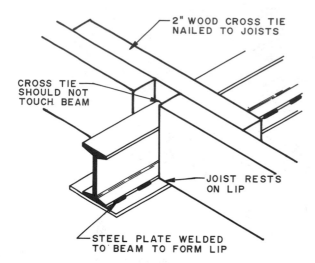

Figure 11-13. *A joist can be framed around a steel beam to give a flush ceiling to the room below.*

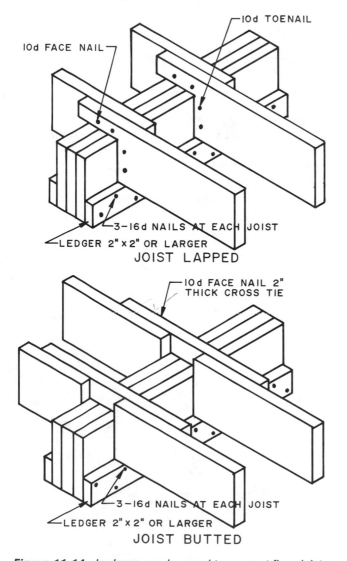

JOIST LAPPED

JOIST BUTTED

Figure 11-14. *Ledgers can be used to support floor joists at the beam.*

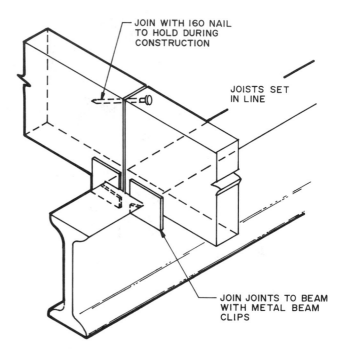

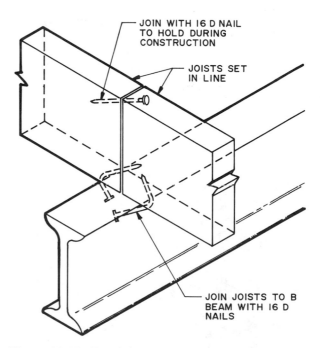

Figure 11-15. *Wood floor joists can be secured to a steel beam with a wood sill by using clinched nails or metal beam clips.*

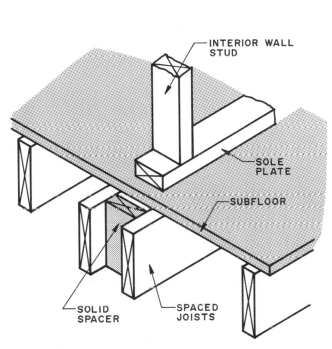

Figure 11-16. *Joists are doubled under interior partitions. They are often spaced out to permit pipes to be run inside the wall.*

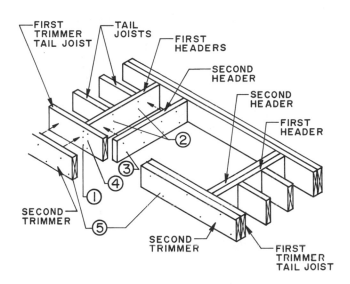

1. NAIL FIRST TRIMMER TO FIRST HEADER.

2. END NAIL HEADER TO TAIL JOIST.

3. NAIL SECOND HEADER TO FIRST HEADER.

4. NAIL FIRST TRIMMER TO FIRST AND SECOND HEADERS.

5. PLACE SECOND TRIMMER AGAINST FIRST TRIMMER AND NAIL TO FIRST TRIMMER.

Figure 11-18. *Openings in floors are framed with double headers and trimmers. This illustration shows the nailing sequence for framing these openings.*

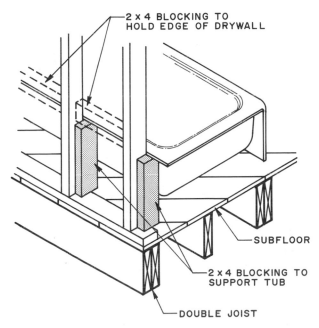

Figure 11-17. *Bathtubs require special framing to carry the concentrated load and hold them in position.*

Trus Joist Floor System

Trus Joist is a manufactured wood member constructed with structural panel webs and MICRO-LAM laminated veneer lumber flanges. The web is glued into a groove in the laminated veneer lumber members. They are used for joists in the same manner as solid wood. These units have long span capabilities and uniformity in load-bearing strength. A typical joist and framing example is in Fig. 11-28.

Typical construction details are in Fig. 11-29. Joists can be butted to each other or to wood joists or beams with approved metal joist hangers. When joists are doubled to carry a heavy load, as in a load-bearing partition, the space between the webs is filled with a 2×8 solid wood member plus $\frac{1}{2}$-in. plywood.

When a load-bearing wall runs perpendicular to the joists 2×4 blocking or TJI joist blocking is used.

When the blocking over the foundation must carry a wall load of over 2000 lb, the TJI joist blocking is doubled. Additional construction details are in manuals available from the manufacturer.

Recommended spans for TJI joists for light construction are in Fig. 11-30.

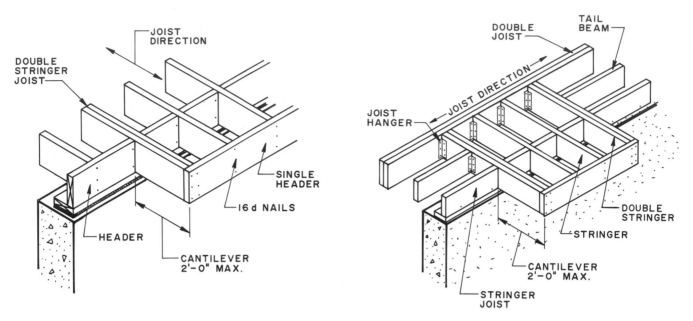

Figure 11-19. *How to frame floor projections parallel with and perpendicular to the floor joists.*

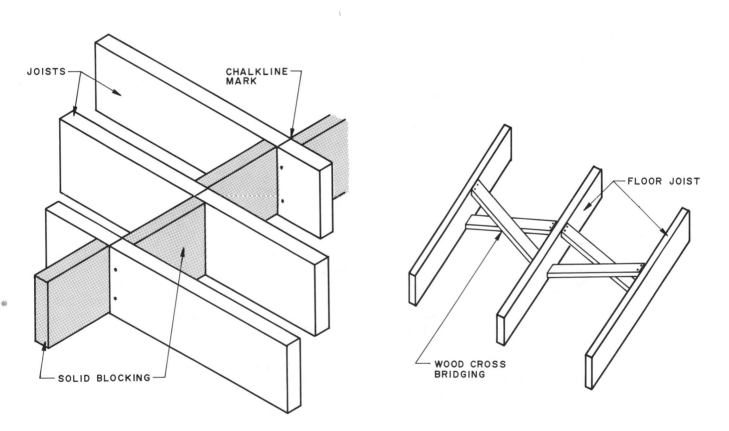

Figure 11-20. *Two types of wood bridging.*

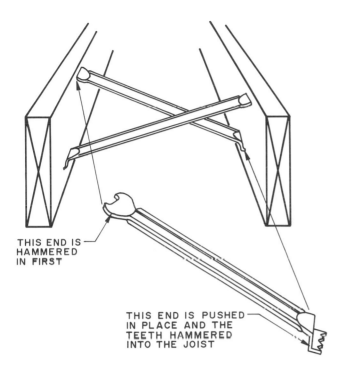

THIS END IS
HAMMERED
IN **FIRST**

THIS END IS PUSHED
IN PLACE AND THE
TEETH HAMMERED
INTO THE JOIST

Figure 11-21. *Typical metal bridging.*

Figure 11-22. *This carpenter is locating rows of bridging. (Courtesy of American Plywood Association.)*

Panel Span Rating (or Group Number)	Panel Thickness (in.)	Maximum Span (in.)
$\frac{24}{16}$[3]	$\frac{7}{16}$	16
$\frac{32}{16}$	$\frac{15}{32}, \frac{1}{2}, \frac{5}{8}$	16[1]
$\frac{40}{20}$	$\frac{19}{32}, \frac{5}{8}, \frac{3}{4}, \frac{7}{8}$	20[2]
$\frac{48}{24}$	$\frac{23}{32}, \frac{3}{4}, \frac{7}{8}$	24
$1\frac{1}{8}''$ Groups 1 & 2[3]	$1\frac{1}{8}$	48
$1\frac{1}{4}''$ Groups 3 & 4[3]	$1\frac{1}{4}$	48

[1]*Span may be 24 inches if $\frac{25}{32}$ inch wood strip flooring is installed at right angles to joists.*
[2]*Span may be 24 inches if $\frac{25}{32}$ inch wood strip flooring is installed at right angles to joists, or if a minimum of $1\frac{1}{2}$ inches of lightweight concrete (or 1 inch of some gypsum concrete products) is applied over panels.*
[3]*Check dealer for availability. Note that a Span Rating of $\frac{32}{16}$ is the minimum recommended on joists spaced 16 inches on center when topped with lightweight or gypsum concrete.*

American Plywood Association

Figure 11-23. *Panel subflooring. (Courtesy of American Plywood Association.)*

Wood Floor Trusses

A variety of wood floor trusses are manufactured that give long spans and reasonably high total loads per square foot of floor area. Data for one type are in Fig. 11-31. They are made in a range of joist sizes. Those most frequently used are 12-, 14-, 16-, 18-, 20-, and 22-in. depths.

Selected designs for these joists are in Fig. 11-32. Decking and ceiling materials can be applied directly to the truss. Generally they are spaced 24 in. O.C., therefore less labor is required. On many structures, they can span from one side of the foundation to the other, eliminating the need for a beam and columns. Heat ducts, plumbing, and electrical lines can be run through the webs, greatly speeding up construction and reducing costs.

Subfloors

Subfloor material for wood-framed floors is usually solid wood or plywood. Stressed skin floor panels are also widely used.

Wood Subflooring

Solid wood subflooring is 1 in. thick and 4 to 8 in. wide. It may be applied perpendicular to the joists or on a 45° diagonal (Figs. 11-33 and 11-34). The ends of the boards must meet on a joist. If finished wood flooring is applied over it, this must be perpendicular to the subfloor boards.

A plywood or hardboard underlayment is applied over the subfloor to produce a smooth surface for carpet or tile.

Diagonal installation is preferred because it allows the finish wood flooring to be laid at right angles or parallel to the joists. It produces a rigid floor because it forms a series of structural triangles.

Plywood subflooring is applied with the grain of the outer ply at right angles to the joists. The panels are staggered so that the end joints occur at different joists (Fig. 11-35). The edge joints between the panels must have blocking below them unless they are tongue and grooved (Fig. 11-36).

Conventional plywood subfloor is covered with an *underlayment*. An underlayment is a plywood or hardboard panel that has a surface smooth enough that vinyl composition tile or carpet can be installed over it. Some types of plywood subfloor are made with the top veneer to serve as the underlayment so the separate layer of underlayment is not needed.

Plywood underlayment is laid with the face grain perpendicular to the floor joists. Stagger the end joints and keep them over a floor joist.

A $1\frac{1}{8}$-in.-thick plywood panel is made for floors using beams for joists. For light construction it will span beams 48 in. O.C. The edges are tongue and grooved so blocking is not needed (Fig. 11-37).

Plywood subfloors can be used in commercial construction where heavy loads are expected. Two thicknesses of 1-in. plywood will support concentrated loads of 23 000 lb and two thicknesses of $1\frac{1}{8}$-in. plywood will support 30 000 lb when beams are spaced 12 in. O.C.

Plywood Subfloor-Underlayment

Span Rating (Maximum Joist Spacing) (in.)	Panel Thickness (in.)
16	$\frac{19}{32}, \frac{5}{8}, \frac{21}{32}$
20	$\frac{19}{32}, \frac{5}{8}, \frac{23}{32}, \frac{3}{4}$
24	$\frac{11}{16}, \frac{23}{32}, \frac{3}{4}$
	$\frac{7}{8}, 1$
48 (2-4-1)	$1\frac{1}{8}$

[1] APA Rated Sturd-I-Floor

[2] *As indicated above, panels in a given thickness may be manufactured in more than one Span Rating. Panels with a Span Rating greater than the actual joist spacing may be substituted for panels of the same thickness with a Span Rating matching the actual joist spacing. For example, $\frac{19}{32}$-inch-thick Sturd-I-Floor 20 O.C. may be substituted for $\frac{19}{32}$-inch-thick Sturd-I-Floor 16 O.C. over joists 16 inches on center.*

American Plywood Association

Plywood Underlayment

Plywood Grades and Species Group	Application	Minimum Plywood Thickness (in.)
Groups 1, 2, 3, 4, 5 APA UNDERLAYMENT INT (with interior or exterior glue) APA UNDERLAYMENT EXT APA C-C Plugged EXT	Over smooth subfloor	$\frac{1}{4}$
	Over lumber subfloor or other uneven surfaces	$\frac{11}{32}$
Same grades as above, but Group 1 only	Over lumber floor up to 4″ wide. Face grain must be perpendicular to boards	$\frac{1}{4}$

When $\frac{19}{32}$ inch or thicker underlayment is desired, APA Rated Sturd-I-Floor may be specified. In areas to be finished with thin floor coverings such as tile, linoleum, or vinyl, specify Underlayment, C-C Plugged or Sturd-I-Floor with fully sanded face.

American Plywood Association

Figure 11-24. *Plywood underlayment. (Courtesy of American Plywood Association.)*

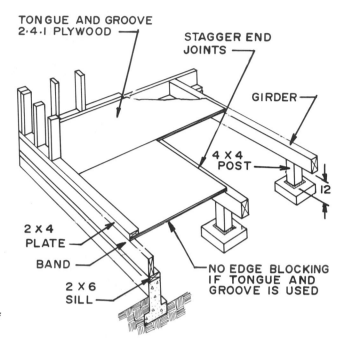

Figure 11-25. *The 2–4–1 flooring system using beams and 1⅛-in.-thick tongue-and-groove plywood. (Courtesy of American Plywood Association.)*

Figure 11-26. *Installing the 2–4–1 flooring system. (Courtesy of American Plywood Association.)*

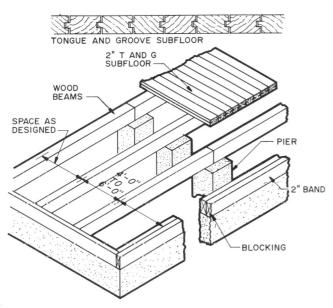

Figure 11-27. *Beam-framed floors with heavy wood decking permits long spans.*

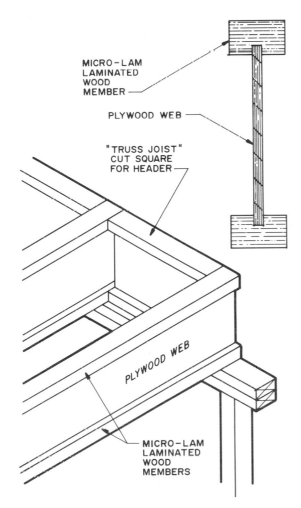

Figure 11-28. *A factory manufactured joist identified as a Residential TJI joist. (Courtesy of Trus Joist Corporation.)*

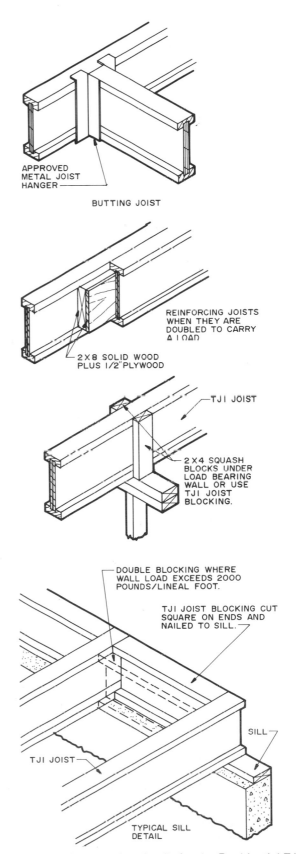

Figure 11-29. *Construction details for the Residential TJI® joist. (Courtesy of Trus Joist Corporation.)*

Joist Depth

O.C. Spacing (in.)	9 1/2	11 7/8	14	16
12	18'–2"	21'–9"	24'–8"	27'–3"
16	16'–6"	19'–9"	22'–5"	24'–10"
19.2	15'–6"	18'–6"	21'–1"	23'–4"
24	14'–4"	17'–1"	19'–8"	21'–7"
32	11'–4"	14'–4"	—	—

Based on a floor load of 40 lb/ft² and 10-lb dead load.

Figure 11-30. *Spans for TJI® floor joists. (Courtesy Trus Joist Corporation.)*

Clear span (ft)	Joist Depth					
	12	14	16	18	20	22
14	108	118	—	—	—	—
16	83	100	—	—	—	—
18	66	79	92	105	117	120
20	53	63	74	85	95	103
22	—	52	61	70	79	88
24	—	—	51	59	67	74
26	—	—	—	50	57	63
28	—	—	—	—	49	55
30	—	—	—	—	—	47

*Pounds per square foot. (Loads may change depending on lumber specie and lumber grade.) Data based on NDS 1986 Edition.

Figure 11-31. *Spans for truss-type floor joists spaced 24 in. B.C. (Courtesy of Alpine Engineered Products, Inc.)*

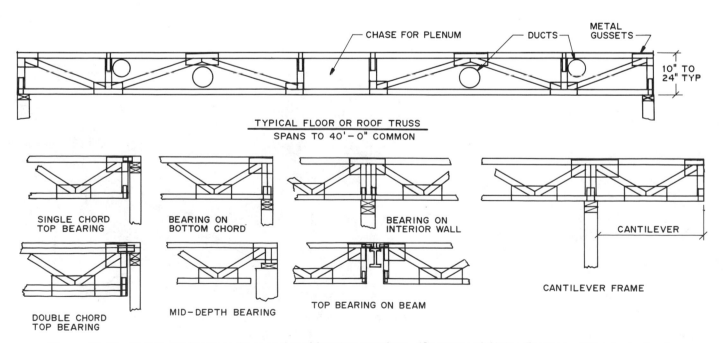

Figure 11-32. *Details for flat truss floor and roof framing members. (Courtesy of Alpine Engineered Products, Inc.)*

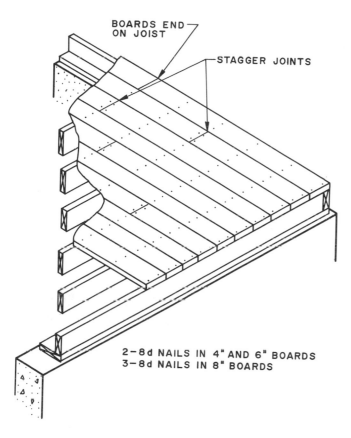

Figure 11-33. Solid wood subflooring can applied at right angles to the joists.

2-8d NAILS IN 4" AND 6" BOARDS
3-8d NAILS IN 8" BOARDS

BOARDS END ON JOIST

STAGGER JOINTS

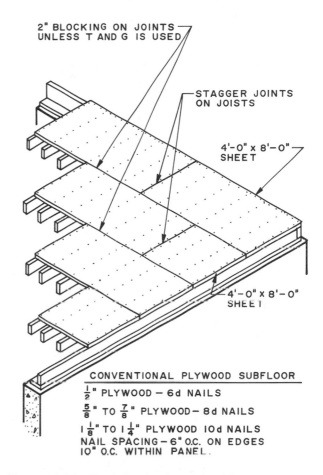

2" BLOCKING ON JOINTS UNLESS T AND G IS USED

STAGGER JOINTS ON JOISTS

4'-0" x 8'-0" SHEET

4'-0" x 8'-0" SHEET

CONVENTIONAL PLYWOOD SUBFLOOR
$\frac{1}{2}$" PLYWOOD — 6d NAILS
$\frac{5}{8}$" TO $\frac{7}{8}$" PLYWOOD — 8d NAILS
$1\frac{1}{8}$" TO $1\frac{1}{4}$" PLYWOOD 10d NAILS
NAIL SPACING — 6" O.C. ON EDGES
10" O.C. WITHIN PANEL.

Figure 11-35. The joints in plywood subfloor sheets must be staggered.

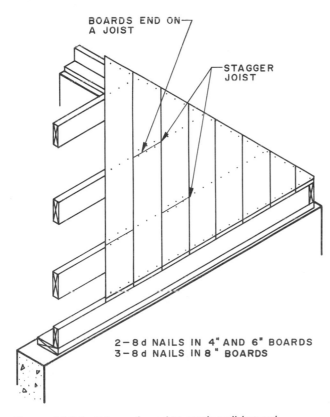

BOARDS END ON A JOIST

STAGGER JOIST

2-8d NAILS IN 4" AND 6" BOARDS
3-8d NAILS IN 8" BOARDS

Figure 11-34. It is preferred to apply solid wood subflooring on a diagonal.

Figure 11-36. Installing a sheet of subfloor–underlayment. (Courtesy of American Plywood Association.)

167

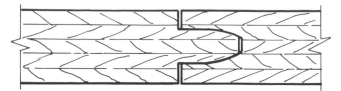

Figure 11-37. *Plywood floor panels have tongue and grooves on their edges.*

Stressed Skin Panels

Stressed skin panels are flat panels with a plywood skin and spaced lumber stringers. They are made with one and two skins (Fig. 11-38). They must be designed properly and manufactured according to strict guidelines. In general, the top skin is $\frac{5}{8}$-in. thick and placed perpendicular to the wood stringers which are 16 in. O.C. When used as floor panels, the top skin is usually thicker than when used as roof panels (Fig. 11-39).

Concrete Floors

The design of concrete floors requires a study of the properties of the soil and the size of the slab. There are four basic designs, unreinforced, lightly reinforced, structurally reinforced and independently supported (Fig. 11-40).

The *unreinforced* slab floor depends upon the soil below for support. It requires stable soil. It may crack during curing because of stresses created by shrinkage. It should be at least 4 in. (102 mm) thick. Seldom are slabs over 32 ft (9734 mm) poured. If a larger slab is needed, control joints are placed between each section.

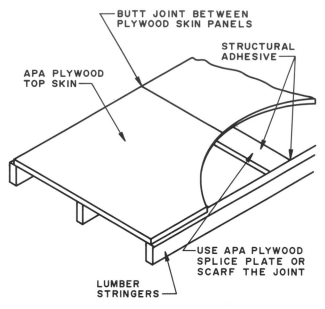

Figure 11-39. *A single skin stressed skin panel.*

Lightly reinforced floor slabs have welded wire fabric imbedded in them. The sizes of welded wire fabric are shown in Fig. 11-41. A commonly used size is $6 \times 6 / W1.4 \times W1.4$. The 6×6 means the wires forming the mesh are spaced 6 in. (152.4 mm) apart both ways. The W1.4 refers to the wire size. Wire W1.4 is the smallest diameter wire used (0.134 in. or 3.4 mm). The wire fabric does not add structural strength to the slab but it does help it resist cracking and when this does occur helps keep the cracks narrow. Lightly reinforced slabs can have perimeter dimensions up to 75 ft (22 680 mm) without a control joint.

Structurally reinforced floor slabs have reinforcing bars

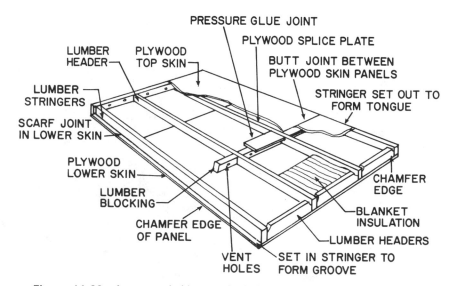

Figure 11-38. *A stressed skin panel with plywood skins on both sides.*

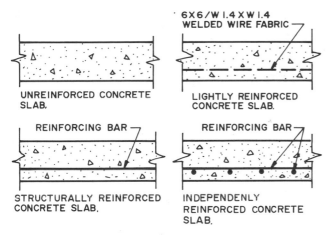

Figure 11-40. *Common types of floor slabs.*

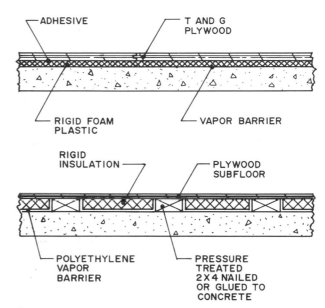

Figure 11-42. *Details for constructing wood floors over a concrete slab floor.*

inserted. While it still depends upon the ground for support, the rebar enables the load to be distributed over a large portion of the slab.

Independently reinforced floor slabs are used where ground support is inadequate and the slab must carry the total load. A mesh of reinforcing bars forming a grid is inserted in the slab. It resembles a concrete beam. The distance it must span and the load it must carry must be known so the amount of reinforcing and slab thickness can be calculated.

When wood floors are to be built over a concrete slab floor the construction in Fig. 11-42 can be used.

The design of the slab at the foundation is shown in the section of this chapter that shows wall construction for buildings with slab floors. Notice that some rest on the foundation. This provides support to the edge of the slab. Others butt the foundation and are relying entirely upon the ground for support. Others have the foundation and floor slab cast monolithically.

Style Designation		Steel Area (in.²/ft)		Weight Approx. lbs. per 100 S.F. (lb/ft³)
New Designation (by W-Number)	Old Designation (by Steel Wire Gauge)	longit.	trans.	
Rolls				
6 × 6–W1.4 × W1.4	6 × 6–10 × 10	0.028	0.028	21
6 × 6–W2.1 × W2.1	6 × 6–8 × 8	0.042	0.042	30
6 × 6–W2.9 × W2.9	6 × 6–6 × 6	0.058	0.058	42
6 × 6–W4.0 × W4.0	6 × 6–4 × 4	0.080	0.080	58
4 × 4–W1.4 × W1.4	4 × 4–10 × 10	0.042	0.042	31
4 × 4–W2.1 × W2.1	4 × 4–8 × 8	0.063	0.063	44
4 × 4–W2.9 × W2.9	4 × 4–6 × 6	0.087	0.087	62
4 × 4–W4.0 × W4.0	4 × 4–4 × 4	0.120	0.120	85
Sheets				
6 × 6–W2.9 × W2.9	6 × 6–6 × 6	0.058	0.058	42
6 × 6–W4.0 × W4.0	6 × 6–4 × 4	0.080	0.080	58
6 × 6–W5.4 × W5.4	6 × 6–2 × 2	0.108	0.108	78
4 × 4–W4.0 × W4.0	4 × 4–4 × 4	0.120	0.120	85

Figure 11-41. *Common stock sizes of welded wire fabric.*

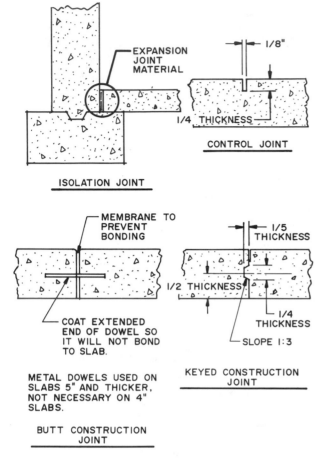

Figure 11-43. *Joints used in concrete floor construction.*

Joints in Floor Slabs

The common joints used in the construction of floor slabs are in Fig. 11-43. The three types are isolation, control, and construction joints. *Isolation joints* are made with an expansion joint material. This keeps the slab from touching the adjoining wall, footing, or column. It allows movement between the slab and fixed parts of a building such as a wall or column. *Control joints* are made at intervals of 10 to 25 ft. If the slab happens to crack, it will crack at a control joint, which help control where the crack will occur. They can be sawed or trowelled after the slab is in place. They can also be formed by inserting a plastic or metal strip in the concrete before it sets up. Fill the joint with silicone joint sealer. *Construction joints* are made between sections of slabs to be cast at different times. They also serve as control joints.

Vapor Barriers

Plastic sheets having a permeance of .20 perms are used below the slab to reduce the passage of water through the slab from the ground below. Usually 6- or 8-mil-thick polyethylene sheets are used.

Exterior Walls

Exterior walls in light construction are commonly made of masonry, frame, and various combinations of these materials. The following sections will show typical design details.

Masonry Exterior Walls

Masonry walls are made from brick, stone, concrete brick and blocks, clay tile, or some combination of these. Masonry exterior walls have the advantages of being weather resistant, fire resistant, and are a good sound transmission barrier. Bricks are clay units made in a variety of sizes, colors, and textures (Fig. 11-44). The lighter colored bricks (pinks) are softer and less weather resistant than the darker red and red-block bricks. Bricks also have an excellent compression rating.

Stone varies widely in size, color, and hardness. It can be cut to rectangular shapes or placed in its natural irreg-

Modular Brick Sizes for Selected Types of Brick

Type	Joint Thickness	Actual Sizes (in.)		
		Thickness	Height	Length
Standard	$\frac{3}{8}$	$3\frac{5}{8}$	$2\frac{1}{4}$	$7\frac{5}{8}$
	$\frac{1}{2}$	$3\frac{1}{2}$	$2\frac{1}{4}$	$7\frac{1}{2}$
Roman	$\frac{3}{8}$	$3\frac{5}{8}$	$1\frac{5}{8}$	$11\frac{5}{8}$
	$\frac{1}{2}$	$3\frac{1}{2}$	$1\frac{1}{2}$	$11\frac{1}{2}$
Norman	$\frac{3}{8}$	$3\frac{5}{8}$	$2\frac{1}{4}$	$11\frac{5}{8}$
	$\frac{1}{2}$	$3\frac{1}{2}$	$2\frac{1}{4}$	$11\frac{1}{2}$
SCR	$\frac{3}{8}$	$5\frac{5}{8}$	$2\frac{1}{4}$	$11\frac{5}{8}$
	$\frac{1}{2}$	$5\frac{1}{2}$	$2\frac{1}{4}$	$11\frac{1}{2}$

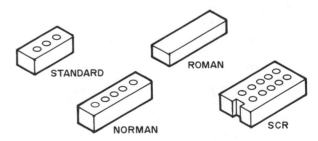

Figure 11-44. *Several of the types of bricks used in building construction.*

Nominal Dimensions of Concrete Masonry Units (in.)*

Height	4, 8
Length	8, 12, 16, 18, 24
Width	2, 3, 4, 6, 8, 10, 12

*Actual sizes ⅜ in. less to allow for mortar joint

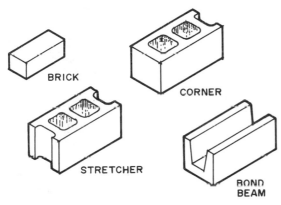

Figure 11-45. *A few of the many concrete masonry units manufactured.*

ular form. Concrete bricks and blocks are made from a variety of concrete mixes. In general, they are strong in compression and make good load-bearing walls. Concrete bricks are made in the same sizes as clay bricks (Fig. 11-45).

There are many special shapes made for use in specific locations. Some of these are sill block for openings and pilaster block and column block for structural use. Special blocks are formed for sashes.

Structural clay tile is made for use in load-bearing and nonload-bearing walls. It is made in many sizes and shapes (Fig. 11-46).

Brick Exterior Walls

Brick exterior cavity walls can be reinforced with reinforcing bars. The spacing of the bars depends upon the building codes and structural requirements. Reinforced walls are used where there are unusual conditions such as high winds or earthquakes. More commonly the wall is built as a cavity wall with the air space filled with insulation. Rigid foam sheets are often used. The two walls are held together with noncorrosive metal ties set in the mortar joints. The cavity must be at least 2 in. wide but not over $4\frac{1}{2}$ in. This same wall can be built with a concrete block backup wall (Fig. 11-47). Solid brick walls can also be built using SCR brick or by joining the two masonry walls with a $\frac{1}{2}$-in. grout layer. The height of the wall should be designed to use the modular size of the brick.

Wall thickness	Height	Length
4 and 8	12	12
	8	8
	8	12
	$5\frac{1}{3}$	12
6	12	12
	8	12
10	12	12
	8	12
	8	16
	$5\frac{1}{3}$	12
	$5\frac{1}{3}$	16
12	12	12
	8	12

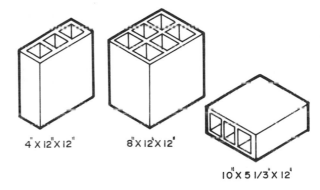

Figure 11-46. *Nominal sizes of selected structural clay tile units (in.).*

The way these walls are shown in section on a drawing is illustrated in Fig. 11-48.

Brick Veneer over Frame

Brick veneer can be applied over wood or metal stud framed walls. The maximum thickness in many codes is 5 in. when applied over structural masonry, concrete, or studs. Typical design details are in Fig. 11-49. The brick veneer is fastened to the frame wall with metal ties set in the mortar joint and nailed to the stud.

Masonry Ties

Masonry walls are made from two vertical rows of masonry units with a cavity between. These walls are held together with some form of cross tie. Metal ties should be noncorrosive. They should be coated with copper, cadmium, zinc, or other metals having corrosion resistant properties. Always consult the local building codes before

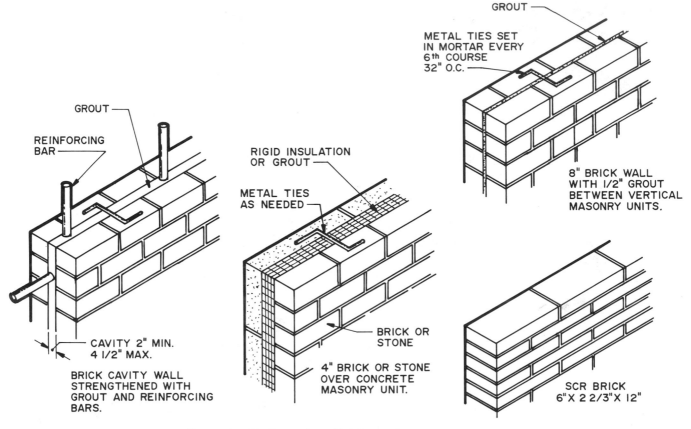

GROUT

REINFORCING BAR

GROUT

CAVITY 2" MIN. 4 1/2" MAX.

BRICK CAVITY WALL STRENGTHENED WITH GROUT AND REINFORCING BARS.

RIGID INSULATION OR GROUT

METAL TIES AS NEEDED

BRICK OR STONE

4" BRICK OR STONE OVER CONCRETE MASONRY UNIT.

METAL TIES SET IN MORTAR EVERY 6th COURSE 32" O.C.

8" BRICK WALL WITH 1/2" GROUT BETWEEN VERTICAL MASONRY UNITS.

SCR BRICK 6"X 2 2/3"X 12"

Figure 11-47. *Examples of brick exterior wall construction.*

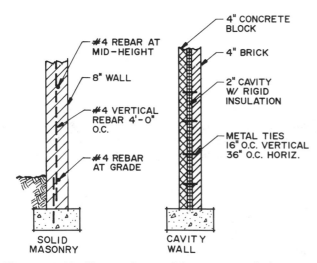

#4 REBAR AT MID-HEIGHT

8" WALL

#4 VERTICAL REBAR 4'-0" O.C.

#4 REBAR AT GRADE

SOLID MASONRY

4" CONCRETE BLOCK

4" BRICK

2" CAVITY W/ RIGID INSULATION

METAL TIES 16" O.C. VERTICAL 36" O.C. HORIZ.

CAVITY WALL

Figure 11-48. *How to draw solid masonry walls in section.*

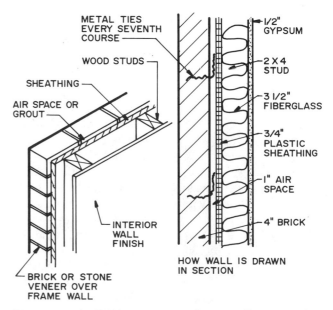

METAL TIES EVERY SEVENTH COURSE

WOOD STUDS

SHEATHING

AIR SPACE OR GROUT

INTERIOR WALL FINISH

BRICK OR STONE VENEER OVER FRAME WALL

1/2" GYPSUM

2 X 4 STUD

3 1/2" FIBERGLASS

3/4" PLASTIC SHEATHING

1" AIR SPACE

4" BRICK

HOW WALL IS DRAWN IN SECTION

Figure 11-49. *Brick veneer over frame wall construction.*

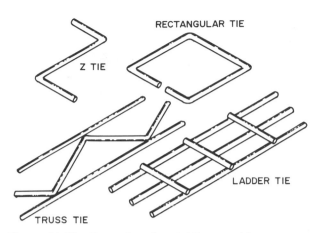

Figure 11-50. *Examples of metal ties used in masonry wall construction.*

Figure 11-51. *Brick header courses can be used as cross ties.*

selecting masonry ties. The ties are spaced according to the engineering design of the wall. A typical spacing specification would be a vertical spacing of 16 in. and a horizontal spacing of 36 in. Some typical types of ties are in Fig. 11-50.

Brick header courses can also be used as cross tics (Fig. 11 51). These are typically placed every seventh course.

Stone Exterior Walls

Stone exterior walls are usually built as a veneer over some type of backup wall. This is usually a wood frame, metal frame, or concrete block wall. The stone can have

a maximum of 5 in. in thickness. Examples are shown in Fig. 11-52. The stone is tied to the backup wall with noncorrosive metal ties or anchors as specified by codes.

Concrete Block Exterior Walls

Exterior structural concrete block walls are usually 6, 8, 10, or 12 in. in thickness. The cores of the block can be left open, be filled with insulation or grout, and have reinforcing bars inserted for greater strength against high

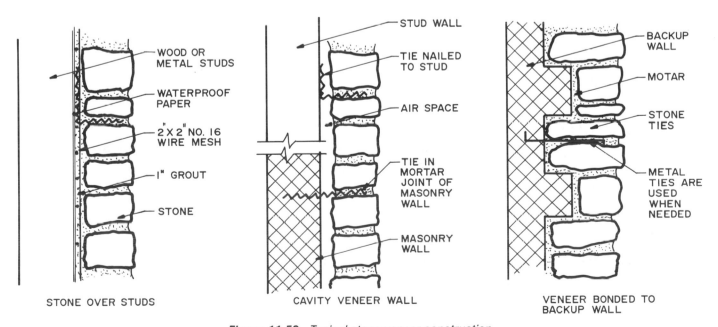

Figure 11-52. *Typical stone veneer construction.*

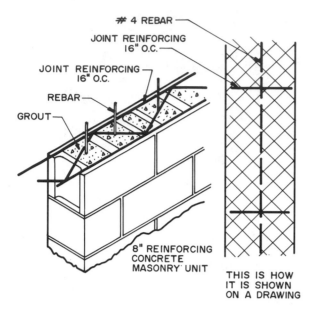

Figure 11-53. *Concrete block walls can be reinforced with rebar, joint reinforcing, and grout.*

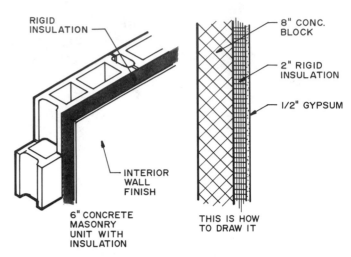

Figure 11-55. *One way to apply insulation and an interior finish wall to concrete block.*

winds and earthquakes (Fig. 11-53). The mortar joints can be reinforced with wire mesh or truss type reinforcing.

When the wall will support a lightweight roof, a 2 × 4 in. or 2 × 6 in. wood plate is bolted to the wall with $\frac{1}{2}$-in. bolts set 6 in. into the grout, filling the core in the top block. The bolts are spaced 4 ft on center. If the wall is to support a heavy load, bond beam blocks are laid as the top row. They are filled with grout and have horizontal reinforcing bars in the grout (Fig. 11-54).

Concrete block exterior walls can be insulated by gluing rigid insulation to the inside. An interior wall finish, as gypsum board, can be glued to the insulation (Fig. 11-55). The wall can also be furred out with 1 × 2 or 2 × 2 wood

members and insulation placed between them. The finish wall material is glued or nailed to the furring strips (Fig. 11-56).

Frame Exterior Walls

Frame exterior walls may be framed using platform framing, balloon framing, braced framing (Fig. 11-57), or post and beam framing. Platform framing is the one most commonly used.

Platform Framing

Platform framing, sometimes called Western framing, has the advantage of providing a flat, sturdy deck upon which the exterior walls can be built. Basically the floor is framed

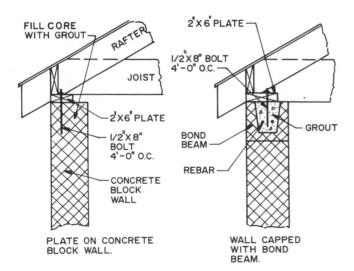

Figure 11-54. *Typical ways to cap a concrete block wall to receive a roof.*

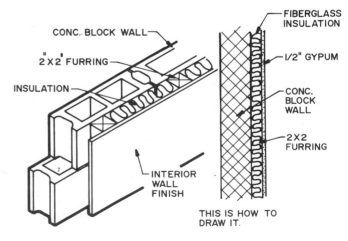

Figure 11-56. *Details for furring out a concrete block wall so it can be insulated and have a finished interior covering.*

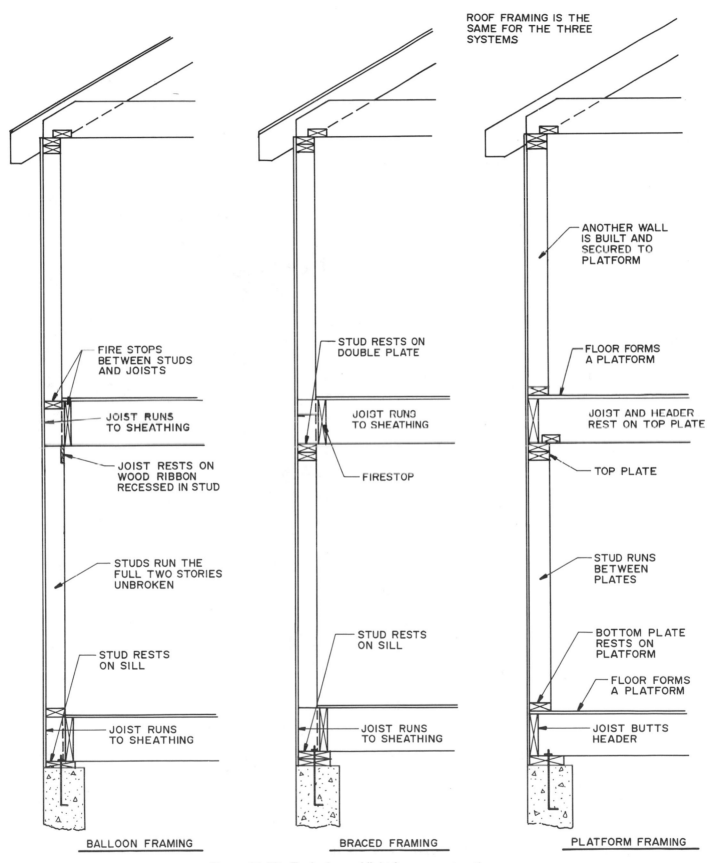

Figure 11-57. *Typical wood light frame constructions.*

and the subfloor is applied. The walls for the first floor are built flat on the subfloor and raised into the vertical position. The second floor joists are set on top of these walls and the subfloor is applied. The walls for the second floor are built and raised in the same manner. The ceiling joists and rafters or trusses are set on top of the second floor wall (Fig. 11-58).

Any openings in the wall as for doors and windows are framed as in Fig. 11-59. Notice the studs are doubled on each side and a header spans the opening. It must carry any roof loads or second floor loads. The header can be built from 2-in. stock and use cripples to fill in to the top plate or be built from 2 × 12 in. stock and fill the entire space (Fig. 11-60). Box beams made from 2 × 4 in. stock and $\frac{1}{2}$-in. plywood can also be used (Fig. 11-61). Recommended carpenter built header sizes are in Fig. 11-62.

Balloon Framing

Balloon framing is used for two-story buildings. It has studs that extend the full two stories. This will reduce the amount of shrinkage and movement that can occur. If a brick veneer wall is built over this frame crackage is less likely to happen. Notice that the second floor joists rest on a ribbon set into the stud. The studs rest on the sill and the first floor joists are placed beside them. The roof is framed in the same manner as platform framing (Fig. 11-63).

Braced Framing

Braced framing at the sill is the same as balloon framing. The studs rest on the sill and the floor joists extend to the sheathing. The studs run only one story in height and have a double top plate like the wall used in platform framing. The second floor joist rests on the top plate and extends to the sheathing. A firestop is set between joists the same as with balloon framing. The second floor wall studs rest on the double top plate. See Fig. 11-57.

Post and Beam Framing

Post and beam framing uses a structure of large wood posts, floor beams and roof beams that span large distances and carry loads greater than the normal 2-in. stock used for platform and balloon framing. The floor and roof decking is 2 to 3 in. thick and usually spans distances of 4 to 8 ft between joists and rafters. This reduces the number of parts to be handled and speeds construction. It also frees the walls built between columns from carrying the roof load. Large expanses of glass can be installed in these walls with no lintels. Typical framing details are in Figs. 11-64 and 11-65.

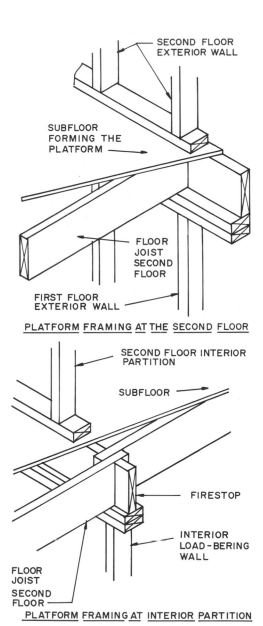

Figure 11-58. *Typical construction details for platform framing at the second floor.*

The roof and floor decking is usually tongue and groove so no support is needed over long spans (Fig. 11-66). The posts can be joined to the roof beam with a metal dowel or metal plates (Fig. 11-67). The post can be joined to the foundation with metal dowels (Fig. 11-68). The inside surface of the roof decking is usually left exposed to form the finished ceiling.

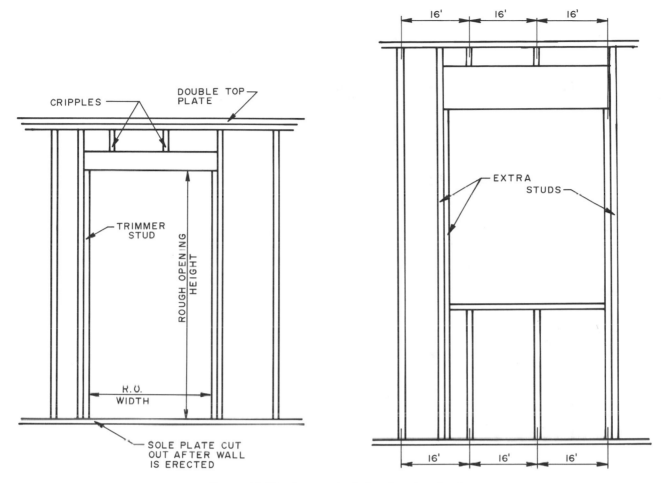

Figure 11-59. *Door and window framing details.*

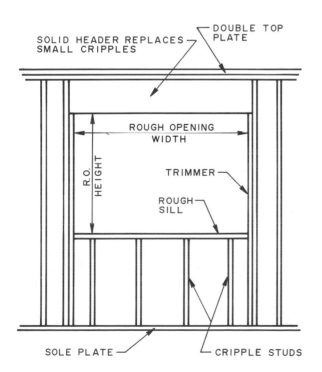

Figure 11-60. *This header is built from 2 X 12 in. lumber eliminating the need for cripples.*

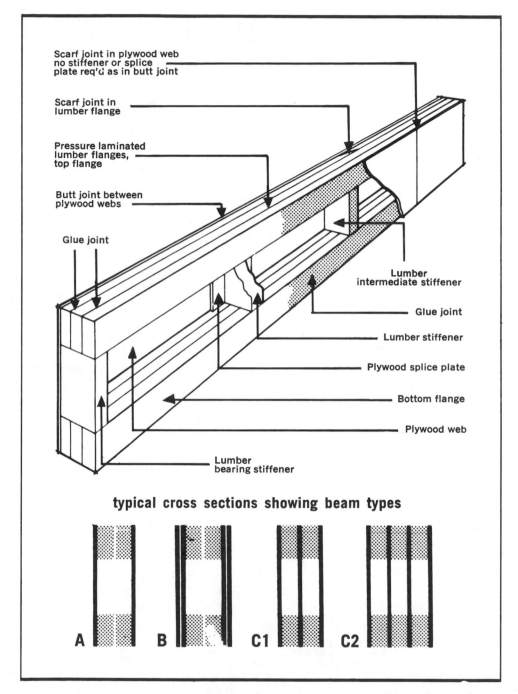

Scarf joint in plywood web
no stiffener or splice
plate req'd as in butt joint

Scarf joint in
lumber flange

Pressure laminated
lumber flanges,
top flange

Butt joint between
plywood webs

Glue joint

Lumber
intermediate stiffener

Glue joint

Lumber stiffener

Plywood splice plate

Bottom flange

Plywood web

Lumber
bearing stiffener

typical cross sections showing beam types

A   B   C1   C2

Figure 11-61. *Box beams are carefully designed and assembled. (Courtesy of American Plywood Association.)*

Material Forming Header (in.)*	Supporting One Floor, Ceiling, and Roof	Supporting Only Ceiling and Roof
2–2 × 4	3'–0"	3'–6"
2–2 × 6	5'–0"	6'–0"
2–2 × 8	7'–0"	8'–0"
2–2 × 10	8'–0"	10'–0"
2–2 × 12	9'–0"	12'–0"

Two pieces this size nailed together to form the header.

Figure 11-62. *Typical wood header sizes and spans for residential construction.*

Lintels

A lintel is a structural member used to span door and window openings and carry the masonry wall above the opening. In some cases it may carry the floor or ceiling load.

Figuring the Lintel Load

The wall area supported by the lintel is called the *spandrel*. To select the proper size steel or concrete lintel it is necessary to figure the total weight of the material to rest on the lintel. This is done by figuring the square feet of material and multiplying this by the weight of the material. Since the span of the lintel is known and the total weight is known, the proper size lintel can be chosen from a chart.

To figure the area to be carried find the area of a triangular spandrel if the distance between openings (as windows) is equal to or greater than the opening width (Fig. 11-69).If the opening is less than the width, figure the area for the rectangular area between them (Fig. 11-70).

If the lintel is to carry floor, roof, or ceiling loads these must be added to the weight of the spandrel.

Concrete Lintels

Concrete lintels may be precast reinforced concrete or precast concrete masonry units. In each case, they must rest 8 in. on each side of the opening.

Reinforced concrete units may be one- or two-piece lintels. One piece lintels are single 8 × 8 in. units. Two piece are made in 4-in. and 6-in. units (Fig. 11-71). Two 4-in. lintels are combined to carry an 8-in. wall. A 4 and 6 are used on a 10-in. wall. Two 6-in. lintels are used on 12-in. walls.

Concrete masonry units use precast concrete lintel blocks filled with cement grout fill and reinforced with reinforcing bars (Fig. 11-72). Sometimes concrete block

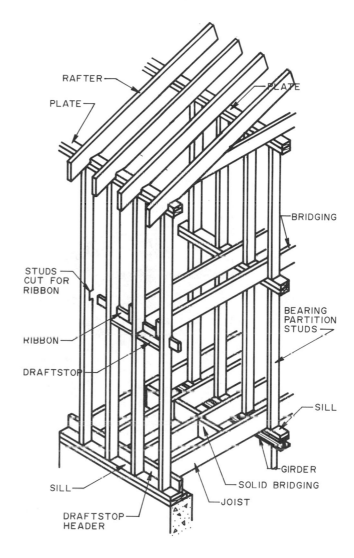

BALLOON FRAMING

Figure 11-63. *Balloon framing as used in residential construction.*

bond beam units are used. Figure 11-73 shows how these are installed in a masonry wall.

Steel Lintels

Steel lintels are usually metal angles or a W-beam with a wide steel plate welded to the bottom. An example of this last example is in Fig. 11-74. The lintel must be designed to carry the imposed loads.

It is more common to use steel angles as lintels. A separate angle is used for each 4 in. of masonry (Fig. 11-75). The size of steel angles is recorded on drawings by giving the length of the two legs followed by the thickness of the metal. For example, a note might read $3\frac{1}{2}" \times 3\frac{1}{2}" \times \frac{1}{4}."$.

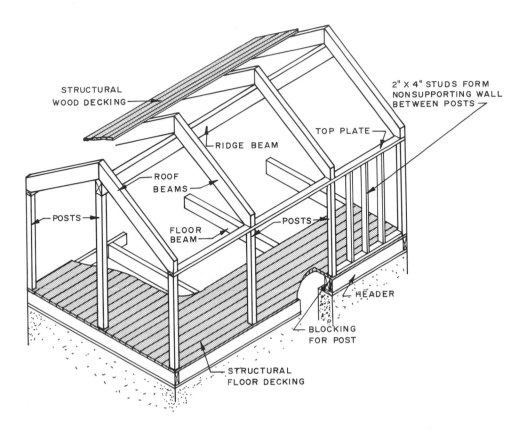

Figure 11-64. *Post-and-beam framing with wood frame members running the width of the building.*

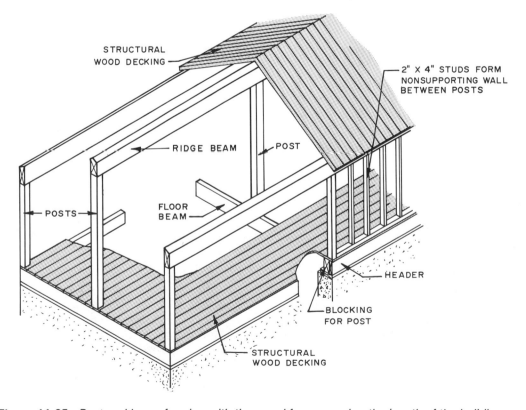

Figure 11-65. *Post-and-beam framing with the wood frame running the length of the building.*

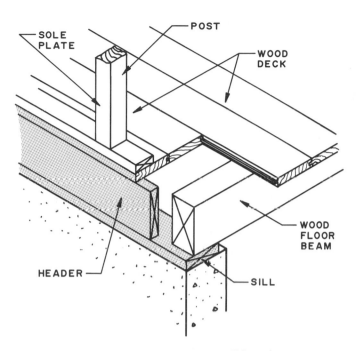

Figure 11-66. One way to frame the sill is to have a header run perpendicular to the floor beams.

The safe carrying load is recorded in steel tables. A few sizes are shown in Fig. 11-76.

Details showing the end bearing construction are in Fig. 11-77. The minimum bearing on the supporting wall is 4 in. Additional bearing is required if loads are heavy.

Frame Exterior Wall Finish

Wood-framed exterior walls can have a wide range of finish material applied. Generally some type of sheathing is nailed to the studs. This is usually plywood, composition

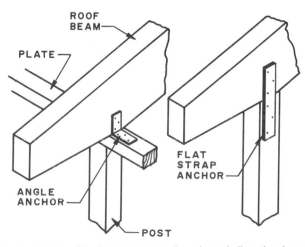

Figure 11-67. Roof beams must be placed directly above a post.

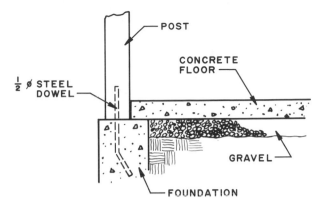

Figure 11-68. Posts can be joined to the foundation with metal dowels.

board, rigid foam plastic sheets, particle board, oriented strand board, waferboard, and occasionally 1-in. solid wood boards. Plywood and solid wood sheathing provide resistance against the wall racking so special bracing is not needed. Nonstructural sheathing, as rigid foam plastic, requires the wall be braced to resist racking. This is usually done by letting in a 1 × 4 diagonal brace at each corner. Another way is to place a sheet of plywood sheathing at each corner (Fig. 11-78).

The common types of finish materials are shingles, solid wood siding, plywood, hardboard, and stucco.

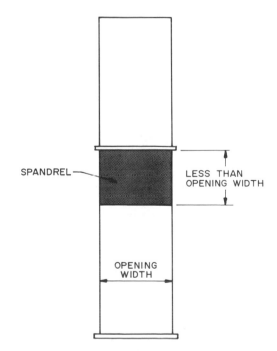

Figure 11-69. When the distance between two openings is less than the opening width, the load on the lintel is the weight of the materials in the spandrel. Floor, roof, and ceiling loads that may be on the lintel are in addition to this.

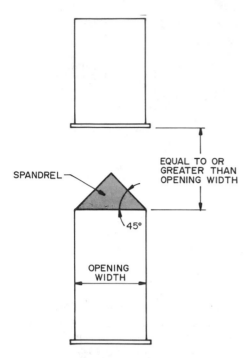

Figure 11-70. *When the distance between two openings is equal to or greater than the opening width, the load on the lintel is equal to the weight of materials in the spandrel area shown. Floor, roof, and ceiling loads that may be on the lintel are in addition to this.*

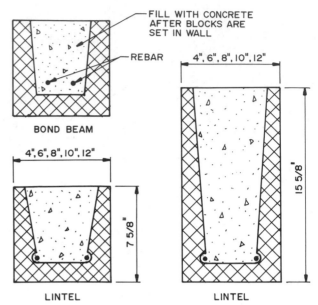

Figure 11-72. *Typical precast concrete masonry lintel blocks.*

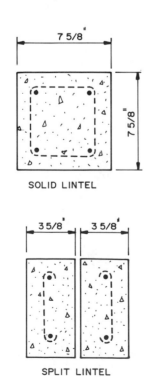

Figure 11-71. *Typical reinforced precast concrete lintels.*

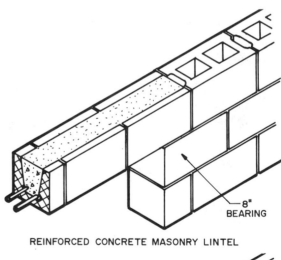

Figure 11-73. *Concrete lintels should have an 8-in. bearing surface on each side of the opening.*

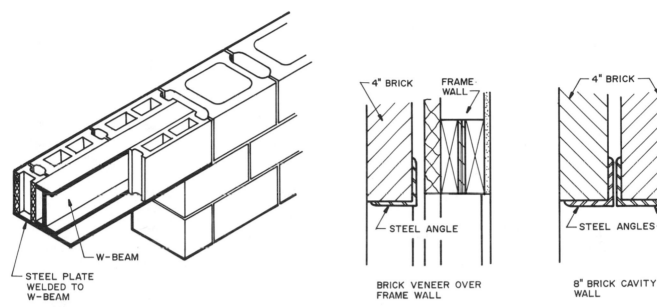

Figure 11-74. Construction details for using a steel beam as a lintel.

Figure 11-75. A typical application using steel angles to form a lintel.

	Wt per foot	Span (ft)				
Angle Size		2*	3	4	5	6
5 × 3 1/2 × 3/8	10.4	15.3	10.3	7.7	6.1	5.1
5 × 3 1/2 × 1/2	13.6	20.0	13.3	10.0	8.0	6.7
4 × 3 1/2 × 5/16	7.7	8.7	5.8	4.3	3.5	2.9
3 1/2 × 3 1/2 × 1/4	5.8	5.3	3.5	2.6	2.1	1.8

*Allowable uniform load in kips.

Figure 11-76. Allowable loads and spans for steel angles serving as lintels.

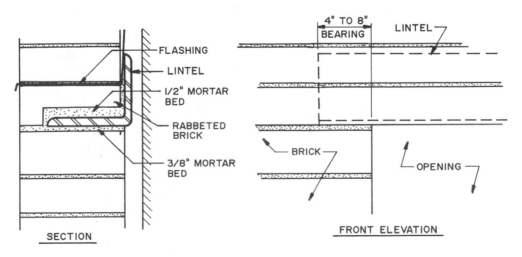

Figure 11-77. End bearing details for steel angles used as lintels.

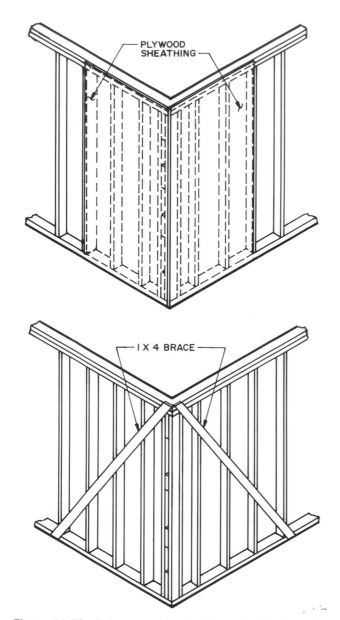

Figure 11-78. *A frame wall can be braced with plywood sheathing at the corners or with 1 X 4 in. wood diagonals let into the studs.*

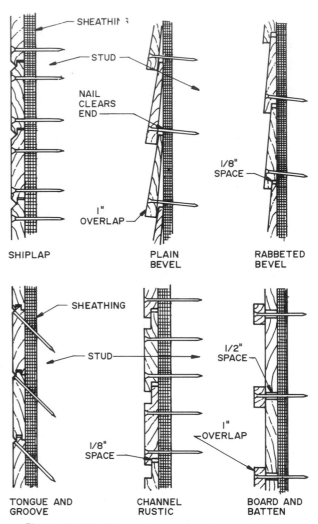

Figure 11-79. *Typical types of solid wood siding.*

Solid wood siding is available in a wide range of sizes and shapes. Some of the common types of siding are shown in Fig. 11-79. *Plywood and hardwood* are also extensively used for exterior siding. They are made in sheets 4 ft wide and 8, 9, and 10 ft long. The most common thicknesses are $\frac{3}{8}$, $\frac{1}{2}$, and $\frac{5}{8}$ in. They are also made in boards for use as horizontal siding. Widths commonly used are 10 and 12 in.

Plywood siding can be applied directly to the studs. If the studs are 16 in. O.C., use $\frac{3}{8}$-in. plywood. Use $\frac{1}{2}$-in. plywood for studs spaced 24 in. O.C. (Fig. 11-80). This has sufficient strength to resist racking so the wall requires no special bracing. If horizontal siding is applied directly to the studs 1 × 4 in. bracing is let into the studs on a diagonal at each corner.

Wood shingles are applied over plywood or solid wood sheathing. They may be applied in single course or double course (Fig. 11-81). The single course provides two thicknesses of shingles on the entire wall. The double course provides considerably more coverage.

Stucco exterior finish is usually made from three coats of stucco. Stucco is made of a portland cement base. The first coat is the scratch coat. It is worked into the wire lath. The second coat is the brown coat. It builds up the thickness and smooths out irregularities in the scratch coat. The final coat is the finish coat. It can be trawled smooth or given a rough textured appearance. Typical stucco finishes are shown in Fig. 11-82.

Exterior Walls on Buildings with Concrete Floors

Design details for typical frame exterior walls on buildings with concrete floors are shown in Fig. 11-83. In some cases the sheathing is shown overlapping the foundation.

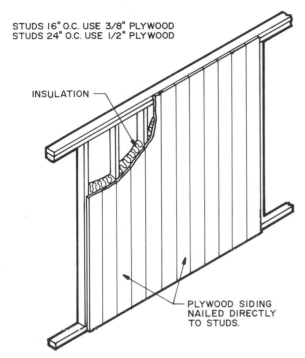

Figure 11-80. *Plywood siding can be applied directly to the studs.*

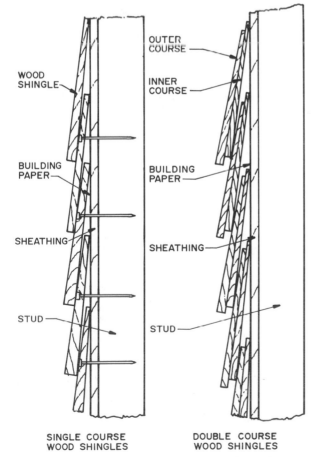

Figure 11-81. *Wood shingles can be used to side a wood-framed building.*

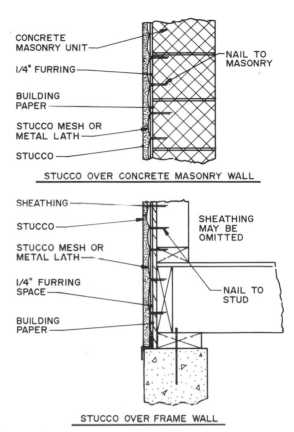

Figure 11-82. *Stucco exterior finish can be applied to a concrete block or wood frame wall.*

In others it is set flush. Either design is acceptable. In Fig. 11-84 are shown details for the construction of masonry exterior walls on buildings with concrete floors. A detail for brick or stone veneer over a frame wall is in Fig. 11-85.

Roof Construction

Roofs for light construction are generally built using individual wood rafters or trusses.

Roof Slope and Pitch

Figure 11-86 shows the terms used when describing the slope and pitch of a roof. The *rise* is the distance from the top of the double plate to the top of the ridge. *Run* is the distance from the outside of the stud wall to the center of the ridge board. *Span* is the distance from the outside of the stud wall on one side to the outside of the wall on the opposite side.

Slope is the term used to specify the angle the roof makes with the horizontal. Slope is specified as the ratio between rise and run. For example, the building in Fig. 11-86 has a rise of 6″-0″ and a run of 12′-0″. This slope is 6 in. of rise for every 1 ft of run. The slope on a drawing always has the run as 12 in. Therefore, this slope is 6/12.

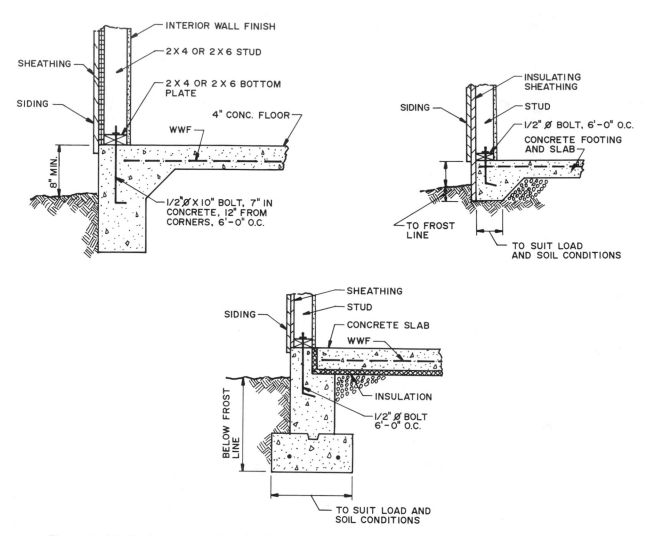

Figure 11-83. *Typical construction details for buildings with wood-framed walls and concrete slab floors.*

The *pitch* is rise over span or 6/24. This is 1 ft of rise to 4 ft of run, or a pitch of 1/4.

Various roofing materials require a minimum slope to be effective. The recommended minimum slopes are in Fig. 11-87. *Wood shingles* are thin, tapered wood pieces sawed from tree trunks. *Wood shakes* are tapered wood pieces formed by splitting rather than sawing. They have rough, textured surfaces. Most are made from cedar or redwood (Fig. 11-88). Fiberglass asphalt shingles are made with a fiberglass base mat, weathering grade asphalt, and ceramic-coated rock minerals. The most common type is slotted twice to appear like three individual shingles (Fig. 11-89). *Slate* shingles are split and trimmed to size. They have holes drilled through them for fastening. *Clay tiles* are either cylindrical or flat. They are formed of clay and fired in a kiln. *Concrete tiles* are formed in much the same shapes as clay tile (Fig. 11-90). Sheet metal roofing is available in lead, copper, aluminum, zinc alloys, and stain-

less steel. These use either a standing seam or a flat seam (Figs. 11-91) and 11-92).

Fire Rating

Roofing materials are grouped into four classes for fire rating.

Class A roof coverings are effective against severe fire exposure. These include slate, clay tile, concrete tile, and fiberglass asphalt shingles.

Class B roof coverings are effective against moderate fire exposure. These include sheet metal roofing and some composition shingles.

Class C roof coverings are effective against light fire exposure. These include most asphalt shingles and fire-retardant treated wood shingles.

Nonclassified roof coverings can be used on agricultural

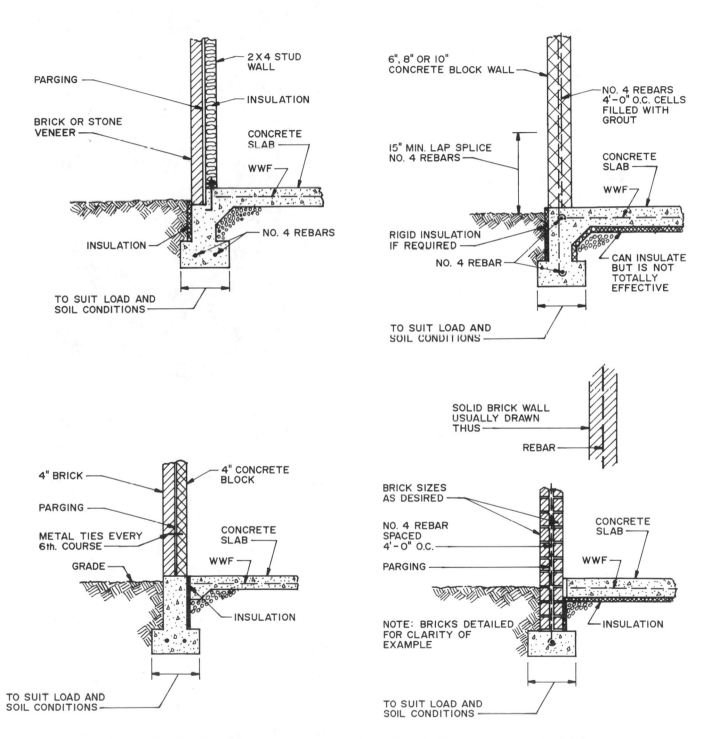

Figure 11-84. Construction details for masonry exterior walls on buildings with concrete slab floors.

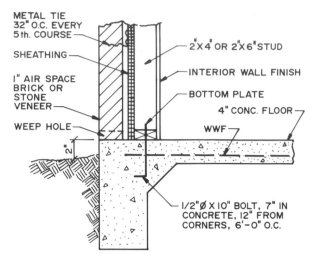

Figure 11-85. Brick or stone veneer over a frame wall on a building with concrete slab floors.

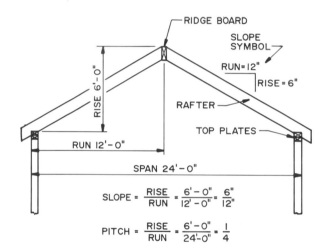

SLOPE = $\dfrac{\text{RISE}}{\text{RUN}}$ = $\dfrac{6'-0''}{12'-0''}$ = $\dfrac{6''}{12''}$

PITCH = $\dfrac{\text{RISE}}{\text{RUN}}$ = $\dfrac{6'-0''}{24'-0''}$ = $\dfrac{1}{4}$

THIS ROOF HAS A 6/12 SLOPE OR A 1/4 PITCH

Figure 11-86. Terms used to specify the angle of the roof with the horizontal.

Material	
Built-up	Under 3-12
Asphalt	
—Regular	4-12
—Heavyweight	3-12
—Locking, selfsealing	2-12
—Cemented*	2-12
Concrete tile	4-12
Wood shingles and shakes	4-12
Asbestos-cement	5-12
Slate	6-12
Metal shingles	3-12
Tile, clay	4-12

*Must have a double layer of no. 15 builders felt.

Figure 11-87. Minimum roof slopes for selected building materials.

(a)

(b)

(c)

(d)

Figure 11-88. Typical patterns for wood shingles. (Courtesy of Cedar Shake and Shingle Bureau.)

Figure 11-89. *Install three-tab asphalt shingles.*

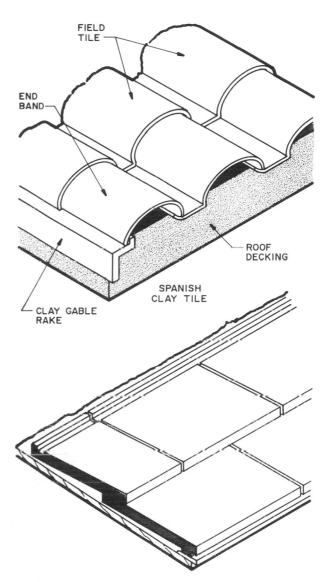

Figure 11-90. *Types of clay tiles used for a finished roof.*

and storage buildings. Untreated wood shingles are in this group.

Roof Flashing

Flashing is used to prevent leaks where the roof is pierced or changes direction. Flashing is made from thin metal sheets, usually zinc, aluminum, or copper. Typical places requiring flashing are skylights, the intersection of the roof and a chimney or dormer, vent pipes, where a roof meets and exterior wall, and roof valleys (Fig. 11-93).

Roof Types

The roof types commonly used in residential and small commercial buildings are shown in Fig. 11-94.

Flat. The flat roof is generally the least expensive to build. It is widely used on small commercial buildings. These roofs are given a slope of $\frac{1}{4}$ to $\frac{1}{2}$ in./ft to provide some drainage. Usually a tar and gravel top coating is used. It is difficult to keep this roof from leaking.

Shed. The shed roof is a flat roof that has been given considerable slope. It is economical to build and drains well.

Butterfly. The roof has two sloping surfaces meeting in a valley. The valley can be sloped to one end to provide drainage. It can also be sloped from each end to the center to a drain pipe that runs in the center of the building. This drain will require frequent cleaning.

Gable. The gable roof has two sloping surfaces meeting at a ridge. It is possibly the most frequently used type. It is easy to build, provides storage or rooms in the attic, and has excellent drainage.

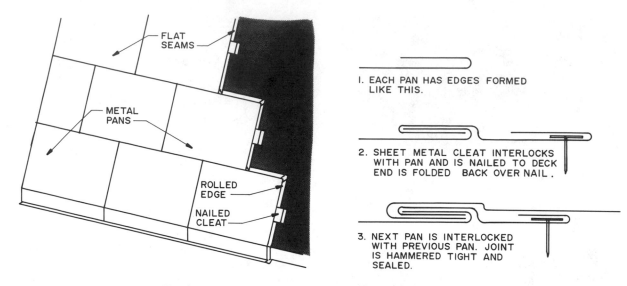

1. EACH PAN HAS EDGES FORMED LIKE THIS.

2. SHEET METAL CLEAT INTERLOCKS WITH PAN AND IS NAILED TO DECK END IS FOLDED BACK OVER NAIL.

3. NEXT PAN IS INTERLOCKED WITH PREVIOUS PAN. JOINT IS HAMMERED TIGHT AND SEALED.

Figure 11-91. Flat seam joint for roofs using metal pans.

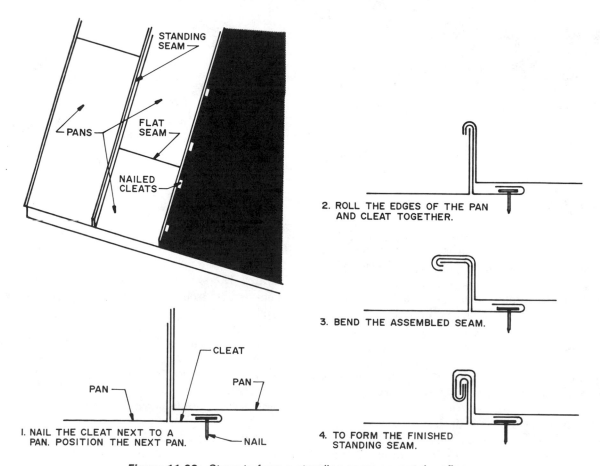

1. NAIL THE CLEAT NEXT TO A PAN. POSITION THE NEXT PAN.

2. ROLL THE EDGES OF THE PAN AND CLEAT TOGETHER.

3. BEND THE ASSEMBLED SEAM.

4. TO FORM THE FINISHED STANDING SEAM.

Figure 11-92. Steps to form a standing seam on metal roofing.

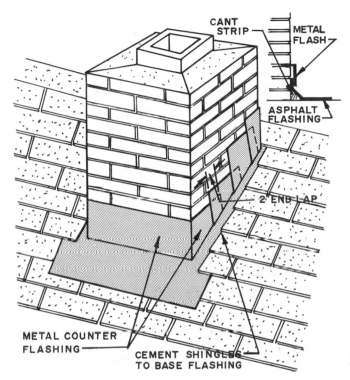

Figure 11-93. Typical flashing at a chimney.

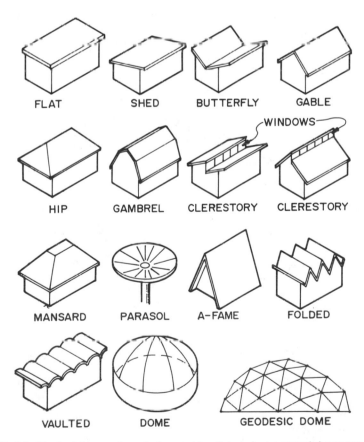

Figure 11-94. Typical types of roofs for residential and commercial construction.

Hip. The hip roof is much like the gable except it slopes to the ridge from all four sides. It is more difficult to build but eliminates the gable end.

Gambrel. The gambrel roof has each side broken into two different pitches. It provides considerable room on the second floor and eliminates the exterior walls needed on the typical two-story building

Mansard. The mansard roof is much like the gambrel except it also slopes toward the ends of the house.

Clerestory. The clerestory roof utilizes the simplicity of the shed roof to admit light and permit ventilation of the building. It can take a sawtooth form or have the roof slope in opposite directions.

Folded. Folded roofs are a series of small gable roofs. They give an unusual appearance to a building.

Parasol. The parasol roof is a round or square roof with a center supporting column. Several can be placed together to cover an area.

A-Frame. This is a variety of the gable roof. The roof extends almost to the ground so the building has no exterior walls on two sides. The framing requires large structural members.

Geodesic Dome. The geodesic dome is framed from members forming triangles. When the triangular sections are joined together, a dome-shaped structure of great strength is formed.

Domes. Domes are roofs that appear like half of a sphere. They are built of preengineered structural members that can span large distances. They are frequently used on convention centers and athletic facilities.

Vault. A vaulted roof is a series of round roofs placed side by side to cover an area.

Conventionally Framed Roofs

Conventionally framed roofs are built on the job piece by piece. The carpenter cuts each rafter and the ridge board and nails them together on top of the walls of the building. Various roof designs require a variety of rafters to be cut. These are shown in Fig. 11-95.

There are many ways a cornice can be built, depending upon the style of the house. Some provide large overhangs to protect the windows from the hot summer sun. Others are short or have no overhang because this suits the architectural style. Figure 11-96 shows several typical cornice designs in connection with solid masonry, masonry over frame, and frame exterior walls. Many other variations of these can be built.

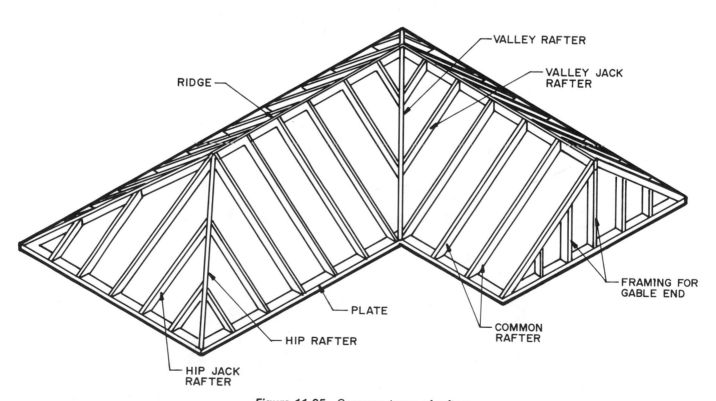

Figure 11-95. Common types of rafters.

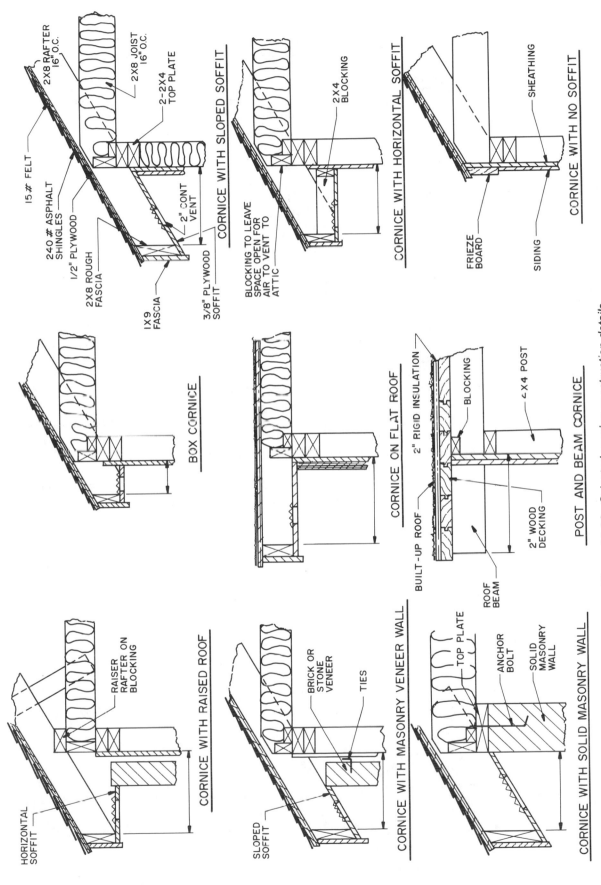

Figure 11-96. Selected cornice construction details.

15# FELT

240 # ASPHALT SHINGLES

1/2" PLYWOOD

2×8 RAFTER 16" O.C.

2×8 JOIST 16" O.C.

2-2×4 TOP PLATE

2×8 ROUGH FASCIA

1×9 FASCIA

2" CONT VENT

3/8" PLYWOOD SOFFIT

CORNICE WITH SLOPED SOFFIT

2×4 BLOCKING

BLOCKING TO LEAVE SPACE OPEN FOR AIR TO VENT TO ATTIC

CORNICE WITH HORIZONTAL SOFFIT

SHEATHING

FRIEZE BOARD

SIDING

CORNICE WITH NO SOFFIT

BOX CORNICE

CORNICE ON FLAT ROOF

2" RIGID INSULATION

BLOCKING

4×4 POST

BUILT-UP ROOF

ROOF BEAM

2" WOOD DECKING

POST AND BEAM CORNICE

HORIZONTAL SOFFIT

RAISER RAFTER ON BLOCKING

CORNICE WITH RAISED ROOF

SLOPED SOFFIT

BRICK OR STONE VENEER

TIES

CORNICE WITH MASONRY VENEER WALL

TOP PLATE

ANCHOR BOLT

SOLID MASONRY WALL

CORNICE WITH SOLID MASONRY WALL

193

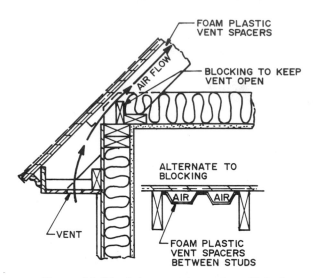

Figure 11-97. Attics must be well ventilated.

the rafters, ceiling joist, and webs for bracing. The entire unit is set on top of the exterior walls. Trusses do not require support between the exterior walls. Therefore, interior walls are nonload bearing. The triangular design used in trusses is very strong. This permits them to be built from smaller members than conventional framing. In Fig. 11-98 is a typical truss. This design is widely used for roof construction in residential and small commercial buildings. There are many other types of trusses in use. (Some examples are shown in Fig. 11-99).

A flat truss is used for both roof and floor construction. These are shown in Fig. 11-32. It is also used for roof construction (Fig. 11-100). Examples of possible cornice designs are in Fig. 11-101.

As the cornice is built it is necessary to provide vents in the soffit to permit air to flow up into the attic. The use of 12 in. or more of insulation in the attic would block the flow of air. It is necessary to provide blocking of some kind to keep air passages open. This can be wood framing or plastic vent spaces (Fig. 11-97).

Tables for selecting rafter and joist sizes are in the Appendix. The things to consider when selecting a rafter are the run, spacing between rafters, roof slope, and snow loads. The tables are set up for various runs, rafter spacing, and slopes. Snow loads vary considerably throughout the United States. Data on snow loads are given in Chapter 10.

Roof Trusses

Roof trusses have the advantage of speeding on-site construction. A roof truss is a factory built unit that includes

Interior Walls

Interior walls are generally wood 2 × 4 studs with plaster or gypsum board finish. Ceilings will be of the same material or some form of tile.

Figure 11-102 shows the installation of gypsum lath on studs. Gypsum lath measuring $\frac{3}{8}''$ × 16″ × 4′-0″ is nailed to the studs. Sometimes a perforated metal lath in sheets 27″ × 8′-0″ are used instead (Fig. 11-103). These serve as the base for the plaster coatings. When gypsum lath is used, pieces of metal lath are nailed over it in the areas most likely to crack. These include the upper corners of door and window openings. Metal corner bead is installed where walls and ceilings intersect.

Three coats of plaster are used over metal lathe. The first coat is the scratch coat. It is roughened to improve the bond with the second coat called the brown coat. The finish coat is a hard layer applied over the brown coat (Fig. 11-104.

When gypsum lath is used, two coats are applied. The

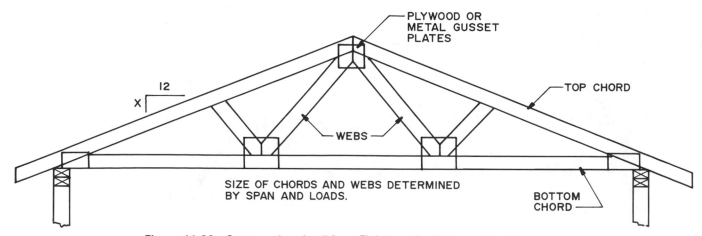

Figure 11-98. Construction detail for a Fink truss for light construction.

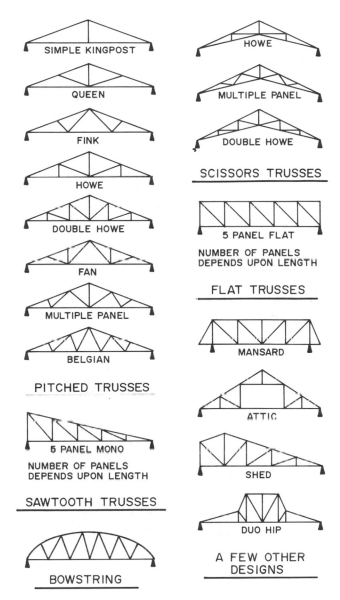

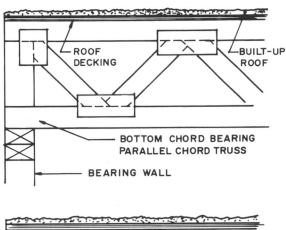

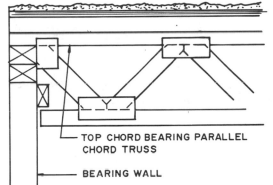

Figure 11-100. *Typical construction details for flatroof trusses.*

Figure 11-99. *A few of the many truss designs in use for light frame construction.*

first coat is a combination of the scratch and brown coats. Then the finish coat is applied over this.

The most frequently used interior finish material is $\frac{1}{2}$-in. gypsum board (called dry-wall) nailed to wood studs. The cracks between the sheets are covered with tape and joint cement. Nails are also covered with joint cement. When sanded and primed, it appears much like a plaster wall.

If gypsum board is applied to metal studs they are fastened with self drilling screws driven with a power screwdriver (Fig. 11-105). Screws can also be used with wood studs. When gypsum lath is applied to metal studs metal clips are sometimes used (Fig. 11-106).

When it is necessary to reduce the transmission of sound through interior partitions the studs can be staggered,

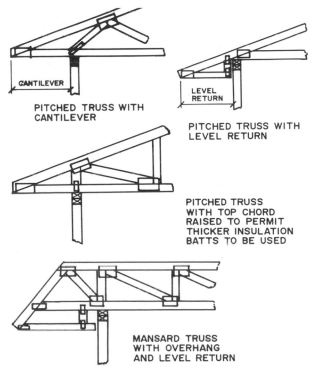

Figure 11-101. *Cornice designs used with wood roof trusses.*

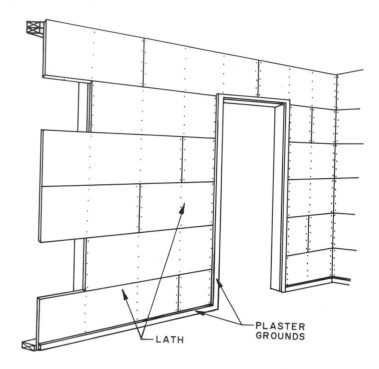

Figure 11-102. *Gypsum lath is applied with its long dimension perpendicular to the studs.*

FASTENER	LATH THICKNESS (in.)	SPACING
Nail 1⅛ in. 13 gauge, ⁹⁄₁₆-in.-diameter flat head, blued	⅜	16-in.-wide lath, 4 nails for support, spaced 5 in. o.c., ⅜ in. from ends and edges. 24-in.-wide lath, 5 nails per support.
Nail 1¼ in. 13 gauge, ⁹⁄₁₆-in.-diameter flat head, blued	½	16-in.-wide lath, 5 nails per support, spaced 4 in. o.c., ⅜ in. from ends and edges. 24-in.-wide lath, 6 nails per support.
Staple ⅞ in. long, ⁷⁄₁₆ in. wide, 16 gauge flattened, galvanized	⅜	Crown parallel with long dimension of stud. 16-in.-wide lath, 4 nails per member, 5 in. o.c., ⅜ in. from ends and edges. 24-in.-width lath, 5 staples per sup- port.
Staple same as above but 1 in. long	½	Same as above. If studs 24 in. o.c., use 5 staples per support at 4 in. o.c. 24-in.-wide lath, 6 staples per support.
Screws to steel studs	½ and ⅝	1-in. type S Bugle Head screws
Screws to wood framing	⅜, ½, and ⅝	1¼-in. type W Bugle Head

Figure 11-103. *Examples of metal lath. (Courtesy of Unimast, Inc.)*

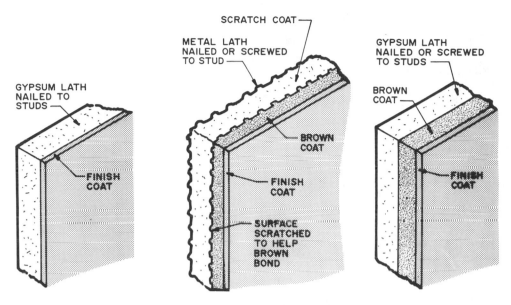

Figure 11-104. *Three frequently used lath and plaster interior wall constructions.*

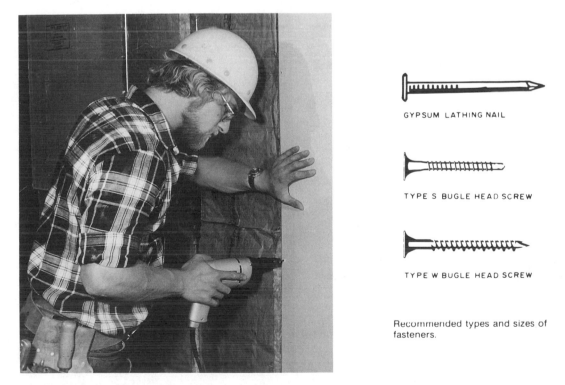

Recommended types and sizes of fasteners.

Figure 11-105. *Gypsum panels can be installed with screw-type fasteners using a power screwdriver.*

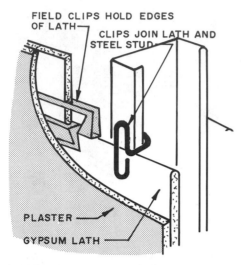

Figure 11-106. *Gypsum lath can be fastened to metal studs with metal clips.*

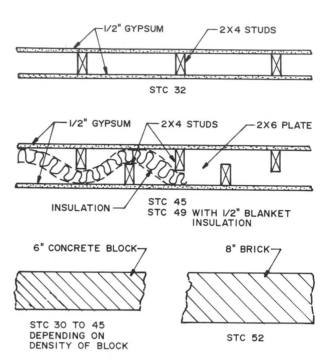

Figure 11-107. *Typical STC ratings for selected wall constructions.*

sound-deading board installed beneath the gypsum board, the cavity can be insulated, or the gypsum board can be applied in double thickness (Fig. 11-107). The ability of a material or assembly of materials to resist the transmission of sound is indicated by its Sound Transmission Class (STC). The higher the STC number the better it is as a sound barrier. Following are examples of STC ratings:

STC Rating

25 Normal speech can be understood easily
35 Loud speech is audible but not intelligible
45 One must strain to hear loud speech
50 Loud speech not audible

Sound transmission data are in the Appendix. It also helps to caulk around the edges of the gypsum board and around openings, such as electrical outlets, with acoustical caulking.

Another type of interior wall sometimes used in buildings with concrete floors is made from 6- or 8-in. concrete block. These walls can be painted, have plaster applied directly to them, or be furred out with wood 2 × 2 stock and have plaster or gypsum board applied as just described (Fig. 11-108). Interior nonload-bearing masonry walls should be designed to carry their own weight plus any superimposed finish and lateral forces.

Truss-Framing System

The Truss-Framing System (TFS) offers a new technology for residential and light commercial building construction. It is made up of a roof truss and a floor truss joined by regular wall studs (Fig. 11-109). These factory assem-

bled units are erected 2 ft O.C. on the foundation and connected with sheathing, producing a wood-framed building which has strength and durability (Fig. 11-110). Windows can be installed in the space between the studs or by installing a conventional header in the truss-framed wall (Fig. 11-111).

TFS requires less structural lumber than conventional construction. Almost all framing is done with 2 × 3 and 2 × 4 stock instead of the more expensive dimensional lumber commonly used for rafters, ceiling joists, and floor joists. Long spans and areas with high winds or heavy snow loads will require the use of 2 × 6 studs in the walls to carry the stresses at the 2 ft O.C. spacing.

Designs include the conventional truss frames, partial truss frame, and two-floor truss frame (Fig. 11-112). While this figure shows a Queen-type truss, almost any type of truss design can be used.

In Fig. 11-113 is a design for a one-story house with a crawl space. The conventional truss frame assembly is used. These units are generally spaced 2 ft O.C. The same application but with a basement is shown in Fig. 11-114. Provisions are made in the floor truss to provide an opening for the stair. The deck shown is field built.

A two-story house is constructed using a two-floor truss frame assembly and adding a partial truss frame on top to form the roof and second story walls (Fig. 11-115). The family room shown is constructed with conventional truss frames over a crawl space. The garage has a concrete floor and the roof and walls use partial truss frame assemblies.

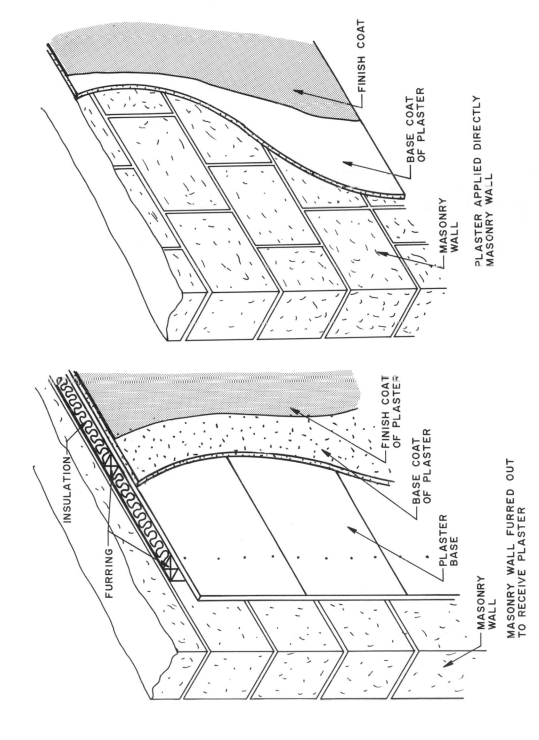

FINISH COAT

BASE COAT OF PLASTER

MASONRY WALL

PLASTER APPLIED DIRECTLY MASONRY WALL

INSULATION

FURRING

FINISH COAT OF PLASTER

BASE COAT OF PLASTER

PLASTER BASE

MASONRY WALL

MASONRY WALL FURRED OUT TO RECEIVE PLASTER

Figure 11-108. Plaster can be applied directly to a masonry wall or the wall can be furred out and plaster base used.

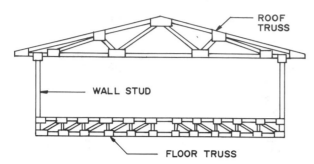

Figure 11-109. *A typical TFS unitized frame.*

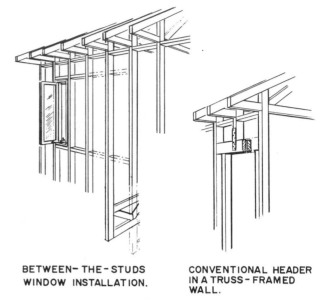

BETWEEN-THE-STUDS WINDOW INSTALLATION.

CONVENTIONAL HEADER IN A TRUSS-FRAMED WALL.

Figure 11-111. *Ways windows can be installed in the TFS exterior wall. (Courtesy of USDA-Forest Service, Forest Products Laboratory.)*

Construction of a light commercial building is shown in Fig. 11-116. Notice the office level truss frames are supported on post foundations. The two-story assembly utilizes the two-floor truss frames having sufficient height to accommodate suspended ceilings. The roof is a single slope truss mounted on panelized exterior wood stud walls. The souvenir shop has a conventional truss frame using a single slope roof truss.

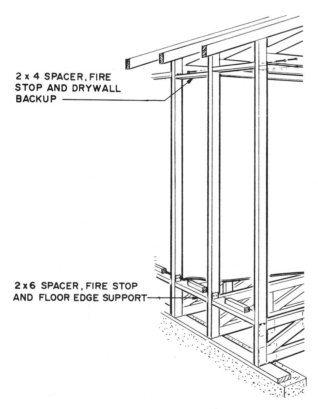

Figure 11-110. *This shows the basic building shell construction. (Courtesy of USDA-Forest Service, Forest Products Laboratory.)*

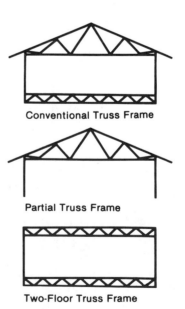

Conventional Truss Frame

Partial Truss Frame

Two-Floor Truss Frame

Figure 11-112. *These are the types of assemblies used in the truss-framed system. (Courtesy of USDA-Forest Service, Forest Products Laboratory.)*

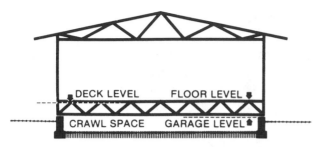

Figure 11-113. *A conventional truss frame is used on this one-story house. (Courtesy of USDA-Forest Service, Forest Products Laboratory.)*

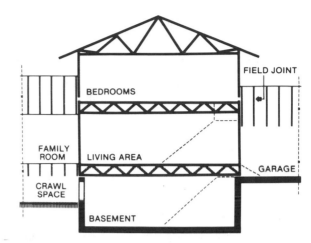

Figure 11-115. *Construction details for a two-story house with one-story additions. (Courtesy of USDA-Forest Service, Forest Products Laboratory.)*

Technical Vocabulary

Following are some important technical terms used in this chapter. Write a brief definition for each.

Joists

Subfloor

Fire cut

Trus joist

Bridging

Stressed skin panels

Isolation joint

Control joint

Construction joint

Vapor barrier

Masonry ties

Lintel

Ledgers

Planking

Spandrel

Rise

Run

Span

Slope

Flashing

Sound transmission class

Truss framing

Roof truss

Study Questions

Answer the following questions without referring to the text. Then check your answers with the text and correct those that were wrong.

1. What adjustment is made to floor joists located below load-carrying interior walls?

2. When must double headers be used on floor openings?

3. What types of bridging are in use?

4. What three types of floor-framing structural members are available for residential use?

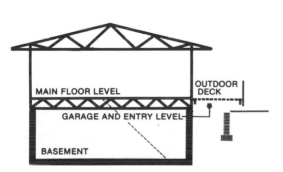

Figure 11-114. *The addition of a basement does not change the use of conventional truss frame assemblies. (Courtesy of USDA-Forest Service, Forest Products Laboratory.)*

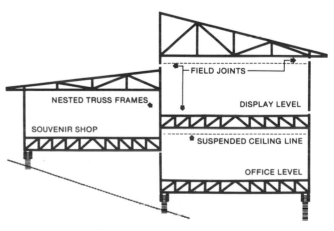

Figure 11-116. *This commercial building utilizes truss-framed construction with some exterior walls built in panelized sections. (Courtesy of USDA-Forest Service, Forest Products Laboratory.)*

5. What are the four basic designs of concrete floor slabs?

6. What types of joints are used in concrete floor slabs?

7. What advantages are attributed to masonry wall construction when compared to wood wall construction?

8. How are masonry cavity walls reinforced?

9. What are the ways frame exterior walls can be built?

10. What is the area of a triangular spandrel 4'-0" wide and 3'-0" high?

11. What stock members are used for steel lintels?

12. What are the common types of exterior finish materials used on residential construction?

13. If a roof has a span of 30'-0" and a rise of 7'-6", what is the slope? The pitch?

14. What are the classes of roofing materials indicating their fire rating?

15. Where is flashing usually needed?

16. What are some of the commonly used roof trusses?

17. What are some ways to decrease the transmission of sound through a wall?

Laboratory Problems

1. Design a floor, wall, and roof system for the retail store building designed in Chapter 8. To help you make a final decision, make freehand wall sections of the following.

Foundation and floor designs:

   A. Concrete slab on grade
   B. Concrete slab over a full basement

Wall designs:

   A. Masonry cavity wall with brick exterior veneer
   B. Metal siding over structural steel framing as used in metal building design
   C. Solid concrete masonry unit wall

Roof designs:

   A. Flat roof
   B. Sloped roof hidden by parapet wall. Include scupper details
   C. Gable roof

2. Design a floor, wall, and roof system for the residence designed in Chapter 8. To help you make a final decision, make freehand wall sections of the following:

Foundation and floor designs:

   A. With a crawl space
   B. With a full or partial basement
   C. Concrete slab floor supported by foundation

Wall designs:

   A. Wood or plywood siding on frame wall
   B. Brick veneer over frame wall
   C. 8-in. solid masonry wall

Roof designs:

   A. Flat
   B. 3-in. 12 slope
   C. 9-in. 12 slope

Cornice design:

   A. Try several different amounts of overhang as 4, 6, 12 in. but be certain it clears the top of the window

Roof design:

   A. Make sketches of the front elevation and try different types of roofs such as flat, shed, gable, and hipped.

12

Floor, Wall, and Roof Construction for Commercial Buildings

This chapter covers the systems commonly used in commercial building construction. There are many variations of these systems. No attempt has been made to get into the structural design of the various components.

Design Considerations

In addition to consideration of the structural aspects of a building, the designer must consider fire-resistive standards and sound transmission. Fire-resistive standards include the fire resistance of materials and assemblies of these materials, flame-spread ratings, and smoke-developed ratings. Sound transmission includes the sound transmission class of materials and assemblies and the impact isolation class.

Fire Resistance Ratings

Building codes specify the materials and systems to be used for fire-resistive purposes. These are specified in the codes in great detail. If a design varies from these it must be approved by the building official after examination of evidence submitted by the designer showing that the construction meets the fire-resistive classification. Selected fire ratings are in the Appendix. Trade publications often contain this information for their products.

The major parts of a building where fire-resistive standards are of major importance include beams, columns, floor-ceiling, roof-ceiling, wall, and partition assemblies. Materials and assemblies are tested using fire tests specified by the American Society for Testing and Materials, National Fire Protection Association, and the Underwriters' Laboratories, Inc.

The fire ratings are given in terms of the *number of hours* the material or assembly will withstand exposure to fire before failing.

Flame Spread

The flame-spread rating is a measure of the rapidity with which a fire will spread across the surface of a material.

Class	Flame-Spread Index
1	0–25
2	26–75
3	76–200

Figure 12-1. *Flame-spread classes and index.*

The rate of flame travel is measured using an ASTM test in which a specified species of wood has a value of 100 and noncombustible cement–asbestos board has a value of 0.

Materials are grouped into three flame-spread classifications. These are shown in Fig. 12-1. The larger the flame-spread index value, the more rapidly the material will permit the fire to spread across its surface. Flame-spread requirements are specified in building codes.

Selected flame-spread classifications for various occupancies are in the Appendix. More detailed information is in building codes and architectural standards publications.

Smoke-Developed Ratings

Smoke-developed ratings are also determined as the flame-spread rating test is made. They classify a material according to the amount of smoke a material gives off as it burns. Any material with a smoke rating over 450 cannot be used inside a building.

Sound Transmission Class

Sound transmission class (STC) ratings are a measure of the effectiveness of an assembly of material to reduce airborne sound transmission. They are based on the potential of the sounds of speech being transferred. When an area, as a movie theater, is being designed, additional considerations must be used because of the electronically developed sound. STC ratings are therefore most useful when planning areas used by people only, such as apartments, hospital rooms, and classrooms. The larger the STC value, the more resistant a material is to the transfer of airborne sound. Examples of STC ratings are in the Appendix.

It is important that all cracks around the edges of wall panels, electrical outlets, and other penetrations of the panel be caulked with acoustical caulking. A poorly fit door or window will also permit transmission of sound.

Impact Isolation Class

Airborne noise is transmitted through floors to the living space below. The sound transmission class ratings apply to these but also requiring consideration is transmission of noise due to impact, such as someone walking. Impact noise is expressed as *Impact Isolation Class* (IIC) ratings. The larger the IIC value, the more resistant a material is to impact noise. These ratings are often given in trade literature involved with various types of floor construction. Examples of floor assemblies and their IIC ratings are in the Appendix.

Preengineered Metal Building Systems

Preengineered metal buildings are designed and manufactured by companies specializing in this type of construction. They are sold and erected by franchised dealers. The dealers work with customers and architects to design buildings to house the required activities. The components are manufactured in a plant and shipped to the site for erection (Fig. 12-2).

These buildings are assembled using preengineered components. Manufacturers have available a large selection of preengineered components and can design and build any needed special parts. Some systems permit the design of both one- and two-story buildings. They have designs that permit a structure to support a crane or to include a balcony or mezzanine (Fig. 12-3).

The structural frame along with the purlins, girts, bracing, and metal skin provide the needed strength and rigidity. The foundation and footings are designed to carry the loads and meet local codes.

There are several basic types of preengineered metal buildings: rigid frame, truss type, post and beam, and sloped roof. These have eave heights of 10 to 24 ft.

Rigid frame buildings are available as a low profile or high profile (Fig. 12-4). The low profile generally has a slope of 1 in. in 12 in. They can be had with clear spans from 30 ft to 130 ft.

Truss type buildings use a preengineered steel structure of columns and beams. The roof structure uses trusses or open web bar joists. This type of building can be erected rapidly and can enclose large areas and have long spans between rows of columns (Fig. 12-5).

Post and beam buildings with one post at the center have spans from 80 to 120 ft, with two posts from 120 to 180 ft, and with three posts from 160 to 240 ft. Bay sizes range from 20 to 24 ft (Fig. 12-6).

Sloped roof buildings use a rigid frame rafter with the top surface sloped. It is supported by columns. Purlins run perpendicular to the rafters and support the roof decking (Fig. 12-7).

Another system uses a Delta Joist™. This triangular joist is designed in 4-ft widths and 2-ft increments in length (Fig. 12-8).

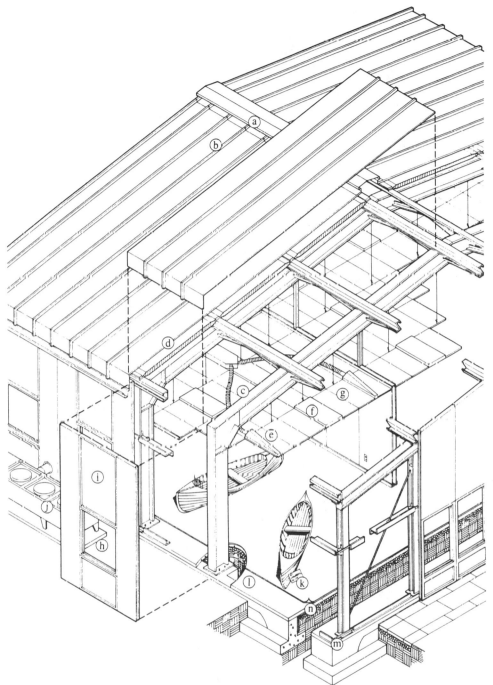

a. *Ridge vent*
b. *Standing seam metal roof*
c. *Rigid steel frame*
d. *Batt insulation*
e. *Ducts and diffusers*
f. *Fluorescent light fixtures*
g. *Suspended acoustical tile ceiling*
h. *Window assembly*
i. *Insulated metal wall panels*
j. *Heat pump*
k. *Carpet*
l. *Slab on grade and concrete foundation*
m. *Dampproofing*
n. *Vapor barrier*

The pre-engineered metal building integrates lightweight structural and envelope components at the connected level, but the result is a structure and envelope that combine to produce a common structural effect; each component adds strength and rigidity to the overall form. The floor slab, often left uncovered in warehouse and industrial applications, unifies the envelope, structure, and interior systems, and is normally the only major site preparation required for erecting the building. The pre-engineered, cold-formed steel componentry is very flexible and can be used for a wide variety of building shapes and sizes. Such buildings can be rapidly dismantled and moved.

The rectilinear nature of such systems usually results in buildings that are easily expanded in the longer dimension. Mechanical and interior systems are meshed in the ceilings, but the mechanical plant (here shown on the ground adjacent to the building, but just as easily roof-mounted) is normally kept on the exterior, sometimes presenting visible integration difficulty. The light weight of the envelope system, which is valuable for shipping, is especially vulnerable to wind uplift and requires great care in design and layout of fastenings. For applications where privacy or sound isolation are issues, the thin sheet steel presents an acoustical problem.

Figure 12-2. *A preengineered metal building using rigid frame construction. Reproduced from "The Building Systems Integration Handbook" copyright 1986, by permission of The American Institute of Architects under license number 92053. FURTHER REPRODUCTION IS PROHIBITED.*

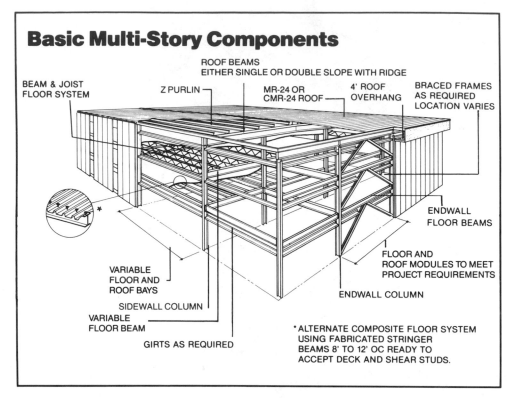

Figure 12-3. *A multistory preengineered metal building. (Artwork provided by and reflecting the products, components and systems of Butler Manufacturing Company, P.O. Box 917, Kansas City, MO 64141.)*

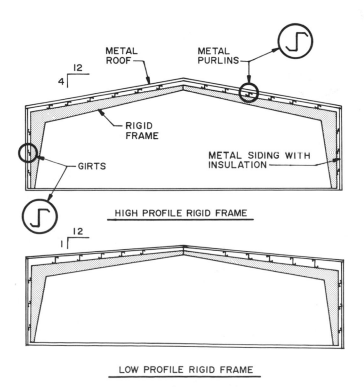

Figure 12-4. *Typical rigid frame wall and roof construction.*

Steel-Framed Structures

Steel-framed structures are built using a variety of structural members. Some are formed by rolling them to shape from steel blooms that are hot. Others are formed by cold rolling flat steel sheets to the desired shapes.

The hot-rolled steel shapes are shown in Fig. 12-9. The *wide-flange*, called W-shapes, have the inner faces of the flanges almost parallel to the outer face. The two general forms of wide-flange shapes are those suitable for beams and a more nearly square shape suitable for columns. The means of designating hot rolled steel members on drawings is shown in Fig. 12-10.

The *American Standard beams*, called S-beams, have the inner face of the flange sloped 1 in 6.

Standard mill beams, called miscellaneous M-shapes, are also available. They are beams that cannot be classified as W, S, or HP.

Angles are available with either equal or unequal legs.

Bearing piles, identified as HP, have parallel flanges and equal flange and web thickness.

Tees are commonly made by cutting the webs of wide-flange and S-beam shapes. They are called *structural tees* and indicated as WT or ST. WT is cut from a wide-flange shape and ST from an S-beam shape.

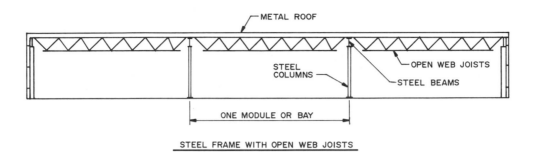

STEEL FRAME WITH OPEN WEB JOISTS

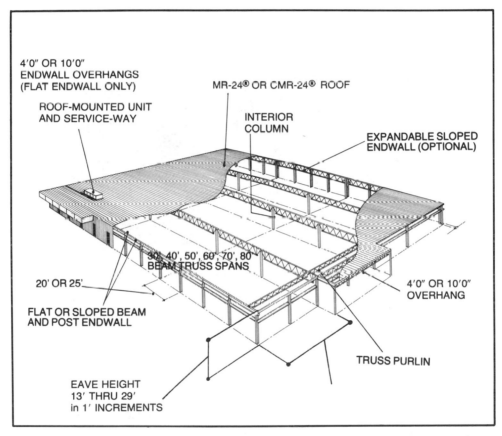

Figure 12-5. *A truss type building uses open web joists or trusses and steel columns. (Artwork provided by and reflecting the products, components and systems of Butler Manufacturing Company, P.O. Box 917, Kansas City, MO 64141.)*

Square, rectangular, and round structural tubular shapes and round pipe are made in a variety of sizes and wall thicknesses. These are widely used as columns. They fit into frame and masonry walls better than pipe or wide-flange columns.

Square and round bars are used for ties, bracing, sag rods, and hangers. They are made in a variety of sizes.

Plates are flat sheets of steel. They are available in square and rectangular shapes and a variety of thicknesses. Plate is indicated on notes as PL.

Cold formed light weight shapes are shown in Fig. 12-11. The sheet steel is bent into shapes desired such as a C-shape and with welding into an I-shape. These are short-span framing members used as studs in partitions and exterior walls and floor structures in smaller buildings. Sheet stock is also rolled into corrugated configurations and serves as floor and roof decking. Typical construction details using cold rolled steel shapes are in Fig. 12-12. The floor and roof decking can be plywood, steel slab form and concrete, steel deck, and concrete or precast concrete.

The system is assembled with self-drilling screws or welding. Plywood decks are fastened using screws or spiral shank nails. Adhesives are often used in conjunction with nails or screws. Welds on galvanized members must be painted to retard rust.

A drawing showing the light weight steel framing in use

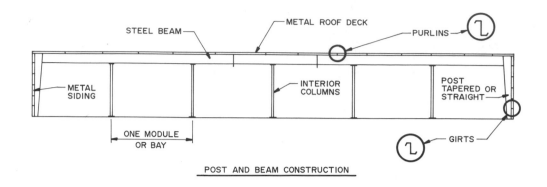

POST AND BEAM CONSTRUCTION

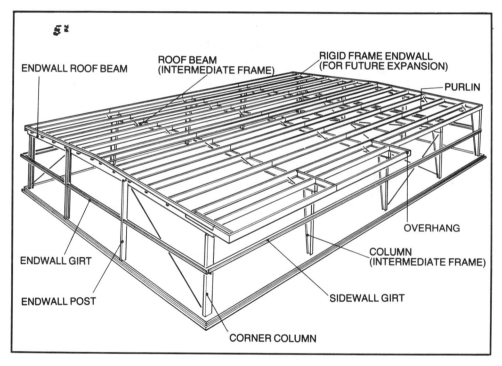

Figure 12-6. *This is a six-bay post and beam frame. (Artwork provided by and reflecting the products, component and systems of Butler Manufacturing Company, P.O. Box 917, Kansas City, MO 64141.)*

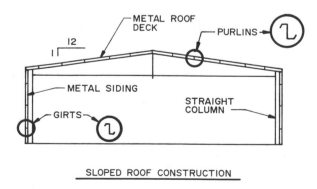

SLOPED ROOF CONSTRUCTION

Figure 12-7. *A sloped roof rigid frame metal structure.*

as the supporting frame for a brick veneer structure is in Fig. 12-13.

Structural steel framing is widely used because it offers a large number of possible combinations of girders, beams, columns, and miscellaneous shapes. Each piece is detailed by a structural designer and made in a steel frabrication shop. They are marked with an identifying number. An erection drawing is made with each piece numbered to correspond with the fabricated pieces. The steel is shipped to the job site for erection.

At the job site, the steel is unloaded and placed in a sequence that will make each piece available when needed for erection. The pieces are lifted into place, connected,

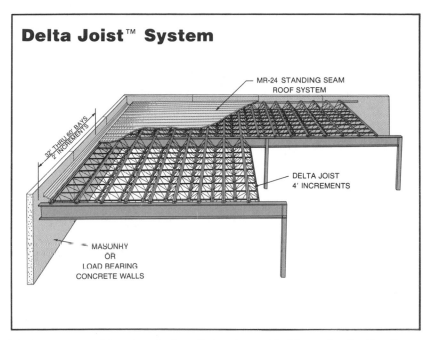

Figure 12-8. *A Delta Joist™ system roof framing design. (Artwork provided by and reflecting the products, components and systems of Butler Manufacturing Company, P.O. Box 917, Kansas City, MO 64141. Delta Joist is a trademark of Butler Manufacturing Company.)*

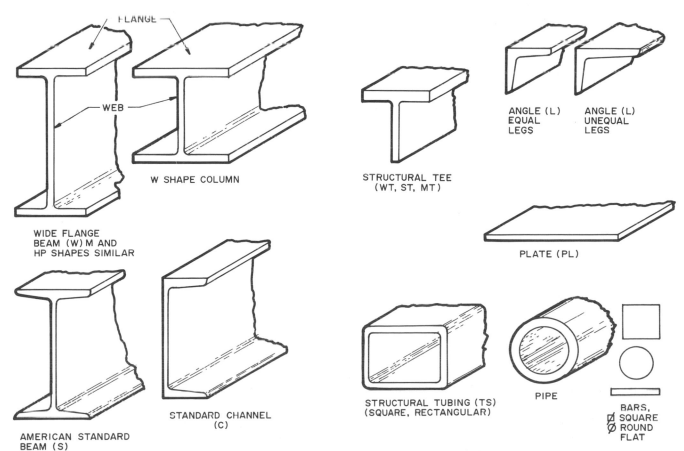

Figure 12-9. *The most commonly used hot-rolled steel shapes.*

Designation	Type of Shape
W18 × 70	W shape
S18 × 70	S shape
M10 × 9	M shape
C12 × 30	American standard channel
MC12 × 45	Miscellaneous channel
HP12 × 74	HP shape
L8 × 8 × 1	Equal-leg angle
L4 × 3 × ½	Unequal-leg angle
WT8 × 25	Structural tee cut from W shape
ST12 × 60	Structural tee cut from S shape
MT4 × 11.25	Structural tee cut from M shape
PL ½ × 24	Plate
Bar 1	Square bar
Bar 1 ½	Round bar
Bar 2 ½ × ½	Flat bar
Pipe3 Std	Pipe
Pipe3X-Strong	
Pipe3XX-Strong	
TS3 × 3 × 0.375	Structural tubing: square
TS4 × 3 × 0.375	Structural tubing: rectangular
TS3 OD × 0.250	Structural tubing: circular

Figure 12-10. *Hot-rolled structural steel shape designations.*

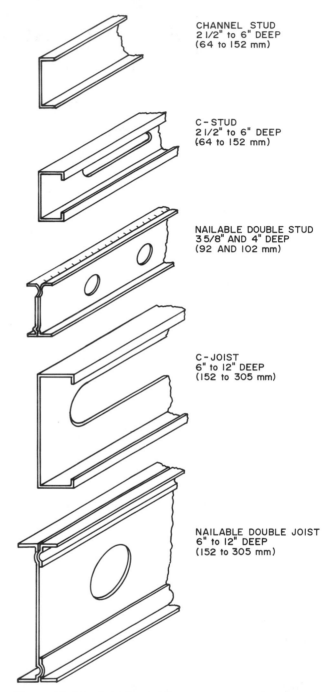

CHANNEL STUD
2 1/2" to 6" DEEP
(64 to 152 mm)

C-STUD
2 1/2" to 6" DEEP
(64 to 152 mm)

NAILABLE DOUBLE STUD
3 5/8" AND 4" DEEP
(92 AND 102 mm)

C-JOIST
6" to 12" DEEP
(152 to 305 mm)

NAILABLE DOUBLE JOIST
6" to 12" DEEP
(152 to 305 mm)

Figure 12-11. *Cold-formed light-gauge steel framing studs and joists.*

plumbed, and guyed with wire cables or turnbuckles. The connections may be bolted, riveted, or welded.

Steel framing permits rapid erection of the structural frame of a building. When steel decking is used it serves as a working surface and becomes the formwork for a concrete floor. The frame permits the use of long uninterrupted clear spans. The steel frame is structurally independent of the exterior walls. The exterior walls are supported by spandrels which transmit the load to the outside columns. A *spandrel* is a wall panel filling the space between the top of the window in one story and the sill of the window in the story above. Electrical and mechanical systems can be run in the space provided by the beams. Steel structural members must be given fire protection (Fig. 12-14).

Generally, steel-framed connections are made using angles, plates, or tees to join the members to be connected. A bolted beam-to-column-flange connection (Fig. 12-15) uses two angles and bolts, rivets, or is welded. The angles are joined to the beam in the steel fabricator's shop and are joined to the column on the job. This type of connection transmits shear from the beam to the column. *Shear* is the vertical forces acting upon the beam. It does not transmit bending moment from the beam to the column because the flanges of the beam are not secured to the column. This can be done by welding the beam flange to

the column or using angles or plates to bolt or rivet them together (Fig. 12-16).

Resisting Lateral Forces

The structural steel framework must be made stable against lateral forces such as wind and earthquake. This is done with diagonal bracing, shear panels, and moment connections (Fig. 12-17). *Diagonal bracing* creates trian-

Construction details

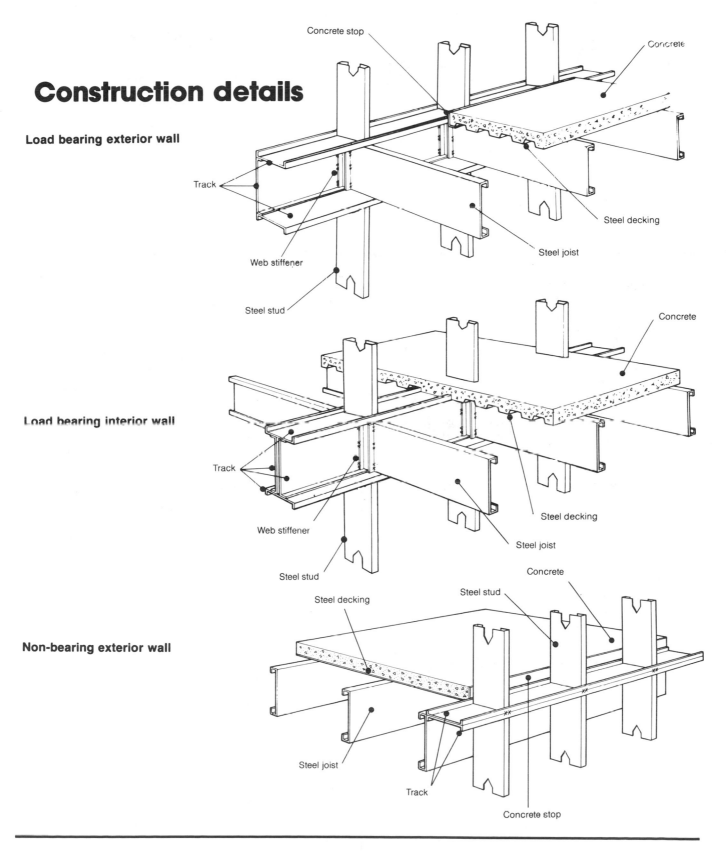

Load bearing exterior wall

Concrete stop

Concrete

Track

Web stiffener

Steel decking

Steel joist

Steel stud

Load bearing interior wall

Concrete

Track

Web stiffener

Steel decking

Steel joist

Steel stud

Non-bearing exterior wall

Steel decking

Steel stud

Concrete

Steel joist

Track

Concrete stop

(a)

Figure 12-12. *Typical construction details for light-gauge metal framing. (Courtesy of Dale/Incor, Inc.)*

Construction details

Typical load bearing wall panel

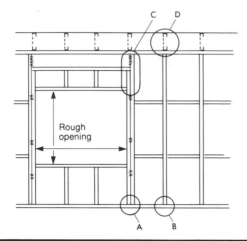

Rough opening

C D

A B

Detail A
Multiple stud and stud to track attachment (single stud to track identical)

Load bearing studs must be seated tight to track web

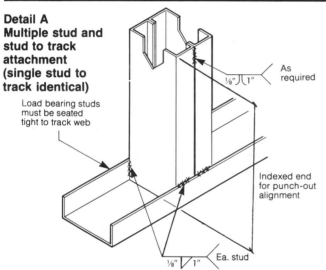

1/8″ 1″ As required

Indexed end for punch-out alignment

1/8″ 1″ Ea. stud

Detail B
Stud to track (alternate to welding)

NOTE: In curtain wall application, only (1) screw required at both sides.

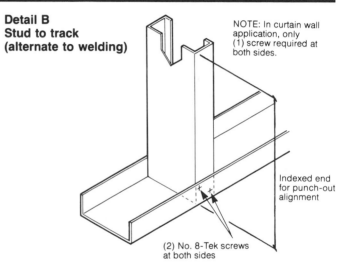

Indexed end for punch-out alignment

(2) No. 8-Tek screws at both sides

Detail C
Header detail

Track

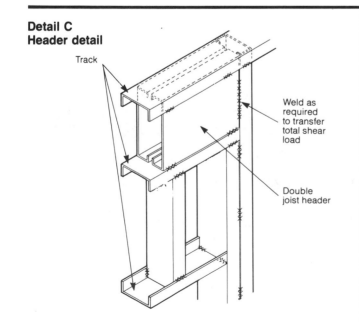

Weld as required to transfer total shear load

Double joist header

Detail D
Joist to track attachment

Steel joist

3/8″ ± 1/8″

Track

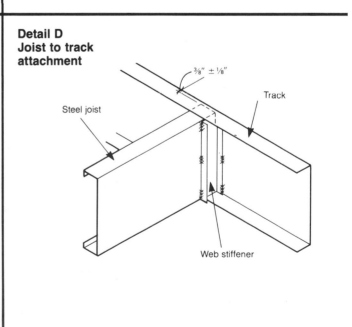

Web stiffener

(b)

Figure 12-12. (Continued)

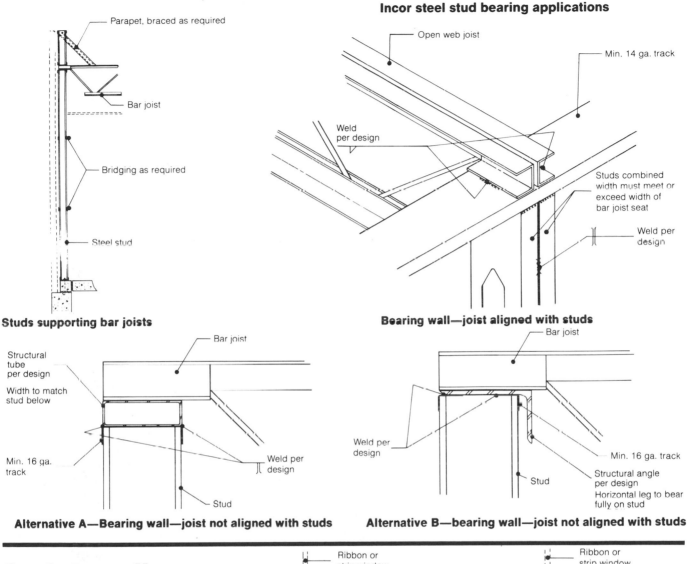

Incor steel stud bearing applications

Studs supporting bar joists

Bearing wall—joist aligned with studs

Alternative A—Bearing wall—joist not aligned with studs

Alternative B—bearing wall—joist not aligned with studs

Curtainwall Construction

Stub wall (base connection to resist overturning due to lateral forces)

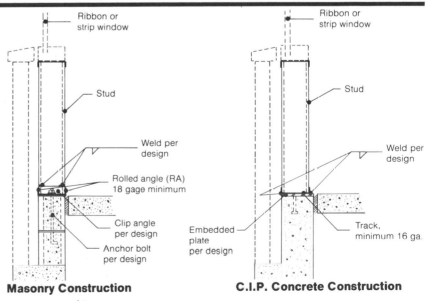

Masonry Construction

C.I.P. Concrete Construction

(c)

Figure 12-12. (Continued)

Curtainwall Construction

Spandrel conditions

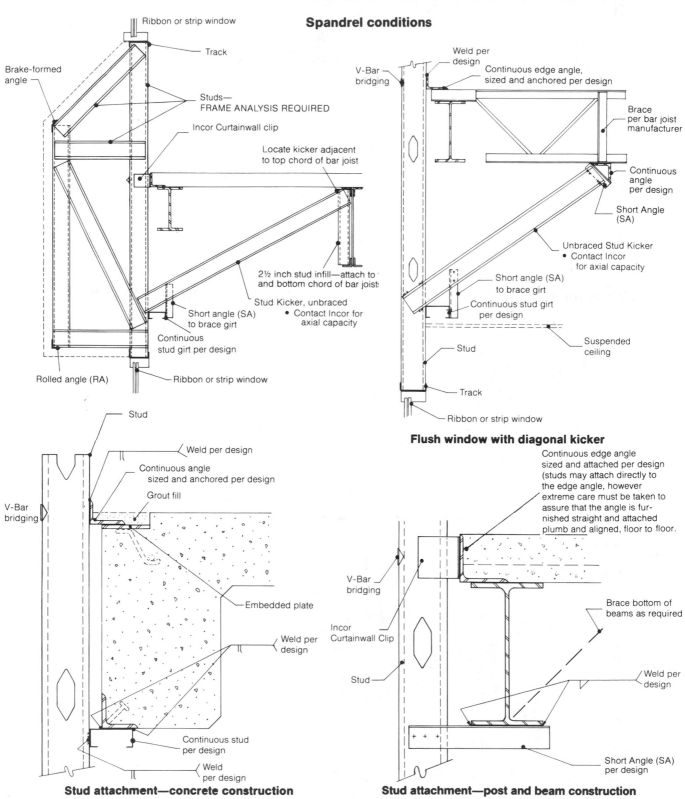

Ribbon or strip window

Track

Brake-formed angle

Studs— FRAME ANALYSIS REQUIRED

Incor Curtainwall clip

Locate kicker adjacent to top chord of bar joist

2½ inch stud infill—attach to and bottom chord of bar joist

Stud Kicker, unbraced
• Contact Incor for axial capacity

Short angle (SA) to brace girt

Continuous stud girt per design

Rolled angle (RA)

Ribbon or strip window

Weld per design

V-Bar bridging

Continuous edge angle, sized and anchored per design

Brace per bar joist manufacturer

Continuous angle per design

Short Angle (SA)

Unbraced Stud Kicker
• Contact Incor for axial capacity

Short angle (SA) to brace girt

Continuous stud girt per design

Suspended ceiling

Stud

Track

Ribbon or strip window

Flush window with diagonal kicker

Stud

Weld per design

Continuous angle sized and anchored per design

Grout fill

V-Bar bridging

Embedded plate

Weld per design

Continuous stud per design

Weld per design

Stud attachment—concrete construction

Continuous edge angle sized and attached per design (studs may attach directly to the edge angle, however extreme care must be taken to assure that the angle is furnished straight and attached plumb and aligned, floor to floor.

V-Bar bridging

Incor Curtainwall Clip

Stud

Brace bottom of beams as required

Weld per design

Short Angle (SA) per design

Stud attachment—post and beam construction

(d)

Figure 12-12. (Continued)

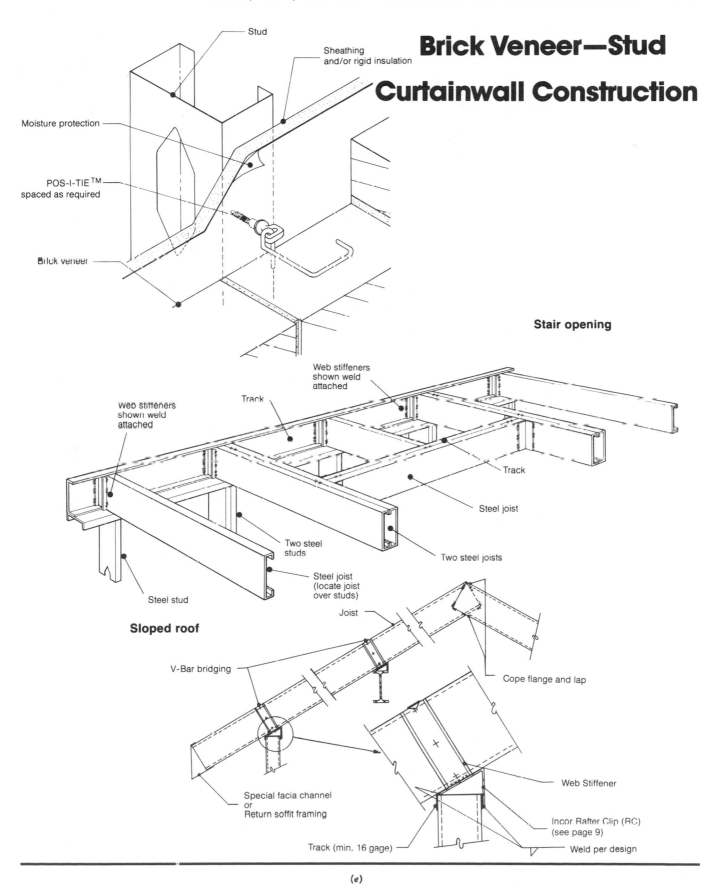

Brick Veneer—Stud
Curtainwall Construction

Stair opening

Sloped roof

(e)

Figure 12-12. (Continued)

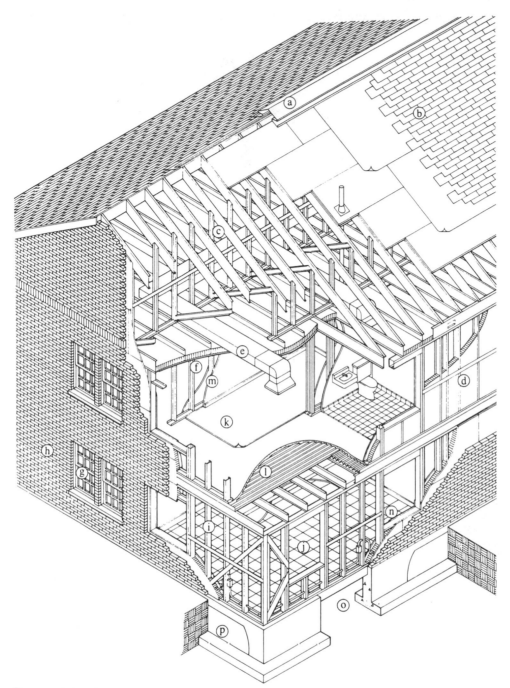

a. *Metal ridge vent*
b. *Roofing*
   - *Roofing felt*
   - *Shingles*
   - *Plywood sheathing*
c. *Metal roof frame*
   - *C-stud brace*
   - *C-rafter*
   - *C-channel*
   - *C-joist*
d. *Batt insulation*
e. *Ducts and diffusers*
f. *Suspended acoustical tile ceiling*
g. *Window assembly*
h. *Brick veneer*
i. *C-stud assembly*
j. *Ceramic floor tile*
k. *Carpet*
l. *Metal floor frame and steel deck and concrete topping*
m. *Drywall*
n. *Resilient tile flooring*
o. *Slab on grade and concrete foundation*
p. *Dampproofing*

Structural, interior, and envelope systems are connected in lightweight steel frame and brick veneer construction, while the mechanical systems are meshed within the structural walls, floor, and roof. Connections between the brick veneer envelope and the cold-rolled steel structural frame are minimal, to permit nearly independent movement of the two systems, each of which expands and contracts in different ways. Care must be taken in detailing at openings, where sills, jambs, and other pieces span both the frame and veneer. The brick veneer is self-supporting and serves almost exclusively as envelope. The lightweight cold-formed steel members are load-bearing, and beams, columns, chan-

nels, headers, and other elements can be built up from standard steel shapes and sections. The rigidity of the frame depends on cross bracing, interior and exterior sheathing, the distance from exterior corner to exterior corner, and on the type and layout of fasteners used. Advantages of cold-formed steel framing include light weight, dimensional stability, speed and ease of assembly, resistance to moisture and decay, and, in some cases, readier availability than wood framing members. Detailing and fastening of the cold-rolled steel frame differs markedly from practices used in wood frame construction, and the technology requires special noncarpentry tools and equipment.

Figure 12-13. *A multistory building using brick veneer over light-gauge steel framing. Reproduced from "The Building Systems Integration Handbook" copyright 1986, by permission of The American Institute of Architects under license number 92053. FURTHER REPRODUCTION IS PROHIBITED.*

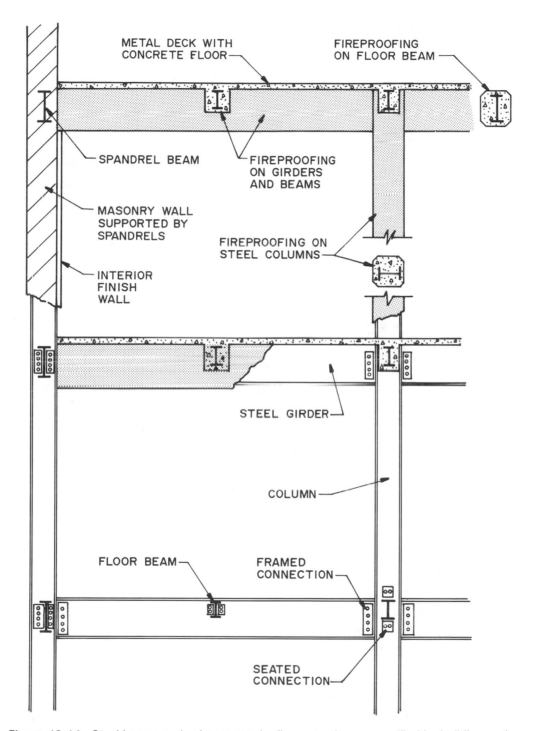

Figure 12-14. *Steel beams and columns require fire protection as specified by building codes.*

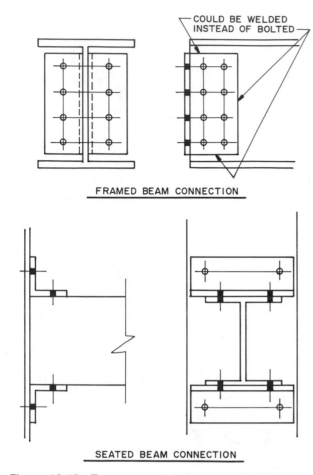

FRAMED BEAM CONNECTION

SEATED BEAM CONNECTION

Figure 12-15. *Two ways to join beams and girders to columns.*

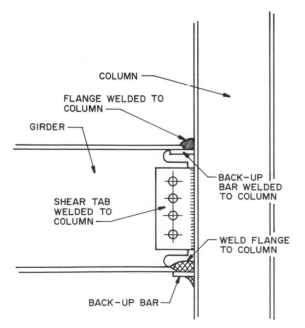

Figure 12-16. *This shows flanges welded to the column providing a moment connection.*

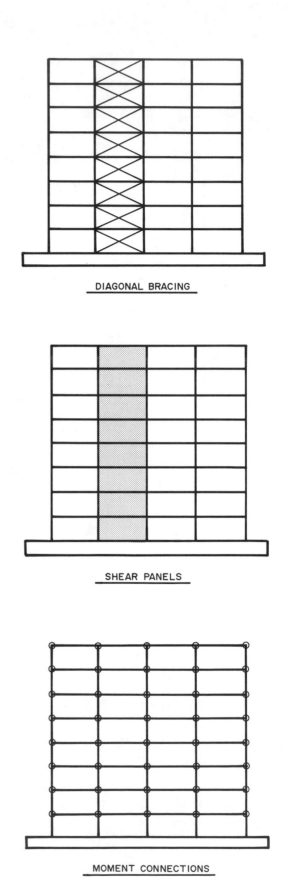

DIAGONAL BRACING

SHEAR PANELS

MOMENT CONNECTIONS

Figure 12-17. *Basic ways to develop lateral stability to a steel framework.*

gular configurations within the rectangular elements of the steel frame. *Shear panels* are braced rectangular panels placed within the rectangular elements of the building frame. They are either steel or concrete. *Moment connections* are used where beams and columns meet. They stabilize the frame against lateral forces, eliminating the need for diagonal bracing or shear panels.

There are two common ways used to stabilize the frame of a multistory building (Fig. 12-18). One uses a *stable core* in the center of the building. The core can contain elevators, stairs, restrooms, and mechanical chases. It is a structural tower braced using diagonal bracing, shear panels, or moment connections. The floors of the structure act as horizontal shear panels, keeping the bays around the core rigid by connecting them to the core.

Another way to stabilize a structure is to make the *outer walls rigid* using diagonal bracing, shear panels, or moment connections. The interior connections must only resist shear. The floor system adds to the rigidity of the structure by connecting with the outer walls. The American Institute of Steel Construction (AISC) defines three types of steel frame construction. These are based upon the manner in which they achieve stability against lateral forces.

AISC Type 1, Rigid Frame construction requires that beam-to-column connections are sufficiently rigid so that the geometric angles between members remain virtually unchanged under load.

AISC Type 2, Simple Frame Construction, assumes shear connections only and requires diagonal bracing or shear panels be used for lateral bracing.

AISC Type 3 is a semirigid construction having connections that are not as rigid as in AISC Type 1, but possess a dependable and predictable moment-resisting capacity to stabilize the building.

A composite drawing of a structural steel building with mechanical and electrical systems, floors, ceilings, and roof construction is in Fig. 12-19.

Another type of steel framing uses *floor-to-ceiling high trusses* spanning between steel columns (Fig. 12-20). These trusses carry the loads of the roof, ceilings, and floors. Notice how the trusses are staggered from floor to floor creating openings for mechanical and electrical systems.

Space frames provide another structural roof system. They provide roof support and large spaces for the installation of mechanical and electrical systems. They are usually covered with a metal deck, insulation, and a built-up roof (Fig. 12-21). The round struts are high-strength extruded aluminum and are joined by solid aluminum hubs. The space frames are usually left exposed and form an attractive, dramatic overhead view. They can be designed to accept clerestory glazing where they meet the exterior wall.

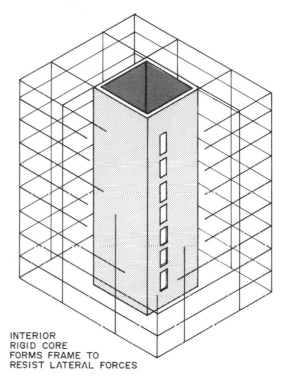

INTERIOR
RIGID CORE
FORMS FRAME TO
RESIST LATERAL FORCES

EXTERIOR
WALLS FORM
RIGID FRAME TO
RESIST LATERAL FORCES

Figure 12-18. Multistory buildings can be stabilized using a stable core or by making the outer walls rigid.

The *tension fabric structure* is an unusual structure (Fig. 12-22). The fabric membrane is a polyester substrate with polyvinyl-chloride-coated outer layer. A stronger fabric is Teflon-coated or silicone-coated fiberglass. The fabric

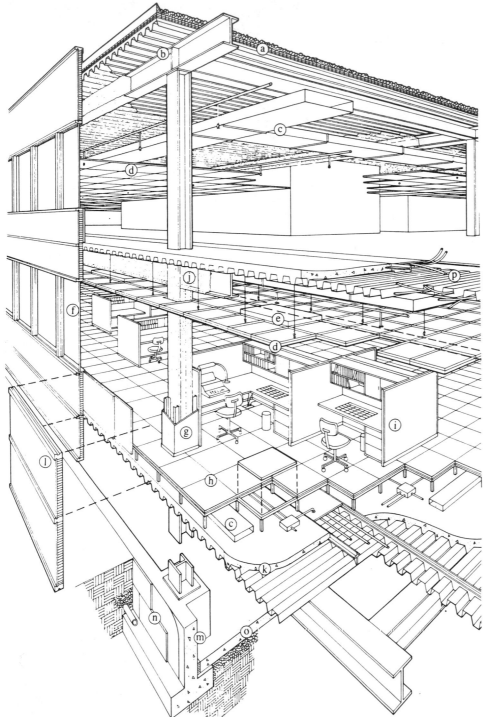

a. Built-up roofing and
    rigid insulation
b. Steel beams and steel
    roof deck
c. Ducts and diffusers
d. Suspended acoustical
    tile ceiling
e. Fluorescent light fixture
f. Window assembly
g. Drywall
h. Carpeted access
    flooring
i. Open office furniture
j. Steel beams and
    columns
k. Steel decking with cast-
    in-place concrete
    topping
l. Insulated spandrel
    panels
m. Slab on grade and
    concrete foundation
n. Waterproofing and
    protective board
o. Vapor barrier
p. Structural/electrified
    floor

Structural steel framing and a steel and concrete floor diaphragm result in relatively long, uninterrupted clear spans. Structural/electrified floors and access floor systems are both shown as possible solutions for a flexible interior environment. The steel frame is structurally independent of the envelope elements, providing great flexibility in the weight and configuration of envelope systems employed. The access floor is touching the composite structural slab and actually provides a redundant floor structure. Mechanical systems are meshed within the space between structural floor and finished floor. The suspended ceiling also provides space for distribution of internal services, but tends to be used principally for overhead lighting and ductwork, which, if placed in the floor, could block the path of wires for power and signal distribution. Fire protection of steel members is eased by use of the cellular concrete deck, although fire compartments may be interrupted by through-floor penetrations and by light fixtures and air grilles in the ceiling.

Figure 12-19. Details for a structural steel framed building. Reproduced from ''The Building Systems Integration Handbook'' copyright 1986, by permission of The American Institute of Architects under license number 92053. *FURTHER REPRODUCTION IS PROHIBITED.*

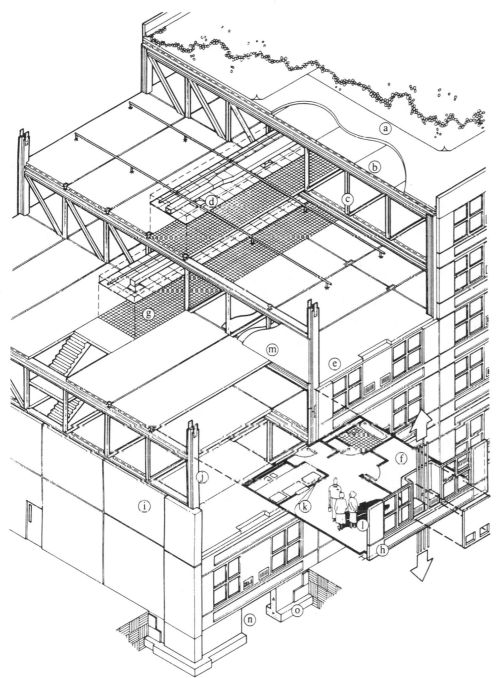

a. *Rigid insulation,
   elastomeric roofing
   and ballast*
b. *Precast hollow core
   concrete plank deck*
c. *Steel truss*
d. *Ducts and sprinkler*
e. *Window assembly*
f. *Utility risers and piping*
g. *Seamless resilient
   flooring*
h. *Precast stiffener beams*
i. *Precast shear panels*
j. *Steel columns*
k. *Carpet*
l. *Precast concrete fascia
   panels*
m. *Drywall*
n. *Concrete foundation*
o. *Waterproofing and
   protective board*

In this example, large floor-to-floor steel trusses serve as load-bearing members for roofs, floors, and ceilings. The layout of the structural trusses, which are staggered in a brick-joint pattern from floor to floor, creates highly regularized compartments or bays and accommodates openings for circulation and mechanical systems. The trusses also serve as the plane for attaching fire-resistive partitioning materials between units or bays, thus integrating structure, envelope, and interior systems within individual spaces. The trusses provide a rigid frame in the direction of the truss axes, while precast floor, roof, and perimeter wall panels stabilize the structure in the direction perpendicular to the trusses and provide the enve-
lope. In this sense, envelope and structure are unified for a portion of the system. Such construction can proceed very rapidly, with most components manufactured off-site and erected quickly by cranes and hoists. Although interior and mechanical systems are for the most part integrated with the structure only at the connected level, the trusses do provide, by means of a special Vierandeel section at the center of a double-loaded corridor layout, an appropriate place for meshing of mechanical and structural systems. Staggered truss construction is most often indicated for double-loaded residential-type occupancies, including hotels, highrise apartments, nursing homes, and hospitals.

Figure 12-20. *A steel framed building using floor-to-ceiling trusses. Reproduced from "The Building Systems Integration Handbook" copyright 1986, by permission of the American Institute of Architects under license number 92053. FURTHER REPRODUCTION IS PROHIBITED.*

221

a. Built-up roofing and
   rigid insulation
b. Metal space frame and
   metal deck
c. Ducts, sprinkler piping
   and electrical conduit
d. Incandescent light
   fixture
e. Glass block panel
f. Concrete masonry
   bearing wall
g. Brick veneer and rigid
   insulation
h. Wood flooring
i. Slab on grade and
   concrete foundation
j. Vapor barrier

Structure and envelope are connected in this example, with the exposed nature of the space frame requiring a high degree of visible integration between the frame's structural components and parts of the mechanical system. The ceiling unifies interior and structural systems, and meshes them with unified mechanical and interior systems. The solid hubs in the frame serve to join the struts and can also accommodate mountings for the envelope system and various types of interior equipment. The space frame permits very long column-free spans with minimal amounts of structural material. Its visual properties can be destroyed if the frame is coated for fire protection; in many cases coating can be forgone if the frame is placed 20 ft or more above floor level.

Figure 12-21. A structure using space frames for the roof supporting structure. Reproduced from "The Building Systems Integration Handbook" copyright 1986, by permission of the American Institute of Architects under license number 92053. FURTHER REPRODUCTION IS PROHIBITED.

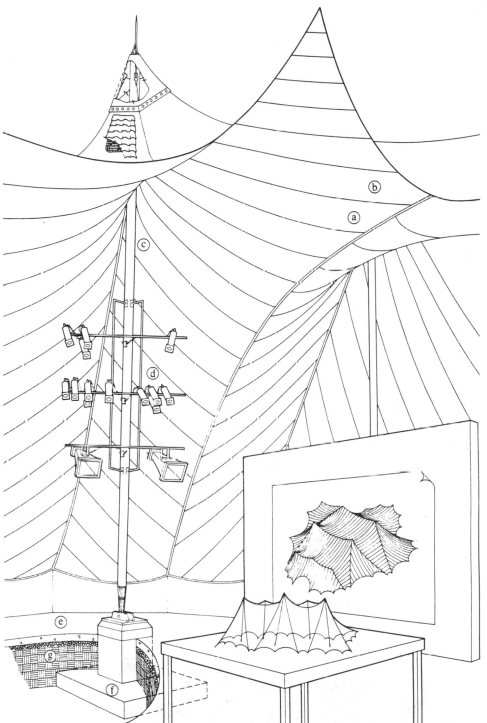

a. *Steel cables in fabric
  sleeves*
b. *Non-combustible fabric
  membrane*
c. *Steel masts*
d. *Incandescent light
  fixtures and sound
  system speakers*
e. *Slab on grade*
f. *Pivoted mast base plate
  and concrete footing*
g. *Vapor barrier*

*Structure, envelope, and interior systems are uni-
fied in fabric buildings. The fabric provides all
three functions and, because it is light-transmit-
ting while blocking direct rays of the sun, also
assumes some functions normal to mechanical
systems. Electrical lighting and other equipment
are difficult to integrate, due to the thinness of the
structural envelope membrane, and are nearly
always attached to the structural masts or placed
on independent, freestanding structures. Tension
fabric construction can conserve time and mate-*
*rial. Fabrics can range in service life from several
years to several decades, but vary accordingly in
cost. Acoustical, thermal, and fire-safety considerations are difficult to accommodate in tension
structures, although their light weight and dy-
namic properties under wind loading make them
very safe from a structural point of view. If areas
of fabric are placed close to the ground or in other
easily accessible locations, vandalism becomes a
concern, as most materials suitable for tensile
structures are easily cut.*

Figure 12-22. *A structure formed by placing a fabric membrane over steel cables supported by steel or aluminum masts.
Reproduced from ''The Building Systems Integration Handbook'' copyright 1986, by permission of the American Institute of
Architects under license number 92053. FURTHER REPRODUCTION IS PROHIBITED.*

membrane is anchored to steel cables which are suspended from steel or aluminum masts to totally enclose the desired area.

Open Web Joists and Joist Girders

Joists are parallel structural members used to support floors and roof. Joist girders are structural members that run between columns and support joists. Open web joists are also called bar joists.

Open web steel joists are used for floor and roof construction. They are usually spaced 2 ft or more and can span distances up to 144 ft. Standard depths range from 8 to 72 in. The size and spacing of the joists depends upon the span, the loads to be carried, and the distance the decking can span under the loads required.

Open web joists are made in three series, H, LH and DLH. The H series is made in depths from 8 to 30 in. and spans to 60 ft. The LH series is made in depths from 18 to 48 in. and spans to 96 ft. The DLH series is made in depths from 52 to 72 in. and spans to 144 ft.

Joist girders are prefabricated trusses used as primary framing members supporting floor and roof joists and other loads as mechanical equipment. They are used instead of wide-flange steel beams and girders when the greater depth of the truss is acceptable (Fig. 12-23).

Floor assemblies with 1- to 4-hr fire ratings and roof assemblies with 1- and 2-hr fire ratings are easily attainable.

Bridging is required to support the top chords against lateral movement during the construction period. It is intended that the roof and floor deck provide lateral support under full loading conditions. Metal standing seam roofs do not provide adequate lateral support and require additional bridging. Bridging for joists spaced under 3 ft O. C. is $\frac{1}{2}$-in. round rod and angles of various sizes are used for wider spacing (Fig. 12-24).

Open web joists are available in a variety of types (Fig. 12-25). They can have either underslung or square ends and have single or double pitched top chords. Standard pitch is $\frac{1}{8}$ in./ft. Typical construction details are shown in Fig. 12-26.

Open web joists with masonry-bearing wall construction are shown in Fig. 12-27. This popular method provides large interior areas free from columns. It gives the designer great freedom to use the interior space without concern for columns or load-bearing walls.

The floor systems commonly used with open web joists are metal decking topped with a concrete slab, precast concrete planks, and plywood. Information on floors can be found later in this chapter.

Cast-in-Place Concrete Structures

Cast-in-place concrete structures use columns and beams that are formed and on the site. The necessary reinforcing steel is set in place and the concrete is poured into the forms forming the column or beam.

Figure 12-23. *A steel framed building using joist girders and open web joists for floor and roof construction. (Courtesy of the American Institute of Steel Construction.)*

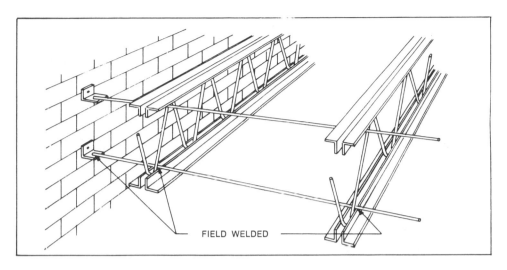

HORIZONTAL BRIDGING

Figure 12-24. One type of bridging used with open web joists. (Courtesy of Vulcraft Division of Nucor Corporation.)

Concrete Columns

Concrete columns can take many shapes with square, rectangular and round being most often used (Fig. 12-28). Vertical reinforcing bars are placed near the surface to provide resistance to bending. Columns are primarily under vertical load (compression). Even though concrete is strong in compression, these forces tend to cause the concrete on the outside of the column to spall off. To stop

this, circumferential reinforcements are placed perpendicular to the vertical reinforcements.

Square and rectangular columns use metal *ties* between the vertical reinforcement. Round columns use *spiral reinforcing* called a spiral hoop (Fig. 12-29). Columns with ties are called *tied columns*. Those with spiral hoops are called *spirally reinforced columns*. These reinforcements also confine the concrete core withing the spiral, reducing the likelihood that the column may suddenly fail. Ties are not as effective as spirals and loads on a tied column are less than on the same size spirally reinforced column.

Another type of concrete column uses a steel member, as a W column, as the core. It is completely encased in concrete and has vertical and spiral reinforcing. Another variation is to use concrete-filled pipe columns instead of a W column.

Concrete Beams and Girders

Beams and girders, when under load, are in tension. Since concrete is weak in tension and steel strong in tension, steel reinforcing is added to the beam. The top of the beam is in compression and the bottom is in tension (Fig. 12-30).

The typical concrete beam is rectangular in shape. Reinforcing to resist tension is placed in the bottom of the beam. If for some reason, such as limited space, the beam must be small and additional compressive strength is needed, reinforcing can be placed in the top of the beam. Since the concrete on the tension side of the beam does little to resist tension, a T-beam can be used. This leaves a wide concrete top to resist compression and a narrower

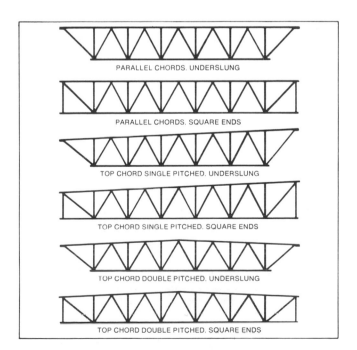

Figure 12-25. Various configurations of open web joists. (Courtesy of Vulcraft Division of Nucor Corporation.)

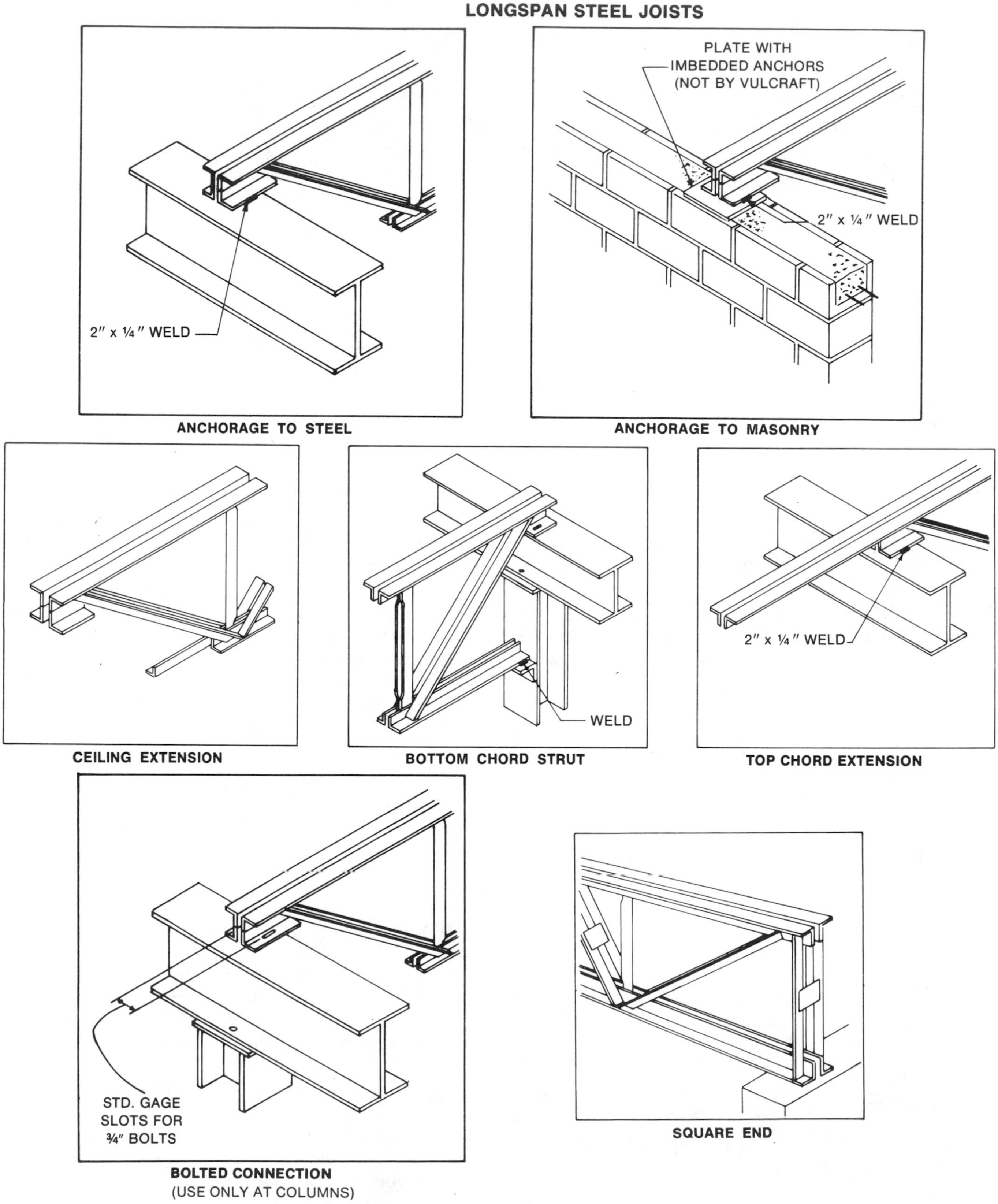

LONGSPAN STEEL JOISTS

2" x ¼" WELD

ANCHORAGE TO STEEL

PLATE WITH
IMBEDDED ANCHORS
(NOT BY VULCRAFT)

2" x ¼" WELD

ANCHORAGE TO MASONRY

CEILING EXTENSION

WELD

BOTTOM CHORD STRUT

2" x ¼" WELD

TOP CHORD EXTENSION

STD. GAGE
SLOTS FOR
¾" BOLTS

BOLTED CONNECTION
(USE ONLY AT COLUMNS)

SQUARE END

Figure 12-26. *Construction details for open web joists. (Courtesy of Vulcraft Division of Nucor Corporation.)*

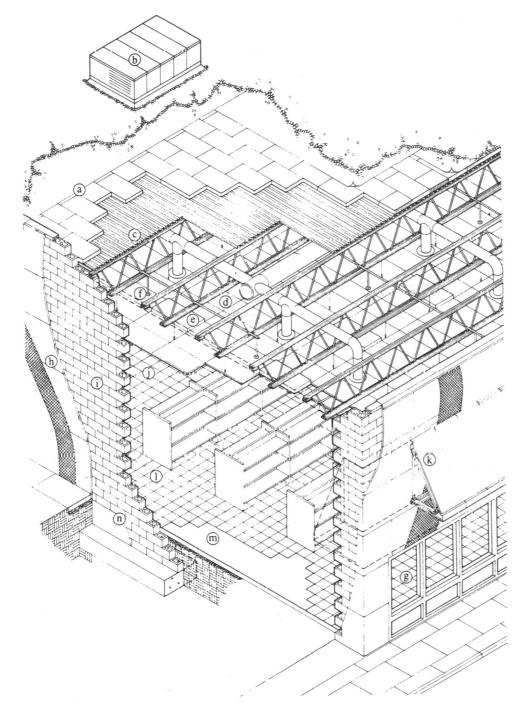

a. Built-up roofing and
   rigid insulation
b. HVAC unit
c. Steel decking and open
   web steel joists
d. Ducts and sprinkler
   piping
e. Fluorescent light fixture
f. Suspended acoustical
   tile ceiling
g. Window assembly
h. Rigid insulation and
   veneer coating
i. Concrete masonry
   bearing wall
j. Glazed face
k. Canopy assembly
l. Resilient tile flooring
m. Slab on grade and
   concrete footing
n. Vapor barrier and
   dampproofing

Bearing wall and bar-joist construction yields buildings that have relatively large interior clearspans and flexible interior layouts. The open webbing of the bar joists provides a lightweight structure that is easily penetrated by mechanical systems. The meshing of mechanical and structural systems in the roof plane also conserves vertical spaces. The bottom chords of the bar joists are used for suspension of interior finishes, lighting fixtures, and air diffusers in finished areas, or may be left uncovered. In this case, the structural, mechanical, and interior systems would be fully meshed. The concrete masonry unit bearing walls are insulated on the exterior to take better advantage of the wall's thermal mass by placing it toward the occupied site. Long-span open-web bar joist roofs can deflect substantially, and the camber of the joists alone is often not sufficient to maintain the necessary slope to roof drains. Beams running in a transverse direction to the joists can block the threading of piping, ductwork, and wiring, and variations in the configuration of perimeter walls should not disrupt the regular pattern of the joist web elements in a manner that will interfere with straight runs for mechanical components.

Figure 12-27. *A building using masonry bearing walls and open web joists. Reproduced from "The Building Systems Integration Handbook" copyright 1986, by permission of the American Institute of Architects under license number 92053. FURTHER REPRODUCTION IS PROHIBITED.*

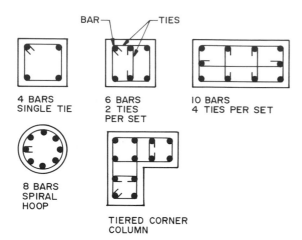

Figure 12-28. Typical reinforced concrete columns.

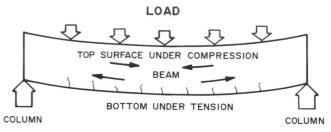

Figure 12-30. A loaded beam responds to tension and compression stresses.

steel reinforced bottom to resist tension. This produces a lighter beam. Stresses near the neutral axis of the beam are very small, so reinforcing by steel or concrete here is not significant (Fig. 12-31).

Concrete beams also must resist shearing stresses. Shearing stresses plus tensile stresses cause diagonal tension stresses that can produce diagonal cracks at the ends of a beam. To prevent this, shear reinforcement is added by using steel U-shaped stirrups vertically in the beam, using tension bars or both (Fig. 12-32).

Stress also tends to cause the reinforcing steel to slip within the beam. This is reduced by using deformed rebars and hooking the ends.

When a cast-in-place beam is to be continuous over several columns, the reinforcing at each support must be considered. A completely reinforced continuous beam is in Fig. 12-33. Horizontal reinforcing is placed in the bottom of the entire length. Some of these bars are trussed over each column to provide for compressive and shear forces. Stirrups and tensile bars are placed at each column.

Concrete floor slabs are usually cast monolithically with the beams and girders. The slab resists compressive and flexural stresses of the upper part of the beam below it at the middle of the span. Near the columns the compressive stresses are in the lower part of the beam. Continuous beams with monolithic floor slabs are therefore like T-beams in the center of the span and reinforced rectangular beams over the columns or other supports.

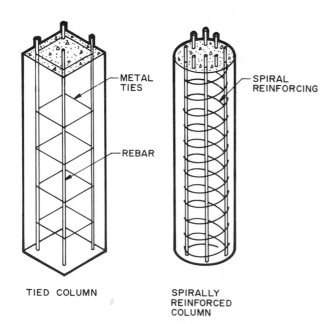

Figure 12-29. Reinforced concrete columns use ties and spiral reinforcing.

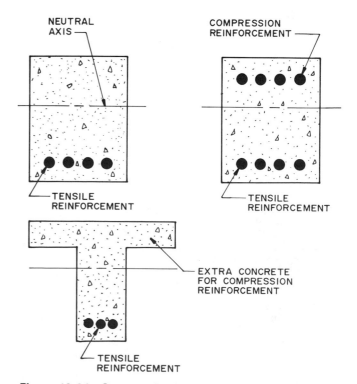

Figure 12-31. Concrete beams are reinforced to control tensile and compression stresses.

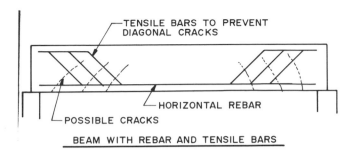

BEAM WITH REBAR AND TENSILE BARS

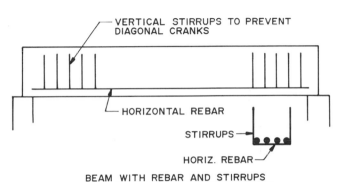

BEAM WITH REBAR AND STIRRUPS

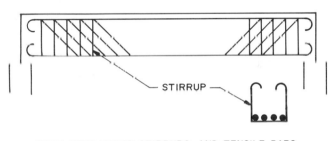

BEAM WITH REBAR, STIRRUPS, AND TENSILE BARS

NOTE: ENDS HOOKED TO INCREASE
RESISTANCE TO SLIPPING.

Figure 12-32. *Stirrups and tensile bars are used to prevent diagonal cracks at the ends of concrete beams.*

Concrete Slab Floors and Roofs

The common types of cast-in-place concrete slabs for floor and roof construction are flat plate, flat slab, one-way solid slab, two-way solid slab, one-way joists with beams, and two-way joists without beams.

Flat Plate Construction

Flat plate slabs are solid, uniform two-way reinforced slabs made without drop panels, column capitals, or interior beams or girders (Fig. 12-34). They are used in buildings having lighter loads and shorter spans such as hotels and apartment buildings. Flat slabs are reinforced in both directions. Since they are relatively thin, usually 6 to 10 in. (152 to 254 mm), they save on building height. The shearing stresses in the slab around the columns are great and

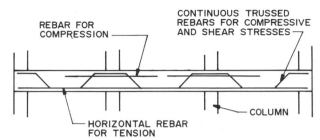

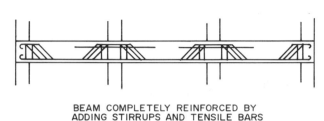

BEAM WITH REINFORCING FOR TENSION AND COMPRESSION

BEAM COMPLETELY REINFORCED BY
ADDING STIRRUPS AND TENSILE BARS

Figure 12-33. *A reinforced beam that runs continuously across several supports.*

limit the loads feasible for this type of construction. Flat plate construction usually requires larger columns than for flat slab construction.

Typical construction details for a building using flat plate construction are in Fig. 12-35. Notice the placement of ducts and electrical work between the slab and the dropped ceiling.

Flat Slab Construction

Flat slabs are solid concrete slabs cast monolithically with drop panels or column capitals (Fig. 12-36). Monolithically

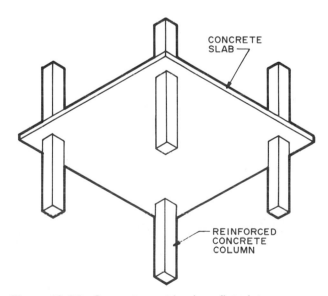

Figure 12-34. *Concrete cast-in-place flat plate construction.*

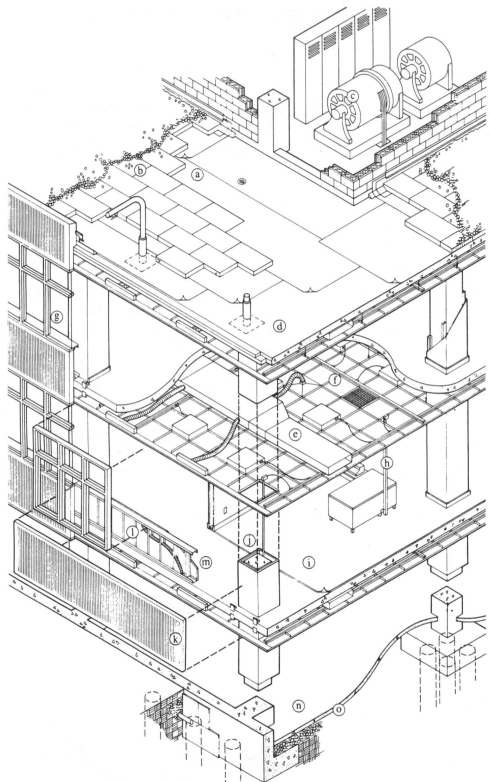

a. *Rigid insulation and ballast*
b. *Protected roof membrane*
c. *Elevator equipment*
d. *Cast-in-place concrete flat plate*
e. *Ducts and diffusers*
f. *Suspended acoustical tile ceiling*
g. *Window assembly*
h. *Power and communications poles*
i. *Carpeting*
j. *Concrete columns*
k. *Precast concrete spandrel panels*
l. *Batt insulation*
m. *Metal stud and drywall assembly*
n. *Slab on grade and concrete pile foundation*
o. *Vapor barrier*

Nearly every element in flat plate construction is integrated at a connected level, except for the interior walls and the ceiling assemblies, where mechanical and interior elements are meshed, and the roof assembly, where elements are touching but not connected. Precast concrete spandrel panels are connected to the structural concrete frame and backed up by a steel-stud and drywall assembly that also allows for a meshed level of electrical and mechanical distribution. Window assemblies connected to the concrete spandrel units complete the exterior envelope.

Figure 12-35. *A building using flat plate construction. Reproduced from "The Building Systems Integration Handbook" copyright 1986, by permission of the American Institute of Architects under license number 92053. FURTHER REPRODUCTION IS PROHIBITED.*

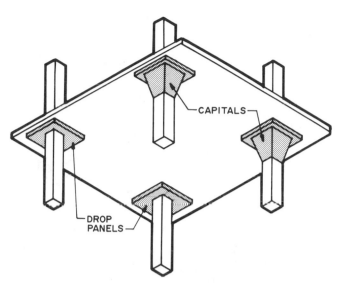

Figure 12-36. *Concrete cast-in-place flat slab construction.*

means the slab and panel or column are cast together at the same time and are a single unit. A *drop panel* is a thickened concrete area surrounding the column. A *column capital* is sloped concrete support at the top of the column used to carry shear stresses (Fig. 12-37). The slab is reinforced in two directions and transfers its loads to the columns without beams or girders. Such a slab is often called a two-way slab. Flat slabs can carry heavy loads with long spans and generally need smaller columns than flat plate slabs. They are most effective when square bays are used.

One-Way Solid Slab Construction

A one-way solid slab is constructed by monolithically casting beams, girders, and the slab (Fig. 12-38). They are used when support for heavy or concentrated loads are expected. Usually spans are less than 20 ft (6096 mm). This construction is costly to build because of the complex formwork. Generally the columns and walls are built and then the formwork for the beams, girders, and slab is constructed. The girders, beams, and slab are reinforced to handle the tension, compression, and shear stresses as well as shrinkage and temperature.

A one-way solid slab with beams and girders is shown in Fig. 12-39. This construction is used when heavy or concentrated loads are needed and wider spans than those normally provided by the design in Fig. 12-38 are required. A span of 30 ft (9149 mm) or less in square bays is generally used.

One-Way Joists with Beams

One-way concrete joist construction has a series of joists which run between beams that connect columns. The slab,

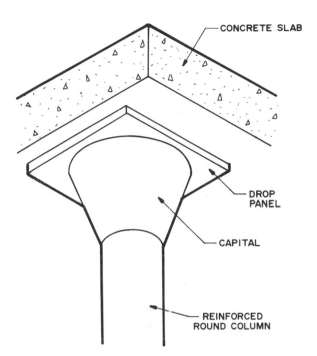

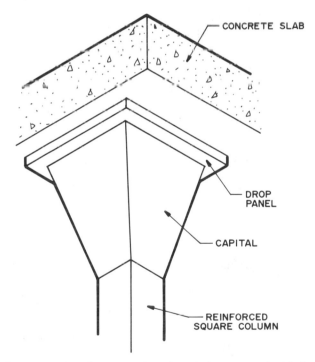

Figure 12-37. *Drop panel and capitals are used with flat plate construction.*

joists, and beams are cast monolithically (Fig. 12-40). The voids between the joists are formed with prefabricated pans. The pans are placed on a plywood deck or a wood strip deck. The joists run in one direction between beams with a distribution rib in the center (Fig. 12-41).

Generally, the pan forms selected are of sufficient depth

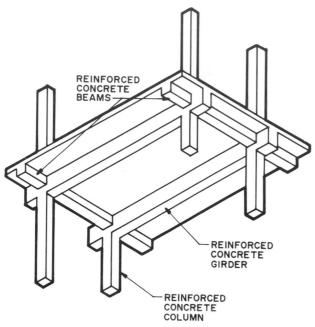

Figure 12-38. *One-way solid slab with beams construction.*

so there is a uniform dimension between beams and joists throughout the structure. The voids are usually 20 or 30 in. (508 to 762 mm) wide and in depths from 6 to 20 in. (152 to 508 mm). The pans telescope so the lengths can vary as needed.

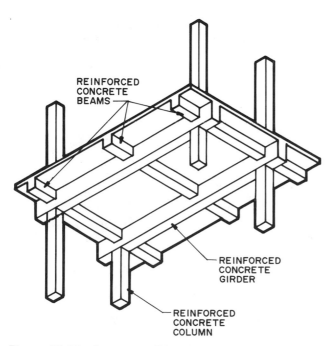

Figure 12-39. *One-way solid slab with beams and girders construction.*

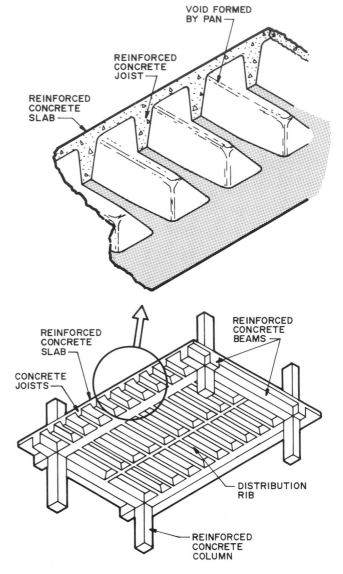

Figure 12-40. *One-way joists with beams.*

Joists are reinforced for flexure in the direction of the span. Temperature reinforcing in the slab can be welded-wire fabric or reinforcing bars.

One-way joist construction is lightweight and permits long spans and heavy loading. For a solid slab to span the same distance, it would have to be very thick and thus heavy. This joist system removes a lot of the nonworking concrete on the bottom of the slab, thus reducing weight. The bottom steel is located in the joists so they become small beams. The floor slab can be rather thin, since it only spans from joist to joist. A 4-in. (100-mm) thickness is often used. A *distribution rib* is formed perpendicular to the joists at midspan to help distribute concentrated loads to more than one joist.

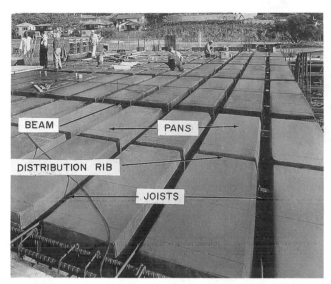

Figure 12-41. Pans and reinforcing being set in place to cast a floor using one-way joists with beams. (Courtesy of Robertson-Ceco Corporation.)

Two-Way Joists Without Beams

This type of concrete construction is often called a concrete waffle slab. It is a two-way slab with evenly spaced joists at right angles to each other. These are cast monolithically with a thin floor slab to form the structural unit (Fig. 12-42). It is built using prefabricated square domes which rest on a plywood deck (Fig. 12-43). Domes are omitted around the columns to form solid heads (Fig.

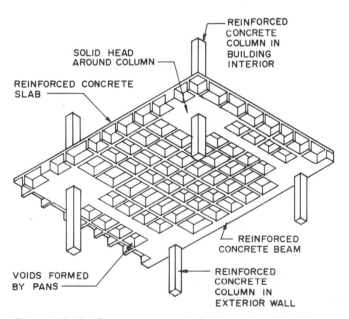

Figure 12-42. Two-way concrete joist construction (also called waffle slab construction).

12-44). Domes are 19 or 30 in. (482 to 762 mm) square and from 6 to 30 in. (152 to 762 mm) in depth. The same size dome is generally used throughout the structure because it is more economical. The joists are reinforced in flexure and the bays are kept square.

Waffle slab construction is much lighter than solid flat slab or flat plate construction. This design permits heavier loads and longer spans. The ceiling is often sprayed with acoustical plaster and left exposed. It produces a very decorative ceiling and can be effectively lighted (Fig. 12-45).

Precast Concrete Construction

Precast concrete members are those cast in separate forms, cured, removed from the form, shipped to the construction site, and set in place. While they are usually cast by a company specializing in that work and shipped to the site, they can be cast on the site if it is more economical. On the site, the completed members are lifted into place by cranes.

Members commonly produced include floor and roof slabs, wall panels, bearing walls and partitions, joists, beams, girders, columns, rigid frames, arches, domes, and piles. These can be used to construct multistory buildings.

Advantages of Precast Members

Precast concrete is generally more economical than cast-in-place concrete when many members of the same size are required. Following are typical advantages:

1. They can be cast in reusable forms, reducing forming costs.
2. The exposed surfaces can be more carefully prepared, reducing or eliminating finishing steps on the site.
3. The quality of the concrete is more carefully controlled.
4. In a casting yard, work can continue even under adverse weather conditions.
5. Members use less job site storage area because deliveries can be scheduled to keep up with the erection schedule.
6. Curing can be carefully controlled.
7. Erection can continue under conditions that would shut down a cast-in-place operation.
8. The erection time is greatly reduced.
9. Under many conditions precast is more economical.

Prestressed Concrete Members

Prestressed concrete is concrete in which internal stresses are introduced to counteract the tensile stress resulting

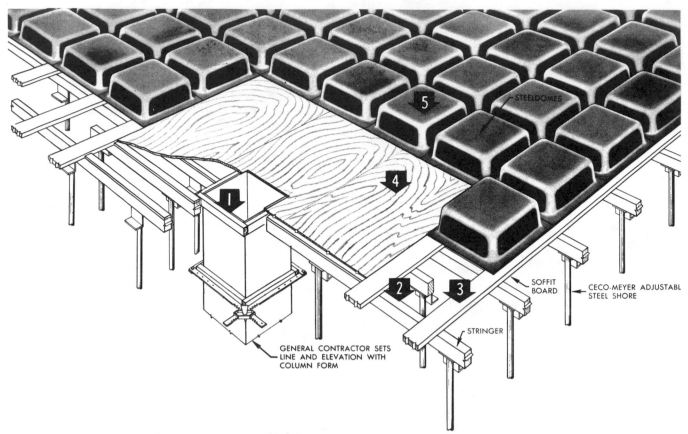

Figure 12-43. *Erection procedure for monolithic, reinforced concrete construction. (Courtesy of Robertson-Ceco Corporation.)*

1. *Forms for columns, beams, and column capitals below the joist level are put into place.*
2. *Wood stringers and metal shores are erected.*
3. *Soffit boards are placed on the stringers and spaced to support the steel forms.*
4. *Flat forms are placed for all solid areas.*
5. *Steel forms are placed and nailed to soffit boards.*
6. *Plumbing sleeves, electrical outlet boxes, and reinforcing steel and mesh are placed.*
7. *Concrete is poured over and between domes.*

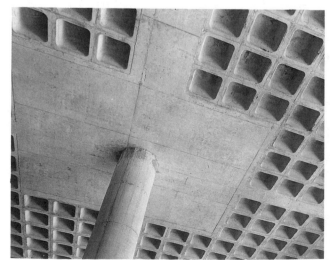

Figure 12-44. *Solid heads are formed at each column. (Courtesy of Robertson-Ceco Corporation.)*

from the loads applied to the member. Concrete members that are not prestressed are referred to as *conventionally reinforced concrete*.

Prestressed concrete members are usually precast. There are two classes, pretensioned and post-tensioned. The difference relates to when the unit is cast and prestressed.

Pretensioned members are cast in a metal form. The reinforcing tenons are placed in the form and tightened to the required tension. Other required reinforcing is also set in place. Then the concrete is poured and cured. The tenons are bonded in the concrete and will not slip.

The forms used are often several hundred feet long so more than one unit can be poured at one time. The tenons are tensioned with jacks. A bulkhead is placed in the forms between members. After the concrete has cured the bulk-

Figure 12-45. *This attractive ceiling was produced by leaving the pan indentions exposed and coating them with acoustical plaster. (Courtesy of Robertson-Ceco Corporation.)*

heads are removed and the tenons cut with a torch (Fig. 12-46).

Post-tensioned members have the tenons placed inside holes cast in the member after the concrete has cured. In some cases, flexible metal tubes are cast in the member and the tenons are placed in these. The tenons in post-tensioned concrete may be *bonded or unbonded*. If they are bonded, cement grout is forced into the space surrounding the tenon after the prestressing has been accomplished. If the tenons are to be unbonded, they are greased to reduce friction and protect them from corrosion. Then

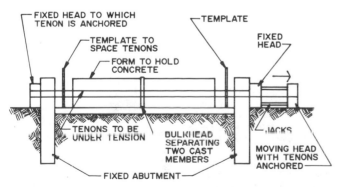

Figure 12-46. *A typical pretensioning bed used for long line casting of several members.*

they are wrapped with heavy plastic and inserted into the holes in the member.

The tenons are anchored to one end of the member and tension is applied to the tenons at the other end with jacks. When the proper tension is reached, this end is then anchored to the end of the member.

A typical post-tensioned building structure is shown in Fig. 12-47. The post-tensioned steel tenons are run through the floor slab. This is a rather dangerous on-site operation and must be accomplished with great care.

Principles of Prestressed Concrete

The lower part of a simple concrete beam is subject to tensile stresses. Since the tensile strength of concrete is low, an unreinforced concrete beam have very little flexural strength. That is why reinforcing steel is added at the lower part of concrete beams. The steel resists the tensile forces while the concrete in the lower portion provides little or no flexural strength.

When the steel tenons are subjected to tensile stresses *before* an external load is applied to the member, compressive stresses are induced in the concrete. Usually the tensile stresses induced in the concrete by an external load are offset by the compressive stresses in the concrete induced by prestressing. The concrete in this situation is

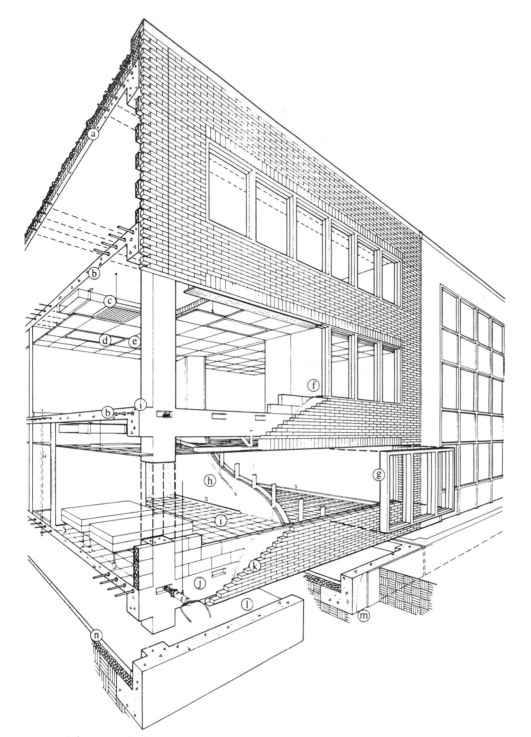

a. *Built-up roofing*
b. *Concrete slab*
c. *Ducts and diffusers*
d. *Fluorescent light fixtures*
e. *Suspended acoustical tile ceiling*
f. *Operable partitions*
g. *Window assembly*
h. *Metal stud and drywall assembly*
i. *Resilient flooring*
j. *Rigid concrete frame*
k. *Brick and concrete masonry and rigid insulation*
l. *Slab on grade and concrete foundation*
m. *Waterproofing and protective board*
n. *Vapor barrier*

Post-tension construction is a highly sensitive integration of the compressive strength of concrete with the tensile strength of steel. Systems integration is influenced greatly by the positioning of the tendons, because this determines the possible locations for through-slab penetrations. Post-tensioning allows shallower beams and slabs, reducing overall building height and permitting longer spans with thinner structural members. Most systems are integrated at the connected level, in part due to the need to maintain the structural system as a distinct element. The resultant structure is quite rigid and less subject to movement and creep than other types, making connection of the unit masonry skin appropriate. The potentially dangerous forces involved in post-tensioning require care and experience on the part of the contractor. Alterations can be difficult and must in any case preserve the integrity of the tensioning elements.

Figure 12-47. *This building uses post-tensioned construction. Reproduced from "The Building Systems Integration Handbook" copyright 1986, by permission of the American Institute of Architects under license number 92053. FURTHER REPRODUCTION IS PROHIBITED.*

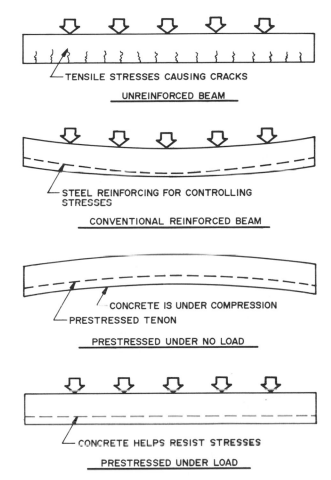

Figure 12-48. *Reinforcing steel and prestressed tenons are used to resist tensile stresses.*

helping to resist tensile forces induced by the load (Fig. 12-48).

Tenons

Tenons used in prestressing may be high-strength steel wires or high-strength alloy steel bars. Wires are formed by winding $\frac{1}{4}$-in. (6-mm) diameter wires spirally around a straight center wire forming the core. The wires may be galvanized to resist corrosion. The diameter of the wire and the number of strands varies according to the design.

High-strength steel alloy bars vary in diameter from $\frac{1}{2}$ in. (12 mm) to $1\frac{1}{8}$ in. (29 mm). These are not generally used in pretensioned members.

Since both steel and concrete creep, part of the prestressing would be lost over a period of time. If the steel bar used was the same as used for conventional reinforcing, the prestressing force would disappear almost completely. This is why it is necessary to use a special steel with a high ultimate strength, yield point, and allowable working stress.

Advantages and Disadvantages of Prestressed Members

Most prestressed members are precast and therefore have the advantages listed for precast concrete. In addition, prestressing has the following advantages and disadvantages.

Advantages

1. Produces smaller members that will carry the same loads.
2. Members have smaller deflections.
3. Members less likely to crack.
4. Supporting columns and walls can be smaller because loads are lighter.

Disadvantages

1. Members cost more to produce.
2. Not cost effective for short spans with low stresses.

Precast Joists, Beams, Girders, and Columns

Some manufacturer's produce a series of preengineered members which they keep in stock. A designer can develop a structure utilizing these units. The manufacturer can also cast any of the special designs prepared by the structural engineer.

Columns

Precast columns are very similar to cast-in-place columns. They are usually square or rectangular in section. Since they are usually under compression loads, flexural demands are small. Prestressing longitudinally can be done if they are to be under large flexural stresses. Details for column-to-column and column-to-base connections are in Fig. 12-49. These are typical of the designs used. The metal fittings are placed in the form before the concrete is poured.

Beams and Girders

The terms beams and girders are often used interchangeably. When each is used in a description those members with longer spans are called girders.

Girders are made as conventional precast and prestressed members. In cross section, they are usually an I, T, L, or rectangular shape. The I-shape is usually cast as a solid rectangle at each end (Fig. 12-50). The projecting ledgers on L-shapes and inverted T-shapes provide direct support for precast slabs. This reduces needed headroom in a building when compared to the use of rectangular

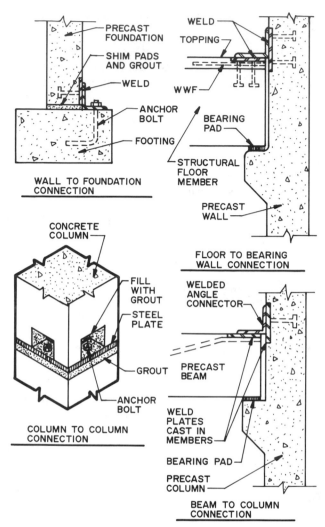

Figure 12-49. *Selected typical connection details for precast concrete structural framework.*

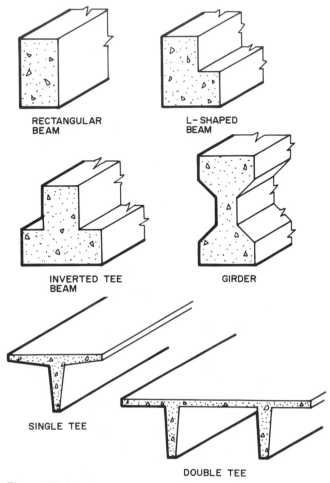

Figure 12-50. *Cross sectional shapes of precast structural members.*

beams with the slab resting on the top (Fig. 12-51). The beams may have stirrups that project above the top of the member to provide a bond to the topping, providing composite structural action (Fig. 12-52).

Beam connections are often made by welding steel plates that were cast as a part of the beam. These are *matching plates*. Sometimes plates are bolted and metal angles are used instead of plates. Beams can be joined end-to-end by welding reinforcing bars that extend beyond the end of the beam. The welded area is then filled with concrete, forming what is called a *wet joint*. Pipe sleeves or holes can be cast in a beam. These fit down over steel dowels cast in the column. The space around the dowels is filled with grout. Examples of connections are in Fig. 12-53. Examples of precast concrete columns are in Fig. 12-54.

Precast prestressed beams and columns are used in low- and high-rise structures. In some, the beams and columns are exposed to view and become an architectural feature.

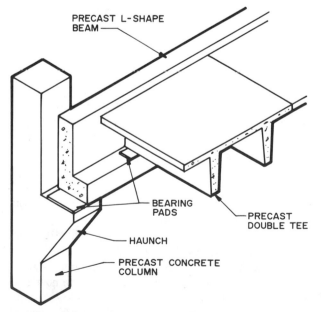

Figure 12-51. *L and inverted tee beams can save headroom when used to support precast tees for floor and roof construction.*

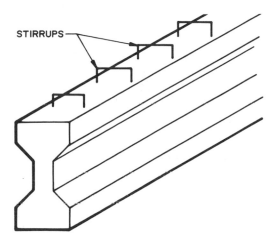

Figure 12-52. *Stirrups can extend above the beam and are bonded in the topping.*

An example of a beam-column framed building is in Fig. 12-55.

Precast Floors and Roofs

There are a number of precast concrete panels and slabs designed for use as floor and roof slabs. Common among

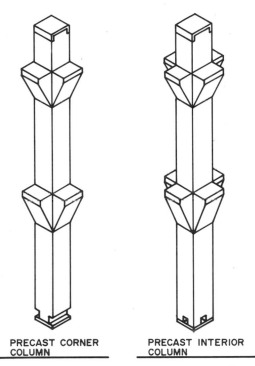

Figure 12-54. *Typical precast concrete columns.*

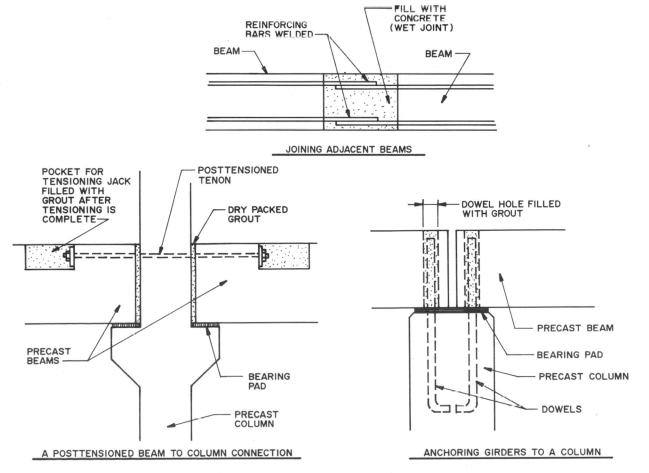

Figure 12-53. *Examples of precast beam connections.*

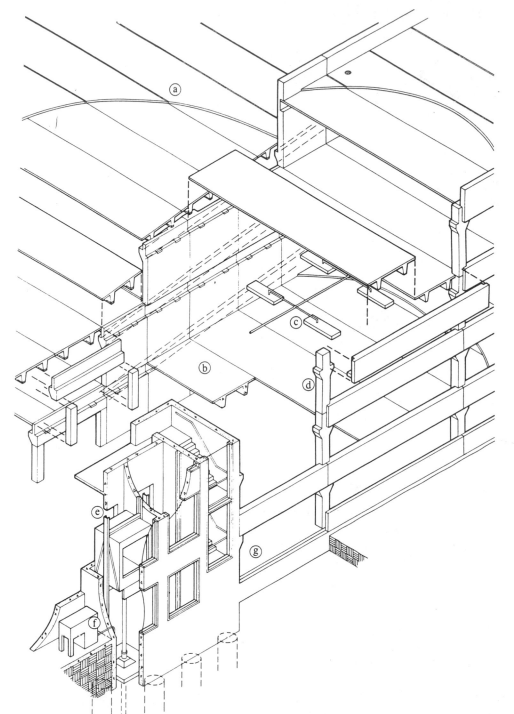

a. Concrete topping
b. Precast prestressed
   concrete double T's
c. Fluorescent light
   fixtures
d. Precast concrete
   columns and spandrel
   beams
e. Elevator and stair core
f. Hydraulic elevator and
   elevator equipment
g. Slab on grade and cast-
   in-place concrete
   piles

Use of a precast concrete frame for an un-enclosed parking facility results in structural, envelope, and interior systems that are unified. Off-site precasting can conserve time and materials for concrete forming, and on-site erection time is considerably faster in comparison with cast-in-place construction. The visible building materials are of one basic kind, thus also leading to natural visible integration. Some mechanical and interior elements are integrated at the connected level (as in the case of curbs, handrails, and signs), but power distribution lines are meshed with the upper surface of the precast floor T's and the concrete topping, as are pipes for surface drainage and supply of fire-sprinkler heads. The site-poured concrete floor topping provides a smooth, tightly sealed surface. The adjacent stairway and elevator envelopes integrate security and life safety considerations with requirements for impermeability to weather, by providing transparent insulated glass viewing panels toward the outside. The cast-in-place walls for these circulation elements also provide lateral stability to the frame.

Figure 12-55. A typical beam–column framed structure using precast prestressed members. Reproduced from ''The Building Systems Integration Handbook'' copyright 1986, by permission of the American Institute of Architects under license number 92053. FURTHER REPRODUCTION IS PROHIBITED.

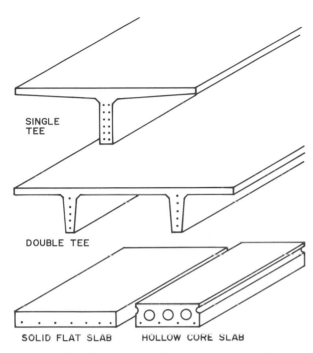

Figure 12-56. *Major types of precast concrete floor and roof construction.*

Figure 12-57. *Prestressed hollow core slabs being installed for floor and roof decking. (Courtesy of the Prestressed Concrete Institute.)*

these are solid flat slabs, hollow core slabs, single tees, double tees, and channels (Fig. 12-56).

Precast floor and roof members can be supported by masonry walls, steel framework, cast-in-place, or precast framework or precast load-bearing walls.

Solid flat slabs are used for short spans requiring minimum depth. Depths of 4 to 16 in. (102 to 152 mm) are common. Some designs require a concrete topping. Spans range from 12 to 24 ft (3660 to 7320 mm) depending upon the thickness and superimposed load.

Hollow core slabs are used for intermediate length spans ranging from 12 to 40 ft (3660 to 12 200 mm). The voids in the center remove areas of concrete that add little to the strength. The voids do help reduce the weight and provide channels to run wiring and plumbing. These are precast pretensioned units (Fig. 12-57).

Single tees and *double tees* are used to span long distances ranging up to 100 ft (30 500 mm) and more. The voids in the concrete forming the tee remove nonworking concrete and reduce space. These are precast pretensioned units.

Generally these all are cast with a rough surface so a concrete topping can be poured on them. The topping is finished to the desired smooth surface. The topping is usually 2 in. (50 mm) thick. When it bonds to the precast members, it adds to the structural integrity of the floor or roof. Since it ties the individual members together, they act as a single structural unit. The topping also provides the opportunity to level the floor and conceal any camber in the prestressed members. Reinforcing bars can be cast

in the topping over the supporting beams and walls. Electrical conduits can be placed on the precast members and covered with the topping.

These are usually joined to beams and girders by welding metal plates cast in the units using dowels or reinforcing rods. Typical connection details are in Fig. 12-58.

These members are cast from normal density concrete or structural lightweight concrete. While lightweight concrete reduces the load on the structure and footings, it is more expensive.

A structural use of precast prestressed exterior and interior load-bearing walls is shown in Fig. 12-59. The transverse load-bearing walls can resist lateral forces and support the floors and roof. The floors and roof are often precast prestressed hollow core planks. The mass production of the repetitive units lowers the cost and speeds construction.

Precast Walls and Partitions

Precast walls and partitions can be load or nonload bearing. Typically these are *solid reinforced slabs* 5 to 8 in.

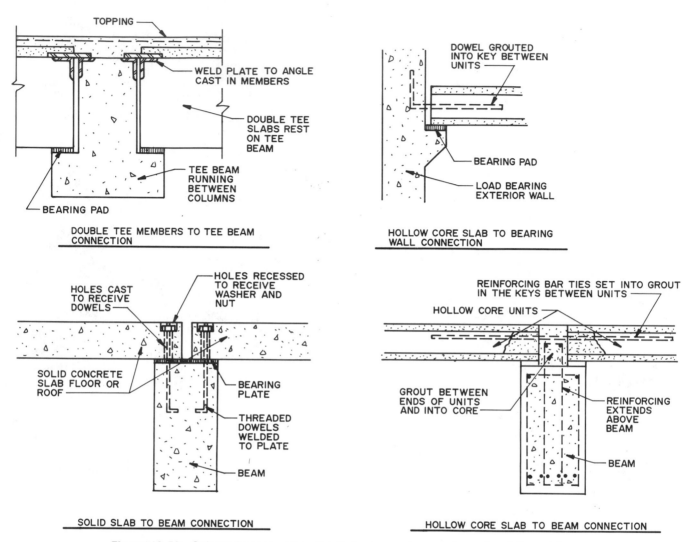

Figure 12-58. *Selected construction details for precast concrete roof and floor slabs.*

(127 to 203 mm) thick that are cast in a horizontal position. They are lifted by cranes to a vertical position and set in place. Door and window openings can be cast in them. Extra reinforcement is placed around the openings (Fig. 12-60).

Sandwich panels are cast for use as exterior nonload bearing walls. They have a core of insulation, usually rigid foam sheets. The two concrete faces are tied together with metal ties (Fig. 12-61).

Precast curtain-wall panels are normally cast in sizes from 20 to 60 ft^2 (1.8 to 5.5 m^2) and from 2 in. (51 mm) thick. If larger units are cast, the thickness and reinforcement must be increased. These panels are cast in mold boxes and reinforced with galvanized, welded wire fabric. These panels are designed to be used in a vertical position and are stored, transported, and hoisted in this position.

Precast curtain-wall panels are mechanically fastened to the structural framework. One system has metal brackets cast into the back of the panel. The brackets can be bolted to a steel framework or have a metal pin set in the mortar joint in a masonry wall (Fig. 12-62).

Precast channels and double tees can be placed vertically to form load-bearing walls. If they are supported in their height and are nonload bearing such as by a second or third floor, they can extend 50 ft (15 250 mm) or more in height (Fig. 12-63).

Tilt-up construction is a technique where walls are cast on the site in a horizontal position, raised to a vertical position, set in place, and secured to form a load-bearing wall. They are economical to build and erect and enable a building to be enclosed very rapidly. While their greatest use is on one-story buildings, they can be used on multi-story designs (Fig. 12-64).

The panels must be carefully designed to carry the im-

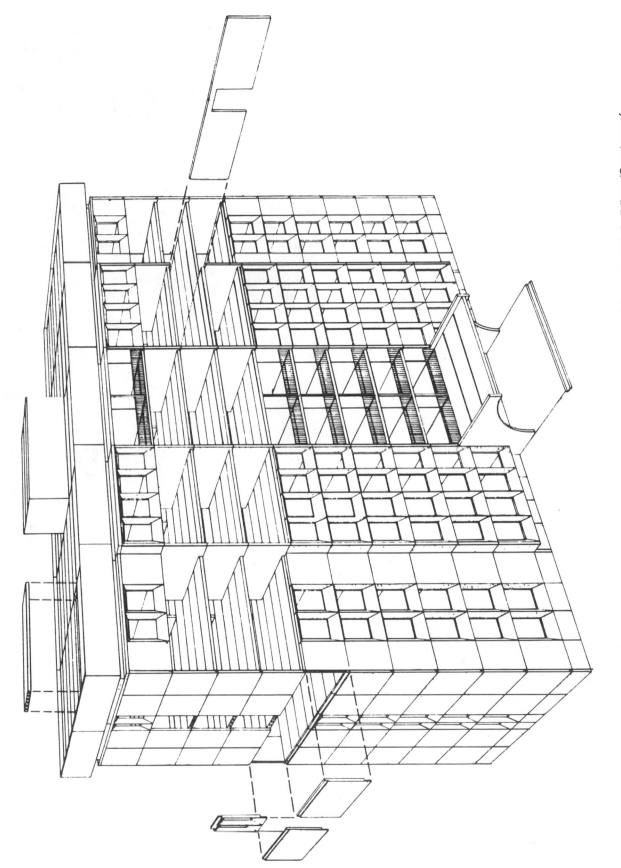

Figure 12-59. Precast prestressed exterior and interior wall units provide the structural frame for this building. (Courtesy of the Precast Prestressed Concrete Institute.)

Figure 12-60. *Precast walls with openings are set in place with a crane. (Courtesy of Precast Prestressed Concrete Institute.)*

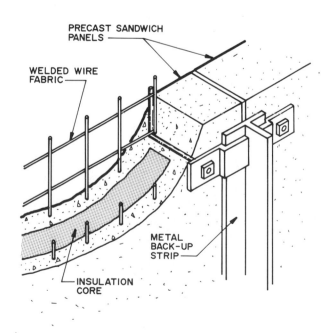

Figure 12-61. *Precast sandwich panels are tied together with metal back-up strips.*

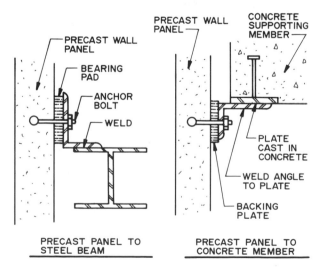

Figure 12-62. *Typical details for fastening precast wall panels to the structure.*

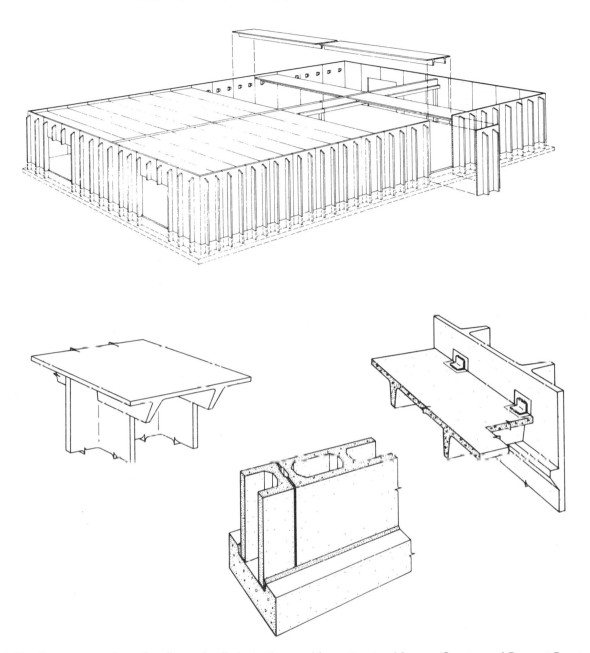

Figure 12-63. *Precast prestressed wall panels eliminate the need for a structural frame. (Courtesy of Precast Prestressed Concrete Institute.)*

posed loads as well as the stresses created when they are lifted. The panels can be load bearing or nonload bearing. They can be set on a continuous foundation or on column footings.

The design must include the location of the points on the panel where it will be lifted. The method of attaching the lifting equipment must be known so stresses can be determined.

Typical designs for roof connections to the panel are in Fig. 12-65.

Typical joints between panels and columns are shown in Fig. 12-66. After the tilt-up panels are in vertical position, the needed columns are formed and poured. The reinforcing is extended beyond the end of each panel and into the space for the column. Panels are always bonded to corner columns. At intermediate columns, the reinforcement is wrapped to prevent it from bonding to the column. This allows for expansion and contraction. Exceptions to this occur in areas where earthquakes occur.

Joints where two panels meet have some form of keyed shape. The exposed corner is molded to form an exposed V-shape.

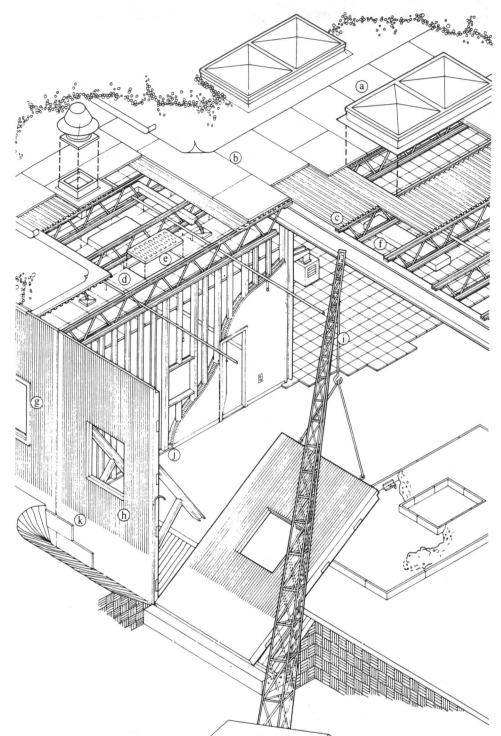

a. *Skylights*
b. *Built-up roofing and rigid insulation*
c. *Steel deck and open web steel joists*
d. *Suspended acoustical tile ceiling*
e. *Radiant heat panels*
f. *Fluorescent lighting*
g. *Window assembly*
h. *Precast concrete panels*
i. *Resilient tile flooring*
j. *Slab on grade and concrete footing*
k. *Dampproofing and protective board*

The wall panels in tilt-up construction unify the envelope, structural, and interior systems. The site-cast panels are the load-bearing elements for the roof members, and provide both interior and exterior finish. These properties and the use of repetitive wall modules offer major advantages in the conservation of time and materials. In the enclosed office area, the mechanical and interior systems are meshed. The suspended ceiling panels incorporate radiant heat panels while duct-work for cooling and ventilation air is threaded through the open-web bar joists. In the open area, gas-fired heating units are suspended from columns and the structure is left exposed. The floor slab, which also integrates envelope and structure at a unified level, serves as a casting surface for the tilt-up wall elements. It is held away from the edge of the building to aid in tilting operations and to permit backfilling of earth against the base of the panel below grade.

Figure 12-64. Tilt-up wall panels are cast horizontally on the job and raised into position with a crane. Reproduced from "The Building Systems Integration Handbook" copyright 1986, by permission of the American Institute of Architects under license number 92053. *FURTHER REPRODUCTION IS PROHIBITED.*

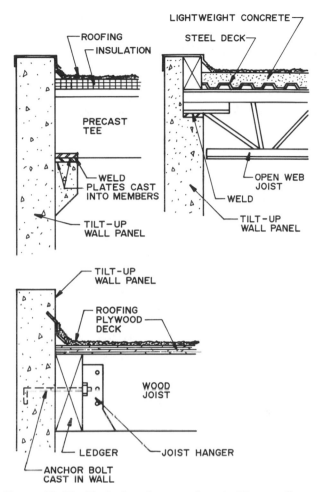

Figure 12-65. *Typical roof connections to tilt-up wall panels.*

Other Precast Units

There are many other types of precast concrete members. Among these are rigid frames, arches, and shell structures.

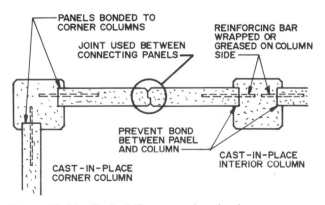

Figure 12-66. *Typical tilt-up panel and column connections.*

Precast Concrete Rigid Frames

Rigid frames are designed to carry all the roof loads through to the foundation. They are in effect a column and rafter type structure. The exterior walls are nonload bearing.

The vertical members of rigid frames are called *legs* and the top members *rafters*. The part of the frame where the leg and rafter meet is called the *haunch* or *knee*. The center of the frame at its top is called the *crown* (Fig. 12-67).

Rigid frames can be designed as single and multiple span units. A variety of roof designs are common. They can have the rafter extended beyond the leg to form a large *canopy*. Rigid frames are excellent for buildings where large open floor areas and high ceiling heights are required.

It is generally necessary to run steel ties under the floor from one leg to the other. These are usually necessary to carry the horizontal thrust exerted on the legs at the foundation.

Arches

Arches are used to cover buildings requiring large open areas. The distance covered by the arch is called the *span*.

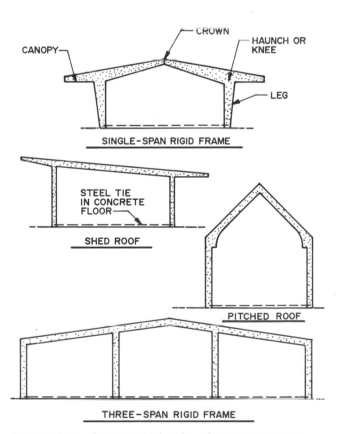

Figure 12-67. *Some typical styles of precast concrete rigid frames.*

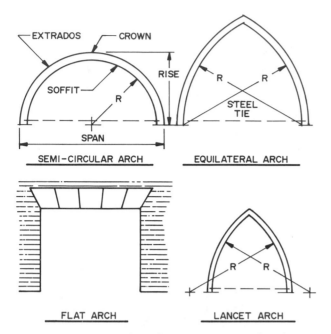

Figure 12-68. *A few of the many types of arches.*

The maximum height of the arch is called the *rise*. The underside of the arch is the *soffit* and the exterior curve of the visible face of the arch is the *extrados*. The highest point in the arch is the *crown* (Fig. 12-68).

An arch can be supported in several ways (Fig. 12-69). A frequently used method of support is to use piers on each end. Usually under these conditions a tie under the floor is required to control horizontal thrust at each end of the arch. It is possible to support the ends of the arch with massive rigid abutments. When arches are supported on

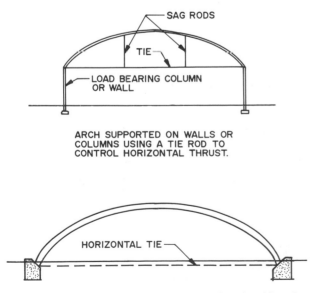

Figure 12-69. *Arches can be supported on load-bearing walls, columns, or large concrete piers.*

walls or columns, a tie is run across the span to control horizontal thrust. Vertical sag rods connect the arch and the tie rod.

Precast Concrete Shell Construction

The folded plate and the barrel shell roofs are the two most common types of shell roofs. They develop their stiffness from the folding of the plate or the arch of the barrel shell. This rigidity makes it possible to keep the concrete thickness to a minimum. These forms may be reinforced when cast or utilize post-tensioning techniques to resist the tensile forces (Fig. 12-70).

Heavy Timber Construction

The large timbers used in heavy timber construction are able to absorb heat and are therefore slower to catch fire than small wood members. When a building fire occurs, the beams will char. The char tends to protect the undamaged wood from the fire, thus reducing its burning potential. Charred timbers will support a load long after steel members subjected to the same fire would have collapsed. Often a charred member does not have to be replaced be-

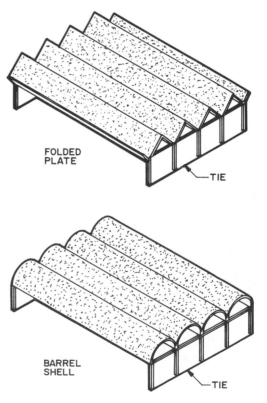

Figure 12-70. *Two frequently used precast concrete shell structures.*

cause the remaining undamaged section is adequate to carry the load. Both solid wood and glued laminated structural timbers provide excellent structural support during fires.

Heavy timber construction requires that the exterior walls be constructed of noncombustible materials and have a fire rating of 2 hr or more. Wood structural members may be solid wood or structural glued-laminated timber. Laminated members are stronger and more dimensionally stable than sawn wood. They are manufactured in a wide range of sizes and shapes and can carry predetermined loads over known distances.

Columns are usually required to be at least 8 in. (203 mm) in the smallest dimension when supporting roof or floor loads. *Floor beams* and *girders* should be at least 6 in. (152 mm) in width and 10 in. (254 mm) in depth. Any *trusses* supporting floor loads must have members at least 8 in. (203 mm) in the smallest dimension.

Timber *arches* or *rigid frames* for roof construction which connect to foundations at the floor line must have members at least 6 in. (152 mm) and width 8 in. (203 mm) in depth in the lower half and not less than 6 in. (152 mm) in the upper half. Arches resting on the tops of walls can have 4 in. (102 mm) by 6 in. (152 mm) minimum size members.

Floors must be tongue-and-groove or splined planks at least 3 in. (76 mm) thick. They are sometimes covered with 1 in. (25 mm) tongue-and-groove flooring laid crosswise or on a diagonal or covered with $\frac{1}{2}$-in. (13-mm) plywood.

Roof decks must be at least 2-in. (51-mm) thick tongue-and-groove or splined planks. They may also be $1\frac{1}{8}$-in. (28-mm) thick plywood with exterior glue. Generally the inside of the roof deck is exposed to view. This means that insulation must be placed on the outside. Rigid insulation is usually used. If the roof is flat it can be finished as discussed for flat roofs later in this chapter. If it is sloped, a nailing deck of plywood must be installed over the insulation so shingles can be installed.

Interior partitions may be of solid wood construction containing at least two layers of 1-in. (25-mm) boards or of laminate construction of 4-in. (102-mm) thickness or other construction having a 1-hr fire rating.

The framework for a typical heavy timber building using solid wood members is in Fig. 12-71.

Building codes specify the required construction details. They require the use of approved wall plate boxes or hangers where wood members rest on concrete or masonry walls. At least 1-in. (25-mm) air space should be left on all sides of the beam on masonry walls to avoid decay. If the beam is pressure treated to resist decay this is sometimes not required by code.

One way to anchor wood beams to masonry or concrete is to use steel beam boxes (Fig. 12-72). Notice the end of

the beam is cut on an angle. This is called a fire-cut. If during a fire the beam fails and falls to the ground, the beam will not bring down the exterior masonry wall (Fig. 12-73).

Solid wood beams rest on top of wood columns. In traditional construction, a malleable iron or steel cap is placed on top of the column. Another design uses bearing blocks and split ring connectors (Fig. 12-74). A *split ring connector* is a round steel ring that is set into circular grooves cut into the two parts to be joined. Half the ring goes into each part and a bolt runs through the center (Fig. 12-75).

Wood trusses also find considerable use in heavy timber construction. Split ring connectors are used to transmit the loads between the overlapping truss members. Notice the use of a long anchor strap on the exterior wall. This permits the weight of the masonry above the anchor bolts to be used to resist wind uplift forces on the roof (Fig. 12-76). Another design using steel rod tension cords is in Fig. 12-77. This is not used in areas with high winds that would cause forces to reverse tensions in the rods.

Glued-Laminated Construction

Glued-laminated members are made by bonding carefully selected and machined wood laminations. This produces a stress-rated product suitable for a wide range of structural applications. Typical products include beams, girders, rigid frames, arches, and domes (Fig. 12-78). Commonly manufactured glued-laminated beams are shown in Fig. 12-79. These are often referred to as glulam members. The beam names describe the top and bottom surfaces of the beam. The words before the dash describe the top surface and those following the dash the bottom surface. The "S" refers to sawed surfaces.

A major consideration is the connections between wood members. The connections shown in the next several illustrations are designed for use with structural glued-laminated timber. The designer must consider the design of connections, vertical and horizontal forces, shear, and the prevention of rotation of the member. These are generic examples and the actual quantities and sizes of bolts and other connectors will depend upon the loads and forces that exist.

Typical *beam to foundation* connections are shown in Fig. 12-80. When vertical and horizontal forces are a major consideration, anchor clips containing two or more bolts are used. *Column to foundation* connections are in Fig. 12-81. Notice the use of heavy steel angle clips and several bolts to resist the horizontal and vertical forces. It is recommended the column sit upon a steel bearing plate. Column-bearing elevation should be a minimum of 3 in. above grade or above the finished floor. *Girder and beam*

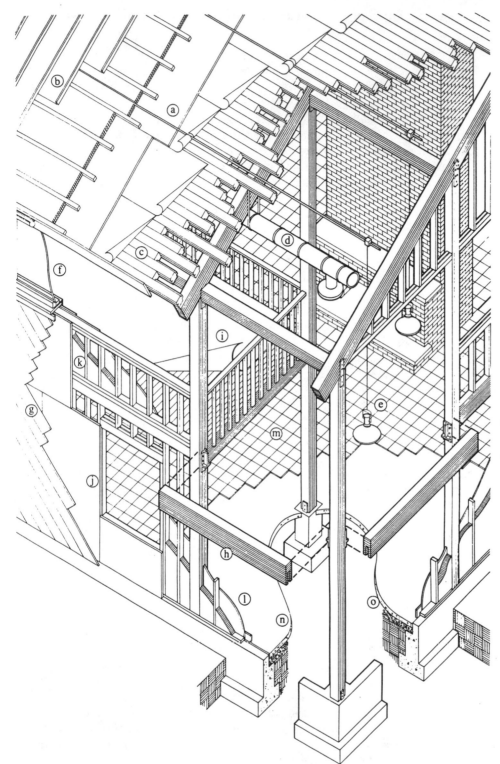

a. *Electrical conduit*
b. *Roofing*
   - *Standing seam roof*
   - *Roofing felt*
   - *Rigid insulation*
c. *Plywood sheathing and wood roof and tongue-and-groove wood decking*
d. *Ducts*
e. *Incandescent light fixture*
f. *Window assembly*
g. *Wood siding*
h. *Glued laminated wood frame*
i. *Carpeting*
j. *Exposed wood frame and plywood sheathing*
k. *Batt insulation*
l. *Drywall*
m. *Clay tile flooring*
n. *Slab on grade and concrete foundation*
o. *Vapor barrier*

Structure and interior are unified in post and beam construction. Because the structural elements in this system are exposed to view in the finished building, as are portions of the mechanical system, care is required in the visible integration of these components and in the design and appearance of hardware used for joinery of the wood members. Certain parts of the mechanical system can be meshed within interior partitions and exterior walls, leaving them concealed. The sizing of structural members and joinery details may be influenced more by considerations of visual proportion and appearance than strictly by the loading and stress conditions involved.

Figure 12-71. *Heavy timber post and beam construction is used on the multistory building. Reproduced from "The Building Systems Integration Handbook" copyright 1986, by permission of the American Institute of Architects under license number 92053. FURTHER REPRODUCTION IS PROHIBITED.*

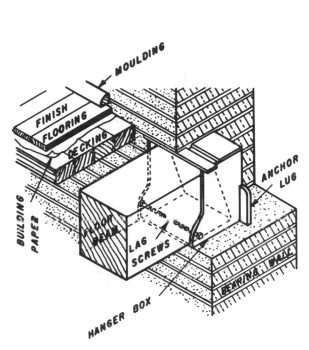

Figure 12-72. *Wood beams can be anchored to masonry walls with a metal hanger box. (Courtesy of National Forest Products Association.)*

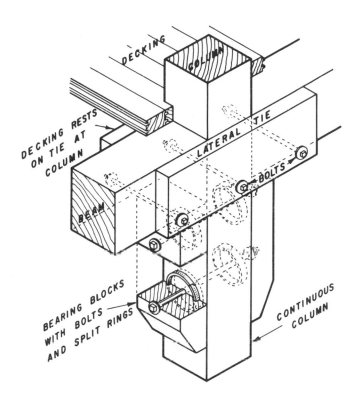

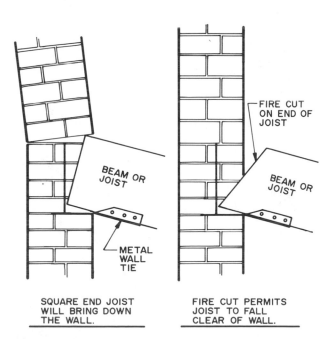

Figure 12-73. *When a timber beam or joist burns through it will most likely bring down the masonry wall unless it has a fire cut on the end.*

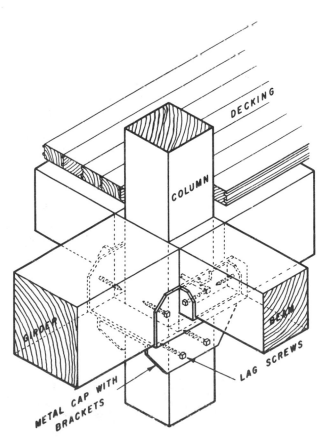

Figure 12-74. *Typical heavy timber floor beams and column framing details. (Courtesy of National Forest Products Association.)*

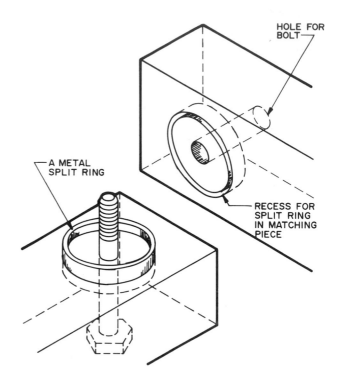

Figure 12-75. *A metal split ring is set half of its width into mating members and secured with a bolt.*

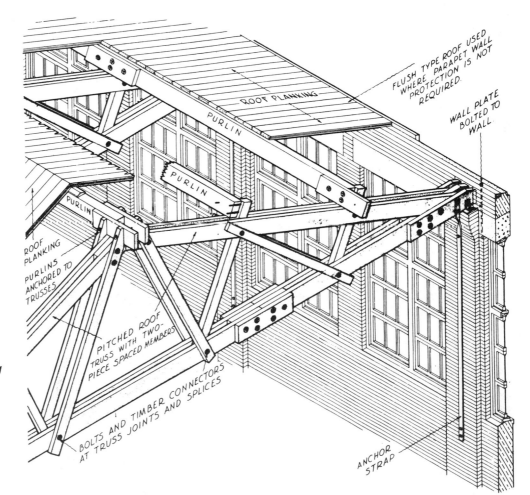

Figure 12-76. *This is a heavy timber roof truss using double members. Split ring connectors are used to transmit the loads between joining members. Trusses of this type with single members are also used. (Courtesy of National Forest Products Association.)*

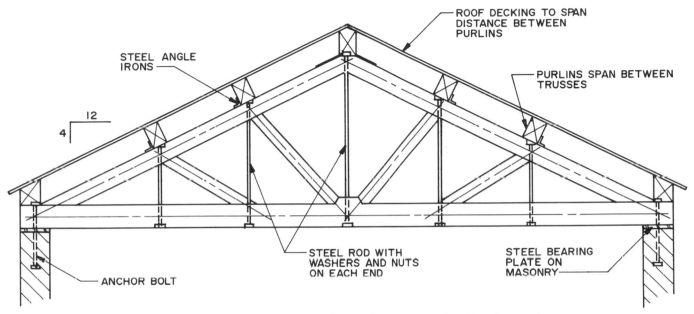

Figure 12-77. *A heavy timber roof truss that uses steel rod tension cords.*

Figure 12-78. *These glued laminated rigid frames and connecting purlins can span long distances. (Courtesy of American Institute of Timber Construction.)*

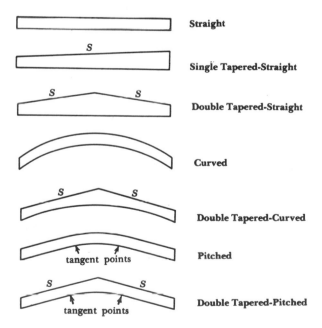

Figure 12-79. *Types of glued-laminated beams. (Courtesy of American Institute of Timber Construction.)*

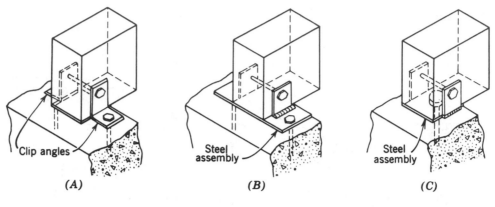

BEAM ANCHORAGES

Figure 12-80. Selected glued-laminated beam to foundation connections. (Courtesy of American Institute of Timber Construction.)

to column connections are in Fig. 12-82. Notice the use of shear plates and pins and steel straps to resist uplift forces.

Roof decking cannot span the long distances between glued-laminated beams so purlins are run between them to support the deck. Also two beams often must be connected. Several *beam to purlin and beam to beam* connection methods are shown in Fig. 12-83. The top of the purlin can be set flush with the beam because the wood members are seasoned. If not seasoned, the purlin must be set above the surface of the beam an amount shown on the drawing. The saddle type connector is used for moderate and heavy loads. These metal connectors can be used to join two beams or a beam and a purlin.

Extensive use of metal hangers provides for easy assembly and prevents rotation of the member. In some cases, consideration for the protection of timber from weathering, decay, and insect attack is necessary. This includes the use of waterproof adhesives on sections exposed to the weather. Metal connectors must be protected from corrosion.

Several building systems utilizing glued-laminated timber are shown in Fig. 12-84. These include using 2-in. (50-mm) decking or plywood sheathing over a system of beams and purlins, heavy decking over laminated beams, and using one and two-sided stressed skin panels.

Several types of arches are built from glued-laminated timber (Fig. 12-85). These are engineered to carry known roof loads over wide distances and provide an attractive interior ceiling.

Selected details for arches are shown in Fig. 12-86. Glued-laminated wood arches can be mounted on steel, masonry, or concrete foundations. Steel shoes are se-

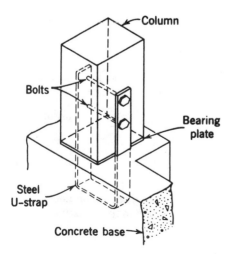

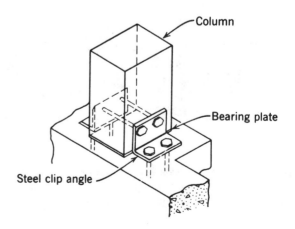

Figure 12-81. Selected glued-laminated column to foundation connections. (Courtesy of American Institute of Timber Construction.)

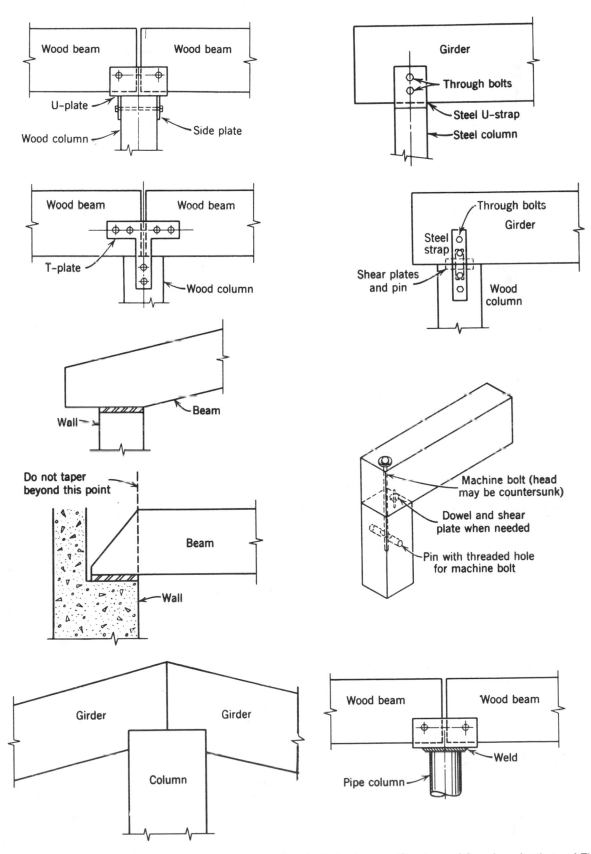

Figure 12-82. *Typical girder and beam connections to wood and steel columns. (Courtesy of American Institute of Timber Construction.)*

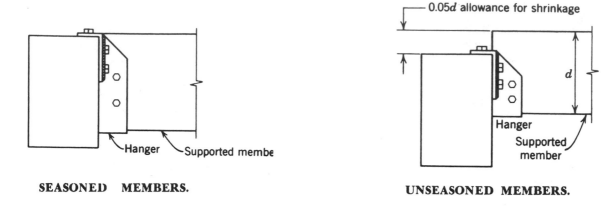

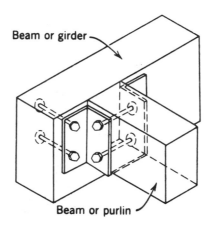

SADDLE TYPE.

Figure 12-83. *Several ways for connecting beams to beams and purlins to beams. (Courtesy of American Institute of Timber Construction.)*

cured to the foundation and the leg of the arch is bolted in place. A metal tie rod is run across the building to control horizontal forces. Several designs showing wall construction are in Fig. 12-87. Flat and sloped roof beam construction is in Fig. 12-88.

Exterior Walls

Exterior walls may be load bearing or nonload bearing. The type used depends upon the structural design of the building. If a structural steel, heavy timber, or concrete structural frame is built, the exterior walls must only enclose the space and protect the interior of the building. If they are load bearing, they must carry roof, floor, snow, wind, and other loads to be transferred to the foundation. There are many types of exterior walls used in commercial construction.

Curtain Walls

Curtain walls form the exterior surface of a building and carry no loads except their own weight. They are fastened to the structural frame and serve to keep out the rain, heat, cold, and wind. They must be watertight and resist deterioration due to exposure to the weather. They consist of panels designed to carry their own weight and resist other forces, as wind, to which they may be subjected. They may be solid panels or contain doors, windows, and other openings. They are available in a wide variety of stock sizes and materials and can be custom-made to meet special design requirements (Fig. 12-89).

Panels are covered with many different facing materials. Commonly used facings include glass, porcelain over steel or aluminum sheet, ceramic tile, thin layers of precast concrete, and plastic-coated inorganic sheets (Fig. 12-90).

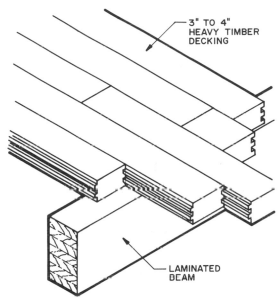

HEAVY TIMBER DECKING ON A LAMINATED BEAM SYSTEM.

Heavy timber decking either laminated or solid 3 or 4 in. nominal thickness is nailed directly to the main laminated beams. The economical span range for the heavy timber decking is 8 to 20 ft depending upon the thickness and loading conditions.

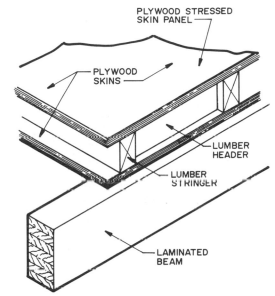

STRESSED SKIN PANELS ON LAMINATED BEAM SYSTEM,

Stressed skin panels, which have a practical span range of 32 ft, are fastened directly to the main laminated timber beams by lag screws or gutter spikes.

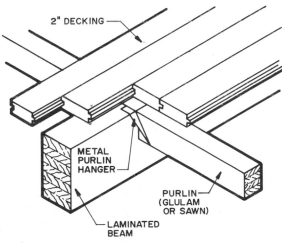

TWO-INCH DECKING ON A LAMINATED BEAM AND PURLIN SYSTEM.

Two-inch nominal thickness decking with an economical span range of 6 to 12 ft is nailed directly to glulam or sawed wood roof purlins, typically on 8 ft centers. Purlins are connected to the main laminated timber beams by metal purlin hangers.

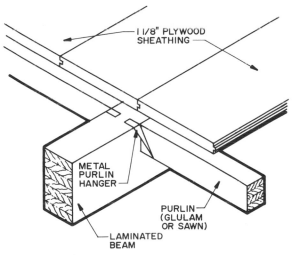

ONE AND ONE-EIGHTH-INCH PLYWOOD ON A LAMINATED BEAM AND PURLIN SYSTEM.

Figure 12-84. *Typical building systems using glued-laminated structural members and heavy timber decking or stress skin panes. (Courtesy American Institute of Timber Construction.)*

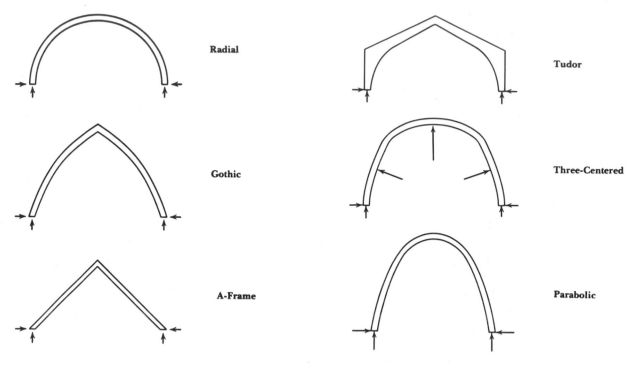

Figure 12-85. *Glued, laminated arches. (Courtesy of American Institute of Timber Construction.)*

Metal Curtain Walls

Metal curtain walls are an assembly of several different materials. The *supporting framework* of horizontal and vertical mullions is usually aluminum protected with an anodic coating. Stainless steel, carbon steel, and bronze are also used.

The *metal curtain wall panels* are an assembly of an interior and exterior skin, insulation, and the necessary structural framework within the panel. Most are laminated panels and the layers are bonded with adhesives. Laminated metal panels have cores of aluminum honeycomb, polystyrene, polyurethane, or foamed glass. Vapor barriers are often placed on the warm side of the panel.

There are three basic types of metal curtain walls—commerical, industrial, and custom. *Commercial* walls are assembled from standard parts produced by a manufacturer. These can be assembled according to stock designs or special designs prepared by the architect. The system involves the use of a structural framework which is secured to the framework of the building. The vertical and horizontal mullions are clearly visible and are a part of the overall design of the wall system. The preassembled panels are fastened to the supporting framework (Fig. 12-91). Commercial curtain walls are generally used for one- and two-story buildings, such as offices and schools. The panels have both interior and exterior finished surfaces and an insulated core.

The *industrial* type has completely assembled panels which may extend the height of the building (Fig. 12-91). They are preformed metal sheets (ribbed or fluted) which are made in stock sizes. They may or may not be insulated or have a finished interior side and can contain stock doors and windows. They are generally used for large, low-cost buildings such as those needed for factories and warehouses (Fig. 12-92).

Custom type curtain walls are those designed specifically for a building. The mullions, panels, windows, and doors are built to the specifications of the architect. Many parts are custom produced for this one project. These are usually used on multistory buildings and often set new directions in architectural design. The vertical and horizontal mullions often are an important part of the design.

Anchors are designed to support the curtain wall panels where they contact the structural frame. These are usually galvanized or bonderized to protect against corrosion.

Sealants are used to close the joints between panels and panels and the frame. They are a critical element, because moisture must be repelled. Moisture inside a panel ruins the insulation and could seep into the building. Freezing and thawing of moisture in a panel can cause considerable damage.

Precast Concrete Curtain Walls

These are discussed earlier in this chapter under precast concrete. They are made from lightweight concrete which reduces the weight and improves their heat insulation

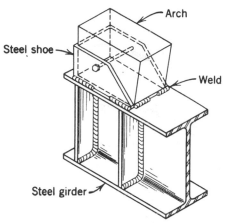

ARCH ANCHORAGE TO STEEL GIRDER. Vertical uplift load and thrust are taken through the weld.

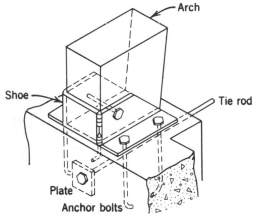

TIE ROD IN CONCRETE. Thrust is taken by anchor bolts in shear into the concrete foundation and tie rod.

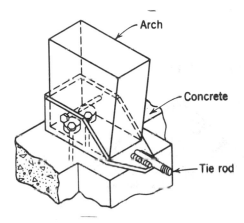

TIE ROD TO ARCH SHOE. Thrust due to vertical load is taken directly by the tie rod welded to the arch shoe.

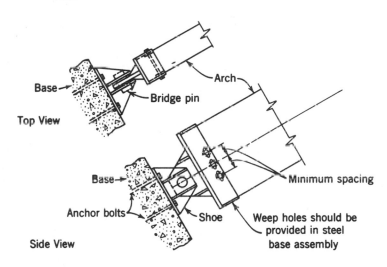

TRUE HINGE ANCHORAGE FOR ARCHES.

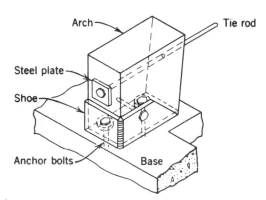

TIE ROD TO ARCH. Thrust due to vertical load is taken directly by the tie rod.

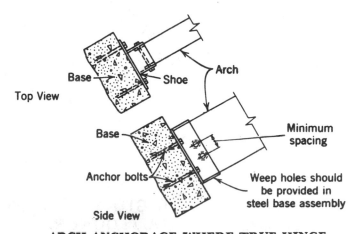

ARCH ANCHORAGE WHERE TRUE HINGE IS NOT REQUIRED.

Figure 12-86. *Construction details for glued, laminated timber arches. (Courtesy of American Institute of Timber Construction.)*

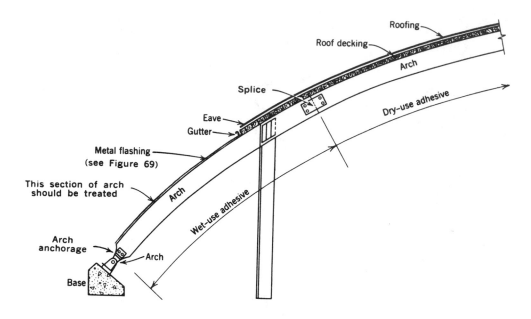

PARTIALLY EXPOSED ARCH.

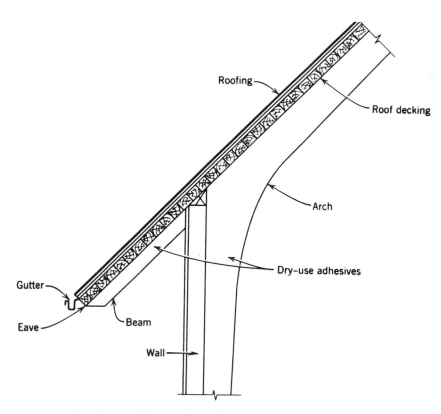

RIGID FRAME WITH PROTECTED OUTLOOKER.

Figure 12-87. *Wall and roof construction details when using structural glued-laminated timber arches and rigid frames. (Courtesy of American Institute of Timber Construction.)*

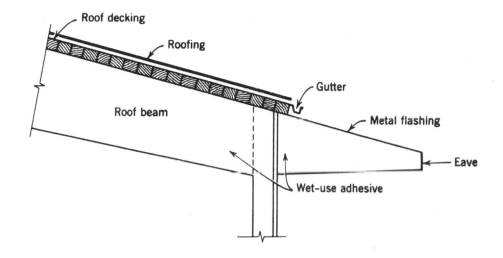

BUILDING WITH UNCOVERED OVERHANG.

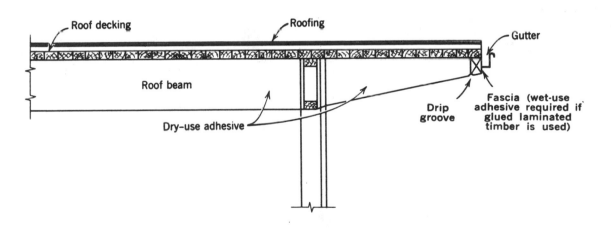

BUILDING WITH COVERED OVERHANG.

Figure 12-88. *Construction details when using structural glued-laminated timbers for flat and sloped roofs. (Courtesy of American Institute of Timber Construction.)*

Figure 12-89. *These walls were built using factory manufactured wall system panels. (Courtesy of Dale/Incor, Inc.)*

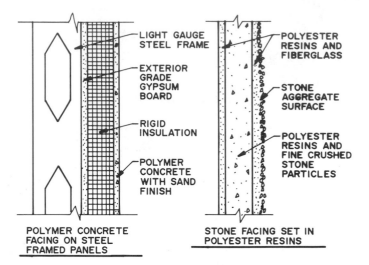

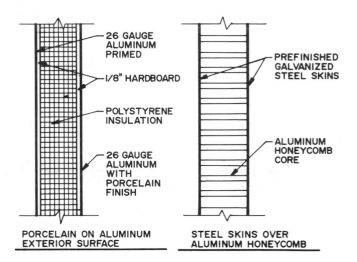

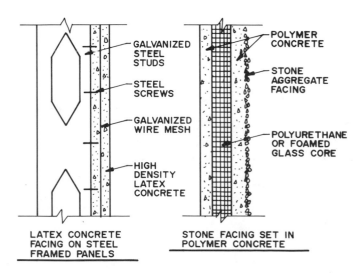

Figure 12-90. *A few examples of panels used in curtain wall construction.*

properties. The facings on the panels can be made from many materials. Typically they have exposed aggregate finish. The aggregate used includes quartz, gravel, marble, and granite. Tile can be cemented to the panel to form a finish. The panel surface can have some of the mortar brushed away, producing a rough surface or it can be ground smooth.

Panels are usually cast square or rectangular but any desired shape can be produced. Insulation qualities can be improved by plastering the interior face with vermiculite or perlite plastic.

Precast tilt-up wall panels are discussed earlier in this chapter.

Solid Masonry Walls

Walls of this type are discussed in Chapter 11. While these are shown for residential buildings, the same basic construction is used for commercial buildings.

Steel Stud Walls

Steel studs are formed from light-gauge steel to standard widths and lengths. They are available in load-bearing and

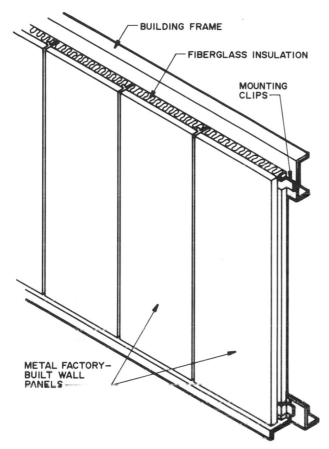

Figure 12-91. Industrial panels can extend 20 ft or more up a wall.

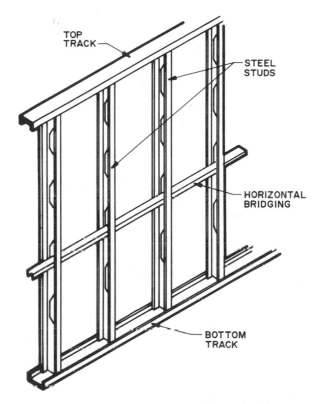

Figure 12-93. A steel stud framed wall.

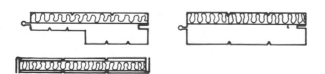

Figure 12-92. Sections through typical industrial type curtain wall panels.

nonload-bearing types, depending upon the gauge of the steel and the width-to-height ratio. *Nonload-bearing studs* are made from 25 and 20 gauge steel and in depths from $1\frac{1}{2}$ in. (38 mm) to 6 in. (152 mm) and lengths from 8 ft (2438 mm) to 20 ft (6096 mm). *Load-bearing studs*, called C studs, are made from 14, 16, and 18 gauge steel and in depths from $1\frac{5}{8}$ in. (41 mm) to 12 in. (305 mm) and in lengths from 7 ft (2133 mm) to 37 ft (11 277 mm). They are available galvanized or painted.

Studs are assembled in C-shaped tracks that serve as top and bottom plates. Special bridging is also produced. They are joined by self-tapping screws or welded. The bottom track can be fastened to concrete floors or steel framing with power-driven fasteners (Fig. 12-93).

The studs have openings in their length to permit running electrical wiring or plumbing. Insulation can be installed between them. Typical finish materials used with steel studs include metal lath and plaster, gypsum lath and plaster, and gypsum drywall sheets.

Windows and Doors

Another part of the exterior enclosure of a building is the doors and windows. An examination of manufacturer's catalogs reveals an extensive range of types and sizes.

Doors

Doors that permit entrance into a building are called *entrance* doors. Doors between rooms are *interior* doors, while those designed for fire protection are called *fire* doors. Examples of other types of doors include revolving doors, garage doors, industrial doors, elevator doors, and storm doors. These are usually hinged, sliding, or run on a track. Doors may be made from wood, metal, glass, or plastic and some are insulated or have glass lights (openings) in them. They can have materials bonded to their faces to improve appearance or provide resistance to damage or weathering. The various types of doors are shown in Fig. 12-94.

Swinging doors may be single acting, double single act-

ing, or single double acting. The double acting door has hinges with springs that keep the door closed when not in use.

Sliding doors run on horizontal or vertical tracks. Some are manually slid while others, such as store entrances or elevators are power operated. Vertical sliding doors may be operated with a cable–pulley arrangement that is manually pulled or electrically opened. These are generally used in industrial buildings for large openings, such as in a shipping area.

Other large industrial doors that open vertically are the canopy, rolling, and vertical track. The *canopy door* is counterweighted and may be manual or electrically opened. The *rolling door* operates like a window shade. It can be manually opened with a chain and pulley arrangement or be electrically operated. The vertical track has four or more leaves hinged along their horizontal edges. The ends of the doors have rollers which run in a metal track. It uses a large coil spring to balance the weight. It may be manually or electrically operated. Small versions of this are commonly used on residential garages.

Folding, bi-fold, and accordion doors run on tracks mounted in the ceiling. They can be used as single doors or in groups to form partitions. Often they will have some type of bottom guide. Doors forming partitions are available up to 20 ft (2438 mm) high and can be expanded to distances of at least 80 ft (24 384 mm).

There are many different stock wood door designs. Wood doors can be flush, have louvers, glass or plastic lights, and wood panels (Fig. 12-95). Standard wood door sizes are in Fig. 12-96. Metal doors have panels and other

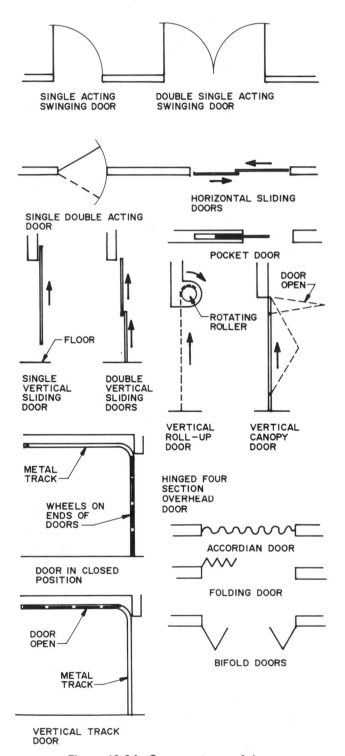

Figure 12-94. *Common types of doors.*

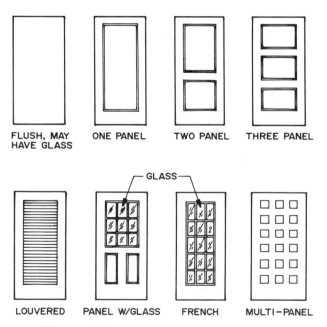

Figure 12-95. *A few of the many door styles.*

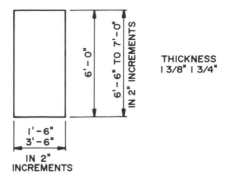

THICKNESS
1 3/8" 1 3/4"

6'-0"

6'-6" TO 7'-0"
IN 2" INCREMENTS

1'-6"
3'-6"
IN 2"
INCREMENTS

FLUSH, HOLLOW CORE DOORS

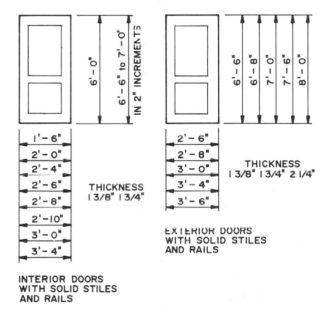

6'-0"

6'-6" to 7'-0"
IN 2" INCREMENTS

THICKNESS
1 3/8" 1 3/4"

1'-6"
2'-0"
2'-4"
2'-6"
2'-8"
2'-10"
3'-0"
3'-4"

INTERIOR DOORS
WITH SOLID STILES
AND RAILS

6'-6"
6'-8"
7'-0"
7'-6"
8'-0"

THICKNESS
1 3/8" 1 3/4" 2 1/4"

2'-6"
2'-8"
3'-0"
3'-4"
3'-6"

EXTERIOR DOORS
WITH SOLID STILES
AND RAILS

Figure 12-96. *Standard door sizes.*

designs stamped into the sheet stock so they appear much the same as wood doors.

The parts of a door include the *stiles* which are the vertical members that run the length of the door. *Rails* are horizontal members running between the stiles. The rails at the top and bottom are the *top rail* and *bottom rail* and those in between are called crossrails or lockrails. A smaller vertical member running between stiles is a *mullion* (Fig. 12-97).

Fire Doors

Fire doors are used to protect vertical and horizontal openings. The fire rating of fire doors is found by testing them in a laboratory. Building codes specify the requirements for fire-resistive assemblies for protection of openings.

Following are descriptions of several types of fire doors.

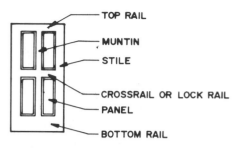

TOP RAIL
MUNTIN
STILE
CROSSRAIL OR LOCK RAIL
PANEL
BOTTOM RAIL

Figure 12-97. *Parts of a wood-framed door.*

Composite doors are flush with a manufactured core and a chemically impregnated wood edge banding, untreated wood face veneers, laminated plastic faces, or surrounded and encased in steel.

Hollow metal doors are formed of 20-gauge or heavier steel. They may have panels stamped into them or be flush.

Metal clad doors (Kalamein) have wood cores, wood stiles and rails, or insulated panels covered with 20-gauge steel.

Sheet metal doors are made using 22-gauge or lighter steel. They may be flush, paneled, or corrugated.

Rolling steel doors are made using an interlocking steel slot design or plate steel construction.

Tin clad doors have a two- or three-ply wood core covered with 30-gauge galvanized steel or terneplate.

Curtain type doors have interlocking steel blades or a continuous spring steel curtain running in a steel frame.

Fire doors are made with the following fire ratings.

3-hr fire doors are used in walls separating buildings or dividing a building into separate fire areas.

$1\frac{1}{2}$-hr fire doors are used in enclosures of vertical openings through a building, such as stairs and elevators, that require a 2-hr wall.

1-hr fire doors are used in openings in walls and other enclosures that require a 1-hr fire rating.

$\frac{3}{4}$-hr fire doors are used on openings in corridor and room partitions which require a 1-hr fire rating.

$\frac{1}{2}$-hr and $\frac{1}{3}$-hr fire doors are used where smoke control is the primary concern.

Under certain conditions, fire doors can have wired glass to provide vision. Glazed panels are not allowed in doors with a fire rating of 3-hr or in $1\frac{1}{2}$-hr doors used in areas of severe fire exposure. Vision panels are limited to 100 in.^{2} (64 500m^2) in $1\frac{1}{2}$-hr rated doors and to 1296 in.^{2} (835 920 m^2) with a maximum dimension of 54 in. (1372 mm) in $\frac{3}{4}$-hr rated doors.

The glazing used is a glass sheet not less than $\frac{1}{4}$ in. (6 mm) thick reinforced with 24-gauge wire mesh forming squares not larger than 1 in. (Fig. 12-98). Laminated plastic panels are under development for glazing purposes in fire doors.

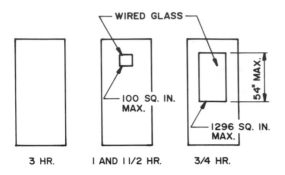

Figure 12-98. *Maximum glazing permitted in fire doors.*

Door Frames

Door frames finish off the opening in the wall left for the door and hold hardware required. They may be wood, steel, aluminum, or stainless steel.

The parts of a wood door frame are shown in Fig. 12-99. The sides are called *jambs* and the horizontal top member is the *head*. Interior door frames have a *door stop* nailed to the jamb. The door closes against it. Exterior doors have the jamb *rabbeted* to received the door. The exterior door has a *brick molding* on the outside. The siding butts against this while a wood casing covers the space between the frame and finish wall on the inside. At the floor is a wood sill.

A typical metal doorframe is shown in Fig. 12-100. There are many design variations and ways to connect the door to the building. In addition there are fire-rated frames for use with fire doors.

Roof Construction

A major function of the roof is to shed water and keep the interior of the building dry. Steeply pitched roofs shed water easily and are in general satisfactory. Many commercial buildings however, have flat or nearly flat roofs. These require a jointless, watertight roof covering. In this

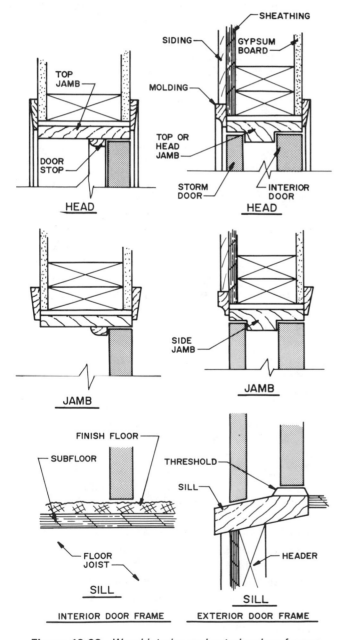

Figure 12-99. *Wood interior and exterior door frames.*

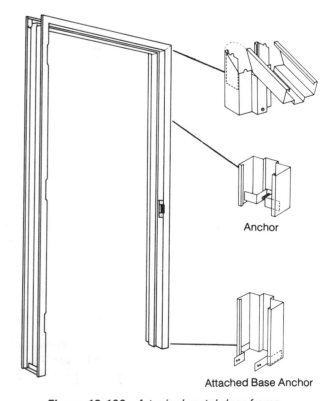

Figure 12-100. *A typical metal door frame.*

chapter, the more frequently used decks and finish roof covering systems will be discussed.

Roof Decks

The roof deck serves two purposes. It transfers the weight of the live and dead loads to the supporting joists, purlins, and subpurlins, acts as a diaphragm, and transmits wind and seismic forces to the structural system of the building.

The roof deck used must provide a surface that is suitable for the application of the desired finish roofing materials. Not all decks can satisfactorily accept all finish materials. In addition, the deck must carry the design loads with a deflection limited to $l/240$ of the span. In some cases, the deflection is limited to $l/360$ of the span. The roof deck must also be compatible with the structural system of the building. It also can provide a degree of insulation. Following are the more commonly used roof decks.

Wood Boards on Wood Joists and Purlins. The boards may be square edge, shiplapped, or tongue-and-groove. Tongue-and-groove is preferred because it makes a more solid deck. The minimum thickness is 1 in. (25 mm).

Plywood on Wood Joists and Purlins. The plywood should have at least five plies and be of waterproof exterior grade. If the sheets are not tongue-and-groove, the joints should be taped with fiberglass tape to prevent the asphalt priming coat from running through the joints. The minimum plywood thickness is $\frac{1}{2}$ in. (13 mm).

Plywood over Tongue-and-Groove Decking. This permits lower grade lumber to be used and the use of a mopped-on roof membrane. The roof is built by nailing the tongue-and-groove decking in place and covering it with unsaturated building paper. Unsanded $\frac{3}{8}$-in. (9-mm) exterior plywood is nailed or stapled over this. The roof felt applied over the plywood is run perpendicular to the long edge of the plywood (Fig. 12-101).

Steel Deck with an Overlay of Plywood, Gypsum Board, or Insulating Board. The steel deck is designed to carry predetermined uniform loads, stress and deflection. Deflection of $l/240$ of the span is permitted unless a dropped ceiling is used. In this case, the deflection is limited to $l/360$ of the span. The spans vary with the type of rib and gauge of the steel.

The steel deck is covered with rigid insulation, plywood, or gypsum board. These are mechanically fastened to the steel deck. Adhesive fastening is not recommended (Fig. 12-102). Steel roof decks are commonly $1\frac{1}{2}$ in. (38 mm) deep and formed in four configurations—narrow rib, intermediate rib, wide rib, and deep rib (Fig. 12-103).

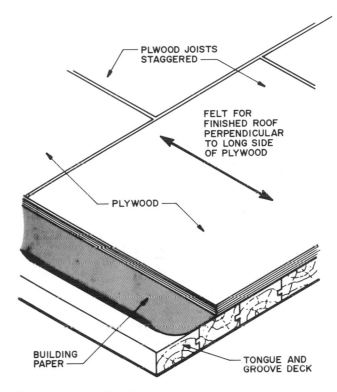

Figure 12-101. *One form of roof using plywood over tongue-and-groove solid wood decking.*

Poured Gypsum. Gypsum roof decks are made from gypsum concrete mixed with either wood fibers or mineral aggregate and water. They are formed by pouring gypsum concrete over permanently installed formboards that are supported by structural steel framing. The poured gypsum is reinforced with welded wire mesh and should be at least 2 in. (51 mm) thick. It should cover the top of the bulb tee at least $\frac{1}{4}$ in. (6 mm). Adequate ventilation must be provided below the slab to remove excess moisture (Fig. 12-104).

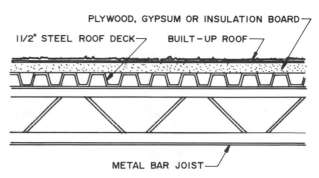

Figure 12-102. *A steel deck with an overlay of plywood, gypsum board, or insulation board.*

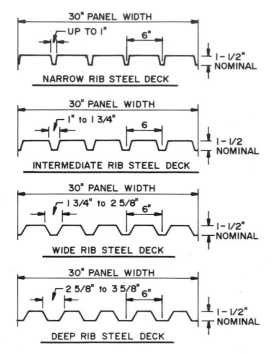

Figure 12-103. *Frequently used types of steel roof decking.*

Precast Gypsum. Precast gypsum planks are made 2 in. (52 mm) thick, 15 in. (381 mm) wide, and up to 10 ft (2540 mm) long. They are reinforced with welded wire mesh and have galvanized steel tongue-and-groove ends and sides. The planks are placed upon the structural members of the roof and attached with clips (Fig. 12-105).

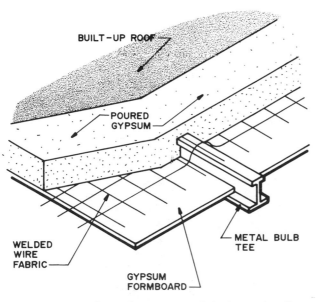

Figure 12-104. *Poured gypsum roof deck construction.*

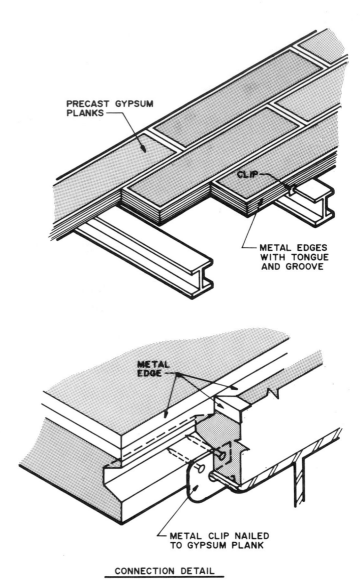

Figure 12-105. *Precast metal edged gypsum planks are used to form roof decks.*

Precast Concrete. Precast concrete roof slabs may be flat, channel slabs, or tees. The *flat planks* are reinforced with galvanized weld wire mesh and have tongue-and-groove edges and sides. Some types can be nailed to supporting members. Some types are square edged while others have tongue-and-groove edges (Fig. 12-106). These commonly are 2 in. (51 mm) to 4 in. (102 mm) thick and span 5 to 8 ft (1525 to 2440 mm). They can be used on flat and sloped roofs (Fig. 12-107).

Channel slabs commonly run $2\frac{3}{4}$ to 4 in. (70 to 102 mm) thick and span 6 to 10 ft (1830 to 2540 mm). Acoustical treatment can be cast on the underside of the slab. These 2-ft (610-mm) wide slabs are fastened to beams and purlins with special metal clips (Fig. 12-108).

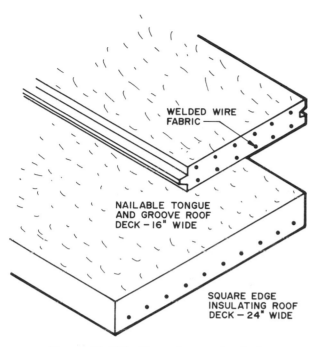

Figure 12-106. *Precast concrete planks.*

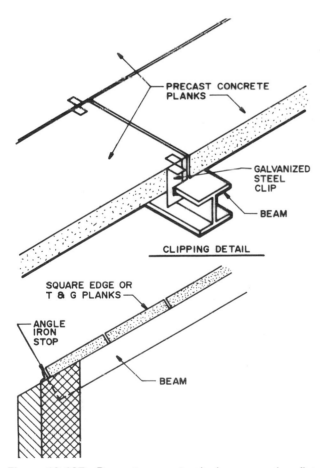

Figure 12-107. *Precast concrete planks are used on flat and sloping roofs.*

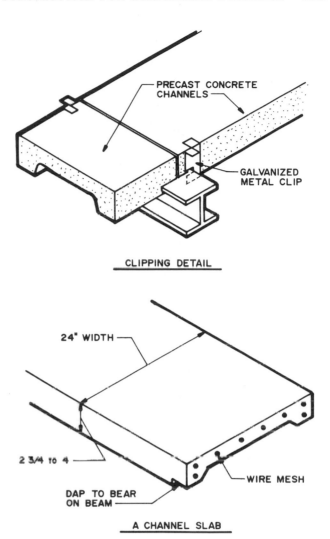

Figure 12-108. *Precast concrete channel slab details.*

The *tees* are available as single and double tees. They are described earlier in this chapter where floors are discussed.

Wood Fiber Decking

There are a number of roof decking materials utilizing wood fibers. One type pressure bonds wood fibers and portland cement to form a substrate with a 1½-hr fire rating. It has polyurethane insulation bonded to the substrate. Builders felt or waferboard is bonded on top of the insulation (Fig. 12-109). The planks have tongue-and-groove edges and are fastened with metal clips. Some types are made with metal channel installed on the groove edge. This enables the decking to span longer distances. Thicknesses of 2 to 4 in. (51 to 102 mm) are common and spans from 3 to 8 ft (915 to 2440 mm) are available (Fig. 12-110).

Figure 12-109. *This is a wood fiber roof deck. (Courtesy of Martin Fireproofing Georgia Inc.)*

Precast Hollow Core Slabs

These precast slabs were discussed earlier in the section on precast floors. They are held together with a grouted key (Fig. 12-111). Since there can be thermal movement in large sections of concrete it is best if the concrete roof slab can be kept in an environment having a relatively stable temperature. When possible, the continuous roofing membrane should be separated from the concrete deck. Control joints should be properly located and waterproofed.

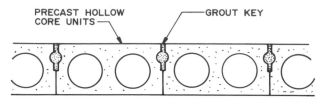

Figure 12-111. *Precast concrete hollow core units are tied together with a grout key.*

Cast-in-Place Concrete Roof Slab

The basic types of cast-in-place concrete slabs were described earlier under cast-in-place floors. When used as roof decks, they permit a wider selection of roofing specifications than the other types mentioned. Generally there are fewer failures of the finished roof over cast-in-place slabs. The slab eliminates roof flutter due to high winds and vibration caused by those installing or providing maintenance on the roof.

Lightweight Insulating Concrete Roof Decks

Lightweight insulating concrete roof decks are designed cast-in-place over galvanized, corrugated metal forms, bulb-tee and formboard systems, and cast-in-place and precast concrete substrates. The deck is at least 2 in. (51 mm) thick. The concrete is produced by combining lightweight aggregates, such a perlite or vermiculite, with

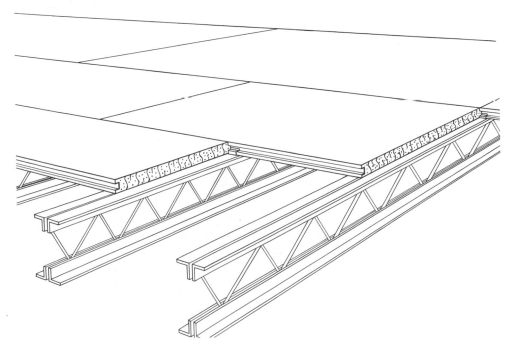

Figure 12-110. *This wood fiber roof deck is held to steel bar joists with metal clips.*

portland cement and water. Insulating decks are produced by blending pregenerated foam with portland cement and water.

Lightweight concrete decks must be vented through the topside, bottomside, or in some cases both sides if built-up roofing is to be applied.

Roof Systems

The type of roofing system selected depends upon many factors such as the desired appearance, type of construction, type of roof deck, availability of an experienced roofing contractor, and availability of the needed materials. The advice of an experienced roof designer is important to success. The selection of the various materials and the installation methods is critical to building a watertight roof. Consideration of fire codes and climatic conditions may influence the choice.

There are four commonly used groups of roof covering—built-up, single-ply, metal, and shingles and tiles.

Built-up Roof System

A built-up roof system is comprised of three elements—felt, bitumen, and surfacing material.

Felts are made of glass, vegetable (wood fiber and rag), or asbestos fibers. They serve as reinforcing much the same as welded wire fabric in concrete. They help resist the tensile forces that pull on the roofing material. They are applied in layers with coats of bitumen between each. The bitumen is the main waterproofing material and the felts permit the application of more of it to the roof. *Bitumen* may be a coal-tar pitch or asphalt. It melds with the felt to form a watertight membrane.

Surface material is applied to the bitumen coat, called the flood coat. It is usually smooth gravel, slag, mineral granules, or a mineral-coated cap sheet. The gravel, slag, or mineral granules are spread evenly over the flood coat and embedded into it. They serve to protect the top coat from damage such as hail or walking on the surface. Some designs use a cap sheet. A cap sheet is a very thick layer of felt that has a mineral granule surface.

The design and application of built-up roofing systems depends upon a number of circumstances, the most important being the decking material. The opinion of experts is necessary to get the most satisfactory combination. Basically most systems use two, three, or four plies of felt with asphalt, bitumen, or coal-tar pitch. They can be applied to most nailable and non-nailable decks. Application can be made to rigid deck insulation or directly to the deck. Typical examples are in Figs. 12-112 and 12-113.

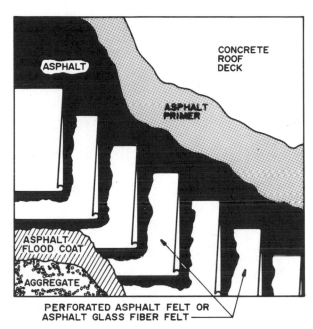

Figure 12-112. *A typical built-up roof over a concrete roof deck.*

Single-Ply Roofing Systems

Single-ply roofing systems have a single membrane applied over the roof insulation. This system is also referred to as *elastomeric roofing*. They can be applied loose-laid and ballasted, partially adhered or fully adhered. The loose-laid membrane has the side and end laps fused or

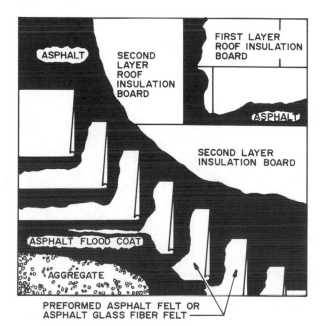

Figure 12-113. *A built-up roof applied over roof insulation board.*

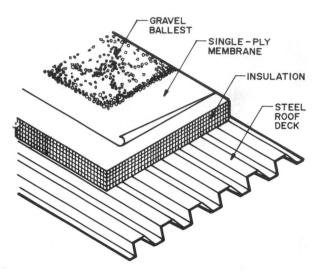

Figure 12-114. *A typical detail for a single-ply roofing system.*

glued to form a single sheet. It is ballasted with $\frac{1}{2}$ in. (12-mm) of stone. The partially adhered sheet has a series of strips or plate fasteners which join it to the deck and structure. Fully adhered systems are bonded to the base according to the manufacturers' directions (Fig. 12-114).

There are three basic categories of single-ply systems—thermosetting, thermoplastic, and composites. In Fig. 12-115 are examples of some of these systems.

There are many conditions that might make a single-ply membrane the wrong choice. The designer must be aware of the experience of others with a particular material before choosing to use it. Even the choice of insulation below the membrane must be carefully considered. Since the

---

Thermosetting Membranes

EPDM (Ethylene propylene)
PIB (Polyisobutylene)
Neoprene (Synthetic rubber)

Thermoplastic Membranes

PVC (Polyvinyl chloride)
CSPE (Chlorosulfonated polyethyene)
CPE (Chlorinated polyethylene)

Composite Membranes

Glass reinforced EPDM/neoprene
Modified bitumen/polyester
Nylon reinforced PVC
Polyester reinforced PVC

Figure 12-115. *The three systems of a single-ply roofing system.*

membrane is very thin and insulation is compressible, foot traffic on the roof is undesirable.

Metal Roof Systems

There are a number of manufacturers producing metal roof systems. They are light weight, available in many shapes and colors, resist deterioration by the sun, and are easily installed in any weather. Metal roof systems can be adapted to many building designs and have a long life. When installed following the manufacturer's directions, they produce a quality, reliable roof. It is important to note that they are designed for use on pitched roofs. Therefore, water drainage is excellent (Fig. 12-116).

Steel metal roofing is surface coated by galvanizing, terne coating (lead–tin alloy) and painting, factory applied enamel, and mastic coatings. Aluminum, copper alloys, and lead-coated copper roofing are also available.

The design of the connections between sheets and the fastening devices allows for expansion and contraction. The sheets are laid over purlins or spaced sheathing. The sheets are designed to span predetermined distances and carry the required roof loads. The actual spacing of purlins will vary with the design of the metal roofing sheets. It can also be laid over solid sheathing or decking. Construction details are in Fig. 12-117.

Metal roof systems are insulated below the metal. The insulation is therefore on the inside of the building. A vapor barrier must be placed below the insulation to keep moisture from penetrating to the metal deck. Often a ventilation system is used to clear the air between the insulation and the metal.

Shingle and Tile Roof Systems

Shingles and tiles are used on sloped roofs. They have excellent watersheding qualities, are easy to install, and have a long life.

Figure 12-116. *A metal roof has a long life and is water tight. (Courtesy of Butler Manufacturing Company.)*

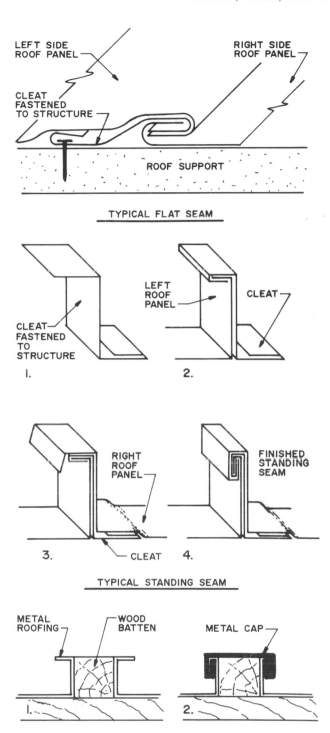

LEFT SIDE ROOF PANEL

RIGHT SIDE ROOF PANEL

CLEAT FASTENED TO STRUCTURE

ROOF SUPPORT

TYPICAL FLAT SEAM

CLEAT FASTENED TO STRUCTURE

LEFT ROOF PANEL

CLEAT

1.

2.

RIGHT ROOF PANEL

FINISHED STANDING SEAM

3.

CLEAT

4.

TYPICAL STANDING SEAM

METAL ROOFING

WOOD BATTEN

METAL CAP

1.

2.

BATTEN SEAM JOINT

Figure 12-117. Typical seams used with metal roof materials.

Shingles are available in asphalt, fiberglass asphalt, wood, slate, and metal. Tiles are made from clay and concrete.

Asphalt shingles are made in a variety of weights and styles. They range from 210 to 385 lb/square. A *square*

is 100 lb/ft². *Fiberglass asphalt shingles* range from 225 to 300 lb/square. They both are made in two- and three-tab and two-layer laminated shingles. *Wood shingles* may be shingle or shake grade. Shakes, which are hand split, thicker, and rougher, are more expensive. *Metal shingles* are either aluminum or steel and have various colored coatings. *Slate shingles* are available in a commercial grade, which is smooth, and a quarry grade, which is rough. They will weight 700 to 3600 lb/square. Therefore, the roof structure needs extra strength. *Clay tile* is made in several styles and weighs from 800 to 1000 lb/square. *Concrete tile* are made as flat shingles and a curved tile shape. They weigh 950 lb/square. The roof structure must be designed to carry the extra load of clay and concrete tile roofing materials.

Most shingle and tile roofs require a roof slope of 4 in. (102 mm) of rise per 12 in. (305 mm) of run. In some cases, 3 in. (76 mm) of rise is acceptable.

Shingles and tiles are shown in Chapter 11.

Flashing

Flashing is used to keep water from penetrating the building in places where the roof membrane is interrupted. It is required in locations such as the roof perimeter, roof penetrations, such as pipes and skylights, and where roofs of various slopes intersect.

Flashing materials are commonly aluminum, copper, lead-coated copper, lead, polyvinyl chloride, butyl rubber, copper-clad stainless steel, stainless steel, zinc alloy, copper alloy, galvanized steel, and asphalt products such as shingles and felt.

The design of the roof system includes careful detailing of the flashing to be used. Following are flashing details for use with built-up roofs. In Fig. 12-118 a typical roof edge detail is shown. Notice the double layer of flashing. Often a roof meets an exterior wall that has a parapet. A *parapet* is an exterior wall extending above the level of the roof. The use of a cant strip, base flashing, and top flashing provides a water-tight seal (Fig. 12-119). A large roof deck will often have an expansion joint. One way to flash this joint is shown in Fig. 12-120.

Fire Resistance and Fire Ratings

When designing a roof system, it is important to remember that the roof is exposed to fire from within the building and from outside. Fires in adjoining buildings can subject a roof to direct heat radiation and falling burning materials. In this case the *external fire threat* is first to the roof membrane, then the insulation, decking, and finally to the structural members. The *internal fire threat* is first to the

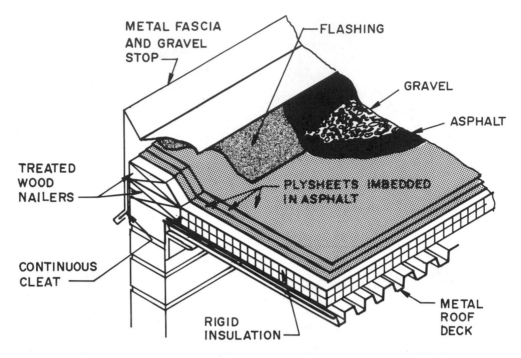

Figure 12-118. *This heavy metal roof edge is used when the deck is supported by the outside wall.*

structural frame, then the deck, and finally the insulation and membrane.

Roofing materials are grouped into four fire resistance classes:

> *Class A* roof materials will resist severe fire exposure. Among these are clay tile, concrete tile, slate, and other materials certified as Class A by an approved testing laboratory.
>
> *Class B* roof materials are effective against moderate fire exposure. Among these are metal roofing and some types of composition shingles.
>
> *Class C* roof materials are effective against light fire exposure. Among these are most asphalt shingles and fire-retardant treated wood shingles and shakes.
>
> *Nonclassified* roof materials include untreated wood shingles and shakes.

The classification required for a particular building is specified by the local building code.

Thermal Insulation in Roof Systems

Much research has been undertaken to try to find the proper type of insulation and how it should be placed in a roof system. Much work is yet to be undertaken before a totally satisfactory solution will be available. There are some basic facts that the designer should consider. The following is a general discussion of these.

Why Insulate a Roof?

Roof insulation is used to satisfy one of the following requirements:

1. To maintain constant interior temperatures.
2. To reduce heat gain, thus reducing cooling costs.
3. To reduce heat loss, thus reducing heating costs.
4. To keep the underside of the deck above the dew point of the outside air to prevent condensation from forming on it.
5. To insulate the roof deck from outside temperatures so expansion and contraction are reduced.
6. To bridge the flutes in steel decks and serve as a base for the roof membrane.

Design Considerations

Steeply sloped roofs permit the installation of insulation batts, blankets, or insulation in loose form in the flat ceiling. A vapor barrier is placed below the insulation and the space between it and the roof deck is ventilated. This work very well because moisture is controlled and removed (Fig. 12-121).

Flat roofs in frame construction are also insulated with

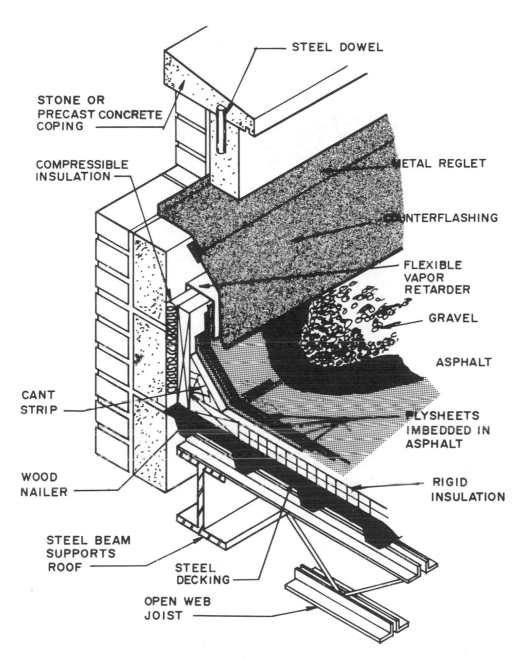

STEEL DOWEL

STONE OR
PRECAST CONCRETE
COPING

COMPRESSIBLE
INSULATION

METAL REGLET

COUNTERFLASHING

FLEXIBLE
VAPOR
RETARDER

GRAVEL

ASPHALT

CANT
STRIP

PLYSHEETS
IMBEDDED IN
ASPHALT

WOOD
NAILER

RIGID
INSULATION

STEEL BEAM
SUPPORTS
ROOF

STEEL
DECKING

OPEN WEB
JOIST

Figure 12-119. *This shows construction of base flashing for non-wall supported roof deck. This allows the wall and roof deck to move independently.*

batts or blankets in the ceiling, leaving several inches of air space between the insulation and the roof deck. This space is ventilated to remove moisture. This type of roof is effective (Fig. 12-122).

In both of these cases, the key to the long life of the deck and roofing material is the elimination of moisture that may get trapped below the roof membrane. Trapped moisture when heated produces great pressures, which cause the membrane to bulge and break.

In many commercial flat roof systems, the insulation is a rigid board type material that is located on top of the deck and below the roof membrane. Commonly used insulation materials include wood or cane fiber, cork, glass fiber, foamed and extruded polystyrene, and foamed polyurethane. Since no installation is perfectly waterproof, there is a chance for water penetration from below and above the insulation. This moisture is trapped in the insulation and due to freezing and high temperatures will eventually destroy the roof covering (Fig. 12-123).

When designing a roof system it is necessary to con-

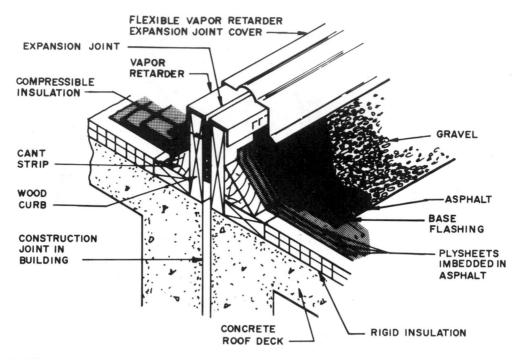

Figure 12-120. *Construction details for an expansion joint. This allows building movement in both directions.*

sider if roof insulation is necessary and if so are there any alternatives. For example, if the building is to have a dropped ceiling, batts or blankets and a vapor barrier could be placed there to control interior temperatures and the roof deck would not need insulation. If the space between the insulation and roof deck was vented, moisture that did

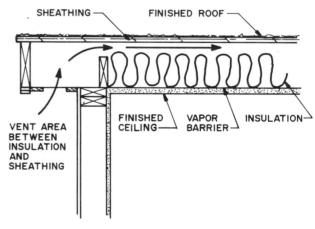

Figure 12-122. *The area between the insulation and sheathing on a flat roof must be ventilated.*

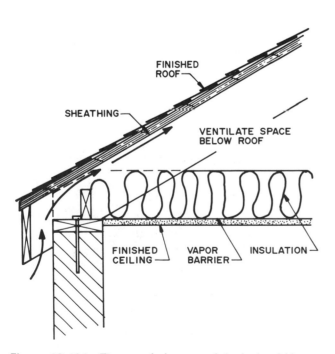

Figure 12-121. *The area below a roof deck should be ventilated to remove moisture.*

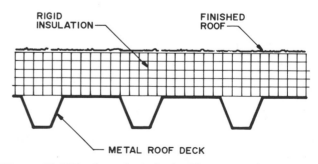

Figure 12-123. *Any minute leak will cause moisture to get trapped between the deck and finish roof, causing severe damage.*

find its way through the ceiling would be removed. Metal decks often have insulation placed on them only because it is needed to bridge the flutes in metal decking so a roof membrane can be installed, not because the insulation is needed. Since this will possibly cause the roof membrane to fail is there an alternative?

Another problem with putting insulation on top of the deck is that the insulation is soft. Invariably there is human traffic on a roof. When they walk on the roof the insulation compresses, and their weight is carried by the roof membrane. Eventually there will be a tear in the membrane. If the roof membrane is installed over a solid deck, as lightweight concrete, there is less chance of damaging the membrane. The use of light colored material on the roof will reduce solar gain because it reflects the heat. Metal roofing can be painted white.

Technical Vocabulary

Following are some important technical terms used in this chapter. Write a brief definition for each.

Fire-resistance ratings
Flame-spread classifications
Smoke-developed ratings
Sound transmission class
Impact isolation class
Preengineered metal buildings
Purlins
Girts
Rigid frame
Truss type metal buildings
Post and beam
Wide flange beams
American standard beams
Standard mill beams
Angles
Bearing piles
Tees
Tubular shapes
Bars
Plates
Spandrel
Shear
Shear panels
Rigid frame construction (AISC Type 1)
Simple frame construction (AISC Type 2)
Semirigid construction (AISC Type 3)
Space frames
Trusses
Tension fabric structures
Open web steel joists
Joist girders

Bridging
Spiral reinforcing
Cast-in-place concrete
Flat plate construction
Drop panel
Column capital
Precast concrete
Prestressed concrete
Pretensioned concrete
Tenons
Wet joint
Matching plates
Precast concrete tees
Curtain wall panels
Heavy timber construction
Split ring connector
Glued-laminated construction
Tilt-up construction
Built-up roof construction
Elastomeric roofing
Flashing

Study Questions

Answer the following study questions without referring to the text. Then check your answers with the text and correct those that were wrong.

1. Where do you find fire-resistance requirements?

2. What are the three flame-spread classifications?

3. How is impact noise classified?

4. What types of footings and foundation are used with preengineered metal buildings?

5. What are the basic types of preengineered metal buildings?

6. How are lightweight steel members joined?

7. How are steel frames of W or S beams joined?

8. How are steel frames braced to resist lateral forces?

9. What are the two common ways to stabilize the steel frame of a multistory building?

10. What are the three series of open web joists?

11. What type of reinforcement is used in round and square concrete columns?

12. What is done to a concrete beam to increase its ability to resist tension?

13. How are concrete beams reinforced to resist shear at the ends of the beam?

14. How do flat plate and flat slab construction differ?

15. What are some advantages of one-way joist concrete floor construction?

16. What is meant by waffle slab construction?

17. What are the advantages of precast concrete construction?

18. What is the difference between pretensioning and post-tensioning?

19. What are the advantages and disadvantages of prestressed concrete members?

20. What types of precast concrete floor and roof members are available?

21. What is meant by tilt-up construction?

22. What are general code requirements for exterior walls for buildings using heavy timber construction?

23. How are heavy timber columns secured to the foundation or a footing?

24. What is the purpose for using curtain walls?

25. What are the fire ratings assigned to fire doors?

26. What are the commonly used roof decking materials?

27. What materials are used for flashing?

28. What are the various fire ratings for roof materials?

Laboratory Problems

1. Design a floor, wall, and roof system for a two-story commercial building 40 ft wide and 120 ft long. Interior ceiling height must be 10 ft clear. It can be divided into 30 to 40 ft bays if necessary.

2. Design a floor, wall, and roof system for the building designed in Chapter 8. It should be energy efficient and have low maintenance.

13

The Title Sheet and Site Plan

The title sheet data and site plan are often placed together on the cover sheet of a set of drawings. If the site plan is large, it is placed on a separate sheet.

The Title Sheet

A complete set of architectural drawings has a cover sheet called a title sheet. While the information appearing on it varies according to the type and size of the project, in general it will contain the following:

Name and location of the project
Name and address of the architect
Name and address of all consulting engineers and designers
An index to drawings
Symbol legend
Site plan
Vicinity map

The name of the project is usually in large letters up to $1\frac{1}{2}$ in. high. The other information is in smaller letters. An attempt is made to produce a pleasing drawing with the information balanced on the sheet. Considerable individual freedom is common when designing and laying out this cover sheet. See Fig. 13-1. The letters are formed using templates or adhesive-backed letters that stick to the sheet. Computer drafting programs provide a variety of decorative letter styles useful for this purpose.

Index to Drawings

The index to drawings gives a descriptive title to each sheet and a drawing number. On small sets of drawing, as for a residence, the drawings are numbered 1, 2, 3, 4, and so on. On large sets that have several sheets devoted to one segment, such as the electrical layout, a descriptive letter and number system is used. Following is one example.

Title Sheet. This is not given a number

A Sheets. These sheets contain architectural drawings such as the foundation plan, floor plan, construction details, schedules, interior and exterior elevations, cabinets, and construction sections. Sheets are number A-1, A-2, and so on.

E Sheets. These sheet contain all electrical information such as electrical layout drawings, electrical schedules, lighting, distribution panel information, and the electrical symbol legend. Sheets are number E-1, E-2, and so on.

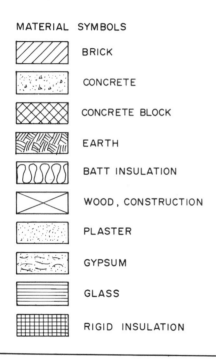

BOND OFFICE BUILDING
CENE, OHIO

J. THOMAS A.I.A.
SENECA, OHIO

J.V. JONES, M.E.
ASH, OHIO

W.C. NATTE, E.E.
ASH, OHIO

MATERIAL SYMBOLS

BRICK

CONCRETE

CONCRETE BLOCK

EARTH

BATT INSULATION

WOOD, CONSTRUCTION

PLASTER

GYPSUM

GLASS

RIGID INSULATION

INDEX

A1 SITE PLAN
A2 FOUNDATION PLAN
A3 FLOOR PLAN AND SCHEDULES
A4 ELEVATIONS
E1 ELECTRICAL PLAN AND SCHEDULES
M1 PLUMBING, HEATING, AND
   AIRCONDITIONING
S1 BUILDING SECTION AND WALL
   SECTION
S2 ROOF FRAMING PLAN, FOOTING
   SCHEDULES, BEAM SCHEDULES

Figure 13-1. A typical title sheet.

M Sheets. These sheets contain all the mechanical information such as the plumbing diagram, heating, air-conditioning and ventilation plan, grille schedule, and small site plan showing entrance of utilities to building. Sheets are numbered M-1, M-2.

S Sheets. These sheets contain all structural information such as roof framing plan, wall framing plans, column and footing schedules, wall and building sections, steel, precast and cast-in-place concrete and heavy timber schedules, and all structural notes. Sheets are numbered S-1, S-2, and so on.

Sometimes a job will give considerable detail of a special feature such as large kitchen equipment layouts which could be identified as K-1, K-2, and so on, or curtain wall details which might be identified as W-1, W-2, and so on.

The Land Survey or Plat Plan

A land survey or plat is shown in Fig. 13-2. It shows the property lines with their bearings and dimensions, streets, easements, and other existing features that need to be indicated. The dimensions are given in decimal feet or meters if it is a metric drawing. The bearings are in degrees, minutes, and seconds from north to south. The existing contours are shown in feet above sea level (or meters) or in relation to a bench mark. A bench mark is some existing

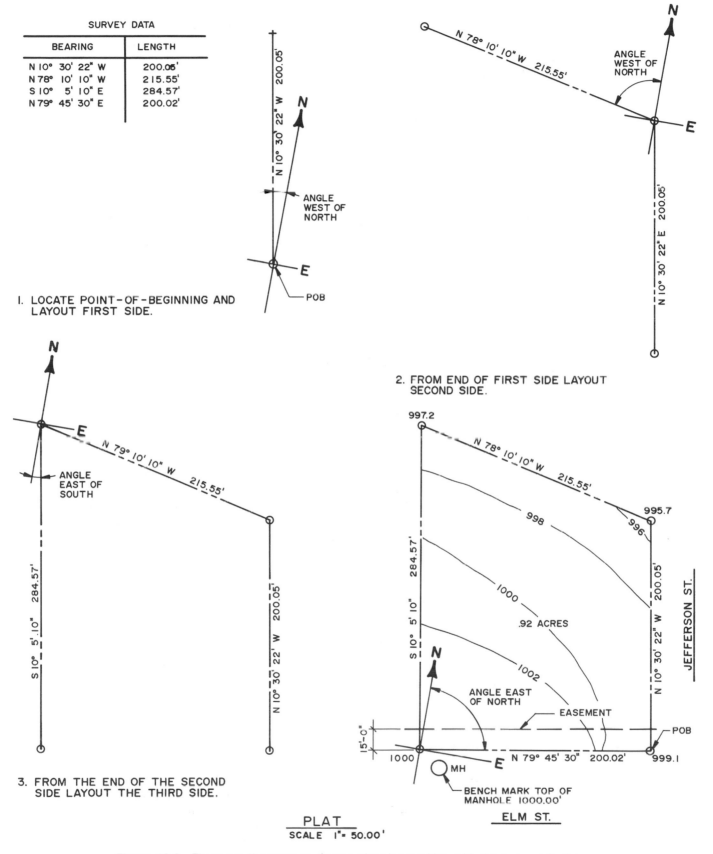

SURVEY DATA

BEARING	LENGTH
N 10° 30' 22" W	200.05'
N 78° 10' 10" W	215.55'
S 10° 5' 10" E	284.57'
N 79° 45' 30" E	200.02'

1. LOCATE POINT-OF-BEGINNING AND LAYOUT FIRST SIDE.

2. FROM END OF FIRST SIDE LAYOUT SECOND SIDE.

3. FROM THE END OF THE SECOND SIDE LAYOUT THE THIRD SIDE.

PLAT
SCALE 1"= 50.00'

Figure 13-2. These are the steps to draw a plat plan working with the surveyor's data.

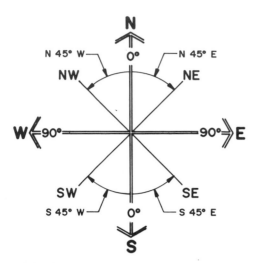

Figure 13-3. *The surveyor takes bearings east and west of the north–south axis.*

point whose elevation is known. In Fig. 13-2 it is the top of an existing manhole. All vertical measurements are made from the bench mark. Sometimes other data are shown, as the name of the surveyor, his or her seal, and the location of the land.

The bearings are indicated by describing the quadrant into which each side falls. See Fig. 13-3. For example, a side that falls in the northeast quadrant is taken from north and lies east of north. It could have a bearing of N 45° 30′ 22″ E meaning the bearing is 45° 30′ 22″ east of north.

To draw the land survey begin at the corner selected as the point-of-beginning. See Fig. 13-2. From this point, draw the first side on the indicated bearing and draw its length to scale. Engineers scales, such as 1 in. = 20 ft, may be used. Continue by locating and drawing each side until you return to the point-of-beginning.

The Site Plan

The site plan is developed from information provided by the surveyor on a plat. The plat contains the physical data about the site as it exists when the building contractor arrives at the job. See Fig. 13-2. The architect uses this information when making decisions about designing the building to fit on the site. The surface of the site can be altered as part of the design. These decisions are shown on the architect's site plan.

Following are things generally found on a site plan:

Original land contours
New land contours required after completion of construction.
Set backs and easements

Buildings and their location on the site
Driveways and sidewalks, their size, and location
Parking areas with stall size data and lot size and location on the site.
Trees, rock out-croppings, and so on, that are to be removed or remain
Size of the site in decimal feet or meters
Compass bearing of each side
Elevations of the corners of site, soil at the corners of the building, finished floor, parking lot surface, and other such areas
Location of utilities
Streets and curbs
The bench mark
Fences
North arrow
Retaining walls
Lights, Flagpole, and so on
Slope on parking lots and driveways
A symbol legend
Drawing title
Scale

Drawing the Site Plan

Site plans are drawn to scale ranging from 1 in. = 10 ft to 1 in. = 100 ft or 1:00, 1:200, or 1:500 mm, depending upon the size of the site and the complexity of the site details. An engineer's scale is used for this drawing when the units used are feet and inches.

The property lines are laid out first using the proper symbol as shown in Fig. 13-4. This is drawn as a thick line. The compass bearings and length must be recorded on each side of the site. The dimensions are recorded in decimal feet or meters if it is a metric drawing.

Now locate the building on the site. This is dimensioned in feet and inches or millimeters. The outline of the building is drawn with a thick, solid line. One corner of the building is located from two sides of the site. Care must be taken if it is not to be parallel with the sides of the site to give adequate dimensions to place it in the desired location. It is not necessary to give the dimensions of the building. The contractor gets these from the floor plan. Now give the elevation of the finished first floor. It will be some predetermines distance above the bench mark on the site. Record this elevation on the building. The bench mark is a marked reference point from which the contours and other heights are taken. It might be a stake in the ground with its top established as a certain height above sea level. All vertical distances on the site and building are measured from this stake.

Now locate all parking lots, driveways, sidewalks, and access roads. These are drawn with thin lines. Dimension

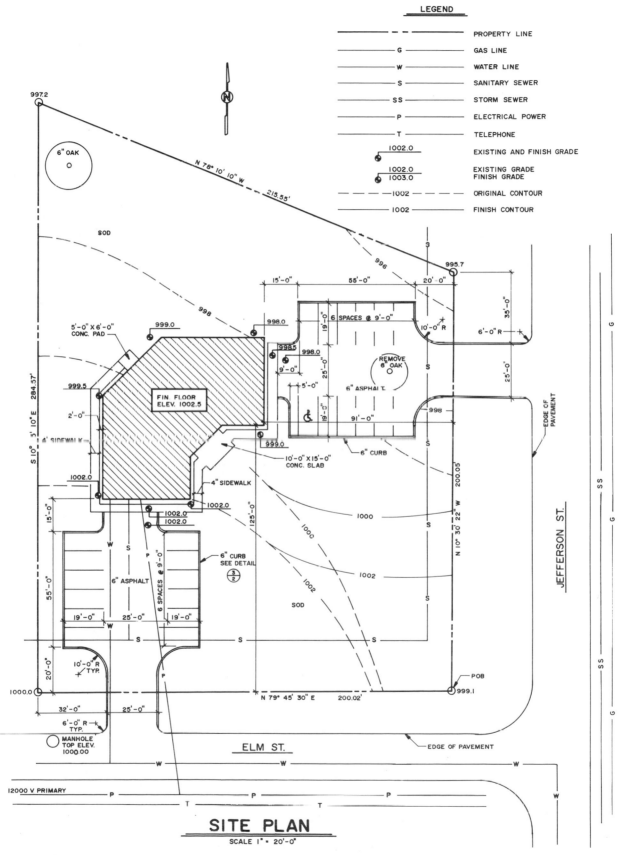

Figure 13-4. *A typical site plan completely describes the site after all construction and adjustments to the site are finished.*

them so their width, radius of curves, and location on the site are given. They are dimensioned in feet and inches or millimeters if it is a metric drawing. Add descriptive notes detailing things as slab material, thickness, and slope. If a concrete curb is to be built, it is indicated. A section through it can be drawn on the same sheet as the site plan. If there are many other site details, such as retaining walls, ramp construction, or light pole footings, these might appear on a separate drawing.

Now locate the original contours using a thin dashed line. The contour line is broken and the height above sea level is lettered in the space. The surveyor will usually keep the same number of feet of drop between contour lines. On very flat property this might be as small as a 1 ft change in grade while on steeply sloped lots, it could be 4 or more ft. On most normal work, a 1- or 2-ft change in grade is used. If an area requires greater accuracy in the final grade, contours could be placed every 1 ft of drop in that area even though the others on the site were greater.

Now the new contours are drawn using a thin solid line. One important reason for adjusting the contours is to provides for controlled surface drainage. These are usually spaced using the same changes in grade as were used on the original contour.

When locating the north arrow before starting the plan, decide which is the best direction to place it on the sheet. North can point in any direction as long as the plan is clearly oriented. North should then be the same on all other plan sheets.

The finishing touches will include an arrow indicating north, locating trees, identifying the utilities, retaining walls, easements, setbacks, and streets. The title and a scale are located below the drawing. The title is usually 1/4 inch high and the scale lettered 1/8 inch high.

Occasionally a building is so large it cannot be adequately detailed in a single sheet of paper. The building is subdivided into several sections and a set of working drawings for each is prepared. These divisions are shown on the site plan. In Fig. 13-5 is a site plan for a shopping center. Notice the building has been divided into three areas labeled Building A, Building B, and Building C. The same site plan is part of the working drawings for each division except the building described in the set is shaded on the site plan to call attention to it.

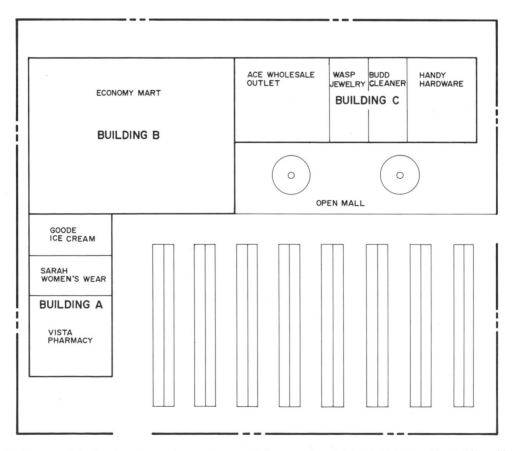

Figure 13-5. *This partial site plan shows how a large building can be divided into several sets of working drawings.*

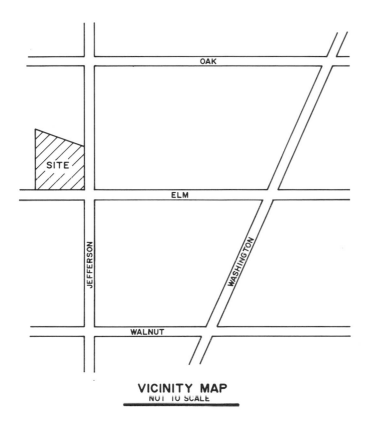

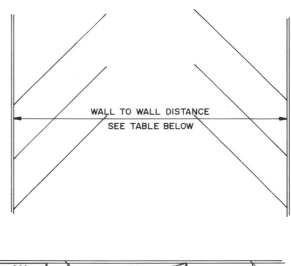

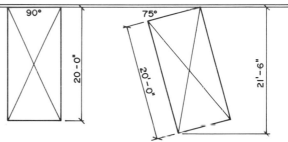

VICINITY MAP
NOT TO SCALE

Figure 13-6. *This is a vicinity map showing streets in the area of the building site.*

Vicinity Map

A vicinity map is a small-scale drawing showing the area surrounding the building site. Generally it is not drawn to scale. See Fig. 13-6

Parking Data

As the site is planned it is necessary to design and locate parking areas, access roads, ramps, and sidewalks. While the width of sidewalks varies considerable, 3 ft is a common size. Data for parking stalls are in Fig. 13-7. Spaces for handicapped parkers are marked on the parking lot layout. An access aisle beside the handicapped parking stall is required because those using vans exit from the side door and need extra space. See Fig. 13-8.

Turning radii for streets and drives vary depending upon the size of the vehicles to use the area. If it is known that buses and large trucks will use the street, larger design sizes must be used. For automobile traffic, a radius of 20 ft at a corner is adequate. In Fig. 13-9 are recommended design sizes for streets, driveways, and cul-de-sacs.

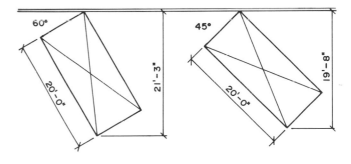

ANGLE TO CURB	STALL WIDTH	WALL TO WALL 2 CARS AND AISLE
45°	8'-6" TO 10'-0"	48' TO 52'
60°	8'-6" TO 9'-0" 9'-6" TO 10'-0"	57' TO 60' 55' TO 58'
75°	8'-6" TO 9'-0" 9'-6" TO 10'-0"	60' TO 62' 58' TO 60'
90°	8'-6" TO 9'-0" 9'-6" TO 10'-0"	62' TO 66' 62' TO 64'

Figure 13-7. *Parking lot design data.*

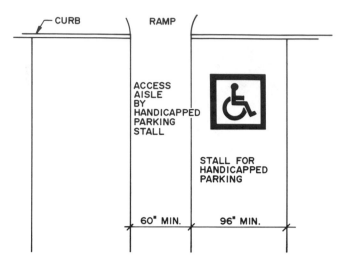

Figure 13-8. Parking spaces designed to accommodate the handicapped driver.

Symbols

Symbols used on site plans are shown in Fig. 13-10. Note that most of these are drawn using a thin line.

Technical Vocabulary

Following are some important technical terms used in this chapter. Write a brief definition for each.

Title sheet
Index to drawings
Site plan
Vicinity map
Plat

Study Questions

Answer the following study questions without referring to the text. Then check your answers with the text and correct those that were wrong.

1. What information is commonly found on the title sheet?

2. How are drawings for large commercial buildings numbered?

3. What is shown on the land survey?

4. What is a bench mark?

5. What is generally shown on the site plan?

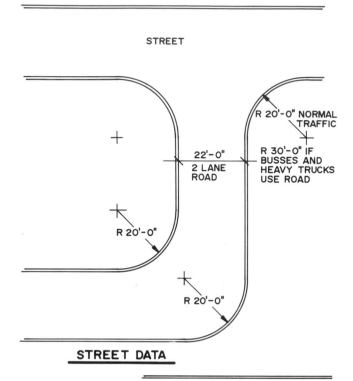

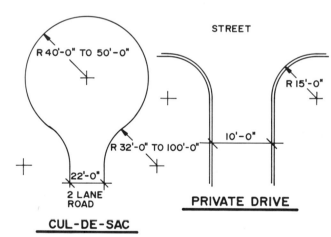

Figure 13-9. Typical street and driveway design data.

6. What scales are used to draw the site plan?

7. What is shown on the drawing of a parking lot?

Laboratory Problems

1. Prepare a title sheet for the residence designed in Chapter 8.

2. Prepare a site plan for the residence designed in Chapter 8.

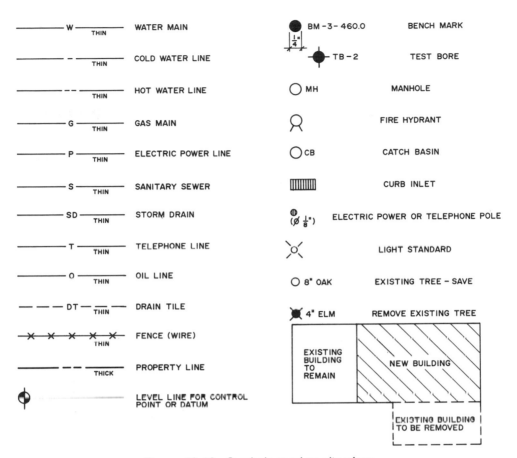

Figure 13-10. Symbols used on site plans.

3. Prepare a title sheet for the retail store designed in Chapter 8. Give the job a name that you like, such as "Economy Camera Shop."

4. Prepare a site plan for the retail store designed in Chapter 8. Use the information from the vicinity drawing included with the problem. Include full data on the parking area designed.

14

Floor Plans

The floor plan is developed first because all of the other drawings are related to it. It is often not completely finished until the other drawings are made because they sometimes will require adjustments in the floor plan. For example, as the structure of a building is developed, it may be decided to move some of the interior walls to enclose and hide a series of columns. The floor plan is possibly the most important drawing because it contains a large amount of information about the building and other drawings depend upon it for their basic information.

A floor plan is a section drawing made by a horizontal cutting plane passing through the building with the upper part removed (Fig. 14-1). In general it is assumed to pass about 3 or 4 ft above the floor. However, this is not strictly followed because it is often necessary to move up to catch a high feature such as a high window or go above cabinets or appliances. Therefore, the actual cutting plane can be raised and lowered as needed to show the information desired.

In Fig. 14-2 are typical examples of how cutting planes pass through buildings. In a single story building it is assumed to pass 3 to 4 ft above the floor. In a two or more story building a plane is passed through each floor in this manner. Sometimes a room is two or more stories high. This will be shown on the upper level floor plans and labeled "open." Split-level buildings present a more difficult choice. The plane must be raised or lowered to show each level. Since there are many possible arrangements for split level buildings the one in Fig. 14-2 is only one example. Split level buildings can split left to right, right to left, front to back, back to front, or have an entrance somewhere in between all of the various floor levels.

A typical floor plan indicates the location of interior partitions, doors, windows, stairs, built-in cabinets, appliances, plumbing fixtures, and on residential drawings, the location of electrical features. All features are drawn to scale. The windows are drawn using symbols and doors open to show the direction of swing. Swinging doors are drawn perpendicular to the wall on which they are hung and the swing is shown with a quarter circle. Doors and windows are indicated by symbols that are shown in the Appendix.

Preliminary Considerations

After the floor plan has been designed and before drawing can begin, it is necessary to select the size of drawing paper to use. Remember, all drawings in a set must be on the same size sheet. The selection of the sheet size is generally determined by the size of the floor plan. Usually the floor plan is the largest single drawing. After you select the scale you can quickly find the overall dimensions of the plan. Remember to allow for exterior items as porches and solar green houses. Then allow about 3 in. on each side for dimensions. The work area available is not the sheet size but what is left after the border and title block is in place. Borders and title blocks are discussed in Chapter 6. Standard sheet sizes are shown in Chapter 1.

Selecting a Scale

Residential floor plans are usually small. Therefore, they are drawn to the scale $1/4'' = 1'-0''$. This reduces the

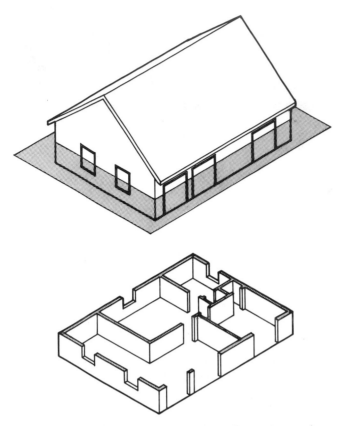

Figure 14-1. *The floor plan is a horizontal section of the building made by a cutting plane passed parallel with the floor and through the center of the windows.*

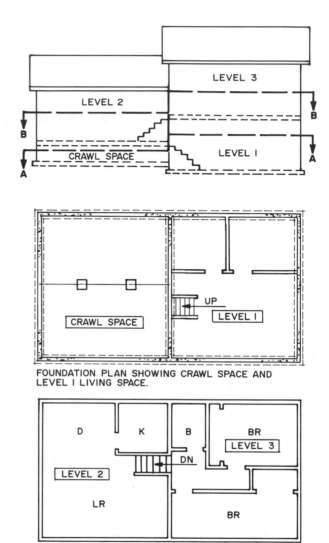

FOUNDATION PLAN SHOWING CRAWL SPACE AND LEVEL I LIVING SPACE.

FLOOR PLAN SHOWING LEVELS 2 AND 3.

Figure 14-2. *Sections are used to draw foundation and floor plans. This is a side by side split level building.*

size 48 times. The foundation plan and elevations use the same scale. Other parts of a set of drawings use larger scales because it is necessary to show great detail. Recommended scales for residential work are in Fig. 14-3.

Since commercial buildings are large they commonly use the scale $1/8'' = 1'-0''$ for the floor plan, foundation plan and elevations. If the building is very large the scale $1/16'' = 1'-0''$ is used or the drawing is made in sections separated by a match line. This is discussed later in this chapter.

Recommended scales for typical commercial drawings are in Fig. 14-4.

How Much Information to Give?

The amount of information given depends upon the size of the project and the complexity of the proposed construction. The plans for a small residence could contain more detailed information than a multistory building because the design is simpler and materials used limited. A major use of the floor plan is to locate partitions, doors, windows, and stairs. This is supplemented by a set of specifications. *Specifications* are a word description of the scope of the work, materials to be used, method of installation, and quality of workmanship required for the building under consideration. They are utilized with the working drawings as part of the construction contract. An outline of a typical specification document is in Chapter 9. There is no need to include on the floor plan detailed information that is in the specifications. Usually a generic term is used on the floor plan to describe an article, such as a water heater. In the specifications this would be described in detail, including its size, electrical or gas requirements, brand, and so on. In fact it could cause great difficulty if this detailed information were placed on the floor plan and in the specifications. If for some reason a decision was made to change something about the water heater and both documents were not changed, conflicting requirements would occur.

U.S. Customary Scales (in.)	
Floor plan	$\frac{1}{4}'' = 1'0''$
Foundation plan	$\frac{1}{4}'' = 1'-0''$
Elevations	$\frac{1}{4}'' = 1'-0''$
Construction details	$\frac{3}{4}''$ to $1\frac{1}{2}'' = 1'-0''$
Wall sections	$\frac{3}{4}''$ to $1\frac{1}{2}'' = 1'-0''$
Cabinet details	$\frac{3}{8}''$ to $\frac{1}{2}'' = 1'-0''$
Site plan	$1'' = 20'$ or $40'$

ISO Metric Scales (mm)	
Floor plan	1:50
Foundation plan	1:50
Elevations	1:50
Construction details	1:20 and 1:10
Wall sections	1:20 and 1:10
Cabinet details	1:50 and 1:25
Site plan	1:100

Figure 14-3. Scales used for residential drawings.

Drawing	U.S. Customary (in.)	SI Metric (mm)
Floor plan	$\frac{1}{8}'' = 1'-0''$	1:100
Foundation plan	$\frac{1}{8}'' = 1'-0''$	1:100
Elevations	$\frac{1}{8}'' - 1'0''$	1:100
Construction details	$\frac{1}{2}''$ to $1\frac{1}{2}''$ $= 1'-0''$	1:25 or 1:10
Interior details	$\frac{1}{2}'' = 1'-0''$	1:25
Building sections	$\frac{1}{4}'' = 1'-0''$	1:50
Framing details	$\frac{1}{8}'' = 1'-0''$	1:100
Lighting, electrical, heating, plumbing, air conditioning plans	$\frac{1}{8}'' = 1'-0''$	1:100
Site plan	$1'' = 20'$ or $40'$	1:100 1:200, or 1:500

Figure 14-4. Scales used for commercial drawings.

Beginning the Drawing

Layout the exterior and interior walls very lightly if you are using manual drafting techniques. They will be darkened and drawn as thick lines later after all details have been located. The computer will indicate these on the screen and they can be changed rapidly and easily when necessary. Remember, exterior and interior walls are drawn with thick, dark lines. All other details such as stairs, doors, cabinets, and dimensions are drawn with thin, dark lines. Remember when using the computer to instruct it to draw the correct line width. The procedure for laying out and finishing a floor plan is in Fig. 14-5. Since many walls are the same width, set a dividers on this width and mark them. This is much faster than measuring each one.

The wall sizes will vary with the design. It is a matter of deciding how each wall is to be constructed and adding the thickness of the materials. Some typical sizes are in Fig. 14-6. Symbols used to indicate wall construction on a plan are in the Appendix.

Draw Doors and Windows

Now draw the doors and windows using the proper symbols. These are drawn with thin, dark lines (Fig. 14-7). When using the computer, you can call up the symbols for doors and windows from the symbol library.

The selection of the style of window is an important feature of the exterior design as well as meeting code requirements for natural light and ventilation. There are available an extensive array of windows utilizing wood, steel, aluminum, and plastic materials. Double and triple glazing is common as is the use of energy efficient glass. Information about doors and windows is in the Appendix. The Sweet's Catalog is the best source for detailed information.

As you locate doors, consider the traffic pattern in the building and the location of other doors, furniture, and door swing. The location of bathroom fixtures must, among other things, leave room for the door to swing into the room. It is best if a swinging door can stand open against a partition. Other types of doors such as pocket, sliding, accordian, and bifold often are most useful.

When selecting windows and doors, record the information you will need for the door and window schedule. This includes unit size, rough opening, and any special features such as plastic cladding or double glazing. Then when doing the schedules, you will not have to find the information about the windows again.

Exterior doors in residential construction range from $2'-6'' \times 6'-8''$ to $3'-6'' \times 8'-0''$. Interior doors range from $1'-6''$ to $3'-4''$ in width and $6'-0''$ to $7'-0''$ high. Standard sizes are in Fig. 14-8. Doors for commercial construction vary widely. They are generally metal and glass. Codes limit the width to $4'-0''$ maximum.

Draw the Details

Now add other details using thin, black lines. This includes things such as stairs, cabinets, appliances, bathroom fixtures, furnace, water heater, fireplace, and counters.

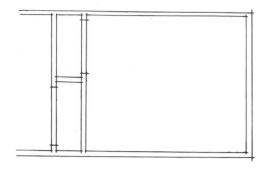

1. DRAW INTERIOR AND EXTERIOR WALLS WITH A THIN, LIGHT LINE.

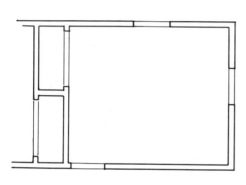

2. LOCATE DOOR AND WINDOW OPENINGS AND DRAW WALLS THICK AND DARK.

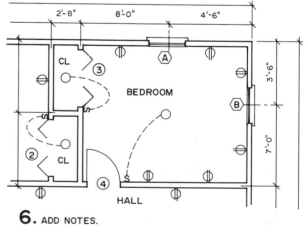

3. ADD DETAILS AS DOOR AND WINDOW SYMBOLS, STARS, AND CABINETS.

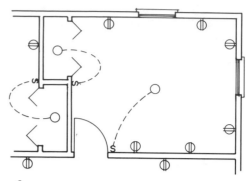

4. ADD ELECTRICAL FEATURES.

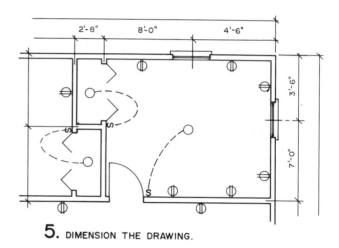

5. DIMENSION THE DRAWING.

6. ADD NOTES.

Figure 14-5. *The steps for laying out a floor plan.*

Wall Construction	Thickness (in.)
Wood-framed wall	
Exterior (2 × 4 stud)	6
Exterior (2 × 6 stud)	8
Interior (2 × 4 stud)	$4\frac{1}{2}$
Interior (2 × 6 stud)	$6\frac{1}{2}$
Brick veneer over frame	10
Brick, 2 courses	8
Brick, 2 courses and air space	9 to 10
Brick, 3 courses	12
Concrete block	8, 10, 12
Metal stud walls	$2\frac{1}{2}$, $3\frac{5}{8}$, 4, 6, 8
Precast concrete double tees	3″ slab with 14″ rib

Figure 14-6. *Typical wall thicknesses.*

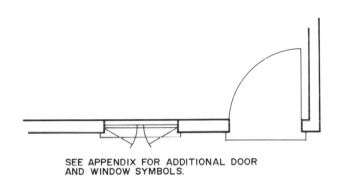

SEE APPENDIX FOR ADDITIONAL DOOR AND WINDOW SYMBOLS.

Figure 14-7. *Door and window symbols are drawn with thin lines.*

Hollow and Solid Core Interior and Exterior Doors

Height	Hollow core interior doors $1\frac{3}{8}$″ and $1\frac{3}{4}$″ thick — Width 1'-6″ 1'-8″ 1'-10″	2'-0″ to 3'-0″ by 2″ increments	Hollow core exterior doors $1\frac{3}{4}$″ thick — Width 2'-8″ to 3'-0″ by 2″ increments	Solid core interior doors $1\frac{3}{8}$″ and $1\frac{3}{4}$″ thick — Width 2'-0″ 2'-4″ 2'-6″ 2'-8″ 3'-0″ 3'-4″	Solid core exterior doors $1\frac{3}{4}$″ thick — Width 2'-4″ 2'-6″ 2'-8″ 3'-0″ 3'-6″
6'-0″		●			
6'-6″	●	●			
6'-8″	●	●	●	●	●
6'-10″	●	●	●		
7'-0″	●	●	●	●	●

Height	Interior wood panel doors $1\frac{3}{8}$″ and $1\frac{3}{4}$″ thick — Width 1'-6″ 2'-0″ 2'-4″ 2'-6″ 2'-8″ 3'-0″ 3'-4″	Height	Exterior wood panel doors $1\frac{3}{8}$″, $1\frac{3}{4}$″ and $2\frac{1}{4}$″ thick — Width 2'-6″ 2'-8″ 3'-0″ 3'-4″ 3'-6″
6'-0″	● ● ● ●	6'-6″	●
6'-6″	● ● ● ● ●	6'-8″	● ● ● ●
6'-8″	● ● ● ● ● ● ●	7'-0″	● ● ● ●
7'-0″	● ● ● ● ● ●	7'-6″	● ● ●
		8'-0″	● ●

Figure 14-8. *Selected sizes for wood doors.*

A stair detail will show a top view of the stair. Draw surrounding walls or railings, treads, and handrails. Then using an arrow indicate if the stair is running up to a floor above or down to a floor below. To a basement it is labeled DOWN. To a floor above it is labeled UP. The tread and riser information is recorded on this arrow or in a clear area beside the stair. See Fig. 14-9.

The width of stair, tread, and riser sizes, and landing sizes are regulated by codes. Stair standards for residential construction are in Fig. 14-10. Stair standards for commercial construction are in Fig. 14-11.

The layout of bathrooms and restrooms must meet standards for space utilization. In Fig. 14-12 are examples of layouts for commercial and residential use. Also shown are examples for facilities for the handicapped. Notice the symbols used to indicate the various fixtures. The range of sizes for bathroom fixtures varies considerably. Refer to manufacturers literature and Sweet's Catalogs for information on various sizes and styles available. Symbols are in Chapter 22. Remember to plan for other features

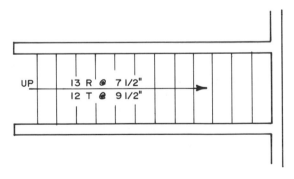

UP | 13 R @ 7 1/2″ / 12 T @ 9 1/2″

Figure 14-9. *Tread and riser data are located on the plan view of the stair.*

such as mirrors, medicine cabinets, soap dishes, towel racks, toilet paper holders, paper towel dispenser and waste container, electric hand dryer, and liquid or powder soap dispensers. Appropriate electrical outlets for hair dryers and electric toothbrushes are also necessary. If natural ventilation is not possible, locate a mechanical ex-

Width	$3'-0''$ with $3\frac{1}{2}''$ handrail
Min. tread (interior)	$9''$
Max. riser	$8\frac{1}{4}''$
Min. tread (exterior)	$11''$
Min. riser (exterior)	$7\frac{1}{2}''$
Landings should be as wide in the direction of travel as the width of the stair.	
Min. headroom main stairs	$6'-8''$

Figure 14-10. Standards for sizing stairs in residential construction.

Width min. 44 in. with $3\frac{1}{2}$-in. handrail and occupant load of 50 or more

Width min. 36 in. with $3\frac{1}{2}$-in. with $3\frac{1}{2}$-in. handrail and occupant load of 49 or less

Min. tread   11 in.

Min. riser   4 in.   max. riser   7 in.

Landings should be as wide in the direction of travel as the width of the stair.

There should be no more than 12 ft vertically between landings.

Figure 14-11. Standards for sizing stairs in commercial construction.

haust fan in the wall or ceiling. Additional information on plumbing design is in Chapter 22.

Kitchen planning involves the arranging of cabinets and appliances to handle three major activities—storage (cabinets, refrigerator), food preparation and clean-up (sink, disposal, compactor), and cooking (stove, oven, microwave). The cabinets may be selected from mass-produced stock sizes (Fig. 14-13) or be custom made. Size specifications for stock cabinets are in Fig. 14-14 and 14-15.

The planning of a kitchen can produce many different arrangements. Typical design solutions include corridor, U-shape, L-shape, and I-shape kitchens (Fig. 14-16). Following are some basic design considerations when planning residential kitchens:

1. The walking distance between the three centers of activity should not exceed 22 ft.
2. Allow at least 3 ft of countertop on each side of a sink.
3. Place the dishwasher and compactor beside the sink.
4. Allow at least 2 ft of countertop on each side of a cooking unit.
5. Allow at least 1 ft of countertop beside the refrigerator and freezer.
6. Use a hood to remove fumes.

7. The countertop height at the sink for the handicapped must be able to be adjusted.

In Fig. 14-17 are graphic symbols used to represent the common cabinets and appliances in kitchens. After the kitchen has been drawn, each kitchen wall is identified by a symbol. This symbol gives the letter that identifies the elevation to be drawn of that wall and gives the number of the sheet upon which it was drawn (Fig. 14-16). These elevations are usually drawn to the same scale as the floor plan, though a larger scale is acceptable. See Chapter 16 for more details.

Many residences and commercial buildings have a variety of built-in units, as bookshelves, counters, and display cabinets. These are shown on the floor plan as simple line drawings shown from the top. They are identified with a note and a symbol giving their elevation identification letter and the number of the sheet upon which the elevation was drawn (Fig. 14-18). See Chapter 22 for details.

Other features as furnaces and water heaters are shown with standard symbols.

Locate Electrical Features

Now show the location of electrical features on residential plans. Larger commercial buildings will usually have a separate electrical drawing which shows the location of each item and the circuitry desired. All these features are shown with symbols. A few of the more frequently used symbols are in Fig. 14-19. Detailed information is in Chapter 22.

Dimension the Floor Plan

Since it will be used to locate walls, windows, doors, and other features, the floor plan must be carefully dimensioned. Even if the drawing is a little out of scale the dimensions must be correct.

Dimensioning Techniques

Architectural dimensions are placed as shown in Fig. 14-20. The distances are recorded in feet and inches above the dimension line. If the drawing is metric, all dimensions are in millimeters. The dimension line is continuous between the extension lines. The extension line goes past the dimension line about $\frac{1}{8}$ in. When arrows or dots are used to indicate the ends of the dimension line, they are stopped exactly on it. When 45° slashes are used, the dimension line extends a little past the extension line. The extension line does not touch the object from which it is

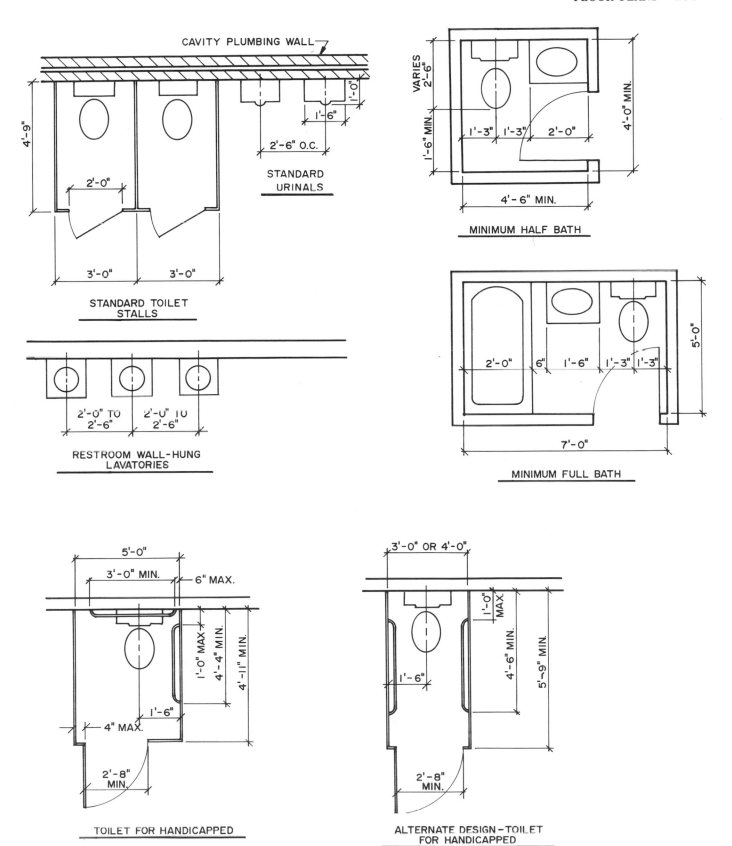

Figure 14-12. Design standards for residential and commercial restroom facilities.

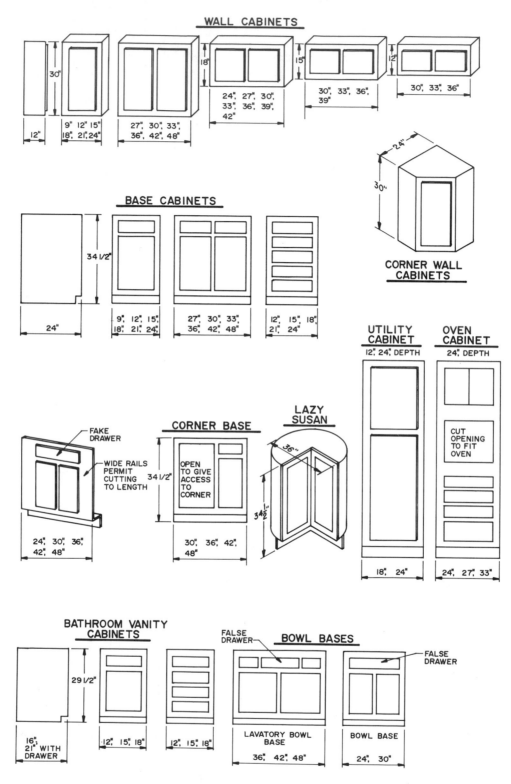

Figure 14-13. *Standard sizes for mass produced kitchen cabinets.*

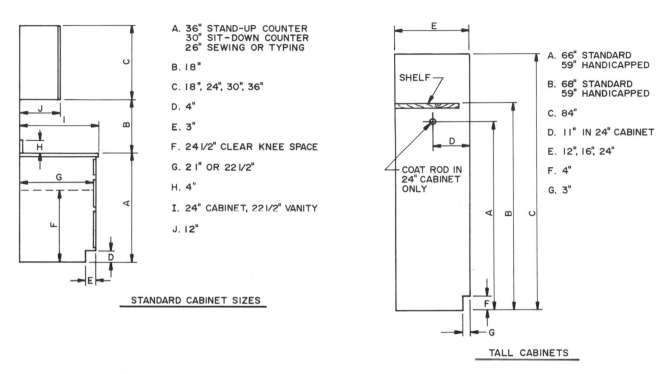

Figure 14-14. Height and depth standards for mass produced kitchen cabinets.

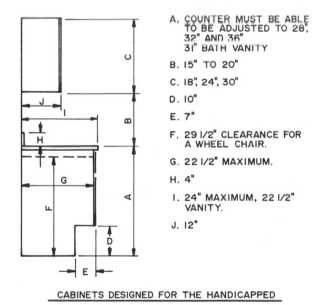

A, COUNTER MUST BE ABLE TO BE ADJUSTED TO 28", 32" AND 36". 31" BATH VANITY

B. 15" TO 20"

C. 18", 24", 30"

D. 10"

E. 7"

F. 29 1/2" CLEARANCE FOR A WHEEL CHAIR.

G. 22 1/2" MAXIMUM.

H. 4"

I. 24" MAXIMUM, 22 1/2" VANITY.

J. 12"

CABINETS DESIGNED FOR THE HANDICAPPED

Figure 14-15. Height and depth standards for kitchen cabinets designed for the handicapped.

drawn. Arrowheads are made about $\frac{1}{8}$ in. long and one-third as wide as they are long. Some prefer to use the 45° type arrowhead (Fig. 14-21).

Dimensions placed in vertical positions are drawn parallel with these surfaces and are read from the right side of the drawing. All notes are lettered so they are read from the bottom of the drawing. They are often directed to some feature with a leader. The leader comes off the beginning or end of the note. It may be a gracefully curved freehand leader or mechanically made (Fig. 14-22). Dimensions and notes are lettered $\frac{3}{32}$ or $\frac{1}{8}$ in. high. Titles are lettered $\frac{3}{16}$ to $\frac{1}{4}$ in. high.

Frame Buildings

Begin by dimensioning the exterior walls. This example is for a frame building. Exterior walls will usually require two or three rows of dimensions on each exterior wall. Begin by examining Fig. 14-23. Here the first row of dimensions locates doors, windows, interior walls meeting exterior walls, and changes in the building shape and is placed 1 to $1\frac{1}{2}$ in. from the exterior wall. It should clear any porches or decks that may project from the building. The second row of dimensions is about 1 in. from the first row. It locates the lengths of the various sections of the exterior wall. This helps the carpenter because it is not necessary to add dimensions to find the wall length. The third row is the overall dimension. It is usually placed on all sides of the floor plan. The overall dimensions run from the outside face of the stud on one wall to the outside face of the stud on the other side of the building. The location of the stud in relationship to the foundation varies depending upon how the house is to be framed. If the stud is set

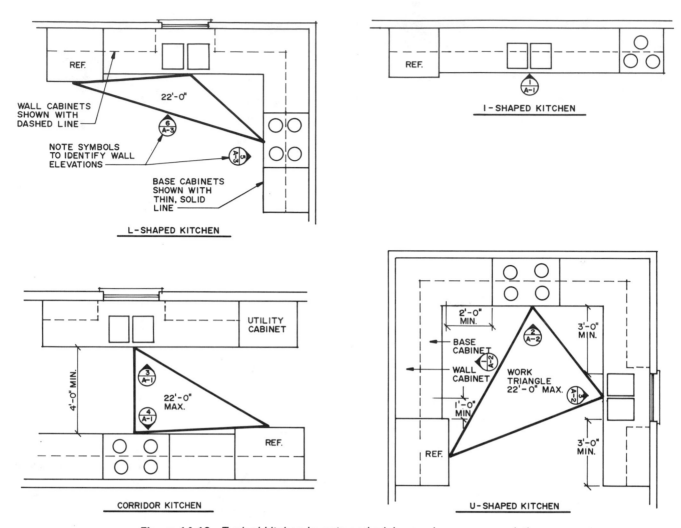

Figure 14-16. *Typical kitchen layouts and minimum size recommendations.*

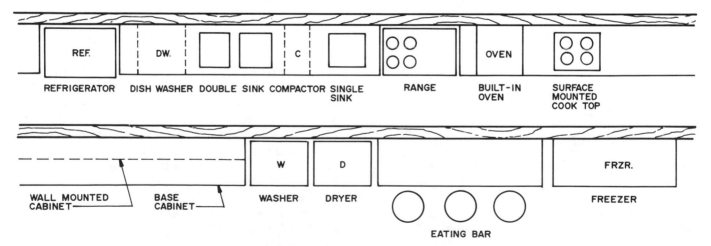

Figure 14-17. *Symbols used to identify kitchen cabinets and appliances.*

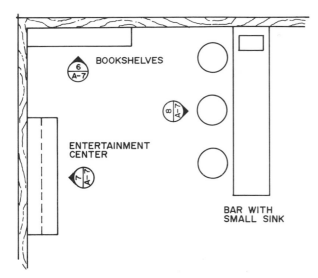

Figure 14-18. Cabinets and built-in units are shown on the floor plan.

of the sheathing shorter than the overall length of the foundation.

Remember, when dimensioning an opening, as doors and windows in a frame wall, dimension to the center of the opening.

Frame interior partitions can be dimensioned to their centerline. When dimensioning from a frame exterior wall, the dimension runs from the outside face of the exterior wall stud to the center of the frame interior partition. Some prefer to dimension interior frame walls to the faces of the stud. When this done, it is necessary to indicate the stud thickness (Fig. 14-25). When possible run dimensions in continuous strings across the building.

Masonry Buildings

If the building has solid masonry walls it is dimensioned as shown in Fig. 14-26. The door, window, and other openings, as vents or access doors, are dimensioned to the sides of the opening. This is the masonry opening needed for installation of the doors and windows. Usually the sizes of doors and windows used in masonry construction are chosen so the openings will follow the masonry block module. This eliminates the need to cut block or bricks around the opening.

When locating interior masonry partitions you can locate to one face if it is part of the exterior string of dimensions. When interior masonry partitions are dimen-

flush with the outside of the foundation, the overall dimension is located as shown in Fig. 14-24B. If the sheathing is to be flush with the foundation, the overall dimension is located as shown at 14-24A. Some put F.O.S. by these dimensions to indicate it is to the face of the stud. When built as at 14-24B, the overall on the floor plan and the foundation are the same length. When built as at 14-22A, the overall on the floor plan is twice the thickness

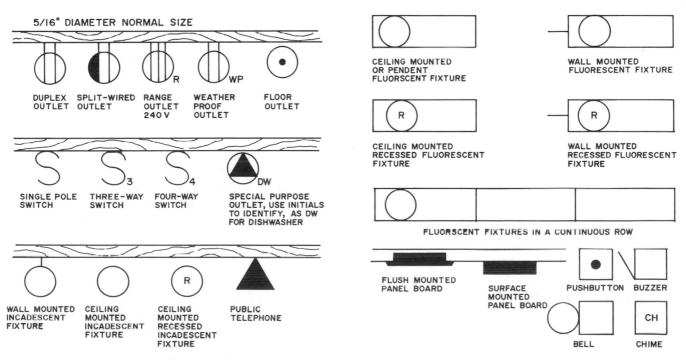

Figure 14-19. Selected electrical symbols used on floor plans.

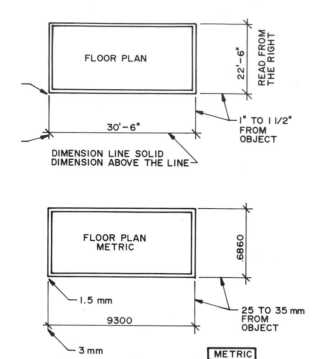

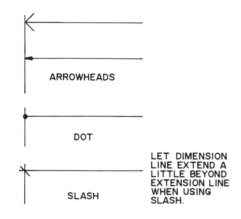

Figure 14-20. *Dimensions are placed above the dimension line.*

Figure 14-21. *Acceptable terminal symbols used on the ends of dimension lines.*

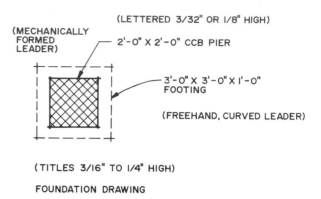

Figure 14-22. *Two types of leaders used on architectural drawings. Generally all of one style are used on a drawing rather than mixing the two styles.*

sioned inside the floor plan they are located to the faces with the wall thickness shown. Wood and steel interior walls in a masonry building are located to their centerline or face as previously described.

Masonry walls often have pilasters. A *pilaster* is a masonry column built into the wall to stiffen it or to hold the end of a beam (Fig. 14-27). Pilasters are located by dimensioning to their centerline. Concrete columns are located the same way. These are located using a column reference grid (Fig. 14-27). The horizontal grid identifies

the location of each row of columns or pilasters by numbering them from left to right. The vertical grid identifies each with a letter beginning at the top. Each pilaster or column can then be identified by its location on the grid, such as column B2.

When dimensioning a floor plan, line up the dimensions across it in strings rather than staggering them or placing them at random. This makes it easier to read the drawing and check it for possible incorrect dimensions.

When an exterior wall has an offset, it can be dimensioned as shown in Fig. 14-28. Some prefer to run a long extension line and line up the dimension with the others across the front. Others prefer to place it close to the location of the offset.

There are other parts of a building that are located off the plan, such as posts or columns. These are located by dimensioning from some part of the structure that will be built before the columns. Columns are then spaced by dimensioning from center to center (Fig. 14-29).

Steel-Framed Buildings

Steel-framed buildings have steel columns and beams that carry the wall, floor, and roof loads. On the floor plan the steel columns will be shown. The entire structural frame will be detailed on a series of structural drawings.

Steel columns are supported on the ground by a large concrete footing (Fig. 14-30). The size and thickness of the footing depends upon the loads to be carried and soil conditions. On the floor plan, steel columns are dimensioned center to center (Fig. 14-31). The concrete footings appear on the foundation plan and are also dimensioned center to center. Therefore, the footing and column location dimensions are the same. Occasionally it is necessary to dimension from the face of the column. Instead

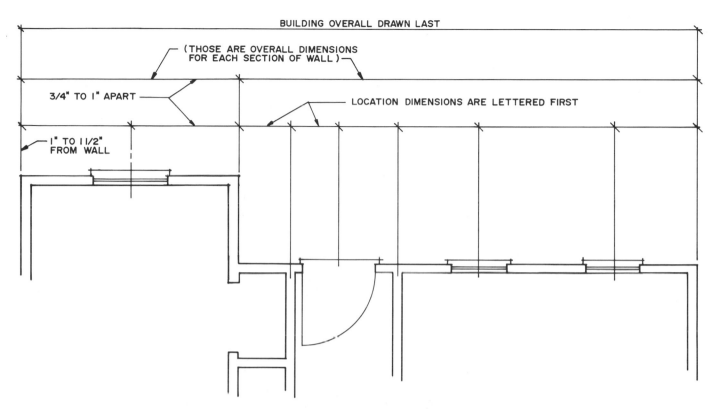

Figure 14-23. *With frame construction, windows and doors are located by their centerline. Partitions meeting exterior walls are located by their centerline.*

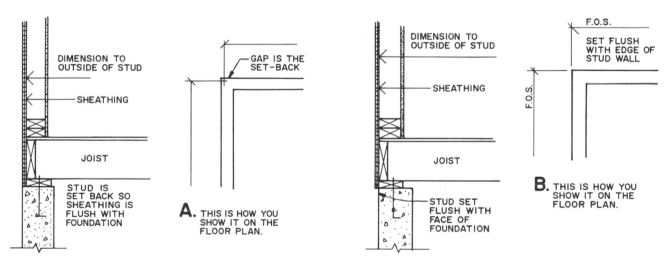

Figure 14-24. *Exterior frame walls are dimensioned to the outside face of the stud.*

of giving the dimension between columns an axial reference plane is used. The engineer usually designs the structure so the columns are the same distance apart. This forms a grid in the same manner as discussed for masonry construction. Each column is identified by its location on the grid, as C-3.

Notes and Identification

Now letter any notes or identification of features. Since the drawing is basically finished, these can be placed in open areas with the knowledge that something, as a dimension, will not be drawn over them.

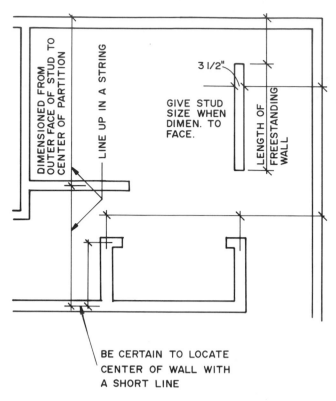

Figure 14-25. *Techniques for dimensioning interior frame partitions.*

Identify each door with a mark. On small buildings, such as a residence, doors could be coded as D-1, D-2, D-3, and so on. All doors that are exactly alike would have the same mark, as D-1, placed by them. If a building had five different types and styles of doors, it would have five different marks. Another system used identifies them with numerals, such as 1, 2, 3, and so on. On large commercial buildings, the rooms are numbered. Whenever possible, the doors are given the same mark number as the room number. If there is more than one door entering a room, the number is followed by a letter, such as 125A, 125B, 125C (Fig. 14-32). Mark numbers are placed inside a circle $\frac{3}{8}$ to $\frac{1}{2}$ in. in diameter.

Windows on small buildings use the same system as doors except the symbol is W-1, W-2, and so on, or by letters such as A, B, C. These are placed inside a circle. Commercial buildings usually identify windows by letters placed inside a hexagon (Fig. 14-33). Door and window marks are used to identify them on the schedules.

On residential drawings, each room is given a name. When several rooms have the same number, such as bedrooms, they are also given a number. On commercial drawings, each space is given a name and a number. This includes rooms, stairs, storage areas, halls, lobbies, and other spaces (Fig. 14-34). These are often $\frac{3}{16}$ in. high letters. The room number is placed inside a rectangular box.

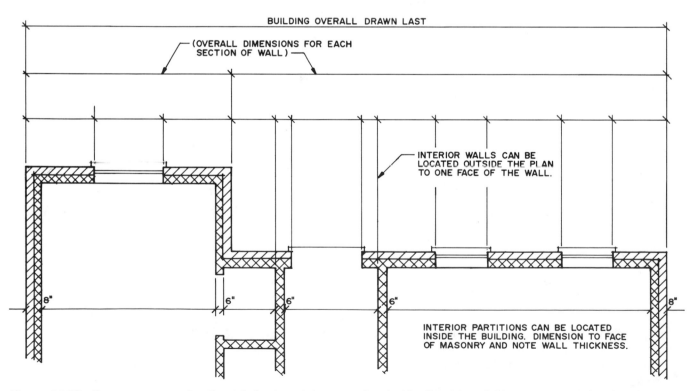

Figure 14-26. *On masonry construction windows and doors are located by the sides of the masonry opening. Interior partitions can be located by one face with the dimensions outside the plan or to their face with the wall thickness given.*

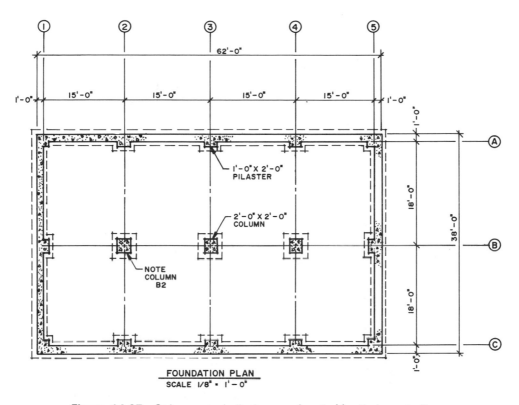

Figure 14-27. *Columns and pilasters are located by their centerlines.*

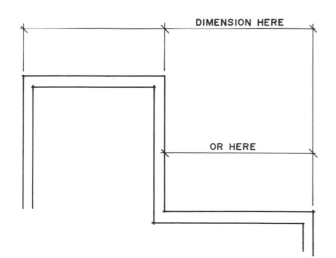

Figure 14-28. *Setbacks in exterior walls can be dimensioned in either of these ways.*

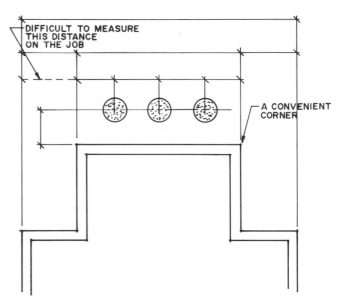

Figure 14-29. *Locate columns from a location that is permanent and near their proposed location.*

Stair data are lettered on the stair when possible. Break the stair tread lines so it is clear. Give the number of risers and the riser size and the number of treads and the tread size. If the stair goes down from the floor plan, place an arrow on it and label it DN. If it goes up, label it UP. Refer back to Fig. 14-9.

Label other things that might not be clear, such as the refrigerator, compactor, dishwasher, water heater, furnace, railing, and bookshelves. Indicate interior elevations with the proper symbol (Fig. 14-35).

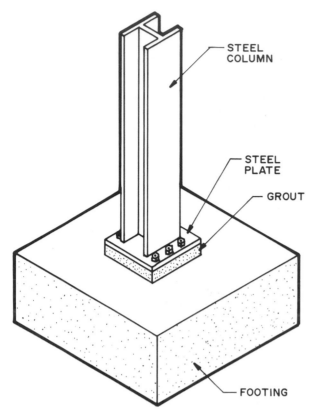

Figure 14-30. A typical steel column and footing.

Indicate sections to be taken through different parts of the building. Sections may be through one feature as a wall or through the entire building. These symbols are shown in the Appendix and applications in Fig. 14-35.

Construction features are noted as a 4-in. concrete porch or garage floor, a redwood deck, column sizes, special floor or wall finish, and other things the designer feels needs a note to clarify a feature.

Using a Match Line

Sometimes a building is so large it is not possible to draw the entire floor plan on one sheet. When this occurs it is broken into two or more parts with match lines. A *match line* is a very thick line composed of long dashes drawn across the floor plan where the building will be divided (Fig. 14-36). The floor plan details are drawn past the match line several inches. When the other half is drawn, it also goes past the match line in the opposite direction. This overlap helps orient the person using the drawing. Dimensions that cross the match line are shown in full size. Some do not put an arrow or terminal symbol on the end of the dimension line crossing the match line while others put a double arrowhead (Fig. 14-37).

Preparing Plans for Buildings Too Large for Use of a Match Line

Some buildings, such as a large shopping center, are so large that the use of match lines is inadequate. These buildings are divided into subunits and each subunit is detailed as a separate building with connections to adjoining subunits indicated (Fig. 14-38). A small-scale drawing of the entire building is made and the subunits identified. This is usually on the cover sheet as part of the site plan. The unit contained in the drawings behind the cover sheet is highlighted on this drawing.

Study Questions

Answer the following study questions without referring to the text. Then check your answers with the text and correct those that were wrong.

1. What is shown on a floor plan?

2. What scales are used for residential floor plans?

3. What scales are used for commercial floor plans?

4. What type of information is included in the specifications?

5. What type of line is used to indicate exterior and interior walls on a floor plan?

6. What type of line is used to draw cabinets and stairs?

7. Sketch the symbols in double hung, fixed, and casement windows.

8. How do you draw window symbols when using the computer?

9. What is shown on the view of the stair?

10. What is the minimum tread and maximum rise for residential and commercial stairs?

11. How can you ventilate a bath that has no exterior wall?

12. What are the three major activities around which the plan of the kitchen is designed?

13. Where can you find information on the variety of types and sizes of bath fixtures?

14. What are the commonly used arrangements of kitchen cabinets and appliances?

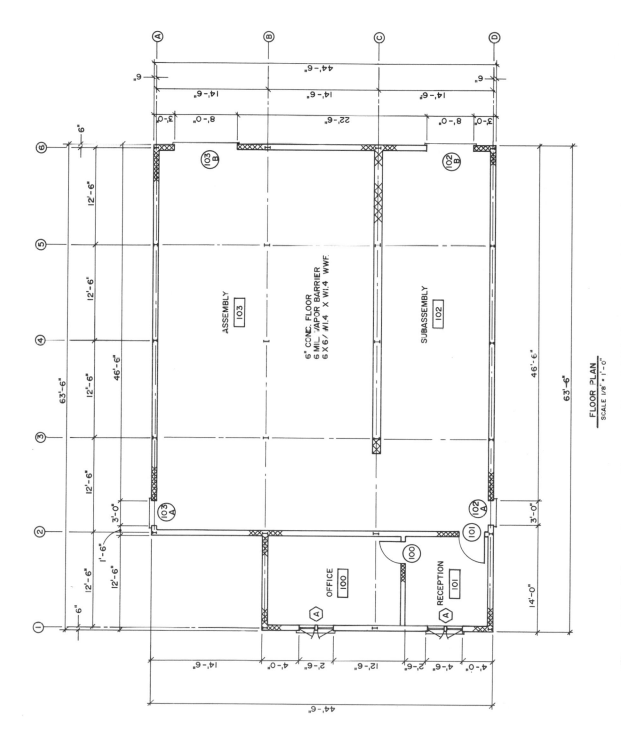

FLOOR PLAN
SCALE 1/8" = 1'-0"

Figure 14-31. Column reference grids are used to establish the locations of the steel columns on this plan.

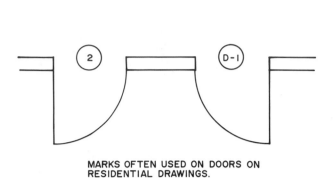

MARKS OFTEN USED ON DOORS ON
RESIDENTIAL DRAWINGS.

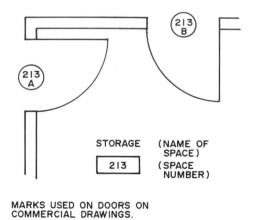

STORAGE (NAME OF
SPACE)

213 (SPACE
NUMBER)

MARKS USED ON DOORS ON
COMMERCIAL DRAWINGS.

Figure 14-32. *Marks used to identify doors on residential and commercial drawings.*

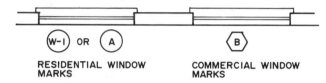

RESIDENTIAL WINDOW
MARKS

COMMERCIAL WINDOW
MARKS

Figure 14-33. *Marks used to identify windows on residential and commercial drawings.*

15. What is the recommended maximum walking distance between the three main centers of activity in a kitchen?

16. How much counterspace should be allowed beside each kitchen appliance?

17. How are the elevations of the walls of a kitchen identified on the floor plan?

18. Sketch the symbols used on the floor plan to indicate the following: duplex outlet, three-way switch, split wired outlet, fluorescent light, door bell, and telephone.

19. What units are used to dimension floor plans when using customary and metric measure?

20. What symbols may be used on the end of a dimension line?

21. Notes on a drawing are lettered parallel to which side?

22. Dimensions on a drawing are lettered parallel to which sides?

23. What is a leader and where is it used?

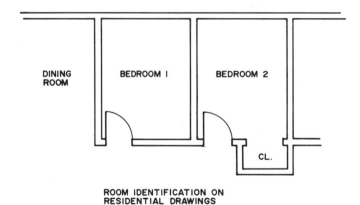

DINING
ROOM   BEDROOM 1   BEDROOM 2

CL.

ROOM IDENTIFICATION ON
RESIDENTIAL DRAWINGS

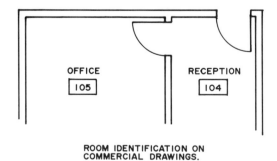

OFFICE   RECEPTION
105   104

ROOM IDENTIFICATION ON
COMMERCIAL DRAWINGS.

Figure 14-34. *Spaces are identified by name and number.*

24. What height letters are used for notes and dimensions?

25. To what point are solid masonry walls dimensioned?

26. How are pilasters and steel or concrete columns located?

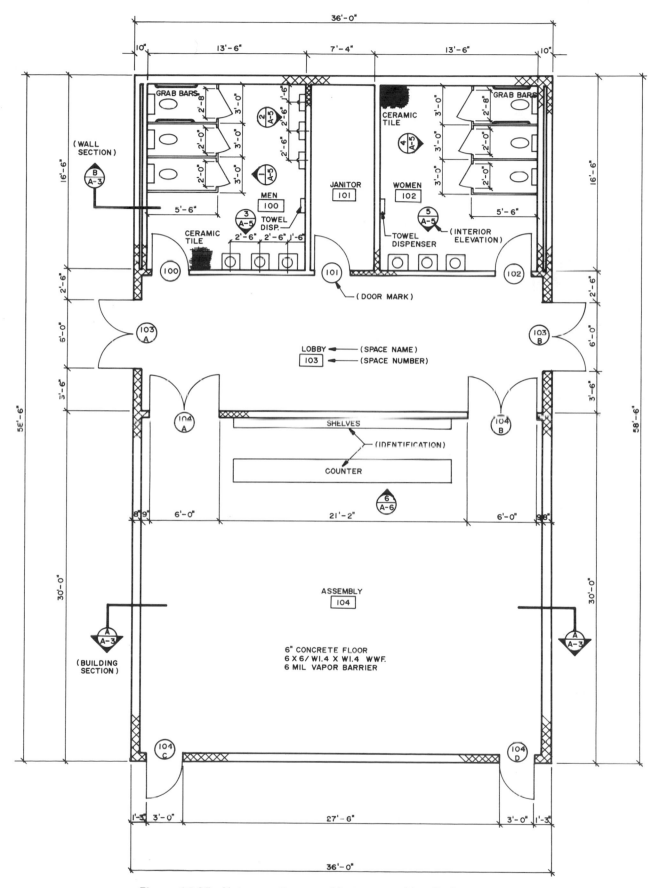

Figure 14-35. *Notes, sections, and features are identified on the drawing.*

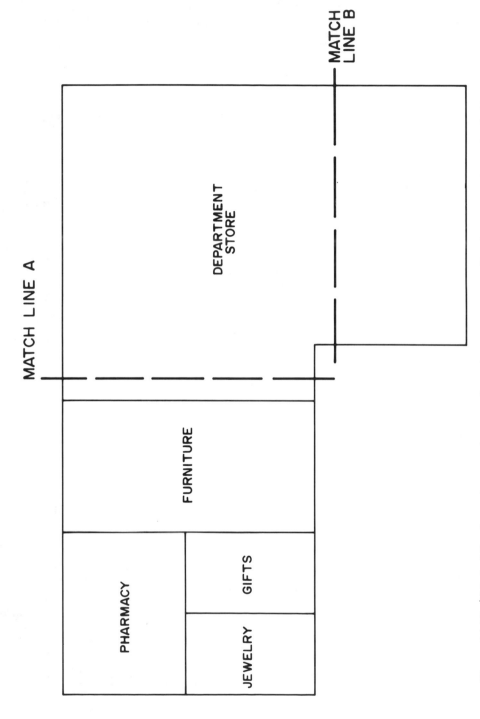

Figure 14-36. *This building is too large to draw the floor plan on one sheet. Therefore it has been divided into three parts with match lines.*

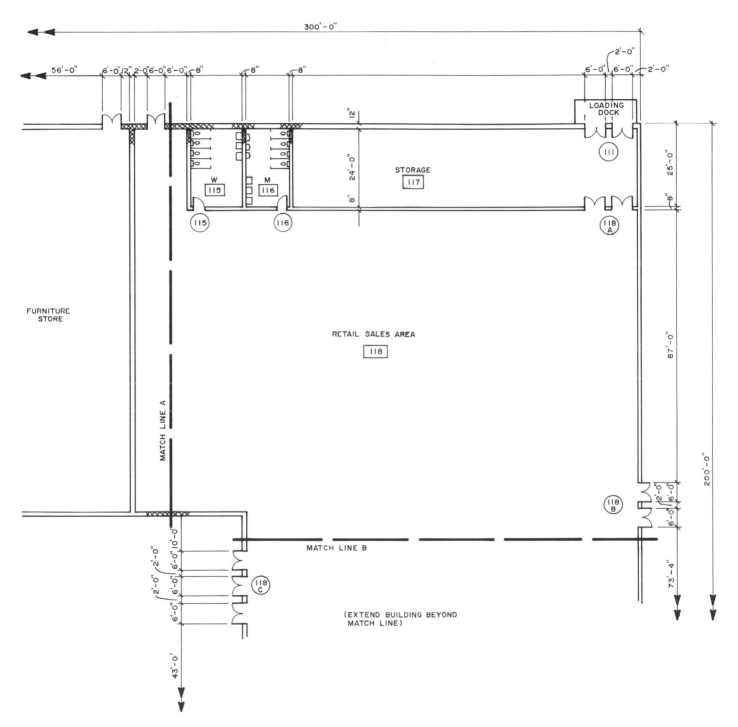

Figure 14-37. *Match lines are used to show where the drawing has been divided.*

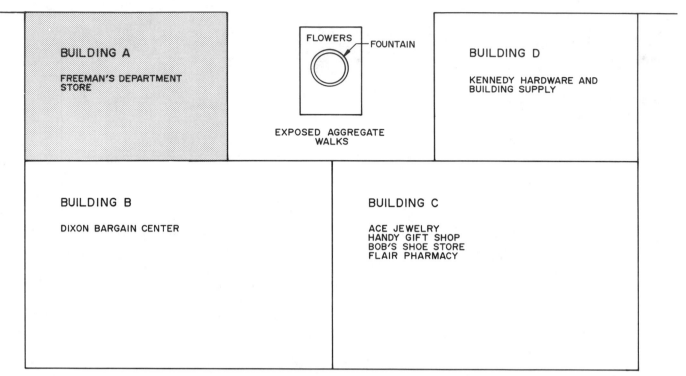

Figure 14-38. *This large building has been divided into subunits each of which is detailed in a separate sheet of working drawings. The drawings for building A are contained in the set which has this drawing on the cover sheet.*

27. What is meant by ''keeping dimensions in strings''?

28. How are doors and windows identified on the floor plan?

29. On floor plans for commercial buildings how are the various rooms, halls, and other spaces identified?

30. How are sections located on the floor plan?

31. What is a ''match line''?

Laboratory Problems

1. Draw a floor plan for the residence designed in Chapter 8. It should be complete in every detail and of the highest quality work.

2. Draw a floor plan for the commercial building designed in Chapter 8. It should be complete in every detail and of the highest quality work.

15

Foundation Plans

The foundation plan is a drawing looking down upon the foundation before the building is built upon it. Since the foundation carries the weight of the building (dead load), things brought into the building (live load), and wind and snow loads, it is very important that it be complete and accurately drawn. It is drawn after the floor plan has been finalized.

Before it can be drawn, a number of engineering calculations must be made. These include the size of the footings, foundation, beams, piers or columns, and pilasters. These are all structural and must carry the loads imposed. Study Chapter 10, Footings and Foundations, for information on soil testing, and the various foundation designs commonly used. The procedures for figuring footing sizes, pier and column footing sizes, and beam sizes are also in Chapter 10.

What Appears on a Foundation Plan?

The actual items to appear on a foundation will vary with the type of foundation. This chapter will discuss three types, basement, crawl space, and concrete slab on grade construction. Following is a check list of items commonly appearing on a foundation plan:

Size of foundation walls
Size of footing
Size and location of beams
Size and location of piers and columns
Size and location of pilasters
Size and location of openings for vents, doors, windows, and access doors
Material symbols
Section symbols
Interior partitions in basements
Furnace and water heater
Electric panel
Electrical features
Plumbing fixtures
Washer, dryer, toilet, lavatories
Notes on unexcavated areas
Notes for floors
Floor joist symbol
Stairs
Fireplace
Chimney
Floor drain
Marks for doors and windows

Drawing a Basement Foundation

A typical foundation plan for a building with a basement is in Fig. 15-1. Refer to this as you read the following comments.

The foundation plan can be laid out by tracing the floor plan or by redrawing it using the design dimensions. If the foundation is redrawn the preliminary layout can be laid over the floor plan as a check for errors. If an error had been made in laying out either plan this would catch it. If an error existed in the floor plan and it was traced, the error would be transferred to the foundation plan.

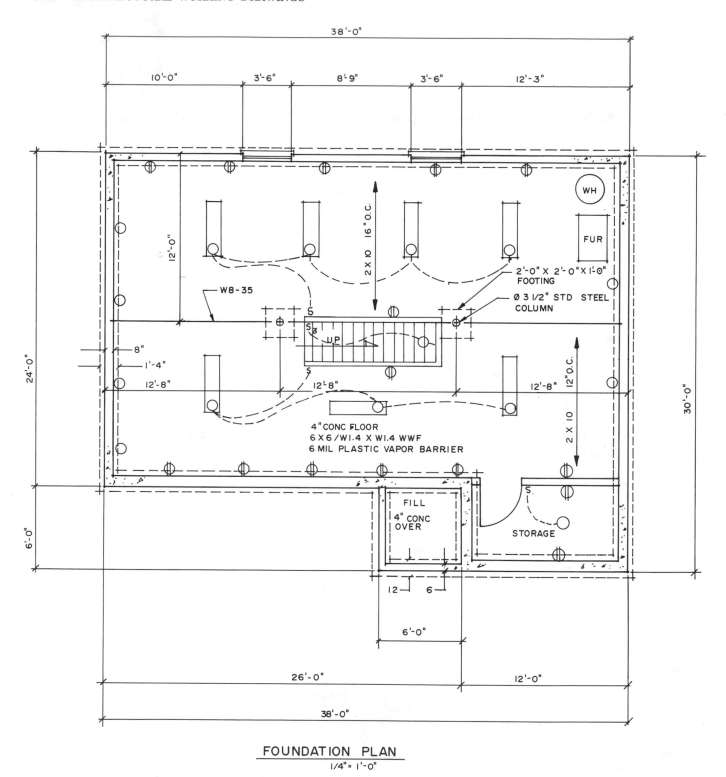

FOUNDATION PLAN
1/4"= 1'-0"

Figure 15-1 *A typical foundation plan for a building with a full basement. Notice the windows in the rear wall.*

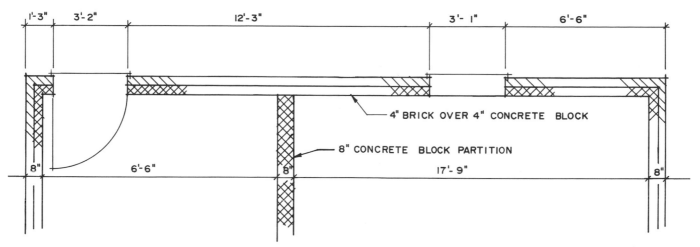

DIMENSIONING MASONRY OPENINGS AND PARTITIONS

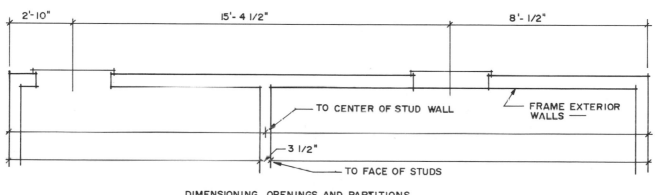

DIMENSIONING OPENINGS AND PARTITIONS
IN FRAME CONSTRUCTION

Figure 15-2. *This is how to locate and dimension frame and masonry interior walls.*

If the floor plan is traced, copy the features that are common to the foundation plan. This could include the outline of exterior walls, stairs, and fireplaces or chimney locations. This means that the scale used is the same as that used for the floor plan. The foundation wall thickness is then drawn. These are drawn with thick lines. Next draw the footings with thin, dashed lines. Dashed lines are used because the footing is below grade and not visible. Now locate beams, using a thick line of long and short dashes. This line represents the centerline of the beam. If the beam requires columns or piers, these are located and drawn. Their footings are drawn with thin dashed lines. Beams are dimensioned by locating them from the outside of the foundation wall. Piers and columns are located by dimensioning to their centerline. Their sizes are given with notes. Pilasters are located by their centerlines on the outside of the basement. The size of the pilaster is given with a note.

Locate door and window openings and vents and access doors in crawl spaces. Door and window openings in ma-

sonry walls are dimensioned to the sides of the opening. Dimensions to all masonry parts of a building are to the face of the masonry. The thickness of the masonry wall must be given in each place it occurs.

If the basement is to be divided into rooms, the walls and doors are drawn and located in the same manner as discussed for floor plans. Wood-framed partitions are located by their center line or to the face of the stud. If dimensioned to the face of the stud, the size of the stud must be indicated. Masonry partitions are located by their face. See Fig. 15-2.

Now add electrical light, convenience outlets, and other electrical features. On large buildings having extensive electrical requirements, a separate electrical drawing of the basement is made. This means the electrical is not shown on the foundation plan. See Chapter 21 for details.

The plumbing fixtures can be added. A separate plumbing drawing of the basement is made. See Chapter 23 for details.

If the heating, ventilating, and air-conditioning units are

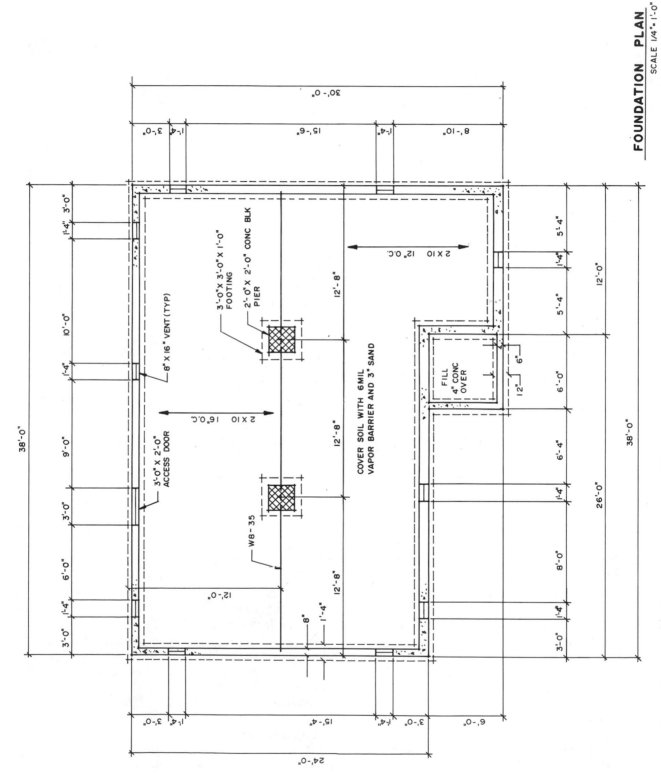

FOUNDATION PLAN

SCALE 1/4" = 1'-0"

Figure 15-3. A typical foundation plan for a building with a crawl space below the wood framed floor. This design shows cast-in-place concrete walls but concrete block foundations are very common.

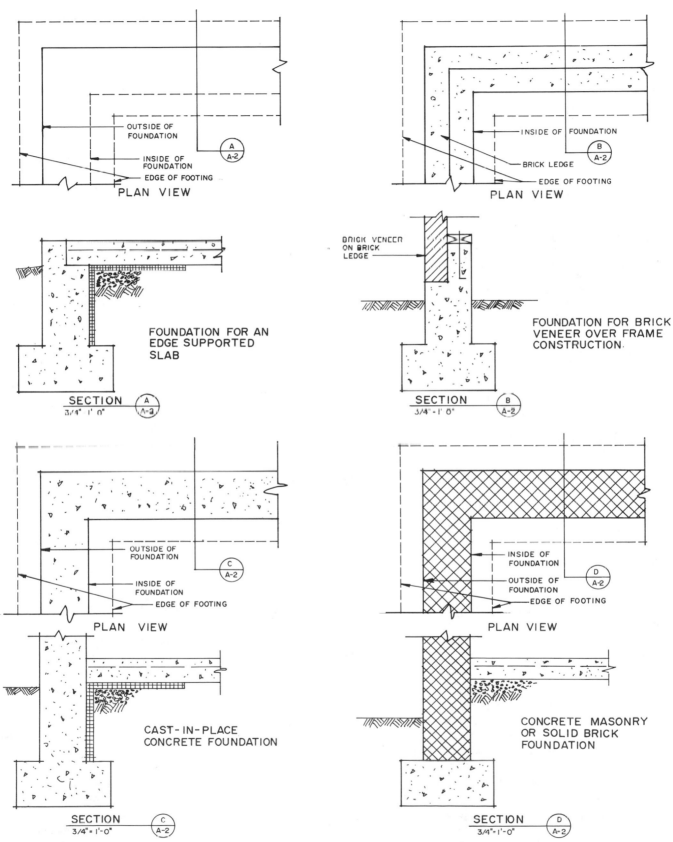

OUTSIDE OF FOUNDATION
INSIDE OF FOUNDATION
EDGE OF FOOTING
A
A-2
PLAN VIEW

FOUNDATION FOR AN EDGE SUPPORTED SLAB

SECTION
3/4" = 1'-0"
A
A-2

INSIDE OF FOUNDATION
BRICK LEDGE
EDGE OF FOOTING
B
A-2
PLAN VIEW

BRICK VENEER ON BRICK LEDGE

FOUNDATION FOR BRICK VENEER OVER FRAME CONSTRUCTION

SECTION
3/4" = 1'-0"
B
A-2

OUTSIDE OF FOUNDATION
INSIDE OF FOUNDATION
EDGE OF FOOTING
C
A-2
PLAN VIEW

CAST-IN-PLACE CONCRETE FOUNDATION

SECTION
3/4" = 1'-0"
C
A-2

INSIDE OF FOUNDATION
OUTSIDE OF FOUNDATION
EDGE OF FOOTING
D
A-2
PLAN VIEW

CONCRETE MASONRY OR SOLID BRICK FOUNDATION

SECTION
3/4" = 1'-0"
D
A-2

Figure 15-4. *Typical concrete slab on grade footing, foundation, and floor constructions showing how they are drawn on the foundation plan and in section.*

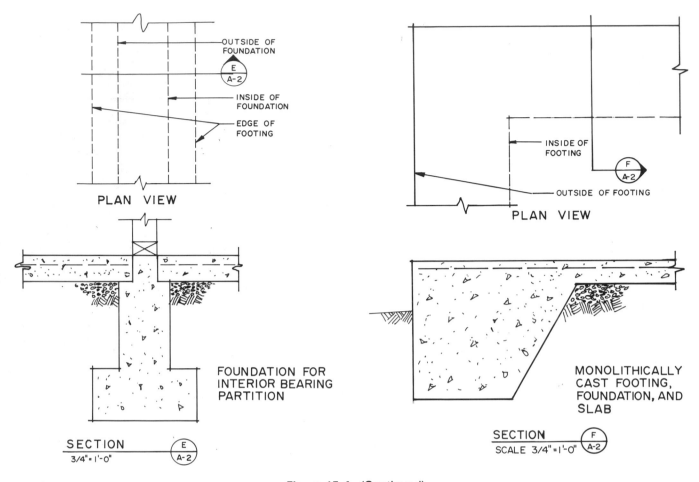

Figure 15-4. (Continued)

in the basement, they are located on this drawing. Separate HVAC drawings are made giving design details. See Chapter 22 for details.

Finally, complete the job by adding notes such as the thickness of the concrete floor with required reinforcing and vapor barrier, room names, and floor joist data. Place material symbols as needed such as on the foundation wall. It is not necessary to completely cover the entire foundation with the symbol. Place some at the corners and where it changes direction.

When dimensioning the foundation, locate the dimensions for doors, windows, and other openings about 1 to $1\frac{1}{2}$ in. from the foundation. Then place the overall dimension about 1 in. outside this. It is customary to place overall dimensions on all sides even when they repeat the one on the opposite side.

All dimensions and features such as stairs, doors, and so on are drawn with thin lines. Foundation walls, interior partitions, and the beam symbol are drawn with thick lines. Some drafters prefer to overlap the lines as they meet at corners. Some prefer to make them meet in a sharp corner. The computer will draw sharp corners.

The title and scale are lettered below the drawing. The title is lettered $\frac{3}{16}$ or $\frac{1}{4}$ in. high while the scale uses $\frac{1}{8}$-in.-high letters.

Drawing a Crawl Space Foundation

This plan is drawn exactly like the foundation plan for a basement just described. See Fig. 15-3. It will have vents in the foundation so the air can be changed below the floor and keep the humidity down. Vents should be placed within 3 to 4 ft of each corner. Additional vents are needed until there is 1 ft^2 of vent opening for every 150 ft^2 of surface area in the crawl space. Every wall should have at least one vent. Typical vent sizes are $5 \times 8\frac{1}{8}$ in., $5 \times 16\frac{1}{2}$ in., and $7\frac{3}{4} \times 16\frac{1}{2}$ in.

An access door in the foundation is needed so repairs can be made in the crawl space. These are usually made from plywood so there is no standard size. A typical size is 32×24 in. This is two concrete blocks long and three high. The access door is located by its sides as are all openings in masonry walls. The size is given by a note.

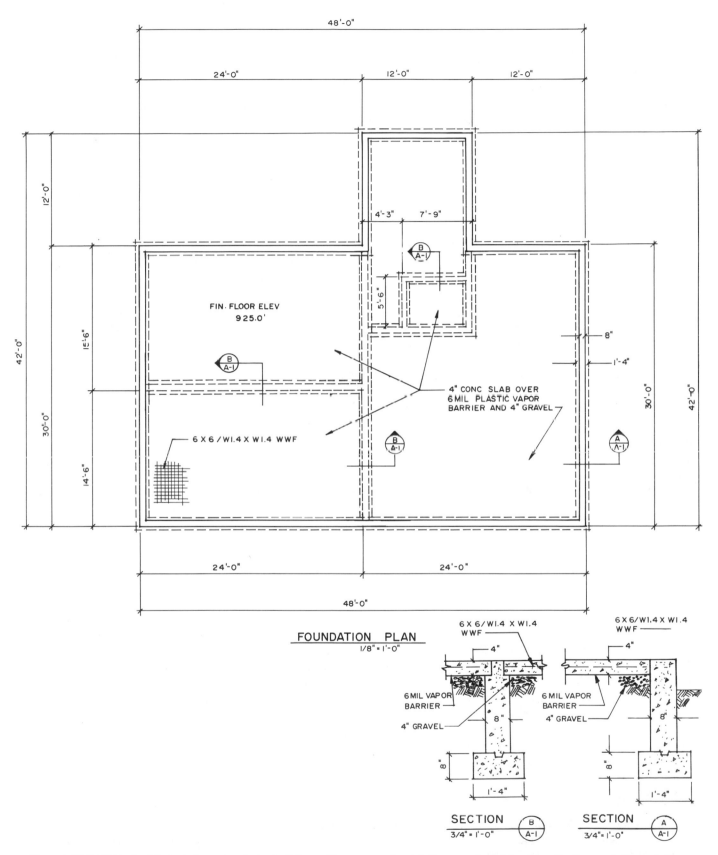

FOUNDATION PLAN
1/8" = 1'-0"

SECTION (B) (A-1)
3/4" = 1'-0"

SECTION (A) (A-1)
3/4" = 1'-0"

Figure 15-5. *A typical foundation plan for a building with a concrete slab floor and cast-in-place footings and foundation for exterior and interior supporting walls. Notice the use of sections to show design details.*

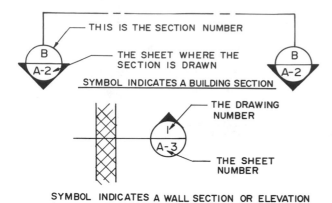

Figure 15-6. *Symbols used to indicate sections on foundation plans.*

Any beam below the floor is usually supported by piers. Piers may be poured concrete or concrete block and are located by dimensioning to their center line. Their size is given with a note. Wood beams are sometimes set on short 4 × 4 or 6 × 6 in. posts that rest on a concrete pier and footing. The beam, pier, and posts are located by their centerline and sizes are given with a note.

If the surface of the earth in the crawl space is to have a vapor barrier placed over it this is shown with a note. If the earth is sloped to one side or corner to a drain this is noted.

The foundation wall and beam are drawn with thick lines and the footings and other features with thin lines.

The plan is dimensioned in the same manner as the basement plan.

Concrete Slab on Grade Foundation

There are several commonly used designs for constructing buildings with concrete slab floors on grade. These are shown in Fig. 15-4. The plan view shows details of how this construction would appear on a foundation drawing. This figure also shows typical sections through this type of construction.

A typical foundation plan for a concrete slab on grad building is in Fig. 15-5. On this building, the slab is not supported on the edges by the foundation. Therefore, both edges of the foundation are visible and drawn with solid lines. The footings are hidden and drawn with dashed lines. Interior load-bearing walls are shown with dashed lines because their footing and foundation are hidden below the slab. They are sized to carry the loads imposed upon them using the same procedures as used for the exterior wall footings. These footings could also be sized to hold equipment often found in commercial buildings.

Notes are used to give floor construction information.

For example, the thickness of the concrete slab is given and the welded wire fabric reinforcing is specified. Also the need for a vapor barrier below the slab is indicated. If the floor has slope, the amount and direction is shown with a note. The elevation of the finished floor is given.

Sections are indicated for interior and exterior load-bearing walls. The meaning of these symbols as used on foundation plans is shown in Fig. 15-6. Additional symbols are in the Appendix. These are also used on basement and crawl space foundations. The slab on grade foundation plan in Fig. 15-7 has the slab and foundation poured monolithically. This means they are poured at the same time. Notice the outside edge of the foundation and footing is visible and is drawn with a solid line. The inside edge of the footing is hidden and drawn with dashed lines. The footings at the sections of thickened slab are drawn with dashed lines. Sections are used to clarify construction.

The foundation plan for a commercial building designed using steel columns to support the floors and roof above is in Fig. 15-8. The basic principles previously discussed for concrete slab construction apply to this plan. The columns are located by dimensioning to their centerline. The same procedure is for wood and cast-in-place and precast concrete columns. Column footing details are clearly shown and located by the same dimensions that locate the columns. Footing and column sizes are indicated with notes.

The design of buildings of this type usually places the columns in orderly rows forming a structural grid. Notice how the vertical grid lines are identified by letters in a circle and the horizontal row uses numbers in a circle. This grid is useful when locating items on the plan. Numerous sections are essential to the complete foundation design. They are indicated using the standard section symbol.

A foundation plan for a multistory building built on piers and grade beams is detailed in Fig. 15-9. The grade beams and piers are drawn with dashed lines. The foundation placed on top of the grade beam is drawn with visible lines. Each pier and grade beam is identified by a mark, such as GB 15, which indicates this is grade beam 15. Design details for each are then drawn on sheets devoted to structural details. Selected examples are shown in Fig. 15-10. The piers are located on a grid with the horizontal and vertical rows identified by letters and numbers.

A building built on piles would have a foundation plan like that in Fig. 15-11. The differences between a pier and a pile is shown by the following definitions. A *pier* is a column designed to support a concentrated load. The pier usually forms an integral part of the wall and is placed at intervals along the wall to provide lateral support or to take a concentrated vertical load. A *pile* is a steel, wood, or concrete column usually less than 2 ft (600 mm) in diameter that is driven or otherwise introduced into the soil to carry a vertical load or to provide lateral support.

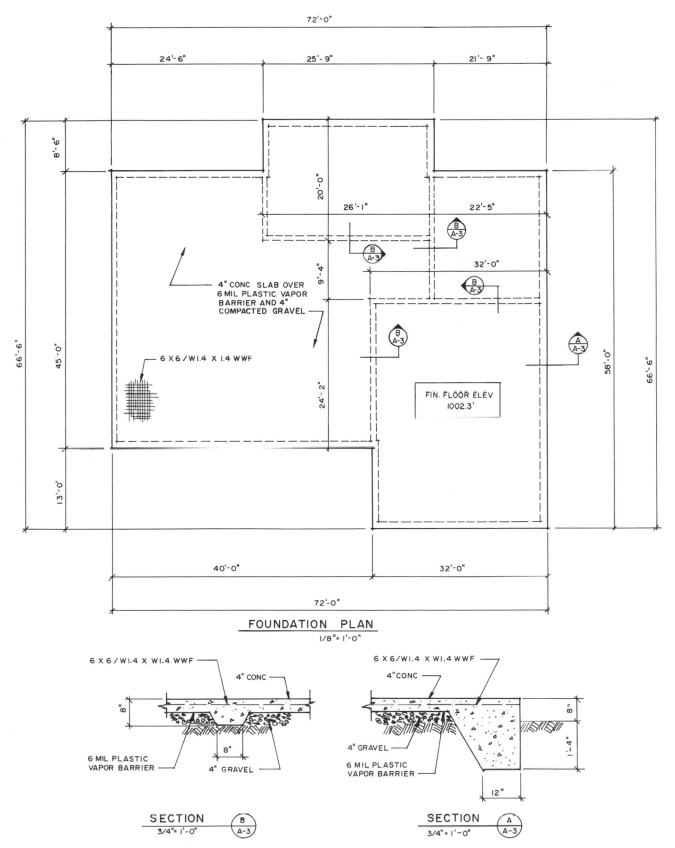

Figure 15-7. *Typical foundation plan for a building with a concrete slab floor and foundation poured monolithically. Note the thickened slab forming footings under nonload-bearing interior partitions.*

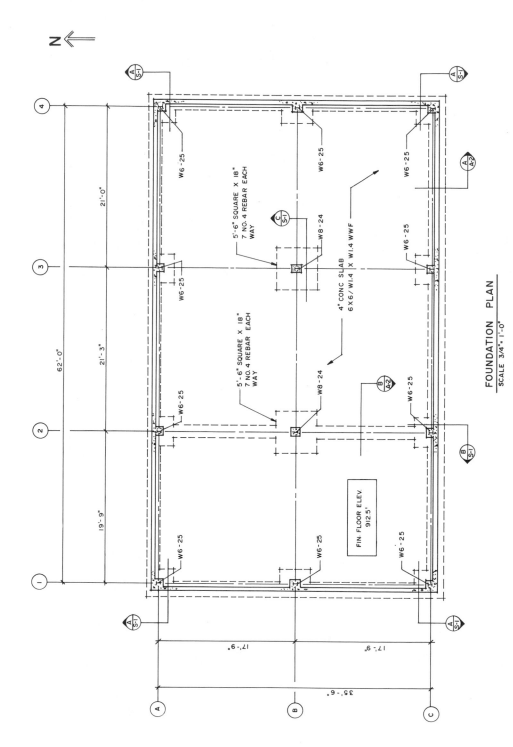

Figure 15-8. *A foundation plan for a building using steel columns to support the floors and roof above the ground. This same technique is used for wood and cast-in-place and precast concrete columns. (Sections shown on next page).*

FOUNDATION PLAN
SCALE 3/4"=1'-0"

N

62'-0"

21'-0"

21'-3"

19'-9"

W6-25

W6-25

W6-25

W6-25

W6-25

W6-25

W6-25

W6-25

W6-25

W6-25

W6-25

5'-6" SQUARE X 18"
7 NO. 4 REBAR EACH
WAY

5'-6" SQUARE X 18"
7 NO. 4 REBAR EACH
WAY

W8-24

W8-24

4" CONC SLAB
6X6/ W1.4 X W1.4 WWF

FIN. FLOOR ELEV.
912.5'

35'-6"

17'-9"

17'-9"

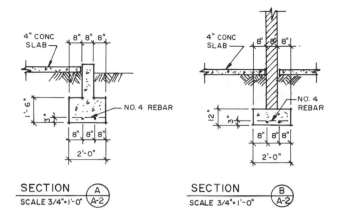

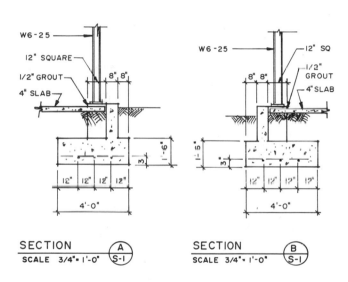

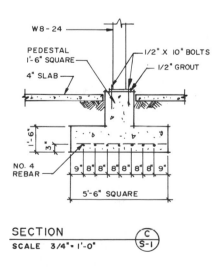

Figure 15-8. (Continued)

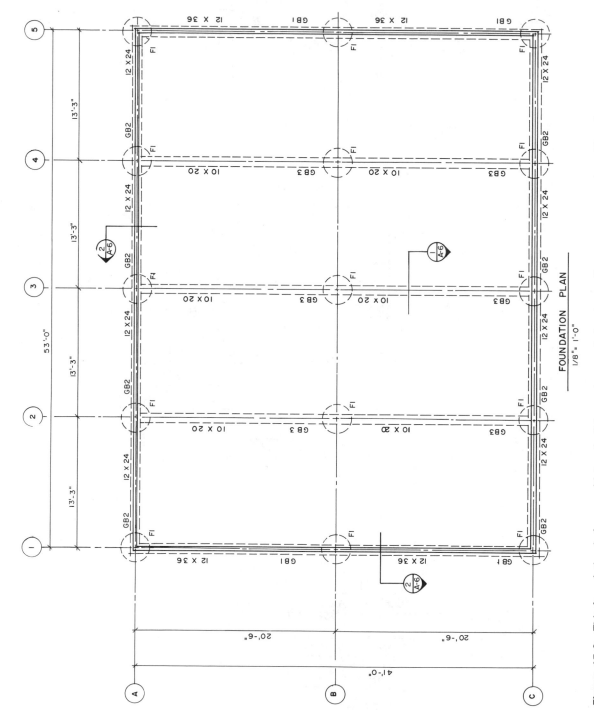

Figure 15-9. *This foundation is for a multistory building using grade beams resting on concrete piers. The piers are set on a grid. Notice how the piers and grade beams are identified.*

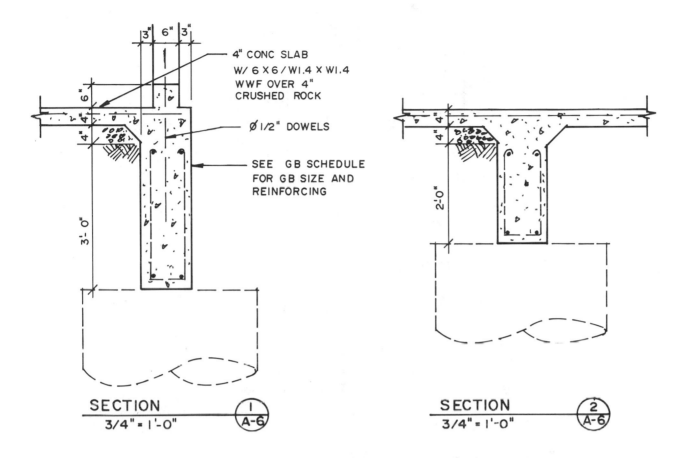

4" CONC SLAB
W/ 6 X 6 / W1.4 X W1.4
WWF OVER 4"
CRUSHED ROCK

Ø 1/2" DOWELS

SEE GB SCHEDULE
FOR GB SIZE AND
REINFORCING

SECTION
3/4" = 1'-0"   ①
              A-6

SECTION
3/4" = 1'-0"   ②
              A-6

GRADE BEAM SCHEDULE

MARK	SIZE	NO.	REINFORCING	TOP BARS			BOTTOM BARS			STIRRUPS				
				HK		HK	HK		HK	NO.	SIZE	LGTH	TYP	SPACING
GB1	12 X 36	4	2-#5 X 20'-6" 2-#6 X 16'-10	7	20'-6"	—	—	16'-10"	—	13	#3	6'-11"	⌴	@18
GB2	12 X 24	8	2-#5 X 13'-3" 2-#7 X 10'-6"	—	13'-3"	—	—	10'-6"	—	12	#3	4'-11"	⌴	@ 12
GB3	10 X 20	6	2-#5 X 20'-6" 2-#7 X 16'-10"	—	20'-6"	—	—	16'-10"	—	13	#3	4'-11"	⌴	@12

COLUMN SCHEULE

MARK	F1
TOTAL NUMBER	15
PIER	36" Ø 8 #9 V. #3 T @18"

Figure 15-10. *Typical sections used with the foundation plan in Fig. 15-9.*

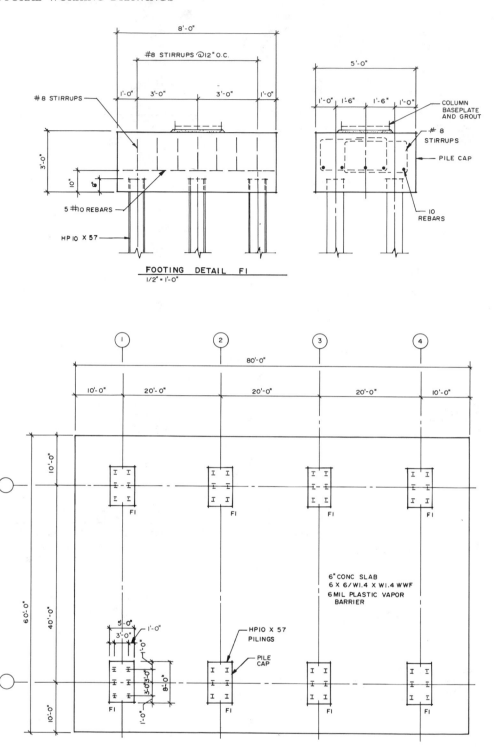

FOOTING DETAIL F1
1/2" = 1'-0"

FOUNDATION PLAN
1/8" = 1'-0"

Figure 15-11. *A foundation plan for a structure supporting columns on pile caps supported by HP piles.*

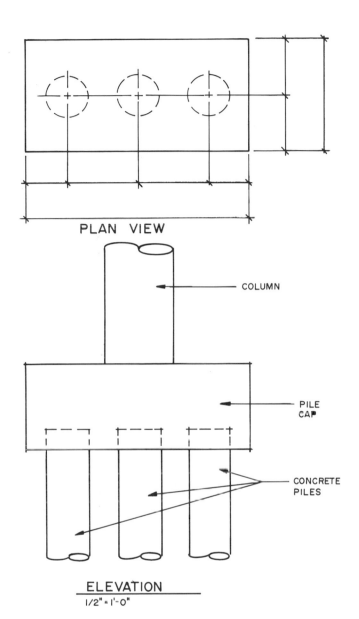

PLAN VIEW

COLUMN

PILE CAP

CONCRETE PILES

ELEVATION
1/2" = 1'-0"

Figure 15-12. Details for a pile cap and precast concrete piles.

In Fig. 15-11 the footing or pile cap is supported by 6 HP piles that are driven until they reach a firm bearing stratum. The pile cap is cast on top of the piles. Piles can be precast concrete, steel H-piles, and steel pipe piles. Concrete piles can be formed by casting in place in holes bored into the earth. A detail for a precast concrete pile is in Fig. 15-12.

Study Questions

Answer the following study questions without referring to the text. Then check your answers with the text and correct those that were wrong.

1. What is shown on the foundation plan?
2. What calculations must be made before the foundation plan can be drawn?
3. What scale is used to draw residential and commercial foundation plans?
4. What type of lines represent the foundation wall and footing?
5. How are beams located and identified on a foundation plan?
6. How are interior walls located on a basement foundation plan?
7. Where is the foundation plan title and scale lettered?
8. What things usually appear on a foundation plan for a building with a crawl space that are not necessary on a basement plan?
9. Sketch various ways foundations can be designed if a concrete slab floor is to be used.
10. How are columns and their footings located on the foundation plan?
11. How are grade beams and piers drawn on the foundation plan?
12. What is the difference between a pier and a pile?
13. What is a pile cap?

Laboratory Problems

1. Draw and dimension a complete foundation plan for the residence designed in Chapter 8. Do the necessary calculations to ascertain footing, beam, pier, and column sizes and attach to the foundation plan drawing.

2. Draw and dimension a complete foundation plan for the small commercial building designed in Chapter 8. For most soil conditions, a spread foot footing would be satisfactory, however design both a spread foot footing and one using piers set into the ground until it reaches load-bearing soil and put a grade beam on top. The grade beam will have to carry the weight of the building between piers. If you have not had a structures class, use an estimated beam size for this project.

16

Architectural Sections

The floor plan shows the layout of rooms, doors, windows, and other features. It does not reveal how the various elements are to be constructed or even show the materials to be used. To give this information, imaginary cuts are made through the area to be described, as a header, and the surfaces revealed are drawn. These drawings are called section drawings. The locations of the sections are indicated with a letter or number and the number of the sheet upon which they are drawn. Likewise, the elevations give additional information including exterior finish materials but do not show construction details.

As the building is being designed, decisions relating to the materials and method of construction are made. These are recorded as freehand sketches and serve as the basis for the drafting of the final sections. It is important that the preliminary sketches be complete and size and material decisions be accurately recorded. Also needed are dimensions relating to the locations and heights of various features such as the bottom of the footing or the distance the subfloor is above the footing. Once these decisions are final and recorded, the finished section drawings can be drafted.

Identification of Sections

Locations where sections are taken are referenced on the floor plan and the elevation. The mark used gives the section identification which could be a letter or a number and

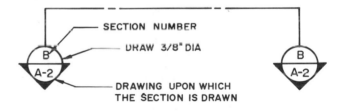

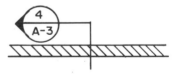

Figure 16-1. Sections are identified by a letter or number and the number of the sheet on which they are drawn.

shows the sheet upon which the section is drawn (Fig. 16-1). The mark will contain a direction arrow which indicates the direction to look when drawing the section. It is important to draw the section looking in the indicated direction.

Sections are indicated on floor plans in a variety of ways. Typical methods are shown in Fig. 16-2. A section through a single element, such as a wall, can have the mark and a short line through the wall locating the section. A directional arrow is used. Sometimes a section may run through a part of a building but not all the way through. This can be shown with the mark on one end and a centerline sym-

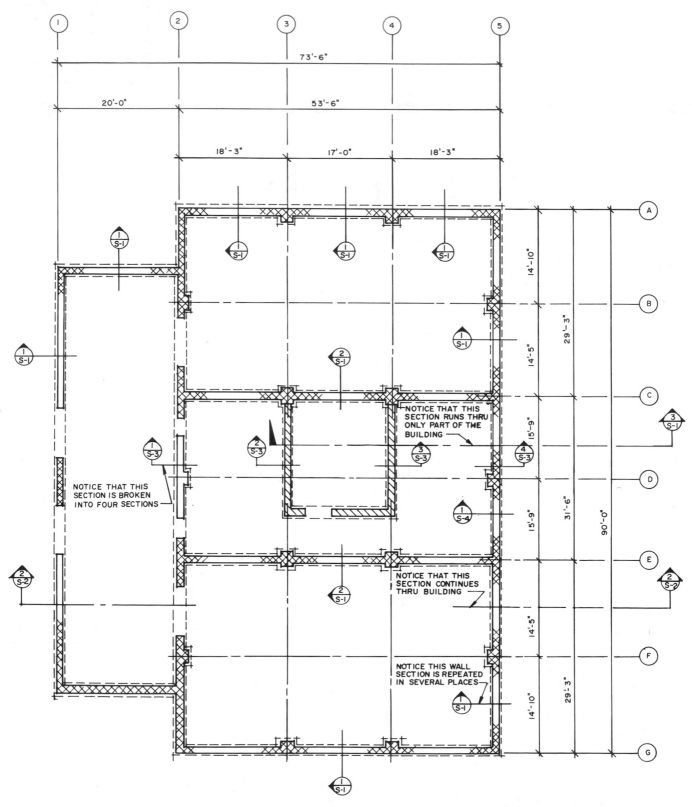

Figure 16-2. *This partially dimensioned plan shows examples of how the location and identification of sections can be drawn.*

bol running to the other end. Sometimes an arrow is placed on this end or another mark could be drawn. The centerline symbol indicating the location of the section is broken when it crosses dimension lines. A section running through an entire building has identical marks on each end. The centerline connecting them need not run through the entire building. If a section is to show some feature, as a series of interior partitions and the exterior walls, marks can be located on each and these walls are drawn lined up from left to right. This is much the same as a full building section but eliminates the construction in between the walls. These various sections are illustrated in Fig. 16-3 through 16-6.

Types of Sections

Plans for small residences and some very simple commercial buildings often are drawn with only a typical wall section. This section shows the construction in detail and implies that all the walls of the structure use this identical construction (Fig. 16-3 and 16-4). If this is not the case, then additional sections need to be drawn.

A building can have full sections cut through its narrow width producing *transverse* sections, or through its length producing a *longitudinal* sections. A full building section is shown in Fig. 16-5. It shows all construction details including floor, roof, and other connecting elements. If it is too large to fit on a sheet small portions that are identical and continuous can be broken out. The major structural features are identified, elevations of major levels (floors, ceiling, roof, etc.) are dimensioned, rooms are identified by name and number, and any other descriptive information necessary can be added. The structural grid is identified. It must match the grid on the floor plan. Sometimes some construction features on a section drawing are too small to be clearly shown. When this is the case, these are drawn as construction details at a larger scale. Typical examples include door and window sections and stair details. These are circled on the section and identified with a mark.

An example of a section through a building that shows structural details of interior and exterior walls eliminating the connecting construction is in Fig. 16-6. Each structural detail is given a different section mark. This permits the section to be drawn to a larger scale, thus showing construction details more clearly. It is important that you do not break out anything that shows a change in methods, materials, sizes, or assembly. If these occur, they must become part of the section drawing.

The scale used to draw building sections varies with the size of the building and the drawing paper. The larger the scale used, the clearer the details. While $1/4'' = 1'-0''$ or metric 1:50 is commonly used, larger or smaller scales are acceptable. If the scale is too small to show certain features, these can be drawn to a larger scale as individual details as indicated on the section in Fig. 16-6. These are explained in Chapter 17.

Steps to Draw a Section

The exact procedure for drawing a section can vary but the following is typical.

1. Examine the freehand sketches of needed sections made during the design process. If they have not been approved by the person responsible for the project have them checked and approved before producing the final drawings. It is helpful if all needed labels, notes, and dimensions can be located on this sketch. This will help when planning the space needed for the finished drawing and give you a chance to arrange them so they are clear of each other.

2. If several sections are to be on a sheet block out the area needed for each. Leave room for dimensions, labels, and notes. This frequently requires 3 to 4 in. of clear space.

If it is to be drawn using a CAD system, you may want to plan out the areas needed on a small piece of paper before starting to draw.

3. Locate the critical levels such as the bottom of the footing, grade, subfloor, concrete floors, top plate or bearing levels of columns and beams, and the ridge if needed or the line of the roof on flat roof buildings (Fig. 16-7). If this produces a section that is too large for the paper, plan to break out some of the walls that have uniform construction.

4. Now block in the details such as footing thickness, width and height of the foundation, studs, joists, concrete floors, sheathing, siding, masonry, rafters, steel or concrete beams, bar joists, and roof decking (Fig. 16-8). See Fig. 16-3 for a typical residential wall section and Fig. 16-4 for a wall section for a small commercial building. If you are using a CAD system, each feature drawn will be to its finished size.

5. Next draw the lines of these features to their final thickness and darkness. These are to be thick, dark lines. Begin at the top of the sheet and work down. If there are several sections on a sheet, layout each lightly before darkening any of the lines. To avoid smears as you darken the lines you can cover parts of the drawing with a sheet of clean paper. This will also help protect the drawing when you add material symbols, labels, notes, and dimensions (Fig. 16-9). When using a CAD system these steps are

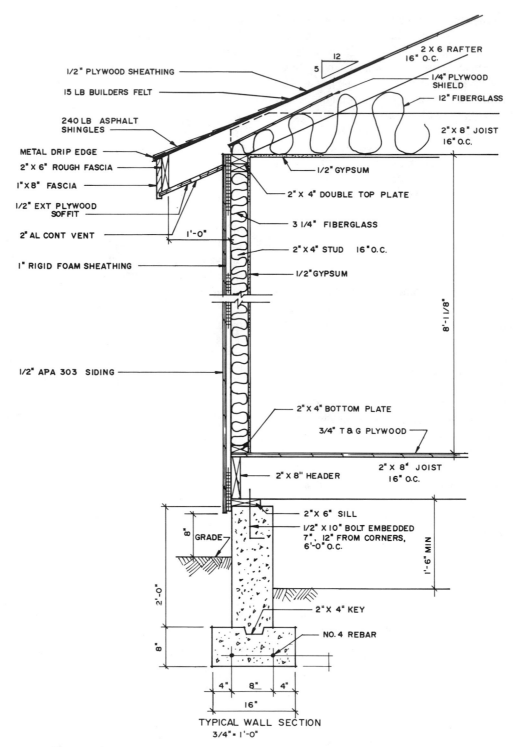

Figure 16-3. *A typical wall section for a residence using frame construction.*

not necessary, because it will draw the finished drawing in total after everything is located on the monitor. The line thickness will depend upon the instructions to the plotter.

6. Now add the material symbols. These materials are in section so use standard symbols for each. You will find there is often more than one symbol in use for some materials. Symbols are drawn with thin, black lines. Recommended symbols are in the Appendix (Fig. 16-10).

7. Now locate and letter the notes and labels as shown on the design sketch. Try to avoid crowding and the cross-

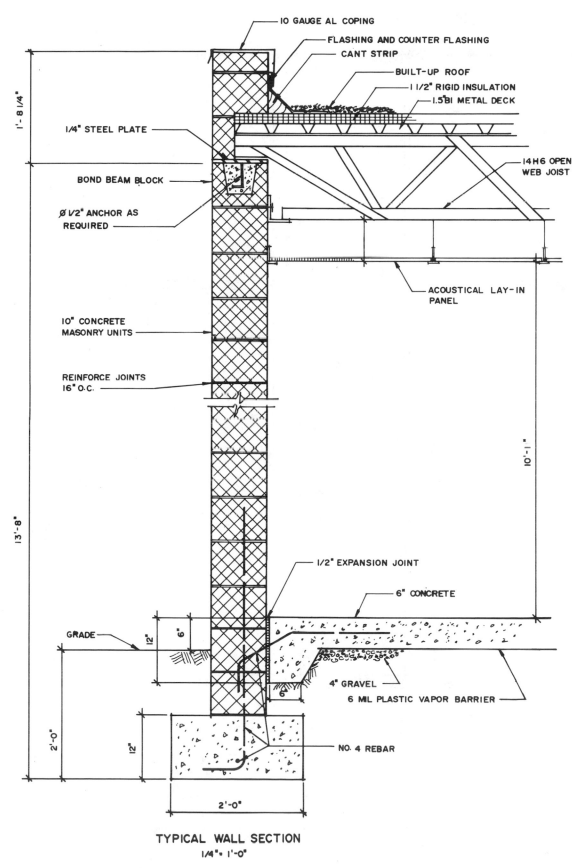

Figure 16-4. *A typical wall section for a small one story commercial building.*

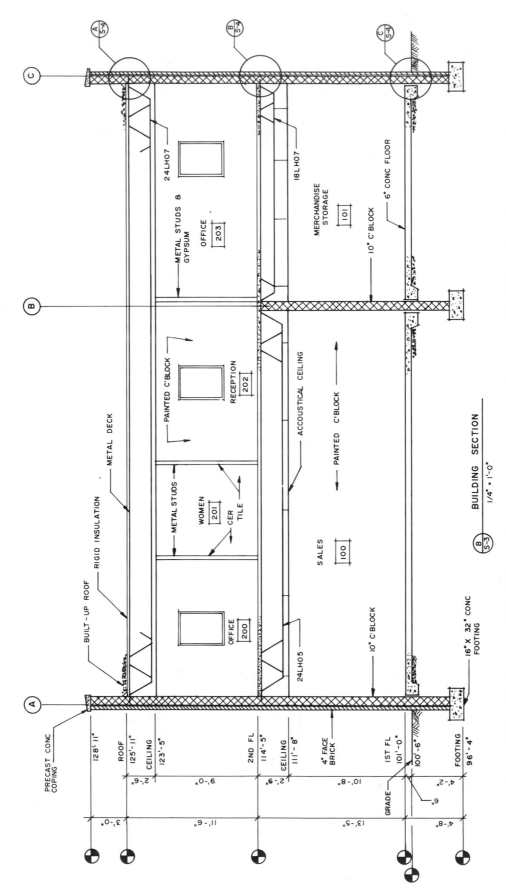

Figure 16-5. *This is a typical full building section showing major structural parts and identifying selected materials. Notice the three structural details referenced to sheet S-4.*

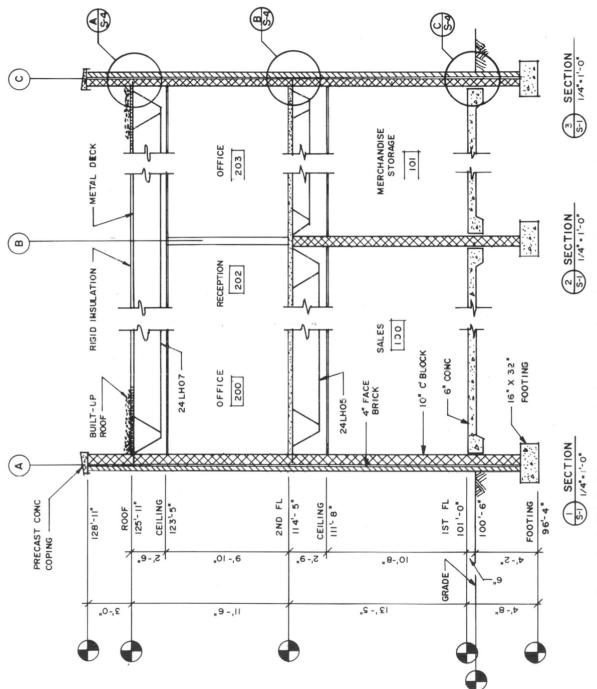

Figure 16-6. *This building section is drawn with the uniform connection areas shortened.*

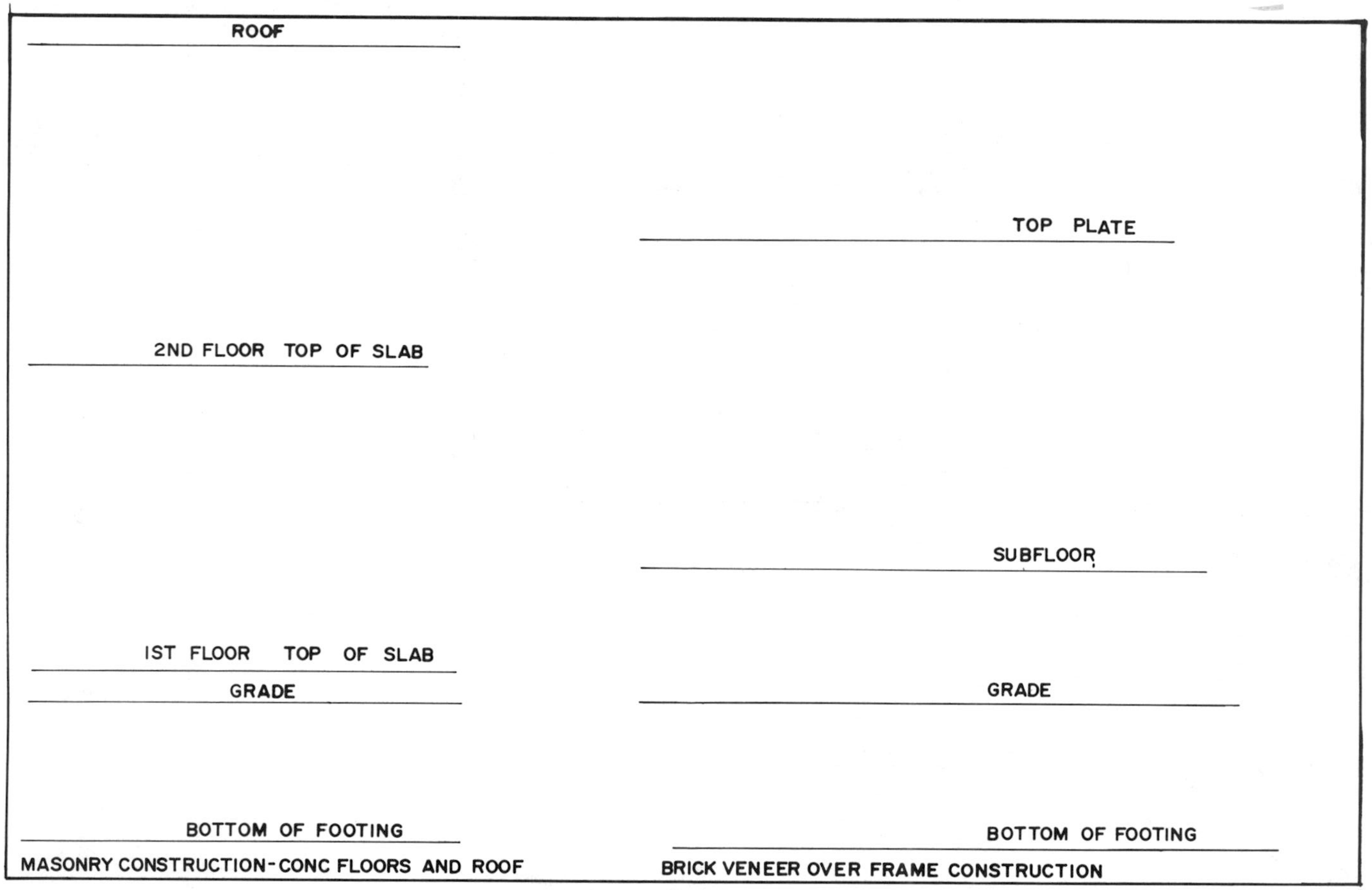

ROOF

TOP PLATE

2ND FLOOR TOP OF SLAB

SUBFLOOR

1ST FLOOR TOP OF SLAB

GRADE

GRADE

BOTTOM OF FOOTING

BOTTOM OF FOOTING

MASONRY CONSTRUCTION-CONC FLOORS AND ROOF

BRICK VENEER OVER FRAME CONSTRUCTION

Figure 16-7. *Begin a section by locating the critical levels of the parts of the building.*

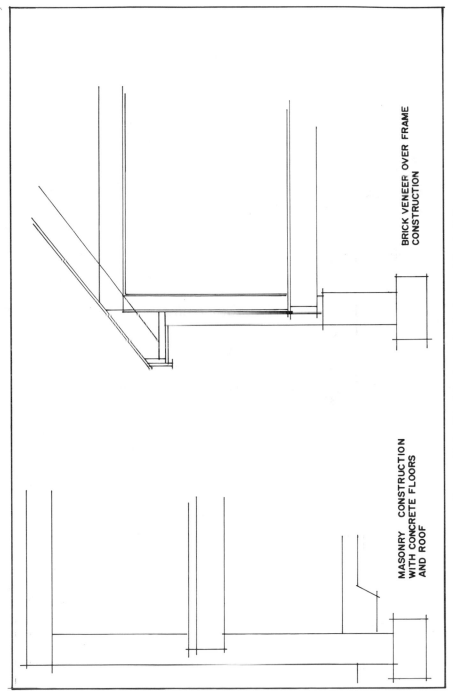

MASONRY CONSTRUCTION WITH CONCRETE FLOORS AND ROOF

BRICK VENEER OVER FRAME CONSTRUCTION

Figure 16-8. Block in the major features of the building.

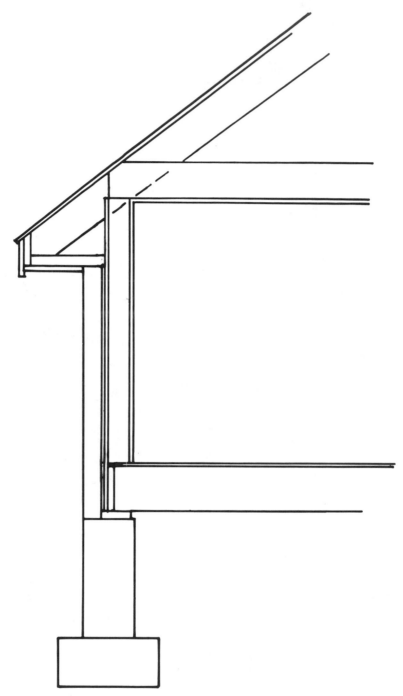

Figure 16-9. *Now draw the lines of the features to their final width and darkness.*

ing of leaders. A label can be used to identify several similar parts if it can be done without confusion. Place the labels far enough away from the drawing to permit an adequate leader to be drawn (Fig. 16-10).

Leaders can be drawn with instruments or freehand. Generally whichever is chosen is used on the entire drawing rather than mixing the two styles. Office drafting stan-

dards may dictate which to use. The ease of drawing them with the computer may also influence the choice. The leader always comes off the beginning or end of the label or note and starts with a short horizontal section.

8. Finally add any needed dimensions. Again these will be shown on the sketch. They should be clear of all notes

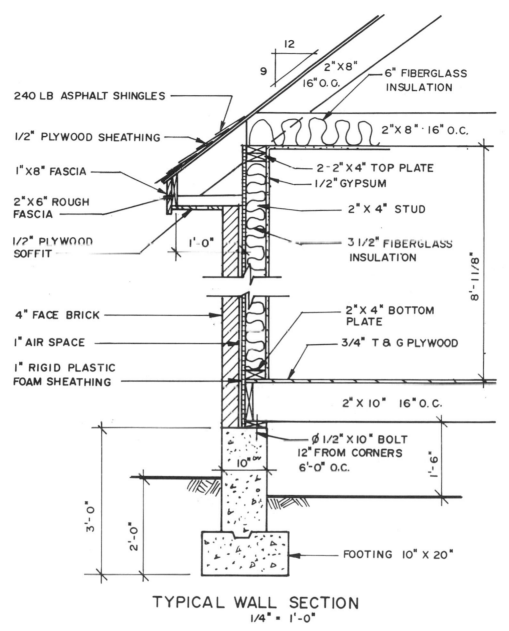

12
9

2"X8"
16" O. C.

6" FIBERGLASS
INSULATION

240 LB ASPHALT SHINGLES

1/2" PLYWOOD SHEATHING

1"X8" FASCIA

2"X6" ROUGH
FASCIA

1/2" PLYWOOD
SOFFIT

4" FACE BRICK

1" AIR SPACE

1" RIGID PLASTIC
FOAM SHEATHING

2"X 8" · 16" O.C.

2-2"X4" TOP PLATE
1/2" GYPSUM

2" X 4" STUD

3 1/2" FIBERGLASS
INSULATION

2" X 4" BOTTOM
PLATE

3/4" T & G PLYWOOD

2" X 10" 16" O.C.

Ø 1/2" X 10" BOLT
12" FROM CORNERS
6'-0" O.C.

FOOTING 10" X 20"

8'-11 1/8"

1'-0"

1'-6"

3'-0"

2'-0"

10"

TYPICAL WALL SECTION
1/4" = 1'-0"

Figure 16-10. *Add material symbols, labels, notes, title, and scale.*

and their leaders. Whenever possible, avoid crossing leaders with dimension or extension lines (Fig. 16-11).

9. Next add any references to details to be drawn relating to the section. These details are enlarged drawings of one small part such as how a door frame or window frame is installed in an exterior wall. These details are indicated on the section by drawing a circle around them and attaching an identifying mark (Fig. 16-12). Also see Fig. 16-6. The drawing of architectural details is covered in Chapter 17.

10. Finish the drawing by adding the title, scale, and the identifying mark as shown on the floor plan.

Study Questions

Answer the following study questions without referring to the text. Then check your answers with the text and correct those that were wrong.

1. How are sections noted on the floor plan?

2. How does the contractor know where in the set of architectural drawings to find each section?

3. What should be done before drawing the final sections?

4. How do you know which way a section should be viewed?

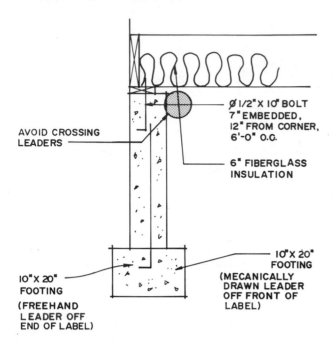

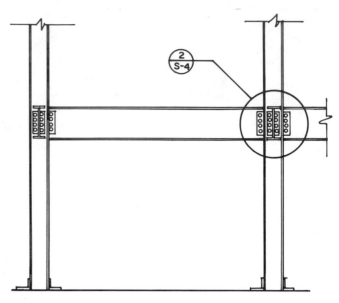

Figure 16-11. *Some tips on locating labels and dimensions.*

Figure 16-12. *The area inside the circle is to be drawn as detail 2 on sheet S-4.*

5. What should be included when you dimension a section?

6. If a section becomes too high to fit on the paper, what can you do to reduce its height?

7. What weight lines are used to draw the features of the section and the material symbols?

Laboratory Problems

1. Draw a finished, dimensioned typical wall section for the residence designed in Chapter 8. Draw additional sections for features that may be different from those shown in the typical wall section.

2. Draw a finished wall section for the commercial building designed in Chapter 8. In addition, draw needed sections to show other features, such as column to footing and beam to column connections.

17

Architectural Details

As indicated in Chapter 16, there are many construction features that appear on various drawings, as might appear on a plan or elevation, which are shown so small it is difficult to interpret them. These details are identified on the smaller scale drawing with a mark and drawn to a larger scale. These larger scale drawings are called architectural details.

Purpose of Details

Details are used to specify exactly how the architect or engineer intends for the structure to be built. Since there are several different ways of doing the same thing, a detail drawing is the clarifying agent. Since the working drawings are part of the legal contract, architectural details are needed so the intent of the designer is absolutely clear. A set of drawings can have many pages of detail drawings.

Selecting Details

There are many factors that make a detail drawing necessary. Most commonly they are used to describe structural details and indicate the materials, sizes, and methods of connection. The shape of parts and dimensions and methods of assembly dictated by codes or various government agencies are recorded. For example, the installation of metal anchoring devices as used on roof construction in areas of high winds, needs to be detailed. Various clearances and tolerances, as space between a chimney and wood framing, need to be shown.

Details can be used to describe desired finishing requirements, such as how to install lath and plaster on an arched opening or some exterior detail as quoins on the exterior corners of masonry buildings. Various aspects of waterproofing and flashing are important detailing subjects. If not detailed, subcontractors will provide whatever they feel is adequate rather than what the designer expected. Details setting forth insulation, vapor barriers, and blockage of air infiltration are increasing in importance.

There are many things that do not require detailing because they are received on the job in a finished, assembled condition. For example, factory built cabinets do not need details showing the size of parts and the method of assembly because these decisions have been made by the manufacturer, while custom built cabinets would require detail drawings.

Detail drawings are also used to check a proposed assembly. Often an assembly can be planned and is assumed to be workable but by drawing it as a large-scale detail, it can be rapidly seen if the assembly will work as planned.

Detail Identification

The feature needing to be drawn as an enlarged detail is enclosed in a large circle where it appears on the plan, section, or elevation drawing. A mark containing a letter or number identifying the detail and the sheet number upon which the detail is drawn is connected to this circle with a leader (Fig. 17-1). This mark is placed with the title of the detail below the finished drawing. Each detail should have a different identifying letter or number.

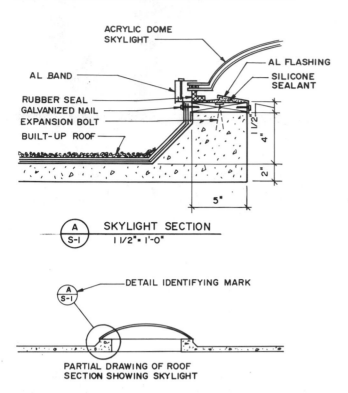

Figure 17-1. *Details are identified by a mark which gives them an identification number or letter and indicates the sheet upon which they are drawn.*

Preliminary Planning

As explained for other types of drawings, the location and placement of details requires some preliminary planning. They may be placed on the sheet with other drawings. If this is done it is helpful to draw details that pertain directly to that drawing. For example, if a wall section drawing indicating a detail of the sill is needed, locate it on the same sheet if possible. On a big job with many details, such as window details, the details are often placed together on a sheet containing only details. As you plan the location, group alike details together. For example, place all window details together on one area of the sheet. Group all door details together and keep structural details together. If you have room, it would be helpful to also place the door and window schedules and the lintel schedule on the same sheet as the door and window details. Remember to allow room for dimensions, notes, and labels (Fig. 17-2).

On large buildings there are many other details that can be grouped together. Structural details are a major part of a set of working drawings. For example, details of the assembly of a steel-framed building can be located with the steel framing drawing. Cast-in-place concrete structures require details showing the size, location, and bends on

the reinforcing bars (Fig. 17-3). Whenever possible, get all drawings that are related together on one sheet.

Scale

The scale to use will vary depending upon the size of the parts in the detail and the overall size of the detail. It should be large enough to clearly show each feature. If it is drawn too large, it is using up space that might be needed for another details. In general, details will be drawn from $1/2'' = 1''-0''$ (1:25 metric) to $3'' = 1'-0''$ (1:4 metric). On occasion, scales of $6'' = 1'-0''$ (1:2 metric) and full size (1:1 metric) are used. Sometimes it is necessary to lightly layout the detail to see how big it becomes. It can be erased if too large or too small. If drawn on a CAD system, it can be quickly drawn to a larger or smaller scale.

Dimensioning

Be certain the dimensions used related to accessible parts of the building. For example, a location dimension is of little value if the point on the building to which it relates is covered up by construction which occurs before the construction of the detail. Details should be dimensioned from parts of the building that will be constructed before the construction on the detail begins. For example, a restroom wall detail that locates the toilet from the lavatory might be useless because the lavatory may not be in place. Locate each from a partition.

Notes and labels should clearly spell out sizes, materials, connection requirements, and other specific requirements.

Drawing the Detail

Before starting the finished drawing, you need a sketch showing the accepted design with all sizes and materials indicated. If the design has been approved by the person responsible for the project, you can proceed with the drawing. There are many standard detail drawings available for reference. A major source is the literature contained in the Sweet's Catalogs and literature from companies manufacturing and selling construction products. For example, door and window manufacturers provide large, scaled, detail drawings of their products showing the design of parts of the door or window and installation details in various types of wall construction. The manufacturers of steel framing materials, precast concrete, roofing systems, and other such products provide extensive detailing information (Fig. 17-4). In addition, there are numerous books showing construction details of all types.

MARK	NUMBER	UNIT SIZE	ROUGH OPENING	TYPE	MATERIAL	REMARKS
W1	6	2'-3 5/8" X 4'-9 7/8"	2'-1" X 4'-8 1/2"	CASEMENT	PINE	DBL GLAZED
W2	2	1'-11 5/8" X 2'-9 7/8"	1'-9" X 2'-8 1/2"	CASEMENT	PINE	DBL GLAZED
W3	1	6'-7 5/8" X 5'-7"	6'-6 3/8 X 5'-5 3/4"	FIXED	PINE	DBL GLAZED
W4	4					
W5	2					

A PARTIAL WINDOW SCHEDULE

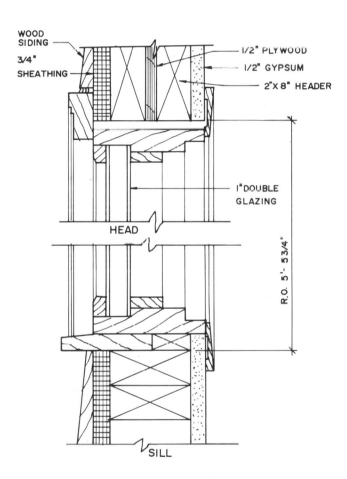

WOOD SIDING

3/4" SHEATHING

1/2" PLYWOOD

1/2" GYPSUM

2"X 8" HEADER

1" DOUBLE GLAZING

HEAD

R.O. 5'- 5 3/4"

SILL

W 3 FIXED WINDOW INSTALLATION
1/4" = 1'-0"

Figure 17-2. *Schedules may be placed on the same sheet as the details relating to them.*

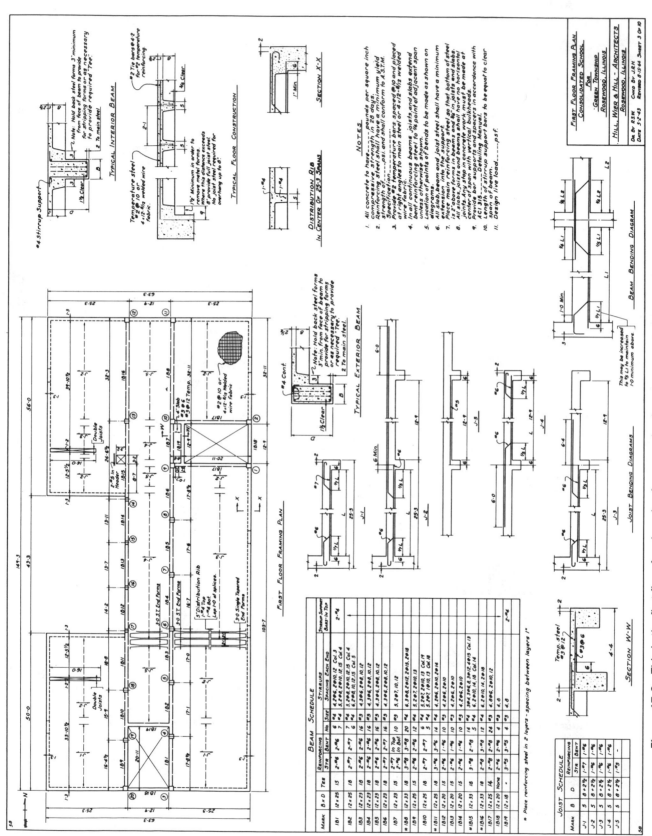

Figure 17-3. This is the first floor framing plan for a cast-in-place concrete building. Notice the enlarged detail drawings show information about the joists. These are identified by the joist identification numbers. (Courtesy of The American Concrete Institute.)

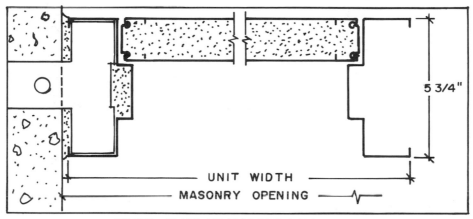

5 3/4"

UNIT WIDTH

MASONRY OPENING

STEEL JAMB AT MASONRY WALL

FIRE DOOR INSTALLATION DETAIL. PEACHTREE DOORS, INC., NORCROSS, GA.

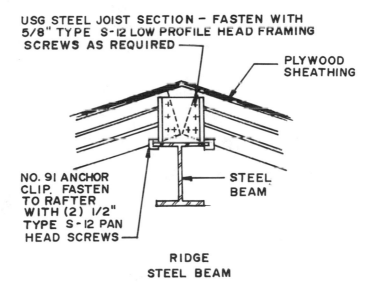

USG STEEL JOIST SECTION – FASTEN WITH 5/8" TYPE S-12 LOW PROFILE HEAD FRAMING SCREWS AS REQUIRED

PLYWOOD SHEATHING

NO. 91 ANCHOR CLIP. FASTEN TO RAFTER WITH (2) 1/2" TYPE S-12 PAN HEAD SCREWS

STEEL BEAM

RIDGE
STEEL BEAM

STEEL FRAMING DETAIL.

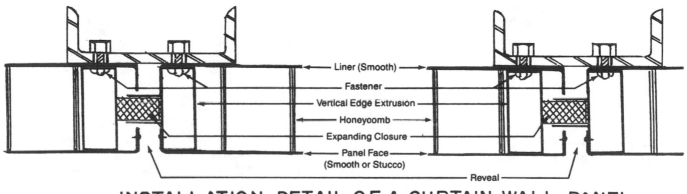

Liner (Smooth)

Fastener

Vertical Edge Extrusion

Honeycomb

Expanding Closure

Panel Face
(Smooth or Stucco)

Reveal

INSTALLATION DETAIL OF A CURTAIN WALL PANEL.

Figure 17-4. *Typical construction detail drawings found in the technical literature of companies manufacturing and selling various products for building construction.*

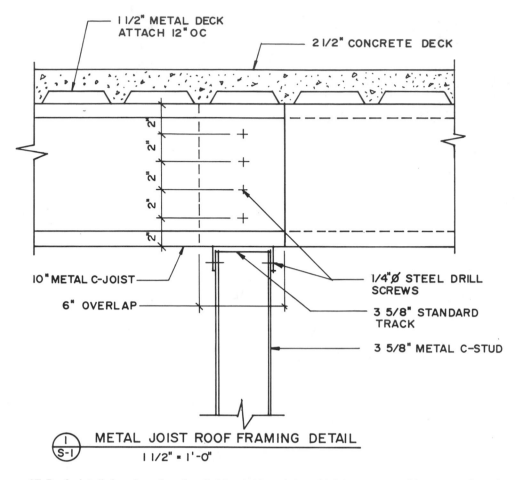

Figure 17-5. *A detail drawing showing lightweight metal roof joists supported by a metal stud wall.*

The steps to produce detail drawings follow:

1. Lay out the features of the detail using light lines. When using a CAD system, these will become your finished lines produced by the plotter. Allow room for dimensions, notes, and labels. If in doubt about the need for a dimension, note, or label, put it on the drawing. Layout lightly all the details to be on the sheet. Use guidelines to locate notes and labels and lightly draw dimension lines.

2. Darken the details beginning at the top of the page and working across and then down. This helps prevent smearing.

3. Add material symbols again starting at the top. You can cover the lower details with a sheet of paper to prevent smears. Standard material symbols are in the Appendix.

4. Add the dimensions, notes and labels.

5. Letter the title, scale, and mark below the drawing.

Selected Detail Drawings

The detail drawings that follow are only examples of typical design solutions. The actual details developed on a set drawings must be directly related to the design, loads, structure, and materials to be used. Figure 17-5 is a drawing showing the roof framing details for a building using metal studs and joists. It shows the design decisions made by the structural engineer. A similar detail showing floor framing details for a building with brick load-bearing walls and precast concrete floor units is in Fig. 17-6. It shows the reinforcing, parging, and concrete topping on the precast floor unit. A detail showing the coping on an exterior wall of a building built using a curtain wall panel is in Fig. 17-7. It shows the exterior glass panel, insulation, plywood interior, and related aluminum coping and flashing.

There are several ways siding can be applied to frame walls used in residential construction. In Fig. 17-8, the detail shows how to make up the studs on the corner and the size and placement of the corner boards. Masonry requires steel lintels to carry it over openings. Details of

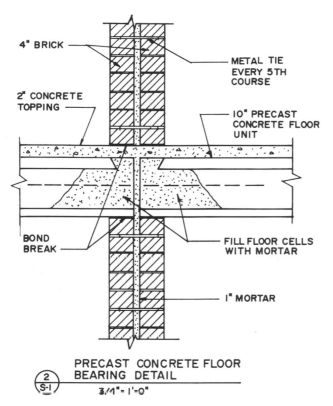

4" BRICK

METAL TIE
EVERY 5TH
COURSE

2" CONCRETE
TOPPING

10" PRECAST
CONCRETE FLOOR
UNIT

BOND
BREAK

FILL FLOOR CELLS
WITH MORTAR

1" MORTAR

PRECAST CONCRETE FLOOR
BEARING DETAIL
2
S-1
3/4"= 1'-0"

Figure 17-6. This drawing shows construction details for supporting precast concrete floor units on solid masonry walls.

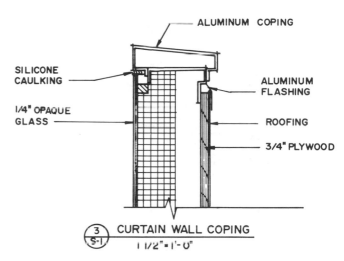

ALUMINUM COPING

SILICONE
CAULKING

1/4" OPAQUE
GLASS

ALUMINUM
FLASHING

ROOFING

3/4" PLYWOOD

CURTAIN WALL COPING
3
S-1
1 1/2"=1'-0"

Figure 17-7. This is a coping detail for manufactured curtain wall exterior panels.

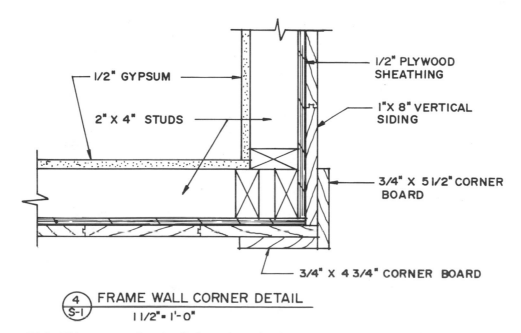

1/2" GYPSUM

2" X 4" STUDS

1/2" PLYWOOD
SHEATHING

1"X 8" VERTICAL
SIDING

3/4" X 5 1/2" CORNER
BOARD

3/4" X 4 3/4" CORNER BOARD

FRAME WALL CORNER DETAIL
4
S-1
1 1/2"= 1'-0"

Figure 17-8. This construction detail shows how the designer wants the corner built on a frame building.

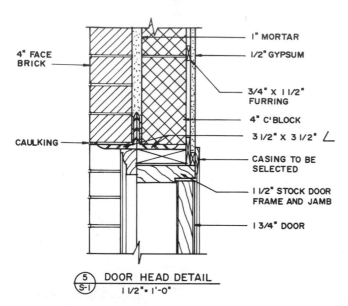

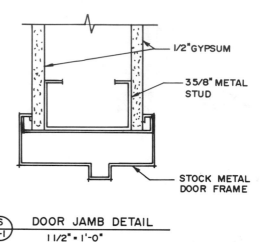

Figure 17-9. *The lintel detail clarifies the construction desired at the head of exterior doors.*

Figure 17-10. *There are many types of metal door jambs available. This detail clearly shows the design of the frame to be used and how it relates to the metal stud and gypsum wall.*

how this is to be constructed over doors is shown in Fig. 17-9. It shows the size and placement of the lintels and the blocking required to install the door in the masonry opening. The jamb details for a metal door frame installed on walls using metal studs is in Fig. 17-10. This leaves no doubt how the construction should be accomplished.

Study Questions

Answer the following study questions without referring to the text. Then check your answers with the text and correct those that were wrong.

1. How are details identified on the drawing from which the enlarged detail will be taken?

2. How should detail drawings be grouped?

3. What scales are commonly used for detail drawings?

4. What must you do before starting to draw the finished, dimensioned detail?

5. Where can you get information to help when designing the features involved in the detail to be drawn?

Laboratory Problems

1. Study your residential plan developed in Chapter 8 and decide which features need an enlarged detail drawing. Draw these using a scale large enough so everything is clearly shown.

2. Study the plan of the commercial plan developed in Chapter 8 and decide which features need an enlarged detail drawing. Draw these using a scale large enough so everything is clearly shown.

18

Elevations

Exterior elevations are shown for each wall of the building. Interior elevations are drawn when needed to clarify the design and materials of interior walls or where special features, as a wall of cabinets, exist.

Exterior Elevations

An exterior elevation describes the finished appearance of the exterior wall of a building. It shows the types of materials used, types of windows and doors, the finished grade, roof slope, foundation, footings, and selected vertical dimensions. Elevations, more than any other drawing, give an easily understood picture of how the finished building will appear.

As the building was being designed it was necessary to develop sketches of the exterior. These helped the designer to see how proposed door and window locations on the floor plan will influence the appearance and show the proportions and mass of the structure. These sketches can be helpful when drawing the finished exterior elevations. Wall section drawings are also made and are necessary when drawing the elevations. If they are drawn to the same scale as the floor plan, they can be used to locate vertical distances. If drawn larger the dimensions shown on them are used to lay out the vertical distances.

Identifying the Elevations

Elevations are drawn looking perpendicular to each side of the building (Fig. 18-1). Each elevation is identified with a title and scale. Generally the elevations are identified as

NORTH ELEVATION, EAST ELEVATION, SOUTH ELEVATION, and WEST ELEVATION. While a wall of the building as shown on the site plan may not face true north, the side oriented most nearly north is so identified. Then the others are titled according to the compass direction they are facing (Fig. 18-2).

If a site for the building has not been chosen the elevations are identified as FRONT ELEVATION, REAR ELEVATION, RIGHT ELEVATION, and LEFT ELEVATION. These are located by facing the front of the building. The end to the right of the observer is the right elevation (Fig. 18-2).

When a floor plan is irregular in shape, inclined walls will appear foreshortened and distorted on normal elevations. Also walls that are part of a recess or courtyard will be hidden. The elevations of these walls must be drawn as separate drawings and show their true lengths. They are identified by a number or letter. The elevations are drawn looking perpendicular to the wall indicated (Fig. 18-3). Often an irregular shaped building will have an *elevation key plan* drawn to show how the elevations drawn relate to the floor plan. This is drawn to a small scale on the first sheet containing elevations (Fig. 18-4).

Drawing Exterior Elevations

First ascertain how the elevations will fit on the sheet. Remember, all sheets in a set of drawings are the same size so it is necessary to use the same size paper as was used for the floor plan.

It is necessary to determine the scale to be used. It is generally the same as that used for the floor plan. For

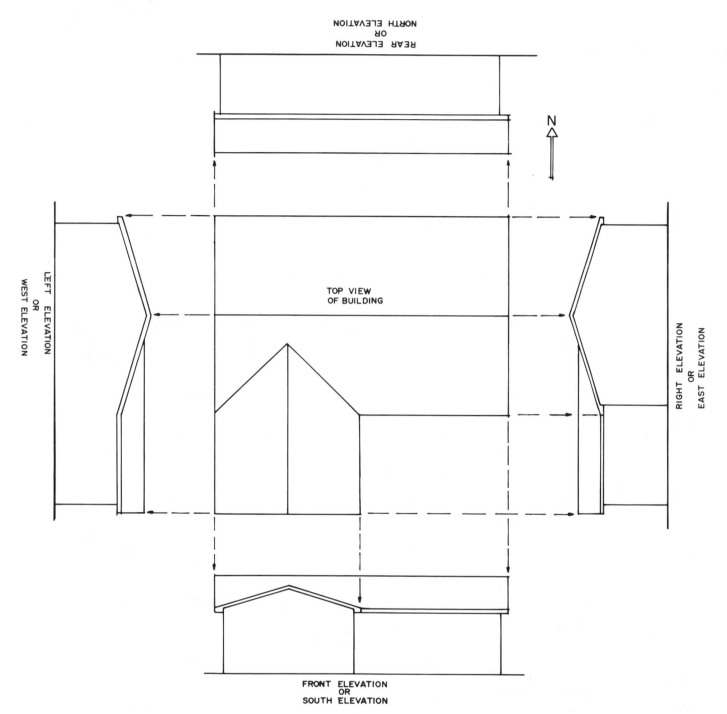

Figure 18-1. *Exterior elevations are drawn by looking perpendicular to each wall of the building.*

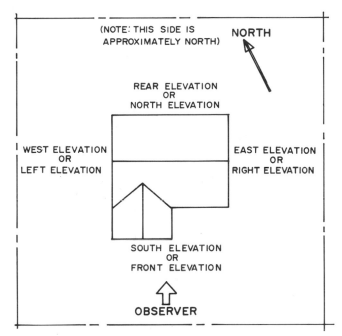

Figure 18-2. *Elevations are identified by compass direction or whether they are the front, rear, right or left sides of the building.*

small buildings, $1/4'' = 1'-0''$ is common. Larger buildings use $1/8'' = 1'-0''$ and in some cases, $1/16'' = 1'-0''$.

Placement on the sheet depends not only upon the sheet size but the size of the building. Small buildings can often have all four elevations on one sheet. The size and location of the title block also influences placement of the views. A good plan is to place the front view and right side view side by side. Below them place the rear view and left side (Fig. 18-5). Other possible arrangements are often necessary. Whenever possible place all elevations on one sheet. This is often not possible. No other drawings should be placed on the same sheet as elevations.

To draw the elevations, follow these steps.

1. Layout the overall length and width of the front and right side views. Leave room between them for vertical dimensions, porches, walls, or other projections. Leave room below them for the title and scale. Layout the areas for the rear and left end elevation (Fig. 18-6). Use very light lines.

2. Tape a drawing of the wall section (if it is the same scale as the elevation) to the right of the drawing. Project horizontally the ridge, fascia, window and door height, ceiling and floor lines, foundation, grade, footing, and any other needed vertical features across the space for the elevation. If a scale wall section is not available, measure the vertical distances and label them lightly (Fig. 18-7). Use very light lines.

3. Now turn the floor plan so the right side is directly above the space for the right elevation. Project down the corners, windows, and other needed features as explained for the front elevation (Fig. 18-8). Locate any roof features, as overhang and gable ends.

4. Turn the floor plan around so the rear wall is facing down. Project needed features to the space for the rear elevation. Then move the wall section down and project the features horizontally as explained for the right elevation.

5. Once more turn the floor plan so the left side is facing down and lined up with the space for the left elevation. Project needed features on the space for the left elevation.

6. Now darken the lines forming the profile of the building. These are thick, dark lines. They make the basic profile stand out. Then darken items such as railings, porches, and steps that fall on top of the elevation. Next draw the foundation and footing. All of these are drawn with thin, dark lines. Then draw in details as doors and windows with thin, dark lines. To help reduce smudging the drawing, start darkening from the top and work to the bottom. If it is necessary to work over an area that has been darkened, cover the area with a sheet of paper to reduce smearing.

Locate and draw the grade line with a thick line. Remember, the footings, foundation, and other features below grade are shown with a thin, dark, dashed line (Fig. 18-9).

7. Next dimension the views. Only the vertical dimensions are given. Horizontal dimensions are found on the floor plan. Typically the following dimensions are necessary: bottom of footing, finished grade, top of foundation, top of subfloor, top of the wall plate, and ridge. Special details such as the height of the chimney, roof overhang, or a connecting wall are also dimensioned. Some prefer to place these dimensions on all elevations, while others place them on the front elevation only. If the elevations are within a few inches of each other, the dimensions could be placed between the view and serve both drawings (Fig. 18-9).

There are two methods for indicating these vertical dimensions. One method uses a vertical dimension line with the distances between features lettered parallel to it (Fig. 18-10). Each extension has a note, as top plate, explaining what it represents. These are the same as used on the wall section drawing.

A second method gives the elevation of each feature, as the top plate, from the elevation established for the finished grade of the soil around the building. The desired finished grade is shown on the site plan as is the elevation

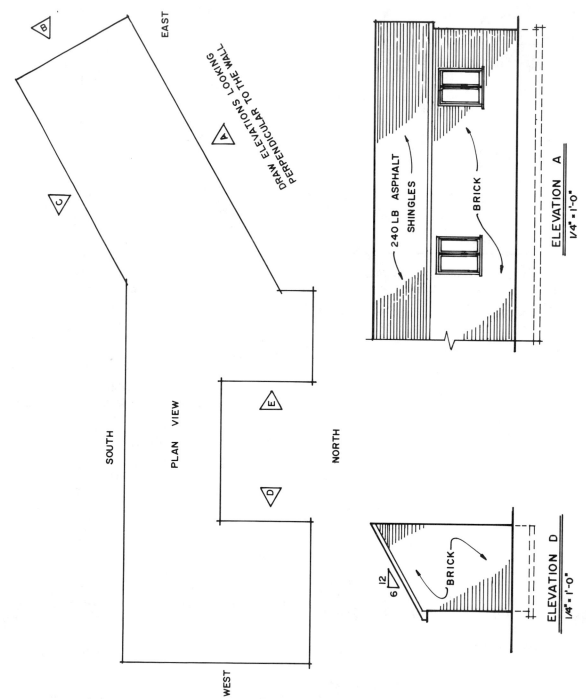

Figure 18-3. Hidden and inclined walls require special elevations.

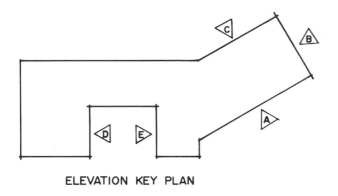

ELEVATION KEY PLAN

Figure 18-4. *An elevation key plan is drawn rather small and located on the first sheet containing elevations.*

of the floor. The elevation of the footing is determined by the required depth below the grade. All vertical distances are indicated above the elevation of the bottom of the footing (Fig. 18-11).

Figure 18-12 shows a partial elevation of a small multistory building on which the heights were shown in feet and inches and the elevations above and below the final grade were also shown.

Finally notes are lettered. These typically include materials, finishes, title, scale, roof slope, and any other features that need to be explained. The height of the lettering is usually $\frac{3}{32}$ or $\frac{1}{8}$ in. Company standards will establish this size. Titles identifying drawings are lettered $\frac{3}{16}$ to $\frac{1}{4}$ in. Usually material are indicated on all elevations though

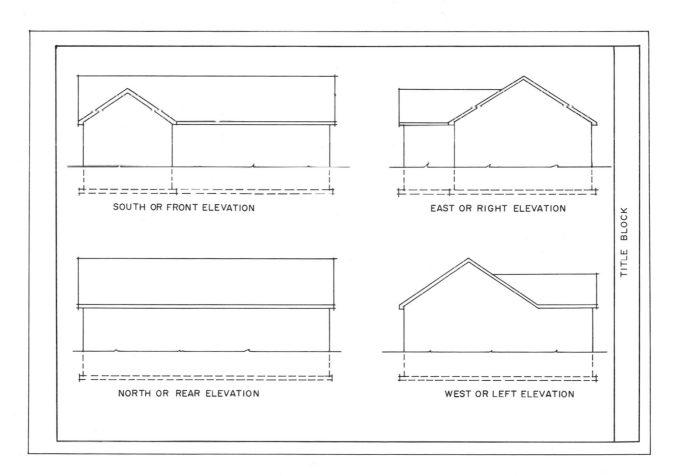

SOUTH OR FRONT ELEVATION

EAST OR RIGHT ELEVATION

NORTH OR REAR ELEVATION

WEST OR LEFT ELEVATION

TITLE BLOCK

Figure 18-5. *This is one way to locate elevations for a small building on a single sheet.*

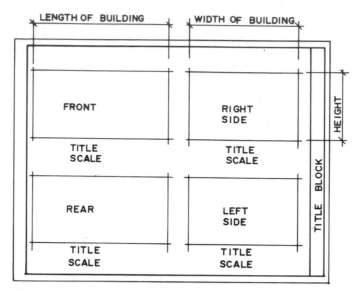

Figure 18-6. *Block in the length and height needed for each location.*

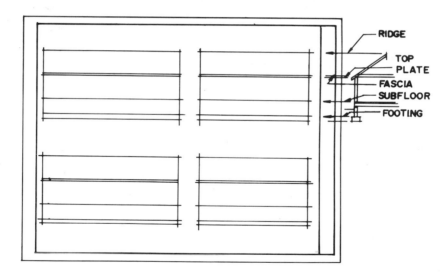

Figure 18-7. *Locate the heights of needed features as fascia, floors, and footing.*

some prefer to show them only on the front elevations. This is often not the case, so identification on all elevations is frequently necessary (Fig. 18-13). When indicating materials, some prefer to simply list a rather generic identification, such as "wood siding," and indicate detailed specifics in the specifications. Others give more detail in the notes on the elevation, such as "$7\frac{1}{2}$" bevel cedar siding." The title and scale are noted below such elevation.

Some drafters like to put the marks on the doors and windows but this is optional, and company drafting practices should be followed. Remember, they must match the marks used on the floor plan (Fig. 18-13). Repeating the marks on the elevation could create a problem because whenever a feature is repeated there is a chance for it to be recorded differently in the second location. This leaves the contractor the problem of deciding which note is correct.

Some architectural firms prefer to indicate the location of wall and building sections on the elevations. This is an optional practice. Once again this is an example of repetitious information which could lead to errors. If this is done they must be in exactly the same location as the in-

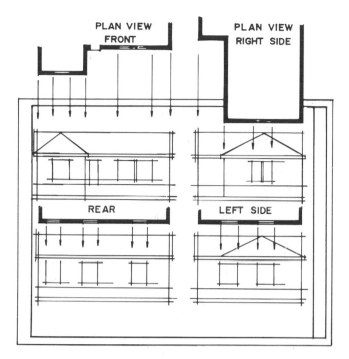

Figure 18-8. *Locate doors, windows, and other features.*

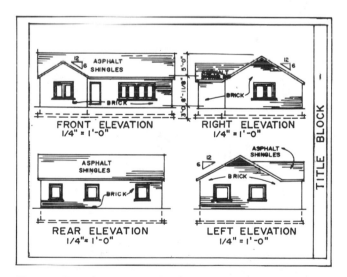

Figure 18-9. *Darken needed lines and erase excess layout lines. Draw to proper width. Add dimensions.*

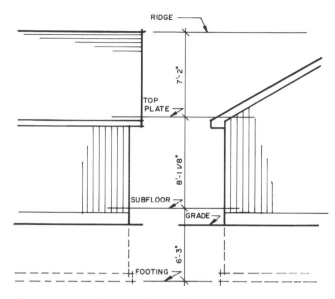

Figure 18-10. *Vertical distances can be indicated in feet and inches from the bottom of the footing.*

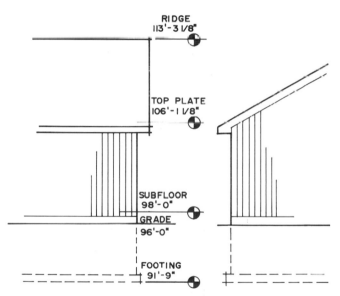

Figure 18-11. *These vertical distances are indicated by giving their elevation above or below the datum used to establish the grade around the building.*

dicated section on the floor plan. The section line need not be drawn through the entire building. A single symbol may be placed at the top or at the top and bottom. The section mark may be nondirectional though directional markings are preferred (Fig. 18-12 and 18-13).

After all notes are lettered, the material symbols are drawn. Various symbols are used to identify materials. they are not intended to replace material notes. The entire surface to receive a material symbol is usually not cov-

ered. Areas with notes are left free of symbols. Various styles of symbol application are used. One technique places the symbol at the ends of a surface and slants the ending on an angle. All symbols on that elevation use the same technique and angle (Fig. 18-14). Another technique places symbols on each end of a surface but drops them out as the center of the area is reached (Fig. 18-15). Another covers the entire area and puts material notes off of the elevation (Fig. 18-16).

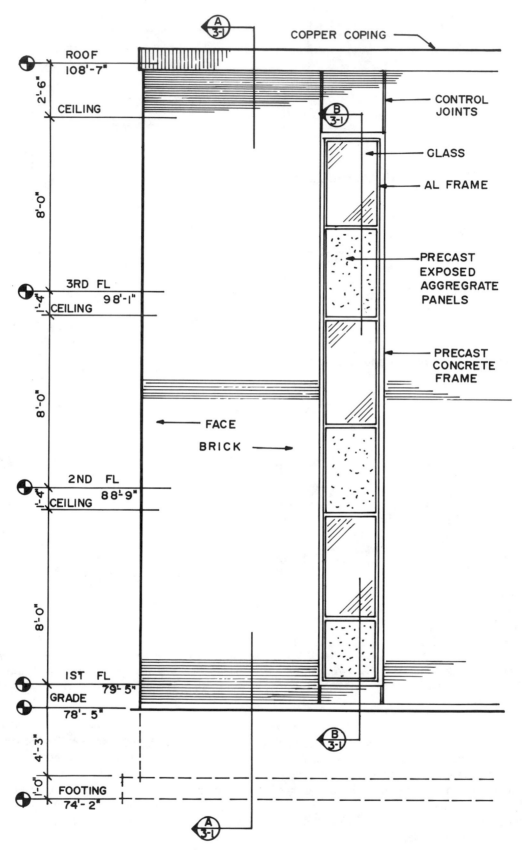

Figure 18-12. *A typical elevation for a small multistory building.*

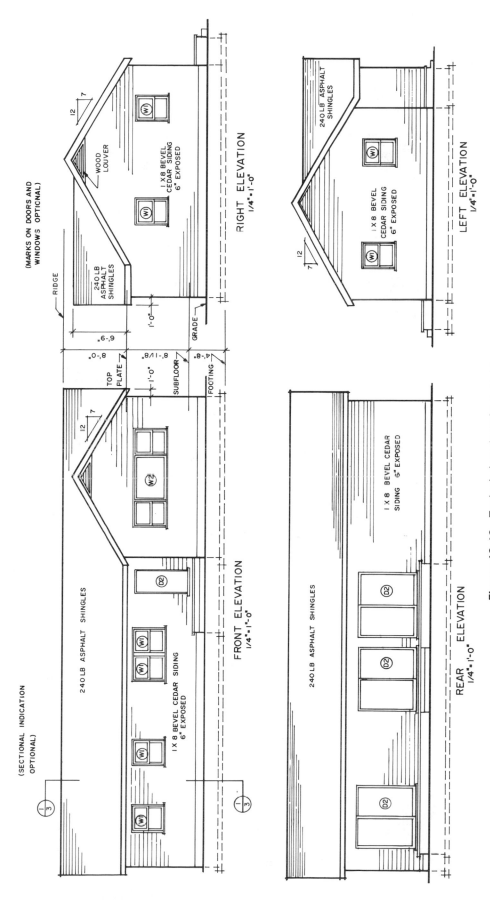

Figure 18-13. *Typical elevations for a residence.*

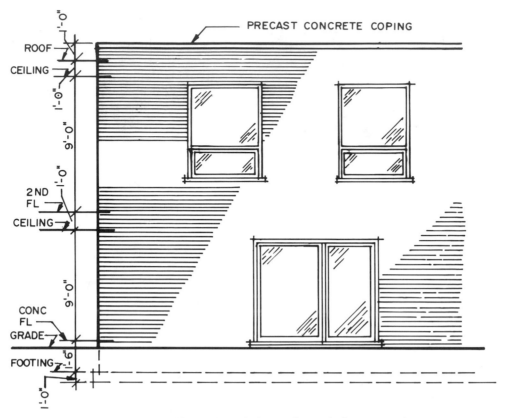

Figure 18-14. *Material symbols can be ended on an angle.*

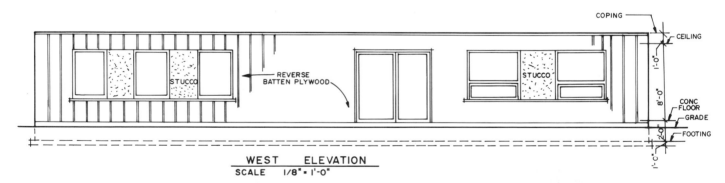

Figure 18-15. *Material symbols can be placed on the ends of each surface leaving the center clear for notes.*

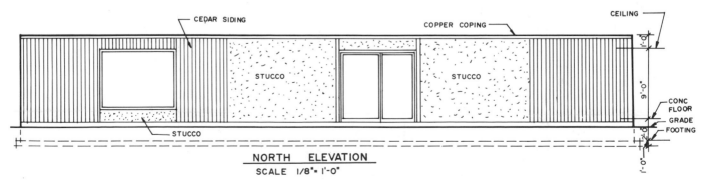

Figure 18-16. *This elevation has material symbols covering the entire wall area.*

Material symbols are drawn with a very thin line. Typical symbols for materials in elevation are shown in the Appendix.

Interior Elevations

Interior elevations are used to show features that need clarification. For example, kitchen cabinets shown on a floor plan give no information about the desired locations of doors and drawers or cabinet widths and heights. Elevations of each wall are used to give this information. In residential work, things such as fireplaces, built-in cabinets, and balconies often require interior elevations. In commercial work, the use of interior elevations is extensive. Large restrooms require elevations showing the location of water closets, lavatories, urinals, soap dispensers, towel dispensers, electric drying units, mirrors, and other planned features. An elevation of each wall is drawn. While there are many other examples of needed interior elevations, the following few will give typical examples. Schools require elevations of classroom walls showing things such as storage units, blackboards, and permanently installed audio and visual equipment. Retail stores have extensive shelving and display areas on their walls which require elevations. Churches need interior elevations of walls in the narthex, nave, and chancel area

Interior elevations show the size and location of the features involved. Often the unit, as a lavatory, is identified at to size and brand by a note. The finish on walls can be noted and special decorative features described.

Drawing Interior Elevations

Interior elevations are usually drawn to the same scale as the floor plan. If necessary to show small details or to correspond to an enlarged section of the plan, they can be drawn larger. The placement on the sheets in a set will vary. In residential work it is desirable to place kitchen elevations on the same sheet as the floor plan if space permits. In this way the plan view of the kitchen, and the elevations of the kitchen cabinets can be studied without flipping sheets back and forth. On commercial work, interior elevations are usually placed together on one or more sheets.

Elevations are identified on the floor plan with a mark. Some coding system, such as letters of the alphabet, or a number, is used to provide this identification (Fig. 18-17). The mark usually gives the elevation, a letter, or number and shows the sheet number upon which it was drawn.

Following are some suggestions for drawing interior elevations.

1. Determine the overall size of each elevation. This will help you to make a neat layout on the sheet and use

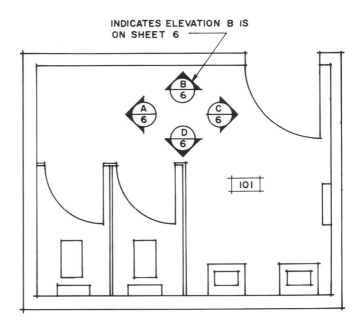

Figure 18-17. *Elevation marks are shown on the floor plan and are recorded with the title of the elevation drawing.*

the space to maximum advantage. Elevations can be as close as 1 in. to each other unless a column of vertical dimensions is necessary. Keep the walls of each room grouped together on the sheet.

2. After the scale layout of each wall has been completed, draw in the details. Some prefer to draw fixed items, such as doors and windows, first. Then the cabinets or other features must be designed to fit into the remaining wall space. The walls, floor, and ceiling are drawn with a single line. No studs, joists, or other structural members are drawn (Fig. 18-18).

When drawing interior elevations, the drafter is assumed to be standing in the center of the room looking perpendicular to the wall to be drawn. Everything that appears on the wall is drawn.

3. After all features are laid out, darken them beginning at the top of the drawing.

4. Finally, add notes detailing things such as location, size, manufacturer, identification of the feature by name, and wall finishes. Each elevation should have a title and scale. The title includes the mark used to identify the elevation on the floor plan.

Figure 18-19 shows the plan view of a small kitchen and the related interior elevations. In this case, if stock cabinets are to be used, the dimensions must match the stock sizes available.

Figure 18-18 shows one wall of a large restroom. Note the location of figures and identification of wall finish.

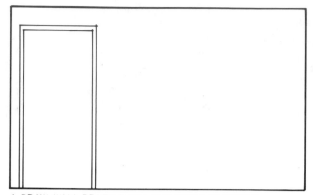

1. DRAW WALL PROFILE AND ADD FIXED FEATURES.

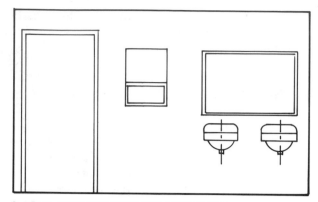

2. DRAW FEATURES THAT ARE ON THE WALL.

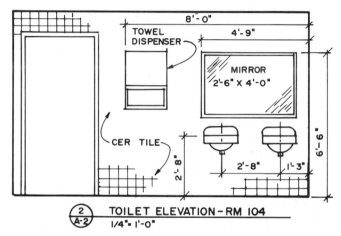

3. DARKEN THE LINES, ADD NOTES, DIMENSIONS, TITLE, AND SCALE.

Figure 18-18. *Suggested steps to draw interior elevations.*

Figure 18-20 shows an interior elevation of one wall of a classroom. If there are several rooms identical to this, their numbers are given and the drawing is considered typical. It is not necessary to redraw the same wall over and over again.

Study Questions

Answer the following study questions without referring to the text. Then check your answers with the text and correct those that were wrong.

1. What is shown on a exterior elevation?

2. How do wall sections help when developing the elevations?

3. How may elevations be identified?

4. How are irregular or inclined exterior wall elevations drawn so they appear true size?

5. What is an elevation key plan?

6. What scale is used when drawing elevations?

7. What other drawings can be placed on the same sheet as elevations?

8. How can the floor plan be used to speed up drawing the elevations.

9. Which lines on an elevation are drawn thick? Which are drawn thin?

10. What notes and dimensions are placed on elevations?

11. What methods are used to indicate vertical heights on elevations?

12. What type of interior elevations are commonly drawn?

13. How are interior elevations identified on the floor plan?

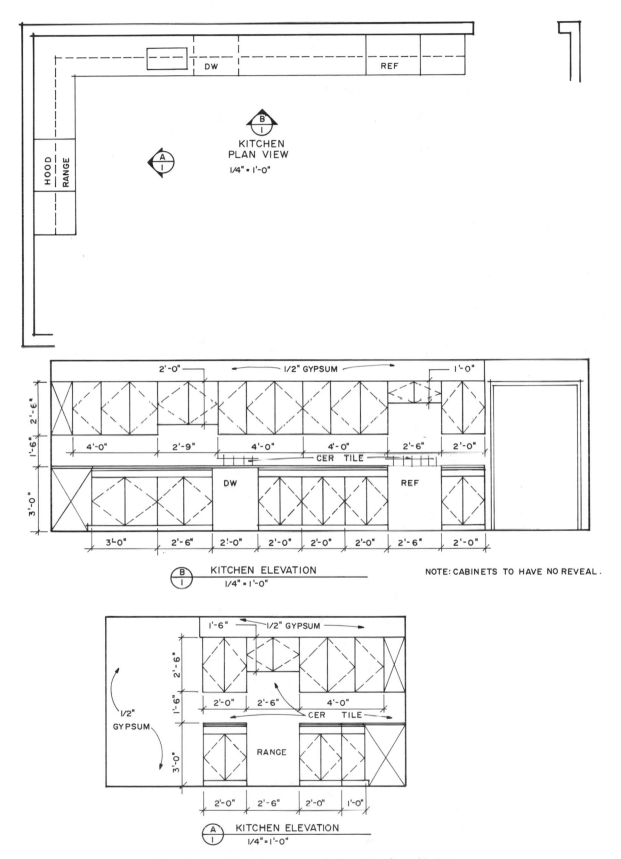

Figure 18-19. *A plan view and elevations for a kitchen.*

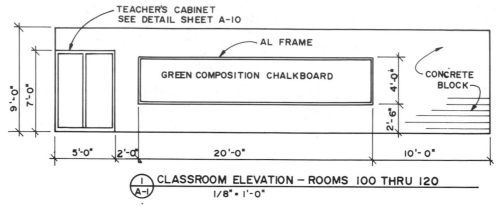

Figure 18-20. *An interior elevation of a classroom wall that is typical for several rooms.*

Laboratory Problems

1. Draw elevations of all sides of the residence designed in Chapter 8. Include necessary notes and dimensions.

2. Draw elevations of all sides of the commercial building designed in Chapter 8. Include necessary notes and dimensions.

3. If assigned by your instructor, draw preliminary elevations with different types of roofs and window styles. This will help you decide on the best one.

19

Roof Plans and Framing Plans

The development of the structural frame of a building is a vital part of the design process. Without a properly engineered structural design, the building will most likely not function as expected. New products and combinations of materials are constantly becoming available for structural use. This includes things such as better methods for the erection of structural steel, the use of laminated materials, including wood glu-lams, and members made from composites (a combination of two or more different materials). The wide spread use of light-weight wood and steel trusses for floor and roof construction has changed the designs used for residential and commercial buildings.

This chapter will discuss the preparation of roof plans and floor, roof, and wall framing drawings. These drawings are made after the designer selects materials and designs the structural system.

Roof Plans

A roof plan is a top view drawing of a finished roof. On small buildings, a simple roof plan may be drawn on the plan view of the building shown on the site plan (Fig. 19-1). This is usually to a very small scale, so complex or detailed plans are generally drawn as separate drawings to a larger scale (Fig. 19-2). The scale to use depends upon the size of the building and the complexity of features to

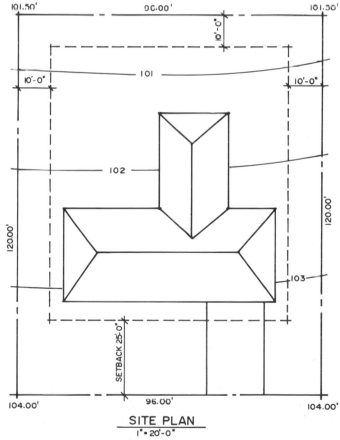

Figure 19-1. *A partially completed site plan showing a roof plan for a building with a hip roof.*

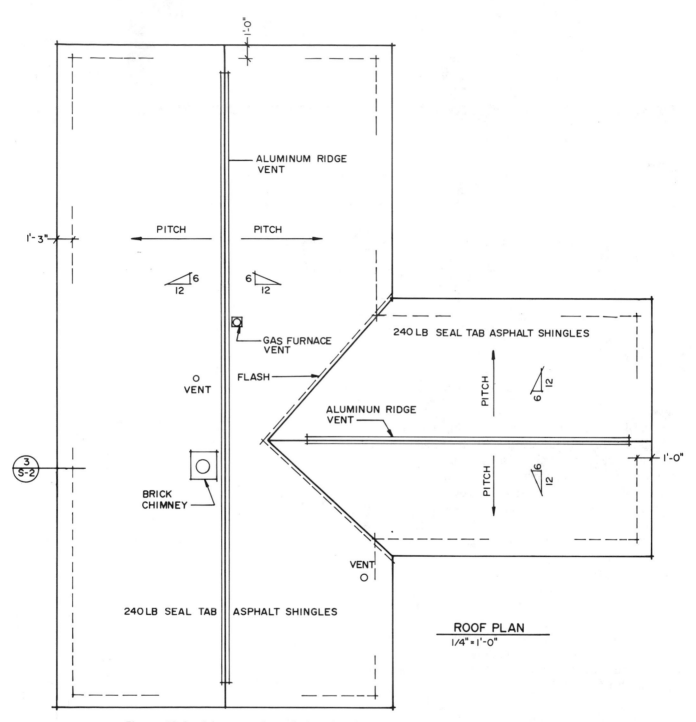

Figure 19-2. *A large-scale roof plan showing complete details of the finished roof.*

be shown. Scales from $1/16'' = 1'-0''$ (1:200 mm) to $1/4'' = 1'-0''$ (1:50 mm) are most commonly used. Select the smallest scale that will clearly show all the needed details. Notice in Fig. 19-2 the outline of the roof, ridges, and valleys are drawn with a thick line. Other details are drawn with a thin line.

Begin the drawing by laying out the outline of the roof

and show all intersections. Locate all features that appear on the roof and dimension them. Identify each with a label. If the roof overhangs the exterior walls, the walls are often shown with a dashed line and the amount of overhang dimensioned. Darken all lines and add notes, section and detail marks, title, and scale to complete the drawing. A roof plan for a small church is shown in Fig. 19-3. The

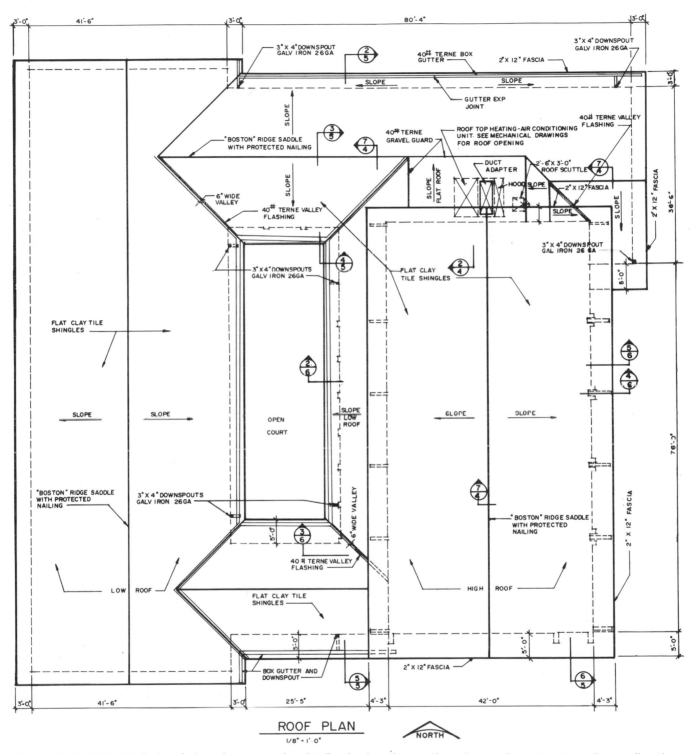

ROOF PLAN
1/8" = 1'-0"

NORTH

Figure 19-3. *This detailed roof plan gives extensive details plus locating sections that are important to understanding the construction details.*

church consists of two main buildings connected with roofed passageways all built around a courtyard. Notice the indication of parts of the heating and air-conditioning system, sections, slope, flashing, and roof covering material. The outline of the major roof is drawn with a thick

line and details on the roof with thin lines. Extensive notes are used to clearly identify all features.

A roof plan for a building with a flat roof is shown in Fig. 19-4. Notice the use of grid markers. These must coincide with those on the floor plan. Slope of roof drains is noted

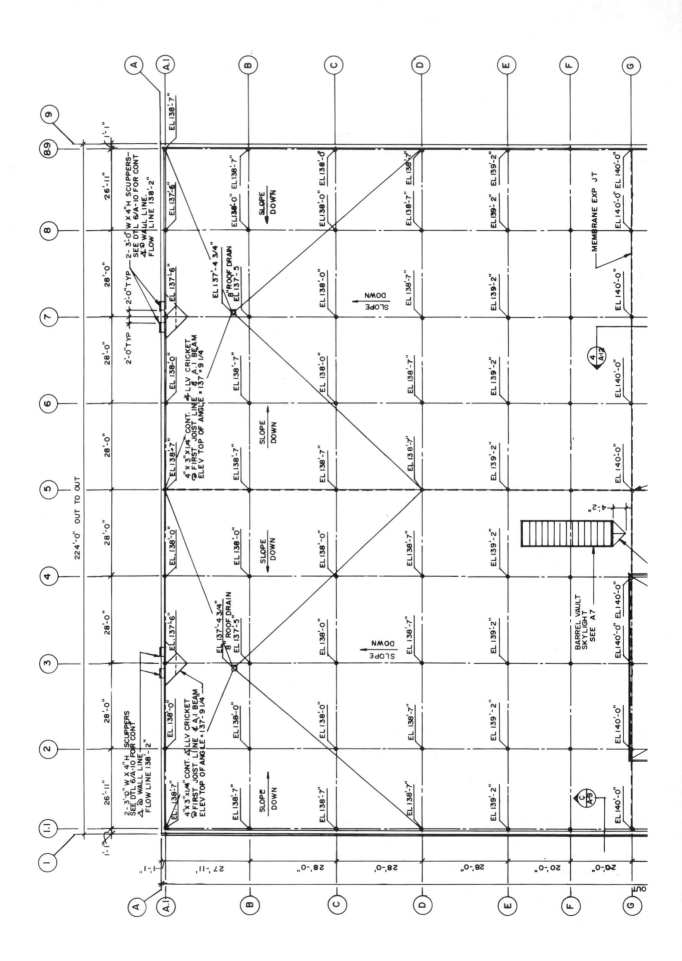

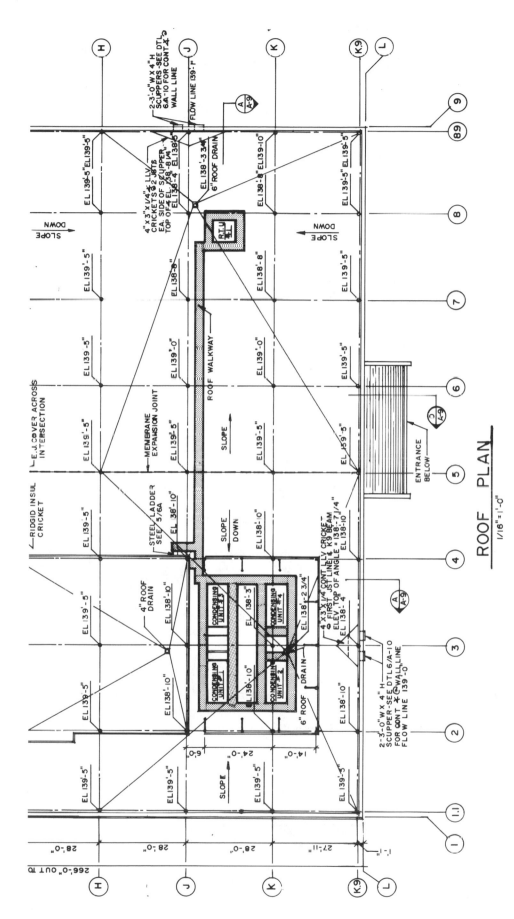

ROOF PLAN
1/16" = 1'-0"

Figure 19-4. This is a roof plan for a building with a flat roof. It uses a grid to record elevations.

and is controlled by the elevations of grid points across the roof. Mechanical equipment and related walkways are noted. These are shaded to give them increased emphasis. Extensive notes and labels are used to identify all design features.

Another form of roof plan that is useful even for small residential buildings is a roof sheathing layout. This plan is a flat view of the roof. For example, if it is a gable roof, each side is drawn actual size as if the roof were flat on the ground. Only half a symmetrical roof need be drawn. Remember to include the overhang. Run the plywood or other sheet type sheathing perpendicular to the rafters. Start with a whole sheet on one end. Lay out 8-ft sheets across the lower (eave) edge of the building. The ends must rest on a rafter so the first sheet usually has to be cut. Start the second row with a partial sheet so the joints between the sheets do not line up. The joints between the ends of sheets must end on a rafter so they can be nailed in place. Continue the layout until the ridge is reached. Usually the last row of sheets have to be cut to width to fit the remaining space. Allow $1\frac{1}{2}$ in. more than the rafter length so the sheathing covers the ridge. (Fig. 19-5).

Framing Systems

The commonly used framing systems are explained in detail in Chapters 10–12. The engineer uses the one that is best suited and most economical for the project being designed. In most types of structures, certain basic principles apply. The roof and floors are generally supported by load-bearing exterior and interior walls or columns or both. the load-bearing walls and columns are supported by footings resting on undisturbed soil or on pilings.

Most buildings have some type of skeleton frame. This frame is tied together with some form of structural sheathing, such as plywood, or diagonal braces tied to the members of the frame. In frame residential walls the diagonals might be a 1 × 4 wood member recessed into wood studs. In steel-framed buildings, it might be metal dowels or angles welded to the vertical structural members. In multistory buildings, the diagonals could even be S or W beams.

This braced structural frame is finally covered with some form of enclosing material such as wood siding, masonry, or curtain wall panels.

Design Loads

As the structural frame is designed it must carry live and dead loads. Dead loads are those that are permanent and apply a pressure on a building that is constant. This includes the weight of all the materials in the building. Live load are those that are variable. They include things brought into the building when it is occupied, such as people and furniture. The stresses caused by snow, wind, and rain are also live loads because they occur intermittently (Fig. 19-6).

As the engineer determines the live and dead design loads and begins to make decisions on structural members, the *strength of the materials* available becomes important. Structural members are subjected to compression, tension, shear, and torsion. Compression stresses tend to squeeze a material as if it were in a vise. Tension stresses tend to stretch a member. Shear stresses are directly opposing forces on a member. Torsion produces a twisting force (Fig. 19-7).

Structural members are made of various shapes. A simple rectangular member, such as a wood floor joist, if laid flat, will have considerable vertical deflection and little horizontal deflection. If stood vertically, it will have reduced vertical deflection but considerable horizontal deflection (Fig. 19-8). Horizontal and vertical deflection can be reduced by combining these two aspects into a single member. The structural angle has reduced deflection because it is a combination of a horizontal and vertical rect-

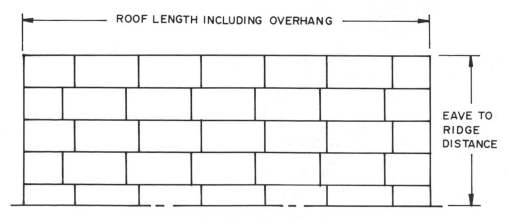

Figure 19-5. A roof sheathing layout.

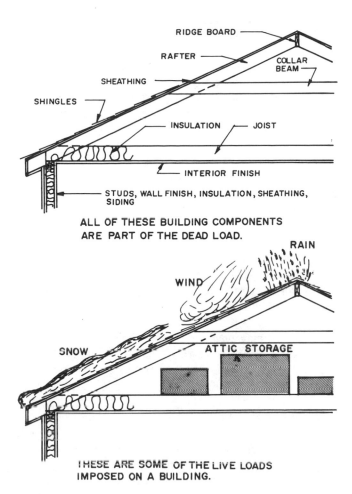

Figure 19-6. *Structures are subjected to live and dead loads.*

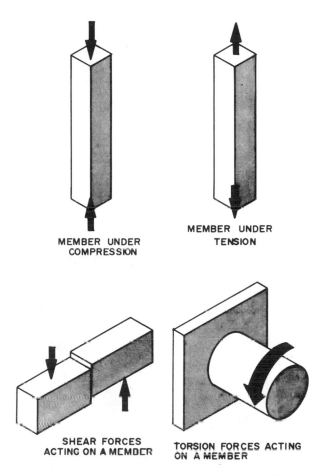

Figure 19-7. *The structural engineer must consider tension, compression, sheer, and torsion when designing a structure.*

angular member. An S or W beam provides additional stability as shown in Fig. 19-8.

The information placed on a framing plan varies considerably with the type of structure—steel, wood, or concrete. The drawings that follow in this chapter are typical of those in use. You will find variations depending upon the actual design of the building and local architectural practices. Publications from the American Institute of Steel Construction and the American Concrete Institute will prove helpful. Also technical information from companies manufacturing structural products, such as preengineered metal buildings, precast concrete structures, and glued-laminated wood structural systems is available.

Framing Plans

A framing plan contains the information needed by the constructor to assemble the roof, floors, or walls of a building. On residential drawings, a roof framing plan is necessary if the roof is complex. They are often not drawn for simple flat or gable roofs. On commercial buildings a framing plan is drawn for all floors and the roof. Often wall framing plans are drawn to clearly show sizes of members, bracing, or special design considerations such as unusual openings, are drawn.

Roof and floor framing plans show the basic outline of the building, exterior, or interior supporting walls and columns, the sizes and spacing of the structural members, and symbols indicating sections and details. Often it is necessary to show equipment located on a roof or floor. This is especially common when designing commercial buildings. Features, such as heating and air-conditioning units, plumbing vents, roof access doors, ducts, and electrical units, such as transformers, are to be located. The designer will have to adjust the roof or floor structural system to carry the additional load and possibly withstand vibration.

Following are selected examples of framing plans with brief explanations.

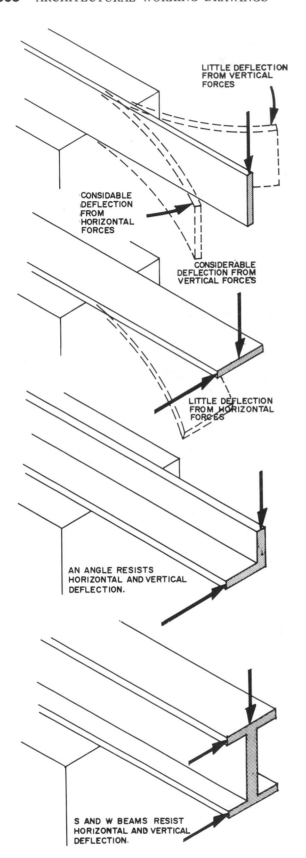

Figure 19-8. *Structural members are designed to resist deflection.*

Wood Structure Framing Plans

Roof framing plans for wood frame construction are drawn by first locating exterior and interior load-bearing walls. These are drawn with a thin, black line. Rafters are represented by thick single lines. Rafters may be represented with double lines but this is time consuming.

If the roof is simple the framing plan can be drawn on the site plan (Fig. 19-9). The site plan should be drawn to a scale large enough to permit adequate detail, dimensions, and notes.

A roof framing plan for a wood-framed building with hip roof construction is shown in Fig. 19-10. The rafter, ridge, and hip rafter sizes are noted. The spacing of rafters and size of the overhang are dimensioned.

A roof framing plan for a wood-framed building having a flat roof is in Fig. 19-11. The spacing and number of rafters are dimensioned. Notice how the overhang is framed on the ends of the house.

A roof framing plan for a frame building with a gable roof is in Fig. 19-12. The overhang on the gable end is constructed using lookouts that run to the second rafter in from the edge of the exterior wall. A valley rafter is used where the two gable roofs intersect. The spacing of rafters, rafter size, and the amount of overhang are dimensioned.

In Fig. 19-13 is a roof framing plan for a one-story building using heavy timber construction. Columns are marked C, beams B, girders G, and purlins P. Notice that a transverse section is indicated.

The beams and girders are drawn with heavier lines than the purlins. Purlins of identical size can be dimensioned using a line with arrows on each end to indicate the purlins of that size. Notice the grid system used to identify the rows of columns that extend through the building. These smaller beams join these larger beams to provide support for the purlins.

The sizes of girders, beams, columns and purlins are given in schedules. Each member has an identifying mark. This is used in the schedule and marked on the actual members to aid in the erection of the building.

This drawing does not indicate the type of roof decking, slope, or finished roofing material. These will show on the section drawing and the roof plan.

A roof framing plan for a building with a sloped roof supported by a double tapered-curved glu-lam beams is shown in Fig. 19-14. The beams provide a sloped roof and span the entire width of the building. Notice the indicated section and detail which give connection information. In one place, the glu-lam roof beams are seated upon square steel columns. The columns are separated by steel lintels which carry the brick and block walls over openings in the walls. The roof overhang on each end is framed by allowing the 4-in.-thick decking to extend beyond the exterior

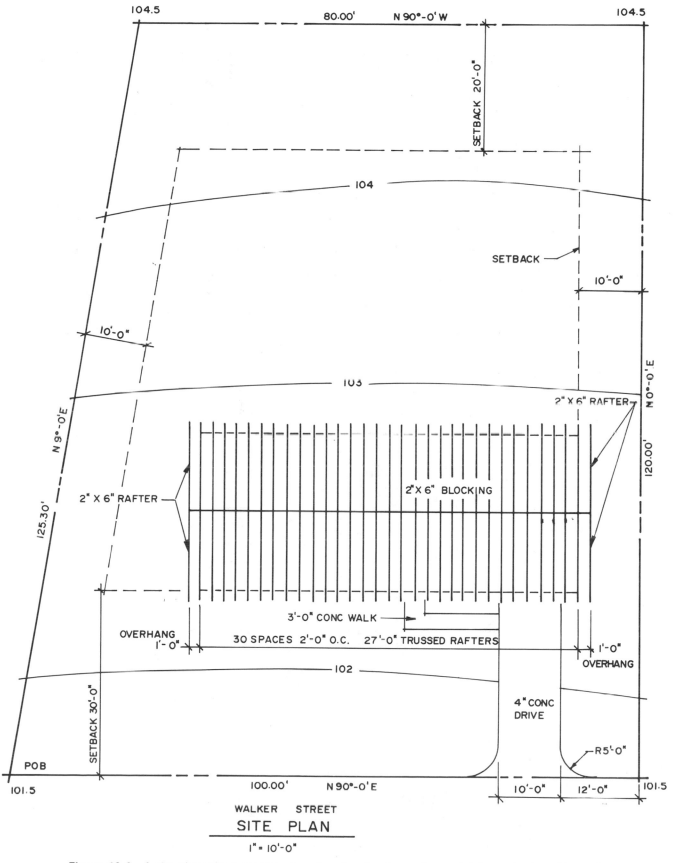

104.5   80.00'   N 90°-0'W   104.5

SETBACK 20'-0"

104

SETBACK

10'-0"

N 0°-0' E

10'-0"

103

2" X 6" RAFTER

2" X 6" RAFTER

2" X 6" BLOCKING

120.00'

N 9°-0' E

125.30'

3'-0" CONC WALK

OVERHANG 1'-0"

30 SPACES 2'-0" O.C.   27'-0" TRUSSED RAFTERS

1'-0" OVERHANG

102

4" CONC DRIVE

SETBACK 30'-0"

R5'-0"

POB

101.5   100.00'   N 90°-0' E   10'-0"   12'-0"   101.5

WALKER STREET
SITE PLAN
1" = 10'-0"

Figure 19-9. *A site plan with a roof framing plan showing truss placement for a simple gable roof.*

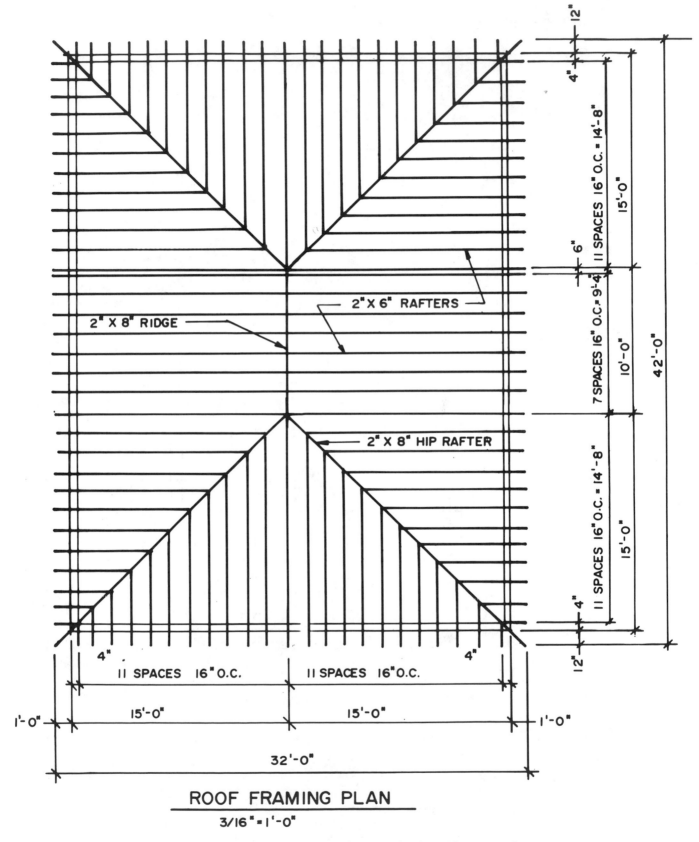

ROOF FRAMING PLAN

3/16" = 1'-0"

Figure 19-10. *A typical roof framing plan for a hip type roof.*

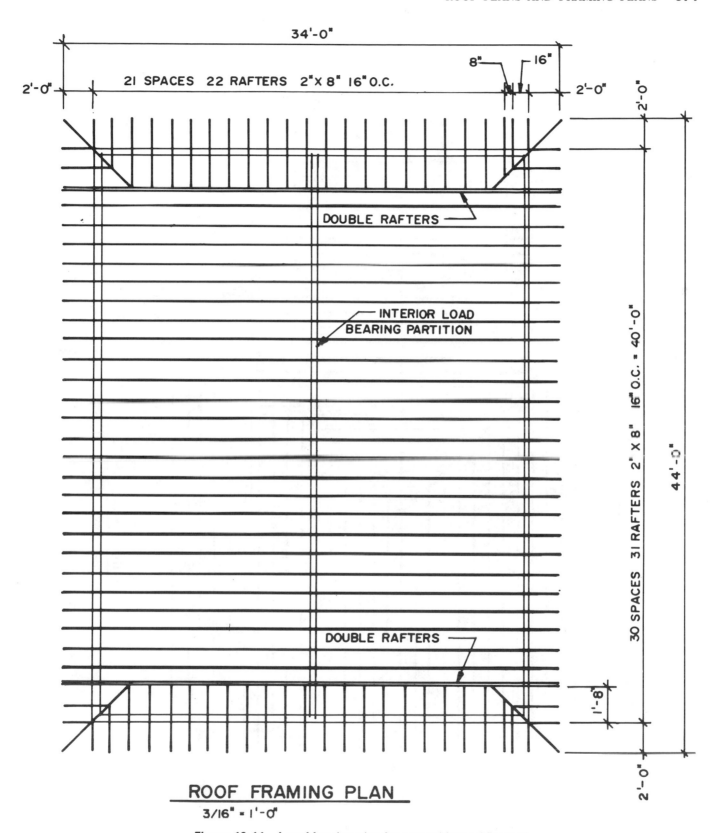

ROOF FRAMING PLAN
3/16" = 1'-0"

Figure 19-11. *A roof framing plan for a wood-framed flat roof.*

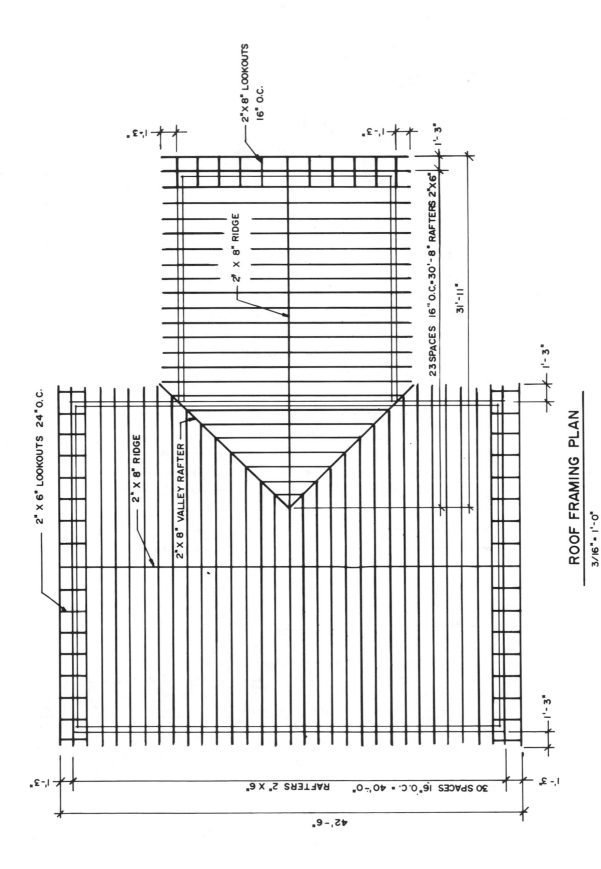

2"x 8" LOOKOUTS
16" O.C.

1'-3" 1'-3"

2" X 8" RIDGE

2" x 6" LOOKOUTS 24" O.C.

2" X 8" RIDGE

2" X 8" VALLEY RAFTER

23 SPACES 16" O.C.=30'-8" RAFTERS 2"x6"

1'-3"

31'-11"

1'-3"

1'-3"

1'-3"

1'-3"

30 SPACES 16" O.C. = 40'-0" RAFTERS 2" X 6"

42'-6"

ROOF FRAMING PLAN

3/16" = 1'-0"

Figure 19-12. *This roof framing plan shows two gable roofs meeting at 90°. It is for a wood-framed roof.*

372

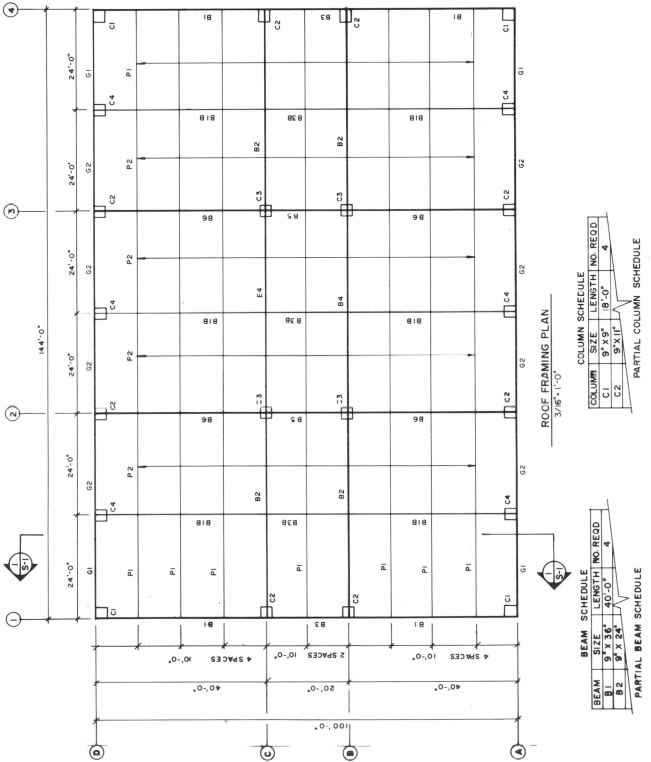

ROOF FRAMING PLAN
3/16" = 1'-0"

COLUMN SCHEDULE

COLUMN	SIZE	LENGTH	NO. REQD
C1	9" x 9"	18'-0"	4
C2	9" x 11"		4

PARTIAL COLUMN SCHEDULE

BEAM SCHEDULE

BEAM	SIZE	LENGTH	NO. REQD
B1	9" x 36"	40'-0"	4
B2	9" x 24"		4

PARTIAL BEAM SCHEDULE

Figure 19-13. *A roof framing plan for one-story heavy timber construction. Sizes of girders, beams, purlins, and columns are given in schedules.*

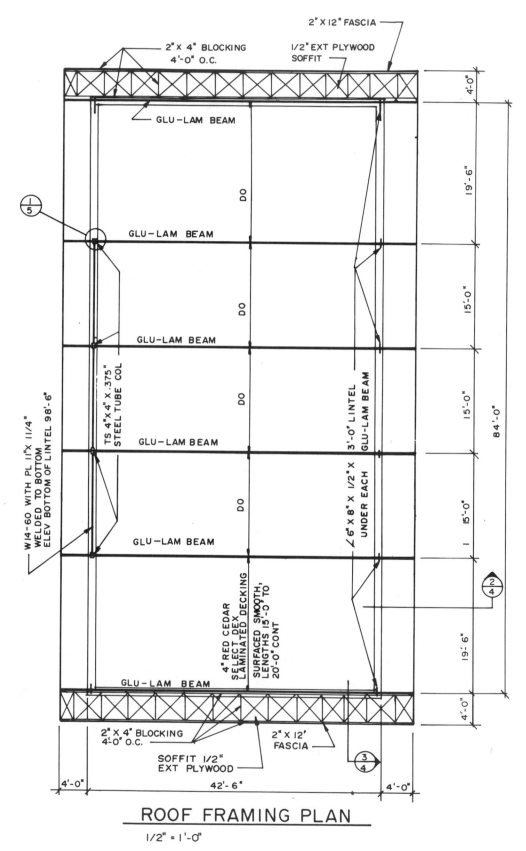

ROOF FRAMING PLAN

1/2" = 1'-0"

Figure 19-14. A roof framing plan for a building using glu-lam beams and 4-in.-thick roof decking.

wall with 2 × 4 in. blocking nailed below the decking to give the roof the desired thickness. A 2 × 12 in. fascia is secured to this and $\frac{1}{2}$-in. plywood is used for the soffit. See the construction details in Fig. 19-15. They will help you interpret the roof framing plan.

Steel Structure Framing Plans

The following illustrations will show a variety of steel framing plans. A roof framing plan for a building with a flat roof that uses open web joists and a W beam for structural

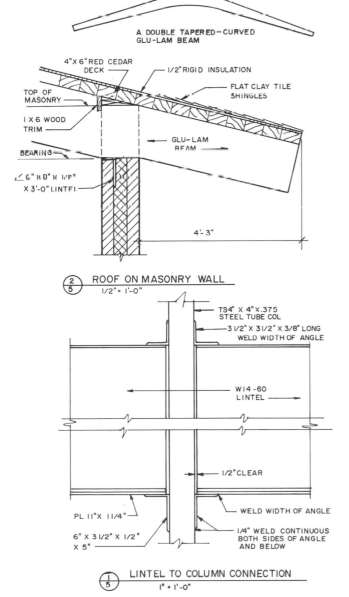

Figure 19-15. *Construction details related to the roof framing plan in Fig. 19-14.*

framing is shown in Fig. 19-16. The joists are shown with a centerline symbol drawn as a thick line although they are sometimes drawn with thick, solid lines. Rather than identifying each joist separately, those of identical description are bracketed by a dimension line. Bridging is noted and the required rows are shown.

In Fig. 19-17 is a framing plan for a flat roof on a steel-framed building. The major girders are W members which are indicated by a thick solid line. Beams are also W members drawn the same way. Columns are indicated and sometimes identified by their mark. Open web bar joists that run between the W beams serve as purlins and support the roof deck. Notice how the roof overhang is indicated. The grid lines are drawn and must be the same as those on the floor plan. The scale is often the same as used to draw the floor and foundation plans.

The framing plan for the floor of a steel-framed building is drawn about the same as the roof plan (Fig. 19-18). This particular plan has W24 × 61 girders connecting the columns and supporting the beams forming the floor structure. Notice the framed opening for a stair. The outer edge is framed with steel channels. This building will be enclosed with a glass and aluminum curtain wall. Several sections are shown in Fig. 19-19. They will help you interpret the framing plan.

A typical roof framing plan for a building using rigid frames for the wall and roof structure and metal "C" or "Z" purlins to support the roof material is in Fig. 19-20. Sometimes the sizes of members are indicated on the drawing. Often they are listed in the specifications instead.

Sometimes it is necessary to draw wall framing plans. A plan for one wall of a small steel-framed building is in Fig. 19-21. In addition to giving the size of each member, they may also be identified by a mark, such as B1. The mark is painted on each member so this drawing can be used as an erection drawing also.

Concrete Structure Framing Plans

Concrete floor and roof framing plans are drawn following details given in the American Concrete Institute publication, *A Manual of Standard Practice for Detailing Reinforced Concrete Structures.* The following examples are from that manual. Figure 19-22 is a framing drawing that shows the general arrangement of the structure, the size of each member, the reinforcing required, and related notes and sections. All design information must be given by a drawing, a note, or in the schedule. This floor framing drawing shows each beam, joist, and cast-in-place floor information. Notice each beam is given a mark which is used in the schedule to identify size and reinforcement

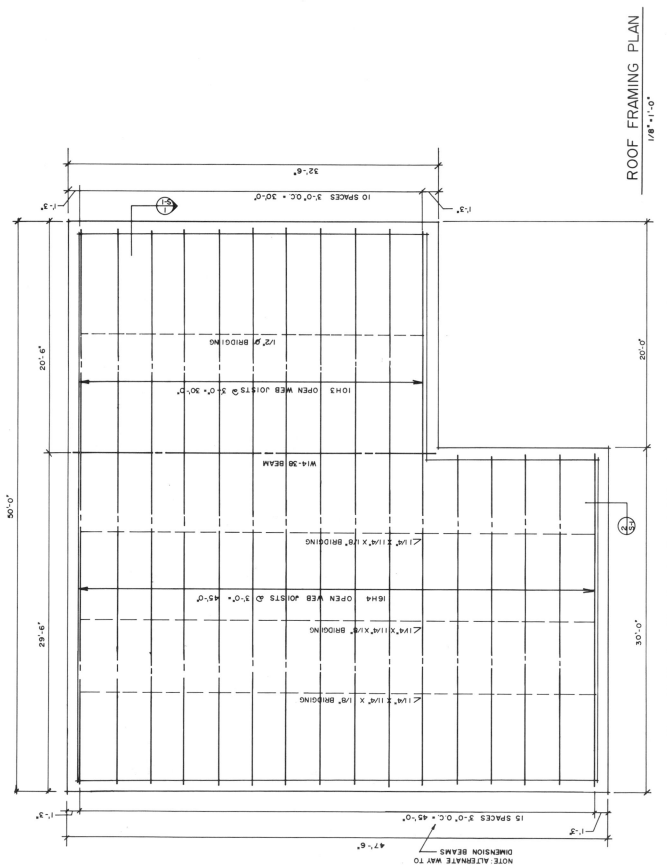

ROOF FRAMING PLAN
1/8" = 1'-0"

Figure 19-16. A roof framing plan for a building using open web steel joists to carry the roof and related loads.

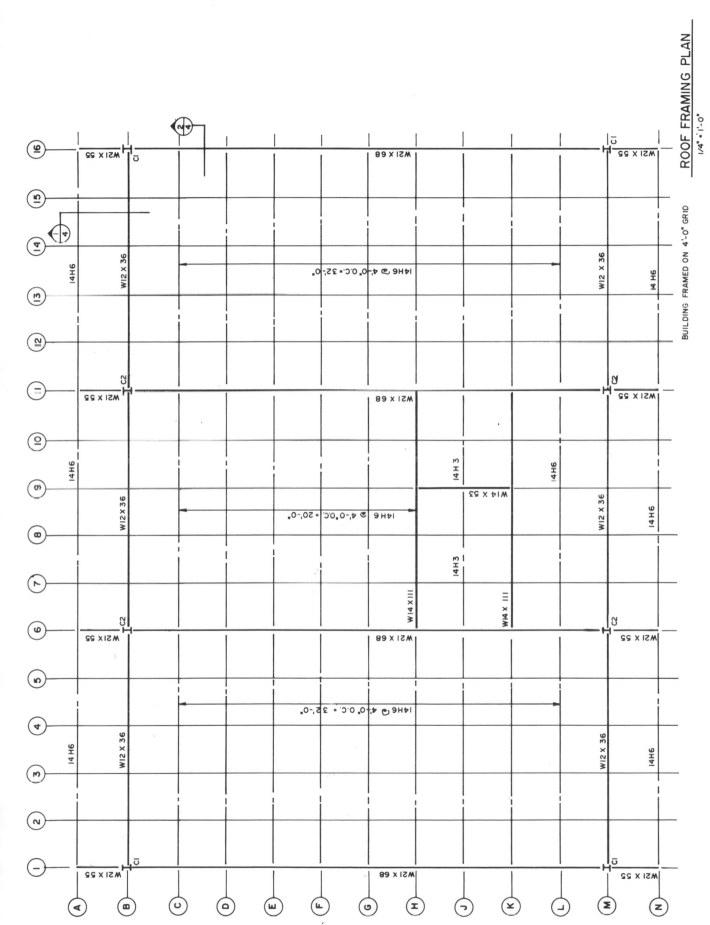

Figure 19-17. *A roof framing plan for a flat, steel-framed roof using W beams and open web joists.*

ROOF FRAMING PLAN
1/4" = 1'-0"

BUILDING FRAMED ON 4'-0" GRID

377

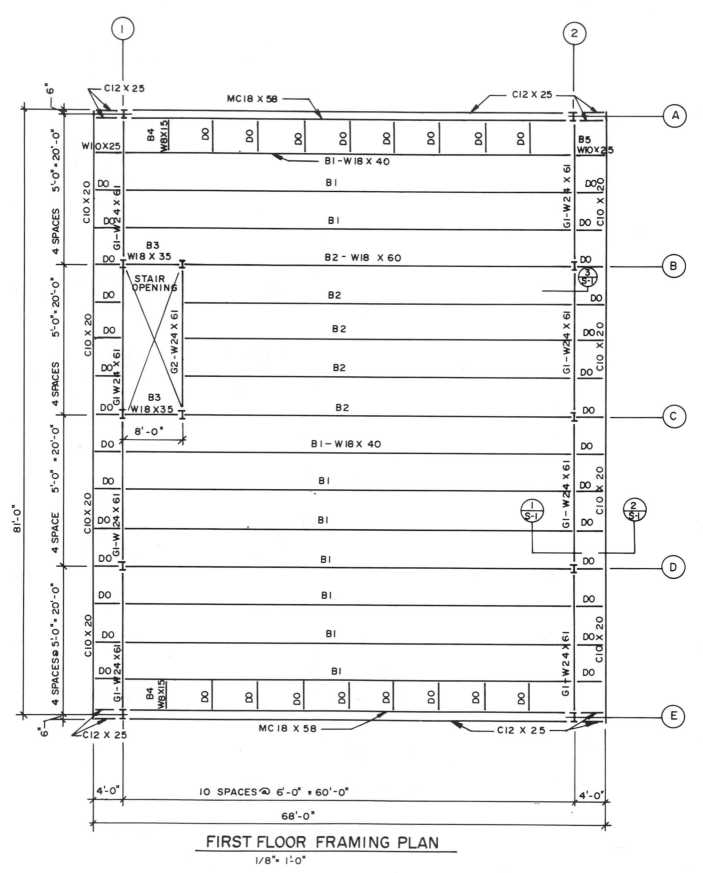

FIRST FLOOR FRAMING PLAN

1/8" = 1'-0"

Figure 19-18. *This is a floor framing plan for a structural steel-framed building.*

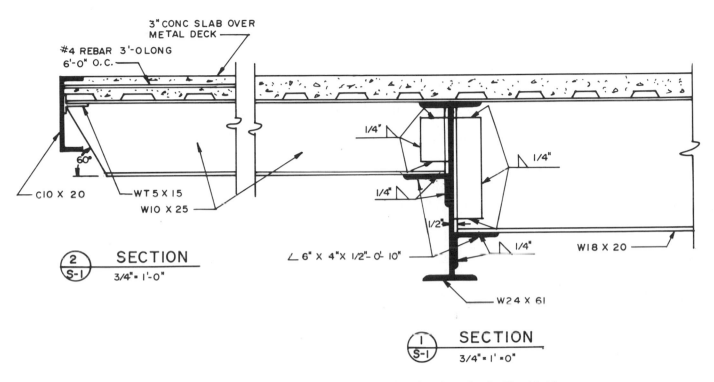

3" CONC SLAB OVER
METAL DECK

#4 REBAR 3'-0 LONG
6'-0" O.C.

60°

C10 X 20

WT 5 X 15

W10 X 25

1/4"

1/4"

1/4"

1/2"

∠ 6" X 4" X 1/2"- 0'-10"

1/4"

W18 X 20

W24 X 61

2
S-1   SECTION
3/4" = 1'-0"

1
S-1   SECTION
3/4" = 1'-0"

Figure 19-19. *Selected sections from the floor framing plan in Fig. 10-18.*

information. On this particular drawing the beam mark, as 1B2, means it is on the first floor and is beam number 2. The schedule shows the 1B2 is 12 × 23 in. and reinforcing is then listed.

A *placing drawing* for the above cast-in-place concrete floor is in Fig. 19-23. It is actually a detail drawing showing the size, spacing, and required bends in the reinforcing bar in each cast-in-place beam and joist. The dimensions shown pertain to the size, shape, and location of the reinforcing bars. Concrete floor slab reinforcement is also shown on this placing drawing.

Precast concrete framing plans are drawn and dimensioned in the same manner as described earlier for steel-framed floors and roofs.

In Fig. 19-24 is a typical framing plan for a floor or roof using precast concrete structural slabs that span from one supporting wall to another. The design of each slab pertains to the span, load it must carry, and the openings required. The slabs are identified by a mark usually established by the company manufacturing the units. Slab specifications are given in a materials list which includes the identifying mark, the number of each member required, thickness, manufacturers code specifications, and the length. A number of details are required to show bearing points and how the slabs are tied to the structure. One example is in Fig. 19-25. Special design data for the various slabs are also shown.

Study Questions

Answer the following study questions without referring to the text. Then check your answers with the text and correct those that were wrong.

1. What is shown on a roof plan?

2. On which of the architectural drawings are roof plans for small buildings often drawn?

3. What scales are used for drawing roof plans?

4. What parts of a roof plan are drawn with thick lines?

5. What is a roof sheathing layout?

6. What loads must the structural frame of a roof carry?

7. What forces act upon roof structural members?

8. Why does a structural steel angle reduce deflection when compared to a steel plate?

9. What is shown on a framing plan?

10. What parts of commercial buildings often require framing plans?

11. What type of line is used to draw load-bearing walls on framing plans for wood-framed structures?

12. How are wood rafters shown on roof framing plans?

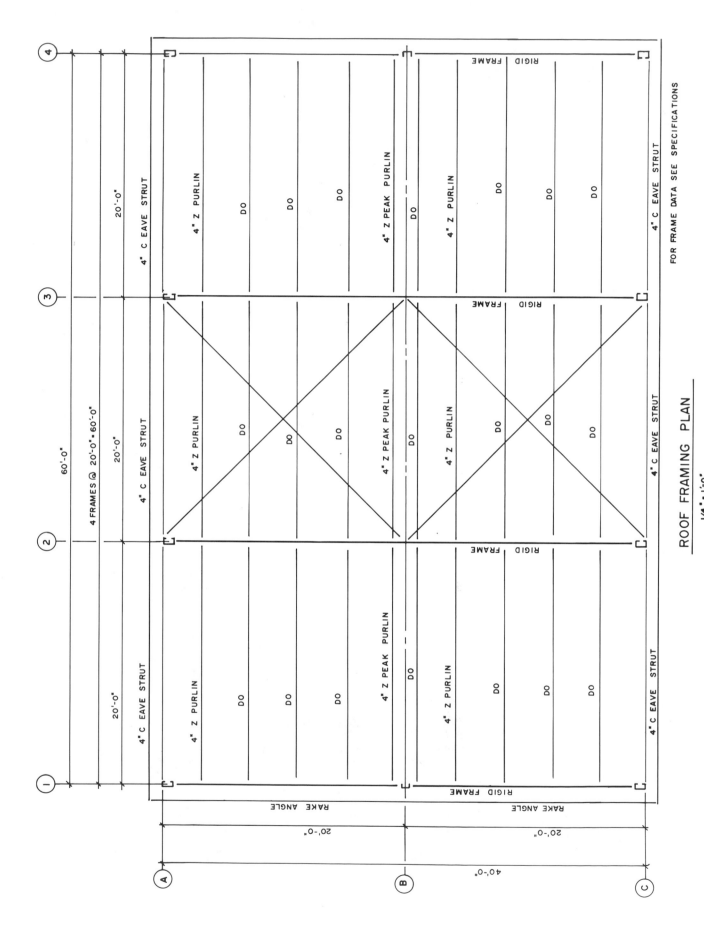

ROOF FRAMING PLAN

1/4" = 1'-0"

Figure 19-20. A roof framing plan for a small structure using rigid frames.

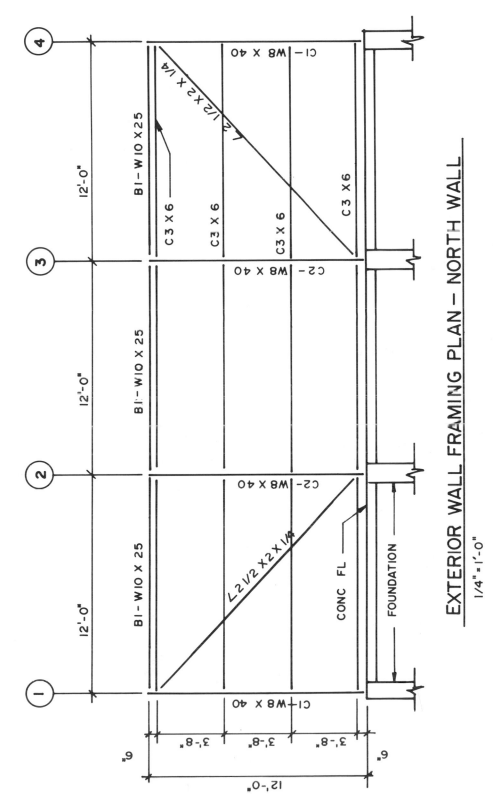

EXTERIOR WALL FRAMING PLAN – NORTH WALL

1/4" = 1'-0"

Figure 19-21. A simple wall framing plan for a steel-framed building.

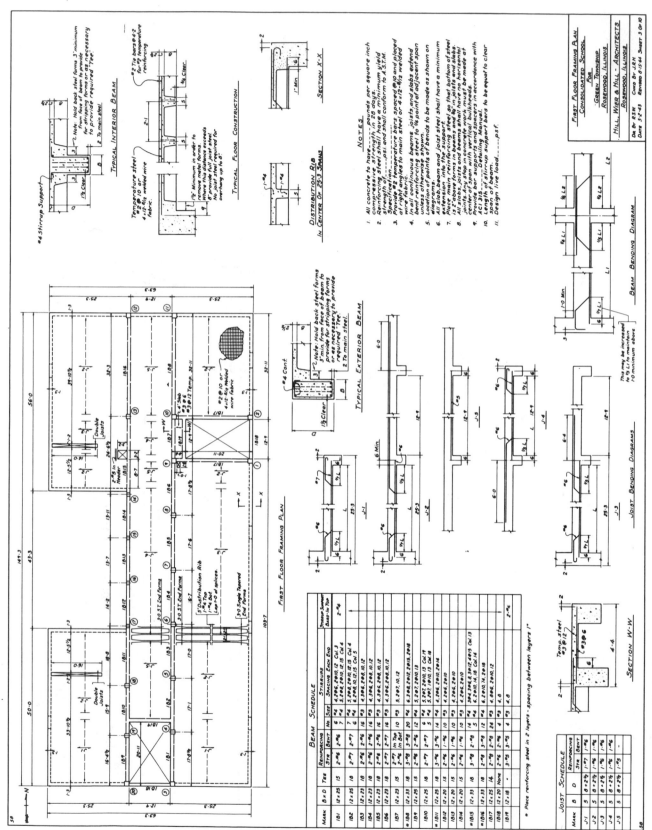

Figure 19-22. This framing plan for a cast-in-place concrete floor uses schedules and sections to give details about size and reinforcing. (Courtesy of the American Concrete Institute.)

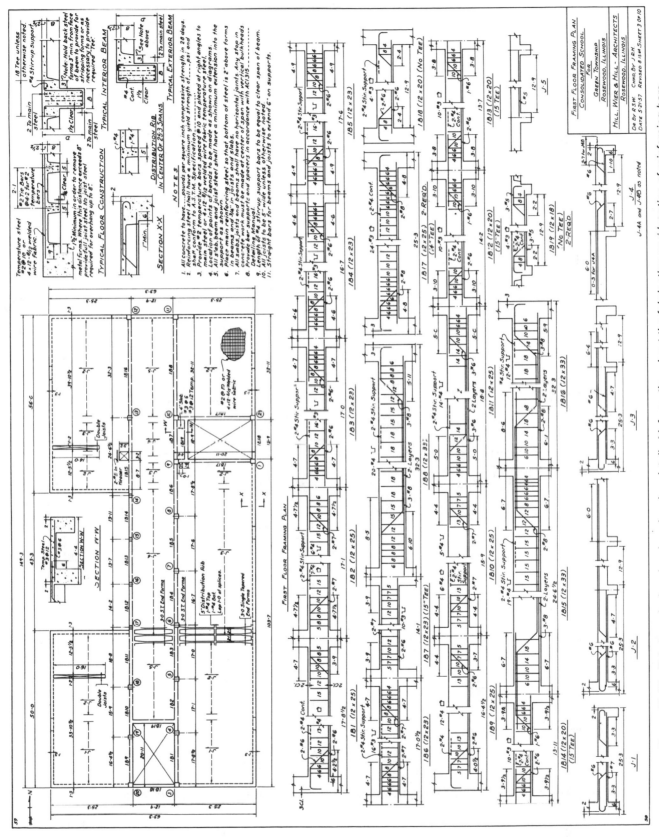

Figure 19-23. This is a placing drawing showing detailed information about the fabrication and location of reinforcing bars for the plan shown in Fig. 19-22. (Courtesy of the American Concrete Institute.)

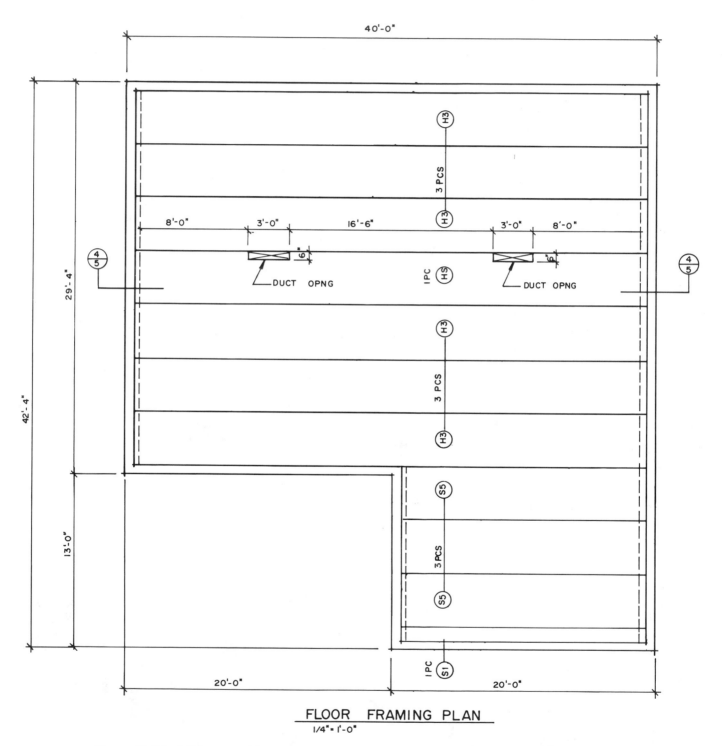

FLOOR FRAMING PLAN
1/4" = 1'-0"

Figure 19-24. *A floor or roof framing plan for a structure using precast concrete structural slabs.*

MATERIAL LIST			
MARK	QTY	UNIT SERIES	LENGTH
S1	1	6" SPANFLOOR UNIT	18'-6"
S5	3	DO	18'-6"
H3	6	12" SPANF~~L~~	

TYPICAL MATERIAL LIST

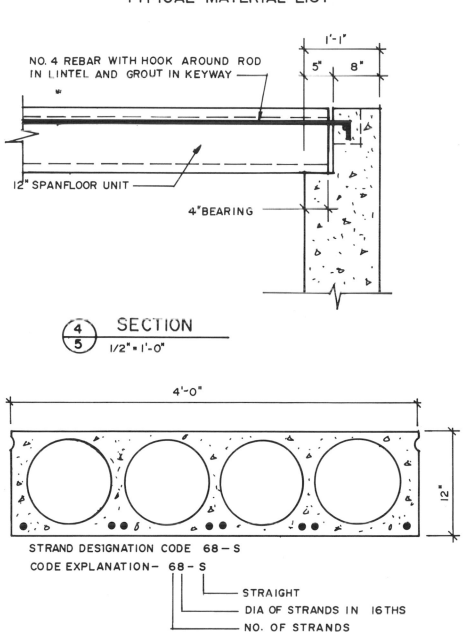

NO. 4 REBAR WITH HOOK AROUND ROD
IN LINTEL AND GROUT IN KEYWAY

1'-1"
5"   8"

12" SPANFLOOR UNIT

4" BEARING

4 / 5 ___SECTION___
1/2" = 1'-0"

4'-0"

12"

STRAND DESIGNATION CODE 68-S

CODE EXPLANATION- 68-S

STRAIGHT
DIA OF STRANDS IN 16THS
NO. OF STRANDS

TYPICAL DESIGN DATA - H3

Figure 19-25. *Typical design data and size specifications for one type of precast concrete structural slab.*

13. What information is given on wood-framed roof framing plans?

14. How are rows of columns identified on a roof framing plan for heavy timber construction?

15. How are the sizes of wood roof members in heavy timber construction shown?

16. How are open web joists indicated on a roof framing plan?

17. How are the sizes of open web joists shown on the roof framing plan?

18. What type of line is used to show beams and girders made from W members?

19. How is design information for concrete structure framing plans shown?

20. What is shown on a placing drawing for cast-in-place concrete structure?

21. How are the specifications for precast concrete structural members shown on the framing plan?

Laboratory Problems

1. Draw a roof framing plan and a roof sheathing layout for the residence designed in Chapter 8.

2. Draw a roof framing plan for the commercial building designed in Chapter 8.

Schedules

Items that appear on architectural drawings, such as doors, windows, and electrical fixtures, are represented with symbols. These only indicate what is to be at a particular location and give no details about the actual item. These specific details are given in *schedules* and written *specifications*. Therefore, it is the purpose of schedules to provide the detailed information. While there are no nationally standardized forms of schedules most architectural offices have standardized sheets for their use. The information shown and the method of organization varies depending upon the degree of detail wanted and the clearest way to show this.

On small commercial and most residential buildings, schedules are rather short and require little time. On large commercial buildings they are extensive and it often requires several sheets to accommodate them. A wide range of features are described in schedules. Among these are doors, windows, lintels, columns, beams, electrical units, plumbing units, heating and air-conditioning units, room finish information, appliances, and footings.

Laying Out Schedules

Once the information has been compiled and the layout of the schedule decided, the finished schedule can be drawn. Some drafters prefer to rough out the schedule and data freehand before starting the finished drawing. The length of each column will depend upon the longest entry. Sometimes the line widths are made wide enough to permit two lines of lettering, thus reducing the length of the schedule. For single line entries a line width of $\frac{3}{16}$ in. is commonly used. Some prefer to use a $\frac{1}{4}$-in. width. Lettering is usually $\frac{3}{32}$ or $\frac{1}{8}$ in. high. When a two-line entry is to be used, a $\frac{3}{8}$ in. wide line is used. Some prefer to start the schedule on the left and complete a vertical row before starting the next row. This has the advantage of permitting the column width to be made wide enough to accommodate the longest entry. Some draw the schedule lines on the back of the sheet.

When just a few schedules are required, an attempt is made to locate them near the drawing containing the symbols being described. For example, the door and window schedules are often located on the same sheet as the floor plan. The electrical schedule can be located on the sheet with the electrical drawing, and so on. Drawings for large commercial buildings often do not permit this and many schedules are grouped together on one or more sheets.

Following are representative examples of several frequently required schedules.

Window Schedules

Information often included on a window schedule includes the mark, sometimes the number required, type, unit size, rough opening, materials, type of glass, and finish. A remarks column provides space for some special information pertaining to one or two of the windows. The mark is the identification lettered by each window on the floor plan. See Chapter 14 for details about marks on floor plans. Window elevations appear on the elevation drawings of the buildings. However, if there are a wide variety of windows and sections are needed to explain how they are to be installed, window elevations may be included beside the window schedule. A typical schedule for a residence is in Fig. 20-1. Since windows designed for use in residences are very standard as far as installation goes installation sections are usually not necessary.

Figure 20-2 has a simple window schedule for a small commercial building with aluminum-framed windows. Notice unit sizes of the windows are given on elevations drawn below the schedule.

Another type of window schedule is the graphic type (Fig. 20-3). Notes are used to provide additional information.

Door Schedules

Door schedules are usually longer than window schedules because most buildings have more different sizes and types of doors than windows. Door schedules for residential

construction usually contain the mark, number required, size, type of door, material, and remarks (Fig. 20-4).

A door schedule using only a graphic representation is in Fig. 20-5. Sizes and fire ratings are given with notes and openings for glazing and louvers are dimensioned. Another type of schedule giving both door and door frame information is in Fig. 20-6. This type of schedule could be stored in the memory of a computer and reproduced on the drawing quickly. It could also be made by having a rubber stamp made or be reproduced on clear plastic film with an adhesive back. These would place the basic framework on the drawing, requiring the drafter to only fill in the needed information. These techniques could be used for all of the basic schedules. Another detailed door schedule with frame information is in Fig. 20-7. It refers to other sources for detailed information. For example, it refers to FR. NO. which would be the marks used for various door frames. Dimensioned sections of each frame must accompany the schedule. Also it refers to H.W. SET. These

WINDOW SCHEDULE

MARK	NO.	UNIT SIZE	ROUGH OPENING	TYPE	MATERIAL	GLAZING	REMARKS
W1	1	5'-0" X 4'-0"	5'-01/2" X 4'-01/2"	FIXED	PINE	DOUBLE	ENGY EFF GL
W2	6	3'-1 5/8" X 4'-9 1/4"	3'-21/8" X 4'-9 5/8"	D. H.	PINE	SINGLE	
W3	2	4'-0" X 3'-6"	4'-01/2" X 3'-6 1/2"	GLIDING	PINE	SINGLE	

Figure 20-1. *A typical window schedule as used on residential architectural drawings.*

WINDOW SCHEDULE

MARK	UNIT SIZE	TYPE	MATERIAL	GLAZING	FINISH	REMARKS
A	4'-0" X 4'-6"	FIXED/HOPPER	ALUM	5/8" INSUL	BRONZE	
B	2'-8" X 4'-6"	DO	DO	DO	DO	
C	4'-0" X 3'-0"	AWNING	DO	DO	DO	1
D	4'-0" X 2'-6"	DO	DO	DO	DO	1
E	4'-0 X 4'-0"	FIXED/HOPPER	DO	DO	DO	
F	4'-0 X 6'-8"	DO	DO	DO	DO	

NOTE: 1. REMOVE HANDLE

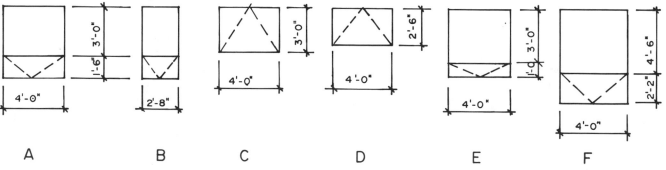

Figure 20-2. *A window schedule showing metal windows for a small commercial building.*

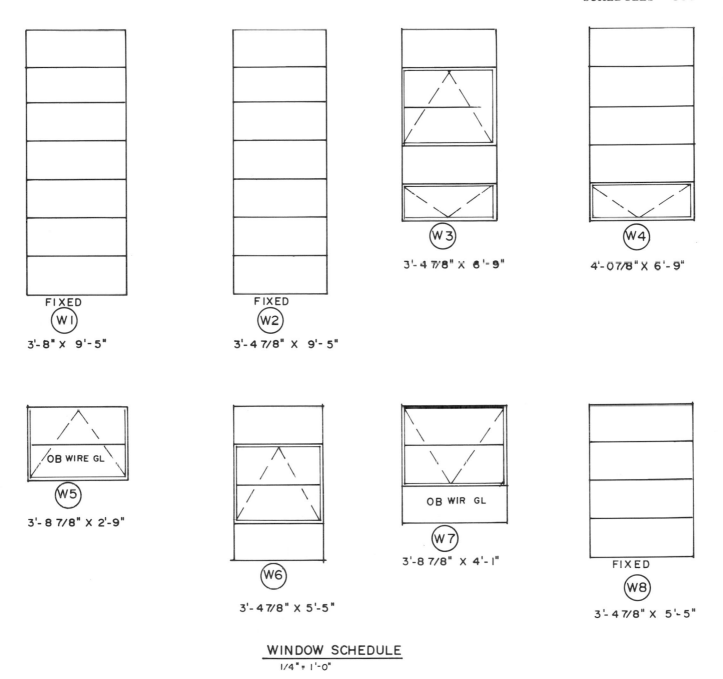

FIXED
(W1)
3'-8" X 9'-5"

FIXED
(W2)
3'-4 7/8" X 9'-5"

(W3)
3'-4 7/8" X 6'-9"

(W4)
4'-07/8" X 6'-9"

OB WIRE GL
(W5)
3'-8 7/8" X 2'-9"

(W6)
3'-4 7/8" X 5'-5"

OB WIR GL
(W7)
3'-8 7/8" X 4'-1"

FIXED
(W8)
3'-4 7/8" X 5'-5"

WINDOW SCHEDULE
1/4" = 1'-0"

NOTES:
1. ALL WINDOWS ARE ALUMINUM
   INTERMEDIATE PROJECTED TYPE.
2. WINDOWS ON SOUTH AND NORTH
   ELEVATIONS TO BE CLEAR "E" OR
   "F" LABEL FIRE WINDOWS WITH CLEAR
   WIRE GLASS EXCEPT WHERE NOTED
   OBSCURE WIRE GLASS.

Figure 20-3. *A graphic window schedule combines elevation view, size, type, and mark on one drawing.*

DOOR SCHEDULE

MARK	NO.	SIZE	TYPE	MATERIAL	REMARKS
D1	1	3'-0" X 6'-8" X 1 3/4"	SOLID CORE, FLUSH	BIRCH	NATURAL FINISH
D2	6	2'-8" X 6'-8" X 1 3/8"	HOLLOW CORE, FLUSH	BIRCH	DO
D3	3	6'-0" X 6'-8" X 1 1/4"	BI-FOLD, PANEL	PINE	PAINT
D4	1	3'-0" X 6'-8" X 1 3/4"	PANEL	PINE	1/4" TEMPERED GL

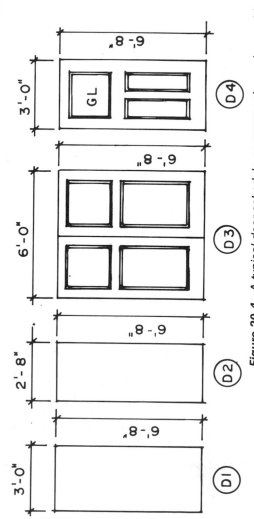

Figure 20-4. *A typical door schedule as commonly used on residential architectural drawings.*

390

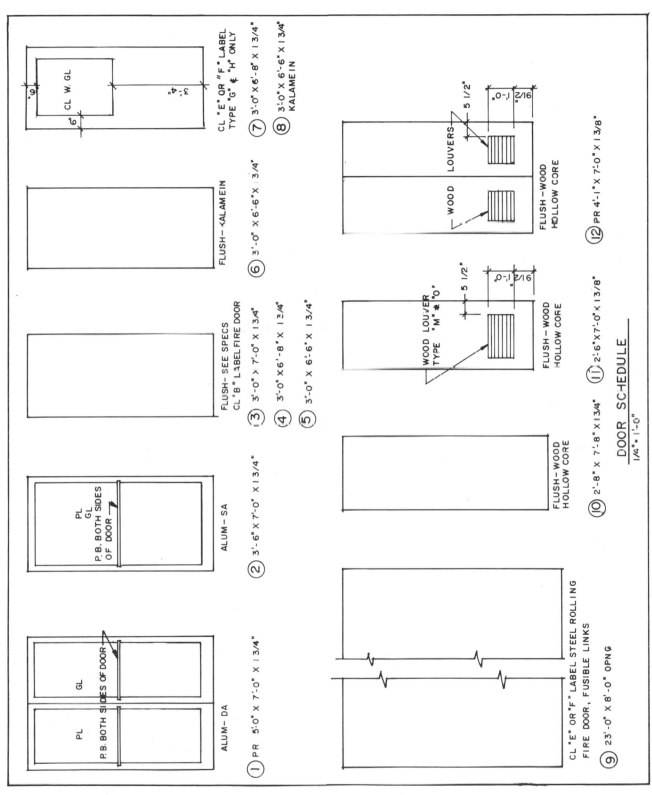

Figure 20-5. A graphic door schedule combining elevation, material, size, type, mark, and special specifications such as fire rating and louvers.

DOOR SCHEDULE

MARK	DOOR														FRAME								
	SIZE			MATERIAL				TYPE													FIRE RATING	HARDWARE SET	REMARKS
	W	H	T	HOL MTL	WOOD S.C.	WOOD H.C.	ALUM & GL	FLUSH	PANEL	OVERHEAD	BI-FOLD	ROLLING	DUTCH	SLIDING	HOLLOW MTL	ALUMINUM	WOOD	METAL	JAMB	HEAD			
1	3'-0"	6'-8	1 3/4"		●			●									●		1 1/16"	1 1/16"	1/3	1	
2	3'-0"	6'-8"	1 3/4"			●		●		●							●		DO	DO		2	1
3	2'-6"	6'-8"	1 3/8"			●		●									●		DO	DO		1	
4	2'-0"	6'-8"	1 3/4"			●		●									●		DO	DO		1	
5	2'-8"	6'-8"	1 3/8			●		●									●		DO	DO		1	
6	3'-0	7'-0"	1 3/4"	●					●						●				1 15/16"	1 15/16"	1 1/2	3	
7	3'-0"	6'-8"	1 3/4"	●					●						●				DO	DO	1 1/2	3	

1. PAIR

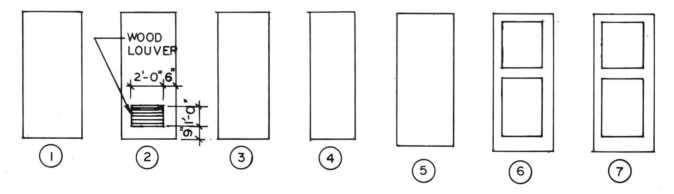

Figure 20-6. *Another form of door schedule with frame information.*

marks refer to a schedule or a listing in the specifications of the various hardware sets required. The "ACTIVE HAND" refers to the direction of swing of the door.

Interior Finish Schedules

Interior room finish schedules vary in complexity depending upon the amount of information needed. For example, for a residence in which all walls of each room will have a common interior, finish can have a rather brief schedule (Fig. 20-8).

Commercial buildings usually have a much wider range of interior wall finish ranging from simple painted concrete block to expensive custom made paneling. In Fig. 20-9 is an example of a more detailed schedule. In commercial buildings rooms are identified by numbers and these are essential when identifying exactly which room is being described. Interior colors and finish material details can be recorded in an interior color schedule (Fig. 20-10). The mark is located on the floor plan with the room identification number.

Sometimes the walls in a room will have different finishes. For example, three walls may be painted and one paneled. To record this type of information each wall of each room is noted on the finish schedule. One way to do

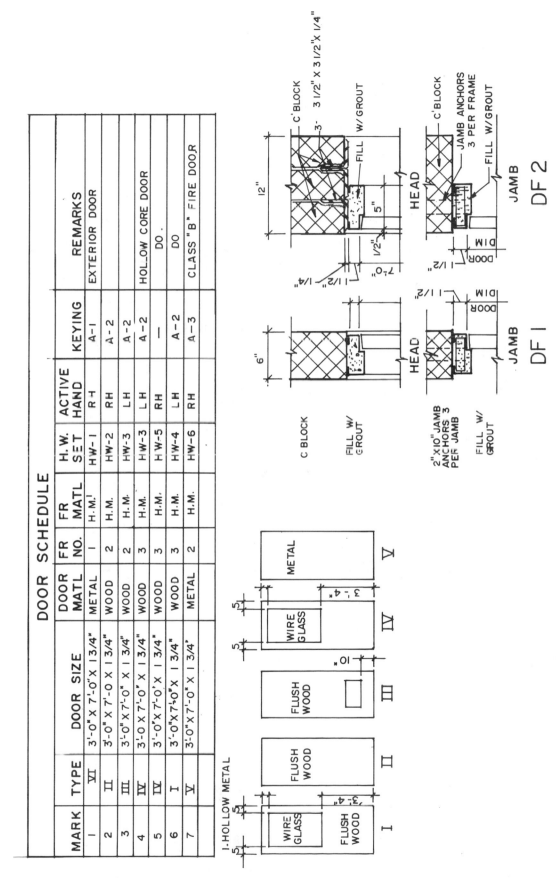

DOOR SCHEDULE

MARK	TYPE	DOOR SIZE	DOOR MATL	FR NO.	FR MATL	H.W. SET	ACTIVE HAND	KEYING	REMARKS
I	VI	3'-0" X 7'-0" X 1 3/4"	METAL	I	H.M.	HW-1	RH	A-1	EXTERIOR DOOR
2	II	3'-0" X 7'-0" X 1 3/4"	WOOD	2	H.M.	HW-2	RH	A-2	
3	III	3'-0"X7'-0" X 1 3/4"	WOOD	2	H.M.	HW-3	LH	A-2	
4	IV	3'-0"X 7'-0" X 1 3/4"	WOOD	3	H.M.	HW-3	LH	A-2	HOLLOW CORE DOOR
5	IV	3'-0"X7'-0"X 1 3/4"	WOOD	3	H.M.	HW-5	RH	—	DO.
6	I	3'-0"X7'-0"X 1 3/4"	WOOD	3	H.M.	HW-4	LH	A-2	DO
7	V	3'-0"X7'-0" X 1 3/4"	METAL	2	H.M.	HW-6	RH	A-3	CLASS "B" FIRE DOOR

1.-HOLLOW METAL

Figure 20-7. This door schedule not only gives door size and type information but includes door frame data, hardware, swing of door, and keying codes.

INTERIOR FINISH SCHEDULE

ROOM	FLOOR MTL	FL FINISH	WALL MTL	WALL FINISH	CEILING MTL	CLG FINISH	TRIM MTL	TRIM FINISH	REMARKS
LIVING RM	CARPET	——	GYPSUM	LATEX PAINT	GYPSUM	LATEX PAINT	PINE	LATEX SEMI—GLOSS ENAM	
BEDROOM 1	CARPET	——	GYPSUM	LATEX PAINT	GYPSUM	LATEX PAINT	PINE	LATEX SEMI-GLOSS ENAM	
BEDROOM 2	CARPET	——	GYPSUM	LATEX PAINT	GYPSUM	LATEX PAINT	PINE	LATEX SEMI—GLOSS ENAM	
BATH	CER TILE	——	GYPSUM-M.R.	CER. TILE	GYPSUM	LATEX PAINT	PINE	LATEX SEMI—GLOSS ENAM	
DEN	T &G OAK	VARNISH	PINE PANEL	YELLOW SHELLAC	APC	——	OAK	CLEAR LACQUER	

Figure 20-8. A simple interior finish schedule. The abbreviation APC refers to acoustical plaster ceiling.

ROOM FINISH SCHEDULE

ROOM	MARK	EXPOSED CONCRETE	VINYL	BRICK	CERAMIC TILE	4" VINYL	4" RUBBER	NO BASE	CONC BLOCK	BRICK	CONCRETE	1/2" GYP BD. FURR OUT	1/4" HDWOOD PANEL	1/2"×12"×12" ACST TILE	WOOD DECKING	1/2" FIRECODE GYP BD	1/2" GYP BD	CEILING HEIGHT
		FLOOR				BASE			WALLS					CEILING				
CLASSROOM	01		•			•			•					•				9'-0"
CLASSROOM	02		•			•			•					•				9'-0"
CLASSROOM	03		•			•			•					•				9'-0"
CLASSROOM	04		•			•			•					•				9'-0"
CORRIDOR	05		•			•				•				•				8'-8"
MEN	06				•		•		•								•	8'-8"
WOMEN	07				•		•		•								•	8'-8"
COATROOM	08		•			•			•								•	9'-0"
LOBBY	09			•				•					•		•			9'-0"
MECHANICAL RM	10	•						•			•					•		12'-0"
SOCIAL HALL	11		•			•						•		•				12'-0"
																		9'-0"
														•				9'-0"
RECEPTION	1			•		•			•			•		•				
OFFICE	2		•			•			•									
OFFICE	3		•			•			•									
OFFICE	4		•															
OFFICE	5																	
MEN	6																	
WOMEN																		

Figure 20-9. A partial room finish schedule for a commercial building.

INTERIOR COLOR SCHEDULE

MARK	MATERIAL	COLOR OF PAINT, STAIN, VARNISH	SPEC	LOCATION
1	WOOD DECKING	LIGHT WALNUT, SUBMIT SAMPLES	6C3	LOBBY
2	GLU-LAM BEAMS	LIGHT WALNUT, SUBMIT SAMPLES	6C3	LOBBY
3	GYPSUM BD	YELLOW # 1200	6E	SOCIAL HALL. COATS
4	GYPSUM BD	YELLOW # 1200	6E	RESTROOMS
5	CONC BLOCK	GREEN # 2300	6D	CLASSROOMS
6	CONC BLOCK	WHITE # 1000	6F	COAT ROOM
7	WOOD DOORS	LIGHT WALNUT, SUBMIT SAMPLES	6C3	EXTERIOR DOORS
8	STEEL WINDOWS	SEMI-GLOSS BROWN	6A	EXTERIOR
9	CHALKBOARD	GREEN	12-1	CLASSROOMS
10	TOILET PARTITIONS	GREEN # 2100	12-3	RESTROOMS

Figure 20-10. *This schedule records interior finish materials and colors.*

ROOM FINISH SCHEDULE

ROOM NAME	FLOOR	BASE	WALL FINISH				CEILING		REMARKS
			NORTH	EAST	SOUTH	WEST	MATERIAL	HT	
SALES ROOM	VINYL TILE	4" VINYL	GYP	GYP	GYP	WD PANEL	ACST TILE	14'-0"	SEE COLOR SCHDULE
MECANICAL ROOM	CONC	NONE	CONC BLK	CONC BLK	CONC BLK	CONC BLK	TYPE X GYP 1/2"	10'-0"	DO
RESTROOMS	CERAMIC TILE	CER.	CER TILE	CER TILE	CER TILE	CER TILE	PLASTER	10'-0"	DO
STOCK ROOM	CONC	NONE	GYP	GYP	CONC BLK	CONC BLK	TYPE X GYP 1/2"	14'-0"	DO

Figure 20-11. *This room finish schedule gives details for each wall and ceiling of each room.*

this is to relate each wall to its orientation. If a wall faces north or a little east or west of north identify it as north. The technique is the same applied to the east, west, and south walls (Fig. 20-11).

There are a variety of symbols used on the floor plan to identify interior finish in each room with the interior finish schedule. One of these is in Fig. 20-12.

Figure 20-12. *This is an example of a symbol used on the floor plan to identify interior finish in each room.*

Schedules Related to Structure

There are a number of schedules commonly used to provide details pertaining to structural features. Among these are lintel, column, and beam schedules. A lintel schedule is in Fig. 20-13. It is often located with the door and window schedules because the lintels relate closely to any sections taken through the head of these units.

A combined column and footing schedule is in Fig. 20-14. This is a useful way to record this information when there are just a few sizes and there are no complex factors involved. A detailed footing schedule is in Fig. 20-15. It includes footing sizes and required reinforcing. A column schedule showing rectangular and round steel columns and a W-column is in Fig. 20-16. It also gives the size of the bottom plate, the detail number, and where to look to find the detail drawings.

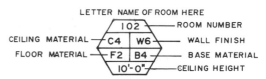

MARK	NO.	DESCRIPTION	LG	REMARKS
1	8	∠ 3 1/2" X 3 1/2" X 1/4"	4'-6"	PRIME
2	1	8" X 8" PRECAST CONC	8'-4"	2 # 5 REBARS

Figure 20-13. *A lintel schedule.*

COLUMN AND FOOTING SCHEDULE

MARK	P1	P2	P3
PIER	42" ∅ 8 #9 VERT #3 TIES @ 18" O.C.	24" ∅ 6 #6 VERT #3 TIES @ 12" O.C.	30" ∅ 6 #7 VERT #3 TIES @ 12" O.C.
FOOTING	42" ∅	24" ∅	30" ∅

NOTE: PIERS TO BEAR ON UNWEATHERED SHALE.
TYPE P1 PIERS PROVIDE 6 #7 DOWELS W/STD HOOKS IN TOP OF GRADE BEAM EXTENDING 3'-0" INTO PIER.

Figure 20-14. *A combined column and footing schedule.*

FOOTING SCHEDULE

MARK	SIZE	REINFORCING
F 1	3'-2" X 3'-2" X 1'-0"	4 #5 BARS X 2'-10" – 10 % E.W.
F 2	4'-1" X 4'-6" X 1'-0"	5 #5 BARS X 3'-6" – 10 % E.W.
F 3	4'-0" X 2'-6" X 1'-0"	5 #4 BARS X 2'-0" 2 #4 BARS X 5'-6"
F 4	7'-0" X 2'-6" X 1'-0"	7 #4 BARS X 2'-0" 2 #4 BARS X 6'-6"
F 5	6'-0" X 2'-6" X 1'-0"	5 #4 BARS
F 6	3'-6" X 2'	

Figure 20-15. A typical footing schedule.

COLUMN SCHEDULE

MARK	SIZE	BOT PL	DETAIL
A	2" X 6" X 1/4" STEEL	1/2" X 7" X 7"	2 / 7 / 7
B1,C1,C2, C7,C9	6" ROUND STEEL	3/4" X 10" X 10"	3 / 7 / 7
D3 , D5	6" ROUND STEEL	3/8" X 7" X 12"	4 / 7 / 7
E 5	W 8 X 31	1/2" X 12" X 12"	5 / 7 / 7

NOTE: ALL BOTTOM PLATES TO RECEIVE 2- 3/4" X 1'-0" BOLTS

Figure 20-16. This column schedule shows details for several types of columns.

BEAM SCHEDULE

MARK	SIZE	SPLICE DETAIL	END BRG DETAIL	TOP BM ELEV
A	W12 X 16.5	1	3	120'-6 1/2"
B	W16 X 45	12	3	121'-3"
C	W16 X 45	12	3	121'-3"

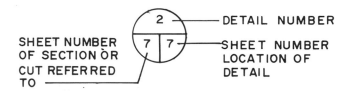

SHEET NUMBER OF SECTION OR CUT REFERRED TO — 2 — DETAIL NUMBER
7 | 7 — SHEET NUMBER LOCATION OF DETAIL

Figure 20-17. This is a schedule for W beams.

schedules are representative of the many types frequently used.

Heating, Air Conditioning, and Ventilation

These systems vary widely in design, fuel used, spaces to be conditioned, and equipment manufactured. The following schedules show how some situations are handled. These are representative only and do not reflect a total coverage of possible schedules.

A unit ventilator schedule is in Fig. 20-20. A *ventilator* is a device, such as an exhaust fan, that removes stale air and circulates fresh air. This schedule shows the mark, number required, cubic feet per minute, the percent fresh air used, gallons of hot water per minute running through the ventilator, total capacity, and tells where each is located. An *exhauster* is a unit used to draw off air or fumes from inside a building. A typical exhauster schedule is in Fig. 20-21. It gives the mark, number required, cubic feet per minute air flow, static pressure developed, horsepower of the motor, and the speed of the fan tips. A convector schedule is shown in Fig. 20-22.

Some industrial environments require extensive use of exhaust fans. They are commonly used in kitchens and baths in residential construction. An exhaust fan schedule for a commercial building is in Fig. 20-23.

A grill and diffuser schedule is shown in Fig. 20-24. A *grill* is a criss-cross grating used over air duct openings. A *diffuser* is an outlet for air from a forced-air heating system.

A schedule for thru-the-wall heating and cooling units is shown in Fig. 20-25. It gives extensive data including cooling, heating, the evaporator coil, the condenser coil, and required electrical service.

A beam schedule for W-beams is in Fig. 20-17. It gives the mark, beam size, elevation of the top of the beam, and where to find details pertaining to splices and end bearing construction.

Grade beams are frequently used in commercial construction. A partial schedule for grade beams is in Fig. 20-18. It not only gives the mark, size, and number required but gives data pertaining to required hooks and overall lengths of reinforcing bars, stirrups, and their spacing.

Cast-in-place concrete structures utilize a series of girders, beams, ribs, and a monolithically cast floor or roof deck. These require careful sizing, spacing, and reinforcing bar selection. A typical rib table for floor ribs for such construction is in Fig. 20-19. Notice the use of section drawings which relate to sizes and placement data in the rib schedule.

Schedules Related to Mechanical Features

The mechanical features of a building include electrical, heating, air conditioning, ventilation, and plumbing. Each of these require a number of schedules to list and describe parts of each system. Drawings for mechanical systems are described in Chapter 21. The following examples of

GRADE BEAM SCHEDULE

MARK	SIZE	NO	REINFORCING	TOP BARS			BOTTOM BARS			STIRRUPS				
				HK	⌣	HK	HK	⌣	HK	NO.	SIZE	LG	TYP	SPACING
GB1	12" X 24"		2-#5 X 26-9 2-#7 X 21-10	7	26'-2"	—	—	21'-10	—	28	#3	4'-11"	⊔	@ 9, 4 CANT
GB2	12" X 24"		2-#6 X 21-10 2-#5 X 12-11	—	21'-10"	—	—	12'-11"	—	8	#3	4'-11"	⊔	@ 18
GB3	12" X 36"		2-#6 X 25-0 2-#5 X 16-5	—	25'-0"	—	—	20'-1"	—	24	#3	4'-11"	⊔	@ 9

Figure 20-18. A partial grade beam schedule.

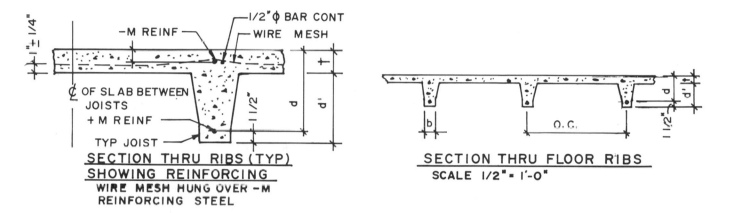

RIB SCHEDULE

RIB NO.	a	-M STL	+M STL	b	d'	d	o.c.	t
R-1	3'-0"	3/4"φ	5/8"φ	3 5/8	8.0"	9.0"	33.625"	3.5"
R-2	2'-0"	3/4"φ	5/8"φ	"	"	"	"	"
R-3	3'-0"	1"φ	3/4"φ	"	"	"	"	"
R-4	3'-0"	3/4"φ	7/8"φ				"	"
R-5	3'-0				"	"	"	"
		4φ	5/8φ	"	"	"	"	"
R-12	2'-6"	5/8"φ	7/8"φ	35/8"	"	"	"	"

T. -M STEEL IS IN ADDITION TO 1/2"φ BAR CONTINUOUS.

Figure 20-19. A partial rib schedule and related details for a cast-in-place floor.

UNIT VENTILATOR SCHEDULE

NO	QTY	CFM STD AIR	% F.A.	GPM	TOTAL CAP. BTU/HR	REMARKS
U-1	4	1200	30	5.5	105,000	RMS 110. 112, 116, 118
U-2	1	1000	30	4.3	85,000	RM 111
U-3	2	1200	50	5.0	95,000	RMS 113, 114
U-4	3	750	40			

NOTE: SCHEDULE IS BASED ON 220° ENTR WATER TEMP & 40° TEMP DROP

Figure 20-20. This schedule is one of several related to the mechanical systems in a building.

EXHAUSTER SCHEDULE					
NO.	NO. REQD	CFM	SP	MOTOR I-P	TIP SPEED
E-1	5	425	1/8	1/15	4000
E-2	2	725	1/8	1/8	3500
E-3	1	730	1/4	1/8	4100
E-4	6	175	1/8	1/20	
E-5				1/8	2900
E-10	3	1475	1/8	1/6	3800

NOTE: ALL EXHAUSTERS TO BE 110V SINGLE PHASE.
ALL EXHAUSTERS TO BE EQUIPPED WITH
BACK DRAFT DAMPERS.

Figure 20-21. This exhauster schedule gives considerable technical information. CPM is cubic feet per minute and SP is the static pressure.

CONVECTOR SCHEDULE					CONVECTOR SIZE		
NO.	QTY	CAP. BTU/HR	GPM	TYPE	LENGTH	HT	DEPTH
C-1	2	8,000	0.7	FR OUTLET FL. STANDING	63"	28	4"
C-2	1	6,000	0.4	SEMI-REC.	24"	32"	10"
C-3	3	12,500	1-4	FULLY-REC.	63"	28"	10"
C-4	1	3,000					

NOTE: SCHEDULE IS BASED ON 220° ENTR WATER TEMP & 40° TEMP DROP.

Figure 20-22. A convector schedule. GPM is the gallons per minute of hot water passing through the convector.

In Fig. 20-26 is a heating/air-conditioning schedule giving specifications for each equipment item. If the drawing was being prepared on a computer this would be composed as fast as a drafter could keyboard it into the memory. There are available long, open-end carriage typewriters that could also be used. Either method is faster and clearer than hand lettering such a schedule.

Plumbing Schedules

Plumbing systems include a variety of fixture sizes and types. Commercial buildings could have the usual restroom fixtures plus other plumbing requirements made necessary by the activities occurring in the building. In addition, there are many pipe and pipe fitting sizes and materials to identify. Figure 20-27 shows a simple schedule for identifying specific fixtures and related pipe sizes. It gives the mark, name of fixture, the number required, manufacturer, the manufacturer's catalog number, the sizes of cold water, hot water and vent pipes, and the trap size. Often the information about the manufacturer or brand is in the specifications rather than in the schedule.

A pump schedule is shown in Fig. 20-28. It gives the mark, manufacturer, model, and technical data such as gallons per minute, the heat in feet, revolutions per minute, pump efficiency, and required electrical service.

EXHAUST FAN SCHEDULE						
MARK	✱ MODEL	C.F.M.	S.P	MOTOR H.P	CURRENT	REMARKS
E-1	TRANE AEB-48	18,000	1/4"	2	208/3/60	MOTORIZED DAMPER
E-2	JENN-AIR 98CR	550	1/8"	1/12	115/1/60	GRAVITY DAMPER
E-3	JENN-AIR 75CR	425	1/8"	1/12	115/1/60	GRAVITY DAMPER

✱ TRANE, JENN-AIR, PENN, OR ACME EQUALLY ACCEPTABLE

Figure 20-23. This exhaust fan schedule indicates the manufacturer, model, and specifications for each fan.

GRILLE & DIFFUSER SCHEDULE					
MARK	FUNCTION	✱ MODEL	SIZE	C.F.M.	COLOR
1	CLG S.A.	S-400 R2 BAO 4 WAY	30"X 30"	2000	OFF WHITE
2	CLG S.A.	S-400 R2 BAO 3 WAY	30" X 30"	2000	OFF WHITE
3	CLG S.A.	S-310 RI BAO 3 WAY	20"X 20"	1000	OFF WHITE
4	CLG SA	S-30 R BAO			
		BAO	14 X 14"	700	OFF WHITE

✱ TITUS, CARNES, KRUGER, AND TUTTLE EQUALLY ACCEPABLE.

Figure 20-24. A mechanical system will require a variety of diffusers and grilles. Specifications for each are shown on a schedule.

THRU THE WALL UNITS		
MARK	AC-A	AC-B
MFG	CARRIER	CARRIER
MODEL	50-ET 218	50-ET 230
CFM	550	850
E.S.P. (IN W.G.)	.2	.47
FAN HP	1/4	1/3
COOLING CAPACITY		
SENSIBLE MBH	—	—
TOTAL MBH	18	27.1
HEATING CAPACITY		
KW	7.5	10.0
NO. CIRCUITS	1	2
EVAP COIL		
ROWS	3	3
FINS/INCH	14	14
FACE AREA/SQ. FT.	2.0	4.2
ELECTRICAL		
VOLTAGE	208/1/60	208/1/60
COMP./RLA	9.3	16.9
COND. FAN/FLA	1.5	1.5
INDOOR FAN/FLA	1.7	2.4
ELEC HEATER FLA	26.8	36.0
SEER (EER)	8.0	8.0
MCA	48.3	48.0
AREA SERVED	APT "A"	APT "B"

NOTES: 1. CAPACITIES BASED ON 80/67°F E.A.T., 95°F O.A.
2. KW SHOWN FOR 240V DERATE FOR 208V.

Figure 20-25. *This is a partial schedule giving details for thru-the-wall heating and cooling units.*

HEATING/AIR CONDITIONING
EQUIPMENT SCHEDULE

1. BOILER – HOT WATER HEATING, 2 REQD, 150 EACH, REFER TO SPECS.
2. BOILER – H.P. STEAM, 125 HP, REFER TO SPECS.
3. CHILLER – ABSORPTION TYPE, 125 TON, REFER TO SPECS.
4. COOLING TOWER – REFER TO SPECS.
5. FUEL OIL TANK – 10,000 GAL., REFER TO SPECS.
6. COOLING TOWER PUMP – 450 GPM   60'-0" HEAD. 220V/3/60 10HP 1750RPM.
7. HEATING WATER PUMP – 400 GPM   60'-0" HEAD. 220V/3/60 10HP 1750RPM.
8. CHILLED WATER PUMP – 300GPM   80'-0" HEAD. 220V/3/60 10HP 1750RPM.
9. UNIT HEATER – VERTICAL HOT WATER TYPE. 1/8 HP 110V MOTOR 1135RPM
      2300 CFM, 78,000 BTU, 200° EWT, 40°TD.
10. COMPRESSION TANK – 2 REQD. 400GAL., 36" DIA. 96" LONG.

Figure 20-26. *Another form of a schedule giving information about mechanical equipment.*

PLUMBING SCHEDULE

MARK	FIXTURE	NO.	MFR	MFG NO.	CW	HW	VENT	WASTE	TRAP
P-1	WATER CLOSET	6	ELJER	091-1500	1"	—	4"	4"	INT
P-2	LAVATORY	6	ELJER	051-3334	1/2"	1/2"	1 1/4"	1 1/4"	1 1/4"
P-3	SERVICE SINK	1	ELJER	222-2200	3/4"	3/4"	1 1/2"	1 1/2"	1 1/2"
P-4	DRINKING FOUNTAIN	3	ELJER	191-0580	3/8"	—	1 1/4"	1 1/4"	1 1/4"
P-5	FLOOR DRAINS	3	—	—	—	—	3"	3"	3"
P-6	URINAL	3	ELJER	161-1000	3/4"	—	2"	2"	2"

Figure 20-27. A typical plumbing schedule.

PUMP SCHEDULE

MARK	MFR	MODEL	GPM	FT. HD.	RPM	HP	EFF.	ELEC	REMARKS
FP-1	AURORA	5-481-15	1000	139'	1770	50	76%	208/3/60	RE: DTL. "I", SHT. MP-9
JP-1	AURORA	934-JP-138.5-5-EO3	5	139'	3500	3/4	●	208/3/60	RE: DTL "I", SHT. MP-9
SP-1	HYDROMATIC	SW25AI	29	12'	●	1/4	●	120/1/60	LOC: ELEVATOR PIT

Figure 20-28. A typical pump schedule.

FIXTURE SCHEDULE

FIXTURE MARK	MFR	CATALOG NO.	NO.	LAMP WATT	LAMP TYPE	FINISH	MOUNTING	REMARKS
(A)	DAY-LITE	R4124-BP	2	40	RS	STANDARD	SURFACE	ON BOTTOM OF ROOF DECK
(B)	DAY-LITE	4F20-714-2	2	40	RS	DO	RECESSED	
(C)	DAY-LITE	4812-8	6	40	RS	DO	PENDANT	14' STEMS
(D)	PRESLITE	8710	4	60	A16	DO	SURFACE	
(E)	STONE	6700	2	150	PA38	DO	SURFACE	SPOT. MOUNT REAR CORNERS

Figure 20-29. An electric light fixture schedule.

Electrical Schedules

Buildings require extensive electrical service including the amount of power, its distribution, and the fixtures, such as lights, pumps, and furnaces, that are part of the overall system. An electrical light fixture schedule is in Fig. 20-29. It shows the mark, which in this case is the electrical symbol appearing on the drawing. This schedule gives the name of the manufacturer, catalog number, number required, wattage and type of lamp, the finish on the fixture, and how it is mounted.

Figure 20-30 shows a portion of a switchboard and feeder schedule. It is divided into circuits with information about the load served, switches, fuses, feeder wires, and conduit sizes. One of the panels, panel "B," in Fig. 20-30 has a schedule made to identify the use of the 20

circuits in the panel. Notice it is a surface mounted panel and has several spare (unused) circuits (Fig. 20-31).

Study Questions

Answer the following study questions without referring to the text. Then check your answers with the text and correct those that were wrong.

1. What information is included on a schedule?

2. What features of a building are frequently described by schedules?

3. How do you decide how long and wide a schedule will be drawn?

SWITCHBOARD FEEDER SCHEDULE

CKT NO.	LOAD SERVED	SWITCH		FUSE	FEEDER			CONDUIT SIZE	REMARKS
		AMPS	POLES	AMPS	NO.	SIZE	TYPE		
S-1	PANEL "A"	400	3	225	4	4/0	THW	2 1/2"	
S-2	PANEL "B"	200	3	200	4	3/0	THW	2"	
S-3	SPARE	60	3	CLIPS ONLY	—	—	—	—	
S-4	AIR HANDLING UNIT	60	3	60	3	6	THW	1"	
S-5	COMPRESSOR 1	600	3	500	6	250MCM	THW	2 1/2"	FEEDER INSTALLED BY OTHERS

Figure 20-30. A switchboard feed schedule.

PANEL "B"

120/208V – 3φ – 4W   100A. M.I.D.   SURFACE   MTD.   EMD = 52A.

CKT NO	LOAD SERVED	V.A.	C.B.	PH	C.B.	V.A.	LOAD SERVED	CKT NO.
1	INSIGNIA LIGHTS	500	20/1	A	20/1	1000	SIGN LIGHTS	2
3	SOFFIT LIGHTS	1200		B		1000		4
5	↓	1500		C		1000		6
7	DOCK LIGHT	200	↓	A	↓	1000	↓	8
9	PARKING LIGHTS	2500	20/2	BC	20/2	2500	PARKING LIGHTS	10
11	SPARE		20/1	C	20/1		SPARE	12
13			↓					14
15		↓	↓		↓		↓	16

Figure 20-31. This schedule gives details for one of the panels in an electrical system.

4. Where are the best places to locate schedules?

5. What items are generally in a window schedule?

6. How are fire ratings for doors shown when using the graphic representation technique?

7. What items are described on an interior finish schedule?

8. If the walls of a room have different finishes, how is this handled on the finish schedule?

9. What type of schedules are used to describe the structural aspects of a building?

10. What type of schedules are often necessary to describe mechanical features?

11. What is included on a plumbing fixture schedule?

12. What is included on a light fixture schedule?

Laboratory Problems

1. Prepare a door, window, and interior finish schedule for the residence designed in Chapter 8.

2. Prepare door, window, and interior finish schedules for the commercial building designed in Chapter 8. Prepare additional schedules as needed to describe your electrical, mechanical, plumbing, and structural features.

21

Electrical Plans

Electrical systems provide power for illumination and to run all of the items, as furnaces, requiring electricity as the source of energy. The requirements vary a great deal from building to building so a careful analysis of the needs is necessary. Those designing electrical systems for commercial and industrial structures require special preparation and often are electrical engineers. They often specialize in this one design area. Small residential system design is often left to the licensed electrical contractor. The location of lights, outlets, and other electrical equipment is noted on the floor plan. The circuitry is designed by the licensed electrical contractor. Commercial buildings require a separate set of electrical drawings.

Electrical contractors and engineers must be familiar with the electrical codes in use in the area where the structure is to be built. The National Electrical Code is a major source. It establishes the requirements such as wire sizes, circuit capacity, and the properties of various conductors.

The actual design of electrical systems is a subject to be studied by itself. The following material covers some basic material necessary to produce electrical drawings of designs prepared by others. It is not intended to be instructions on how to design an electrical system.

Electrical Terminology

Following are definitions of terms which are basic to an understanding of electrical systems.

Branch Panel. A panel containing circuit breakers that is fed off the main service panel and located in an area some distance from the main service panel. Individual circuits are run from the branch panel to the lights, outlets, and other devices in its proximity.

Circuit. A system of electrical conductors through which an electric current can flow. It is made of two or more wires that carry the electricity from a source to an electric device and back to the source.

Circuit Breaker. An electric device that automatically opens a circuit when it senses an abnormally high current. It can be reset and reused after the source of trouble has been corrected.

Conductor. A wire or device offering low resistance to the flow of electric current.

Conduit. A tube in which electric wires are run. It is used to protect the wires.

Convenience Outlet. An electrical outlet mounted on the wall to supply electricity for lamps and other devices plugged into it.

Current. The flow of electricity through a conductor in a circuit. The measure of flow is the ampere.

Fixture. An electrical device secured to a wall or ceiling that holds light bulbs or tubes.

Ground. A wire that connects an electric circuit to the earth to minimize shock and damage to an electrical system from lightning.

Resistance. The physical property of an electrical conductor causing it to resist the flow of current. Resistance is measured in ohms.

Service Entrance. The wires, conduit, meter, and fittings that bring electricity into a building.

Service Panel. A panel inside the building that receives the electricity from the service entrance and distributes it to various parts of the building through circuits. It contains the circuit breakers.

Switches. A device used to control (on and off) the flow of electricity.

Voltage. The unit of electrical pressure or potential difference produced by the source of electrical energy. It is measured in volts. One volt applied across a resistance of 1 ohm produces a current flow of 1 ampere.

Service Entrance and Service Panel—Residential

The service entrance for residential construction will usually be 200 to 400 A (ampere) brought in overhead to a weatherhead mounted on the building or with an underground cable (Fig. 21-1). The electric meter is mounted at eye level on the outside of the building. It should be easily accessible.

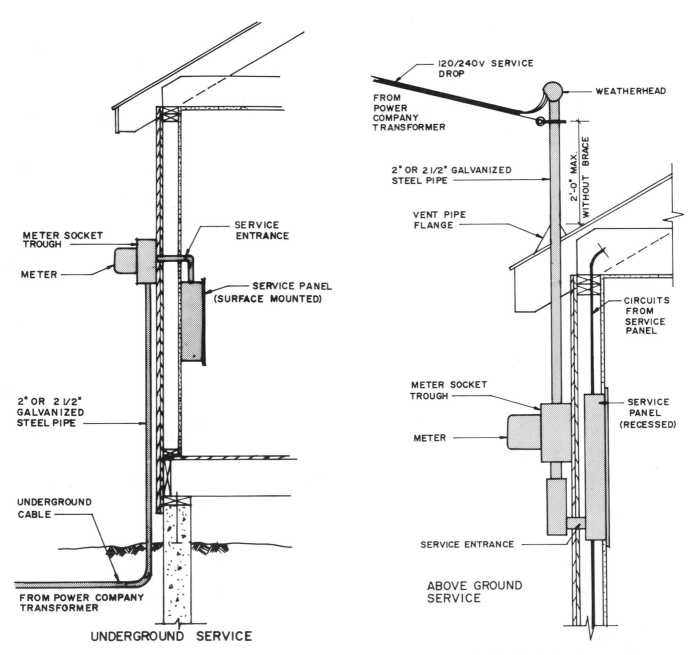

Figure 21-1. *The service entrance can be above the ground through a weatherhead or below the ground.*

The service panel should be mounted inside the building as near to the meter as possible. A cable connects the meter to the service panel. From this main service panel, wiring is run to *branch panels* located in other parts of the building and to individual circuits. The locations of panels is an important part of the early planning of the building. Provision must be made to run the wires to each keeping them concealed.

Wires for telephone service, cable television, television antennas, burglar alarms, intercoms, and smoke alarms also need to be run. Since they use small diameter wires, it is easier to provide runs for them.

The size of the service entrance can be found by first estimating the total load in watts. Then divide this by the entrance voltage, usually 240 V, to get the amperage required. For example, a house with 30,000-W load would require 125 A.

$$\text{amperes} = \frac{\text{watts}}{\text{volts}} = \frac{30,000}{240} = 125 \text{ A}$$

If you allow 20% for future expansion, this would require 129.1 × 0.20 = 25.8. Total service entrance 125.1 + 25.8 = 150.9 A. A 150-A service entrance would be acceptable.

Service Entrance and Electrical Rooms—Commercial

Commercial buildings require large amounts of current and have one or more transformers, meters, and a panel of switchgear to distribute power to interior wiring panels and circuits. The location and size of these vary depending upon the practices of the utility company, building design, codes, and judgment of the electrical engineer designing the system.

Electric power companies economically transmit power at high voltages. Transformers at the building step this down to the lower voltages needed by fixtures and equipment in the building. This is usually 120/208 V or 115/230 V. Some machinery requires 480/277 V.

The primary transformers are usually mounted on concrete pads inside or outside the building. The outside location is preferred. Oil-filled transformers inside a building are placed in a fireproof transformer vault that has two exits. Dry-type transformers do not need a vault and are placed in the electrical room. Switchgear, consisting of disconnect switches, secondary switches, circuit breakers, and fuses, are also housed in the electrical room. This room must be ventilated to disperse the heat generated by the transformer. The electrical room may also contain

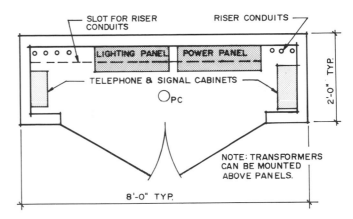

Figure 21-2. *An electrical room will contain lighting and power panels, telephone and signal cabinets, and sometimes transformers.*

lighting, power, telephone, and signal cabinets. Typical designs are in Fig. 21-2.

Some buildings require an emergency generator to furnish electricity if a power failure occurs. These are usually fueled with propane or diesel oil. They require considerable air for combustion and cooling and an exhaust to remove gases produced. The best location is outside the building on the ground housed in a small building. It should be near the switchgear room. They can be placed inside the building next to an outside wall.

Conductors run from the switchgear in the electrical room to electric panels or electrical closets located throughout the building. From these the individual circuits are run to the lights, convenience outlets, and electrical equipment in that area. Schematics are shown in Fig. 21-3.

Fixtures

Incandescent electric fixtures are indicated on a drawing with a $\frac{3}{16}$-in.-diameter circle. Fluorescent fixtures are drawn with a $\frac{1}{8}$-in.-wide rectangle drawn to correct length (on 1/4″ = 1′-0″ scale drawings). These symbols do not specify a particular design or brand of fixture. This information is given in a fixture schedule. See Chapter 20 for information on schedules. There are many types of fixtures available and manufacturer's catalogs provide extensive information. Some provide direct lighting, while others indirect lighting. They may be surface mounted, recessed, or hung on a pendant. They can be mounted on walls, ceiling, in a cove, or behind a valance. See Fig. 21-4. Fluorescent lamps are available in 18-, 24-, 36-, 48-, and 96-in. lengths.

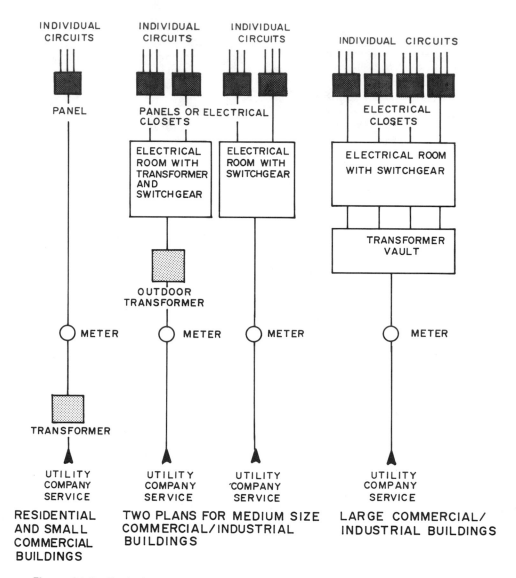

Figure 21-3. *Typical systems of electrical service for buildings of different sizes.*

Switches

Switches are indicated on a drawing with the letter S. Switches are mounted on walls to control lights, fans, ventilators, and other such units. Under most circumstances, they simply turn lights on and off. Dimmer switches are used to vary the intensity of the light. A delayed action switch will turn a light or other unit off a minute or two after the switch is thrown. Another switch will vary the speed of fans.

Switches are usually located 4 ft above the floor and on the latch side of doors. Usually they are inside the room they control. A single pole switch opens one wire and is used to control one light. A three-way switch is used to control one light from two locations. A four-way switch

controls one light from three locations (Fig. 21-5). The wiring connecting switches and fixtures is drawn solid because it is to be concealed in the ceiling and wall. If it was in a concrete floor, it would be a dashed line.

Convenience Outlets

Convenience outlets are shown on drawings with a $\frac{1}{8}$-in.-diameter circle crossed by two or three lines. Two lines indicates it is a 120-V outlet, while three lines show a 240-V outlet for an electric range. Outdoor outlets are marked WP (weatherproof) beside the symbol. Examples of drawing convenience outlets are in Fig. 21-6.

Convenience outlets usually have two openings and are

The number of outlets on a circuit is limited by the capacity of the wire used in the circuit. A typical general-purpose circuit would use No. 12 copper wire and be rated at 20 A. This will carry eight duplex convenience outlets.

Circuits

In residential construction, electricity is distributed throughout the building on branch circuits. A *branch circuit* connects the service panel to the electrical device or devices it will supply with power. This could be a single device, such as a water heater or multiple devices, such as a series of convenience outlets.

Large commercial work would require long runs to reach everything, resulting in a heavy voltage drop. To reduce voltage drop, *feeder circuits* are run from the service panel to a subdistribution panel located near the area where power is needed. A large diameter wire carries power from the service panel to the subdistribution panel. Branch circuits are run from it to the devices needing power.

The capacities of the branch circuits will vary depending upon the requirements and wire size. Electrical conductors (electric wiring) are selected for current capacity, jacket and insulation type, voltage class, voltage drop, and mechanical strength. They are usually specified by number and size of conductor, insulation type, and voltage class. An example for a single conductor is (1/c) No. 10 RUH 600 V. This reads, a single conductor, number 10 gauge, heat-resistant latex rubber, 600 V. Single conductors No. 8 American wire gauge or smaller are called wires. A single No. 6 or larger conductor or several conductors of any size assembled into a single unit are referred to as a cable.

The conductor current capacity (amperes) is determined by the maximum operating temperature the insulation is designed to withstand and the maximum safe temperatures of the bare metal conductors. In Table 21-1 are selected examples. More detailed tables are to be found in electrical design manuals.

Residential construction uses three types of circuits—general purpose, special purpose, and appliance circuits. Following are descriptions of each.

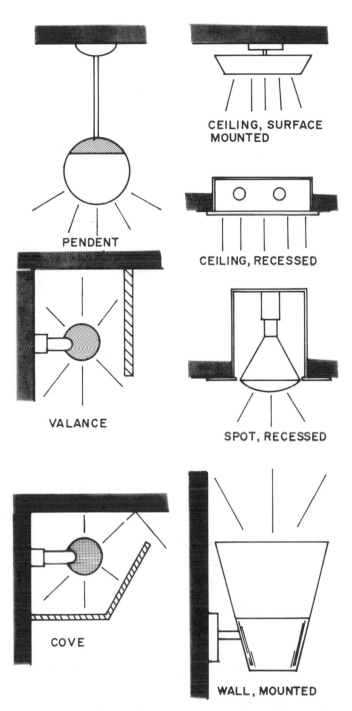

Figure 21-4. *Some of the more commonly used types of lighting.*

often referred to as duplex outlets. They are placed along the wall about 12 to 18 in. above the floor. While the spacing between outlets can vary, they are usually 8 to 10 ft apart in rooms and 15 ft apart in halls and on stairs. Special outlets are located for equipment such as dryers, computers, and other equipment requiring special consideration.

General-Purpose Circuit

2400 W maximum
Amperage: 20 A
Voltage: 120 V (also 110, 115 in same places)
Wire size: No. 12 copper
Uses: Lights, (maximum 120 V–1500 W per circuit), convenience outlets (8 per circuit)

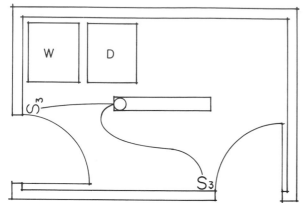

ONE FLUORESCENT FIXTURE CONTROLLED BY TWO SWITCHES. SOLID CONNECTING LINES INDICATE WIRES ARE TO BE CONCEALED IN CEILING AND WALLS.

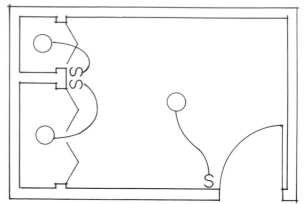

ONE CEILING MOUNTED INCADESCANT FIXTURE CONTROLLED BY ONE SWITCH. TWO CLOSET FIXTURES EACH CONTROLLED BY SEPARATE SWITCHES. SOLID CONNECTING LINES INDICATE WIRES ARE TO BE CONCEALED IN CEILING AND WALLS.

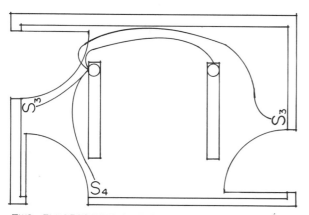

TWO FLUORESCENT FIXTURES CONTROLLED BY THREE SWITCHES.

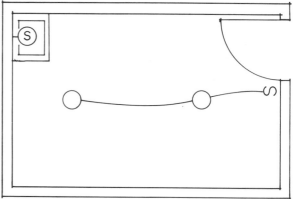

TWO CEILING MOUNTED INCADESCANT FIXTURES CONTROLLED BY ONE SWITCH. FIXTURE OVER LAVATORY CONTROLLED BY AN INTERGRAL SWITCH.

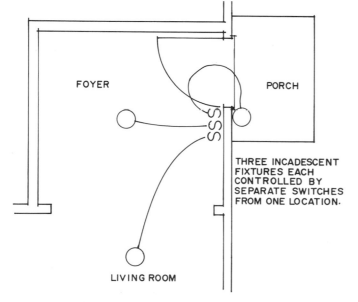

THREE INCADESCENT FIXTURES EACH CONTROLLED BY SEPARATE SWITCHES FROM ONE LOCATION.

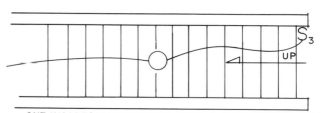

ONE INCADESCANT FIXTURE OVER A STAIR CONTROLLED BY TWO SWITCHES. THE SWITCH SHOWN ABOVE APPEARS ON THE FIRST FLOOR PLAN. THE OTHER SWITCH IS ON THE SECOND FLOOR PLAN.

Figure 21-5. *Examples of electrical fixture and switch connections as shown on architectural drawings.*

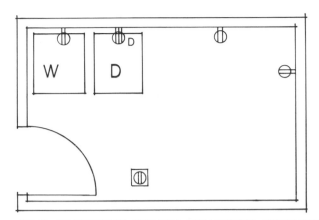

120-V CONVENIENCE OUTLETS ARE LOCATED ALONG THE WALLS. A 240-V OUTLET IS PLACED FOR THE DRYER. A DUPLEX FLOOR OUTLET IS NEAR ONE WALL.

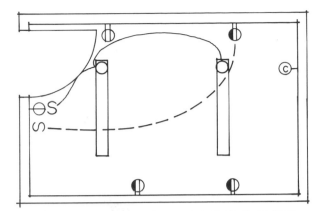

ONE SPLIT-WIRED CONVENIENCE OUTLET IS SWITCH CONTROLLED. THE OTHERS ARE NOT CONTROLLED. THE CONNECTION IS DASHED BECAUSE THE WIRES ARE TO BE IN THE CONCRETE FLOOR. THE FLUORESCENT FIXTURES ARE CONTROLLED BY A SWITCH WITH A SINGLE OUTLET. A CLOCK HANGER OUTLET IS ON ONE WALL.

Figure 21-6. *Examples of convenience outlet symbols as used on architectural drawings.*

Table 21-1: Allowable Current Carrying Capacities for a Cable with no More Than Three Conductors

Conductor Size	Temp 60° C T, TW, or RUW*		Temp 85° C V, MI*	
	Amperes		Amperes	
	Copper**	Aluminum	Copper	Aluminum
14	15	—	25	—
12	20	15	30	25
10	30	25	40	30
8	40	30	50	40
6	55	40	70	55
4	70	55	90	70
3	80	65	105	80
2	95	75	120	95
1	110	85	140	110
0	125	100	155	125

*Insulation Designation

    T = thermoplastic
  TW = moisture-resistant thermoplastic
RUW = moisture-resistant latex rubber
    V = varnished cambric
  MI = mineral insulation with metal sheath

**Typically used in residential construction

LIGHTING OUTLETS

○ INCADESCANT FIXTURE, SURFACE OR PENDANT

Ⓡ RECESSED INCADESCANT FIXTURE

▭ o o o o ▭ INCADESCANT LIGHTING TRACK

Ⓓ DROP CORD

⊗ EXIT LIGHT AND OUTLET BOX, DIRECTIONAL ARROWS TO EXIT, SHADED AREA IS THE FRONT.

Ⓙ JUNCTION BOX

Ⓛ PS LAMP HOLDER WITH PULL SWITCH

Ⓛ OUTLET CONTROLLED BY LOW VOLTAGE SWITCHING WHEN RELAY IS IN OUTLET BOX

▭ B EMERGENCY BATTERY PACK AND CHARGER. HAS SEALED BEAMS.

SINGLE FLUORESCENT FIXTURE, SURFACE MOUNTED

EMERGENCY SERVICE FLUORESCENT FIXTURE

SINGLE RECESSED FLUORESCENT FIXTURE,

CONTINUOUS ROW FLUORESCENT FIXTURE, SURFACE MOUNTED

RECESSED CONTINUOUS ROW FLUORESCENT FIXTURE

SINGLE BARE LAMP FLUORESCENT FIXTURE

CONTINUOUS BARE LAMP FLUORESCENT FIXTURE

RECEPTACLE OUTLETS[1]

⊖ SINGLE RECEPTACLE OUTLET, 120V

⊖ DUPLEX RECEPTACLE OUTLET, 120V

⊕ TRIPLEX RECEPTACLE OUTLET, 120V

⊕ QUADRUPLEX RECEPTACLE OUTLET, 120V

⊖ DUPLEX RECEPTACLE OUTLET, SPLIT WIRED, 120V

⊕ TRIPLEX RECEPTACLE OUTLET, SPLIT WIRED

△ SINGLE SPECIAL PURPOSE OUTLET[2]

△ DUPLEX SPECIAL PURPOSE OUTLET[2]

⊕ 240 V OUTLET[2]

▲ SPECIAL PURPOSE CONNECTION[2]

Ⓒ CLOCK HANGER RECEPTACLE

Ⓕ FAN HANGER RECEPTACLE

⊖ SINGLE FLOOR RECEPTICAL

⊖ DUPLEX FLOOR RECEPTACLE

◁ SPECIAL PURPOSE FLOOR RECEPTACLE[2]

SWITCH OUTLETS

S SINGLE POLE SWITCH

S₂ DOUBLE POLE SWITCH

S₃ THREE-WAY SWITCH

S₄ FOUR-WAY SWITCH

Sₚ SWITCH WITH PILOT LAMP

Sₖ KEY-OPERATED SWITCH

Sₗ SWITCH-LOW VOLTAGE SYSTEM

Sₗₘ MASTER SWITCH-LOW VOLTAGE SYSTEM

Sₜ TIME SWITCH

S_D DOOR SWITCH

S_DM DIMMER SWITCH

S_D AUTOMATIC DOOR SWITCH

Ⓢ CEILING PULL SWITCH

⊖_S SWITCH WITH SINGLE RECEPTACLE

⊜_S SWITCH WITH DOUBLE RECEPTACLE

S_CB CIRCUIT BREAKER SWITCH

RESIDENTAL SIGNALING SYSTEM

▣ PUSHBUTTON

▭ BUZZER

▭◖ BELL

D ELECTRIC DOOR OPENER

CH CHIME

BELL AND BUZZER

▭ INTERCONNECTION BOX

BT BELL-RINGING TRANSFORMER

R RADIO OUTLET

TV TELEVISION OUTLET

◀ OUTSIDE TELEPHONE

◁ INTERCONNECTING TELEPHONE

MISCELLANEOUS SYMBOLS

——▬—— FLUSH MOUNTED SERVICE PANEL

——▬ SURFACE MOUNTED SERVICE PANEL

WIRING CONCEALED IN WALL AND CEILING

- - - SURFACE MOUNTED WIRING

WIRING CONCEALED IN THE FLOOR

Ⓘ SMOKE DETECTOR

1. OUTLETS REQUIRING SPECIAL IDENTIFICATION MAY BE INDICATED BY LETTERING ABBREVITIONS BESIDE THE STANDARD SYMBOL AS, WP FOR WEATHERPROOF OR EP FOR EXPLOSIONPROOF.
2. USE NUMERAL OR LETTER BESIDE SYMBOL KEYED TO A LEGEND OF SYMBOLS TO INDICATE THE TYPE OF RECEPTACLE OR ITS USE.

Figure 21-7. *Standard electrical symbols.*

Special-Purpose Circuit (One Circuit for One Appliance)

Amperage: 30 A
Voltage: 240 V (220 or 230 in same places)
Wire size: No. 10 copper
Uses: Dryer, air conditioner, range, oven, water heater

Appliance Circuit (Will Have Fewer Convenience Outlets per Circuit)

Amperage: 20 A
Voltage: 120 V
Wire size: No. 12 copper
Uses: To operate small appliances in kitchen, laundry, dining area

In commercial work the lighting and convenience outlet circuits generally follow the same loads as given for residential. However, the needs for other items such as heating, air conditioning, and equipment used to manufacture products, call for a wide range of loads, wire sizes, transformers, and circuitry. These are designed by an electrical engineer.

Drawing the Residential Electrical Plan

Generally the residential electrical plan is drawn on the floor plan. If the building is large or complex, a separate, undimensioned floor plan is drawn and the electrical plan is drawn upon it. This is explained in the next section covering commercial electrical plans.

The fixtures, outlets, and other electrical features are shown on the plan with symbols. Some of the more frequently used symbols are shown in Fig. 21-7. It is recommended that the electrical symbols be drawn on the floor plan before it is dimensioned or many notes are lettered on it. Invariably a symbol will fall on top of a dimension requiring it to be moved. It is suggested that you run a blueline print of the floor plan and work out the desired electrical plan on it before drafting it on the finished drawing.

Following are some things to be done as the electrical plan is designed and drawn:

1. Locate the meter and the service panel. If branch panels are to be used, locate these. Branch panels are often used in areas such as a home workshop where special power requirements exist.

2. Locate the convenience outlets. Remember to indicate any special requirements such as weatherproof (WP), split-wired, range, or a special-purpose connection.

3. Locate light fixtures. A study of lighting techniques will help decide which to use. Commonly these are ceiling

or wall mounted. As decisions are made, record these (manufacturer, type, etc.) for use when the fixture schedule is drawn.

4. Locate switches and connect to the device they are to control (fixtures, duplex outlets, door openers). Remember to indicate three-way and four-way switches. Switches are connected to the devices they control with a smooth curved line. Use an irregular curve to get a neat drawing. The connecting line may be drawn solid or dashed. If the wires are to be concealed in the walls or ceiling, draw it solid. If they are to be in the floor, draw with long dashes. If the wires are to be exposed, draw the curve with short dashes. The connecting curved line should hit the fixture or outlet symbol in such a manner that it would pass through the center if continued (Fig. 21-8).

5. Next locate and identify if necessary, other electrical devices such as garage door openers, telephone, TV antenna or cable outlets, doorbells, and alarm systems.

6. An electrical symbol legend is sometimes placed near the floor plan. If only the commonly used symbols are used, this is often omitted on residential drawings.

7. Construct and letter the fixture schedule. See Chapter 20 for details. Add the title and scale below the floor plan.

A finished electrical plan for a small residence is shown in Fig. 21-9.

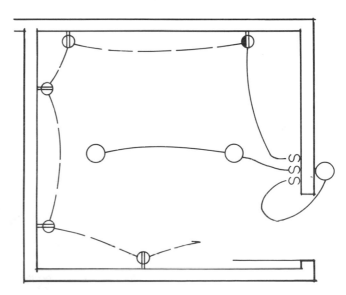

Figure 21-8. *Curved lines representing wiring connections point toward the center of the circle.*

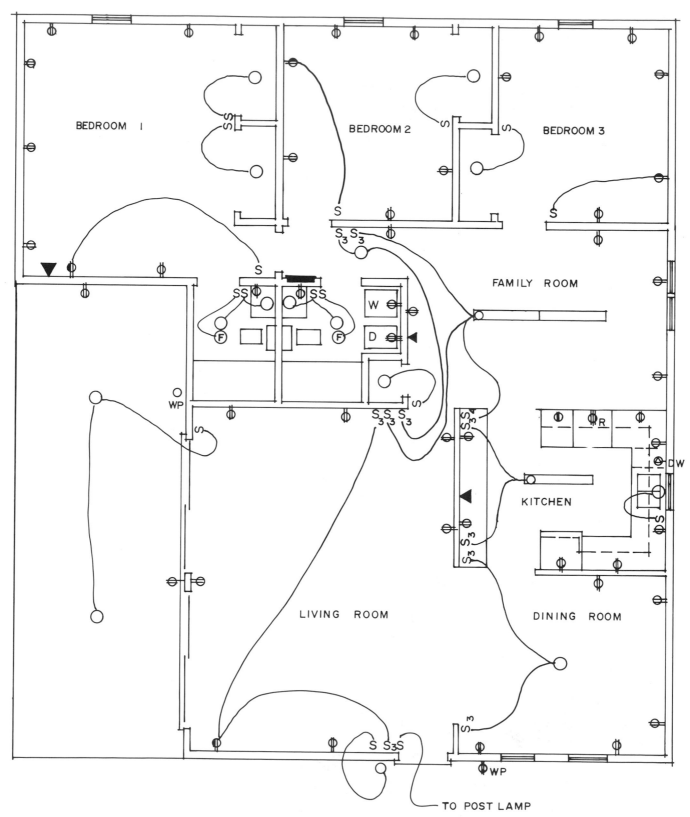

Figure 21-9. *A partially finished floor plan showing the electrical requirements.*

Drawing the Commercial Electrical Plan

Since commercial buildings are large and electrical requirements varied and complex a separate electrical plan is drawn for each floor of the building. Following are suggested steps:

1. Trace the floor plan. Show all interior and exterior walls, stairs, and large devices (as furnaces, air exchangers, pumps) requiring power. Draw the walls with a thin, dark line so they do not dominate the drawing.

2. Locate the meter or meters, service panel or panels, branch panels, electrical room if required, and transformers.

3. Following the procedure suggested for residential work locate fixtures, outlets, switches, and other electrical devices.

4. Connect the switches to the fixture or fixtures they are to control. Connect all of the fixtures that are to be on a single circuit with a smoothly drawn curved line. The number connected depends upon the wattage of each fixture and the capacity of the wires to be used in each circuit. From the last fixture in the circuit, run a lead toward the service panel or branch panel. This is called the home run. It has arrows on the end with numbers. Each number represents a circuit. The crosslines on the wire indicate the number of wires represented by the line. See Fig. 21-10.

5. Connect the convenience outlets that are to be on a single circuit with a smooth, curved line and from the last outlet direct a line with an arrow toward the service or branch panel. Again the number of outlets on a circuit depends upon the design of the system. See Fig. 21-10.

6. Run leads from the various other electrical devices. Many of these will require their own circuit or more than one circuit. Indicate the circuit numbers on the arrows.

7. Letter the symbol legend. This is important on commercial drawings because of the large number of different symbols used.

8. Letter a fixture schedule and other schedules of electrical devices as required.

9. Remember to add the title and scale below the drawing.

A partial drawing of a separate electrical plan is in Fig. 21-11.

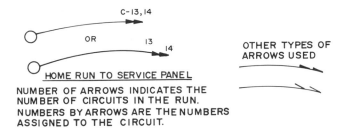

OTHER TYPES OF ARROWS USED

HOME RUN TO SERVICE PANEL
NUMBER OF ARROWS INDICATES THE NUMBER OF CIRCUITS IN THE RUN. NUMBERS BY ARROWS ARE THE NUMBERS ASSIGNED TO THE CIRCUIT.

NUMBER OF CROSSLINES INDICATES THE NUMBER OF WIRES IN THE RUN. NO CROSSLINES MEANS TWO WIRES. THREE CROSSLINES MEANS THREE WIRES, FOUR MEANS FOUR WIRES, ETC.

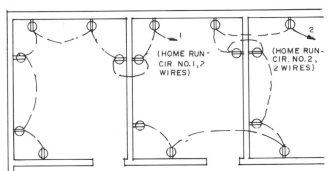

(HOME RUN-CIR NO.1,2 WIRES)
(HOME RUN-CIR. NO.2, 2 WIRES)

CIRCUITS NO. I AND 2 EACH HAVE 8 CONVENIENCE OUTLETS. SINGLE DASHED (LONG DASHES) LINE INDICATES A TWO-WIRE CIRCUIT CONCEALED IN THE FLOOR. ARROW IS HOME RUN TO SERVICE PANEL

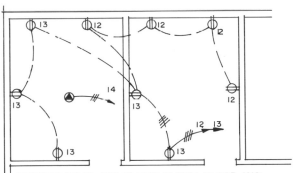

CIRCUITS NO. 12 AND 13 RUN IN THE FLOOR AND COME TOGETHER AT ONE OUTLET ON THE NO. 13 CIRCUIT. FROM THERE THEY RUN AS 4 WIRE CABLE TO THE SERVICE PANEL. THE SPECIAL PURPOSE OUTLET IS ON ITS OWN CIRCUIT.

Figure 21-10. Circuitry for duplex outlets as used on commercial electrical plans.

Technical Vocabulary

Following are some important technical terms used in this chapter. Write a brief definition for each.

Branch panel
Circuit
Circuit breaker
Conductor

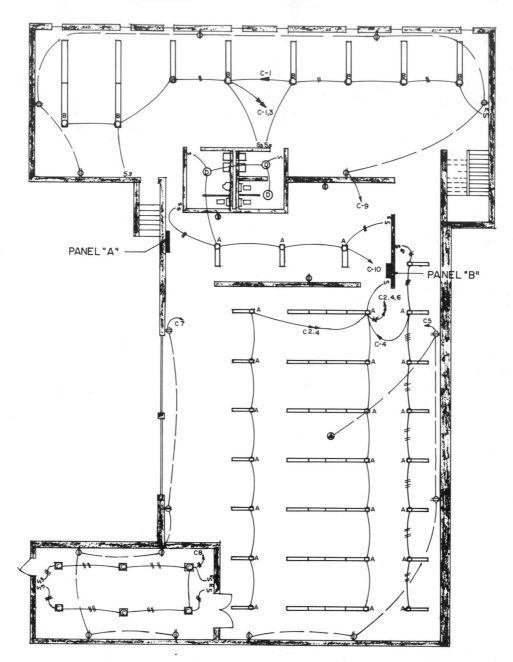

BRANCH CIRCUIT PANEL SCHEDULE

PANEL	TYPE			BREAKER				ACT	SP	REMARKS	MOUNTING	MAIN LUGS
DESIGNATION	VOLT	Ø	W	CIRC. NO.	A.	P.	V.	IVE	ARE			
PANEL "A"	120/208	3	4	1-18, 20, 21, 24	20	1	120	✓			SURFACE	225 A
				19	40	2	208	✓				
				22 - 23	50	1	120	✓				
				25 - 28	20	1	120		✓			
PANEL "B"	120/208	3	4	1-20, 26, 27, 29, 30	20	1	120	✓			FLUSH	225 A
				21 - 23	20	2	208	✓				
				24	50	2	208	✓				
				28	50	3	208	✓				
				32 - 33	20	1	120		✓			
				31	30	2	208	✓				

Figure 21-11. *A partial commercial electrical plan.*

FIXTURE SCHEDULE

FIXTURE	MANUFACTURER	CAT. NO.	LAMP			FINISH	MOUNTING	REMARKS
			NO.	WATT	TYPE			
A	SMITHCRAFT	DMA 1-40	1	40	T-12	STANDARD	CEILING	
B	SMITHCRAFT	DMA 2-42	4	40	T-12	STANDARD	CEILING	
C	LIGHTOLIER	7825	1	150	A	STANDARD	RECESSED	
D	LIGHTOLIER	4362	2	75	A	STANDARD	CEILING	

ELECTRICAL SYMBOLS

○   INCAND LT AND FXTR (CEILING OR PEND.)

▣   INCAND LT AND FXTR (RECESSED)

▭   FLUOR LT AND FXTR (SURFACE MOUNTED

S, S₃   WALL SWITCH, S.P.S.T., 3-WAY

⊖   GND TYPE DUPLEX RCPT

⬤   FLUSH FLOOR RCPT

▬   SERVICE PANEL

Figure 21-11. (Continued)

Conduit
Convenience outlet
Current
Fixture
Ground
Resistance
Service entrance
Service panel
Switches
Voltage

Study Questions

Answer the following study questions without referring to the text. Then check your answers with the text and correct those that were wrong.

1. What guide must be followed when designing an electrical system?

2. What are the two ways the service entrance cable can be brought into a residence?

3. What wiring systems besides basic electrical power must be considered when planning the electrical system?

4. What size service entrance is required for a building with a total load of 75,000 W?

5. Where are primary transformers needed for large commercial buildings usually located?

6. What precautions must be taken if an oil-filled transformer is placed inside a building?

7. What electrical devices are placed in the electrical room in commercial buildings?

8. What provisions are made to provide electrical service if a power failure occurs?

9. How does a dimmer switch differ from a delayed action switch?

10. Where are switches normally located?

11. What is a three-way switch?

12. What type of appliances require special outlets?

13. How many convenience outlets will be placed on a 20-A circuit?

14. What is the difference between a branch circuit and a feeder circuit?

15. What three types of circuits are used in residential construction?

16. Where are the electrical requirements shown on residential plans?

17. Where are the electrical requirements shown on commercial plans?

Laboratory Problems

1. Record the electrical requirements on the floor plan of the residence designed in Chapter 8. If your instructor directs, prepare a separate electrical plan.

2. Draw an electrical plan for the commercial building designed in Chapter 8.

22

Heating and Air-Conditioning Systems

Introduction

There are a wide range of heating and air-conditioning systems in use in residential and commercial buildings. The choice of a fuel is a basic decision and depends upon local availability and cost. For example, in some parts of the country, natural gas is readily available and the choice of most people for heating. Cooling is commonly done by compressive refrigeration units powered by electricity. Large commercial buildings often use chilled water cooling systems.

The sizing of units to heat and cool building interiors depends upon a number of factors. One factor is the amount of heat lost or gained through the walls, ceiling, doors, and windows of a building. Air infiltration through cracks around doors and windows and poorly constructed walls influences the size of heating and cooling units. The use of the interior space is still another factor. In a residence a family of 3 or 4 people does not create as much of a problem as a school room with 30 or more students. Factories, offices, stores, and other commercial and industrial users present even more complex sizing situations. The volume of space to be conditioned, the climate,

orientation to the sun and winds, and need for artificial ventilation are other factors for the designer to consider. The American Society of Heating, Refrigerating and Air-Conditioning Engineers, Inc., has extensive design information that is used by those designing heating and air-conditioning systems.

Residential heating systems fall into three groups: (1) forced air; (2) hot water; and (3) electric resistance.

Forced Air Heat

This system uses hot air blown by an electric fan through supply ducts to the rooms to be heated or cooled. The air is admitted into the spaces through registers (also called diffusers). The fuel used is oil, natural gas, propane, electricity, or solar energy. The design of the system is basically the same regardless of the fuel used.

A forced air system has ducts that return air from the rooms to the furnace where it is reheated or cooled and recirculated through supply ducts. The size of the ducts depends upon the required volume of air needed for each space. Air volume is specified in cubic feet per minute (cfm). Ducts are usually circular because they give the best performance. Rectangular ducts are used when necessary, as to run between studs in a wall. The heat and cool air emitting registers are usually placed below windows on the outside walls of the room. This provides a curtain of conditioned air flowing up the wall where temperature conditions are the greatest. In most cases, the register is located in the floor or in the wall a few inches above the floor. Some systems require the registers to be in the ceiling (Fig. 22-1).

The furnace can be located in any of a number of places. It could be in a utility room, a closet, the attic, the crawl space, basement, garage, and in some cases, outside the building. It should be as centrally located as possible so the ducts to the room are as short as possible.

The air return ducts are located on inside walls. When heating is more important than cooling, as in cold climates, they are high on the wall. When cooling is more important, they are near the floor. It is best if every room has a return duct except the kitchen and bathrooms (Fig. 22-2).

Forced Air Furnaces

The types of forced air furnaces include downflow, upflow, and horizontal (Fig. 22-3). Downflow furnaces are used on systems where the ducts are in concrete floors or below the floor joists in crawl spaces. Upflow furnaces are used in basements or where ducts are in the attic. Hori-

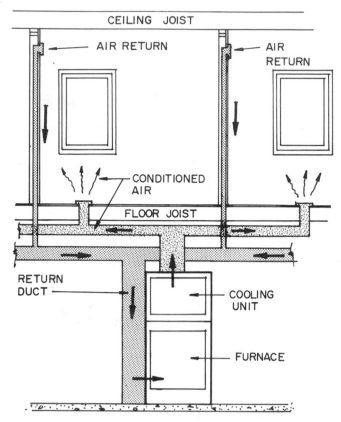

Figure 22-2. *Return ducts are located on inside walls while registers are on outside walls.*

zontal furnaces can be placed in the attic or hung below the floor joists.

In Fig. 22-4 is a gas-fired upflow, hot-air furnace. The box is steel and is insulated to keep exterior temperatures low. It has operating controls that provide automatic safety shut off if something is wrong. The gas control valve has an automatic safety pilot, pilot and bleed gas filtration, automatic electric valve, and gas pressure regulation. The air-conditioning cooling coil is placed on top of the unit.

A highly efficient gas-fired forced-air furnace is the Lennox pulse furnace. An explanation of how it works is in Fig. 22-5. The waste products of combustion have so little heat left in them they are vented outdoors by a 2-in. PVC pipe run either horizontally through a wall or vertically through the roof.

Forced-Air Systems

The common types of forced air systems are perimeter loop, perimeter radial, individual duct, and extended plenum systems. The *perimeter loop system* is shown in Fig. 22-6. In this design, a downflow furnace is used. The heated or cooled air is blown down into supply ducts that

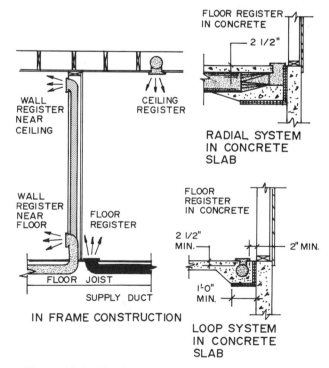

Figure 22-1. *Registers are located in the wall or floor.*

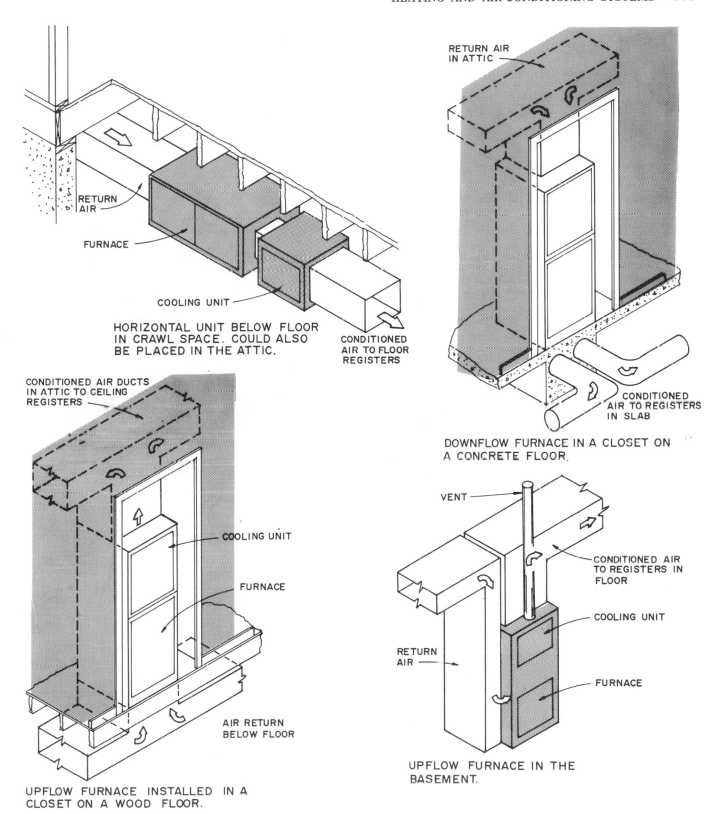

RETURN AIR IN ATTIC

RETURN AIR

FURNACE

COOLING UNIT

HORIZONTAL UNIT BELOW FLOOR
IN CRAWL SPACE. COULD ALSO
BE PLACED IN THE ATTIC.

CONDITIONED
AIR TO FLOOR
REGISTERS

CONDITIONED
AIR TO REGISTERS
IN SLAB

DOWNFLOW FURNACE IN A CLOSET ON
A CONCRETE FLOOR.

CONDITIONED AIR DUCTS
IN ATTIC TO CEILING
REGISTERS

COOLING UNIT

FURNACE

AIR RETURN
BELOW FLOOR

UPFLOW FURNACE INSTALLED IN A
CLOSET ON A WOOD FLOOR.

VENT

CONDITIONED AIR
TO REGISTERS IN
FLOOR

COOLING UNIT

RETURN
AIR

FURNACE

UPFLOW FURNACE IN THE
BASEMENT.

Figure 22-3. *Typical types of hot air furnaces.*

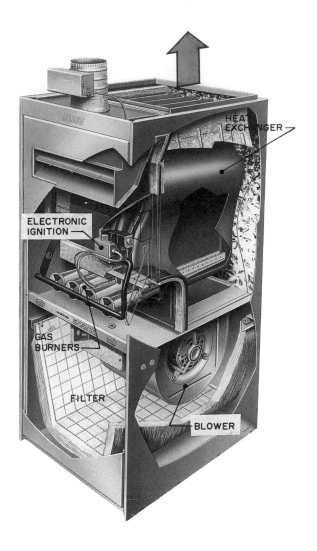

Figure 22-4. *A gas-fired upflow hot air furnace. (Courtesy Lennox International, Inc.)*

feed ducts running around the perimeter of the building. Registers are placed in these ducts as needed. The return air system would be a separate set of ducts running through the ceiling and back down to the furnace. Since it is a downflow furnace, return ducts would be near the ceiling. This system is commonly used in concrete slab construction. The *perimeter radial system* is also used in concrete slab construction but could also be used with a basement or crawl space (Fig. 22-7). It also uses a downflow furnace.

The *individual duct system* and the *extended plenum systems* are most often used with crawl space or basement construction. With a crawl space, a downflow or horizontal furnace below the floor is used. An upflow furnace is used with basement construction (Fig. 22-8).

An attic system is shown in Fig. 22-9. Ducts in the attic or below the floor must be insulated.

The Heat Pump

The heat pump is another form of forced air heating and cooling. The most common system is an air-to-air system. It operates much like your refrigerator. When it is in cooling mode, the circulating air in the space to be cooled is carried to an indoor unit where a refrigerant absorbs the heat in the air. The refrigerant is carried to a compressor where it is elevated to a high temperature. The high temperature refrigerant is moved to the outdoor unit where the heat is discharged to the outside air.

The heating cycle is just the reverse. The refrigerant absorbs heat in the outside air and discharges it inside the space to be cooled (Fig. 22-10). An internal view of the outdoor unit containing the compressor is in Fig. 22-11.

Two other types of heat pumps are finding limited use. These are air-to-water and earth coil heat pumps. The air-

How Lennox' New Pulse Combustion Furnace Works

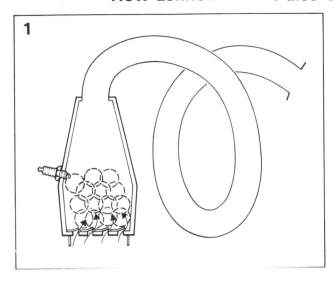

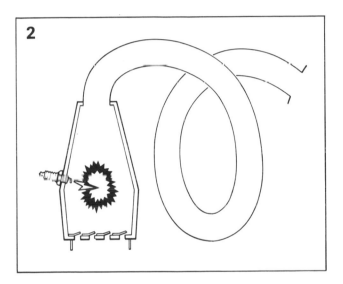

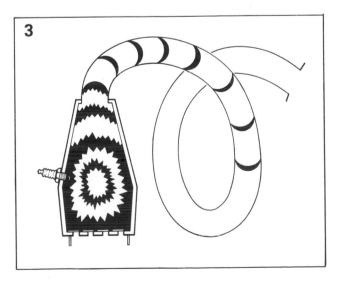

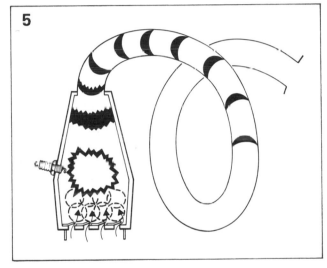

Lennox' new G14 gas furnace operates on the principle of pulse combustion. The process begins when small amounts of gas and air are induced into a combustion chamber through flapper valves (1). This mixture is ignited by a spark plug, causing the first pulse (2). Each pulse produces 1/4 to 1/2 of a Btu of heat. The first pulse causes the flapper valves to close forcing the products of combustion down the tailpipe (3). The length of the tailpipe is designed so that as the shockwave from the pulse reaches the end, it is reflected back to the combustion chamber. Meanwhile, the negative pressure created in the chamber has allowed the flapper valves to open again, admitting more gas and air (4). When the reflected wave re-enters the chamber, there is sufficient flame to ignite the new mixture causing the second pulse and the process starts all over again (5). Once combustion is started, it becomes self perpetuating allowing the combustion blower and spark igniter to be turned off. This happens 68 times a second.

Figure 22-5. *How the Lennox pulse combustion furnace operates. (Courtesy Lennox International, Inc.)*

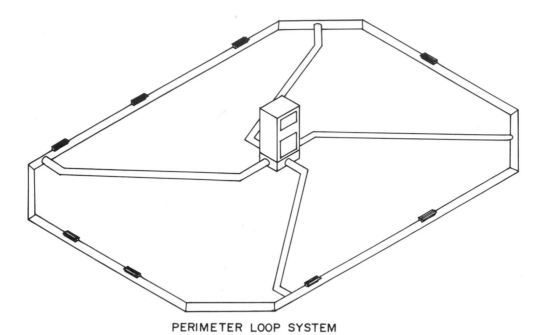

PERIMETER LOOP SYSTEM

Figure 22-6. *A perimeter loop duct system.*

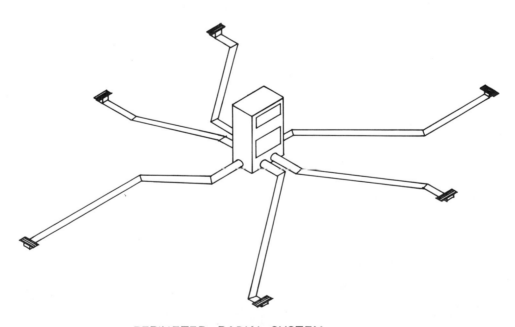

PERIMETER RADIAL SYSTEM

Figure 22-7. *A perimeter radial duct system.*

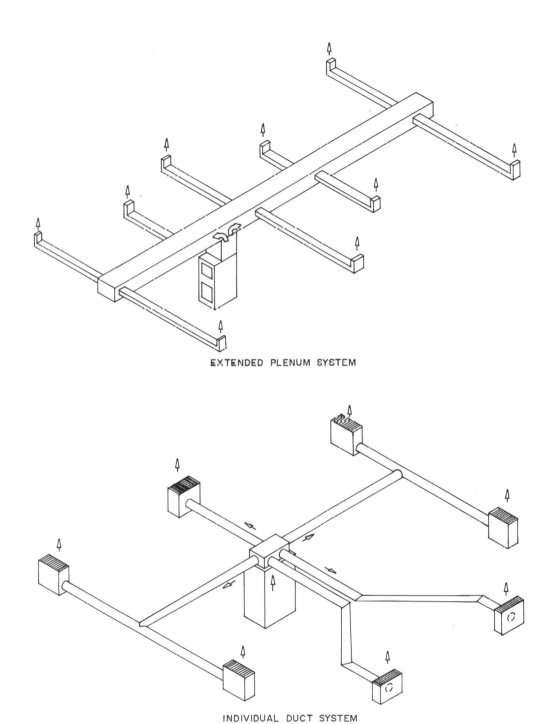

EXTENDED PLENUM SYSTEM

INDIVIDUAL DUCT SYSTEM

Figure 22-8. *Individual duct and extended plenum systems are used when basements are built or a horizontal furnace is hung below the floor or in the attic.*

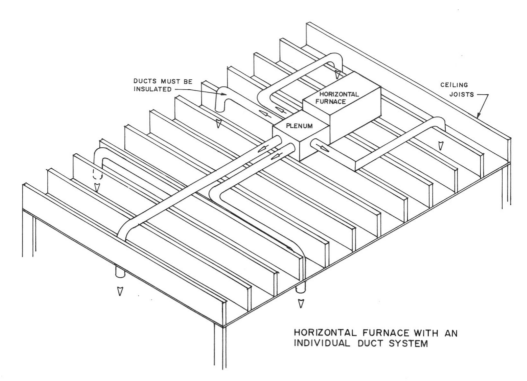

DUCTS MUST BE
INSULATED

HORIZONTAL
FURNACE

PLENUM

CEILING
JOISTS

HORIZONTAL FURNACE WITH AN
INDIVIDUAL DUCT SYSTEM

Figure 22-9. A horizontal forced air furnace can be installed in an attic or below the floor joists.

to-water system removes heat from water, such as a well or lake, and cools by discharging heat to the water. The earth coil system uses a plastic pipe that is buried in the earth. It takes advantage of the relatively stable ground temperatures by circulating a heat transfer fluid (water) through the plastic pipe (the earth coil) buried in the soil. The soil temperature controls the water temperature, providing a source of heat and cooling.

The typical heat pump installation involves locating the outdoor unit containing the compressor on a concrete pad on grade. The indoor unit containing the coils, filters, and fan can be located in a crawl space, basement, or on the floor of the building. Typical installations are shown in Fig. 22-12. Single unit heat pumps contain the compressor, coils, fans, filters, and other parts of the system in a single cabinet (Fig. 22-13). For large installations, they can be mounted on a roof, in an attic, or on a slab on grade. They are connected by ducts to the spaces to be conditioned (Fig. 22-14). Very small single-unit heat pumps are used for small spaces, such as motel rooms. They are placed in an opening in an outside wall and blow cooled or heated air directly into the space without the use of ducts (Fig. 22-15). These are often referred to as thru-the-wall units.

The efficiency of a heat pump to cool is indicated by its Seasonal Energy Efficiency Rating (SEER). The higher the SEER number, the more efficient the system. The SEER is an index of the BTU's of heat moved per watt of elec-

trical energy input. Its efficiency as a heating system is indicated by its Heating Seasonal Performance Factor (HSPF). The higher the HSPF number, the more efficient the heating system.

Preparing Drawings for Forced Air Systems

A forced air heating system drawing is made on a copy of the floor plan that has no dimensions and notes except those related to the forced air system. The designer must calculate the size of each duct, decide how it is to be run, and locate and size the registers. A typical example is in Fig. 22-16. Selected symbols commonly used on this and other heating and air conditioning drawings are in Fig. 22-17. Often a legend of symbols and abbreviations is placed beside the drawings. Sections are drawn when necessary. Following are suggested steps for drawing a forced air heating plan:

1. Trace the exterior and interior walls from the floor plan. Draw all with thin lines because the walls are secondary in importance to the heating system to be drawn over them.

2. Locate the furnace, air conditioner, or heat pump units.

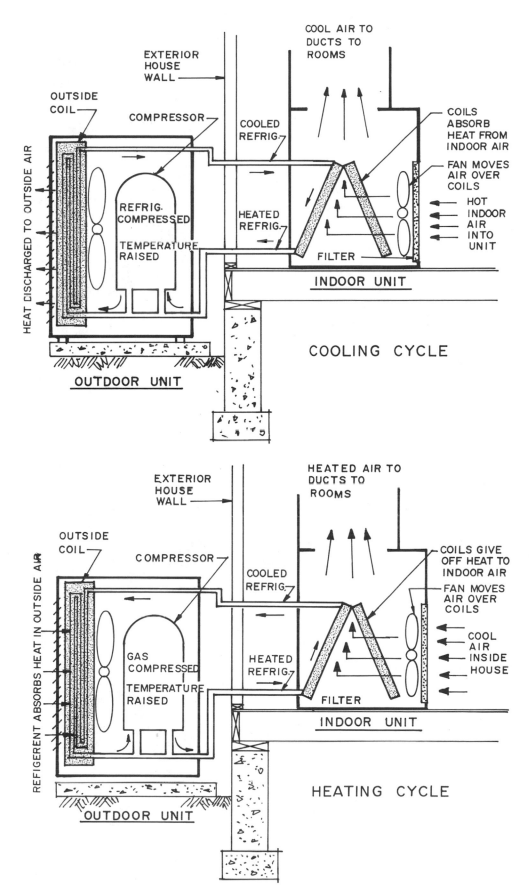

Figure 22-10. *Typical air-to-air heat pump heating and cooling cycles.*

Figure 22-11. *This is the outdoor unit of a heat pump containing the compressor and controls. (Courtesy of Lennox International, Inc.)*

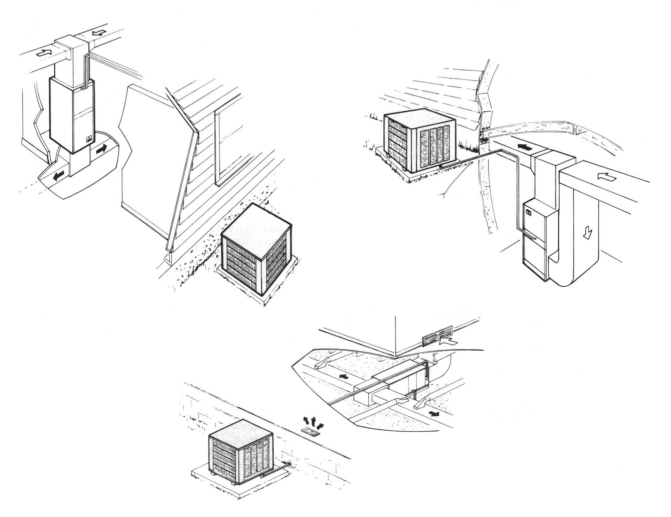

Figure 22-12. *Typical heat pump installations. (Courtesy of Lennox International, Inc.)*

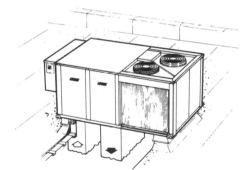

Figure 22-13. *A single-unit heat pump. (Courtesy of Lennox International, Inc.)*

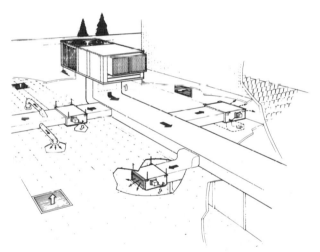

Rooftop Installation with Optional
Blower Powered Mixing Damper Boxes.

Rooftop Installation with
Double Duct Air Distribution System

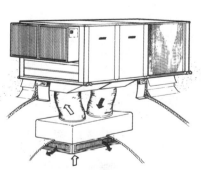

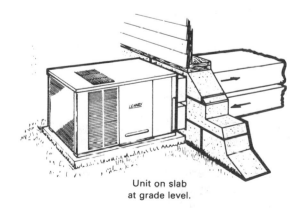

Rooftop Installation with
Combination Ceiling Supply and Return Air System

Unit on slab
at grade level.

Figure 22-14. *Typical applications using a single-unit heat pump. (Courtesy of Lennox International, Inc.)*

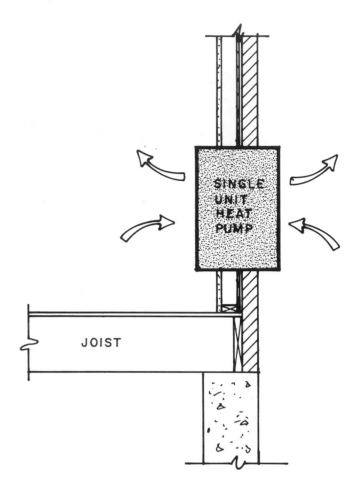

Figure 22-15. *A small single-unit heat pump in a thru-the-wall installation.*

3. Locate registers in each room. Connect with supply ducts. Locate air return registers and air return ducts. Letter needed notes by each such as size, manufacturer, and air flow volume. Sometimes these are given in a schedule and a mark is placed by each register and duct. Note direction of air flow. Sometimes the ducts are shaded to provide emphasis.

4. Locate controls such as the thermostat.

5. Complete the symbol legend.

6. Add the title block and other needed information.

Hot Water Systems

Hot water systems (hydronic) use a boiler to heat water which is circulated by a pump through pipes to radiators, convectors, or baseboard heat-emitting units. A series of pipes are used to return the cooled water back to the boiler (Fig. 22-18). Hot water heat provides a steady uniform heat and keeps heat at the heat emitters for a longer period of time than occurs with hot air systems. While the boiler is much smaller than a forced air furnace and pipes are easier to run than ducts, a separate air cooling system must be installed. This requires the installation of ducts. Large systems for commercial buildings run chilled water through the system for air cooling, thus using the same pipe used for heating.

The most commonly used systems are the one-pipe and two-pipe (Figs. 22-19, 22-20, and 22-21). The one-pipe system requires less pipe than the two-pipe systems but is limited in size because of increased resistance of the diverter fittings. The two-pipe direct-return requires more pipe than the one-pipe system and less than the two-pipe reverse return. It also requires balancing devices to regulate the flow through each radiator. It is not commonly used. The two-pipe reverse-return system makes it easier to balance the flow through the system but requires the most pipe. It is the best choice for large buildings. A building can be divided into heating zones which enable temperatures to be varied within the building (Fig. 22-22).

The most commonly used convector is the fin tube baseboard type. They can be wall hung or recessed in the floor. Various types of floor and wall-mounted convectors and radiators are shown in Fig. 22-23

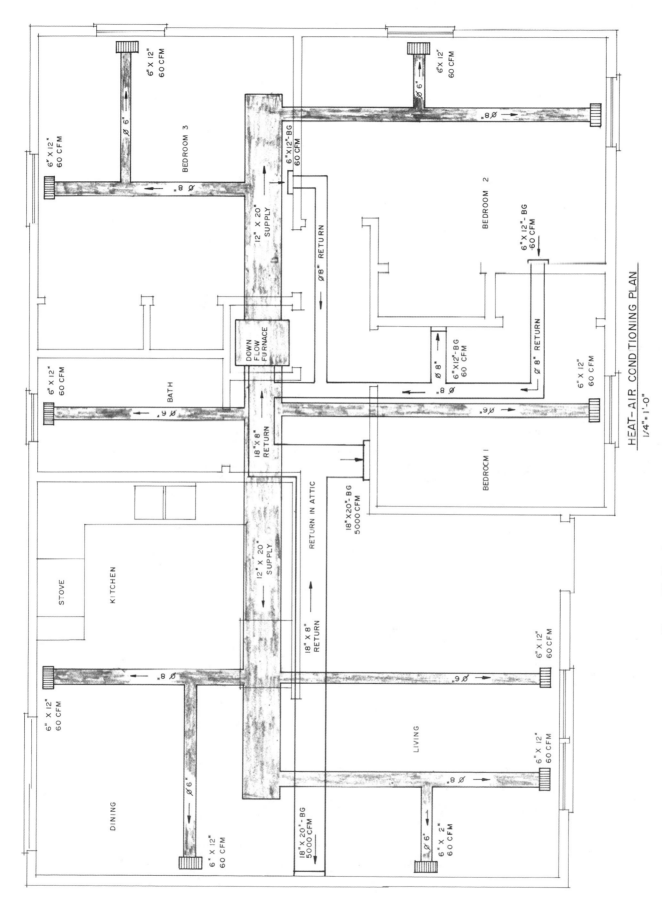

Figure 22-16. A typical forced air heating and air-conditioning plan.

HEAT-AIR CONDITIONING PLAN
1/4" = 1'-0"

429

HEATING AND AIR CONDITIONING SYMBOLS

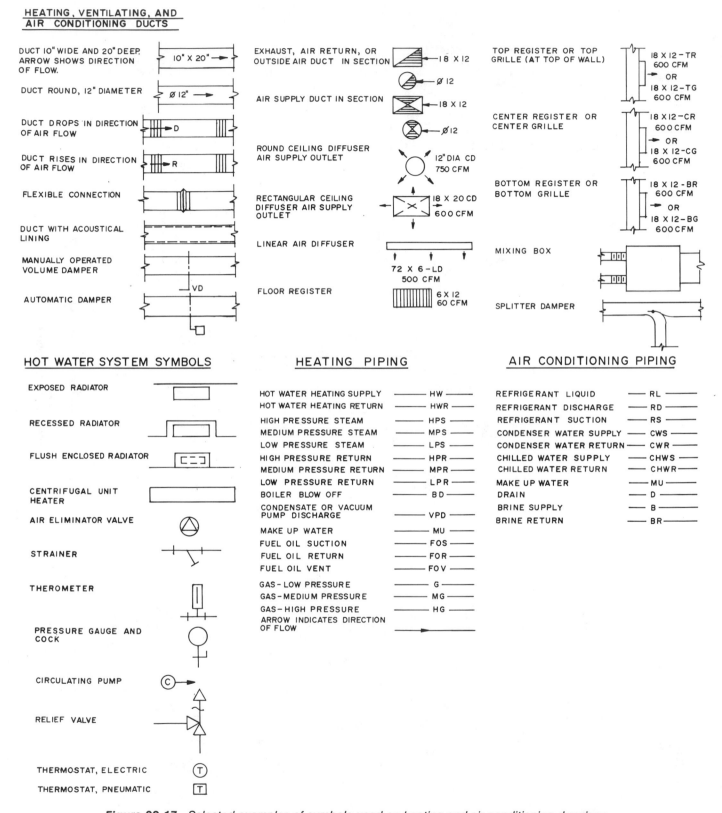

Figure 22-17. *Selected examples of symbols used on heating and air conditioning drawings.*

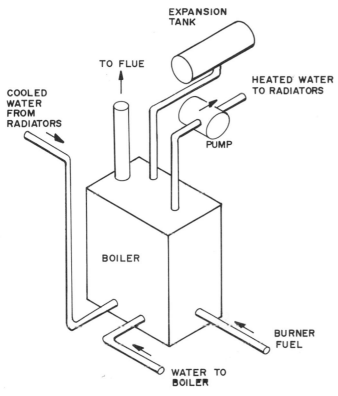

Figure 22-18. The boiler heats the water which is then pumped to radiators in the various rooms.

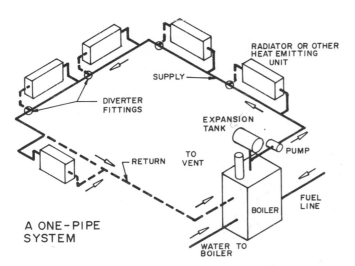

A ONE-PIPE SYSTEM

Figure 22-19. A one-pipe hot water heating system.

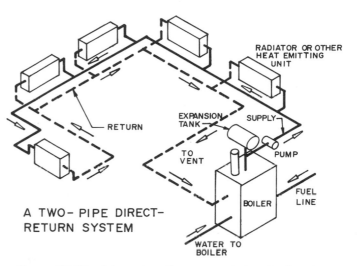

A TWO-PIPE DIRECT-RETURN SYSTEM

Figure 22-20. A two-pipe direct return hot water heating system.

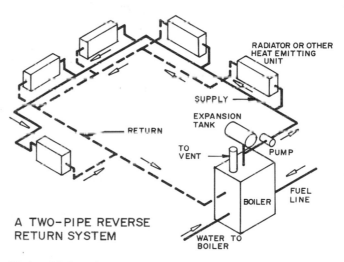

A TWO-PIPE REVERSE RETURN SYSTEM

Figure 22-21. A two-pipe reverse return hot water heating system.

are indicated, and the unit heaters are identified by a mark. The pipe fittings, as elbows and tees, are indicated the same way as used for plumbing diagrams. These are shown in Chapter 23. To complete these drawings, it is necessary to include various schedules such as for convectors, ventilators, exhausters, and other such units needing complete specifications. Schedules are discussed in Chapter 20.

Radiant Heating

Radiant heating provides heat to the air in a room by warming panels in the ceiling, walls, and floor. Most of the heat is given off by radiation rather than convection. The most frequently used methods for heating the panels

A hot water heating plan for a small residence is shown in Fig. 22-24. This is a simplified plan showing convectors and pipe sizes. The procedure for drawing it is the same as described for forced hot air systems. In Fig. 22-25 is a more detailed partial plan for a large commercial building. Notice the multiple pipes are identified, the connections

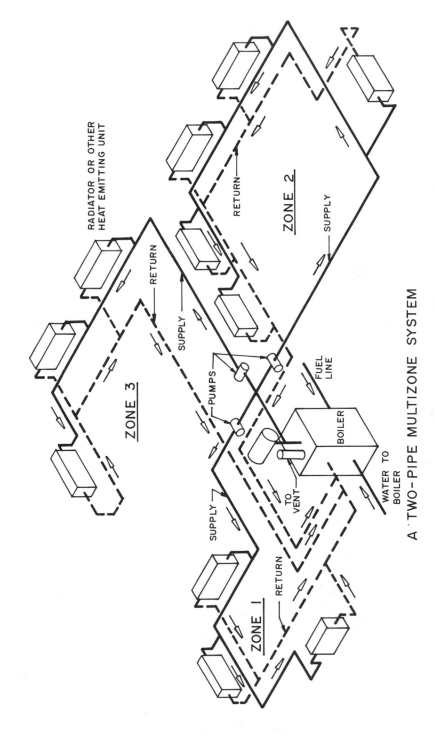

RADIATOR OR OTHER
HEAT EMITTING UNIT

ZONE 3

ZONE 2

ZONE 1

RETURN

SUPPLY

SUPPLY

RETURN

SUPPLY

RETURN

PUMPS

FUEL
LINE

TO
VENT

BOILER

WATER TO
BOILER

A TWO-PIPE MULTIZONE SYSTEM

Figure 22-22. *A pictorial illustration of a two-pipe multizone hot water heating system.*

432

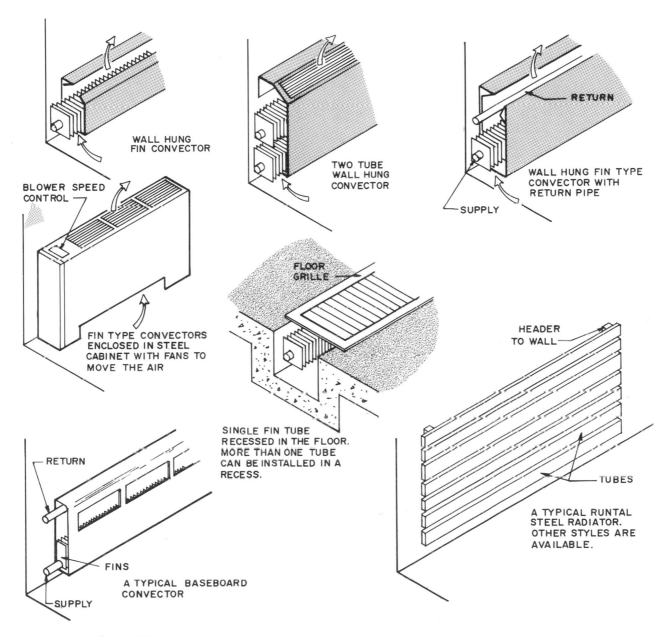

Figure 22-23. *Examples of floor and wall mounted hot water convectors and radiations.*

include hot water circulated in copper pipes in the floor or embedded in plaster in the ceiling and walls, passing warm air through hollow floor tiles or passages in the ceiling, and electric heating cable embedded in plaster in ceilings or on a concrete floor covered with $1\frac{1}{2}$ in. of concrete. The slab must be some type of concrete (Fig. 22-26).

Hot water flowing through the tubes warms the ceiling and floor surfaces. Since the surfaces are warm, they will not pull body heat from those in the room. A room will be comfortable at lower temperatures. A slab heat of around 85°F is adequate to keep a person comfortable even if the air temperature is in the 60°F range. The system can have

separate pipe loops for each room so temperatures can be controlled by rooms. This is often referred to as zoned heating.

The system works best if it is kept operating full time. It is slow to heat up the exposed surfaces, and so does not produce rapid heating.

To design a hot water radiant heating system an analysis of the heat loss for each room is necessary. The radiant output per lineal foot of coil is used to determine the lineal feet of coil needed for each room to replace the heat loss plus capacity to raise the room temperature to desired levels. A typical radiant heating plan is shown in Fig. 22-27.

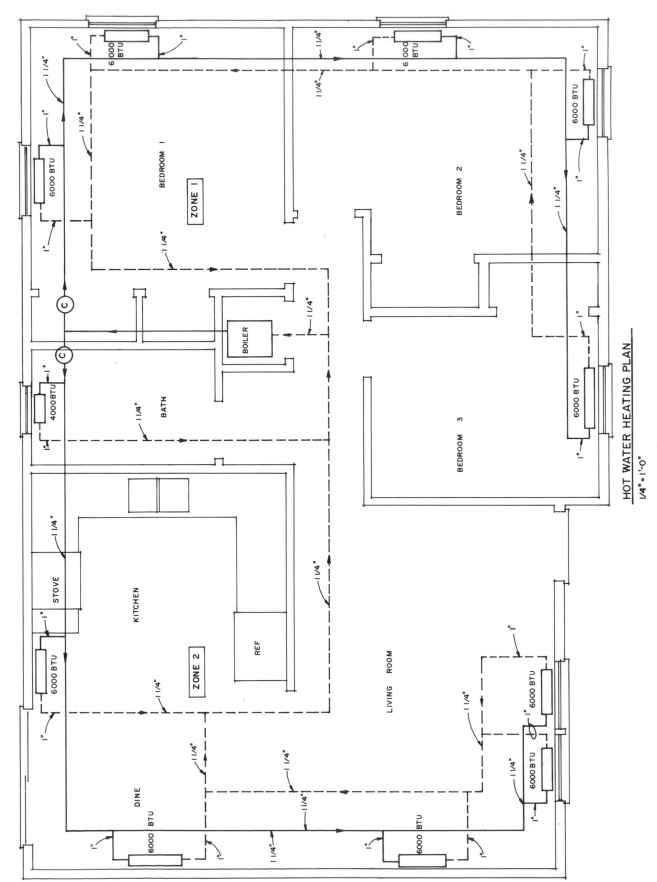

Figure 22-24. A typical hot water heating plan for a residence.

HOT WATER HEATING PLAN

1/4" = 1'-0"

434

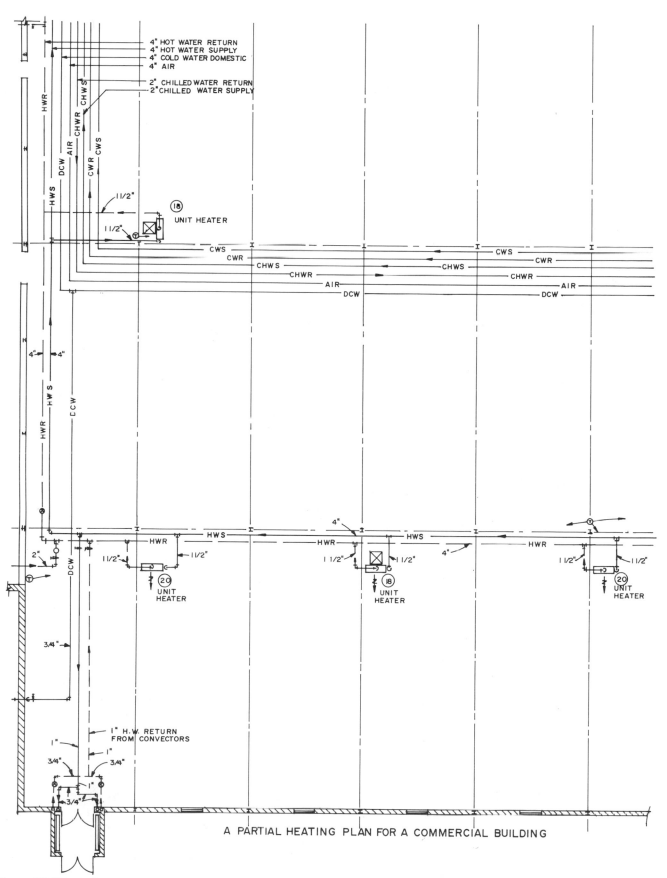

4" HOT WATER RETURN
4" HOT WATER SUPPLY
4" COLD WATER DOMESTIC
4" AIR

2" CHILLED WATER RETURN
2" CHILLED WATER SUPPLY

UNIT HEATER

CWS
CWR
CHWS
CHWR
AIR
DCW

HWS
HWR

UNIT HEATER

UNIT HEATER

UNIT HEATER

1" H.W. RETURN
FROM CONVECTORS

A PARTIAL HEATING PLAN FOR A COMMERCIAL BUILDING

Figure 22-25. *A drawing showing a small part of a hot water heating system with chiller pipes for cooling that is typical of designs used in commercial buildings.*

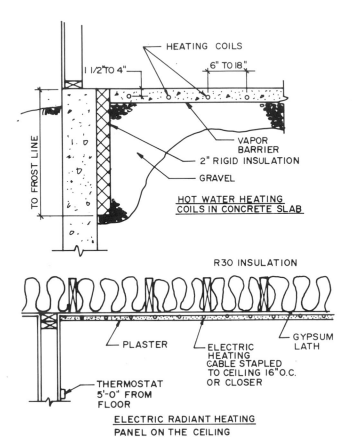

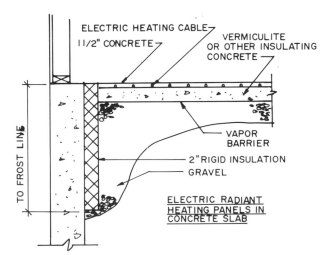

Figure 22-26. *Examples of designs for radiant heat in floors and ceilings.*

Electric Heating Systems

Electric heating systems produce heat by passing electrical energy through wires that have a high resistance to electrical flow. This resistance causes the wires to get hot just like the wires in your toaster. The heat is moved to the various rooms by a blower forcing the heated air through ducts. This is one form of forced air heat. Other electric heaters use baseboards and other forms of floor and wall-mounted units (Fig. 22-28). These are inexpensive to install and require no ducts or vents. They provide fast heat but have limited means of air circulation, filtration, humidity control, and provide for no air cooling. Each room can have a thermostat, thus providing individual temperature control.

Electric radiant systems embed resistance wiring in the ceiling and floor. These function the same as explained for radiant hot water system.

Generally no special drawings are made specifically for electric heat. Notations are made on the floor plan or the electrical plan showing the location of electric panels and sections of resistance wiring.

Cooling Systems

The typical residence or small commercial building uses electricity to power a refrigeration unit made up of a compressor, evaporator, condenser, refrigerant, valves, fans, and controls (Fig. 22-29). The refrigeration cycle uses fans to move the hot air inside a building through the evaporator coils where the refrigerant is a vapor. The refrigerant absorbs heat from the air and is drawn into the compressor where its pressure and temperature are increased. The compressed refrigerant is discharged into the condenser coil located outside the building where it gives up the latent heat it absorbed in the evaporator and returns to a liquid state. From here it passes through an expansion valve turning once again into a vapor and the cycle repeats itself.

The most frequently used configuration is a split system. It is made of two major parts, the compressor and condenser coil, which are located outside the building. They can be on a ground level concrete pad or on the roof. The ground location is preferred because it is often shaded and cooler than roof locations.

The evaporator coil is located inside the building, usually on top of the furnace. The furnace blower moves air past the coil and into the ducts. The same blower is used to move heated air during the months when the furnace burner is used. The condensing unit on the outside is connected to the evaporator coil with two refrigerant lines. One line is for the cold refrigerant and the other the hot refrigerant. The cold line will be insulated (Fig. 22-30).

A *single-package* air conditioner has all of the components in single cabinet. It can be located out of doors on a concrete slab or on the roof. The duct system is connected to the end of the unit (Fig. 22-31).

In large buildings it is not practical to remove the large

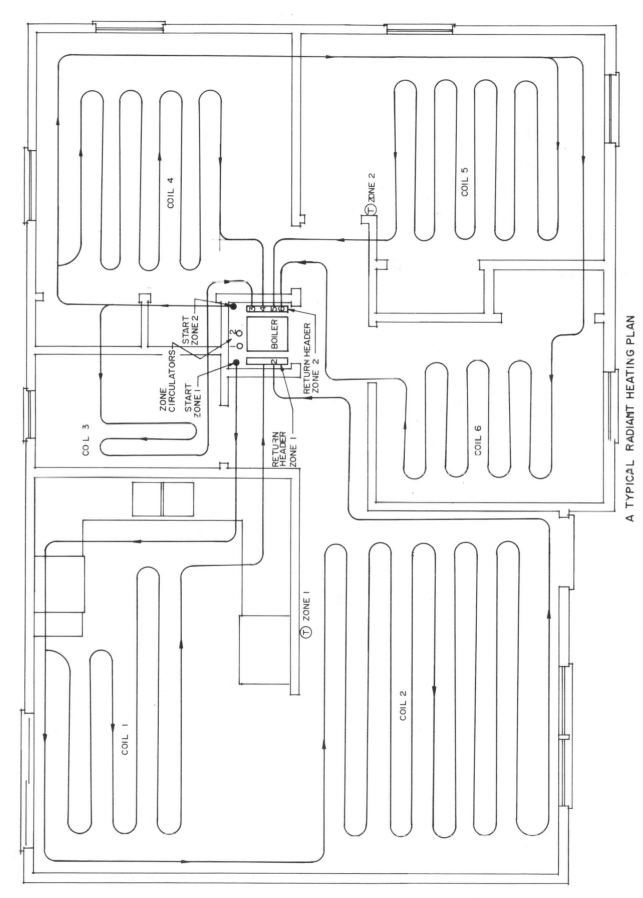

A TYPICAL RADIANT HEATING PLAN

Figure 22-27. *A typical two zone hot water radiant heating system in a concrete slab.*

437

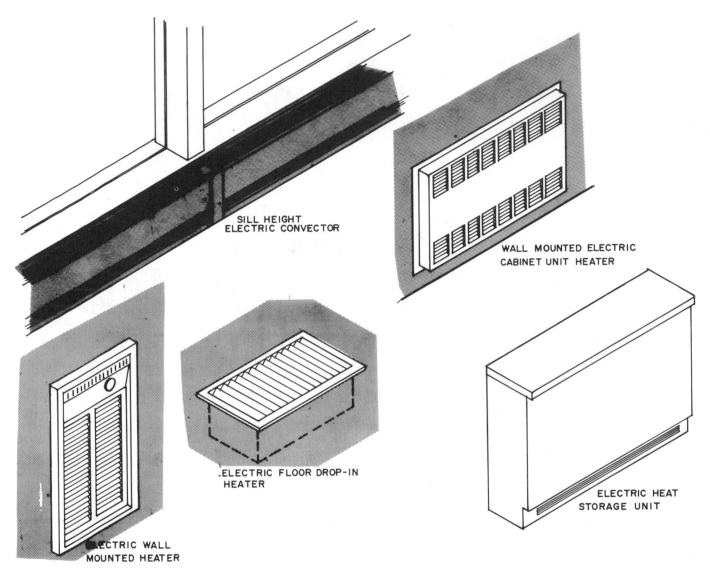

Figure 22-28. *Examples of individual electric heating units.*

amounts of heat required by moving air alone. The ducts would be too large to be practical.

In a typical central cooling system for a large building the evaporator is in a water tank forming a chiller. The chilled water is pumped through cooling coils in an air handler. The cooled air in the air handler is moved through ducts to rooms. The refrigerant picks up heat from the water as it returns to the chiller, it is compressed, and moves to a condenser also in a water tank. The water absorbs the heat from the refrigerant and the cooled refrigerant cycles back to the evaporator. The water in the condenser tank is pumped to a cooling tower outside the building. Here the water is sprayed in the tower and looses much of the heat picked up from the condenser (Fig. 22-32). The water is then recycled back to the condenser.

A variation of this system pumps chilled water to small air-handling units located in each room. These use fans to blow room air plus some fresh air brought in from outside over the evaporator coil where the air is cooled and blown directly into the room (Fig. 22-33). No ducts are needed with this system. This system can also be used to heat a building. A boiler can be added and heat emitting units are placed in the air handler. The hot water from the boiler heats the heating coils which heat the air passed over them (Fig. 22-34).

Solar Heating

Solar heating uses the energy from the sun to heat the interiors of buildings. The two basic systems are active and passive.

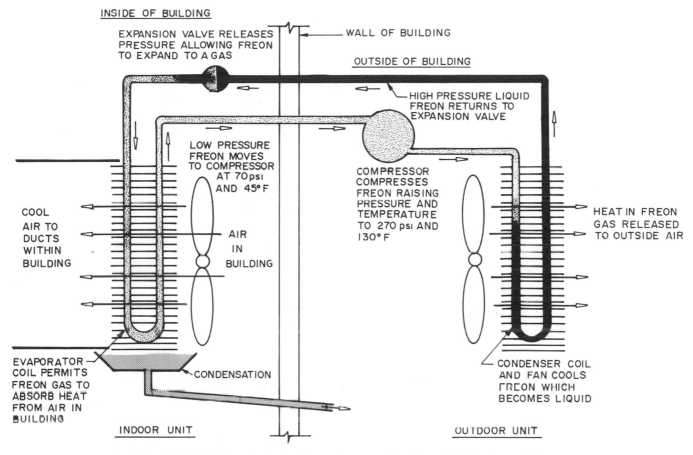

Figure 22-29. *This schematic shows the operation of an electric air conditioner.*

Active Solar Heating

An active system is made up of solar collectors, a transport system to move heat from the collectors to storage, and a distributions system to move the heat from storage to the spaces to be heated. It requires pumps, pipes, ducts, and electric controls (Fig. 22-35). The most noticed features are the solar collectors which are usually mounted on the roof of the building facing about 20° of true south and sloped at an angle to the horizontal of up to 15° more than the latitude of the site. The collectors may utilize a liquid to absorb heat or move heated air trapped in the collector. Heated liquid is moved by a pump to a storage tank below the building. The heated liquid can be moved by pumps to registers in the spaces to be heated and returned cooled to the storage tank (Fig. 22-36).

The warm air system moves heated air from the collector to storage through ducts. The storage is often a rock-filled bin. The heated rocks store the heat which is moved when needed through ducts to the spaces to be heated (Fig. 22-37).

Active solar heat is feasible only in areas where there is considerable sunlight during the winter months. Even

then it is not cost effective when compared with conventional heating methods because it is a costly system to install. It also requires that a backup conventional heating system be installed. In addition, a separate air-cooling system is needed. Often a heat pump is installed to draw heat from storage when it is at rather low temperatures and distribute it at higher temperatures to the spaces to be heated.

Passive Solar Heating

Passive solar heating utilizes glass areas in the walls and roof of a building to admit the heat from the sun into the space to be heated. This means the glass areas must face south. The heat is stored in concrete or masonry floors and walls or in large tubes of water inside the area exposed to the sunlight. When the sun is not entering the space and the air temperature drops below the temperature of the storage material, it gives off heat to the space.

This is an economical means of heating since it requires no fuel or special equipment. Sometimes the construction of glass panels is costly but if cost is controlled, this is a viable system. It does have the disadvantage of not being

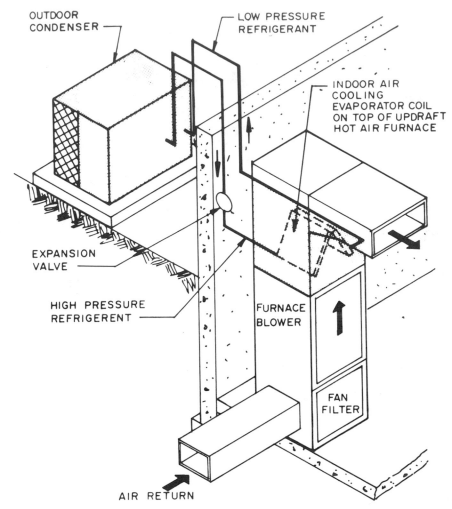

OUTDOOR CONDENSER

LOW PRESSURE REFRIGERANT

INDOOR AIR COOLING EVAPORATOR COIL ON TOP OF UPDRAFT HOT AIR FURNACE

EXPANSION VALVE

HIGH PRESSURE REFRIGERENT

FURNACE BLOWER

FAN FILTER

AIR RETURN

Figure 22-30. *A typical residential forced air electric cooling system mounted on a forced air furnace.*

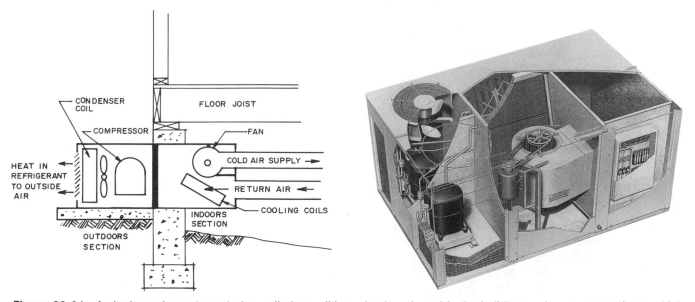

CONDENSER COIL

FLOOR JOIST

COMPRESSOR

FAN

HEAT IN REFRIGERANT TO OUTSIDE AIR

COLD AIR SUPPLY →

RETURN AIR ←

COOLING COILS

INDOORS SECTION

OUTDOORS SECTION

Figure 22-31. *A single package through-the-wall air conditioner is placed outside the building and connects to ducts which run to the rooms. (Courtesy of Lennox International, Inc.)*

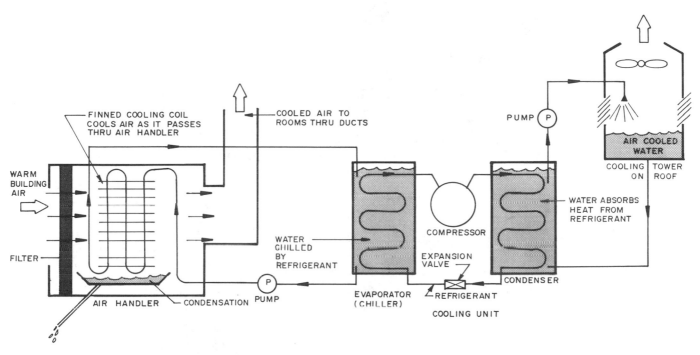

Figure 22-32. *A chilled water air cooling system used for large buildings.*

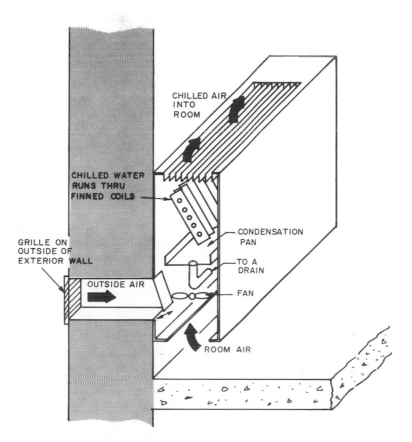

Figure 22-33. *This is a section through a wall-mounted air-handling unit with a small exterior grille to bring in fresh air.*

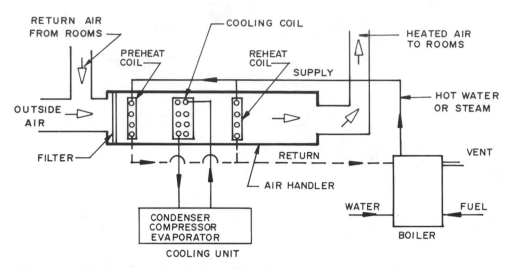

Figure 22-34. *A hot water heating system combined with a cold water chiller for cooling providing year-around service.*

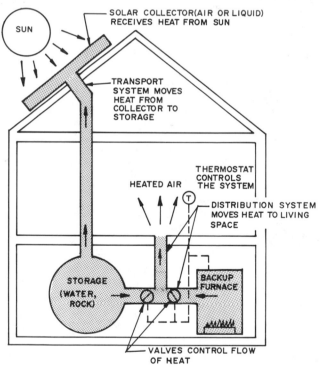

Figure 22-35. *The major parts of an active solar heating system.*

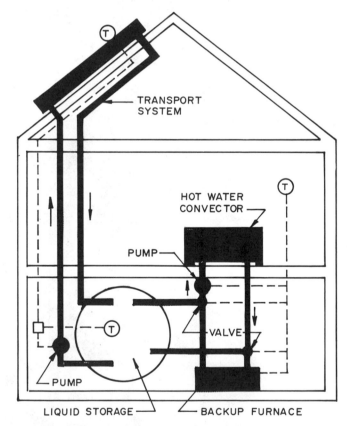

Figure 22-36. *A warm water active solar system.*

able to control the large swings in room temperature. At times the space is too hot, while at other times a backup heating system is needed. Such a system requires that shades, insulated curtains, and awnings be adjusted to attempt to control temperatures. In the summer, it is essential that solar windows be shaded by a roof overhang, insulated curtains, awnings, and other means. A separate air-cooling system is also needed. Several typical passive solar designs are in Fig. 22-38.

Technical Vocabulary

Following are some important technical terms used in this chapter. Write a brief definition for each.

Perimeter loop
Perimeter radial

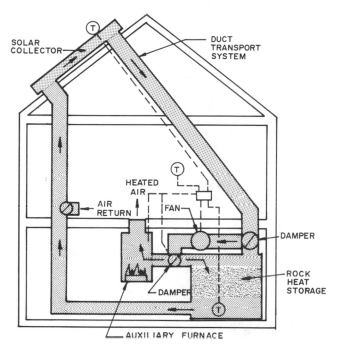

Figure 22-37. *A warm air active solar system.*

Individual duct
Extended plenum
Heat pump
Hydronic
SEER
HSPF
Radiation
Convection
Active solar
Passive solar

Study Questions

Answer the following study questions without referring to the text. Then check your answers with the text and correct those that were wrong.

1. What fuels are used with forced air heating systems?

2. Where are the registers usually located in forced air heating systems?

3. Where can a forced air furnace be located?

4. Where are return air ducts in a forced air system located?

5. What are the commonly used types of forced air systems?

6. How does a heat pump cool and heat the air?

7. What is the most commonly used type of heat pump?

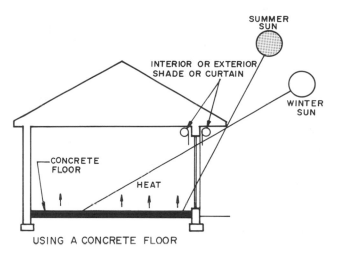

USING A CONCRETE FLOOR

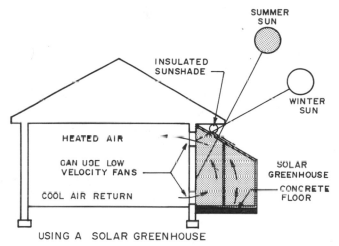

USING A SOLAR GREENHOUSE

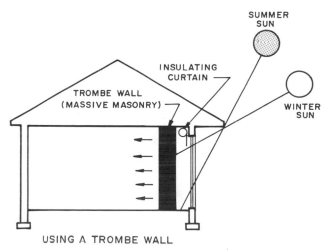

USING A TROMBE WALL

Figure 22-38. *Typical passive solar systems.*

8. What is a thru-the-wall heat pump?

9. What does the SEER rating on a heat pump indicate?

10. What is the HSPF rating on a heat pump?

11. What is a hydronic heating system?

12. What are the common types of hot water heating systems?

13. How are details concerning convectors, ventilators, and exhausters shown on a heating and air-conditioning plan?

14. How does radiant heat warm the air in a room?

15. How does an electric furnace move the heat to the rooms in a building?

16. What types of electric heating systems are available?

17. How does an electric air conditioner cool the air in a building?

18. Where is the evaporator coil in an electric air conditioner usually located?

19. How does a central cooling system using chilled water cool the air in a building?

20. What are the two major solar heating systems in use today?

21. What parts are required by an active solar system?

22. What are the two basic types of active solar systems?

23. How does a passive solar system bring heat into a building?

24. How is heat in a passive solar system stored?

25. Which of the two commonly used solar systems is the least expensive to install and operate?

Laboratory Problems

1. Draw a complete heating and air-conditioning plan for the residence designed in Chapter 8. If you have had a course in designing heating and air-conditioning systems, indicate the size of the ducts or piping.

2. Draw a complete heating and air-conditioning plan for the commercial building designed in Chapter 8. If you have had a course in designing heating and air-conditioning systems, indicate the size of the ducts or piping.

23

Plumbing Plans

Architectural working drawings include various plumbing and piping plans giving specific information about the system. Drawings for small residential buildings often do not have a plumbing plan but leave it up to the plumbing contractor to design and install the system to meet codes. Commercial buildings always have a detailed plumbing and piping plan. The plan can include a variety of systems such as water, sewer, sprinkler, and special systems as may be required for the use of the building.

The water distribution system consists of the supply pipes that bring water from the water main or well into the building and to the fixtures such as dishwasher, toilets, bathtubs, water heater, sinks, and lavatories. A considerable amount of this water must be removed from the building by the water disposal system. These water-carried wastes (sewage) are carried from the fixtures within the building to the public sewer system or private sewage disposal field.

Plumbing Codes

The design of plumbing systems is done by persons trained in design who know the requirements of the plumbing code used in their area. Four of the major codes in use are:

The BOCA National Plumbing Code
Building Officials and Code Administrators International, Inc.
4051 W. Flossmoor Road
Country Club Hills, Ill 60477-5795

National Building Code of Canada
Associate Committee on The National Building Code
National Research Council
Ottawa, Ontario, KIA OR6

Standard Plumbing Code
Southern Building Code Congress International
900 Montclair Road
Birmingham, AL 35213-1206

Uniform Plumbing Code
International Conference of Building Officials
5360 South Workman Mill Road
Whittier, CA 90601

The Water System

Water from a central water system reaches a building through an underground service pipe. This is buried deep enough so it will not freeze. A corporation valve is in the line as it leaves the water main. When it reaches the property, a curb valve is installed. This valve is reached by a long handled tool and is used to turn off the water at the street. In cold climates, the meter is placed inside the building. A third valve is placed inside the building before the line reaches the meter (Fig. 23-1). These valves are often referred to as cocks. In some areas, an electronic readout is mounted outside the building and connected to the meter so the meter reader does not need to enter the building. In warmer climates, the meter is below grade at the street with the curb valve (Fig. 23-2).

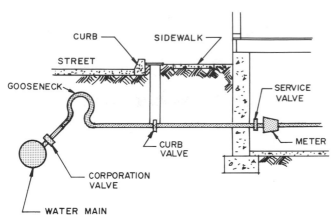

Figure 23-1. *A typical water service connection from the public water main to the house meter.*

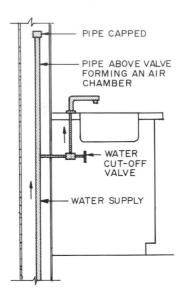

Figure 23-3. *An air chamber above the faucet prevents a banging noise when the water is turned off.*

From the meter, the cold water is run to the water heater and to all the fixtures through copper or plastic pipe. The size of the pipe depends upon the amount of water needed by each fixture. If the water has a heavy concentration of calcium ions, a water softener is installed in the cold water line before it reaches the water heater. The water heater may be gas, oil, or electrically operated. Some solar water heaters are also in use. From the water heater hot water lines are run parallel with the cold water lines to those fixtures needing hot water. Keep water pipes out of exterior walls in cold climates and insulate them if they run through a crawl space to prevent freezing.

In rural areas the water supply may be a well. A water pump is used to move water from the well to the building. It keeps a storage tank full and under pressure.

It is wise to design the water system so it can be shut off and drained. This requires one or more drain valves at the lowest points in the system. A section of pipe is run above the level of the pipe to the faucets. This provides an air chamber that prevents the banging noise that often occurs when the water is turned off quickly (Fig. 23-3).

A typical water system is shown in Fig. 23-4. The pipe sizes shown are typical of those used in small residential buildings. A final design would be based on the amount of flow needed at each unit with an allowance for the possibility that several fixtures on one line may be turned on at the same time. This is the work of a person trained in plumbing design.

The Waste Piping System

A typical waste disposal system is in Fig. 23-5. Notice the waste leaves the fixture, such as a lavatory, through a trap. The *trap* holds water, providing a seal between the waste opening in the fixture and the waste stack. A toilet has a built-in water trap. Sewage produces considerable noxious gas and the trap prevents this gas from entering the building through the waste lines (Fig. 23-6). The trap connects to *waste pipes* that are sloped slightly away from the fixture. Since the waste system relies on gravity to work, the waste lines must be sloped. The slope used varies from $\frac{1}{8}$ to $\frac{1}{2}$ in./ft. The waste pipe connects to a vertical waste stack or soil stack. A waste stack carries liquid waste that does not include human excrement. If a toilet is connected to a vertical stack, the stack is called a soil stack. Soil stacks in residential work are normally 4 in.

The waste and soil stacks carry the material down to the house drain from which it flows to the house sewer and on to the city sewer system or a private waste disposal system, such as a septic tank with a drain field. Notice that each fixture except the toilet has a vent pipe. This pipe connects with a vertical vent stack which runs through the roof. This keeps the system under atmo-

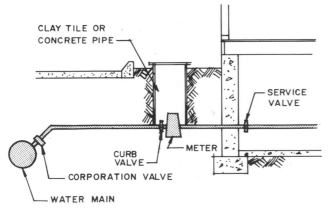

Figure 23-2. *In some areas the water meter is located in a clay tile or concrete pipe beside the curb.*

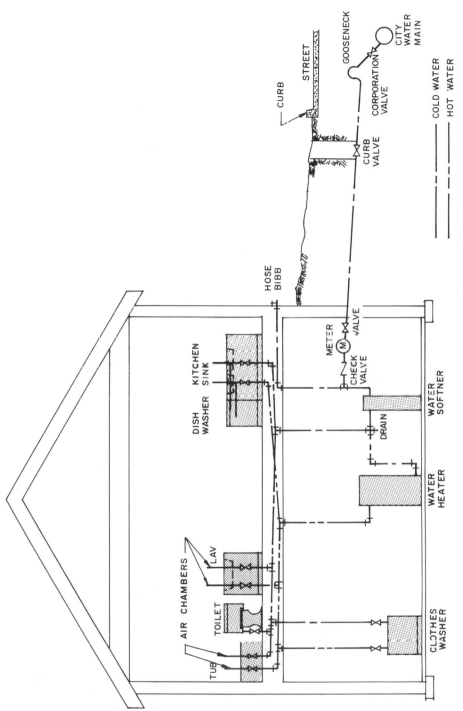

Figure 23-4. A typical water supply system in a small residence.

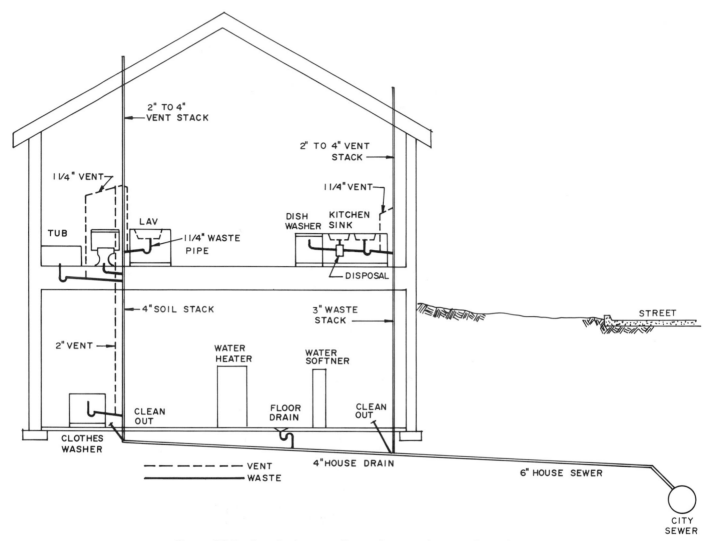

Figure 23-5. *A typical waste disposal system in a small residence.*

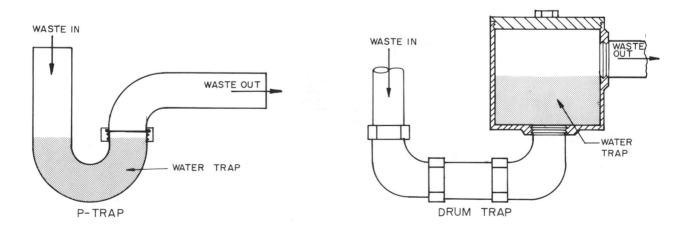

Figure 23-6. *Traps are used to block the flow of sewer gases into the building.*

spheric pressure. If this was not done a sudden rush of water, as flushing a toilet, could produce a vacuum and suck the water out of a nearby trap, thus permitting the entry of sewer gases. Vent stack sizes vary, depending upon the number of fixtures connected and the size of the soil or waste stack. In residential work $1\frac{1}{2}$- to 2-in.-diameter vents are common. In climates having heavy snow vents are often enlarged to 4 in. where they pierce the roof. The vent pipes from the individual fixture are commonly $1\frac{1}{4}$ to 2 in. in diameter. Plumbing codes regulate the distance they can be from the traps and the horizontal distances they can run to reach the vertical vent stack.

A waste system requires that a number of clean-outs be installed in the house drain. These permit the house drain to be cleaned as necessary. Commonly these are placed at the bottom of each vertical waste and soil stack.

Waste, soil, and vent piping is commonly 4 in. or larger in diameter and is more difficult to install between studs and floor joists. A plumbing wall made of 2 × 6 studs is commonly used in residential construction. This will handle the larger diameter pipes. It is economical and good planning to arrange several fixtures along a plumbing wall. They can use the same space and tie into a single waste or soil pipe and use a common vent (Fig. 23-7). If bathrooms and restrooms can be located directly above each other in a multifloor building, this is a great saving. Commercial buildings having large restroom facilities will have a plumbing wall 12 to 16 in. wide. This is large enough to contain the supply, waste, and vent piping. When possible these should be stacked above each other. A typical restroom facility is in Fig. 23-8).

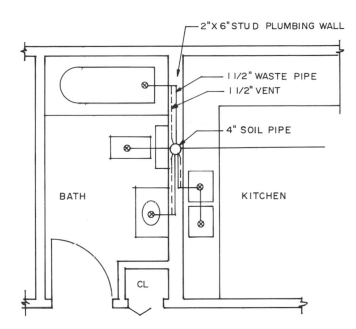

Figure 23-7. *When possible arrange plumbing fixtures along a common plumbing wall.*

Fixture Requirements

The number and type of fixtures required in residential and commercial buildings are specified in plumbing codes. Following are examples typical of those in the codes.

the publication, ANSI A117.1, *Specifications for Making Buildings and Facilities Accessible to and Usable by Physically Handicapped People*, American National Standards Institute, Inc., 1430 Broadway, New York, N.Y. 10018. A typical example of a toilet stall is in Fig. 23-9.

Septic Tanks

A septic tank and drain field are used to dispose of waste when public sewer systems are not available. Septic tanks are precast concrete or steel tanks usually 1000 to 1500 gal (4000 to 6000 l) in capacity. The size is determined by the expected volume of discharge. The sewage is discharged into the tank which is buried in the ground. It is

Type of Building	Water Closets	Urinals	Lavatories	Bathtubs or Showers	Drinking Fountains
Educational secondary schools	1 per 40 students	1 per 35 males	1 per 40 males		1 per 75
Restaurant	1 to 50	1 to 150	1 to 50		
Single-family dwelling	1 per dwelling		1 per dwelling	1 per dwelling	
Office	1 per 15		1 per 15		1 per 75

Special design standards have been accepted for restroom facilities for the handicapped. These are detailed in

digested by anaerotic action after which the effluent flows by gravity to a disposal field consisting of open-jointed or

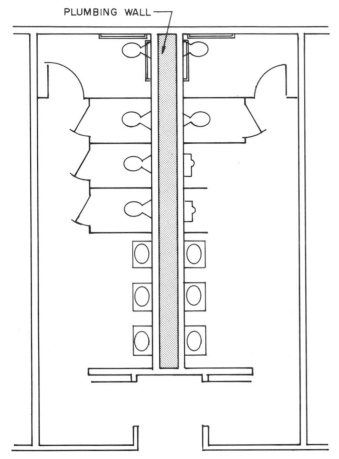

PLUMBING WALL 12" (300mm) WIDE WHEN FIXTURES ARE ON ONE SIDE. 18" (450mm) WIDE WHEN FIXTURES ARE ON BOTH SIDES.

PLUMBING WALL

Figure 23-8. Commercial buildings having a larger number of plumbing fixtures use a wide plumbing wall to contain water and waste disposal pipes.

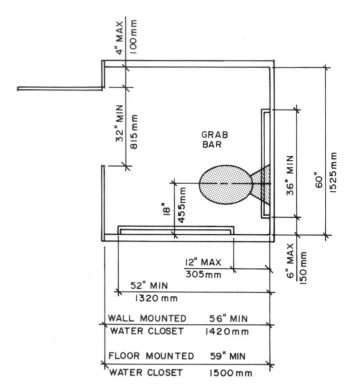

GRAB BAR

WALL MOUNTED	56" MIN	
WATER CLOSET	1420mm	
FLOOR MOUNTED	59" MIN	
WATER CLOSET	1500 mm	

Figure 23-9. This is a toilet stall designed to accommodate a handicapped person in a wheel chair.

perforated pipe laid in a bed of gravel below the surface of the ground. The number of lineal feet of pipe depends upon the expected volume of liquids and the capacity of the soil to accept it. This system must be designed by a registered sanitary engineer and approved by local authorities (Fig. 23-10 and 23-11).

This system is shown on the site plan. Its location must be approved by local health authorities.

Gas Service

Natural gas service is available in many areas. It is distributed by gas lines located below the street or up the easement on the front of lots along the street in the same manner as the water supply is made available. It is run from the gas main to the house by an underground pipe and piped within the house to the various gas fired appliances such as the furnace, water heater, clothes dryer, and cooking stove.

Where natural gas is not available, liquid propane gas is used. It is stored in a tank outside the building and filled by a tanker truck as needed. The tank may be above or below ground. The gas flow from the tank to the building runs through a pressure regulator and an evaporator and into the piping system within the building. Gas piping within the building is made of threaded black iron or steel pipe and fittings.

Sprinkler Systems

Sprinkler systems are used to provide fire protection. They require a piping system and guaranteed water supply. A typical sprinkler head can cover 144 ft² (13.4 m²) of floor area. The system pipe size and location of sprinkler heads must be designed by a person who specializes in this work. The horizontal piping to each sprinkler is small in diameter and should be protected from freezing. This means it must be below the insulated roof. Often they are run in the space directly above a suspended ceiling. The vertical risers are larger in diameter and must be on the warm side of wall insulation. The system requires valves and alarm fittings where it joins the domestic water system. Often a backup water supply is required. This can be a gravity tank high in the building, an air-pressurized water tank, or a water reservoir, such as a lake, and a pump. When a backup water supply is necessary, it is tied into the system at the same point it connects to the domestic water supply. Often a sprinkler system is drawn as a separate drawing from the plumbing system.

Plumbing Drawings

Plumbing and piping drawings are made on a floor plan drawing consisting of room layouts but free of all of the other details commonly found on a floor plan. The wall lines are drawn thin and the piping and symbols thick so they are the dominant element.

There are an extensive array of symbols used for fixtures, piping, and fittings. Some of the most frequently used symbols on plumbing drawings are in Fig. 23-12. Refer to standards manuals for a complete listing. In Fig. 23-13 are symbols used on piping drawings. Many industrial buildings have in addition to standard plumbing systems, piping systems related to the manufacturing pro-

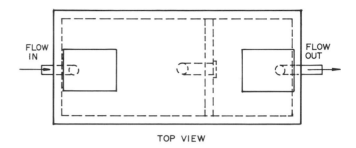

TOP VIEW

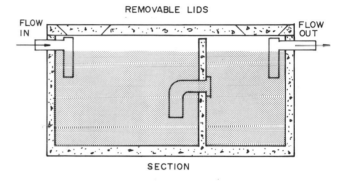

SECTION

Figure 23-11. *A precast concrete septic tank design.*

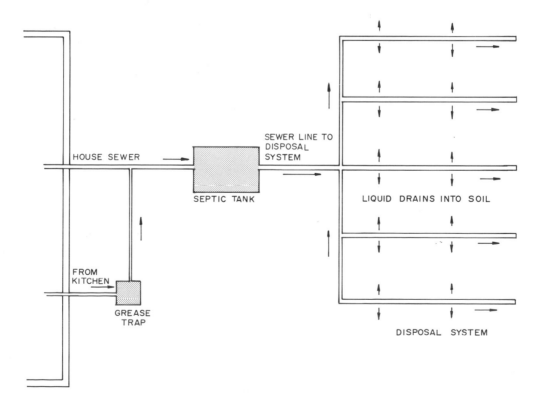

Figure 23-10. *A typical septic tank and disposal field layout.*

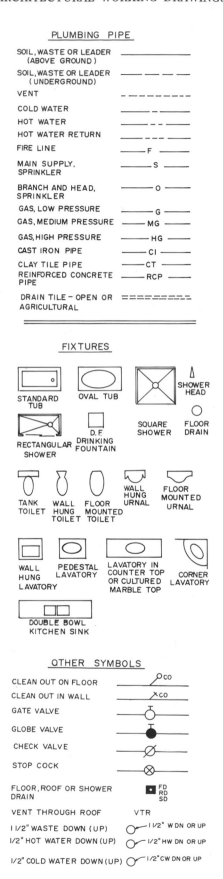

Figure 23-12. *Commonly used plumbing symbols.*

cesses to occur within the building, such as a chemical process. These require extensive piping drawings which are made separate from the conventional plumbing drawings. Some of the symbols used on these drawings are in Fig. 23-13.

A plumbing plan for a small residence is shown in Fig. 23-14. A legend is usually lettered beside the drawing. Since the drawing would be very crowded, some prefer to draw separate water supply and waste disposal drawings.

A small section of a plumbing plan for a commercial building is in Figs. 23-15 and 23-16. The first floor is shown in Fig. 23-15, while Fig. 23-16 shows the area of the second floor directly above. Study these and notice the relationship between water and waste lines on how this influences the drawing.

The walls and fixtures are to be drawn with a thin light line (this is not possible to show in this book). The plumbing details are drawn with a thicker dark line. This makes the drawing easier to read.

On the first floor is shown a mechanical room (Room 123). It has a boiler and chiller. The piping for these units is shown on the mechanical plan. The plumbing plan shows the hot and cold water lines for the plumbing fixtures and the waste, soil, and vent lines. Notice that some of these are marked "UP." This means they run up to the restroom, RM 110, on the second floor that is directly above the mechanical room. The second floor plumbing plan, Fig. 23-16, shows the fixtures and required piping. Here lines that connect directly to those below are marked "DN" (down). Fixtures are identified by marks and are described in detail in a fixture schedule.

A plumbing venting diagram, Fig. 23-17, is laid out by floors with the roof and ceiling lines indicated. This is sometimes called a plumbing section. A space is allowed for identifying the room in which the piping occurs as well as the fixture involved. The mark used on this drawing is the same as used on the plumbing drawing and in the fixture schedule. This drawing is not usually to scale. Standard piping symbols are used to indicate the piping structure. Also notice the drafting technique when drawing vent pipes. When two pipes intersect, they must meet. The connection should not hit the gap between the dashes. Waste and soil lines are drawn solid and also must meet where they join. When possible avoid crossing lines. Vent pipes crossing each other or waste lines should be drawn so the gap between dashes is on the line. When waste lines cross but do not join a gap is left (Fig. 23-18).

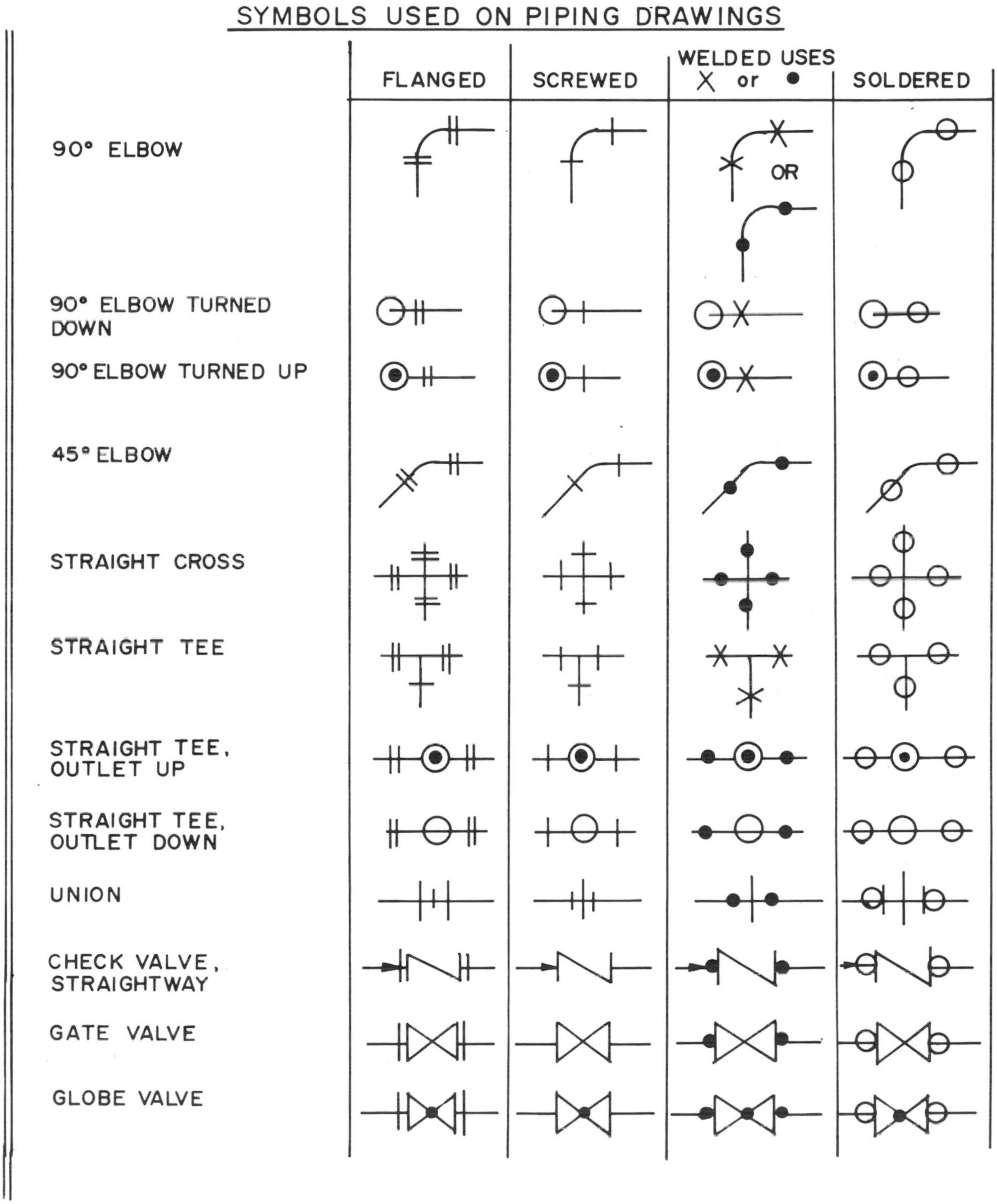

SYMBOLS USED ON PIPING DRAWINGS

	FLANGED	SCREWED	WELDED USES X or ●	SOLDERED
90° ELBOW				
90° ELBOW TURNED DOWN				
90° ELBOW TURNED UP				
45° ELBOW				
STRAIGHT CROSS				
STRAIGHT TEE				
STRAIGHT TEE, OUTLET UP				
STRAIGHT TEE, OUTLET DOWN				
UNION				
CHECK VALVE, STRAIGHTWAY				
GATE VALVE				
GLOBE VALVE				

Figure 23-13. Symbols used on piping diagrams.

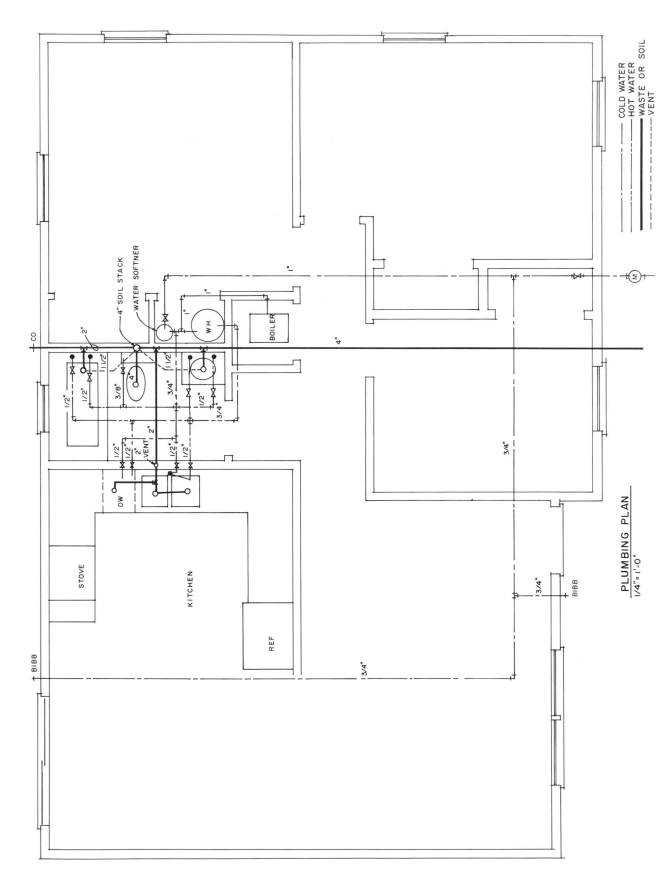

Figure 23-14. *This drawing shows both the water supply and the waste disposal system.*

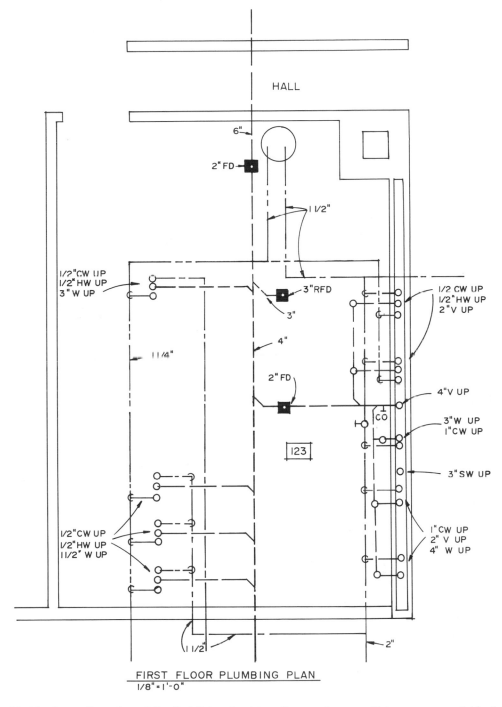

HALL

6"

2" FD

1 1/2"

1/2"CW UP
1/2"HW UP
3"W UP

3"RFD

3"

1/2 CW UP
1/2"HW UP
2"V UP

4"

1 1/4"

2" FD

4"V UP

CO

3"W UP
1"CW UP

123

3"SW UP

1/2"CW UP
1/2"HW UP
1 1/2"W UP

1"CW UP
2"V UP
4"W UP

1 1/2"

2"

FIRST FLOOR PLUMBING PLAN
1/8"=1'-0"

Figure 23-15. *A small section of the first floor plumbing diagram for a multistory commercial building.*

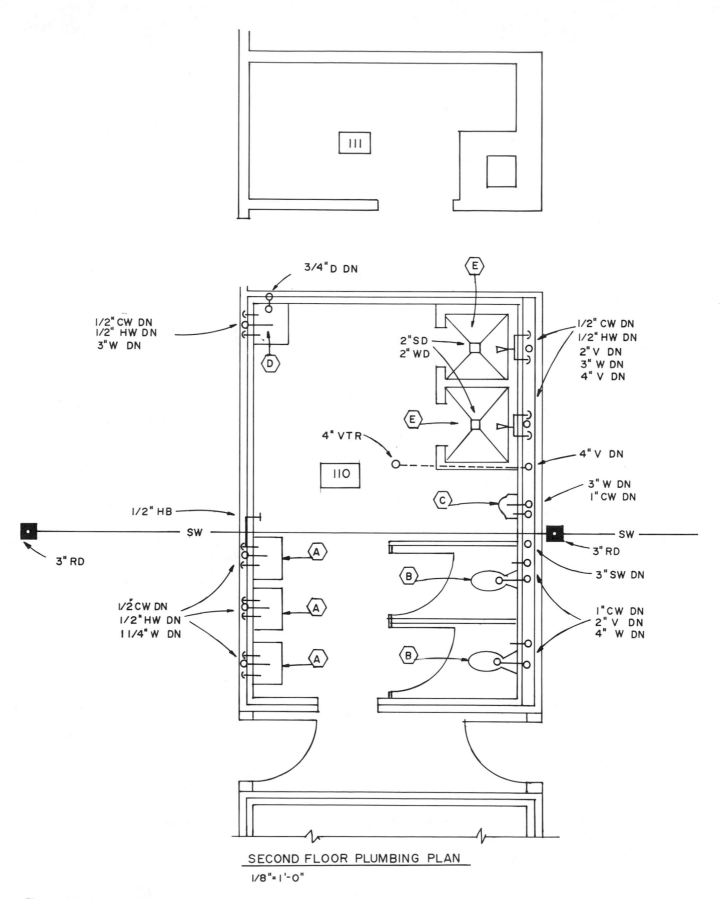

Figure 23-16. A small section of the second floor plumbing diagram that is directly above the plan shown in Figure 23-15. Can you match up the parts of the systems between floors?

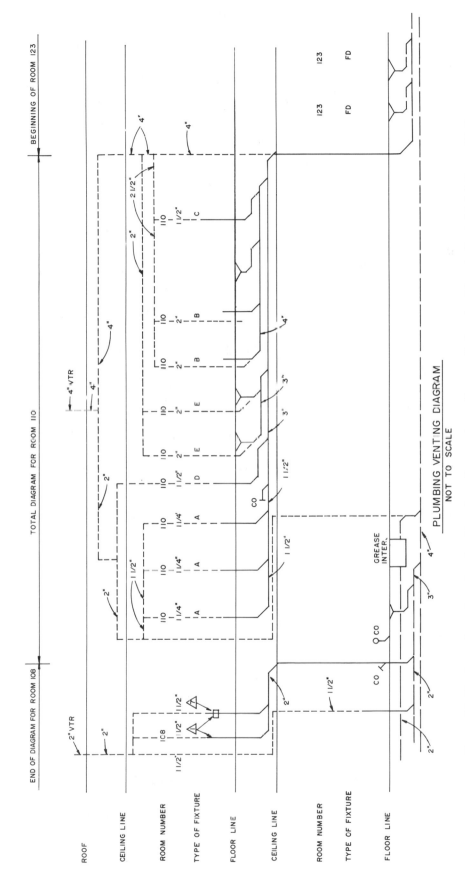

Figure 23-17. A small section of a plumbing riser diagram (sometimes called a plumbing section). Match it up with the floor plans in Figs. 23-15 and 23-16.

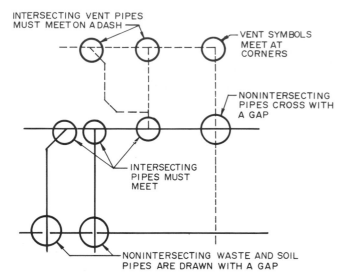

Figure 23-18. *Drafting techniques for drawing plumbing pipe symbols.*

Technical Vocabulary

Following are some important technical terms used in this chapter. Write a brief definition for each.

Trap
Water softener
Waste pipe
Soil stack
Waste stack
Plumbing wall
Sprinklers

Study Questions

Answer the following study questions without referring to the text. Then check your answers with the text and correct those that were wrong.

1. What are the two separate plumbing systems that must be installed in a building?

2. How do local governments regulate the design and installation of plumbing systems?

3. What are the main sources of pure water supply?

4. Why does a waste system require venting?

5. How is waste disposed of if a central sewer system is not available?

6. Where can you find standards pertaining to designing for the physically handicapped?

7. What plumbing system is used to provide fire protection?

8. What is contained in the legend that accompanies the plumbing drawing?

9. What is shown on a plumbing venting diagram?

Laboratory Problems

1. Make a plumbing drawing for the residence designed in Chapter 8.

2. Make a plumbing drawing for the commercial building designed in Chapter 8.

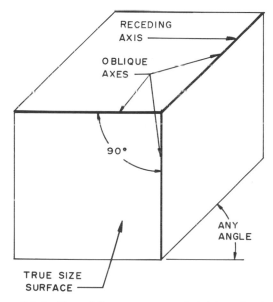

Pictorial Drawing

The types of pictorial drawing commonly used help present information in a form that is easy to understand as oblique, isometric, and perspective.

Oblique Drawings

Oblique drawings have a vertical plane, such as the front of a building or cabinet, parallel with the drawing surface where it is true size and shape. The other sides of the object recede at any convenient angle. The drawing is built around three axes. Two oblique axes are at right angles to each other while the third is the receding axis (Fig. 24-1). All distances are measured along the oblique axes. If a line is on an angle locate each end and connect the points (Fig. 24-2).

The length of the receding side can vary as needed. If it is made shorter than true size the object appears more lifelike because objects appear smaller as they recede in the distance (Fig. 24-3).

This type of drawing is especially useful when an object has circular elements because if these are placed in the front surface they are drawn as circles. Circular elements in the receding surfaces are elliptical (Fig. 24-4). The steps to draw circles on oblique receding surfaces are shown in Fig. 24-5.

Isometric Drawings

Isometric means equal measurement which is reflected by the fact that the isometric axes are 120° apart (Fig. 24-6). These axes can be placed in any position as long as

Figure 24-1. *Two oblique axes are at right angles to each other and the third is the receding axis.*

they are kept 120° apart. The choice of which axes to use depends upon what part of the object is to be seen and the position it is to assume (Fig. 24-7).

The isometric axes represent true length lines; therefore all measurements must be made on them or on lines parallel with them. Inclined lines are drawn by locating each end on an isometric line and connecting the ends (Fig. 24-8).

Circular elements in isometric appear elliptical on all surfaces. The steps to draw isometric circles are in Fig. 24-9. Curved corners or arcs can be drawn as shown in

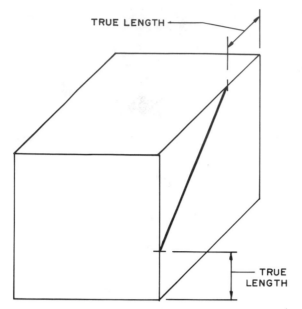

Figure 24-2. *All measurements are taken on the oblique axes.*

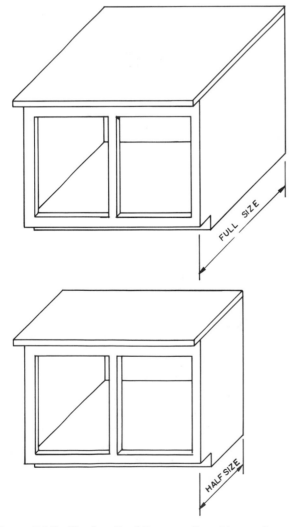

Figure 24-3. *The length of the receding side can be varied as needed.*

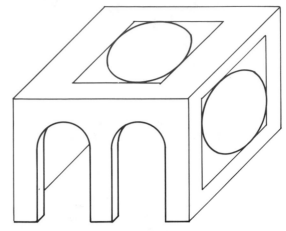

Figure 24-4. *Circular elements are elliptical when they appear on the receding sides.*

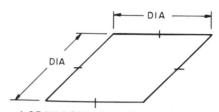

I. DRAW A SQUARE WITH SIDES EQUAL TO THE DIAMETER OF THE CIRCLE.

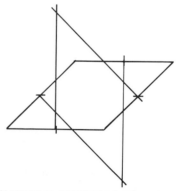

2. MARK THE CENTER OF EACH SIDE AND DRAW PERPENICULARS TO SIDE AT THAT POINT.

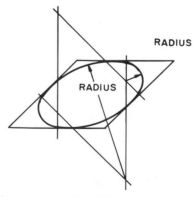

3. WHERE THE PERPENICULARS INTERSECT ARE THE CENTERS FOR DRAWING THE ELLIPSE.

Figure 24-5. *How to draw circles on the receding sides of an oblique drawing.*

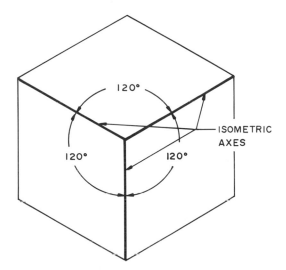

Figure 24-6. *Isometric axes are an equal distance apart.*

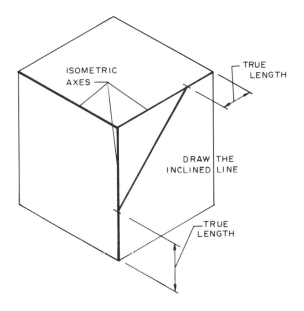

Figure 24-8. *Measurements on isometric drawings are made parallel with or on the isometric axes.*

Fig. 24-10. The easiest way to draw circles in isometric is to use an isometric circle template (Fig. 24-11).

To make an isometric drawing (Fig. 24-12).

1. Lay out the isometric axes.
2. Draw an isometric box the overall size of the object.
3. Locate features parallel with isometric axes.
4. Locate circular features.
5. Remove unneeded lines and darken visible lines.

Hidden edges are not usually shown on pictorial drawings.

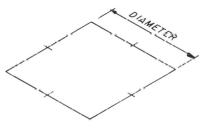

1. DRAW THE ISOMETRIC SQUARE AND LOCATE MIDPOINTS.

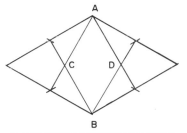

2. CONNECT MIDPOINTS WITH VERTEX LOCATING CENTERS C AND D.

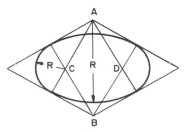

3. DRAW THE SIDES OF THE CIRCLE USING A-B-C-D AS CENTERS.

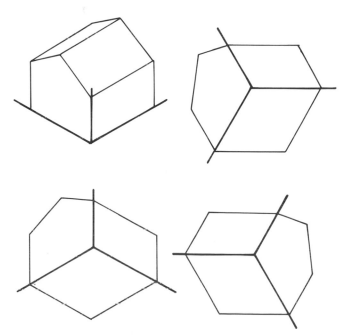

Figure 24-7. *Isometric axes can be positioned in a number of ways to change the view of the object.*

Figure 24-9. *How to draw circular elements on isometric drawings.*

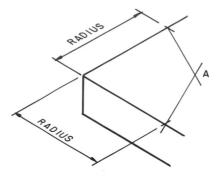

1. MARK THE RADIUS OF THE ARC AND DRAW PERPENDICULARS TO EACH.
2. WHERE THEY CROSS IS CENTER OF THE ARC (A).

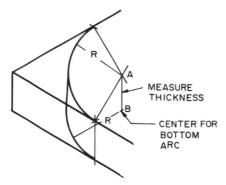

MEASURE THICKNESS

CENTER FOR BOTTOM ARC

3. SWING THE ARC FROM A. LOCATE LOWER CENTER (B) AND DRAW THE LOWER ARC.

Figure 24-10. How to draw arcs on isometric drawings.

Perspective Drawings

A perspective drawing is more life-like than oblique or isometric drawings because it diminishes the size of the object as it recedes into the distance. In oblique and isometric drawings the projectors of the sides are parallel, while in perspective they are not parallel.

The principles of perspective drawing are shown in Fig. 24-13. The person viewing the object is standing at the *station point*. The eye of the observer is the distance above the *ground line*. The object rests on the ground line. The viewer looks at the object which is shown by nonparallel visual rays from the station point to the object. These rays penetrate a plane of projection called the *picture plane*. It represents the drafting paper. The *horizon* is the line in the distance on which visual rays meet. Its location above the ground line varies to suit the needs of the observer. The position of the horizon directly influences the appearance of the perspective. The *vanishing points* are points on the horizon where the visual rays of each side of the object meet the horizon.

Types of Perspective Drawings

The three types of perspective drawings are parallel or one-point, angular or two-point, and oblique or three-point (Fig. 24-14).

Parallel or One-Point Perspective

The one-point perspective has one surface parallel with the viewer. The receding sides extend to a single vanish-

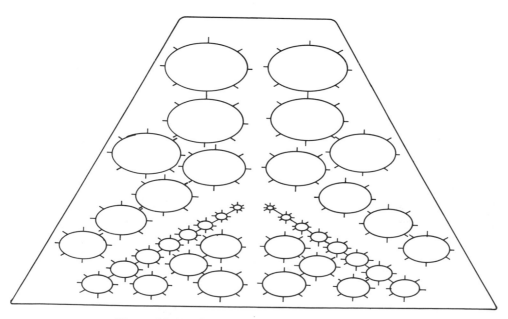

Figure 24-11. A typical isometric circle template.

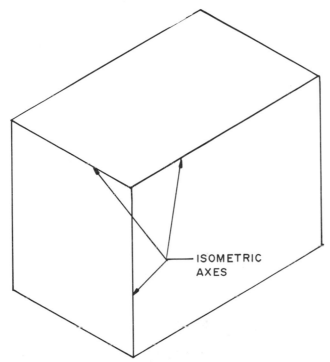

1. LAY OUT AN ISOMETRIC BOX THE OVERALL SIZE
   OF THE OBJECT.

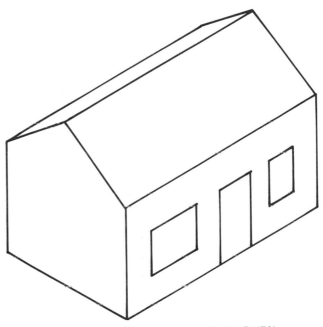

3. REMOVE CONSTRUCTION LINES. DARKEN
   VISIBLE LINES.

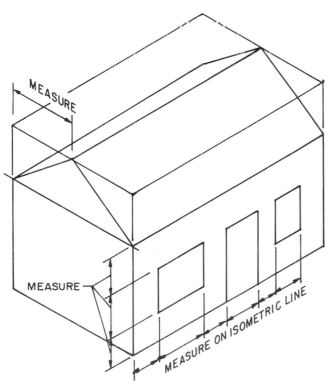

2. BLOCK IN THE DETAILS BY MEASURING ON
   ISOMETRIC LINES.

Figure 24-12. *The steps to layout an isometric drawing.*

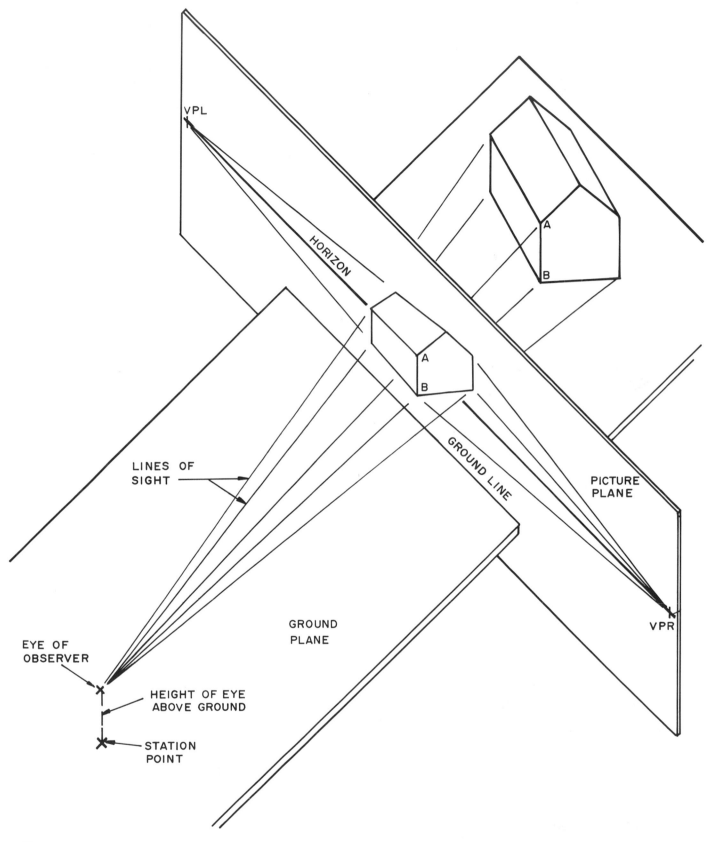

Figure 24-13. *The lines of sight on a perspective drawing begin with the eye of the observer and the image is formed where they pierce the picture plane.*

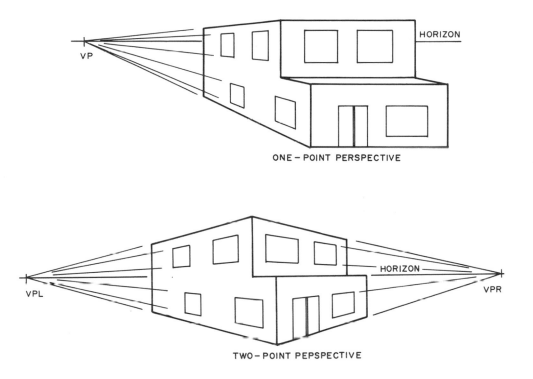

ONE – POINT PERSPECTIVE

TWO – POINT PERSPECTIVE

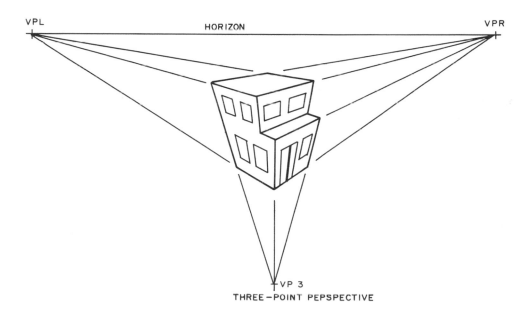

THREE – POINT PERSPECTIVE

Figure 24-14. *The three types of perspective drawings.*

ing point. One-point perspectives are frequently used for drawings of room interiors.

The steps to draw a one-point perspective are in Fig. 24-15. A top view and front view are drawn.

1. Locate the *ground line* in the front view.

2. Locate the *picture plane*. This is an edge view of the drawing paper. The distance between these is not important other than leaving room for the layout needed.

3. Draw the *plan view* of the object in the top view. The front surface will touch the picture plan.

4. Draw the *horizon* in the front view. It can be any distance above the ground line desired. Its location will influence the appearance of the perspective as shown in Fig. 24-16. Normally this will be 6 to 8 ft above the ground line.

5. Locate the *station point* in the top view. Generally it is about in the center of the object. As it is moved it changes the appearance of the perspective (Fig. 24-16).

6. Project the *width* from the top view to the ground line in the front view.

7. Draw the *front view* true size and shape on the ground line. All true size measurements are made in the plane of this view.

8. Project a line from the station point to the horizon. This locates the *vanishing point.*

9. Draw lines from the front view to the vanishing point.

10. Project lines from the station point in the top view to the various corners and parts of the object. Where these projectors cross the picture plane, project lines down to the front view. This locates these points on the perspective. Locate all the corners from the top view to the front view. Where they cross the lines running to the VP forms the sides of the perspective.

Angular or Two-Point Perspectives

Two-point perspectives are useful for interior and exterior perspectives. The steps for making a two-point perspective are divided into (1) making the top view layout, (2) making the front view layout, (3) forming the perspective drawing.

Making the Top View Layout

1. In the top view locate the *picture plane*. It will be near the top of the drawing paper (Fig. 24-17).

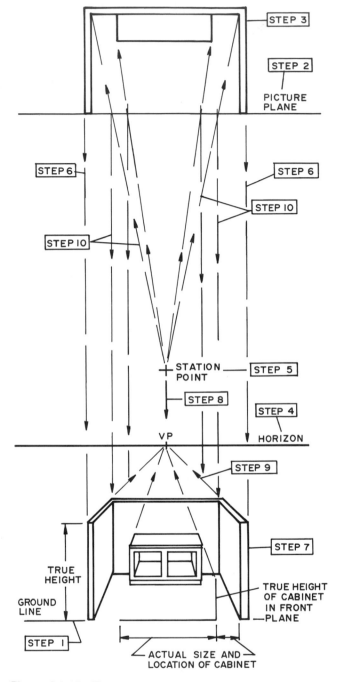

Figure 24-15. *The steps to draw a one-point perspective drawing.*

2. Draw the *outline of the object*, as the floor plan. The corner of the object will touch the picture plane and it can be placed on any angle desired. Angles from 15 to 45° are commonly used. The object will be drawn to scale. The scale used will influence the size of the final perspective.

3. Locate the *station point* by projecting a line from the corner touching the picture plane. Typically this is

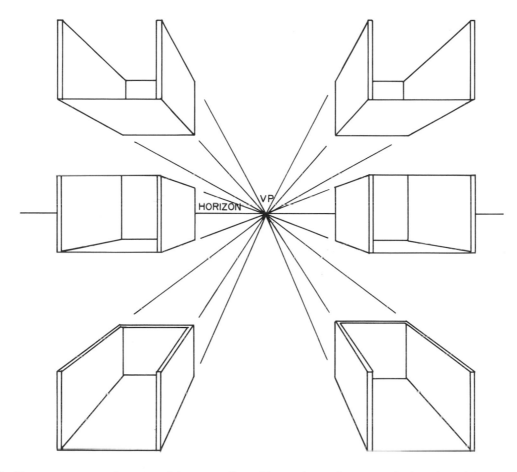

Figure 24-16. *The appearance of a one-point perspective will vary depending upon the location of the horizon and station point.*

drawn perpendicular to the picture plane but it changes the perspective some if it is moved right or left. The distance the station point is located from the picture plane can vary, but a distance of 100 ft is good. The appearance of the perspective will vary as this distance is varied. Experience is helpful in choosing this distance.

4. Locate the *vanishing points* by running lines from the station point parallel with the sides of the object until they strike the picture plane. This produces right and left vanishing points. This completes the layout of the top view.

Making the Front View Layout

5. Locate the *ground line* (Fig. 24-17). It is the surface upon which the object is resting. Place anywhere but usually it is near the bottom of the page.

6. Locate the *horizon.* This is the height of the viewers eye above the ground. It can be any distance. The higher it is placed the more the top of the object, as the roof, is seen and less of the front and sides. Six to eight feet is commonly used.

7. Project the vanishing points from the top view to the horizon.

Forming the Perspective Drawing

8. Project lines from the station point to the corners of the object (*A, B, C*) (Fig. 24-18).

9. Where these cross the picture plane (*A', B', C'*) in the top view drop perpendiculars to the front view. Corner *B* is touching the picture plane so it is true size. All other lines are foreshortened. *All vertical measurements are made on this true length line.*

10. Measure to the scale being used the true height of this corner.

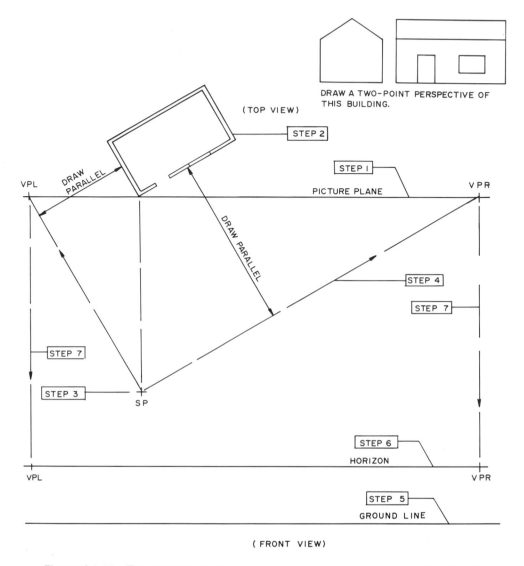

Figure 24-17. *This is the basic layout for starting a two-point perspective drawing.*

11. Project lines from the true length corner to the two vanishing points.

12. Where the lines to the vanishing points cross the lines projecting the sides down from the top view set the size and location of these corners.

13. Repeat these steps to locate other parts of the object. In Fig. 24-19 a window and a door are sighted from the station point. Where they cross the picture plane they are projected to the front view.

14. In the front view the vertical sizes of the window and door are located on the true length corner and projected to the vanishing points. Where these line cross establishes the size and location of each.

Roofs in Perspective

Two problems that occur in drawing roofs is to locate the height and overhang. One procedure is shown in Fig. 24-20.

1. Draw the roof overhang and ridge on the top view.

2. Project the ridge until it touches the picture plane in the top view. Project this intersection to the ground line in the front view. Here it becomes a *true length line*.

3. Measure the height of the ridge on this line and project it to the proper vanishing point.

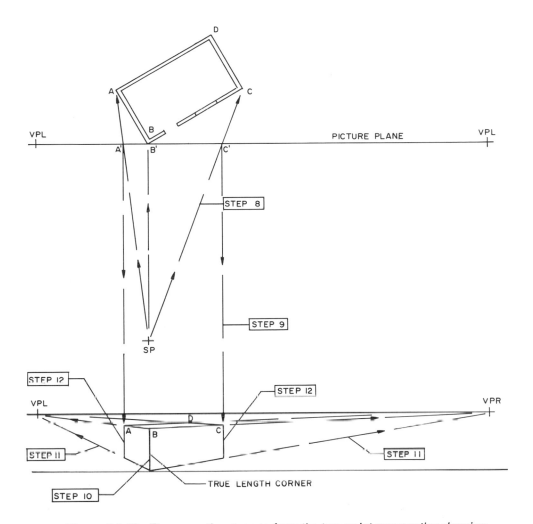

Figure 24-18. *These are the steps to form the two-point perspective drawing.*

4. Find the length of the ridge, *D–E*, by sighting it from the station point as was done with other edges and project it to the front view.

5. The overhang, point *R*, projects through the picture plane. To locate it on the perspective project it back to the picture plane (points). Project this to the front view. The true height of the overhang above the ground can be measured here (points).

6. Run projectors from the true height locations of the overhang (points) to each vanishing point.

Arcs in Perspective

Arcs in two-point perspectives are drawn by locating points along the arc in the top view. Then project each point to the perspective in the usual way. Connect the points with an irregular curve (Fig. 24-21).

Perspective Drawing Aids

There are a variety of products available that will speed up the drafting of perspectives. *Perspective charts* are available that will speed up the drafting of perspectives. *Perspective charts* are printed sheets with lines in true perspective. The perspective chart is placed under the vellum and the printed lines guide the drafter to the vanishing points. They are available in various scales and available with a number of distances of the station point from the object (Fig. 24-22).

A perspective drawing board system will also draw true perspectives. It uses a special board with various scales and vanishing points and a T-square that works on concave curves on the surface. In addition CAD systems have software that is used to produce a variety of pictorial architectural drawing.

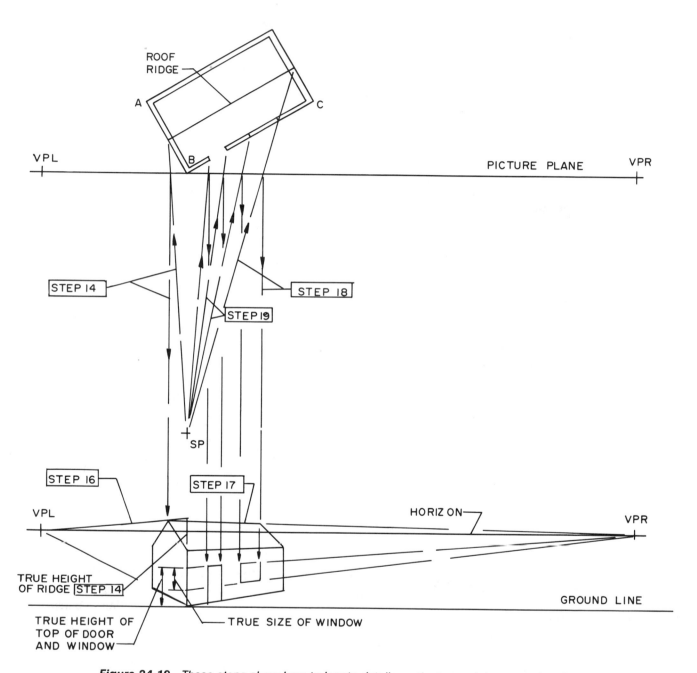

Figure 24-19. *These steps show how to locate details on the two-point perspective drawing.*

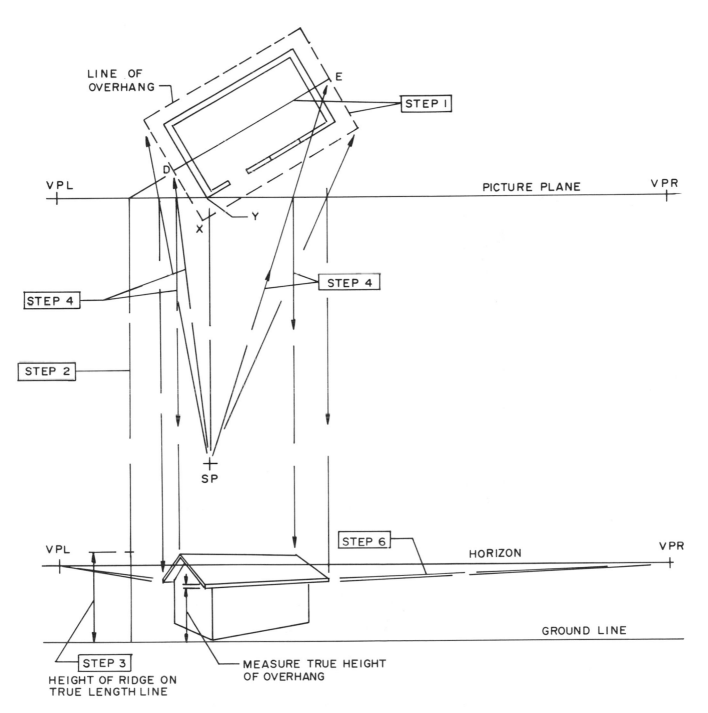

LINE OF
OVERHANG

E

STEP 1

D

VPL   PICTURE PLANE   VPR

Y

X

STEP 4   STEP 4

STEP 2

SP

STEP 6   HORIZON   VPR

VPL

GROUND LINE

STEP 3   MEASURE TRUE HEIGHT
                                          OF OVERHANG
HEIGHT OF RIDGE ON
TRUE LENGTH LINE

Figure 24-20. *The drawing of the roof in perspective requires additional sightings and projections.*

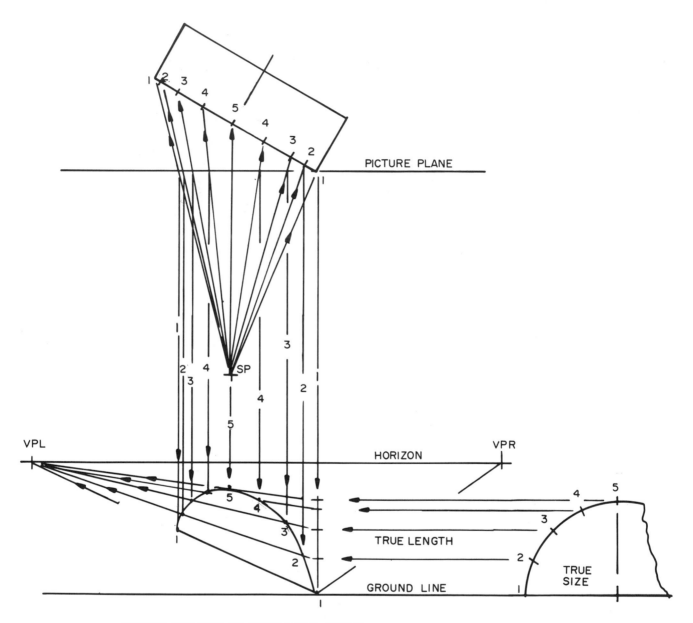

PICTURE PLANE

VPL

HORIZON

VPR

TRUE LENGTH

GROUND LINE

TRUE SIZE

REPEAT PROCESS TO DRAW REAR CURVE

Figure 24-21. *Circles are drawn in perspective by sighting and projecting points on the curve.*

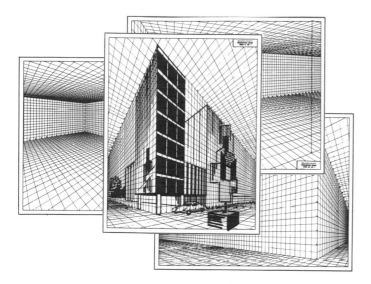

Wide-Angle Perspective Charts

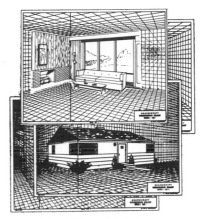

Normal Perspective Charts

EXPANDED PERSPECTIVE GRIDS

Figure 24-22. These charts are used to rapidly draw perspective drawings. (Courtesy of © Graphic Craft, The Color Wheel Company.)

Technical Vocabulary

Following are some important technical terms used in this chapter. Write a brief definition for each.

Oblique drawing
Isometric drawing
One-point perspective
Two-point perspective

Station point
Horizon
Picture plane
Vanishing points

Study Questions

Answer the following questions without referring to the text. Then check your answers with the text and correct those that were wrong.

1. At what angle is the receding axis of an oblique drawing drawn?

2. How many degrees separate the isometric axes?

3. Where do you measure true length distances on isometric drawings?

4. When making a preliminary layout for a perspective drawing what features must be located and drawn?

5. What are the three common types of perspectives used for architectural pictorial drawings?

Laboratory Problems

1. Find a picture of a small building in a magazine and draw it as a two-pint perspective.

2. Draw a one-point perspective of a room interior. Find an example in a magazine or use your drafting room.

3. Draw an oblique drawing of cabinets copying details from a magazine or catalog.

4. Make an isometric drawing of some type of construction detail such as a wall section or fireplace.

APPENDIX

Abbreviations

Standard Abbreviations List

Above finished counter	AFC	Balcony	BALC
Above finished floor	AFF	Basement	BSMT
Above finished grade	AFG	Baseplate	BP
Acoustic	AC	Bathroom	B
Acoustic plaster	AC PL	Bathtub with shower	BTS
Acoustic tile	AC T	Batten	BATT
Actual	ACT	Beam	BM
Additional	ADD	Beam, standard	S BM
Adhesive	ADH	Beam, wide flange	W BM
Adjustable	ADJ	Bearing	BRG
Aggregate	AGGR	Bearing plate	B PL
Air conditioning	AIR COND	Bedroom	BR
Air conditioning unit	ACU	Bench mark	BM
Alternating current	AC	Between	BET
Aluminum	AL or ALUM	Beveled	BEV
Amount	AMT	Bidet	BDT
Ampere	AMP or A	Block	BLK
Anchor bolt	AB	Blocking	BLKG
Angle (in degrees)	⊀	Blower	BLO
Angle (structural)	∟	Board	BD
Approximate	APPROX	Board feet	BD FT
Architectural	ARCH	Both sides	BS
Area	A	Both ways	BW
Area drain	AD	Bottom	BOT
Asbestos	ASB	Boulevard	BLVD
Asphalt	ASPH	Bracket	BRKT
Asphaltic concrete	ASPH CONC	Brass	BR
Assembly	ASSEM	Brick	BRK
At	@	British thermal unit	BTU
Automatic	AUTO	Broom closet	BC
Avenue	AVE	Building	BLDG
Average	AVG	Building line	BL
		Built-in	BLT-IN
		Built-up	BU

Buzzer	BUZ	Cubic	CU
By (used as 2 × 4)	×	Cubic feet	CU FT
		Cubic feet per minute	CFM
Cabinet	CAB	Cubic yard	CU YD
Candela	cd		
Candlepower	CP	Damper	DMPR
Carpet	CPT	Decibel	db
Cast iron	CI	Deep, depth	DP
Cast in place	CIP	Degree	° or DEG
Catch basin	CB	Department	DEPT
Caulking	CLKG	Detail	DET
Ceiling	CLG	Diagonal	DIAG
Ceiling diffuser	CD	Diagram	DIAG
Celsius	C	Diameter	DIA
Cement	CEM	Diffuser	DIFF
Cement plaster	CEM PLAS	Dimension	DIM
Center	CTR	Dining room	DIN RM
Center to center	C to C	Direct current	DC
Centerline	₵ or CL	Dishwasher	DW
Centimeter	cm	Disposal	DISPL
Ceramic	CER	Distance	DIST
Ceramic tile	CT	Ditto	DO
Chalkboard	CHKBD	Divided or division	DIV
Chamfer	CHAM	Door	DR
Channel (structural)	C	Double	DBL
Check	CHK	Double-hung	DH
Cinder block	CIN BL	Double-strength (glass)	DS
Circle	CIR	Douglas Fir	DF
Circuit	CKT	Dowel	DWL
Circuit breaker	CIR BKR	Down	DN
Class	CL	Downspout	DS
Classroom	CLRM	Drain	D or DR
Cleanout	CO	Drawing	DWG
Clear	CLR	Drinking fountain	DF
Closet	CLO or CL	Dryer	D
Clothes dryer	CL D	Drywall	DW
Cold water	CW	Duplicate	DUP
Column	COL		
Combination	COMB	Each	EA
Common	COM	Each face	EF
Concrete	CONC	Each way	EW
Concrete block	CONC B	East	E
Concrete masonry unit (concrete block)	CMU	Elbow	ELL
Construction	CONST	Electric(al)	ELECT
Continuous	CONT	Electric panel board	EPB
Contractor	CONTR	Elevation	EL or ELEV
Contractor furnished	CF	Elevator	ELEV
Control joint	CJ	Enclosure	ENCL
Copper	COP or CU	Engineer	ENGR
Corridor	CORR	Entrance	ENT
Counter	CTR	Equal	EQ
Countersink	CSK	Equipment	EQUIP
Courses	C	Estimate	EST
Cover	COV	Excavate	EXC
Cross section	X-SECT	Exhaust	EXH

Existing	EXIST'G	Glass	GL
Expansion bolt	EB	Glass block	GL BL
Expansion joint	EXP JT	Glazed structural unit	GSU
Exposed	EXPO	Glue-laminated	GLUELAM
Extension	EXT	Government	GOVT
Exterior	EXT	Grade	GR
Exterior grade	EXT GR	Grade beam	GB
		Grating	GRTG
Fabricate	FAB	Gravel	GVL
Face brick	FB	Grille	GR
Face of studs	FOS	Ground	GRND
Fahrenheit	F	Grout	GT
Feet	' or FT	Gypsum	GYP
Feet per minute	FPM		
Fiberglass-reinforced plastic	FRP	Hall	H
Figure	FIG	Hardboard	HBD
Finish(ed)	FIN	Hardware	HDW
Finished all over	FAO	Hardwood	HDWD
Finished floor	FIN FL	Head	HD
Finished floor elevation	FFE	Header	HDR
Finished grade	FIN GR	Heater	HTR
Finished opening	FO	Heating	HTG
Firebrick	FBRK	Heating/ventilating/air conditioning	HVAC
Fire extinguisher	F EXT	Heavy duty	HD
Fire extinguisher cabinet	FEC	Height	HT
Fire hose cabinet	FHC	Hexagonal	HEX
Fire hydrant	FH	Highway	HWY
Fireproof	FP	Hollow core	HC
Fitting	FTG	Hollow metal	HM
Fixture	FIX	Horizontal	HORIZ
Flammable	FLAM	Horsepower	HP
Flange	FLG	Hose bibb	HB
Flashing	FL	Hospital	HOSP
Flexible	FLEX	Hot water	HW
Floor	FLR	Hot water heater	HWH
Floor drain	FD	Hour	HR
Floor sink	FS	House	HSE
Flooring	FLG	Hundred	C
Fluorescent	FLUOR		
Folding	FLDG	Illuminate	ILLUM
Foot	' or FT	Incandescent	INCAND
Footing	FTG	Inch	" or IN.
Forward	FWD	Inflammable	INFL
Foundation	FND	Information	INFO
Four-way	4-W	Inside diameter	ID
Frame	FR	Inside face	IF
Front	FR	Inspect(ion)	INSP
Full size	FS	Install	INST
Furnace	FURN	Insulate(d)(ion)	INS
Future	FUT	Interior	INT
		Interior grade	INT GR
Gallon	GAL		
Galvanized	GALV	Jamb	JMB
Galvanized iron (galvanized steel)	GI	Janitor's sink	JS
Gauge	GA	Janitor's closet	JC

Joint	JT	Mirror	MIRR
Joist	JST	Miscellaneous	MISC
Joist and plank	J & P	Modular	MOD
Junction	JCT	Molding	MLDG
Junction box	J-BOX	Mullion	MULL
Kelvin	K	Noise reduction coefficient	NRC
Kiln dried	KD	Nominal	NOM
Kilogram	kg	North	N
Kilovolt	KV	Not applicable	NA
Kilowatt	KW	Not in contract	NIC
Kitchen	KIT	Not to scale	NTS
Kitchen cabinet	KCAB	Number	NO. or #
Kitchen sink	KSK		
Knockout	KO	Oak	O
		Office	OFF
Laboratory	LAB	On center	OC
Laminate(d)	LAM	One-way	1-W
Landing	LDG	Open web	OW
Latitude	LAT	Opening	OPG
Laundry	LAU	Opposite	OPP
Lavatory	LAV	Opposite hand	OPH
Left	L	Ounce	OZ
Length	LGTH	Outside diameter	OD
Level	LEV	Outside face of concrete	OFC
Library	LIB	Outside face of studs	OFS
Light (pane of glass)	LT	Overhead	OH
Linear feet	LIN FT		
Linen closet	L CL	Painted	PTD
Linoleum	LINO	Pair	PR
Live load	LL	Panel	PNL
Living room	LR	Parallel	PAR or ∥
Location	LOC	Partition	PTN
Long	LG	Passage	PASS
Longitude	LNG	Pavement	PVMT
Lumber	LBR	Penny (nail size)	d
		Per	/
Manhole	MH	Percent	%
Manufacture(r)	MFR	Perforate	PERF
Marble	MRB	Perimeter	PERIM
Mark	MK	Perpendicular	PERP or ⊥
Masonry	MAS	Piece	PC
Masonry opening	MO	Plan	PLN
Material	MAT	Plaster	PLS
Maximum	MAX	Plasterboard	PL BD
Mechanical	MECH	Plastic	PLAS
Medicine cabinet	MC	Plastic tile	PLAS T
Medium	MED	Plate	PL or ℔
Membrane	MEMB	Plate glass	PL GL
Metal	MET	Platform	PLAT
Metal lath and plaster	MLP	Plumbing	PLMB
Meter	m	Plywood	PLY
Millimeter	mm	Polished	POL
Minimum	MIN	Polyethelyne	POLY or PE

Polystyrene	PS	Second	s or SEC
Polyvinyl chloride	PVC	Section	SECT
Position	POS	Select	SEL
Pound	LB or #	Select structural	SS
Pounds per square foot	PFS	Self-closing	SC
Pounds per square inch	PSI	Service	SERV
Precast	PRCST	Sewer	SEW
Prefabricated	PREFAB	Sheathing	SHTHG
Preliminary	PRELIM	Sheet	SHT
Premolded	PRMLD	Sheet metal	SM
Property	PROP	Shower	SH
Public address system	PA	Siding	SDG
Pull chain	PC	Sill cock	SC
Pushbutton	PB	Similar	SIM
		Single-hung	SH
Quantity	QTY	Single-strength (glass)	SS
Quarry tile	QT	Sink	SK
Quart	QT	Slop sink	SS
		Socket	SOC
Radiator	RAD	Soil pipe	SP
Radius	RAD	Solid block	SLD BLK
Random length and width	RL&W	Solid core	SC
Range	R	South	S
Receptacle	RECP	Specifications	SPEC
Recessed	REC	Square	□ or SQ
Redwood	RDWD	Square feet	SF or ⊔
Reference	REF	Square inches	SQ IN or ⊞
Refrigeration	REF	Stainless steel	SST
Refrigerator	REFRIG	Stairs	ST
Register	REG	Stand pipe	ST P
Reinforced, reinforcing	REINF	Standard	STD
Reinforcing bar	REBAR	Station point	SP
Required	REQ	Steel	STL
Resilient	RES	Stirrup	STIR
Resistance	RES	Stock	STK
Return	RET	Storage	STO
Revision	REV	Storm drain	SD
Revolutions per minute	RPM	Street	ST
Right	R	Structural	STR
Right hand	RH	Structural clay tile	SCT
Riser	R	Substitute	SUB
Road	RD	Supply	SUP
Roof	RF	Surface	SUR
Roof drain	RD	Surface four sides	S4S
Roofing	RFG	Surface two edges	S2E
Room	RM	Suspended ceiling	SUSP CLG
Rough	RGH	Switch	S or SW
Rough opening	RO	Symbol	SYM
Round	RD or φ	Symmetrical	SYM
Rubber base	RB	Synthetic	SYN
Rubber tile	RBT	System	SYS
Schedule	SCH	Tack board	TK BD
Screw	SCR	Tangent	TAN

Tar and gravel	T & G	Vestibule	VEST
Technical	TECH	Vinyl	VIN
Tee	T	Vinyl base	VB
Telephone	TEL	Vinyl tile	VT
Television	TV	Vinyl wall covering	VWC
Temperature	TEMP	Vitreous clay tile	VCT
Temporary	TEMP	Volt	V
Terra-cotta	TC	Volume	VOL
Terrazzo	TZ		
Thermostat	THERMO	Wainscot	WSCT
Thickness	THK	Wall cabinet	WCAB
Thousand	M	Wall vent	WV
Thousand board feet	MBM	Waste stack	WS
Three-way	3-W	Water	W
Threshold	THR	Water closet (toilet)	WC
Toilet	TOL	Water heater	WH
Tongue and groove	T & G	Waterproof	WP
Top of wall	TW	Watt	W
Tread	TR	Weatherproof	WP
Two-way	2-W	Weephole	WH
Typical	TYP	Weight	WT
		Welded wire fabric	WWF
Undercut door	UCD	West	W
Underwriters' Laboratory, Inc.	U.L.	Wet bulb	WB
Unfinished	UNFIN	White pine	WP
Urinal	UR	Wide flange (structural)	W
Utility	UTIL	Window	WDW
		With	w/
V-joint	VJ	Without	WO
Vanishing point	VP	Wood	WD
Vanity	VAN	Working point	WPT
Vapor barrier	VB	Wrought iron	WI
Vent through roof	VTR		
Vent stack	VS	Yard	YD
Ventilation	VENT	Yellow pine	YP
Ventilator	V		
Vertical	VERT	Zinc	ZN
Vertical grain	VG		

Selected Metric Conversion Factors

WHEN YOU KNOW		YOU CAN FIND	IF YOU MULTIPLY BY
LENGTH	inches	millimeters	25.4
	feet	millimeters	300.48
	yards	meters	0.91
	miles	kilometers	1.61
	millimeters	inches	0.04
	meters	yards	1.1
	kilometers	miles	0.6
AREA	square inches	square centimeters	6.45
	square feet	square meters	0.09
	square yards	square meters	0.83
	square miles	square kilometers	2.6
	acres	square hectometers (hectares)	0.4
	square centimeters	square inches	0.16
	square meters	square yards	1.2
	square kilometers	square miles	0.4
	hectares	acres	2.5
MASS	ounces	grams	28.0
(Weight)	pounds	kilograms	0.45
	tons (short)	metric tons	0.9
	grams	ounces	0.04
	kilograms	pounds	2.2
	metric tons	tons (short)	1.1
VOLUME	bushels	cubic meters	0.04
	cubic feet	cubic meters	0.03
	cubic inches	cubic centimeters	16.4
	cubic yards	cubic meters	0.8
FLUID VOLUME	ounces	milliliters	30.0
	pints	liters	0.47
	quarts	liters	0.95
	gallons	liters	3.8
	milliliters	ounces	0.03
	liters	pints	2.1
	liters	quarts	1.06
	liters	gallons	0.26
TEMPERATURE	degrees Fahrenheit	degrees Celsius	0.6 (after subtracting 32)
	degrees Celsius	degrees Fahrenheit	1.8 (then add 32)
POWER	horsepower	kilowatts	0.75
	kilowatts	horsepower	1.34
PRESSURE	pounds per square inch (psi)	kilopascals	6.9
	kilopascals	pounds per square inch	0.15
VELOCITY	miles per hour	meters per second	0.45
(Speed)	miles per hour	kilometers per hour	1.6
	kilometers per hour	miles per hour	0.6

APPENDIX

Basic Symbols Used on Architectural Drawings

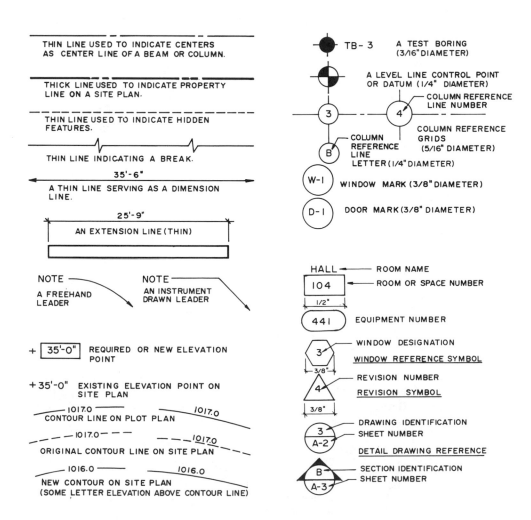

THIN LINE USED TO INDICATE CENTERS AS CENTER LINE OF A BEAM OR COLUMN.

THICK LINE USED TO INDICATE PROPERTY LINE ON A SITE PLAN.

THIN LINE USED TO INDICATE HIDDEN FEATURES.

THIN LINE INDICATING A BREAK.

35'-6"

A THIN LINE SERVING AS A DIMENSION LINE.

25'-9"

AN EXTENSION LINE (THIN)

NOTE — A FREEHAND LEADER

NOTE — AN INSTRUMENT DRAWN LEADER

+ | 35'-0" | REQUIRED OR NEW ELEVATION POINT

+35'-0" EXISTING ELEVATION POINT ON SITE PLAN

1017.0 — 1017.0
CONTOUR LINE ON PLOT PLAN

— 1017.0 — — — — 1017.0
ORIGINAL CONTOUR LINE ON SITE PLAN

1016.0 — 1016.0
NEW CONTOUR ON SITE PLAN
(SOME LETTER ELEVATION ABOVE CONTOUR LINE)

TB-3 A TEST BORING (3/16" DIAMETER)

A LEVEL LINE CONTROL POINT OR DATUM (1/4" DIAMETER)

COLUMN REFERENCE LINE NUMBER

3 4 COLUMN REFERENCE GRIDS (5/16" DIAMETER)

B COLUMN REFERENCE LINE LETTER (1/4" DIAMETER)

W-1 WINDOW MARK (3/8" DIAMETER)

D-1 DOOR MARK (3/8" DIAMETER)

HALL — ROOM NAME

104 — ROOM OR SPACE NUMBER
1/2"

441 EQUIPMENT NUMBER

WINDOW DESIGNATION
3
WINDOW REFERENCE SYMBOL
3/8"

REVISION NUMBER
4
REVISION SYMBOL
3/8"

3 DRAWING IDENTIFICATION
A-2 SHEET NUMBER
DETAIL DRAWING REFERENCE

B SECTION IDENTIFICATION
A-3 SHEET NUMBER

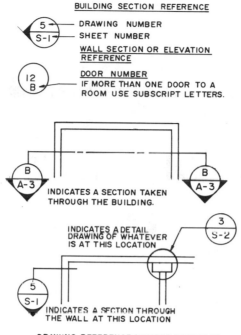

BUILDING SECTION REFERENCE

5 —— DRAWING NUMBER
S-1 —— SHEET NUMBER
WALL SECTION OR ELEVATION
REFERENCE

DOOR NUMBER
12
B —— IF MORE THAN ONE DOOR TO A
ROOM USE SUBSCRIPT LETTERS.

B
A-3   INDICATES A SECTION TAKEN
THROUGH THE BUILDING.

B
A-3

INDICATES A DETAIL
DRAWING OF WHATEVER
IS AT THIS LOCATION

3
S-2

5
S-1   INDICATES A SECTION THROUGH
THE WALL AT THIS LOCATION

DRAWING REFERENCE NUMBER EXAMPLES

APPENDIX

Symbols for Materials in Section

EARTH

EARTH (ALTERNATE)

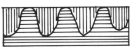

ROCK

GRAVEL, POROUS FILL

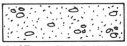

CAST-IN-PLACE AND PRECAST CONCRETE

LIGHTWEIGHT CONCRETE

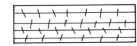

SAND, MORTAR, GROUT AND PLASTER

CLAY TILE

COMMON AND FACE BRICK

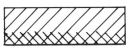

FIRE BRICK

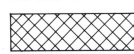

CONCRETE BLOCK

STRUCTURAL FACING TILE

GYPSUM WALL BOARD

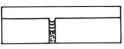

CAULKING

SLATE, BLUESTONE, FLAGGING, SOAPSTONE

RUBBLE

ROUGH CUT STONE

MARBLE

ALUMINUM

BRASS AND BRONZE

CAST IRON

STEEL

END GRAIN, CONSTRUCTION LUMBER

BLOCKING

LAMINATED WOOD

PLYWOOD

HARDBOARD

END GRAIN, FINISH LUMBER

STRUCTURAL GLASS

GLASS BLOCK

INSULATION, RIGID

INSULATION BATTS
OR LOOSE

INSULATION, SPRAY
AND FOAM

STANDARD GLASS

TILE, CERAMIC

TILE, ACOUSTICAL

METAL LATH AND
PLASTER

CARPET AND PAD

TERRAZZO

TERRA COTA

PLASTIC

RESILIENT FLOORING
AND PLASTIC LAMINATE

TILE, STRUCTURAL
CLAY

Symbols for Materials in Elevation

BRICK

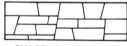

CONCRETE BLOCK, RUNNING BOND

CONCRETE BLOCK, STACK BOND

CONCRETE OR PLASTER

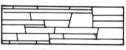

SPLIT STONE

SMOOTHED STONE

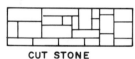

CUT STONE

RUBBLE STONE

MARBLE

GLASS

FLASHING

PLYWOOD

HORIZONTAL SIDING

VERTICAL SIDING

BOARD AND BATTEN OR VERTICAL GROOVE SIDING

CERAMIC TILE

ROOF SHINGLES

APPENDIX

6:

Symbols for Walls In Section

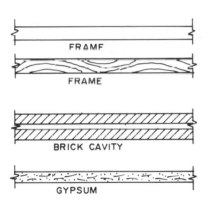

FRAME

FRAME

BRICK CAVITY

GYPSUM

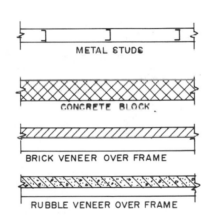

METAL STUDS

CONCRETE BLOCK

BRICK VENEER OVER FRAME

RUBBLE VENEER OVER FRAME

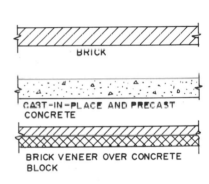

BRICK

CAST-IN-PLACE AND PRECAST CONCRETE

BRICK VENEER OVER CONCRETE BLOCK

APPENDIX

7:

Door and Window Symbols in Plan View

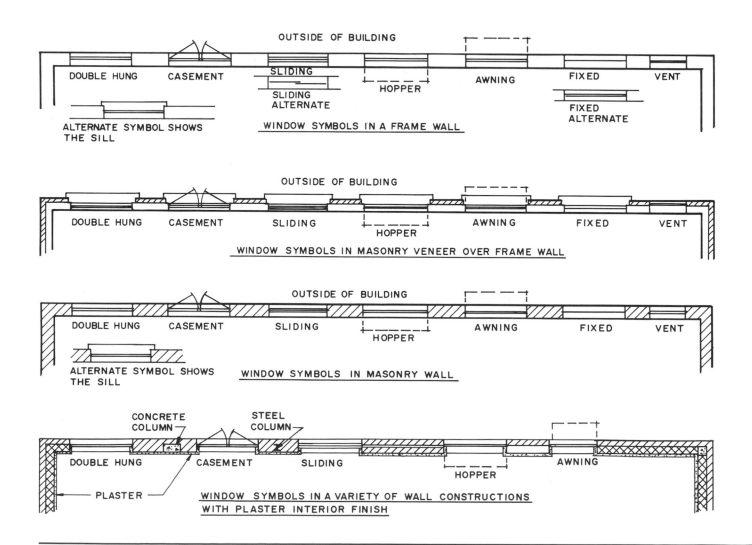

OUTSIDE OF BUILDING

DOUBLE HUNG   CASEMENT   SLIDING   HOPPER   AWNING   FIXED   VENT

SLIDING ALTERNATE

FIXED ALTERNATE

ALTERNATE SYMBOL SHOWS THE SILL

WINDOW SYMBOLS IN A FRAME WALL

OUTSIDE OF BUILDING

DOUBLE HUNG   CASEMENT   SLIDING   HOPPER   AWNING   FIXED   VENT

WINDOW SYMBOLS IN MASONRY VENEER OVER FRAME WALL

OUTSIDE OF BUILDING

DOUBLE HUNG   CASEMENT   SLIDING   HOPPER   AWNING   FIXED   VENT

ALTERNATE SYMBOL SHOWS THE SILL

WINDOW SYMBOLS IN MASONRY WALL

CONCRETE COLUMN   STEEL COLUMN

DOUBLE HUNG   CASEMENT   SLIDING   HOPPER   AWNING

PLASTER

WINDOW SYMBOLS IN A VARIETY OF WALL CONSTRUCTIONS WITH PLASTER INTERIOR FINISH

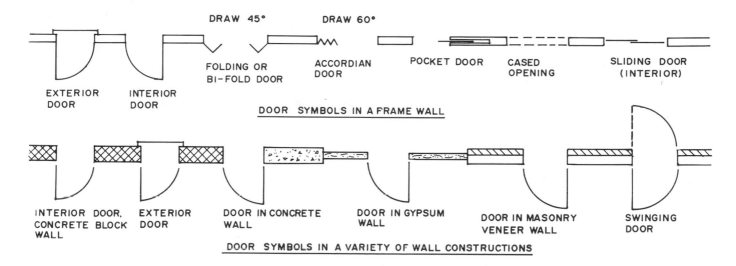

DOOR SYMBOLS IN A FRAME WALL

DOOR SYMBOLS IN A VARIETY OF WALL CONSTRUCTIONS

Elevation Views of Typical Doors and Windows

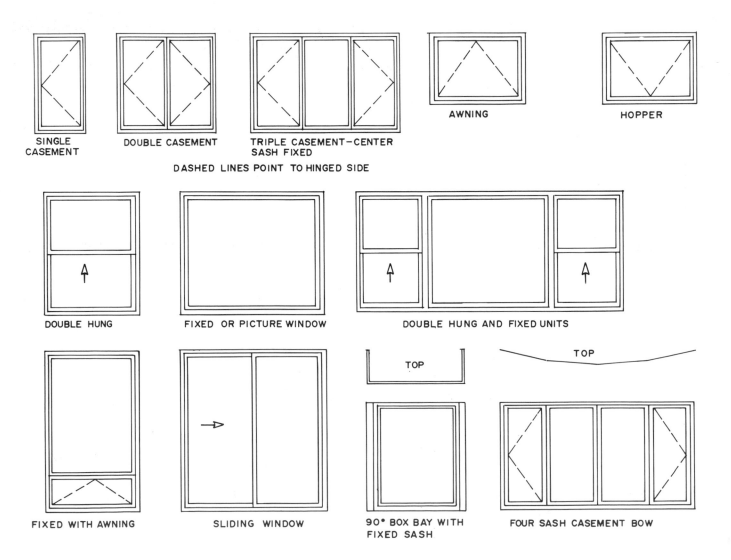

SINGLE CASEMENT

DOUBLE CASEMENT

TRIPLE CASEMENT–CENTER SASH FIXED

DASHED LINES POINT TO HINGED SIDE

AWNING

HOPPER

DOUBLE HUNG

FIXED OR PICTURE WINDOW

DOUBLE HUNG AND FIXED UNITS

FIXED WITH AWNING

SLIDING WINDOW

90° BOX BAY WITH FIXED SASH

FOUR SASH CASEMENT BOW

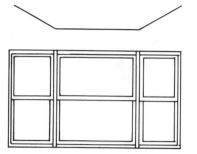

30° ANGLE BAY WITH DOUBLE
HUNG WINDOWS. 45° BAY AVAILABLE.

SLIDING   DOOR

TYPICAL EXTERIOR
DOOR

FRENCH DOORS

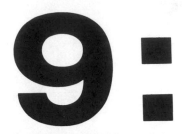

Fire Ratings and Sound Transmission Classes for Selected Partitions

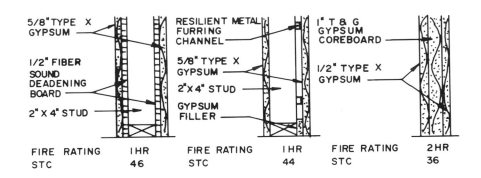

5/8" TYPE X GYPSUM
1/2" FIBER SOUND DEADENING BOARD
2" X 4" STUD

FIRE RATING   1 HR
STC   46

RESILIENT METAL FURRING CHANNEL
5/8" TYPE X GYPSUM
2" X 4" STUD
GYPSUM FILLER

FIRE RATING   1 HR
STC   44

1" T & G GYPSUM COREBOARD
1/2" TYPE X GYPSUM

FIRE RATING   2 HR
STC   36

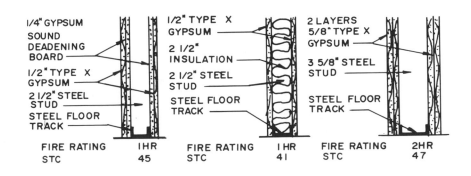

1/4" GYPSUM SOUND DEADENING BOARD
1/2" TYPE X GYPSUM
2 1/2" STEEL STUD
STEEL FLOOR TRACK

FIRE RATING   1 HR
STC   45

1/2" TYPE X GYPSUM
2 1/2" INSULATION
2 1/2" STEEL STUD
STEEL FLOOR TRACK

FIRE RATING   1 HR
STC   41

2 LAYERS 5/8" TYPE X GYPSUM
3 5/8" STEEL STUD
STEEL FLOOR TRACK

FIRE RATING   2 HR
STC   47

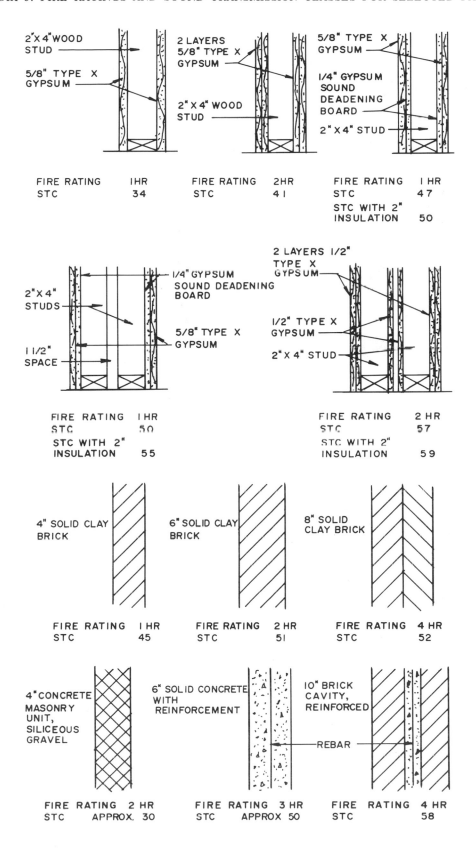

2"X 4" WOOD STUD
5/8" TYPE X GYPSUM

FIRE RATING   1HR
STC   34

2 LAYERS 5/8" TYPE X GYPSUM
2" X 4" WOOD STUD

FIRE RATING   2HR
STC   41

5/8" TYPE X GYPSUM
1/4" GYPSUM SOUND DEADENING BOARD
2" X 4" STUD

FIRE RATING   1 HR
STC   47
STC WITH 2" INSULATION   50

2" X 4" STUDS
1 1/2" SPACE
1/4" GYPSUM SOUND DEADENING BOARD
5/8" TYPE X GYPSUM

FIRE RATING   1 HR
STC   50
STC WITH 2" INSULATION   55

2 LAYERS 1/2" TYPE X GYPSUM
1/2" TYPE X GYPSUM
2" X 4" STUD

FIRE RATING   2 HR
STC   57
STC WITH 2" INSULATION   59

4" SOLID CLAY BRICK

FIRE RATING   1 HR
STC   45

6" SOLID CLAY BRICK

FIRE RATING   2 HR
STC   51

8" SOLID CLAY BRICK

FIRE RATING   4 HR
STC   52

4" CONCRETE MASONRY UNIT, SILICEOUS GRAVEL

FIRE RATING   2 HR
STC   APPROX. 30

6" SOLID CONCRETE WITH REINFORCEMENT
REBAR

FIRE RATING   3 HR
STC   APPROX 50

10" BRICK CAVITY, REINFORCED

FIRE RATING   4 HR
STC   58

REFER ARCHITECTURAL STANDARDS AND MANUFACTURERS
CATALOGS FOR ADDITIONAL INFORMATION.

Fire Ratings and Sound Transmission Classes for Selected Floor Assemblies

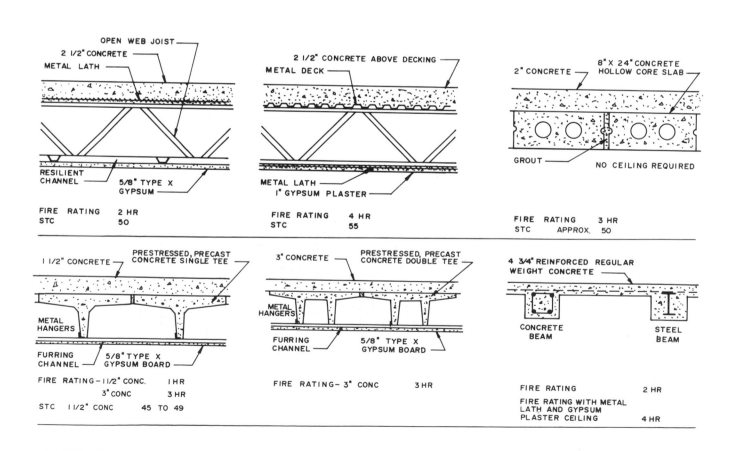

Top row, left:
OPEN WEB JOIST
2 1/2" CONCRETE
METAL LATH
RESILIENT CHANNEL
5/8" TYPE X GYPSUM

FIRE RATING 2 HR
STC 50

Top row, center:
2 1/2" CONCRETE ABOVE DECKING
METAL DECK
METAL LATH
1" GYPSUM PLASTER

FIRE RATING 4 HR
STC 55

Top row, right:
2" CONCRETE
8" X 24" CONCRETE HOLLOW CORE SLAB
GROUT
NO CEILING REQUIRED

FIRE RATING 3 HR
STC APPROX. 50

Bottom row, left:
1 1/2" CONCRETE
PRESTRESSED, PRECAST CONCRETE SINGLE TEE
METAL HANGERS
FURRING CHANNEL
5/8" TYPE X GYPSUM BOARD

FIRE RATING—1 1/2" CONC. 1 HR
3" CONC 3 HR
STC 1 1/2" CONC 45 TO 49

Bottom row, center:
3" CONCRETE
PRESTRESSED, PRECAST CONCRETE DOUBLE TEE
METAL HANGERS
FURRING CHANNEL
5/8" TYPE X GYPSUM BOARD

FIRE RATING— 3" CONC 3 HR

Bottom row, right:
4 3/4" REINFORCED REGULAR WEIGHT CONCRETE
CONCRETE BEAM
STEEL BEAM

FIRE RATING 2 HR
FIRE RATING WITH METAL LATH AND GYPSUM PLASTER CEILING 4 HR

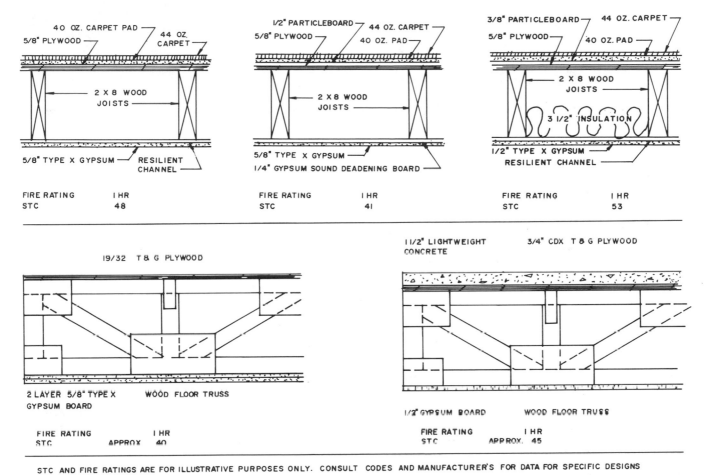

STC AND FIRE RATINGS ARE FOR ILLUSTRATIVE PURPOSES ONLY. CONSULT CODES AND MANUFACTURER'S FOR DATA FOR SPECIFIC DESIGNS AND MATERIALS.

Weights of Building Materials

Brick and Block Masonry	lb/ft²
4″ brickwall	40
4″ concrete brick, stone or gravel	46
4″ concrete brick, light weight	33
4″ concrete block, stone or gravel	34
4″ concrete block, lightweight	22
6″ concrete, stone or gravel	50
6″ concrete block, lightweight	31
8″ concrete block, stone or gravel	55
8″ concrete block, lightweight	35
12″ concrete block, stone or gravel	85
12″ concrete block, lightweight	55

Concrete	lb/ft³
plain, slag	132
plain, stone	144
reinforced, slag	138
reinforced, stone	150

Lightweight concrete	lb/ft³
concrete, perlite	35–50
concrete, pumice	60–90
concrete, vermiculite	25–60

Wall, Ceiling and Floor	lb/ft²
acoustical tile, 1/2″	0.8
gypsum wallboard 1/2″	2
plaster, 2″ partition	20
plaster 4″ partition	32
plaster, 1/2″	4.5

	lb/ft²
plaster on lath	10
tile, glazed 3/8″	3
tile, quarry 1/2″	5.8
terrazzo 1″	25
vinyl composition floor tile	1.4
hardwood flooring, 25/32″	4
Flexicore 6″, lightweight concrete	30
Flexicore 6″, stone concrete	40
plank, cinder concrete, 2″	15
plank, gypsum, 2″	12
concrete reinforced, stone, 1″	12.5
concrete reinforced, lightweight, 1″	6–10
concrete plain, stone, 1″	12
concrete plain, lightweight, 1″	3–9

Partitions	lb/ft²
2 × 4 wood studs, gypsum wallboard 2 sides	8
4″ metal stud, gypsum wallboard 2 sides	6
6″ concrete block, gypsum wallboard 2 sides	35

Roofing	lb/ft²
built-up	6.5
concrete roof tile	9.5
copper	1.5–2.5
steel deck alone	2.5
shingles, asphalt	1.7–2.8
shingles, wood	2–3

	lb / ft²
slate, 1/2"	14–18
tile, clay	8–16

Stone Veneer

	lb / ft³
2" granite, 1/2" parging	30
4" limestone, 1/2" parging	36
4" sandstone, 1/2" parging	49
1" marble	13

Structural Clay Tile

	lb / ft²
4" hollow	23
6" hollow	38
8" hollow	45

Suspended Ceilings

	lb / ft²
acoustic plaster on gypsum lath	10–11
mineral fiberboard	1.4

Wood

	lb / ft²
ash, white	40.5
birch	44
cedar	22
cypress	33
Douglas fir	32
white pine	27
pine, southern yellow	26
redwood	26
plywood, 1/2"	1.5

Residential Assemblies

	lb / ft²
wood framed floor	10
ceiling	10
frame exterior wall, 4" studs	10
frame exterior wall, 6" studs	13
brick veneer of 4" frame	50
brick veneer over 4" concrete block	74
interior partitions with gypsum both sides (allowance per sq ft of floor area—not weight of material)	20

Recommended Live Loads For Design Purposes

Residential	lb / ft²
Living Areas	40
Sleeping Areas	30
Attic, No Storage	10
Attic, Limited Storage	20
Attic, With Pull Down Stair	30
Garage and Carports	50
Balconies and Porches	60
Stairs	60
Sidewalks and Driveways	250
Stairs and Corridors in Apartments	60
Rooms Open To Public	100

Commercial	lb / ft²
Assembly Areas and Balconies	
Interior, Fixed Seating	50
Interior, Moveable Seating	100
Corridors	100
Dining Room, Restaurant	100
Garages, Auto Repair	100
Gymnasiums	100
Hospital	
Operating Room	60
Laboratories	60
Private Rooms	40
Wards	40
Corridors	80

Kitchens, Commercial	150
Laboratories, Scientific	100
Laundry	150
Library	
Reading Room	60
Stacks	150
Office Buildings	
Offices	50
Business Machine Room	100
Lobbies	100
Corridors	80
Computer Rooms—based on analysis of equipment	
Hotels	
Guest Rooms	40
Public Rooms	100
Public Corridors	100
Rest Rooms, Public	60
Schools	
Classrooms	40
Corridors	80
Stairs and Exitways	100
Warehouses	
Light	125
Heavy	250
Stores	
Retail	75
Wholesale	100

13:

Flame-Spread Requirements for Interior Wall and Ceiling Finish *

USE	Enclosed Vertical Exitways	Other Exitways	Rooms or Areas
Assembly buildings	1	2	3
Storage and sales areas for combustible goods	1	2	3
Restaurants less than 50 occupants Retail gasoline stations	1	2	3
Schools	1	2	3
Factories, warehouses, not using highly flammable material	1	2	3
Hospital, nursing home	1	2	2

USE	Enclosed Vertical Exitways	Other Exitways	Rooms or Areas
Hotels, apartments	1	2	3
Residential, single and multifamily	3	3	3
Storage, handling or sale of highly flammable or explosive materials	1	2	3
Auto repair garages	1	2	3
Nurseries	1	2	2
Private garages, carports shed, agricultural buildings	no restrictions		

Generalized examples. See local codes for specific requirements.

14:

Selected Sound Transmission Class (STC) Ratings for Various Occupancies*

Offices	45–52
Conference room	45
Hotel and motel rooms	48–50
Hotel and motel bathrooms	52–55
Apartments	48–55
Single family residence bedroom	40–50
Single family bathroom	45–50
Single family exterior wall	45–40

Generalized examples. See local codes for specific requirements.

Sound Transmission Class Recommendations for Various Occupancies*

Room Occupancy	STC
Conference rooms, doctor's offices, high privacy areas	50–55
General offices, conference rooms low privacy areas	45–50
Large offices, customer areas as in banks	40–50
Mechanical equipment rooms	50–60
Classrooms	50
school music rooms, drama rooms, industrial arts shops	60
Apartment buildings	
Bedrooms	48–55
Bathrooms	55–60
Kitchens	50–55
Living rooms	50–55
Halls	50–55

Generalized examples. See local codes for specific requirements.

Rafter Span Tables

Maximum Spans given in feet and inches

Rafters — 20 psf live load, 10 psf dead load, $\ell/240$, $C_D = 1.15$[1]

No finished ceiling: Low slope (3 in 12 or less)

Size inches	Spacing inches on center	Dense Select Structural	Select Structural	NonDense Select Structural	No. 1 Dense	No. 1	No. 1 NonDense	No. 2 Dense	No. 2	No. 2 NonDense	No. 3
2 x 6	**12.0**	16-4	16-1	15-9	16-1	15-9	15-6	15-9	15-6	14-9	**12-11**
	16.0	14-11	14-7	14-4	14-7	14-4	14-1	14-4	14-1	13-5	**11-2**
	19.2	14-0	13-9	13-6	13-9	13-6	13-3	13-6	**13-2**	12-8	10-2
	24.0	13-0	12-9	12-6	12-9	12-6	12-3	12-6	**11-9**	11-4	9-1
2 x 8	**12.0**	21-7	21-2	20-10	21-2	20-10	20-5	20-10	20-5	19-6	**16-5**
	16.0	19-7	19-3	18-11	19-3	18-11	18-6	18-11	18-6	17-9	**14-3**
	19.2	18-5	18-1	17-9	18-1	17-9	17-5	17-9	**17-0**	16-3	13-0
	24.0	17-2	16-10	16-6	16-10	16-6	**16-2**	**16-5**	15-3	14-7	11-7
2 x 10	**12.0**	✳	✳	✳	✳	✳	✳	✳	✳	24-6	19-5
	16.0	25-0	24-7	24-1	24-7	24-1	23-8	**23-10**	22-3	21-2	16-10
	19.2	23-7	23-1	22-8	23-1	**22-7**	21-9	21-9	20-4	19-4	15-4
	24.0	21-10	21-6	21-1	**21-4**	**20-3**	19-5	19-5	18-2	17-4	13-9
2 x 12	**12.0**	✳	✳	✳	✳	✳	✳	✳	✳	✳	23-1
	16.0	✳	✳	✳	✳	✳	✳	✳	✳	25-1	20-0
	19.2	✳	✳	✳	✳	✳	✳	✳	23-10	22-10	18-3
	24.0	✳	✳	✳	**25-1**	**24-1**	**23-1**	**23-1**	21-4	20-5	16-4

These spans are intended for use in covered structures or where the moisture content in use does not exceed 19 percent for an extended period of time.

Design Criteria: Based on 1991 NFPA Span Tables for Joists and Rafters, and 1991 SPIB Grading Rules.
  Deflection—Based on 20 pounds per square foot (psf) live load only, and limited to span in inches divided by 240.
  Strength—Based on 20 psf live load, plus 10 psf dead load.

✳ Maximum span is 25'-5'' or greater. Check sources of supply for availability of lumber in lengths greater than 20'.

(1) Spans shown in **regular type** (e.g. 18-1) are controlled by deflection. Spans shown in **bold italics** (e.g. **12-2**) are controlled by bending. Allowable bending design values used in calculations include the two-month load duration factor, C_D, of 1.15 for snow loads as permitted in the National Design Specification.'' This may be a conservative assumption for structures qualifying for the seven-day load duration factor, C_D, of 1.25 for construction loads. Designers applying an additional load duration increase for bending-controlled spans in this publication must verify that deflection limits are not exceeded.

*Maximum Spans
given in feet and inches*

Rafters — 30 psf live load, 15 psf dead load, $\ell/180$, $C_D=1.15$[1]

No finished ceiling: High slope (over 3 in 12): Heavy roofing

Size	Spacing	Grade										
inches	inches on center	Dense Select Structural	Select Structural	NonDense Select Structural	No. 1 Dense	No. 1	No. 1 NonDense	No. 2 Dense	No. 2	No. 2 NonDense	No. 3	Standard
2 x 4	12.0	10-0	9-10	9-8	9-10	9-8	9-6	9-8	9-6	**9-0**	7-2	**6-1**
	16.0	9-1	8-11	8-9	8-11	8-9	8-7	**8-9**	**8-3**	**7-10**	6-2	**5-4**
	19.2	8-7	8-5	8-3	8-5	8-3	**8-0**	**8-0**	**7-6**	**7-2**	5-8	**4-10**
	24.0	7-11	7-10	7-8	**7-9**	**7-5**	**7-2**	**7-2**	**6-8**	**6-4**	**5-0**	**4-4**
2 x 6	12.0	15-9	15-6	15-2	15-6	15-2	14-10	**14-8**	13-7	**13-1**	10-6	
	16.0	14-4	14-1	13-9	**13-11**	**13-6**	**12-11**	**12-8**	**11-9**	**11-4**	9-1	
	19.2	13-6	13-3	13-0	**12-9**	**12-4**	**11-9**	**11-7**	**10-9**	**10-4**	8-4	
	24.0	12-6	12-3	12-0	**11-5**	**11-1**	**10-6**	**10-4**	**9-7**	**9-3**	7-5	
2 x 8	12.0	20-9	20-5	20-0	20-5	**19-8**	**18-8**	**19-0**	**17-7**	**16-10**	13-5	
	16.0	18-10	18-6	18-2	**17-10**	**17-0**	**16-2**	**16-5**	**15-3**	**14-7**	11-7	
	19.2	17-9	17-5	17-1	**16-3**	**15-6**	**14-9**	**15-0**	**13-11**	**13-3**	10-7	
	24.0	16-6	16-2	15-10	**14-7**	**13-11**	**13-2**	**13-5**	**12-5**	**11-11**	9-6	
2 x 10	12.0	＊	＊	＊	24-8	**23-4**	**22-5**	**22-5**	**21-0**	**20-0**	15-10	
	16.0	24-1	23-8	23-2	**21-4**	**20-3**	**19-5**	**19-5**	**18-2**	**17-4**	13-9	
	19.2	22-8	22-3	21-10	**19-6**	**18-5**	**17-9**	**17-9**	**16-7**	**15-10**	12-7	
	24.0	21-0	20-8	**19-8**	**17-5**	**16-6**	**15-10**	**15-10**	**14-10**	**14-2**	11-3	

These spans are intended for use in covered structures or where the moisture content in use does not exceed 19 percent for an extended period of time.

Design Criteria: Based on 1991 NFPA Span Tables for Joists and Rafters, and 1991 SPIB Grading Rules.
  Deflection—Based on 30 pounds per square foot (psf) live load only, and limited to span in inches divided by 180.
  Strength—Based on 30 psf live load, plus 15 psf dead load.

＊ Maximum span is 25'-5'' or greater. Check sources of supply for availability of lumber in lengths greater than 20'.

(1) Spans shown in **regular type** (e.g. 18-1) are controlled by deflection. Spans shown in ***bold italics*** (e.g. **12-2**) are controlled by bending. Allowable bending design values used in calculations include the two-month load duration factor, C_D, of 1.15 for snow loads as permitted in the National Design Specification. This may be a conservative assumption for structures qualifying for the seven-day load duration factor, C_D, of 1.25 for construction loads. Designers applying an additional load duration increase for bending-controlled spans in this publication must verify that deflection limits are not exceeded.

Tables Courtesy Southern Pine Marketing Council.

Ceiling Joist Span Tables

*Maximum Spans
given in feet and inches*

Ceiling Joists — 10 psf live load, 5 psf dead load, $\ell/240$

Drywall ceiling: No attic storage: Roof slopes 3 in 12 or less

Size (inches)	Spacing (inches on center)	Grade										
		Dense Select Structural	Select Structural	NonDense Select Structural	No. 1 Dense	No. 1	No. 1 NonDense	No. 2 Dense	No. 2	No. 2 NonDense	No. 3	Standard
2 x 4	12.0	13-2	12-11	12-8	12-11	12-8	12-5	12-8	12-5	11-10	11-7	9-11
	16.0	11-11	11-9	11-6	11-9	11-6	11-3	11-6	11-3	10-9	10-0	8-7
	19.2	11-3	11-0	10-10	11-0	10-10	10-7	10-10	10-7	10-2	9-2	7-10
	24.0	10-5	10-3	10-0	10-3	10-0	9-10	10-0	9-10	9-5	8-2	7-0
2 x 6	12.0	20-8	20-3	19-11	20-3	19-11	19-6	19-11	19-6	18-8	17-1	
	16.0	18-9	18-5	18-1	18-5	18-1	17-8	18-1	17-8	16-11	14-9	
	19.2	17-8	17-4	17-0	17-4	17-0	16-8	17-0	16-8	15-11	13-6	
	24.0	16-4	16-1	15-9	16-1	15-9	15-6	15-9	15-6	14-9	12-1	
2 x 8	12.0	✳	✳	✳	✳	✳	✳	✳	✳	24-7	21-8	
	16.0	24-8	24-3	23-10	24-3	23-10	23-4	23-10	23-4	22-4	18-9	
	19.2	23-3	22-10	22-5	22-10	22-5	21-11	22-5	21-11	21-0	17-2	
	24.0	21-7	21-2	20-10	21-2	20-10	20-5	20-10	20-1	19-2	15-4	
2 x 10	12.0	✳	✳	✳	✳	✳	✳	✳	✳	✳	✳	
	16.0	✳	✳	✳	✳	✳	✳	✳	✳	✳	22-2	
	19.2	✳	✳	✳	✳	✳	✳	✳	✳	✳	20-3	
	24.0	✳	✳	✳	✳	✳	✳	✳	24-0	22-9	18-1	

These spans are intended for use in covered structures or where the moisture content in use does not exceed 19 percent for an extended period of time.

Design Criteria: Based on 1991 NFPA Span Tables for Joists and Rafters, and 1991 SPIB Grading Rules.
   Deflection—Based on 10 pounds per square foot (psf) live load only, and limited to span in inches divided by 240.
   Strength—Based on 10 psf live load, plus 5 psf dead load.

✳ Maximum span is 25'-5'' or greater. Check sources of supply for availability of lumber in lengths greater than 20'.

Maximum Spans
given in feet and inches

Ceiling Joists — 20 psf live load, 10 psf dead load, $\ell/240$

Drywall ceiling: No future sleeping rooms, but limited storage available

Size	Spacing	Grade										
inches	inches on center	Dense Select Structural	Select Structural	NonDense Select Structural	No. 1 Dense	No. 1	No. 1 NonDense	No. 2 Dense	No. 2	No. 2 NonDense	No. 3	Standard
2 x 4	12.0	10-5	10-3	10-0	10-3	10-0	9-10	10-0	9-10	9-5	8-2	7-0
	16.0	9-6	9-4	9-1	9-4	9-1	8-11	9-1	8-11	8-7	7-1	6-1
	19.2	8-11	8-9	8-7	8-9	8-7	8-5	8-7	8-5	8-1	6-5	5-6
	24.0	8-3	8-1	8-0	8-1	8-0	7-10	8-0	7-8	7-3	5-9	4-11
2 x 6	12.0	16-4	16-1	15-9	16-1	15-9	15-6	15-9	15-6	14-9	12-1	
	16.0	14-11	14-7	14-4	14-7	14-4	14-1	14-4	13-6	12-11	10-5	
	19.2	14-0	13-9	13-6	13-9	13-6	13-3	13-3	12-4	11-9	9-6	
	24.0	13-0	12-9	12-6	12-9	12-6	12-0	11-10	11-0	10-6	8-6	
2 x 8	12.0	21-7	21-2	20-10	21-2	20-10	20-5	20-10	20-1	19-2	15-4	
	16.0	19-7	19-3	18-11	19-3	18-11	18-5	18-9	17-5	16-7	13-3	
	19.2	18-5	18-1	17-9	18-1	17-9	16-10	17-2	15-10	15-2	12-1	
	24.0	17-2	16-10	16-6	16-8	15-11	15-1	15-4	14-2	13-7	10-10	
2 x 10	12.0	*	*	*	*	*	*	*	24-0	22-9	18-1	
	16.0	25-0	24-7	24-1	24-5	23-2	22-2	22-2	20-9	19-9	15-8	
	19.2	23-7	23-1	22-8	22-3	21-1	20-3	20-3	19-0	18-0	14-4	
	24.0	21-10	21-6	21-1	19-11	18-11	18-1	18-1	17-0	16-1	12-10	

These spans are intended for use in covered structures or where the moisture content in use does not exceed 19 percent for an extended period of time.

Design Criteria: Based on 1991 NFPA Span Tables for Joists and Rafters, and 1991 SPIB Grading Rules.
   Deflection—Based on 20 pounds per square foot (psf) live load only, and limited to span in inches divided by 240.
   Strength—Based on 20 psf live load, plus 10 psf dead load.

* Maximum span is 25'-5'' or greater. Check sources of supply for availability of lumber in lengths greater than 20'.

Tables Courtesy Southern Pine Marketing Council.

Floor Joist Span Tables

*Maximum Spans
given in feet and inches*

Floor Joists — 30 psf live load, 10 psf dead load, ℓ/360

Sleeping rooms and attic floors

Size inches	Spacing inches on center	Grade									
		Dense Select Structural	Select Structural	NonDense Select Structural	No. 1 Dense	No. 1	No. 1 NonDense	No. 2 Dense	No. 2	No. 2 NonDense	No. 3
2 x 6	12.0	12-6	12-3	12-0	12-3	12-0	11-10	12-0	11-10	11-3	10-5
	16.0	11-4	11-2	10-11	11-2	10-11	10-9	10-11	10-9	10-3	9-1
	19.2	10-8	10-6	10-4	10-6	10-4	10-1	10-4	10-1	9-8	8-3
	24.0	9-11	9-9	9-7	9-9	9-7	9-4	9-7	9-4	8-11	7-5
2 x 8	12.0	16-6	16-2	15-10	16-2	15-10	15-7	15-10	15-7	14-11	13-3
	16.0	15-0	14-8	14-5	14-8	14-5	14-2	14-5	14-2	13-6	11-6
	19.2	14-1	13-10	13-7	13-10	13-7	13-4	13-7	13-4	12-9	10-6
	24.0	13-1	12-10	12-7	12-10	12-7	12-4	12-7	12-4	11-9	9-5
2 x 10	12.0	21-0	20-8	20-3	20-8	20-3	19-10	20-3	19-10	19-0	15-8
	16.0	19-1	18-9	18-5	18-9	18-5	18-0	18-5	18-0	17-1	13-7
	19.2	18-0	17-8	17-4	17-8	17-4	17-0	17-4	16-5	15-7	12-5
	24.0	16-8	16-5	16-1	16-5	16-1	15-8	15-8	14-8	13-11	11-1
2 x 12	12.0	✳	25-1	24-8	25-1	24-8	24-2	24-8	24-2	23-1	18-8
	16.0	23-3	22-10	22-5	22-10	22-5	21-11	22-5	21-1	20-3	16-2
	19.2	21-10	21-6	21-1	21-6	21-1	20-8	20-10	19-3	18-6	14-9
	24.0	20-3	19-11	19-7	19-11	19-6	18-8	18-8	17-2	16-7	13-2

These spans are intended for use in covered structures or where the moisture content in use does not exceed 19 percent for an extended period of time.

Design Criteria: Based on 1991 NFPA Span Tables for Joists and Rafters, and 1991 SPIB Grading Rules.
   Deflection—Based on 30 pounds per square foot (psf) live load only, and limited to span in inches divided by 360.
   Strength—Based on 30 psf live load, plus 10 psf dead load.

✳ Maximum span is 25'-5'' or greater. Check sources of supply for availability of lumber in lengths greater than 20'.

*Maximum Spans
given in feet and inches*

Floor Joists — 40 psf live load, 10 psf dead load, ℓ/360

All rooms except sleeping rooms and attic floors

Size inches	Spacing inches on center	Grade									
		Dense Select Structural	Select Structural	NonDense Select Structural	No. 1 Dense	No. 1	No. 1 NonDense	No. 2 Dense	No. 2	No. 2 NonDense	No. 3
2 x 6	**12.0**	11-4	11-2	10-11	11-2	10-11	10-9	10-11	10-9	10-3	9-4
	16.0	10-4	10-2	9-11	10-2	9-11	9-9	9-11	9-9	9-4	8-1
	19.2	9-8	9-6	9-4	9-6	9-4	9-2	9-4	9-2	8-9	7-5
	24.0	9-0	8-10	8-8	8-10	8-8	8-6	8-8	8-6	8-2	6-7
2 x 8	**12.0**	15-0	14-8	14-5	14-8	14-5	14-2	14-5	14-2	13-6	11-11
	16.0	13-7	13-4	13-1	13-4	13-1	12-10	13-1	12-10	12-3	10-3
	19.2	12-10	12-7	12-4	12-7	12-4	12-1	12-4	12-1	11-7	9-5
	24.0	11-11	11-8	11-5	11-8	11-5	11-3	11-5	11-0	10-6	8-5
2 x 10	**12.0**	19-1	18-9	18-5	18-9	18-5	18-0	18-5	18-0	17-3	14-0
	16.0	17-4	17-0	16-9	17-0	16-9	16-5	16-9	16-1	15-3	12-2
	19.2	16-4	16-0	15-9	16-0	15-9	15-5	15-8	14-8	13-11	11-1
	24.0	15-2	14-11	14-7	14-11	14-7	14-0	14-0	13-2	12-6	9-11
2 x 12	**12.0**	23-3	22-10	22-5	22-10	22-5	21-11	22-5	21-9	20-11	16-8
	16.0	21-1	20-9	20-4	20-9	20-4	19-11	20-4	18-10	18-2	14-5
	19.2	19-10	19-6	19-2	19-6	19-2	18-8	18-8	17-2	16-7	13-2
	24.0	18-5	18-1	17-9	18-1	17-5	16-8	16-8	15-4	14-10	11-10

These spans are intended for use in covered structures or where the moisture content in use does not exceed 19 percent for an extended period of time.

Design Criteria: Based on 1991 NFPA Span Tables for Joists and Rafters, and 1991 SPIB Grading Rules.
        Deflection — Based on 40 pounds per square foot (psf) live load only, and limited to span in inches divided by 360.
        Strength — Based on 40 psf live load, plus 10 psf dead load.

Tables Courtesy Southern Pine Marketing Council.

Appendix

Glossary of Selected Construction and Architectural Terms

Acoustics. The qualities of a room that determine the audibility or fidelity of sounds in it.

Adobe. A sun dried clay brick.

Admixture. A material added to concrete or mortar that alters its characteristics as slowing its setting time.

Aggregate. Inert, granular material, such as sand and crushed stone, used in concrete.

Air-dried lumber. Lumber stored out of doors to dry.

Air-entrained concrete. Concrete having an air-entraining admixture added that produces millions of tiny air bubbles that increase workability, resist deterioration due to freezing and thawing, and reduce the amount of water required.

Ampere. A unit of the rate of flow of electric current. A force of 1 V acting across a resistance of 1 ohm results in a current flow of 1 Am.

Anchor bolts. Bolts used to fasten the wood sill or steel, wood or concrete columns to a concrete or masonry foundation.

Apron. A trim board placed below the window sill on the inside wall. Also a paved area such as where a drive meets the garage.

Arch. A curved construction which spans an opening such as for a door or window.

Areaway. An open area below grade used to admit light and air such as to a basement window.

Awning window. A window that swings toward the outside and is hinged at the bottom.

Balloon framing. A system of wood frame construction in which the studs are continuous from the sill to the roof of two-story buildings.

Baluster. A vertical member that supports the handrails on a stair.

Base. Molding installed where the wall meets the floor.

Batten. Narrow strips of wood or metal used to cover joints as between sheets of plywood.

Beam. A horizontal load-bearing structural member.

Blocking. Wood pieces used to secure, join, or reinforce other wood members.

Break line. A line symbol used on drawings to indicate a portion of the drawing has been removed.

Building section. A cross section through part of a building showing structural details.

Building permit. Written authorization to allow a contractor to proceed with construction.

Cant strip. A triangular strip used to avoid sharp turns in the roofing material.

Cantilever. A condition where structural members extend beyond the support, such as a roof overhang.

Casement. A window having the sash hinged on the verticle side.

Caulking. A waterproof material used to seal the space between two joining surfaces.

Cavity wall. A hollow wall formed by leaving a space between the inner and outer masonry layers forming the wall.

Certificate of occupancy. A document issued by the local government certifying that the building has been completed as specified and is ready to be occupied.

Circuit breaker. An electric device for opening and closing a circuit that opens automatically if an unusually high flow of current is detected.

Coefficient of expansion. The change in dimension of a material per unit of dimension per degree change in temperature.

Coefficient of thermal transmission. The amount of heat transferred through a unit area of a partition per hour, per degree temperature difference between the air on the two sides.

Collar beam. A horizontal member connecting two opposite rafters above the top plate.

Column. A vertical load-carrying structural member.

Computer-aided drafting. Preparing drawings using a computer and drafting software.

Concrete block. A rectangular masonry unit made from concrete.

Contour line. A line on a site plan or land survey connecting points having the same elevation.

Control joint. A groove cut into concrete slabs to provide a way to regulate cracks.

Construction documents. A set of legal documents that set forth graphically and in written form what is required for a specific construction project.

Cul-de-sac. A circular turnaround located at the end of a dead end street.

Counterflashing. Flashing held in a masonry joint that is turned down over the regular flashing.

Details. Enlarged drawings of a portion of a drawing at a smaller scale or a structural feature.

Duct. A pipe used to move heated or cooled air from a furnace to rooms within the building.

Double-glazing. A window with two panes of glass with a sealed air space between them.

Drywall. Wallboard made from gypsum.

Duplex outlet. An electric convenience outlet with two plug receptacles.

Datum. A level surface from which the surveyor takes measurements when measuring elevations.

Decking. Thick wood boards used for structural roofing and flooring.

Design strength. The load-bearing capacity of a member to carry allowable stresses.

Diffuser. A device to scatter light or sound from a source.

Dormer. A structure housing a window and projecting from a sloping roof.

Easement. A right to have access to or go through land owned by another, such as right to install city sewer lines on private property.

Eave. The low part of a roof that projects over the wall.

Efforescence. A white powder that forms on the surface of masonry walls. It is caused by water-soluble salts from the mortar.

Egress. The place to exit from a building.

Ell. A part of a building at right angles to the main structure.

Facade. The front of a building.

Fascia or fasia. The flat board mounted on the outer face or the cornice or the end of the rafters.

Firecut. An angular cut on the ends of joists that are in solid masonry walls.

Fire door. A fire-resistant door, frame, and hardware capable of providing a specified degree of fire protection.

Firewall. A fire-resistant wall capable of providing a specified degree of fire protection.

Flashing. The application of a material, usually metal, to protect the joint between two surfaces from penetration by water.

Flame-spread rating. A numerical designation indicating the ability of a material to resist flaming combustion over its surface. The lower the number the better the material resists the spread of flame.

Flue. An incombustible heat-resistant pipe in a chimney that carries away the products of combustion.

Frost line. The depth frost will penetrate the soil.

Furring. Wood strips mounted on a surface providing an airspace when covered with finished wall or flooring material.

Gable. A vertical, triangular end of the roof of a building having a double sloping roof.

Gambrel roof. A gable roof with two pitches.

Girder. A major horizontal beam used to carry concentrated loads at isolated points along its length.

Glazing. Glass in a frame or the act of installing the glass in the frame.

Glue-laminated beams. Beams made of layers of wood glued together.

Grade beam. Part of the foundation supporting the exterior wall. Usually bears on piers.

Grade line. The line at which the soil meets the foundation.

Grout. A fluid mixture of sand, water, and cement used to fill joints and cavities in masonry walls.

Gussett. A plate used to join wood members, as parts of a truss.

Gypsum. A hydrated sulfate of calcium used to make plaster and wallboard.

Hand. The direction, left or right, of the swing of a door when viewed from the side considered outside.

Hardboard. A sheet material manufactured by compressing wood fibers.

Head. Top of a window or door frame.

Hearth. The floor of a fireplace including area of fire-resistant material on the floor in front of it.

Heat gain. The net increase in heat within a space.

Heat load. The total heat per unit time that must be supplied in order to maintain a specified temperature in a room or building.

Hose bibb. An outside water faucet.

Humidistat. A device that senses changes in humidity and automatically corrects the relative humidity to the desired amount.

Insulation. Materials used to reduce the transmission of heat or cold through walls, floors, and ceilings.

Interior elevation. A drawing showing the details of one or more interior walls.

In situ. In place, undisturbed, as soil in situ in undisturbed soil.

Jamb. The vertical side part of a door or window frame.

Jetting. Sinking piles by use of a water jet run through the center of the pile.

Joist. Parallel wood structural members used to support floors and ceilings.

Junior beams. A standardized series of I-shaped beams made from hot-rolled sheet steel.

Kiln dried lumber. Lumber that has been dried in a kiln.

Lally column. A standard, round steel column.

Lath. A material fastened to a wall or ceiling that acts as a base for plaster.

Lavatory. A washbasin in a bath or a room containing restroom facilities.

Ledger. A horizontal member fastened to a beam to support joists.

Light. A single pane of glass or the opening for this glass.

Lintel. A horizontal structural member that spans openings, as doors and windows, and supports wall and roof weights.

Live load. A movable load on a structural member such as snow, furniture, and people.

Lookout. Framing members used to support the roof overhang at the gables.

Louver. An assembly of sloping, overlapping slats used to admit air.

Masonry. Construction materials of burned clay or concrete such as brick, stone, and concrete block.

Masonry veneer. A layer of masonry units covering a frame or masonry wall.

Mechanical ventilation. Supplying outdoor air into a building or removing inside air by mechanical means, such as fans.

Millwork. Finished wood building products made in a plant such as doors, windows, moldings, and interior trim.

Modular construction. Construction in which prefabricated units are assembled on the job site.

Modulas of elasticity. The ratio of the unit stress to the corresponding unit strain. A measure of stiffness.

Moisture barrier. Sheet material that retards the penetration of water vapor into walls, ceilings, and floor.

Monolithic concrete. Reinforced concrete poured with no joints other than construction joints.

Mullion. A vertical divider in the frame between windows or doors.

Muntin. A thin bar in a window that separates panes of glass.

Nonbearing wall. A wall that carries no load other than its own weight.

Nominal size. The call-out size rather than the actual size, as a 2×4, which is actually $1\frac{1}{2} \times 3\frac{1}{2}$ in.

Occupancy. The intended use of a building.

On Center (O.C.). Means the spacing of the feature, as studs, is taken from the center of the stud.

Overhang. The horizontal distance a roof projects beyond the exterior wall.

Parapet. A portion of an exterior wall that extends above the edge of the roof.

Parge. To apply a thin coat of cement mortar to a masonry wall.

Pier. A masonry or concrete pillar used to support a load such as a beam.

Pilaster. A rectangular pier that is built as an integral part of a concrete or masonry wall.

Pile. A concrete, wood, or steel column driven into the soil to carry a vertical load.

Pitch. The incline of the roof. It is a ratio of the rise to the span.

Posttensioning. A method of prestressing reinforced concrete in which the metal tenons are tensioned after the concrete has hardened.

Precast. A building unit made of concrete that was formed, poured, and cured in a location other than its final position.

Prefabricate. To build components before they are installed at the job site, such as a length of wall.

Purlins. Horizonal roof framing members laid on top of and often perpendicular to other roof framing members.

Rafter. A structural member forming the roof that supports the sheathing and finished roof.

Reference bubble. A symbol used on drawings to tie detail drawings to the drawing upon which they originally occurred.

Reinforced concrete. Concrete masonry in which steel reinforcing is placed to assist in resisting forces.

Reinforced masonry. Masonry units in which steel mesh or rods are inserted to assist in resisting forces.

Ridge. The horizontal line formed by the intersection of the upper edges of two sloping roof surfaces.

Riser. The vertical face of a stair step.

Rough opening. An opening in the framework of a building to receive a unit as a door or window.

Sandwich panel. A panel made by bonding facing sheets, as plywood, to a core material.

Sash. A frame constructed to hold glass as for a window.

Scupper. An opening in the parapet to allow water to flow off a roof.

Shear wall. A wall designed to resist lateral forces such as produced by the wind.

Sheathing. A material covering studs or rafters over which the finish exterior material or shingles are applied.

Site plan. A drawing that shows the ground upon which the building is to be built along with information detailing how it is to be developed.

Soffit. The exposed undersurface of an overhead part of a building, such as a cornice or balcony.

Soil stack. The vertical pipe into which waste from the fixtures flows.

Solar orientation. Placing a building in relation to the sun.

Specifications. A written document describing in detail the scope of work, materials, method of installation, and quality of workmanship.

Stud. A vertical structural member erected in rows to form walls and support floors and roofs.

Subfloor. A flooring over joists providing the surface upon which the finished floor is installed.

Termite shield. A metal sheet placed on top of the foundation to block the passage of termites.

Tension. The condition of being stretched.

Top plate. The top horizontal member on a stud wall.

Thermal expansion. The change in length or volume when a material is heated.

Thru. On drawings is an abbreviation for through.

Trap. A section of the plumbing waste disposal system that blocks sewer gases from entering a building.

Tread. The horizontal part of a step.

Truss. A framework of wood or metal members used to span between supports and carry loads.

Valley. A trough formed by the intersection of two inclined planes of a roof.

Vapor barrier. A material applied to walls, floors, and ceilings to prevent water vapor from passing into them.

Vent stack. The vertical pipe in a plumbing system that runs out through the roof and provides ventilation and pressure equalization.

Vert. On drawings is the abbreviation for vertical.

Wallboard. A rigid sheet made of gypsum or wood fibers.

Water stop. A material, usually plastic, used to provide a waterproof connection between a concrete wall and floor.

Weep hole. A small hole in a wall through which water may drain to the exterior.

Western (platform) framing. A method of wood framing in which the studs are one floor high terminated with a double plate upon which the second floor is constructed.

Index

513